SOUTH ASIAN LANGUAGES

Structure, Convergence and Diglossia

MLBD SERIES IN LINGUISTICS

General Editor
DHANESH JAIN

Volume III

SOUTH ASIAN LANGUAGES

Structure, Convergence and Diglossia

EDITOR

Bh. Krishnamurti

ASSOCIATE EDITORS

Colin P. Masica

Anjani K. Sinha

MOTILAL BANARSIDASS

Delhi Varanasi Patna Madras

Publication partially subsidised with funds from the Department of Linguistics, Osmania University, out of grants provided by the University Grants Commission under the Programme of Special Assistance.

Head Office: Bungalow Road, Delhi 110 007
Branches: Chowk, Varanasi 221 001
Ashok Rajpath, Patna 800 004
6, Appar Swamy Koil Street, Mylapore
Madras 600 004

First Edition: Delhi, 1986

ISBN: 81-208-0033-8

Printed in India by Narendra Prakash Jain at Shri Jainendra Press
A-45 Naraina, Phase I, New Delhi 110 028 and published by
Shantilal Jain for Motilal Banarsidass, Delhi 110 007

To

THOMAS BURROW

MURRAY B. EMENEAU

CHARLES A. FERGUSON

AND

SUMITRA M. KATRE

CONTENTS

SECOND INTERNATIONAL CONFERENCE ON SOUTH ASIAN LANGUAGES AND LINGUISTICS

Department of Linguistics, Osmania University
Hyderabad 500 007, (A. P.), India
January 9-11, 1980

INTERNATIONAL PLANNING COMMITTEE :

Dr. R. E. Asher, U. of Edinburgh, UK

Dr. George Cardona, U. of Pennsylvania, USA

Dr. M. W. Sugathapala De Silva, U. of York, UK

Dr. Edward Dimock (Jr.), U. of Chicago, USA

Dr. Charles A. Ferguson, Stanford U., USA

Dr. Nikita Gurov, Academy of Sciences, USSR

Dr. Hans Henrich Hock, U. of Illinois, USA

Dr. Braj B. Kachru. U. of Illinois, USA

Dr. T. Kandiah, U. of Peradeniya, Sri Lanka

Dr. Ramawatar Yadav, Tribhuvan U., Nepal

ORGANISING COMMITTEE

DIRECTOR

Bh. Krishnamurti

JOINT DIRECTORS

H. S. Ananthanarayana
C. Ramarao

SECRETARIES

B. Lakshmi Bai
B. Ramakrishna Reddy
Anjani Kumar Sinha
Arun Kumar Sharma

PREFACE

The Second International Conference on South Asian Languages and Linguistics (IInd ICSALL) was held in Hyderabad, January 9-11, 1980, hosted by the Department of Linguistics, Osmania University. It was attended by 250 scholars from U.S.A., U. S. S. R., Japan, Thailand, Sri Lanka and Nepal. Nearly 200 of them were from various Indian universities and Institutes of higher learning.

As many as 102 abstracts were received and 67 of these were selected for presentation at the Conference. Of the papers that were revised and submitted for publication, only 30 have been selected for publication in this volume. Two areas were selected for the plenary sessions of the Conference, viz. (1) South Asia as a Linguistic Area, and (2) Diglossia in South Asia, chaired by Professor C. P. Masica and Professor Charles A. Ferguson, respectively. A number of sectional meetings were held on the following themes: Syntax and Semantics, Linguistics and Literacy, Language and Social Interaction, Phonetics and Phonology, Englishization of South Asian Languages, Language Contact and Language Change, Minor Languages of South Asia, Expression and Script. When the papers were organized, we found that they could be published as a single volume with the current title. The papers which did not fall within the scope of either 'Convergence' or 'Diglossia' were given a general title 'Structure'. The abstracts of the selected papers as well as details of presentation schedule were printed in the Conference Souvenir, published on the first day of the Conference.

Since the Conference was held over five years ago, we regret the inordinate delay in the publication of this volume. There were delays in submitting the revised versions of the invited articles, in negotiating with a press to undertake printing on a subvention basis, in editing the papers, etc. The publishers actually started printing the volume in 1982. Since we decided that the authors should also read the page-proofs besides the editor (s) it took a lot of time for certain papers to be proofread and returned by the authors. We are happy that the volume is out finally.

We record here our deep sorrow at the sad and premature death of two of the contributors to this volume—Professor M. W. Sugathapala De Silva (May, 1980) and Professor Suhas Chatterji (May, 1985). The editors send their heartfelt condolences to the bereaved families.

Both in the holding of the Conference and in the preparation of this volume, several agencies and individuals have helped us. We are grateful to the American Institute of Indian Studies and particulary to its Chairman, Professor Edward Dimock, who negotiated with the Smithsonian Institution for the award of travel grants to scholars (both American and Indian) from U.S.A. The Director of the American Institute of Indian Studies,

Dr. Pradeep Mehendiratta, has helped us in more than one way. We are thankful to him for arranging the travel of the scholars from U.S.A., for providing files for the Conference, and for sharing the subvention for the printing of this volume. The teachers and staff of the Department of Linguistics at Osmania University deserve our thanks for their whole-hearted cooperation. We owe a special debt of gratitude to Professor Ramesh Mohan, Director of the Central Institute of English and Foreign Languages, and Professor S. K. Verma, Professor of Linguistics who extended their fullest cooperation in making the Conference a success. The main venue of the Conference was the Central Institute of English and Foreign Languages. We also record our thanks to the University Grants Commission whose financial support under the Special Assistance Programme to the Linguistics Department at Osmania has covered part of the expenditure of the Seminar as well as of the publication of this volume.

We thank the authorities of Osmania University, particularly the then Vice-Chancellor, Professor G. Ram Reddy, for the cooperation we received.

Professor Thomas Burrow (Oxford), Professor M. B. Emeneau (California, Berkeley), Professor C. A. Ferguson (Stanford) and Professor S. M. Katre (Deccan College, Pune, and the University of Texas, Austin) have contributed significantly to the growth of South Asian linguistics. The indebtedness of South Asian scholarship to their work is evident from the articles in the volume. To these four eminent South Asian Scholars we dedicate this volume with gratitude, love and respect.

THE EDITORS

COMMENTS ON "CONVERGENCE" (PART II)

By

COLIN P. MASICA

The South Asian area has become established, particularly since Emeneau's 1956 article in *Language* ("India as a linguistic area"), as a classic locus for convergence phenomena, that is, of the sharing of characteristics by genetically unrelated by geographically contiguous languages. It is only fitting that this volume contain a section devoted to the subject. While some of the papers in this section (those of Masica, Klaiman, Lakshmi Bai, Meenakshi, and Singh, Subbarao and Bandyopadhyay) address topics related to the area as a whole, others (those of Gair, Kachru, Kanittanan, Pandharipande, Patnaik and Pandit, and Steever) deal with more specific instances of convergence between individual neighboring languages or dialects, examples of which also abound in the South Asian area, and which afford good opportunities to study the phenomenon of convergence at close range.

To briefly summarize the content of the papers in this collection in the order in which they are printed, the first (pp.123-46), which is my own (MASICA's), seeks to identify the types of definiteness-marking that are characteristic of South Asia, in the context of an attempted sketch of a general typology of the semantics and typical formal devices of definiteness marking as a motivating factor. I conclude that the use of incipient indefinite articles to mark unidentified-specific status in "marked" environments (e.g., subject), complemented by accusative case-marking of identified objects (the latter strongest in the northwest), is the dominant South Asian pattern. (For further discussion of this problem in the context of Indo-Aryan, see Indira Junghare's article in *Indian Linguistics* 44. 1-4 : 43-53, March-December 1983.)

JAMES W. GAIR's paper on focused sentences in Sinhala (pp. 147-64) describes the contemporary functions and sketches some of the historical development of a construction with no Indo-Aryan but significant South Dravidian parallels, and concludes that it was indeed most probably taken over from the latter in a rudimentary form, but subsequently underwent extensive internal development and systematization in Sinhala and became an important part of its grammar. YAMUNA KACHRU in her paper on Dakkhini syntax (pp. 165-73) suggests Marathi influence behind a periphrastic causative construction in Dakkhini and both Marathi and Dravidian influence on its relative clause constructions.

WILAIWAN KANITTANAN (pp. 174-78) discusses some of the word order characteristics of Kamti (also known as Khamti), the only Tai language participating in the Indian convergence area. Refining the description implied by Greenberg's crude classification of Khamti as SOV-Pr, and comparing it with other Tai languages, she shows how these characteristics throw light on the switch from an earlier SVO typology. Of particular interest is evidence that postpositions may develop in a language (under appropriate areal pressures) first through the agency of definite object markers. M. H. KLAIMAN in her paper on semantic parameters in the Indian linguistic area (pp. 179-94) proposes that common conceptual characteristics may underlie cases of formal convergence among areal languages, and stresses the importance of accurate identification of these in a proper account of areal phenomena. She offers two examples, both involving properties of subjects. The first is a volitional/nonvolitional distinction, illustrated primarily from Bengali but which she suggests may be found to underlie the formal direct-/dative-subject contrast that has been observed in many languages in the area. The second is the affective/effective distinction, identified earlier in Tamil (by Paramasivam) and in the Munda language Gorum (by A. Zide), which Klaiman extends to Hindi-Bengali and offers as a better explanation of certain problems in the description of causative constructions in South Asian languages generally than the positing of a a third or 'ingestive' class of verbs as was done by me (half in jest, as far as the name was concerned) in 1976.

B. LAKSHMI BAI (pp. 195-208) explores another formal-cum-semantic parameter in the Indian area, namely that between existential and equational sentences, and concludes that the maintenance of such a distinction formally (i.e. by the use of two distinct 'be' verbs, negative and positive, one of which may be zero in the positive in some languages in the Present), is—in the area, at least—a Dravidian feature which has spread to some modern Indo-Aryan languages (of which it was not originally and is still not universally characteristic) as well as to some Munda languages. While the BE verbs at least involve mostly cognate forms within each language family, K. MEENAKSHI'S study (pp. 209-18) of the history of quotative markers in Indo-Aryan deals with meanings and functions represented by different forms at different periods even within the same family: the Sanskrit comeplementizer-quotative *iti* has been replaced by several other forms by the time of the modern languages, some of them semantically (as well as syntactically) parallel to those of Dravidian (i.e. based on verbs of 'saying'). At the same time she attempts to make the case that the modern clause-initial complementizer *ki* (Hindi-Panjabi), *ke* (Gujarati), *kī* (Marathi) comes directly from a Middle Indo-Aryan form *kiṁti/kiti* (<Sanskrit *kim iti*) rather than from Persian *ke* (or *ki*) as is often assumed. (In this connection, it might be noted that the older Marathi spelling is *kīṁ*.) She also deals with Bengali/Oriya *je*, in which connection the reader might note the discussion of *je* also in the Patnaik-Pandit paper.

RAJESHWARI PANDHARIPANDE'S study of the Nagpur variety of Marathi (pp. 219-31) sets out to demonstrate that peculiarities of Nagpuri Marathi, spelled out in the course of her article, area features shared, not surprisingly perhaps, with Hindi, a neighboring language in the Nagpur region, and are attributable to local Marathi-Hindi bilingualism. Although many of the features listed involve lexical borrowing, either straightforward or in the form of calquing or domain-extension, some involve importation of syntactic and grammatical features (employing Marathi morphemes—really also a form of calquing) which serve to complicate rather than simplify the grammer. This in turn raises important questions for historical linguistic explanations and assumptions. B. N. PATNAIK and IRA PANDIT'S paper on English influence on written Oriya (pp. 232-43) is a reminder that in these latter days English also has become an important ingredient in the already rich South Asian linguistic stew. Some modern Oriya constructions seem to have been imported, directly or indirectly from English, while others, already present in the language, have expanded their domains as a result of English influence. The conclusion is inescapable that the syntax of all the other modern South Asian languages needs similarly careful historical and descriptive study from this point of view.

The paper on polar verb classification jointly authored by U. N. SINGH, K. V. SUBBARAO, and S. K. BANDYOPADHYAY (pp. 244-69) examined the compound verb phenomenon in several Indo-Aryan languages and one Dravidian language (Telugu) from a point of view not usual in such studies, namely the main ('polar'—that is, lexically "full") verb and its combinatorial possibilities with the various explicator ('vector') verbs in use in the language. According to the authors themselves, the study is tentative in the sense that a larger corpus would be expected to alter the data somewhat. In spite of this, and in spite of the fact that comparisons with other studies (e.g., Hook's) are somewhat vitiated by the use of a different (though overlapping) set of languages in each case, and in spite of the difficulty in following all the statistical permutations of the data by the authors, the study adds a new dimension to our picture of the compound verb and of the South Asian verb in general, upon which further studies could be based. (The authors suggest semantic studies.) Further material pertaining to the South Asian compound verb will be found in the Pandharipande paper and in the Steever paper.

The last paper in the collection, by SANFORD STEEVER (pp. 270-85), examines a miniature convergence area, involing object-incorporation phenomena in South Munda and South Central Dravidian languages in Southern Orissa. He concludes, on the strength of attempted rule-based syntactic and morphological reconstruction, that neither may be said to have directly influenced the other, despite the striking areal coincidence of the phenomena, which remains to be explained. In the course of his discussion, Steever highlights the basic differences between the superficially similar South Munda and South Central Dravidian systems— a reminder that, in our enthusiasm for convergence phenomena, we should not forget important differences that remain between unrelated "convergent" languages—at least those that have not reached the stage of complete morpheme intertranslatability. (A brief discussion of object-incorporation in Munda will also be found in my paper on definiteness-marking.)

COMMENTS ON 'DIGLOSSIA' (PART III)

By
BH. KRISHNAMURTI

CHARLES A. FERGUSON concluded his classic paper on 'Diglossia' with the statement, 'Perhaps the collection of data and more profound study will drastically modify the impressionistic remarks of this paper, but if this is so the paper will have had the virtue of stimulating investigation and thought' (1959; repr. 1964:437). No other concept in sociolinguistic literature has stimulated so much thinking and discussion as 'Diglossia' has during the intervening twenty-six years.[1] Diglossia has come to mean different things to different scholars (see in this volume, Moag, p. 350; De Silva for some modification of the defining features, p. 306). Gumperz and Fishman have used diglossia to mean 'functionally differentiated' societal bilingualism or multilingualism (Fishman 1968; repr. 1972:136). Although the papers included in this volume seek to propose certain modifications and refinements to the definition of 'Diglossia', they have not made out a case either to change or challenge the original concept.

E. ANNAMALAI (pp. 289-293) draws attention to some typical syntactic differences between spoken and written Tamil. Spoken Tamil unlike written Tamil, drops performatives, makes an extensive use of direct speech and favours the tag type of relative clauses; all these, according to Annamalai, involve less 'syntacticization' or fewer transformations. Annamalai wonders if it is the choice of social styles—informal (oral) vs. formal (written)—that determines such grammatical choices. The differences that Annamalai shows between spoken and written Tamil do not have counterparts in the other literary Dravidian languages like Telugu and Kannada. Telugu uses all the three types of relativization—the tag type, the correlative type and the participial type—in both spoken and written styles for different stylistic and

1. Ferguson himself conducted the seminar on diglossia in three sessions on January 10,1980 during the 2nd ICSALL at Hyderabad. Of the eight papers included in this volume, seven were selected from among those presented at the seminar. Gair's (pp. 322-334) was, however, presented at the 1st ICSALL at the University of Illinois in 1978 and was invited for inclusion in this volume. Although it is not relevant to South Asia, we included 'Diglossia in Africa' by Bruce C. Johnson (pp. 337-349) for its theoretical insights and data from another continent to facilitate comparison with South Asian case material. Professor Johnson was specially invited by Professor Ferguson to participate in the seminar.

rhetoric effects. Could such differences be attributed to Tamil diglossia? Annamalai does not, however, address himself to this problem. But, some of his illustrations of written Tamil have their structure rooted in the classicial format.

SUHAS CHATTERJI (pp. 294-303) says that *Sadhu Bhasa* (SB: Pedantic language) and *Colit Bhasa* (CB: current language) can each be distinguished as High and Low varieties in terms of their function and structure. He maintains that High Colit Bhasa (HCB) which is the widely used literary medium is closer in form to High Sadhu Bhasa than to LSB or LCB. He does not discuss the differences between High and Low Sadhu Bhasa. He seeks to show that Ferguson's defining features of diglossia are applicable to HCB and LCB and not to SB and CB. In Ferguson's classification modern standard Bengali does not qualify for diglossia, since it is based on the educated variety of Calcutta metropolis. The fact that a standard language draws its lexical items from earlier literature does not change its situation. The grammar of Colit standard is distinctly different from that of Sadhu bhasa (see also Edward Dimock 1960). Bengali sociolinguists should reflect on the interesting observations of Suhas Chatterji.

The language situations in Bengali and Telugu are similar in that organized efforts were made by traditionalists to create diglossia by superposing the literary language of the classical poetic genre on to modern prose meant to play extended roles in a changing society. Both Bengali and Telugu earlier had traditions of written varieties, though highly restricted, based on contemporary educated spoken language. Counter movements spearheaded by such stalwarts as Rabindranath Tagore (for Bengali) and Gidugu Ramamurthy (for Telugu) led to the increased use and recognition of modern standard languages based on selected regional varieties (see Krishnamurti 1979). One might naively call them cases of 'defeated diglossia' or 'shortlived diglossia', but they do not qualify Ferguson's definition of diglossia which must be a 'stable language situation' with unbroken tradition and commanding wide acceptance by all segments of the society.

SUGATHPALA DE SILVA's paper (pp. 304-311) seeks to set up a typology of languages having 'diglossia' in terms of the number of Ferguson's eight defining features fully or partly shared by them (p. 305). Tamil and Arabic qualify all the eight; Telugu and Sinhala, according to De Silva, have literary varieties which are (1) divergent, (ii) highly codified, (iii) vehicles of respected body of written literature, (iv) learnt through formal education, (v) not used by any sector for ordinary conversation, but are used only in written literature and not for even some of formal spoken purposes. He then rewords Ferguson's definition (p. 306) to accommodate Sinhala-Telugu-Kannada situations also. He speaks of stable and unstable diglossia, the latter characterizing Telugu and Sinhala, because the instability is a 'consequence of the values attributed to different varieties', to start with. Telugu has 'diminishing diglossia' while Sinhala has developed 'indeterminate diglossia' and Kannada 'ambivalent' diglossia. He further emphasizes the point that what are considered formal roles in one language may not be the same for others. In languages with stable diglossia the 'classical format constituted the undisputed literacy model' (p. 308). 'In unstable diglossic situations... an attitude of ambivalence prevails in the sphere of literacy' (p. 308).

'Correct writing' in Tamil has a classical bias, but only 10% accept the classical norm for correctness in Telugu (p. 309). According to De Silva, 'Telugu Diglossia has changed from an "unstable" diglossia to a "steadily diminishing" one (p. 309), but Sinhalese, 'has not changed to a diminishing one'. He proposes that 'the vernacular' must be the medium of literacy, otherwise it will remain an 'elitist activity' (p. 310). It would be interesting to compare the sharp differences between De Silva's characterisation of Sinhala Diglossia with Gair's (pp. 322-336).

MADHAV DESHPANDE (pp. 312-321) gives an authentic account of Sanskrit-Middle Indic diglossia with profuse quotations from ancient grammarians and commentators to show that Sanskrit stood in the same relation to Prakrit and Apabhraṃśa as Latin to Romance languages (Ferguson 1964:436). Sanskrit apparently evolved as the superposed high variety used for both written and formal spoken roles. He quotes an interesting case where some sages used Sanskrit (H) for religious purposes but spoken Sanskrit (L) and Prakrits at home in informal discourse (p. 315). What was considered 'pure' was based on sociolinguistic criteria which are a product of social history of the speech community (p. 320).

JAMES GAIR (pp. 322-336) states that there is an impressive rate of literacy in Sinhala, i.e., 78.1% (1971 Census) despite 'diglossia'. Between Literary (H) and Colloquial (L) there is Formal Spoken, sharing the lexicon and a few grammatical features of Literary, but is closer to Colloquial in syntax. Formal spoken is intermediate between Ferguson's H & L (p. 324). Gair says that 'some form of Literary Sinhala should be used for any serious written purpose' (p. 326). Some of Ferguson's H functions are accomplished by Formal spoken also.

After reading both De Silva's and Gair's papers, one wonders if the formal spoken and written Sinhala is qualitatively different from the situation of a standard-language-with-dialects, as it happens in English, Bengali and Telugu. In all languages where there is a standard language with dialects, the standard written and spoken varieties do differ from the colloquial of any segment of the population, particularly in lexicon and in morphophonemics. In classical diglossia, there is a considerable number of people who control the use of H, as is the case in Arabic, Greek and Tamil. In the case of Sinhala, as it is with Telugu and Bengali, the intermediate varieties are created by hybridizing H & L (p. 330). The question is whether mere allegiance to H without any segment of population having a complete command of it in writing and speech can be called a stable language situation. Gair further notes that the degree of stability is different between Type I diglossia (where H is an older form of the same language) and Type II (where H is brought from another speech community) owing to different sociocultural and political pressures. He concludes that in 'Sinhala' there is a growing tendency toward strengthening the Literary. De Silva differs from Gair in considering Sinhala 'diglossia' fluid.

Bruce Johnson (pp. 337-349) presents an overview of African diglossia and proposes a typology similar to Gair's based on the source of H. In 'Classical diglossia', H originates in an earlier period; in 'Creole diglossia' H originates in another speech community, and 'L is a creole based on the language of which H is the standard variety' (p. 339). In 'Border diglossia', the recognition of H 'depends on the definition of boundaries between speech communities'. German is H in Swiss German area in a diglossic situation, but it is a standard-with-dialects in Germany (p. 339). Arabic and Geez belong to Type I; Geez was H while Amharic was L, but the situation has changed during the 19th and 20th centuries and it is currently post-diglossic (p. 341). Many cases of Creole diglossia are cited based on European languages as H, viz. English, French, and Portuguese (pp. 341-342). Swahili and Afrikaans are given as cases of 'Border Diglossia'. Hindi could be called a case of 'border diglossia' by Johnson's classification. In States like Bihar and Rajasthan it is a superposed H with Maithili, Magahi, Mewari, etc. as L but in the Western Hindi area where it originated, it is a standard language with dialects. Johnson uses the expression 'triglossia' to denote a language situation involving the functional differentiation of three languages, particularly where the functions of H are split between a superposed Lingua franca and a modern world-language for internal communication (p. 346). In Tanzania, there are 100 vernaculars, Swahili is the Lingua franca (official language, i.e. H) and English is used in higher education and administration (p. 346). By this approach multilingualism of former colonial countries will have to be called 'triglossic', as it is true of South Asia with English sharing some of H functions of a standard language. Johnson predicts a continued spread of triglossia for the emerging African nations (p. 348).

Rodney Moag (pp. 350-370) shows how diglossia differs from bidilectalisms, although both language situations may involve the same language as H. Standard Hindi (SH) is the High variety used for all written and formal spoken purposes in Fiji, where Fiji Hindi is L. In contrast to this situation, in some districts of Eastern Uttar Pradesh in India, the use of standard Hindi does not bear the same relationship to spoken varieties. He enlarges Ferguson's original eight defining features into 13 to 15 distinctive features and arranges them in a matrix. In a diglossic situation these features tend to be what he calls 'digital' (binary, with ± values), whereas in a bidialectal situation they tend to be mostly analog (scalar, or one of degree).

Moag has also taken the linguistic features into account although he rightly realizes 'that pure linguistic differences are reflexes of...socio-linguistic and social differences and not vice versa' (p. 350).

Finally, SCHIFFMAN and AROKIANATHAN (pp. 371-379) have presented their results in a hitherto unexplored area of characterizing how colloquial Tamil, which is distinct from formal spoken Tamil, is represented in written form in film scripts and fiction. Since Tamil is diglossic, a number of factors mediate between a pure literary format and what a fiction writer conceives as the spoken counterpart of the literary form. The factors influencing the 'phoneticization' of forms thought out in a literary format are identified and presented. These produce different degrees of 'phoneti-cization'. The mediating factors influencing such phoneticization between H and L styles are presented in a Figure on p. 379. The factors identified as 'readability', 'generality', 'non-native speech' and 'stereotypicalization' may be relevant to distinguish between spoken and written media even in the case of non-diglossic languages like Telugu, Bengali, Hindi, and perhaps Sinhala.

In the discussion following his paper at Georgetown Round Table in 1962, Ferguson commented (1963; repr. 1971 : 81). 'that the original definition of diglossia was based almost completely on factors outside pure linguistics. That is, they were social factors, or factors of function rather than structure'. Ferguson says that, in a diglossic situation, the H variety is never used in ordinary conversation (Arabic, Greek, Tamil), but in the case of a standard-with-dialects, there may be a substantial number of people who use the standard language even for ordinary conversation (Persian, Italian, Bengali, Telugu, etc.) (p. 82). Standard Hindi in Fiji is apparently never used for conversation, whereas in India, there are places like Delhi where Khaṛi boli is used for ordinary conversation by literate persons. It appears to me that an equally important situation is that in which a variety is only used for written purposes but never for any formal spoken, like literary Sinhala, classical Telugu, and Bengali Sadhu bhasa. This diagnostic feature should exclude them from 'diglossia'. The fact that formal written and spoken are heavily influenced by the literary variety of an earlier era (particularly in the lexicon) should not lead us to class these situations as 'diglossic', because even standard languages with dialects draw on the literary usage of a bygone age to different degrees for stylistic effects. Another diagnostic feature of 'diglossia' is that both H and L varieties are identified as forms of the same language. The extension of 'diglossia' to societal bilingualism where H and L functions are fulfilled by different languages is not so much a refinement as distortion of both the original concept and the term used for it by Ferguson. When he wrote the paper in 1959 Ferguson was familiar with multilingual situations where a colonial language was used for 'certain functions of H' in the Middle East and South Asia (Ferguson 1964: 436). 'Diglossia' is one of the ways a standard language emerges in literate societies, and Ferguson chose this term only for that concept.[2]

REFERENCES

Dimock, Edward C. 1960. 'Literary and colloquial Bengali in modern Bengali prose'. In *Linguistic diversity in South Asia*, ed. by C. A. Ferguson & J. J. Gumperz, pp. 43-63. Bloomington: Indiana University.

Ferguson, C. A. 1959. 'Diglossia', *Word* 15.325-340 (1964: repr. in Dell Hymes, ed. *Language in culture and society*, pp. 429-445. New York: Harper & Row. Also 1971 in *Language structure and language use. Essays by Charles A. Ferguson* (selected and introduced by Anwar S. Dil), pp. 1-26. California: Stanford University Press).

Ferguson, C. A. 1963. 'Problems of teaching languages with diglossia', *Georgetown University Monograph Series on Languages and Linguistics* 15. 165-77. Also 1971, repr. in *Language structure and language use. Essays by Charles Ferguson*, pp. 71-86.

Fishman, Joshua, A. 1968. 'Societal bilingualism: stable and transitional', repr. 1972. *Language in sociocultural change. Essays by Joshua A. Fishman* (selected and introduced by Anwer S. Dil), pp. 135-152. California: Stanford University Press.

Krishnamurti, Bh. 1979. 'Classical or modern—a controversy of styles in education in Telugu'. In *Language movements in India*, ed. by E. Annamalai, pp. 1-29. Mysore: Central Institute of Indian Languages.

2. During his visit to Osmania in 1980, Ferguson said that he was planning a comprehensive volume on 'Diglossia' taking into account the entire sociolinguistic literature which had appeared since the publication of his classic paper in 1959 (personal communication).

PART I
Structure

HINDI *-KAR*: THE PROBLEM OF MULTIPLE SYNTACTIC INTERPRETATION

Alice Davison

In this paper I want to discuss the role of the Hindi conjunctive participle marker *-kar/-kee* in indicating relations between clauses in the syntax of Hindi.* This construction, which has analogues in other Indo-Aryan languages and in the Dravidian languages (cf. Lindholm 1975), is particularly interesting theoretically to linguists interested in stating the systematic relations between form and meaning, because the same syntactic construction expresses three different semantic and pragmatic relations, each of which may also be expressed in syntactically distinct ways in Hindi. For example:

(1) 'Coordinate' relation

a. *baniee- kee beeTee-nee ciTThii likh-kar*
shopkeeper of obl. son-obl. erg. letter write-conj. part.

Daak-mẽẽ Daalii.
postoffice in drop-perf.

'The shop-keeper's son wrote a letter and mailed it at the postoffice'.
(Bailey 1956 : 146)

b. *baniee-nee ciTThii likh lii aur phir beeTee-nee*
shopkeeper obl. erg. letter write take-perf. and then son-obl. erg.

Daak-mẽẽ Daalii.
Post Office-in drop-perf.

'The shopkeeper wrote a letter and his son mailed it at the postoffice'.

(2) 'subordinate' relation

a. *mujhee un-ciizõõ- koo deekh-kar bahut gussaa*
me-Dat. those-obl. things Dat. see conj. part. great anger

aayaa.
come perf.

'When I saw those things, I became very angry'.

'Having seen those things, I became very angry'.

b. *un- ciizõõ-koo deekhnee- par, mujhee bahut*
those-obl. things. obl. Dat. see-inf. obl. on me-Dat. great

gussaa aayaa.
anger come-perf.

'I got very angry when I saw those things'.

*I am very grateful to Rajeshwari Pandharipande for suggesting examples to me and for lending me her intuitions about the sentences discussed in this paper. I would also, like to acknowledge a long-standing debt to Jim Lindholm's work on the Tamil adverbial participle, which has had an influence on my ideas on subordination in general and Hindi *-kar* in particular. Many thanks to Rodney Moag for information and some useful examples.

(3) 'Adverbial' relation

a. *dauR-kee jaaoo varnaa naaraaz hũũgaa.*
run-conj. part. go-imper.fam. or else annoyed be-fut. lpsm.
'Go quickly or I will be annoyed'.

b. *jaldii-see calee jaaoogee too mujhee acchaa*
hurry-with go along-perf. go-fut.2ppl then me-Dat. good

nahīī lageegaa
not strike-fut. 3ps.
'If you leave in a hurry, I won't be pleased'.

The sentences (1)-(3)a, each contain an example of the conjunctive participle in one of its uses, while the sentences (1)-(3)b represent very similar sentences to the (a) versions, where the relations between the constituents are expressed by means of some syntactic construction other than *-kar*. In (1b), the construction is the coordinate linking of finite clauses with the conjunction *aur phir* 'and again', 'and then'. In (2b), it is an infinitive construction with the post-position *-par* 'on' indicating a subordinate time (cause) relation. In (3b), the conjunctive participle of (3a) corresponds to an adverbial formed from a nominal *jaldii* 'haste, hurry' and the instrumental post-position. Of course, sentences (1)-(3)a *could* have other interpretations. (1)-(3)b are not the *only* syntactic patterns which could be substituted, and this is a point which will be taken up later in the paper.

I will discuss three alternative ways of describing the properties of *-kar*, concluding that the first two are unsatisfactory. One position might be called an extreme *syntactically* based position, resting on the assumption that any difference of semantic interpretation reflects a difference of underlying structure, in which syntactic as well as semantic relations are expressed. (I will take up the questions as to whether subordination is a semantic or pragmatic relation, or both.) With these assumptions, it would be necessary to derive the *-kar* surface structures from three distinctly different underlying syntactic/semantic structures, as in the diagrams (4)-(7).

(4) Approximate surface structure

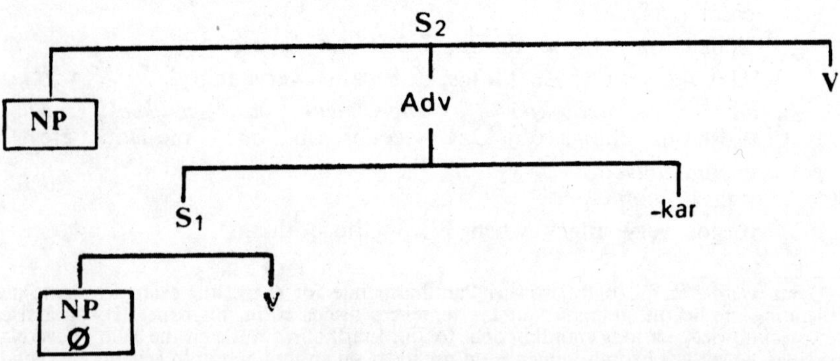

(The boxed NPs are identical in reference. I assume the deleted NP to be in the subordinate clause because the ergative post-position on the subject is expressed if the higher verb belongs to the class of *-nee* transitive verbs.)

(5) Hypothetical underlying structure : coordinate relation

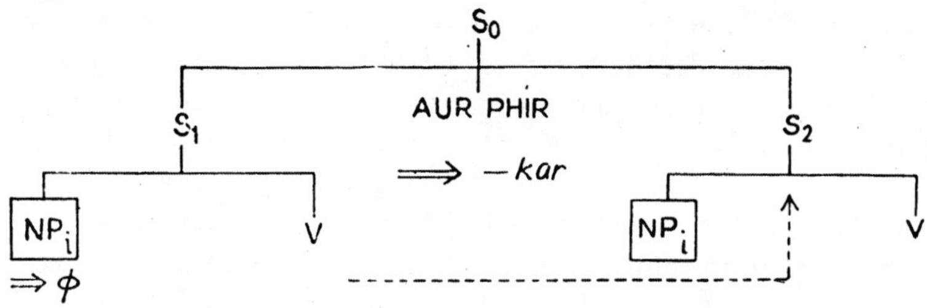

(6) 'Subordinate' relation

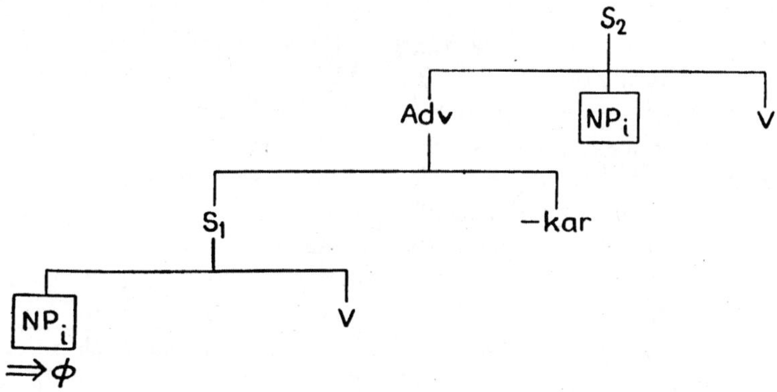

(7) a. 'Adverbial' relation

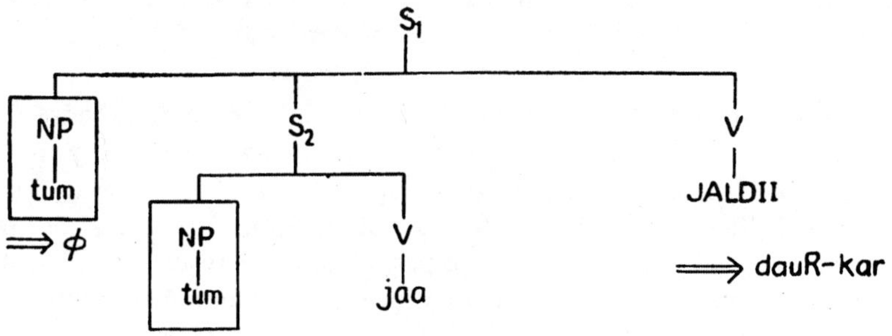

b.

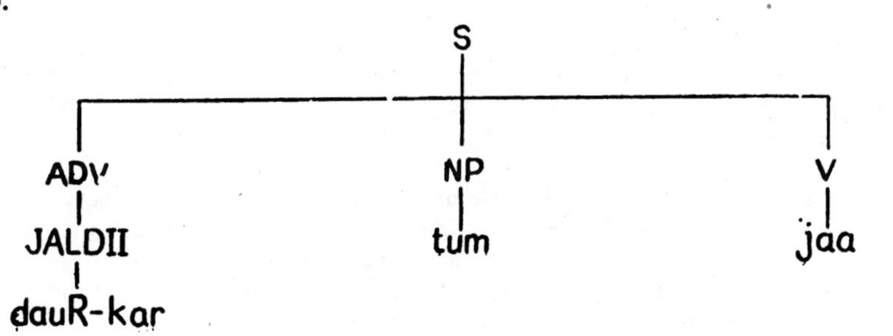

To make this kind of description work, it would be necessary to postulate various transformational operations which turn the underlying structures (5) - (7) into the surface structure (4). In the case of the hypothetical coordinate structure, the first conjunct clause would have to become part of the second clause, with deletion of a coreferential NP. The conjunction would be encoded as the affix *-kar* on the verb of S-. In the case of the subordinate relation, the minimum amount of change would have to take place, assuming that subordinate clause originates in left-most position in the higher clause, the unmarked position for subordinate clauses in SOV languages.[1] Aside from NP deletion in the lower clause, the only transformational operation would be an optional, stylistically related movement rule moving the *-kar* clause to position after the subject of the higher clause. In the case of the adverbial non-clausal structure, there are two possibilities. If we assume that adverbials originate as predicates, in the manner suggested by Lakoff (1971), then the structure (7a) has to be more or less turned inside out, with the lower clause becoming the main clause, and the higher clause getting adjoined with *-kar* and placed in the left-most position. If we assume just some abstract adverb of manner, as in (7b), then this abstract adverb is encoded as a verb stem plus *-kar*. The same encoding will have to take place after the dominance reversal altering (7a).

The transformational operations necessary to sustain these analyses might be possible rules of the Hindi grammar, although most operations proposed as transformations in Hindi simply move constituents—such as Extraposition and Topicalization or Left and Right Dislocation—or change case relations, such as Passive, Raising and Dative Subject Marking. Some deletion by identity rule would also have to apply, though this rule is not particularly controversial, except as to whether the coreferential NPs must be subjects at the initial stage of derivation. This is a question independent of the issues discussed here, however.[2]

While these underlying forms could, in principle, be accommodated in the syntax of Hindi, perhaps requiring the loss of some generality in rule operations, we might wonder if this approach is at all justified. There seems to be little evidence, if any, for such derivations, in spite of the fact that alternative syntactic structures do paraphrase the relations which *-kar* can express. Many sentences with *-kar* have, as I mentioned earlier, two or more interpretations. Sentences like (8) would be syntactically ambigu-

1. This is true without exception for 'strict' SOV languages like Japanese, not so absolute for 'non-strict' SOV languages like Hindi, which allows extraposition of *ki* 'that' complements and permits variation in the position of relative clauses under some conditions.

2. The same range of exceptions occur in both Hindi and Tamil. There is some indeterminacy of case marking in Hindi at least, so that dative experiencer subjects are not distinct in form from dative specific/animate objects. But Tamil also allows the adverbial participle in some cases with datives rather than nominatives. For the purposes of this paper, it is important only that two NPs are coreferential.

ous, and would therefore be derived from two or three different underlying forms:

(8) *us-nee* [*sooc-kar*] *kaam kiyaa*
3 ps. obl. erg. think c. part. work do-perf.
a. 'He/she thought and then did the work'.
b. 'Having thought, he/she did the work'.
c. 'He/she did the work carefully'.

The differences between (8)a, b and c seem to be in how 'prominent' *sooc-kar* appears in relation to the proposition *us-nee kaam kiyaa.* What is important here is that the differences are not ones which can be related to truth conditions. What is described by (8)a or b could be regarded as entailments of (8)c—*thinking* is a precondition of being careful—though one might regard (8)a, b as describing a sequence, and (8)c as two overlapping acts, taking place in the same span of time. One answer to this might be that carefulness expressed by (8)c is a *result* of thinking prior to the event described in the second clause. There need not be any difference of time reference, therefore, between (8)a, b and c. Except for this issue, and the question of pragmatic prominence to be discussed later, the case for real semantic differences among the three readings is not at all convincing. The case for three different underlying syntactic representations is also weak.

Adverbial subordinating conjunctions in many languages may typically be negated or questioned. Leaving aside the problem of negation in connection with-*kar* for a later section, we may note here that in Hindi subordinating conjunctions of time and cause may be in the scope of a yes/no question. That is, the question may have as its object the entire complex sentence, or just the conjunction—was it *after* X happened that Y occurred, was it *because* of X that Y occurred?

(9) *kyaa aap- nee šiilaa-see milnee- kee baad khaanaa*
question you. form. erg. N. with meet-inf. obl. of after food
khaayaa?
eat-perf.
'Did you eat after meeting Shila?'

(10) *kyaa us-nee ghar pahũc-tee hii aap-koo Teelifoon*
question 3ps erg. house arrive-imperf. obl.emph you-dat. telephone
kiyaa?
make-perf.
'Did he call you as soon as he arrived home?'

(11) *kyaa woo vyast hoonee kee kaaraN nahĩĩ aayaa*?
question 3ps. busy be-inf.obl. of-obl. cause not come-perf.
'Did he not come because he was busy?'

The equivalent -*kar* versions are not equivalent, if the scope of the question is the connective, that is, the time sequence :

(12) ?**kyaa aap-nee šiilaa-see mil-kar khaanaa khaayaa*?
meet-conj.p.
'Did you eat after having met Shila?/Did you eat having met Shila?'

(13) ?**kyaa us-nee ghar jaa-kar aap-koo Teelifoon kiyyaa*?
go-conj. part.
'Did he call you after going home?/Did he call you having gone home?'

(14) **kyaa woo vyast hoo-kar nahĩĩ aayaa*?
'Did he not come having been/become busy?'

Likewise, the corresponding assertions (sentence (12)-(14) without *kyaa*) cannot be taken as assertions *about* time and causal sequence.

The hypothetical subordinate structure (6) predicts, incorrectly, that the scope of a question could be the connective alone, or the entire structure, but not the subordinate clause alone. The coordinate structure (5) predicts that the scope of a question would be the entire structure, but not just one of the conjuncts. Neither structure makes the correct predictions about the following sentences, where the import or focus of the question is on the proposition expressed in the subordinate *-kar* clause.

(15) *woo bartan saaf kar-kee hii gaii thii na*?
3ps. pots clean make-conj. part. emph. go-perf. be.past fem not.
'She cleaned the pots before she left, didn't she? (Bailey 1956 : 145)

For (15) I have no real context of utterance, but it is not stretching the imagination to say that the speaker of (15) would not be much concerned with whether someone had left but whether that person had done her job. The higher clause expresses unimportant or redundant information whose communicative function is to express a state or event at a particular reference time—it bears tense/aspect information. The function of *-kar* in these sentences is to express perfectiveness relative to some other reference time, such as a present state or future event.

The hypothetical syntactic derivation of *-kar* which I have sketched has yet another defect, the grave fault of missing generalizations. All cases of *-kar* discussed so far have included clauses in which a NP constituent has been deleted by identity with a NP constituent in the higher matrix sentence. If the syntactic derivations were correct, then it would be simply an unexplained fact as to why, in all three cases, exactly the same condition on NP identity must hold. The underlying structures (5) and (6) require no constituent identity; in principle, the contents of the two conjoined propositions could be entirely unlike. In the case of the adverbial reading, it is less easy to imagine an act done by X which is done in a manner defined by Y's act, but surely it is possible.

The *-kar* equivalents of (1)-(3)a are ungrammatical because the subject NPs are not identical in reference:

(16) **baniyaa ciTThii likh-kar beeTee-nee Daak mẽẽ Daalii.*
'The shopkeeper having written the letter, his son mailed it at the post office'.

(17) **maĩ un-ciizõõ-koo deekh-kar maataa jii-koo bahut kroodh aayaa*
'Because of my seeing those things, mother got very angry'.

(18) **Raam dauR-kar tum jaaoo...*
'Raam having run, you go...

The same meaning can be expressed with coordinate or subordinate conjunctions, but *-kar* cannot be used in these cases without some identity of NP constituents.

Another generalization about *-kar* in all its uses concerns the class of verbs used as aspectual modifiers of a main verb, or as indicators of the speaker's attitude toward the event described (including who the action benefits). These 'conjunct' verbs or 'vector' verbs (cf. Hook 1974) occur with main verbs in coordinate clauses, and with verbs in embedded infinitive or participial constructions (all the following examples are cited from Hook 1974):

(19) Coordinate construction:
kabhii kabhii woo bhay-see kããp uThtii aur pachtaatii.
sometime-sometime 3p. fear-with tremble rise-p. and regret-imperf.
(Hook 1974 : 22)
'From time to time she would start trembling with fear and she regretted (everything)'.

(20) Subordinate participial construction:
kaam kartee kartee ham mar miTee par natiijaa kuch na
work do-imperf. imp. we die be obliterated but result some not
huaa
become-perf.
'We killed ourselves working on it, but there was no result' (Hook 1974:37)

(21) Subordinate infinitive construction:
khiRkii kee baahar sããjh utar aanee par jhõõpRii mẽẽ raat
window of outside evening descend come-inf. on hut in evening
ghiir aatii hai.
come imperf. is (Hook 1974:21)
'When evening descends outside the window, it rushes into the hut'.

These verbs may occur in coordinate structures (19), participial modifiers (20), and subordinate constructions indicating time sequence (21), exactly the three uses of *-kar* and the range of underlying structures from which *-kar* constructions would be derived by the hypothetical syntactic analysis which I am criticising. But *-kar* constructions do not allow conjunct verbs except in a few cases, where the combination has been lexicalized or where essential meaning would be lost if the second element were deleted.[3] The hypothesis that there are three underlying structures which are neutralized and realized as the same surface structure provides no explanation for the fact that conjunct verbs may not appear with *-kar*.

3. R. Pandharipande brought such examples to my attention. Lexicalization is discussed in Hook (1974) and Bhatia (1978).

These derivation are not impossible, of course. If the transformations involved did not delete any conjunct verbs that appear, a surface filter, *V V-*kar*, might apply to all instances of *-kar*. But the conjunct verb restriction, like the facts of negative and a question scope (12)-(16), actually suggest that *-kar* constructions are not exactly *like* any other constructions in Hindi, whether coordinate or subordinate. *-Kar* constructions, though subordinate in form, differ in certain respects from other subordinate constructions. Besides the fact that the conjunction itself cannot be questioned or negated, and the fact that conjunct verbs cannot appear, the complement of *-kar* is not always assumed to be true. *-Kar* clauses can be hypothetical as in

(22) *aisee kar-kee tum kuursii tooR doogee*
so do-conj. part. you chair break give-fut. 2p.fam.
'If you do that, you'll break the chair'/ 'If you do things that way, you'll break the chair.'

That is, one possible interpretation of *-kar* clauses, especially with a future main verb, is that of conditional clauses, and not of '*when*' '*before*' or '*after*' type temporal clauses which strongly implicate that their complements are true.

Such facts suggest that it is wrong in the first place to consider a number of different sources for *-kar* clauses, sources which are based on other constructions which also occur as such, as surface structures in Hindi. An alternative analysis would be to say that *-kar* constructions are derived from a single underlying structure. This structure would be generated by phrase structure rules, and would be identical to the surface structure except that possibly the NP which is deleted in the surface by identity with a main clause NP, is represented. There would then be semantic interpretation rules, two or three of them, which would translate the basic structure (23) into (5), (6) or (7):

(23) Putative single underlying structure:

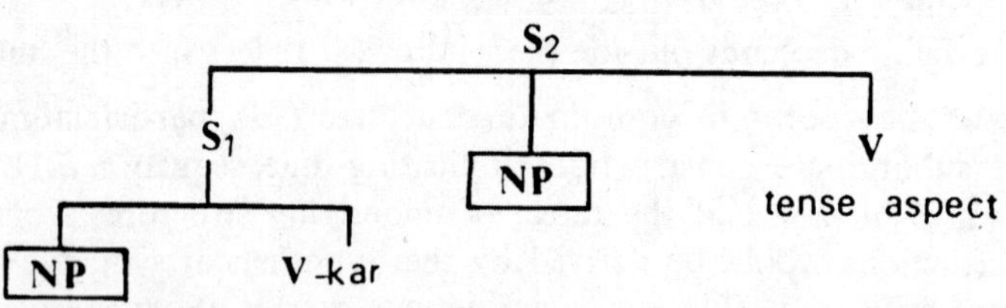

The semantic interpretation rules would be inverses of the transformations needed for the syntactic analysis given earlier. The output of the interpretive rules would be like the input of the transformational rules. Since there is only one underlying structure, the restrictions just discussed would follow automatically for all the interpretations, assuming that the like NP condition and the restriction on conjunct verbs hold for (23) in some way.

The semantic interpretation analysis falls on two counts. First, it provides no way of discriminating among the possible interpretations of *-kar*. It predicts that every *-kar* construction has three possible interpretations, since there is no syntactic or semantic feature apart from *-kar* itself which uniquely marks a subordinate adverbial use as distinct from a manner adverbial use or a coordinate construction. The only criteria for picking out the most likely or most suitable interpretation are world knowledge (i.e. knowledge of what words refer to in general) and knowledge of the context of utterance. These are pragmatic, not syntactic and semantic factors. It is not the case that all *-kar* constructions are semantically three ways ambiguous. The three interpretations actually do not depend on different truth conditions, except possibly in the speaker's perception of whether one single event is referred to (the manner adverbial case) or two closely sequential events, and it is possible to consider this distinction a matter of speaker's beliefs and communicative intentions rather than a difference which can be discriminated by truth conditions.

The second fact about *-kar* which the semantic analysis fails to account for is the indeterminacy of clause relations referred to in the discussion of (14). The semantic analysis would translate the *-kar* sentence into a coordinate structure, where both clauses had equal rhetorical importance, or a subordinate structure, where the main clause had more rhetorical prominence than the subordinate *-kar* clause. This too is a matter of world knowledge, and probably also of knowledge of the context of utterance. The fourth possible interpretation, not predicted by the rules deriving the other three, could probably also be derived by some rule of interpretation, making the structure now four ways ambiguous.

There is a fifth interpretation, an adversitive one which is pretty clearly induced by the presence of negation, and usually also by the presence of the emphatic marker *bhii*:

(24) *tum ustaad hoo-kar bhii yah nahĩĩ jaantee?*
you.f. teacher become-conj part. also this not know-imperf.pl.
'You don't know this even though you are a teacher?' (Bailey 1956:146)

(25. *woo skuul na jaa-kar muuvii gaii.*
she school not go conj.part. movie go-perf.
'She went to the movies instead of going to school'.

This could be described by making up another interpretive rule which is sensitive to negation, or *hii* but not specifically to the presence of *-kar*. As (26) shows, the adversitive interpretation is more general, since it is associated with infinitive *-par* clauses also:

(26) *icchaa na hoonee-par bhii gaanee lagaa.*
desire not become-inf. on also sing-inf. obl. strike-perf.m.s.

'He began to sing although he didn't want to'. (Porizka 1963:343) There is a specific problem about adversitive (or negative) *-kar* sentences, which has to do again with world knowledge and contextual factors, rather than with semantics. Some negative *-kar* sentences are simply ill-formed:

(27) a. *raajaa aa-kar kitaab paRhnee lagaa.*
king come-conj.part. book read-inf.obl. strike-perf.
'Having come, the King began to study the book (Bhatia 1978:142)

b. **raajaa na aa-kar kitaab paRhnee lagaa.*
'Having not come, the King began to study the book' (Ibid:143)

According to Bhatia (1978), (27b) as well as (28b) are ill-formed, while (29b) is well-formed.

(28) a. *woo patra paRh-kar boolaa.*
3ps letter read-conj. speak-perf.
'He spoke after reading the letter'.

b. **woo patra na paRh-kar boolaa.*
'He spoke after not reading the letter'.

(29) a. *woo ghaas khaanee kii jagah pattee khaa rahaa hai.*
3ps. grass eat-inf.obl. of place leaves eat remain is
'He is eating leaves in place of/instead of eating grass.' (Bhatia:159)

b. *woo ghaas na khaa-kar pattee khaa rahaa hai.*
3ps. grass not eat-conj. leaves eat remain is
'Instead of eating grass, he is eating leaves'.

Again the difference between the illformed negative *-kar* clauses (27b,-28b) and the well-formed (29b), seems to be based on world knowledge, rather than grammatical knowledge. In the acceptable cases, it seems that the two clauses express some combination of incompatible but mutually relevant states or events. In the unacceptable cases, it is hard to imagine how the events expressed *could* be incompatible, though perhaps with the right context, I imagine that the unacceptable cases could become acceptable.

The semantic approach has become quite cumbersome and complex in view of all the interpretations it must provide. In any case, it seems that the success of this approach is dependent on extra-grammatical factors such as world knowledge, information that linguists would not want to have to represent in the grammatical description of a language. Let us drop the semantic interpretation rules along with the syntactic transformations, and look at another kind of analysis which makes deliberate use of world and contextual knowledge. I want to propose an analysis which makes use of a certain amount of syntactic and semantic information. This is supposed to state what is common to all the uses of *-kar*, and thus does not explicitly describe differences among them, either transformationally, or semantically. Instead, I will propose that the differences of use can be inferred from the speaker's and hearer's world knowledge, and the context in which the sentence is uttered. It is thus a pragmatically based proposal, which makes use of some grammatical (syntactic and semantic) information combined with principles of conversational inference, such as those described in Grice (1975) according to which conveyed meaning is worked out.

The basic structure I want to propose is the one given in (23), repeated here with more detail:

(30)

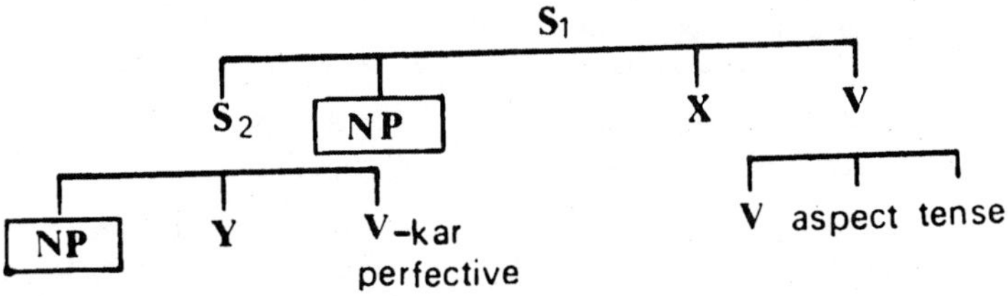

In this analysis, *-kar* is treated as both an affix on the verb which marks perfective aspect and as a clause connective. It therefore resembles the other members of the class of aspect markers which are combined with verb stems, with the stipulation that another clause too must follow. This is like the stipulation associated with the clitic connective *too*. I have considered the construction to be basically a subordinating one, because of the like NP condition which requires that some constituent of the -kar *clause* be identical to another NP constituent of the higher other clause (these are usually subjects). But it is obligatory for one of these NPs to be deleted. Since the NP which remains takes the case role determined by the tense-bearing verb (-absolutive, *-nee* ergative or *-koo* dative) for its subject, I conclude that it is the lower subject which is deleted. Another transformational rule optionally moves the *-kar* constituent to a position following the subject NP. The derived structure is thus:

(31)

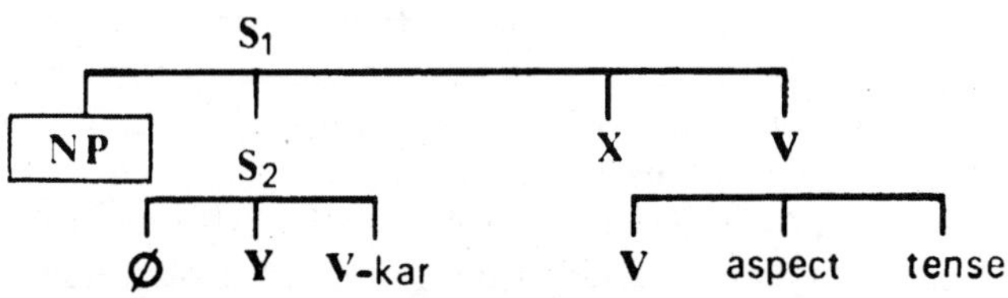

On the basis of patterns observed in many other languages, I am making the assumption that among the *syntactic* markers of subordination are (1) that deletion of constituents occurs in a subordinate clause by identity with other constituents, particularly if the deleted element precedes its antecedent', and (2) that a subordinate construction may be wholly contained within a superordinate constituent. These two criteria are met in this case.

I would now like to discuss the features of (30) and (31) in relation to the properties of *-kar* constructions which were not accounted for in a general way by the other two hypothetical analyses. First, the *-kar* clause is not part of an adverbial constituent (cf. (6)). Its constituent structure would therefore differ from the structures where temporal and causal conjunctions are possible. These conjunctions can be asserted, negated and questioned *per se*, while *-kar* cannot.

Second, the semantic content of *-kar* is 'perfective', that is, is a single very general, aspectual meaning, rather than some collection of aspectual, temporal, causal, conditional or manner advervial meanings. That *-kar* does express perfective aspect can be seen indirectly, in sentences where V V combinations are seen as being derived from V-*kar* V underlying combinations, In positive sentences (see discussion in Hook 1974:104-108). (32)a, b are more or less synonymous, while (33) a and b are nearly equivalent, differing in a way which will be discussed shortly.

(32) a. *pulis-nee coorõõ-koo aa pakRaa.*
police-erg. thieves-obl. dat. come seize-perf.

'The police nabbed the crooks'. (Hook 1974: 52)

b. *pulis-nee coorõõ-koo aa-kar pakaR liyaa.* (*ibid*)
come-conj. seize take-perf.

(33) a. *us-nee apnee pati koo saraabii banaa chooRaa thaa.*
3ps obl. erg. reflex. husband-dat. drunkard make abandon-perf. be-past.

'She irresponsibly /recklessly turned her husband into a drunkard'. (Hook 1974:106)

b. *us-nee apnee pati-koo saraabii banaa-kar chooR diyaa thaa.* (*Ibid*)
make-conj. part. abandon give-perf. be-past

'She made her husband into a drunkard and then left him'.

A '*-kar* deletion' transformation is proposed by Bahl (1964) to derive sentences like (32a) from (33b), more or less preserving meaning (that is, if we assume that the 'beneficiary' information conveyed by *leenaa* 'take' is redundant in cases like these). One of Bahl's conditions is the presence of perfective aspect in the second clause verb phrase. This condition reflects his observation that the deletion of *-kar* and the main verb's 'vector' verbs occurs in the presence of perfective aspect.[4]

If the *meaning* of *-kar* is 'perfective', then its deletion with a perfective main verb is just a case of deletion of redundant information—in a subordinate clause. Furthermore, the application of *-kar* deletion results in the compacting of the bi-clausal sentence into a derived surface structure which resembles a single main clause structure with a vector verb modifying the proposition. This structure exactly fits the interpretation of (33b) in contrast to (33a). In (33b) *chooR* 'abandon' is a modifier, conveying that the act of making the husband a drunkard constitutes abandonment of him, as a reckless or irresponsible action. In (33a) the presence of *-kar* separates

4. Hook (1978) notes a number of parallels between the syntactic behavior of conjunct sequences (*-kar* AD) and compound verbs (p. 103). But in his discussion of Bahl's rule (195) he notes the connection between *-kar* deletion and perfective aspect while disclaiming any proposal which explains the connection.

the two verbs, just as the two events of first driving the husband to drink and then abandoning him are perceived as separate. This distinction actually parallels the distinction discussed earlier between the 'coordinate' reading and the 'manner adverbial' reading, though here it is the second verb rather than the first which has been perceived as a modifier. I would like to suggest that in both cases, a difference of this sort is inferred, and not directly conveyed. Note that (32a, b) are perceived as synonymous, from which we may conclude that the difference of form does not necessarily indicate a difference of sense. It does so in (33a, b) because we can more easily imagine separate events than for (32). This sort of inference is related to the coordinate-subordinate distinction discussed earlier, and to the perception of the syntactically subordinate *-kar* clause as being the 'main' clause rhetorically. That is, in all these cases, it is the prominence of the clause in discourse (as determined by context and world knowledge) which pragmatically determines the inferences from the basic structure (32). (In fact, many criteria for defining subordinate constructions are actually pragmatic; eg. it 'expresses a less important idea' as summarized in Davison (1979).)

The representation of *-kar* need not include temporal and causal information. The sequence of clauses gives information about the sequence and relation of the events or states referred to (as Grice pointed out (1975) and has been observed in many languages). The simple conjunction of two clauses invites very strongly the inference that the conjunction indicates relatedness and the order of utterance indicates the sequence of things referred to. This inference, combined with the perfective aspectual meaning and the tense-aspect information on the main verb is enough, to account for the range of temporal and causal (including conditional) relations which *-kar* may express,

'Relatedness' in time seems, however, to be more loosely construed for coordinate and other conjunctions than it is for *-kar*. In (34a) a sequence of events is described which cannot also be expressed with a *-kar* construction (34b):

(34) a. *mistrii* *aaj* *sanduuq* *banaaeegaa* *aur* *kal* *lee*
carpenter today box make-future and tomorrow take
aaeegaa.
come-future

'The carpenter will make the box today and bring it tomorrow'
(Bailey 1956:141).

b. **mistrii aaj sanduuq banaa-kar kal lee aaeegaa*

I do not know whether the difference between *aaj* and *kal* in time is what makes (34b) unacceptable, or if it is the independent modification of the subordinate clause with a time adverbial. Both these factors seem not to make any difference in (35) and (36a) (suggested by R. Pandharipande):

(35) *aaj* *aisee* *kaam* *kar-kee* *woo* *kal* *pachtaaeegaa.*
today this way work do-conj.prt. 3ps in future regret-future 3ps.

'If he does his work that way today, he will regret it in the future'.

(36) a. *aaj ham sTaak khariid-kar tiin saal kee baad beec*
today we stocks buy-conj.prt. three years of after sell
dẽẽgee.
give-fut

'Today we bought stocks to sell in three years'.

b. *pichleee saal ham sTaak khariid-kar tiin saal kee baad beec dẽẽgee.*
last year we stocks buy-conj.part. three years of aftersell give-fut.

'Last year we bought stocks to sell after three years'.

It is possible that proximity of time referred to the time of speaking is the crucial factor. In both (34a) and (36b), the temporal reference of the first clause is not the time of speaking.

To return to the theoretical problem posed at the beginning of the paper, we can say that to explain how it is that a construction can appear to be both coordinate and subordinate at the same time, it is necessary to reexamine what kinds of criteria we use to define subordination. By strictly syntactic criteria, the *-kar* constructions of all sorts are subordinate, though not identical to adverbial subordinate constructions which have similar discourse function. The other criteria were semantic—that is scope information relating to negation and questions, or pragmatic, relating to prominence in discourse, perceptions on the part of the speaker and hearer which are dependent of world knowledge and context of utterance. In this analysis, I have separated a syntactic and semantic core representation from all the conveyed meanings and discourse functions that sentences containing *-kar* may have. I propose that the latter may be calculated from the former, by the use of Grice's conversational principles, which do not have to be stated as part of any grammar, as they are very general and govern more activities than just speaking. But in particular, Gricean inferences may be inferences from the form that an utterance has, so that it is important to recognize that word order and other features are iconic (in Jim Lindholm's term), and while they convey meaning, the conveyed meanings are not necessarily what these grammatical features actually mean.

REFERENCES

Bahl, K.C. 1964. *A study in the transformational analysis of the Hindi verb.* U. of Chicago: South Asian Language and Area Center.

Bailey, T. Grahame. 1963. *Urdu.* London: English Universities Press.

Bhatia, T.K. 1978. A syntactic and semantic description of negation in South Asian languages. U. of Illinois dissertation.

Davison, A. 1979. Some mysteries of subordination. *Studies in the Linguistic Sciences* 9:1. 105-28.

Grice, H.P. 1975. Logic and conversation. In *Syntax and Semantics,* Vol. 3, Speech Acts ed. by P. Cole and J.L. Morgan. New York: Academic Press. 41-58.

Hook, P. 1974. *The compound verb in Hindi.* Michigan Series in South and Southeast Asian Languages and Linguistics, no. 1.

Lakoff, G. 1971. *Irregularity in Syntax.* New York : Holt Rinehart

Porizka, V. 1963. *Hindiustina, Hindi Language Course.* Prague: Státnī pedagogické nakladatelství.

Schmerling, S. 1975. Asymmetric conjunction and rules of conversion. In *Syntax and Semantics* Vol. 3, Speech acts. 211-31. ed. by P. Cole and J. L. Morgan, New York: Academic Press.

"*P*-ORIENTED" CONSTRUCTIONS IN SANSKRIT

Hans Henrich Hock

Recently there has been a revival of interest in Sanskrit diachronic syntax, especially as it relates to the "*P*-oriented"[1] antecedents for the Modern Indo-Aryan ergative constructions. This paper tries to critically evaluate recent claims—and to come to a better understanding of the developments affecting these constructions in Sanskrit. My findings are still somewhat tentative, since outside the Ṛg Veda and Atharva-Veda, the only texts I have been able to work through are the Taittirīya Saṃhitā and much of the Śatapathabrāhmaṇa. For other texts I had to rely on the evidently incomplete data in Delbrück 1888 and Oertel 1929, 1939.

The Sanskrit constructions which I will be concerned with are preliminarily exemplified in (A), (B), and (C) below. The three constructions share the fact that with transitive verbs they show agreement between the verb and the underlying object or patient (*P*), which appears in the nominative case, while the underlying subject or agent (*A*) is demoted to instrumental.

(A) Passive:	*devadattena*	*kaṭaḥ*	*kriyate* /	*kaṭāḥ*	*kriyante*
	sg.I	sg.N	sg.3	pl.N	pl.3
	'by Devadatta a mat is made / mats are made'				
(B) *ta*-pple.:	*devadattena*	*kaṭaḥ*	*kṛtaḥ* /	*kaṭāḥ*	*kṛtāḥ*
	sg.I	sg.N	sg.N	pl.N	pl.N
	'by D. a mat has been made / mats have been made'				
(C) Gerundive:	*devadattena*	*kaṭaḥ*	*kartavyaḥ* /	*kaṭāḥ*	*kartavyāḥ*
	sg.I	sg.N	sg.N	pl.N	pl.N
	'by D. a mat is / mats are to be made'				

---

*Research on this paper has been in part supported by 1978-80 grants from the University of Illinois Research Board. I also gratefully acknowledge the support from the University of Illinois Traveling Scholars Fund, The National Endowment for the Humanities (through the American Council of Learned Societies), and the Smithsonian Institution (through the American Institute of Indian Studies) for attending the Conference in Hyderabad. Finally, I am especially grateful to William Wallace, my research assistant, for his help in collecting Ṛg Vedic data, and to George Cardona, Myriam Klaiman, Rocky Miranda, and S.N. Sridhar for stimulating and challenging comments on the various versions of this paper. Needless to state, the responsibility for any errors and omissions in this paper remains mine entirely.

1. For a definition of this term, cf. Comrie (1978). As will be seen from the subsequent discussion, although the term is accurate for the early Vedic period, in late Vedic and Classical Sanskrit it is not entirely accurate. For convenience's sake, however, I continue using the term for this later period also.

In traditional western literature all three types are referred to as passive, with type (B) often called a perfect or past passive participle. Two recent generative accounts (Pray 1976, Anderson 1977) are no exceptions. Not all traditional scholars, however, have accepted this view. Debrunner (1954) points out that in origin at least, type (B) seems to be neither specifically passive, nor past-tense, nor even participial: Unlike other participles, which are formed from specific tense stems (such as the perfect participles in (1a) and (b) below), the *ta*-participle is made directly from the root or general verb stem. It can have not only past, but also present value. It has a passive-like quality only for transitives, not for intransitives. Even this distinction is not absolute, however, for as (1c) shows, some transitive *ta*-participles can have both *P*- and *A*-orientation. Finally, while the other participles have voice distinctions (cf. the active/medio-passive distinction in the perfect participles of (1b)), there is no such contrast in the *ta*-participles.

(1) a. *bhū-taḥ* 'having been, being' (vs. perf. *ba-bhū-vas-*)
b. *kṛ-taḥ* '(having been) done' (vs. perf. mid.-pass. *ca-kr-āṇaḥ* act. *ca-kṛ-vas-*)
c. *pī-taḥ* 'having (been) drunk), *bhuk-taḥ* 'having (been) eaten' *drug-dhaḥ* 'harming 'vs. *akṣa-drug-dhaḥ* 'harmed by the dice'

As suggested by Klaiman (1978) as well, evidence like this shows that Anderson's (1977) view according to which the modern ergative reflects a Sanskrit use of the *ta*-participle as a perfective (or periphrastic) passive must be considered dubious. Pray's (1976) "passive" starting point for the modern ergative is subject to the same reservations. However, his contribution does raise certain issues which are of interest, namely the fact that in [Classical] Sanskrit, "*P*-oriented" constructions do not exhibit any constituent movement (as compared to their active counterparts) and the agents, not the surface subjects, of these constructions control absolutive formation. As will be seen later, these are in fact valid generalizations for late Vedic and Classical Sanskrit. However, they do not yet hold for the early language of the mantras and yajus. Rather than providing part of the explanation for the development of the modern ergative, they themselves are in need of an explanation.

A very different approach is taken by Klaiman (1978). She starts out by accepting the traditional definition of ergativity, as codified by Dixon,[2] as obtaining in systems which mark the patients of transitives the same way as the subjects of intransitives. According to this definition, the *ta*-participle is an ergative construction. since it marks transitive patients and intransitive subjects identically, as nominatives; cf. (B1) below beside (B) above.

2. Since then published as Dixon (1979).

(B1) *ta*-pple. (itr.): *devadatto rājā bhūtaḥ / te rājāno bhūtāḥ*
sg.N (sg.N) sg.N pl.N (pl.N) pl.N
masc. masc. masc. masc.
'D. has been/become a king / they have been/become kings'

The passive and the gerundive, however, do not meet this definition, since here transitive agent and intransitive subject are marked alike, as instrumentals (cf. (A1) and (C1) beside (A) and (C)).

(A1) Passive (itr.): *devadattena rājñā bhūyate / tai rājabhir bhūyate*
sg. I (sg.I) sg.3 pl.I (pl.I) sg.3
masc. masc.
'king-being is going on, with D. / them as agent(s)'

(C1) Gerundive (itr.): *devadattena rājñā bhavitavyam / tai rājabhir bhavitavyam*
sg.I (sg.I) sg.N pl.I (pl.I) sg.N
masc. neut. masc. neut.
'D./ they should be king(s)'

Klaiman further claims that the ergative *ta*-participle, as well as the gerundive, predate the finite passive, and that the latter is an innovation, modeled off on the other two constructions to round out the system of passive-like constructions.

A final question tackled by Klaiman without coming to definite conclusions, is why the *ta*-participle eventually replaced the finite past tense in late Sanskrit, Middle Indo-Aryan, and Modern Indo-Aryan[3] (where it results in the so-called ergative past), and why it did so at the expense of the "active" type in *-tavant-*. She tentatively concludes that the reason lies in the fact that the *tavant*-participle had to be derived by means of the possessive suffix *-vant-* from an already productive *ta*-participle. The very productivity of the latter prevented the *tavant*-type from successfully competing with it.

(D) *tavant*-pple.: *devadattaḥ kaṭaṃ kṛtavān*
sg.Nmasc. sg.A sg.Nmasc.
'D. has made a mat'

This last conclusion perhaps has some merit, although other factors may have played a more important role. The most crucial of these may well be the one suggested below, namely the general convergent behavior of the Sanskrit "*P*-oriented" constructions. Klaiman is certainly correct, however, in pointing out that the *ta*-participle is ergative, not passive, and has been that way since Proto-Indo-European times. She is also on the right track when she suggests convergent behaviour for our constructions by claiming that the passive was modeled off on the other two "*P*-oriented" constructions. However, the specific claim that the passive is an innovation

3. Except for a few isolated dialectal relics, mainly in the verb 'to be',

is not supported by the data. Her other conclusions likewise require modification and further discussion.

Let me begin this discussion with a brief summary of the features which characterize—and differentiate—the three constructions under discussion[3a]:

(3)	Passive (A) trans.	Passive (A) intr.	*ta*-pple. (B) trans.	*ta*-pple. (B) intrans.	Gerundive (C) trans.	Gerundive (C) intrans.
(a) Inherited from PIE ?	√ (as category)		√		?	
(b) *P*-promotion?	√		√	No	√	No
A-demotion?	√	(√)	√	No/(√)	√	(√)
(c) Contrasting active?	√		No		No	
(d) Finite?	√		No		No	
(e) Agent:	Instr.		Instr. Gen.		Instr. Gen. Dat.	

The evidence and arguments in support of the feature chart in (2) are as follows:

(a) Contrary to Klaiman, the passive is not an innovation, but it is inherited as category from Proto-Indo-European. The only innovation is the development of a morphological distinction between middle voice and passive. This development, however, is not limited to the present, but is found also in the imperfect (built on the present stem) and in the third singular aorist. Elsewhere, middle voice forms continue to serve also as passives. In the early Vedic language, even present, imperfect, and third singular aorist passives frequently are still expressed through middle-voice forms, as in RV 9.38.3 *yābhir... śúmbhate* 'by whom he is made beautiful'. Also the *ta*-participle is inherited from Proto-Indo-European. In the case of the gerundive, however, it is not quite clear whether it is of Proto-Indo-European origin. For the gerundives of Greek and Latin do not morphologically match the earliest gerundives of Sanskrit (and Indo-Iranian in general). Thus, while we can reconstruct a medio-passive and a *to*-participle on both morphosyntactic and phonological grounds, this is not possible for the gerundive. At the same time, however, the gerundive is firmly established as a category, even in early Vedic.

(b) As far as grammatical relations are concerned, all three types share *P*-orientation in early Vedic, i.e., the appearance of transitive patients as surface subjects. In intransitive constructions, however, there is a difference, and that difference is different from what Klaiman observed by looking only at the later language: Passives are barred from intransitives, i.e., there is as yet no demotional passive of the type (A1). On the other hand, not only do the *ta*-participles here show active, non-demotional constructions,

3a. Parenthesized check-marks in (5) indicate later Sanskrit innovations.

also the gerundives do; cf. RV 1.89.10 *áditir jātám áditir jánitvam* 'Aditi is the born, Aditi is that which is [yet] to be born'.[4] That is, by the usual definition of ergativity, both the *ta*-participle and the gerundive are ergative at this stage. The only difference between these two is pragmatic: Unlike the *ta*-participles, intransitive gerundives are exceedingly rare (11 out of a total of 275 Ṛg Vedic gerundive attestations) and are confined to just two roots (*bhū*- 'be, become' and *jan*- 'be born'). Agent[5]-demoting passives and gerundives from intransitives are an innovation of Vedic prose, with agent demotion obligatory for the passive and the most productive gerundive subtype, that in *-tavya-*. It is this stage of the language which Klaiman's description fits, and it is only at this stage that the *ta*-participle is the sole ergative constructio —given the definition of ergativity which she accepts.

(c) Given a different and, to my mind, preferable definition, the gerundive is ergative also at this later stage. This definition has been advocated by Comrie and characterizes ergativity as "passive" morphology and /or syntax without the existence of a corresponding and more basic "active". In fact, since the *tavya*-gerundive at this stage is obligatorily "passive", even in the intransitives, it can be considered "more" ergative than the *ta*-participle, which is obligatorily "passive" only for transitives. Only the passive has a corresponding, more "basic" active. Thus, (3) below is the active corresponding to (A).

(3) *devadattaḥ kaṭaṃ karoti / devadattaḥ kaṭān karoti*
sg.N sg.A sg.3 sg.N pl.A sg.3
'D. makes a mat / mats'

On the other hand, all three past tenses have their own active/passive distinctions which do not involve the *ta*-participle; cf. (4). And the formations coming closest in value to the gerundive—but without being fully identical with it—, namely the optative, imperative, and future, likewise have their own active/passive distinctions which do not involve the gerundive; cf. (5).

(4)	impf.	*devadattaḥ kaṭam akarot*	:	*devadattena kaṭo 'kriyata*
	aor.	*devadattaḥ kaṭam akaḥ*	:	*devadattena kaṭo 'kāri*
	perf.	*devadattaḥ kaṭaṃ cakāra*	:	*devadattena kaṭaś cakre*
(5)	opt.	*devadattaḥ kaṭaṃ kuryāt*	:	*devadattena kaṭaḥ kriyeta*
	impe.	*devadattaḥ kaṭaṃ karotu*	:	*devadattena kaṭah kriyatām*
	fut.	*devadattaḥ kaṭaṃ kariṣyati*	:	*devadattena kaṭaḥ kariṣyate*

The *ta*-participle and the gerundive further agree on not being finite, as well as on permitting—beside the instrumental—the genitive as case for the agent. In the early language, the gerundive also permits the dative:

(B2) Gen. *púruhūta jánānām* (RV 9.52.4) 'O much-praised-one by the people'

4. Note that the verb 'to be born' is intransitive, not passive in Sanskrit.

5. From now on, I will follow Sanskrit grammatical tradition by using the term agent for the underlying subjects of both transitives and intransitives.

(C2) Gen. *mánor yajñīyas* (RV 10.36.10) 'to be worshiped by Manu'

(C3) Dat. *sákhā sákhibhya íḍyaḥ* (RV 9.66.1) 'a friend to be invoked by friends'

There is here, then, at least potentially a clear distinction between all three formations. Over the long run, however, we can observe a convergence in the behaviour of the three categories. First, the gerundive loses its dative agent marking by the time of Vedic prose. At this stage, the figures in Oertel (1939) suggest a certain increase in popularity for the genitive agent; but these figures seem to be highly inflated. Moreover, in the new, productive use of the *ta*-participle and the gerundive as main verbs (i.e., as the equivalent of finite verbs), instrumental agents clearly predominate. (In the gerundives, the ratio of genitive to instrumental agents in such main-verb constructions is 6 : 40.) Pāṇini accords only marginal status to the genitive agent (cf. sūtra 2.3.69 vs. 2.3.67). In Classical Sanskrit and Middle Indo-Aryan, finally, genitive agents are exceedingly rare. (Thus, in a sample of the Vetālapañcaviṃśati, I found a ratio of 3 genitives vs. 73 instrumentals). That is, the pattern of the passive, with its exclusive use of the instrumental as agent marker, has in effect been generalized also to the *ta*-participle and the gerundive.

Also in other respects an increasing convergence between some or all of these formations can be observed.

Thus both the passive and the gerundive in Vedic prose develop a variant with *A*-demotion even for intransitives:[6]

(6) Type (A1): *mithunena caryate* (ŚB 1.9.2.8) 'a copulation takes place'
sg.I sg.3 (lit, 'it is gone by a copulation')
Similarly ŚB 4.6.7.9,10; TS 1.7.6.4; JB 128

Type (C1): *paśúvratena bhavitavyam* (MS 1.8.7) 'one should be cattle-like'
sg.I sg.N neut.
Similarly ŚB 7.1.2.11, 9.5.1.62, etc. Altogether 24x

It should be noted that these 'impersonal' constructions at this stage are much more commonly attested for the gerundives than for the passives, suggesting that the gerundives provided the starting point for this innovation.[7] If this conclusion is correct, then we must assume that *A*-demotion in the passives is the result of secondary generalization.

The increasing use of the *ta*-participle and gerundive as main verbs, which can be observed in Vedic prose and especially in the later language,

---

6. Also the *ta*-participle develops such a variant. However, compared to the inheirted, non-demoting and "active" type (B1), this variant remains rare and marked. It will therefore be ignored in this paper.

7. Although the details of this development are not entirely clear, one may speculate that *A*-demotion arose in the gerundives in conjunction with the development of the new and productive formation in *-tavya-*. Perhaps the noted rarity of intransitive gerundives in the early language was another factor in this change.

may be considered a case of convergence in syntactic behavior between these non-finite formations and the finite passive. Perhaps this is the major reason that out of a plethora of participial formations (also including active, middle, and passive present participles and active and medio-passive aorist, perfect, and future participles), all of which could occasionally be used in main-verb function in the early language, the "*P*-oriented" *ta*-participle and gerundive were singled out for generalization as main verbs. This may also explain why the *ta*-participle, with *P*-orientation for transitives and thus agreeing with the passive, ultimately ousted the *A*-oriented *tavant*-participle. This is not to deny the possible presence of other factors. Thus in the case of the gerundive, the lack of any finite formation fully corresponding to it in function may have been a strong motivation. In this respect, it is interesting to note that Oertel's (1939) data for Vedic prose show a higher ratio of main-verb uses for the gerundive than for the *ta*-participle, suggesting that the former is in the vanguard of the development.[8] For the *ta*-participle, a further motivation may have lain in the diglossic situation between Sanskrit and early Middle Indo-Aryan. These two dialect continua showed quite divergent developments in the finite past-tense formations: Sanskrit tended to lose the category of aorist and to use perfect and imperfect interchangeably, while Middle Indo-Aryan was in the process of losing its perfect and of merging aorist and imperfect into a single, new category. This formal differentiation, one may speculate, proved too excessive within the diglossic super-system and therefore was alleviated by the increasing use of the one *shared* past-tense formation, the *ta*-participle.

Convergent behaviour can also be seen in the following change. While in early Vedic the surface subject normally occurs as the first constituent in "*P*-oriented" constructions, the later language shows the underlying *agent* in that position. Compare (7) vs. (8)

(7) *eṣá devó vipanyúbhiḥ ... mṛjyate* (RV 9.3.3)
S A V

'this god is being groomed by the praisers'

sákhā sákhibhya ī́ḍyaḥ (RV 9.66.1) 'the friend is to be invoked by friends'
S A V

(8) *devadattena kaṭaḥ kriyate* (cf. act. *devadattaḥ kaṭaṃ karoti*)
A S V A (=S) O V

That is, in the later language the agents of "*P*-oriented" constructions are treated exactly like the subjects/agents of active constructions; the notion subject has been replaced by the notion agent.

A parallel development has taken place as far as the normal control of absolutive constructions is concerned. Although the evidence for the early

8. The ratio is 7 : 1 for gerundives vs. 1 : 5 for the *ta*-participles. Note however that since *ta*-participles are used more frequently, the actual number of main-verb uses (100 out of a total of 604) is slightly higher for the *ta*-participles than for the gerundives (with 84 out of a total of 95).

language of the mantras and yajus is limited for absolutive constructions controlled by a "*P*-oriented" higher clause, all the examples which I have been able to find show identity between the surface *subject* of the higher clause and the subject of the absolutive; cf., for instance (9)

(9) *sarváṃ parigŕ̥hya sūyā íti*
Abs. Pass.

(ŚB 5.2.3.1 (2x); yajus; recurs, partly with different objects of *pari-grah-*, at 5.2.3.6, 8; 5.2.4.1 (2x), 4; 5.2.5.14 (2x).)

'having encompassed the all, may I be consecrated'

In Vedic prose, however, it is the *agent* of the higher clause which normally controls absolutives, even if that agent is generic and unspecified:

(10) Type (A): *ná vā́ áhiṅkṛtya sāma gīyate* (ŚB 1.4.1.1)
(neg.)Abs. S Pass.
'the sāman is not sung without [one's] making the sound *hiṅ*'
Similarly ŚB 14.8.1.1, etc; altogether 6x.

Type (B): *(u)petya pṛṣṭhāny upetya chandomān mahāvratam asyopetaṃ bhavati*
Abs. Abs. S *ta*-pple.
(JB 2.309) 'having undertaken the pṛṣṭhas, having undertaken the chandomas, the mahāvrata is undertaken by him'
No other examples

Type (C): *hiraṇyaṃ suvarṇam upāsyā 'gnir ādheyaḥ* (MS 1.6.4)
Abs. S Ger.
'having thrown a piece of pure gold on (it), the fire should be replenished'
Similarly TB 1.4.3.4.5; altogether 31x.

And this holds true also for Pāṇini (cf. his sūtra 3.4.21), as well as the later, Classical language. In fact, it is probably this change from subject-oriented to agent-oriented syntax which is in large part responsible for the fact that Pāṇini's grammar does not employ the notion of subject, but only that of agent.

It may be noted that at all stages, Sanskrit can also have various other constituents as controllers of absolutive formation (cf. (11) below). However, such constructions are rare deviations from the (subject-oriented or, later, agent-oriented) norm.

(11) *strīyaṃ dṛṣṭvāya kitaváṃ tatāp(a)* (RV 10.34.11)
Abs. O act. V
'seeing his wife, it burns the gambler'

The majority of other apparent deviations in the later language, such as (12), where the subject (*sa*) of the absolutive (*upakrīya*) is the subject, not the agent of the main verb (*avalokitaḥ*), can be explained by bracketing: Here the immediately higher, controlling "clause" is *A*-oriented *gacchan* (pres. act. pple.) 'going', not the *P*-oriented *avalokitaḥ* 'was seen'. (13) shows that bracketing also applies in cases where the higher clause is *P*-oriented: The subject of *ānīya* 'having carried off' is the agent (*śyena-* 'hawk') not the subject (*sarpa-* 'snake') of the passive present participle *khādyamāna-* 'being eaten'.

(12) *sa yajñārthe...chāgam upakrīya...gacchan dhūrtatrayeṇāvalokitaḥ* (Hitopadeśa 43.5-6) 'he, having bought a goat for the purpose of sacrifice ..., (as he was) going was noticed by a trio of rogues'

(13) *ity eva kāle śyenenānīya khādyamānasya sarpasya garalam taddravye nipatitam* (Vetālapañcaviṃśati 76.11-13)
'at that very time, the venom of a snake being eaten by a hawk, after having carried it off, fell into his food'

There remain a few occasional exceptions in the later language where there appears to be genuine control by the surface subject of a "*P*-oriented" construction (cf. (14)). However, in virtually all cases the "*P*-oriented" verbs of such constructions are USED as existential verbs or copula, i.e. the SEMANTIC equivalents of the verb 'to be'. That is, semantic, rather than purely formal-syntactic factors seem to govern absolutive control. Genuine exceptions like (15) are exceedingly rare.

(14) *tadā rākṣasī nijakāntayā saha ramamāṇam ālokya prakupya tatraiva*
S ... Abs. Abs.
bhramarī bhūtvā puṣpaghrāṇasya vyājena vidyate (Vetāla. 136.3-5)
Abs. ... Pass.
'then the ogress, seeing him dallying with his own wife, becoming angry, immediately becoming a bee, is found=IS as if drawn by the smell of a blossom'

(15) *kṛtvā api na nibadhyate* (Bhagavadgītā 4:22b)
Abs. Pass.
'though acting, he is not tied down'

What remains to be explained is how this development from subject-oriented to agent-oriented syntax came about. Perhaps the following speculation may provide an answer.[9]

In Vedic prose it is above all the gerundives which are attested with agent control over absolute formation (cf. the statistics in (9) above). And as noted above, at this stage the gerundives are more advanced along the road to main-verb status than are the *ta*-participles. Moreover, it is the gerundives which most lack a functionally corresponding active and/or finite counterpart. (Recall that none of the active formations of (5) fully corresponds to the functions of the gerundive.) It is therefore the gerundives which

9. Timberlake (1976) notes similar changes from subject-oriented to agent-oriented syntax in Northern Russian dialects. However his speculative explanation for the phenomenon, namely that the case marking used for the agent is also elsewhere associated with subject properties, does not seem applicable to Sanskrit.

are most clearly ergative; and gerundive agents therefore most clearly correspond in function to the subjects of active sentences. Finally, as noted earlier, it is the gerundives which are most advanced in the development of a new, demotional variety, made from intransitives, i.e. a variety lacking any surface subjects. At the same time, in Vedic prose the use of absolutive formation as a subordinating device is markedly on the rise. Given these circumstances, speakers must have been confronted with the difficulty of not being able to use a productive and highly favored subordinating device with the new and very productive demotional gerundive used in main-verb function, since the latter lacked the surface subject required for controlling absolutive formation. The noted functional equivalence of the (ergative) gerundive agents with the subjects of active constructions then seems to have provided for the solution, namely to also syntactically equate gerundive agents with transitive subjects, for the purposes of absolutive formation. Once this equation was made, however, it was possible to extend it also to other syntactic phenomena, such as major constituent order.

What is remarkable is that here as elsewhere, the common "*P*-orientation" of our three constructions seems to have been sufficient to very soon lead to convergent syntactic behavior, with *A*-oriented syntax being generalized not only to the other ergative construction (the *ta*-participle), but also to the passive.

It is only in the area of pragmatics that the three constructions come to differ in a meaningful sense: In late Sanskrit and Middle Indo-Aryan, the *ta*-participle has become a general, unmarked past tense, while the gerundive and passive have more specialized functions, such as indicating deference; cf. e.g. (16) below. This difference is reflected in the frequency with which these constructions are attested (e.g. 53 *ta*-participles vs. 9 gerundives and 8 passives in a sample from the Vetālapañcaviṃśati).

(16) *bhavatā pratītya araṇyaṃ nirvāsyatām* (Vetāla. 24.20)
'by your lordship, having concerned yourself, (she) should be banished to the forest' = 'may it please your lordship ...'

Given this pragmatic difference, it is perhaps not surprising that it is the *ta*-participle which is most generally reflected as a distinct, ergative pattern in Modern Indo-Aryan, as in (17) below. And given that also the Sanskrit gerundive is ergative, it might not be too surprising to find some direct ergative reflexes also for this construction, although with greater dialectal restrictions; cf. (18). In both cases, than, we might say that the modern ergative constructions simply CONTINUE earlier ergatives, rather than replacing earlier passives. This would be a conclusion very similar to that of Klaiman. There is, however, evidence that also some passives are reflected as modern ergatives, not as passives.[10] This is the evidence

10. Generally, however, the old passive—to the extent that it survives at all—either continues to be used as a passive (with different agent marking) or is lexicalized or grammatically reinterpreted. I intend to treat these and related questions elsewhere.

of constructions like that in (19), where forms like *pāhijet* reflect an earlier passive in *-(i)ya-*. These constructions generally are limited to just one or two verbs in a given language. Koṅkarī, however, offers an open-ended construction, which can be used for ALL verbs, as in (20).

(17) Hindī *mɛ ne kitāb paṛhī / kām kiyā*
Ag.[11] fem. fem. masc. masc.
'I read a book, did the work'

(18) Older Marāṭhī: *myā uṭhavẽ*
Ag. neut.
'I (masc. or fem.) should rise'

(19) Mar. *tyā ne gānī mhaṇṭlī pāhijet*
Ag.
'he should sing songs'

(20) Koṅk. *tā-ṇe māriyet*
Ag.
'he can/may strike'

This leads to the conclusion that the modern ergative constructions reflect BOTH OLDER ERGATIVES AND OLDER PASSIVES. That is, neither the traditional passive-origin hypothesis (as recently espoused by Pray and Anderson), nor Klaiman's ergative hypothesis is fully adequate.

Perhaps even more important is the conclusion that here as elsewhere in the history of Indo-Aryan (i.e. in Sanskrit), we find convergent behavior of our three "*P*-oriented" constructions, which suggests that their common "*P*-orientation" ultimately is more important than the difference between ergative and passive. This raises a more general question, which can be answered only by the investigation of other languages: Is this convergent behavior of "*P*-oriented" constructions just a peculiarity of Indo-Aryan, or is it a general feature of languages with "split ergativity"?

REFERENCES

Textual references generally are to the traditional divisions (chapters, etc.) of the Sanskrit texts. There are only two exceptions:

Hitopadeśa: References are to page and line numbers in Lanman's (1884) selections from this text.

Vetālapañcaviṃśati: References are to page and line numbers in Emeneau 1934.

Anderson, Stephen R. 1977. *On mechanisms by which languages become ergative. Mechanisms of syntactic change*. ed. by Charles N. Li. 317-63. Austin: University of Texas Press.

Comrie, Bernard. 1978. *Ergativity. Syntactic typology*, ed. by W.P. Lehmann, 329-95. Austin: University of Texas Press.

11. Ag. here refers to Agentive (i.e. non-nominative) case.

Delbrück, Bertold. 1888. *Altindische Syntax*. (Repr. 1968), Darmstadt: Wissenschaftliche Buchgesellschaft.

Debrunner, Albert. 1954. *Altindische Grammatik* 2:2. Göttingen: Vandenhoeck & Ruprecht.

Dixon, R.M.W. 1979. Ergativity. *Language* 55.59-138.

Emeneau, Murray B. 1934. *Jambhaladatta's version of the Vetālapañcaviṃśati* ... New Haven: American Oriental Society.

Klaiman, Myriam H. 1978. Arguments against a passive origin of the IA ergative. Papers from the 14th Regional Meeting of the Chicago Linguistic Society, 204-16.

Lanman, Charles Rockwell. 1884. *A Sanskrit reader*. Cambridge: Harvard University Press.

Oertel, Hanns. 1929. *The syntax of cases in the narrative and descriptive prose of the Brāhmaṇas*, 1. Heidelberg: Winter.

———. 1939. *Zu den Kasusvariationen in der vedischen Prosa*, 3. (Sitzungsberichte der Bayerischen Akademie der Wissenschaften, Phil.-hist. Abteilung, 1939:6.)

Pray, Bruce. 1976. *From passive to ergative in Indo-Aryan. The notion subject in South Asian languages*, ed. by Manindra K. Verma, 195-211. (South Asian Studies Publication Series, 2.) Madison: University of Wisconsin.

Timberlake, Alan. 1976. *Subject properties in the North Russian passive*, *Subject and topic*, ed. by Charles N. Li, 545-70. New York: Academic Press.

CASE OF CAUSEE*

Kashi Wali

INTRODUCTION

This paper argues that the current syntactic (Aissen 1974, Comrie 1974, 1976; Cole 1976a) and semantic (Cole 1976a, b, c) analyses of the causee's case and grammatical relation are neither universal, nor unitary. They are inadequate at both observational and explanatory levels. In particular they fail to explain many special features of the causee which differentiate it from the indirect object and other oblique NP's which it superficially resembles. Moreover, both proposals treat the causee's case as an isolated factor, being a function of some extraneous grammatical principle such as Comrie's Case Hierarchy and Cole's Agency gradation.

The present paper claims that the causee's special features stem from a pragmatic function inherent in the causal verb itself: namely, *the activity of appointing or employing an agency to get a certain task done* as suggested by the ancient Indian grammarians of the Pāṇinian school. It is this aspect which distinguishes the causal verb from all others and marks the causee from the true indirect object and other oblique NP's. More crucially it explains the fixed hierarchical order found amongst the multiple causees in the rare repeated causatives, unnoticed so far, that exist in Marathi, Gujarati, and some other languages. The current theories have no such power. An extra bonus of the proposed analysis is that, unlike the current proposals, it treats the causative, the causer, and the causee as a single coherent unit.

SYNTACTIC ANALYSES

In the recently proposed analyses of causee's case it has generally been assumed that: (a) causatives are underlying bisentential with a structure such as $[_s$ X cause $[_s$ Y to do something (run, jog, hit Z ..) $]_s]_s$ (b) the causative merger with its complement verb erases the grammatical relation of the complement subject; and (c) the case of the derived NP (i.e. causee) emerging from the complement subject is determined by some universal grammatical principles of higher order. On the basis of a cross language study Comrie, for example, has suggested that the case of the causee follows from two main syntactic principles: the Doubling constraint and the Case Hierarchy (CH). The doubling constraint

*Research in this paper has been supported by a grant from The Senate Research Committee, Syracuse University. I am thankful to Professor Ritchie, Syracuse University, Professor Shibatani, USC and Professor Alice Davison, University of Illinois for their helpful comments and suggestions. Many thanks are also due to my informants Akiko Okuda, Yukio Otsu, Dr. Bhatia, Dr. Moneti, and Dr. Kachru.

prevents the primary subject and object relations from duplicating in simple structures. The case hierarchy, which feeds on the doubling constraint, demotes the causee to Direct, Indirect or Oblique Objects (DO, IO,OO) position with each increase in the number of complement arguments of the causative construction. Thus if the complement clause is without an object the causee positions itself as DO, if the complement DO is already present the causee moves to IO, and if both DO and IO positions are filled, the causee demotes to OO NP whose nature under CH is unspecified. Turkish supposedly represents a paradigm of this operation.

(1) Hasan Ahmet'i güldürdü
(DO) laugh-cause-past
'Hasan made Ahmet laugh.'

(2) Hasan Ahmet'e mektup yazdirdi
(IO) letter (DO) write-cause-past
'Hasan made Ahmet write a letter.'

(3) Hasan-a mektub-u Ahmet-tarafindan gönder-t-tim
IO DO 00(by-agent) send-cause-pas
'I made Ahmet send the letter to Hasan.'

(Note: (3) is only marginally acceptable. It has been included here to illustrate the paradigm.)

A primary problem with the doubling constraint is that it is inadequate even at the observational level. For example, in both Sanskrit (e.g. 4) and Hebrew the causee duplicates itself on the DO while in Italian and French it does so on the IO position (see Wali 1979b for details). The simple structures which causatives resemble after merger at times allow two or more DO's, but two IO cases are almost unheard of. The occurrence of two IO's thus remains mysterious under the present analysis.

Cole in his analysis of Hebrew discards the doubling constraint and suggests that the causee's case results from an interaction of a Ranking and a Place holder principle. The ranking principle based on the Accessibility Hierarchy (AH), $S \geq DO \geq OO$ states that in the merged causal structure the complement subject which is the highest ranking NP next to the main subject moves naturally to DO, the second highest ranking position on the AH. The function of the Place Holder (PH) principle is to confer tenure on the NP's already bearing a given grammatical relation to the complement verb. These NP's cannot be displaced by the complement subject. According to Cole if the ranking principle takes precedence the complement subject becomes a DO causee as in Sanskrit and Hebrew. If the place holding principle takes precedence the complement subject will successively demote to DO, IO, or OO causee as in Turkish.

Notice that the choice between AH and PH is arbitrary and not a governed one. The reformulated hypothesis is still inadequate to resolve the complexity of duplication. First, the result of the AH application is not universally predictable. In Hebrew, for example, AH demotes the original

DO as evidenced by its inability to passivize and cliticize. These properties are now transferred to the derived DO as noted in Cole (1976a). In Sanskrit the derived DO is treated on par with the original DO. Both these DO's undergo passivization as has been documented in most Sanskrit grammars and more recently in Comrie (1974: 17).[1]

(4) Baṭum odanam bhojayati
boy-DO rice-DO eat-cause-tns
'He makes the boy eat the rice.'

(5) Baṭur odanam bhojyate
boy-sub rice-DO eat-cause-passive
'The boy is made to eat the food.'

(6) Baṭum odano bhojyate
boy-DO rice-sub. eat-cause-passive
'The rice is made to eat to the boy.' (Literal translation).
'The rice is made for the boy to eat.'

Secondly, even if the DO duplication is somehow ironed out, the IO duplication still remains problematic. Neither AH nor PH has any way of predicting it.

Consider now the oblique form of the causee. According to both CH and PH the OO causee is triggered by the complement IO. The presence of the complement IO, however, is not strictly necessary for the IO causee to occur. In Marathi, Finnish, Gujarati, Sanskrit and many other languages the OO causee is obligatory with certain verbs irrespective of the presence of the complement IO at any level.

Marathi :

(7) Minine Harikaḍun kapaḍe dhuvavle
-OO clothes wash-caus-past
'Mini caused Hari to wash the clothes.'

Finnish :

(8) Mina rakennutin talo -n muurarei -lla
I build-caus house-DO bricklayers-OO
'I make the bricklayers build the house.'

A mysterious thing about the OO causee in all the cases without exception is that it invariably centers around the semantic concept of a second order agent, its form ranging from a demoted passive agent to an instrumental or some other oblique agent NP. An explanation of this important feature of the causee is beyond the bounds of both the CH and AH-PH principles. These have no way of predicting the class to which the OO causee should belong. The OO causee under these principles turns out to be at best a stylistic variation of the IO causee.

1. It has been brought to my attention by Prof. Shibatani that in German the derived DO looking causee does not demote the original DO. The Sanskrit and the German case together cast doubt on the AH principle.

A superficial similarity of the OO causee with the demoted passive agent NP in some languages has given rise to the hypothesis that the OO causee results from passive application on the complement level.[2] Passive as the source of the oblique causee however confronts many problems as pointed out by Cole and Sridhar (1976), and others. A serious complication with this analysis is that it makes wrong predictions about the causee's case in the rarely found, and so far unnoticed, higher level repeated causatives that exist in Marathi, Gujarati, and some other languages. These causatives are not commonly used but they have been reported in some grammar books such as those of Marathi and Kashmiri. They are also readily accepted by many native speakers and as such should be considered as part of their linguistic competence. These higher level causatives are generated by repeated causative embeddings which result in producing multiple causees in the derived structure (See 9a, b, and c).

(9) a. Mini-ne Lilli-kaḍun Sushice-karvi Vinay-laa patra lih-av-avle
causee$_1$ causee$_2$ IO DO write-caus-caus
'Mini caused Lili caused Sushi to write a letter to Vinay.'

b. Agent Causee$_1$—OO Causee$_2$—OO (IO) (DO) V+caus+caus.
(9c is proposed as the underlying structure of (9a or b))

c. $[_s$Su $[_s$Su $[_s$Su (IO) (DO) V] cause$]_s$ cause $]]]_{s\,s\,s}$

Consider now the result of the cyclic application of Passive on (9c). The repeated applications of Passive should produce identical oblique case markings on all causees. This prediction, however, is not borne out as seen in (9a). In most languages that allow repeated causatives the causees bear separate case markings, as exemplified below in Hindi, Punjabi, Gujarati, and Kashmiri. The only exception as far as I know comes from Japanese which marks all its causees in repeated causatives by *ni*.

(10) H Shilaa-ne Raamke dwaaraa Umaa-se kapḍe dhulwaaye

(11) P Shilaa-ne Raam-vallo Umaa- to kapre tulvaae

(12) G Shilaa-e Raam-paase Umaa-dwaaraa kapaḍaa dhuwaraavyaa
Agent- causee$_1$ causee$_2$ clothes wash-caus-caus-tns
'Shila caused Ram caused Uma to wash the clothes'.

(13) K Shilian leekhinav Raamani-zaryi Umas-athi chiṭh
Agent write-caus causee$_1$ causee$_2$ letter.
Shila caused Ram caused Uma to write the letter.

(14) J Taroo wa Akiko-ni Jiroo-ni sono hon o yom-ase-saseta
Taro caused Aiko caused Jiro to read the book

Finally even in French where the OO causee has been argued to be derived by Passive by Aissen (1974) and others, Pinkham (1974) has pointed

2. This view has been advocated by Comrie, Andrew Radford, and also by the proponents of the Relational Grammar. The causative analysis proposed in the Relational framework has not been considered in this paper.

out that the OO *par* NP does not always correlate with the corresponding passive of the complement clause. More significantly, the causative of the stative and perception verbs do not allow *par* causees *even though these can be passivised*

(15) Les gardes lui ont tiré dessus
'The guards shot at him.'

(16) *Il a été tire dessus par les gardes
'He was shot by the guards.'

(17) Le capitain lui a fait tirer dessus par les gardes
'The captain had the guards shoot at him.'

(18) Les enfants ont vu le film
'The children saw the movie.'

(19) Le film été vu par les enfants
'The movie has been seen by the children'

(20) *Antoine fera voir ce film par ses enfants
'Antoine will make his children see this movie.'

Notice that the semantic agent class universally reflected in the oblique causee is diametrically opposed to the object class This fact in itself casts doubt on the current popular assumption (see Comrie 1976: 269) that IO is the most natural position for the complement subject of the transitive verb to occupy. The IO causee assumption has been based on the *surface case* of the causee in certain languages. No one to my knowledge has compared the deep properties of the causee IO to that of the true IO [3]. A preliminary comparison drawn from widely unrelated languages indicates that the behavioural properties of the causee IO differ considerably from that of the true IO.

Consider coreference first. In most languages the true IO can be a coreferent of the subject NP and has the potential of being reflexivised. The IO causee on the other hand must be nonidentical with the primary agent, the causal subject. No language to my knowledge including Turkish, Italian, French, and Japanese allow the causee to be reflexivised irrespective of its IO/OO form. There appears to be a universal constraint which prohibits the causer causee (IO/OO type) identity.

In Japanese the verb may be marked for both subject and direct object honorification. In bitransitive constructions however the honorification goes to the indirect object only, completely bypassing the direct object as

3. An exception to this claim comes from Harris's analysis of Georgian. She has argued that in G. the causee IO acquires many properties of the true IO while the original IO seems to have lost them. The problem of retention, acquisition, and loss of properties in the dual objects (i.e. DO, DO, IO, IO) appears to be a separate issue by itself. In some languages the newly formed object appears to oust the original one as in G. and Hebrew. In some others the original one appears to retain all the properties. In German, for example, as pointed out to me by Prof. Shibatani, the derived DO causee cannot be passivized. In Sanskrit on the other hand both the DOS can be passivized.

noted by both Harada (1976), and Aiko Okuda (1978) (cf 21, 22). This special IO property cannot be transmitted to the IO causee as is evidenced by the star on (23).

(21) *Watasi wa otooto ni Yamada sensei o *go*-syookai si-ta
I brother-IO teacher-DO obj Hon; introduce obj. Hon. past
'I introduced Prof. Yamada to my brother'.

(22) Watasi wa Yamada sensei no otooto o go-syookai si-ta[4]
'I introduced my brother to Prof. Yamada.'

In (21) the object honorific cannot refer to the teacher, the direct object, though the teacher is superior to the brother.

(23) *Taroo wa kareno sensei ni suisen-joo- o o -kak-ase-si ta
his teacher-IO recommendation letter DO Hon. write-cause-Hon.-past
'Taroo made his teacher write a letter of recommendation.'

In Marathi the auxiliary *gheṇe*, literally *to take*, treats causatives differently from the bitransitives with IO. This auxiliary belongs to a special subset of explicator verbs that are specific to Indic languages. The usual function of these verbs is to enhance the meaning of the main verb by adding aspectual notions such as completion and continuation. An interesting feature of *gheṇe* is that its use relates to the subject NP instead of the main verb. The use of *gheṇe* indicates that the agent itself is the topic of the verb with the suggestion that the action affects the agent. The relevant feature of *gheṇe* in the present context is that its use is blocked in the presence of an IO. It is, however, readily accepted in the presence of a causee, which in Marathi is realised as an OO as noted earlier.[5]

(24) *Minine Ravilaa pustak devun ghetle
-IO book give take-past
'Mini gave a book to Ravi.'

(25) Minine Ravikaḍun kapḍe dhuvavun ghetle
-OO clothes wash-caus take-past
'Mini had Ravi wash the clothes.'

So far I have argued on a cross linguistic basis that the behavioural features of the causee do not always correlate with those of the true IO. In fact the data suggests that the causee is some type of a second order agent and is only masquerading as an IO in some languages, having its low level surface coding property. The IO/Agent duality inherent in the causee suggests an area of strong syntactic-semantic overlap. A pure syntactic approach is naturally inadequate and suggests a need for incorporating a semantic-pragmatic account in the universal grammar.

---

4. I am thankful to Prof. Shibatani for examples (21, 22).

5. I have also learned that the parallel explicator in Hindi, Punjabi, and Gujarati behave in a similar fashion. For more examples on causee IO and true IO distinction see Wali (1979b).

SEMANTIC ANALYSIS

A need for a semantic account of the case of causee has been realised for some time as is evidenced by Cole (1976a, b, c). According to Cole the case of causee is determined by the semantic role of the complement subject vis-a-vis the predicate of the complement clause. Cole relates the grammatical role of the causee with the agentive nonagentiveness of the complement subject. The variation in the agentivity of CS determines the causee's role. The subject of an action verb has the highest degree of agentivity followed by the subject of an experiencer verb. The experiencers are typically nonagents but necessarily animate and therefore potentially agentive. These are midway on a scale of agency between patients and typical agents. (For details see Cole 1976c.)

(26) Agent $\rangle$ experiencer $\rangle$ patient

A proposal such as Cole's which tries to predict the grammatical relations of the causee on the basis of its underlying agentivity creates a host of problems which are not easily resolvable. It is not clear, for example, why the agentive nonagentiveness is crucial for the causal verb alone while it appears to play no role in other predicates such as *force*, *order*, and *tell*. The grammatical relation of the CS in this group remains invariant and appears to be indifferent to the semantics of the complement verb. The proposal also fails to explain why the causee's grammatical relation is not affected by the agentivity of the intransitive complement. The causee in this case is almost universally realized as DO irrespective of the agentivity and even the animacy of the CS. In Sanskrit and many other languages the intransitive complements group themselves with the experiencer verbs as noted in Cardona (1978). The causee in both these groups turns up as DO violating the agency scale in (26). The intransitive-transitive distinction which feeds CH also appears to be irrelevant for this grouping.

Notice that the central issue that needs to be crucially focussed upon is the grammatical relation of the emerged CS, the causee, *in connection with the causal verb itself and not in isolation or autonomously* as done in the proposals by both Comrie and Cole. It is the causal verb that enters into a syntactic and semantic relation with its NP's. The syntactic-semantic relations of the NP's are necessarily tied up with their governing predicates and have no existence in isolation. This is particularly crucial for the causal verb because, as is well known, this verb does not allow the complement verb to exert its independent existence. This is evidenced by the universal inapplicability of the passive at the complement level. Both Comrie and Cole seem to have disregarded this central point. The issue however has been explicitly addressed to by the ancient Indian grammarians of the Pāṇinian school. According to these grammarians the primary meaning of the causal morpheme is: *the activity of appointing or employing an agency to get a certain task done* (see Cardona 1967). I claim that it is this aspect of meaning which distinguishes the causal verb from all others and marks the causee from the inherent receiver, the true IO. According to the

Sanskrit grammarians a causal verb form expresses two activities: the base activity denoted by the verb root and the causation denoted by the affix. Corresponding to these two activities they posit two agents: the *kartṛ*, agent of the base activity; and the *hetu*, agent of causation. The latter is regarded as the principal agent also called a *prayojaka* (a planner), and the former is taken to be the subsidiary agent, a *prayojya*, 'a mediator, the causee'. The recognition of these proper though intricate relationships between the causal verb, the causer, and the causee readily resolves some of the dilemmas inherent in the treatment of the causee mentioned above.

Consider, for example, the universal non-identity constraint between the primary agent and the causee in both IO and OO form. Employment of oneself is semantically odd though it is possible to force or tell oneself. The constraint is clearly related to the causee's employee function. The function also governs the bypassing of the causee in honorification in both Japanese and Korean. The compatibility of the *gheṇe* type auxiliary with the causal verb in Marathi and other Indic languages appears to be tied to the notion of appointing an agency to get a certain task done. The employment is in the interest of the primary agent and the action is not directed towards any IO as in the case of bitransitive verbs. The employee function also explains why the IO causee often transforms into an instrumental or a demoted passive agent without invoking the *ad hoc* machinery of the passive rule. Notice that under the complement agentivity hypothesis of Cole these important features of the causee remain completely unexplained and mysterious.

The semantic-pragmatic function of the employment of the agency to get a certain task done draws a natural distinction between factitive causative and other causatives which originate in the verbs of perception, cognition, or emotion. The cross linguistic causee of these experiencer verbs manifests itself as DO/IO (object category) and naturally aligns itself with the causee of the intransitive complements as mentioned earlier. Expressions such as *X employed Y to see Z*, or *be angry with*, or *to run* are semantically odd. Traditionally, causation governing these verbs is thought to be direct or what Xolodovic has recently called *contactive* (see Cormie 1976b). The causee of the contactive causation turns up as a patient or experiencer belonging to the direct/indirect object category. Some languages such as Bolivian Quechua (see Cole 1976b, c) differentiate experiencer causee from the patient causee of the intransitive complements while some others such as Sanskrit suppress this distinction. The significant thing is that the causee of this group does not emerge as an agent or employee.

In support of the employee-agency feature of the causee consider again the repeated causatives mentioned earlier. An intriguing feature of these is that the postpositions accompaning the multiple causees occur in a fixed order and cannot be switched around even though the language has more or less a free word order.

The PP structure:

(27)	Agent	$causee_1$	$cause_2$
M.	ne	kaḍun	karvi
H.	ne	dwaaraa	se
P.	ne	vallo	to
G.	e	paase	dwaaraa
K.	an	zaryi	athi
J.	wa	ni	ni

The fixed order of these PP's suggest that there is a chain of agent hierarchy, the primary agent representing the supreme planner while the executor occupying the last position. This follows naturally from the Indian Grammarian's insight into the causer-causee relationship.

(28) Agent Hierarchy: Agent > $Causee_1$ > $Causee_2$
(*Hetu*) (*Prayojya*$_1$) (*Prayojya*$_2$)

A final big bonus of the posited semantic function is that it makes historical predictions; namely, if a language has an object causee in the expected agent causee position the object causee will be reanalysed as an agent causee in the course of time. In short the general trend will be towards the agent causee in noncontactive situations. I know of at least one language where this prediction appears to have come true. In Sanskrit during the Vedic period the causee of the intransitive, and cognition verbs as well as verbs of eating and doing was expressed as DO. In the post-Vedic period, however, the causee of the 'eating' and 'doing' group began to appear as an oblique agent causee which was being used for other factitive verbs (see Cardona 1978 for details). This transition from DO to OO causee only in the 'eating' and 'doing' verbs and not in the cognition verbs with the same transitive formula reflects the power of the semantic principle. Clearly the deciding factor in the reanalysis of DO to OO was not transitivity but the abstract semanticity of the agentive function of the causee.

REFERENCES

Aissen, J. 1974. The syntax of causative constructions. Doctoral dissertation, Harvard University.

Cole, P. 1976a. "Causative construction in modern Hebrew: Theoretical implications." *Studies in Modern Hebrew Syntax & Semantics*. Amsterdam: North Holland.

———. b. "A note on the grammatical role of the cause in the universal grammar." *Proceedings of the Mid-America Linguistics Conference*. Univ. of Minnesota.

———. c. The causee in universal grammar: Syntax or semantics. Unpublished MS

———. & S.N. Sridhar. 1976. "Clause union and relational grammar: Evidence from Hebrew and Kannada" *LI* VII:4.

Comrie, B. 1974. "Causatives and universal grammar". In *Transactions of the Philological Society*. London: Basil Blackwell.

———. 1976a. "The syntax of causative constructions: Cross language similarities and divergences." In *Syntax and Semantics* Vol. 6, N.Y.: Academic Press,

———. b. "Review of Tipologija Kauzativnyx Konstrukcij", ed. by Xolodovic. *Language* 52:2.

Cardona, G. 1967. "Cause and causal agent, the Pāṇinian view". *Journal of the Oriental Institute*. Baroda.

———. 1978. Relations between causatives and passives in Indo-Iranian. Collitz lectur, LSA Institute. MS.

Damle, M.K. 1965. *Shastriy Marathi Vyakaran* (A Scientific Grammar of Marathi). 3rd edition. Pune, India: R.D. Yande Publisher.

Harada, S.I. 1976. "Honorifics." *Syntax & Semantics* vol. 5, NY: Academic Press.

Harris, A. 1976. Grammatical relations in Modern Georgian. Doctoral dissertation. Harvard University.

Kachru, B. 1974. *An introduction to spoken Kashmiri*. Urbana, Il.: University of Illinois

Okuda, A. 1978. A performative analysis of Japanese honorifics. MA Thesis. Syracuse University.

Pinkham, J. 1974. Passive and faire-par causative construction in French. Senior Essay, Harvard University.

Radford, A. 1978. "Agentive causatives in Romance: Accessibility versus passivization." *Journal of Linguistics* 14.

Shibatani, M. 1976. "Causativisation." *Syntax & Semantics* Vol. 5.

———. 1977. "Grammatical relations and surface cases". *Language*. 53:4.

Wali, K. 1979a. "Two Marathi reflexives and the causative structure." *Studies in Language*. 3:3.

———. b. "Case of causee". *Descriptive and Applied Linguistics*. 12. Tokyo, Japan: ICU.

———. 1980. "Oblique causee and the passive explanation." *Linguistic Inquiry* 11.1.

———. Cause, causer & causee : A semantic perspective (An enlarged version of the present article).

SUBJACENCY : COUNTER-EVIDENCE FROM KANNADA

K. S. Yadurajan

1. Chomsky (1977) states the Subjacency Condition as follows:

(1) A cyclic rule cannot move a phrase from position Y to position X (or conversely) in:

$$... X ... \left[_{A} ... \left[_{B} ... Y ... \right] ... \right] ... X ...$$ where A and B are cyclic nodes. (p. 73)

The cyclic nodes are S and NP

The Subjacency Condition is one of several other conditions applying to cyclic rules. Movement rules are said to be subject to Subjacency, the Propositional Island Condition (PIC)[1] and the Specified Subject Condition (SSC), among others. Rules of 'Construal' are subject only to the SSC and the PIC and not to Subjacency.

It is evident that the Subjacency Condition would be immediately contradicted by rules like Question Formation in English where the *wh-* element can be moved to a position arbitrarily far away from the extraction site. Chomsky, therefore, assumes a successive-cyclic analysis of this rule; i.e. the *wh-* element instead of being directly moved into its target position (=COMP) as in (2) is moved from COMP to COMP as in (3). Further, *wh-* movement is said to underlie various other unbounded processes like Topicalization, Cleft-Formation, Comparative Deletion, Tough-Movement, etc. In fact these rules are all dispensed with in favour of one rule, Move *wh-* phrase. This analysis meets some of the strongest objections to the initial proposals about Subjacency (Chomsky, 1973) as in Bach and Horn (1976). The analysis, if tenable, is a remarkable simplifiaticon of the syntax of English.

1. Formerly the Tensed-S Condition; now the Nominative Island Condition (NIC)

(2)

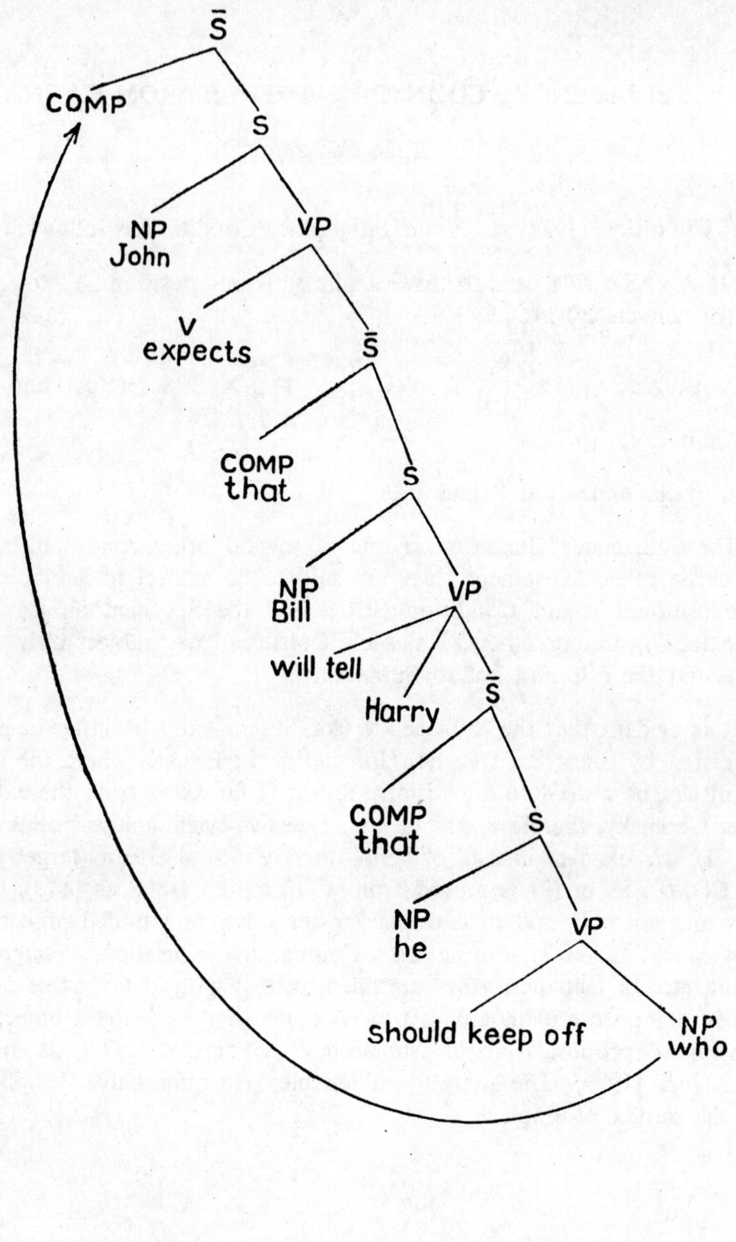
S̄
COMP
S
NP
John
VP
V
expects
S̄
COMP
that
S
NP
Bill
VP
will tell
Harry
S̄
COMP
that
S
NP
he
VP
should keep off
NP
who

(3)

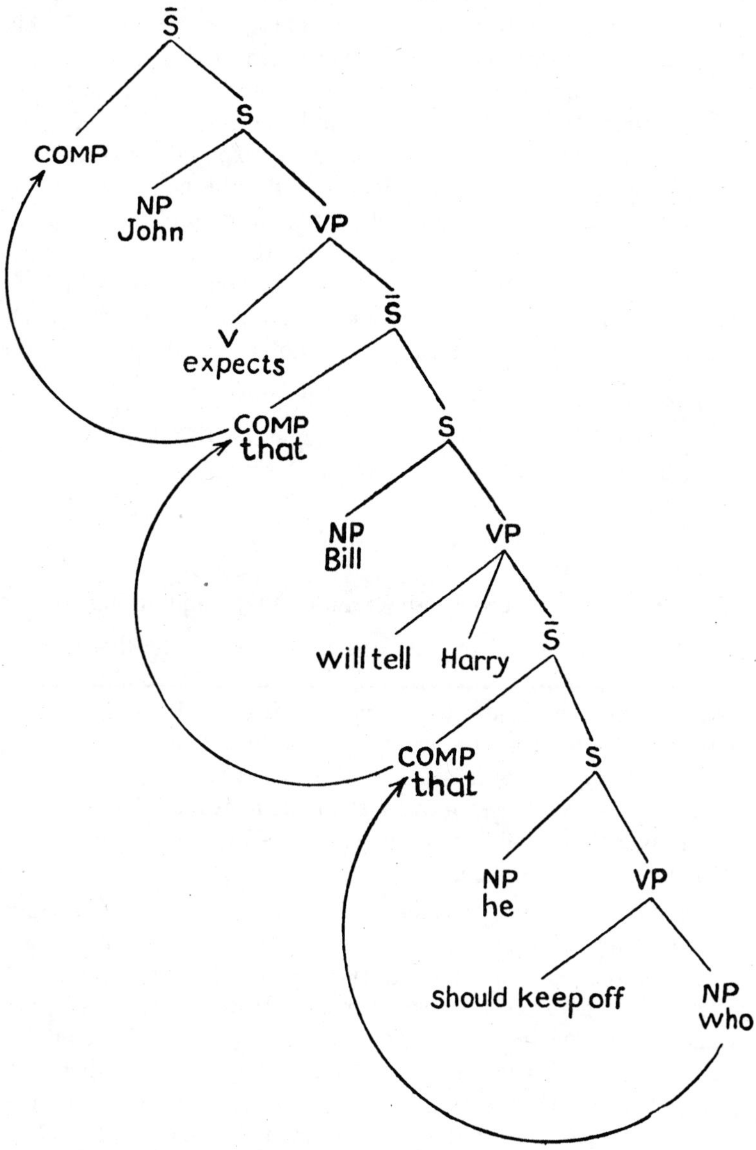
S̄
COMP
S
NP
John
VP
V
expects
S̄
COMP
that
S
NP
Bill
VP
will tell
Harry
S̄
COMP
that
S
NP
he
VP
should keep off
NP
who

However this might be, one may still ask whether the Subjacency Condition is tenable. Subjacency (and the associated conditions) are offered as an improvement on Ross (1967). Chomsky claims that in his analysis "...the island constraints ... can be explained in terms of general and quite reasonable 'computational' properties of formal grammar." As against this "... such conditions as CNPC and the independent *wh-* island Constraint seem very curious and difficult to explain" (1977:89). The claim would be sustained if, in fact, there was no alternative way of accounting for the Ross constraints in a satisfactory manner and the Subjacency Condition accounted for *all* cases of CNPC violation. The latter situation would obtain if all rules subject to CNPC were movement rules. The successive-cyclic analysis of movement would then explain, under the Subjacency Condition, why CNPC could not be violated.

To illustrate: Given (4)

(4) $[_{\bar{S}}$ COMP$_1$ $[_{S}$ I believe $[_{NP}$ the rumour $[_{\bar{S}}$ COMP$_2$ that $[_{S}$ John will divorce who $]]]]]$

we cannot derive

(5) *Who do you believe the rumour that John will divorce ?

The *wh-* can be moved into the lower COMP on the first cycle; it cannot be moved on the next cycle as NPs have no COMPs. Movement into the higher COMP on the third cycle is prevented by the Subjacency Condition as the *wh-* has to cross the two cyclic nodes NP and S. Thus Question Formation in English observes CNPC because it is a movement rule. Additionally, the rule involves moving a *wh-* element into COMP but this movement into COMP would not arise if, in the first instance, Question Formation did not involve movement.

Implicit in Chomsky's claim about Subjacency is the assupmtion that the rules subject to CNPC are all movement rules (in which case they can all be analysed as involving a successive-cyclic *wh-* movement). It also follows that there are no deletion rules obeying CNPC. All such cases of apparent deletion will involve an 'underlying' *wh-* movement. (cf. Chomsky's analysis of Comparative Deletion and Comparative Subdeletion.) Interpretive and construal rules, too, on this analysis, do not observe CNPC.

In a series of important papers Bresnan (Bresnan 1975, 1976a, b, 1977) has questioned some of these conclusions. Bresnan's arguments[2] (especially in Bresnan, 1977) are quite compelling, as noted by Partee (1977).

2. Recall that Ross also had suggested the possibility of deletion rules obeying CNPC (Ross 1967:226) in connection with his discussion of Relativization in Japanese. Since then apparently unbounded deletion rules obeying CNPC have been proposed in connection with various other languages but, apparently, the possibility of an iterated movement of some element over an unbounded context followed by a 'local' deletion of the item cannot be ruled out in these cases, at least in principle.

Nevertheless, arguing against subjacency with data from English is difficult *as rules which observe CNPC in English also observe the wh- island constraint.* In principle, at least, this opens up the possibility of analysing all rules observing CNPC as involving a *wh-* movement. But if there are rules in a language which observe CNPC but not the *wh-* island constraint, there will be no motivation for adopting a successive-cyclic analysis of such rules in that language, especially when the rules in question involve no overt movement. The fact that they observe CNPC would then go unaccounted for by the Subjacency Condition.

The claim, then, of this paper is that the Subjacency Condition accounts for only those cases of CNPC violation where the rule in question also observes the *wh-* island constraint. It cannot account for cases of CNPC violation in a language which has no *wh-* island constraint. When such languages are taken into account, the Subjacency Condition cannot be said to be a satisfactory generalization of CNPC.

These points will now be established in connection with the Participial Relative Clause in Kannada (KPR).

2.

2.1 The principle mode of restrictive relativization in Kannada utilizes a participial structure as in (6).

(6) *raamanu bareda kaadambariyu baha La čennaagide*
Rama (Nom.) write (Participle) novel (Accu.) very good
(The novel which Rama wrote is very good.)

The underlying structure is usually represented as in (7). (cf. Nadkarni 1970.)

(7) $[_{S}\ [_{NP}\ [_{S}$ *raamanu* *kaadambariyannu* *baredanu* $]$ $[_{NP}$ [*kaadambariyu*] $]]$ $[_{VP}$ *bahala čennaagide* $]]$

The relativized NP (singly underscored) is assumed to be deleted under identity with the matrix NP (doubly underscored) and the verb in the relative clause is replaced by its participle form.

We are not concerned with the details of the analysis here. (A different analysis will be sketched towards the end of this paper.) What we are mainly concerned with is to show that no movement is involved in the operation of this rule. This is usually taken for granted but in the context of the present discussion the point must be established. We shall also show that the rule observes CNPC but not the *wh-* island constraint.

2.2

2.2.1 We first establish that Question Formation in Kannada does not involve any *wh-* movement.

It shows none of the properties which Chomsky (1977) has given as 'diagnostic' for *wh-* movement. Chomsky gives the following cluster of properties:

(8) a. it leaves a gap
b. when there is a bridge there is an apparent violation of Subjacency, the PIC and the SSC
c. it observes CNPC
d. it observes the *wh-* island constraints.

(9) is an example of a question in Kannada:[3]

raamanu *eenannu* *tandanu?*
Rama what brought + number + person marker
(nom.) (accu.)
('What did Rama bring?')

Notice that there is no gap; the *wh-* word is in place. Nothing more need be said about (a). As for (b) it has been suggested (Koster 1978) that generally clauses are islands and it is only in some languages that elements can escape from a clause across a bridge (in the sense of Erteschik 1973). COMP-to-COMP movement is a special characteristic of such languages (like English). This accounts for *wh-* movement in (10):

(10) Who do you believe that John will marry?

No such parallel construction is possible in Kannada. (11a) is impossible:

(11) a. **raamanu maduve maaDikoLLuttaane endu niinu*
Rama marriage Do + future CZR you
nambuttiye yaarannu?
believe who

The correct form is (11b).

(11) b. *raamanu yaarannu maduve maaDikollluttane endu niinu nambuttiye?*
(Who do you believe that Rama will marry?)

Consider now (c). Questions can go freely into relative clauses; that is, question, in Kannada, does not observe the complex NP constraint (cf. 17b) and (18b). We illustrate here with 'headed' NP clauses:

(12) a. *raamanu Šaaliniyannu maduve maaDikoLLuttaane*
Rama Shalini (accu.) marriage
emba sangati avana taayiyannu kheeda goLisitu
CZR news his mother (accu.) sad made
(The news that Rama would marry Shalini made his mother sad.)
b. *raamanu yaarannu maduve maaDikoLLuttaane emba sangati avana taayiyannu kheedagoLisitu?*
*(Who did the news that Rama would marry make his mother sad?)

We now come to the final point i.e. (8d). It is not possible to test directly, the way we can in English, whether Kannada has a *wh-* island constraint.

3. Besides the type of question cited in the text Kannada also has an 'yes-no' question: *raamanu bandana*? 'Did Rama come?' *adu nijava*? 'It it true?' This type of question is formed by adding the morpheme *a* to the verb in the sentence. The usual tests for maintaining a *wh* analysis of yes-no question in English, fail in the case of Kannada. This supports the conclusion of section 2.2.1 that questions in Kannada involve no *wh*-movement.

The interaction of Question with Question as in (13) shows that English has a *wh-* island constraint.

(13) *What did he ask who saw?

Such sentences are out in Kannada also:

(14) **yaaru nooDidaru endu KeeLidanu avanu eenannu?*

But this is because of the general fact noted with (8b) above. However, English also provides an indirect way of testing the existence of the *wh-* island constraint: since Question moves the *wh-* element into COMP and Relativization also moves an element (= *wh*) into COMP, the interaction of Relativization with Question is ungrammatical. Given (15)

(15) John asked who had seen the girl

we cannot now relativize *the girl* in the embedded question:

(16) *The girl who John asked who had seen. . .

But in Kannada we can: (17a) corresponds to (15) and (17b) to (16):

(17) a. *yaaru huDugiyaannu nooDidarendu raamanu KeeLidanu*
Who (nom.) girl (accu.) saw+CZR asked

b. *yaaru nooDidarendu raamanu keeLida huDugiyu pooliisarige sikkiddaaLe.*
(*The girl whom John had asked who had seen has been found by the police.)

Again (18a) corresponds to (15), and (18b) to (16):

(18) a. (*goopiyu pustakavannu yaaru baredaru endu keeLidanu*
Gopi book who wrote CZR asked
(nom.) (accu.) (nom.)

b. *goopiyu yaaru baredaru endu keeLida pustakavu bahaLa beleyuL-Laddu*
(*The book which Gopi asked who wrote is very expensive.)

Additional evidence of the same type is also available from the interaction of Question and Focussed Constructions. Contrast (19) with (20):

(19) *John, to whom has written

(20) a. *yaarige barediddaane, goopi?*
(Gopi, who has he written to?' or: Gopi, to whom has he written?)

b. *goopi, yaarige barediddane?*

Notice also: an NP in a relative clause cannot be relativized. Embedding (21) in (22) and relativizing the underlined NP in the relative clause of (21) results in the ungrammatical (23).

(21) *vigrahavannu kadda KaLLanu sikkibiddanu*
idol (accu.) stole (participle) thief (nom.) caught

(22) *vigrahavannu pratiSTHe maaDuttaare*
install do+will .

(23) **kadda kaLLanu sikkibidda vigrahavannu pratiSTHe maaDuttaare*

(*The idol which the thief who stole was caught will be installed.)

Similarly, Focus cannot apply to a construction to which it has already applied:

(24) a. *kaLLanu kaddanu, vigrahavannu*

'The idol, the thief stole'

b. **kaddanu, vigrahavannu kaLLanu*

(*The thief, the idol, stole.)

Now how do we interpret the data (17) - (24)? The possibilities are: (i) Relativization (also Focus) involves (*wh-*) movement but not Question; (ii) Question involves *wh-* movement but not Relativization (or Focus); (iii) none of the rules examined involve any movement. We claim that the correct conclusion is the last one which supports what we are trying to establish that Questions in Kannada do not involve *wh*-movement. The alternative at (ii), although it supports the main point we are trying to make (that Relativization involves no movement), has to be rejected as implausible in the light of the evidence presented so far about Questions. This leaves us with (i), which also suggests that Questions involve no *wh-* movement. We take it, then, that Questions in Kannada involve no *wh-* movement and examine the possibility whether Relativization involves any movement.

2.2.2 If question involves no *wh-* movement, it is highly unlikely that Relativization involves any movement (cf. Schwartz 1971).[4] However, Relativization does exhibit some of the properties described by Chomsky as diagnostic for *wh-* movement; it leaves a gap; it observes CNPC. So we must examine whether there is any plausible movement analysis of this rule.

The possibilities are:

(i) There is an underlying *wh-* word which is moved and is subsequently deleted. This, in the light of the discussion so far must be rejected. To assume that Relativization (or Focus) will involve a *wh-* movement when question does not will go counter to the whole spirit of Chomsky's (1977) analysis where rules which involve no overt *wh-* movement are analysed as having an underlying *wh-* movement *because* they observe the *wh-* island constraint; i.e., they cannot cross the island formed by *wh-* movement in questions. A more direct evidence also is available. Besides the participial relative clause discussed so far, Kannada has a non-participial relative clause as in:

(25) *yaava kaadambariyannu raamanu baredanoo aa kaadambariyu bahaLa čennaagide*

which novel (accu.) wrote+particle particle+novel (nom.) very good

(Which novel Rama wrote that novel is very good.)

4. Cited in de Rijk (1972:118).

This mode of relativization utilizes the relative correlative *yaava - aa*. The particle *aa*, which elsewhere functions as a distal demonstrative appears in the determiner of the matrix NP and the interrogative pronoun *yaava* appears in the determiner of the relativized NP. The verb in the relative clause is finite and takes on the suffix *oo*.

The point to notice is that when relativization does involve a *wh-* word, the *wh-*is *in place*; it is not moved at all. It is also of interest that this mode of relativization came late into the language, a borrowing from Indo-Aryan.[5]

(ii) There may be no *wh-* movement but some type of *NP movement* might be involved. For this to happen we should assume that either the top NP is deleted and the lower NP is moved into that position; or the lower NP is deleted and the top NP is moved into that position. (It is also possible that there is a base-generated *e* ⟨=empty node⟩ into which movement takes place, either way.)

But this suggestion, implausible on independent grounds, gives no support to Subjacency; it actually constitutes a refutation of that condition. Since there is no COMP-to-COMP movement and all intervening NP nodes may be filled, the movement (either way) will have to be an unbounded one, under the Structure Preserving Condition (cf. Emonds 1976). If so, it disconfirms the Subjacency Condition as the base and target nodes may be separated by more than one cyclic node. (Notice, also, that if some sort of deletion is to be assumed, any further movement analysis becomes redundant and the unbounded deletion rule would also constitute a disconfirmation of Subjacency.)

But, as noted above, the movement analysis is implausible on quite general grounds; movement into the lower NP position (assuming that *e* ⟨or the deletion site⟩ is in the lower clause) goes against the constraint proposed by Schwartz that elements are moved into higher nodes; not lower (Schwartz 1972). Movement into the higher NP position is made implausible by the fact that, in general, SOV languages have no such right-movement rules and unbounded right movement is, in any case, very suspect (cf. Ross 1970). We conclude that neither question nor relativization involves movement in Kannada.

2.3 Earlier on we listed (23) as showing that KPR observes CNPC. As Chomsky has rightly pointed out, such examples do not in themselves establish that CNPC is being observed. To show that the constraint being observed is CNPC we must first show that the rule in question is not subject to the weaker Complex Phrase Constraint. Consider (26-27):

(26) $[_{S}\,[_{NP}\,[_{S}\,[_{S}\,[_{S}$ *goopiyu ameerikadinda tanda endu* $_{S}]$
šaradeyu barediruva Lu endu $_{S}]$
raamu heeLida $_{S}]$ *gombeyu* $_{NP}]$ *čennagide* $_{S}]$

5. cf. Caldwell (1956:520): Narasimhia (1941:179).

(The doll which Ramu says that Sharada has written that Gopi brought from America is very good.)

(27) *[S [NP [S [NP [S *goopige lotariyalli banditu* S]
Gopi (dative) lottery in got

emba suddiyu NP] *huDugiyannu*
CZR news girl (accu.)

čaKitagoLisida S] *haNavu* NP] *kaLeduhooyitu* S]
surprised (participle) money lost

*'The money which the news that Gopi got in a lottery surprised the girl was lost.'

(26) and (27) have exactly the same number of intervening cyclic nodes. Yet (26) is good while (27) is bad. This clearly shows that KPR observes CNPC.

3. We have established that KPR is a non-movement, unbounded operation subject to CNPC, but not the *wh-* island constraint. This disconfirms several of Chomsky's assumptions and conclusions.[6]

(i) Chomsky has maintained that constraints like CNPC are observed only by movement rules (1977:118). Challenging Bresnan's claim (Bresnan 1975) that constructions like

(28) Who was planning to buy what

which involve no movement, still obey the CNPC as seen in

(29) *Who was arguing about a plan to buy what?

Chomsky argues that, at best, they only obey the Complex Phrase Constraint and not the Complex Noun Phrase Constraint (1977:117-118). But there is a crucial difference between the data we have considered and the data examined by Chomsky. While no movement is involved in either of the cases, the data we have examined involve *gaps.* The correct position, then, would seem to be that non-movement rules which do not leave gaps do not obey CNPC; but non-movement rules which involve gaps observe CNPC.

(ii) The Subjacency Condition can account for the observance of CNPC by a rule only if the rule in question is a movement rule. It follows that the Subjacency Condition cannot explain why KPR observes CNPC. This, in turn, implies that Subjacency is not a satisfactory generalization of CNPC, contrary to Chomsky's claim.

(iii) The *wh-* movement analysis presented in Chomsky (1977) does not hold good across languages. In Kannada, as in English, elements of a relative clause (Participial) cannot be topicalized but this is not because of any *wh-* movement underlying topicalization. There is none. (cf. Woolford, 1978 for a similar observation about Topicalization in Tok pisin.)

6. KPR is not an isolated rule. Other rules, too, like Topicalization, for example, show the same properties. Hence these rules also would contradict the Subjacency Condition and the other assumptions and conclusions of Chomsky (1977) noted in the text.

These conclusions suggest that the Subjacency Condition (and the associated successive-cyclic analysis of *wh-* movement) may be the wrong devices to account for the facts in question.[7] Nor can we fall back on Ross's CNPC which, besides being descriptively inadequate (cf. Horn 1975) is a totally *ad hoc* condition, as Chomsky has rightly noted. Quite obviously the facts of CNPC must follow from some larger principles.

It is beyond the scope of this paper to present an alternative to Subjacency. For an extensive discussion of the topic and a proposed alternative see Yadurajan (1980).

As for the facts of Kannada relativization, I take it that Relativization (KPR) as also Topicalization (and other rules involving 'gaps') fall under a general rule of construal, specifically, a rule of *Coindexing*. A base-generated *e* is coindexed with a matrix NP. This coindexing rule (we may call it the *NP-gap Binding Rule*) is subject to the Open Path Condition. This condition assures that under certain cirumstances, e.g. when a complex NP intervenes, the NP-gap Binding is ruled out.[8]

REFERENCES

Bach, E. and G.M. Horn. 1976. "Remarks on Conditions on Transformations". *Linguistic Inquiry* 7. 265-299.

Bresnan, J. 1975. "Comparative Deletion and Constraints on Transformations". *Linguistic Analysis* 1. 25-74.

———. 1976a. "On the Form and Functioning of Transformations." *Linguistic Inquiry* 7. 3-40.

———. 1976b. "Evidence for a Theory of Unbounded Transformations." *Linguistic Analysis* 4. 353-394.

———. 1977. "Variables in the Theory of Transformations." In *Formal Syntax*. ed. by P. Culicover, T. Wasow and A. Akmajian. New York: Academic press.

Caldwell, R. 1956. *A Comparative grammar of the Dravidian Languages*. Madras. (3rd edition)

Cattell, R. 1976. "Constraints on Movement Rules." *Language* 52. 18-50.

de Rijk, R.P.G. 1972. "Relative Clauses in Basque: a guided tour." In *The Chicago which hunt*. Chicago Linguistic Society.

Chomsky, N. 1973. "Conditions on Transformations." In *Festschrift for Morris Halle*. ed. by S. Anderson, and P. Kiparsky. New York: Holt, Rinehart and Winston.

———. 1977. "On *Wh*-Movement." In *Formal Syntax*. ed. by P. Culicover T. Wasow, and A. Akmajian. New York: Academic Press.

Emonds, J.E. 1976. *A Transformational Approach to English Syntax : Root, Structure-Preserving and Local Transformations*. New York: Academic Press.

Koster, J. 1978. "Conditions, Empty Nodes, and Markedness." *Linguistic Inquiry*, 9. 551-593.

---

7. The argument developed in this paper against the Subjacency Condition is only one of several others that can be constructed against this condition. cf. Koster (1978).

8. For details see Ragarajan (forthcoming). The open pain condition is formulated in Yadurajan (1980).

Nadkarni, M.V. 1970. NP-embedded Structures in Kannada and Konkani. Unpublished doctoral dissertation. UCLA.

Narasimhia, A.N. 1941. *Grammar of the Oldest Kanarese Inscriptions.* Mysore.

Ross, J.R. 1967. Constraints on Variables in Syntax. Unpublished doctoral dissertation, MIT, Cambridge, Massachusetts.

Schwartz, A. 1972. "Constraints on Transformations." *Journal of Linguistics*, 8. 35-86.

Woolford, E. 1978. "Topicalization and Clefting without *Wh-* movement", in M.J. Stein ed., *Papers from the Eighth Annual Meeting of the North Eastern Linguistic Society,* University of Massachusetts at Amherst, Massachusetts.

Yadurajan, K.S. 1980. Constraints on Movement Rules in English. Unpublished doctoral dissertation. CIEFL.

———. (forthcoming). "NP-gap Binding in Kannada."

TREATMENT OF HOMONYMY IN PĀṆINI'S AṢṬĀDHYĀYĪ

H.S. Ananthanarayana

Morphemes may be defined as phonemic sequences of the expression system and as units of meaning belonging to the content system. The relation between the phonemic sequences and the meanings is unique in that each sequence of phonemes conveys a distinct meaning and, conversely, meaning differences must be matched with difference in phonemic sequences. This neat situation is not always to be found in any language. One often finds that the same phonemic sequence in a language may convey more than one meaning, or, one and the same phonemic sequence may be said to have different functions in the grammar of that language. We may however think of having, in such situations, as many morphemes as there are different meanings, although they may all appear to be alike, phonemically. Instances of this kind are referred to by the term 'homonymy'. Morphemes may include lexical units as well as grammatical units and homonymy may be found equally among both of them. One of the problems of the linguist is to distinguish them formally in a grammar.

Homonymy may refer to situations in which two or more morphemes are pronounced the same way but are spelt differently in writing (e.g., Eng. *site* and *sight*; *rite* and *right*). It may also refer to situations in which morphemes are pronounced as well as spelt the same way (e.g., Eng. *ear* 'organ of hearing' and *ear* 'head of corn'; *mole* 'animal' and *mole* 'excrescence on skin'). We may also note that two or more forms which are spelt in the same way may however be pronounced differently (e.g., Eng. *lead* 'metal' and *lead* 'dog's lead'). The latter is called 'homography', the former, 'homophony'. The writing system used for Sanskrit allows representation of word sequences without junction features so that no distinction is recognized between, for example, *na tena likhito lekhaḥ* 'he did not write the letter' and *natena likhito lekhaḥ* 'bowing, he wrote the letter'. This kind of device has been exploited by writers for the construction of various types of Puns and riddles based on alternative divisions of the piece.

Homonymy results in ambiguity. In order to disambiguate such expressions we need to know the intention of the speaker. Among the Indian writers, Bhartṛhari (7th cent. A.D.) was probably the first to discuss this question, systematically. He lists in his *Vākyapadīya* (II.314) six factors which may be used as helpful cues in correctly interpreting the intended sense. They are: *vākya* 'syntactic construction', *prakaraṇa* 'context', *artha* 'goal', *aucitya* 'propriety', *deśa* 'place', and *kāla* 'time'. To illustrate only one of them, say context, the sentence *saindhavam ānaya* may be understood either meaning 'bring a horse', or 'bring salt', since the word *saindhavam* is here a homonym. However, on hearing the sentence, the listener will interpret it correctly considering the context, viz., whether the speaker uttered this sentence while taking his food, or while getting ready to go to a battle field. Thus, the homonymic situation may be resolved in favour of a single interpretation by resorting to the non-linguistic context.

Western linguists too (e.g., Katz and Fodor 1964) have been concerned with ambiguity in sentences based on lexical items having more than one semantic specification. Thus, the sentence *The bill is large* is ambiguous since it has two 'readings' resulting from the two meanings of *bill.* The sentence can, however, be disambiguated if we extend it with ... *but need not be paid.* Similarly, a word like *bachelor* would have to be distinguished between four meanings, by what are called 'markers' at the level of words.

Although homonymy is a recognized device, it has generally been restricted to only lexical units. Western linguists have not treated homonymous suffixal elements. However in modern times, we may note that writers on semantics have referred to suffixal homonyms. Thus, for instance, Palmer (1977:70ff) observes, "multiplicity of meaning is not confined to the words of the dictionary. It is also found with grammatical elements - the English past tense has two different meanings, past tense and unreality. So do prefixes; *in-* usually means 'not', but this is not so in *inflammable.*" In Sanskrit one comes across discussion on homonymy among the suffixes. Pāṇini (6th cent. B.C.) treats them in his *Aṣṭādhyāyī.* It is the purpose of this paper to show that Pāṇini realised the necessity of representing each semantic specification by a different morphological specification. He introduced certain formal distinctions to their underlying representation and then dropped these characteristics after they were phonetically realized. The paper also attempts, while discussing a homophonous suffix in Sanskrit, to focus on the descriptive techniques of Pāṇini's analysis.

There are five different suffixes involved in our discussion, viz., the primary derivative, the secondary derivative, the denominative, the passive, and the intensive. We will not discuss here the case-ending *ya* substituted for *ṅe* of the dative singular (7.1.13 e.g., *rāmāya*), the *uṇādi* affix *yak* applied to the root *han* 'to kill' to form the Vedic word *aghnya*, the augment *yak* added to the affix *ktvā* in Vedic (7.1.47 e.g., *dattvāya*), or the affix *yak* which derives roots from *kaṇḍū* and others (3.1.27 e.g., *kaṇḍūyate*). We will discuss each one of the suffixes and point out the differentiation made between them in the grammar.

1.The primary or *kṛt* affixes are applied to roots to form verbal derivatives. Suffixes other than *tiṅ* are termed *kṛt* (3.1.93). They are given by Pāṇini in the senses of different *kāraka* relations. Further, he states that if no other meaning is specifically assigned to a *kṛt* affix, then it should be understood that its sense is that of 'an agent of the verbal activity' (3.4.67). The *kṛt* affixes are exhaustively treated by Pāṇini in *sūtras* 3.1.91 to 3.4.117. We will however be concerned here only with four of them, *kyap*, *ṇyat*,

yat, and *lyap*, all of which are realized as *ya*. Of these four affixes, *lyap* is enjoined as a substitute for the gerundive termination *ktvā* in a compound where the first element is not a 'negative' (7.1.37 e.g., *prakṛ-tya* but *akṛ-tvā*). The other three are also termed *kṛtya* when the sense to be indicated by these affixes is 'should be done' (3.1.95). The affix *kyap* is treated in 16 *sūtras* (3.1.106-121), *ṇyat* in 11 *sūtras* (3.1.122-132) and *yat* in 10 *sūtras* (3.1.97-106). The final (1.3.3) as well as the initial consonants (1.3.5-8) in all these suffixes are termed *it* (1.3.2) which are finally dropped (1.3.9).

The affix *kyap* is added in the sense of 'verbal activity' (3.3.95) to derive feminine forms(3.3.94)from roots *vraj*, *yaj*, etc., (3.3.98 e.g., *vrajyā*, *ijyā*).[1] It is also added to roots *vad*, *bhū*, *han*, etc., when preceded by certain *upapadas*, in the sense of 'should be done' (3.1.106 e.g., *brahmavadyam*). The affix *ṇyat* is added to derive potential passive participles from roots ending in ṛ or any consonant (3.1.124 e.g., *kāryam*, *vākyam*). It indicates 'necessity of the activity' when added to a root ending in *u* (3.1.125). The palatal sounds, *c* and *j*, get the substitution of the corresponding velar sounds when bases are formed by the addition of this affix to the roots ending in palatal sounds (7.3.52 e.g., *pākyam*). However, the velar substitution is not made (7.3.59) when the base so formed is employed in the sense of 'necessity' (7.3.65 e.g., *avaśyapācyam*). The affix *yat* also derives potential passive participle and is added to roots in a final vowel (3.1.97 e.g., *geyam*, *peyam*). Final *ā* of stems gets the substitution of *ī* when this suffix is added (6.4.65 e.g., *deyam*, *dheyam*).

By making use of two final *it*-symbols, a two-way distinction is made of these affixes, *kyap* and *lyap* forming one set and *ṇyat* and *yat* forming another. Within each set a further differentiation is made by employing a different initial consonant. The final *it*-symbol in *lyap* signals an *anudātta* 'grave' accent to the affix by a general rule (3.1.4) while in *kyap* it indicates that the affix receives *udātta* 'acute' accent by a special rule (3.3.96). This symbol indicates further that when a *kṛt* affix with a *p*-symbol as its final *it* is applied to a root ending in a short vowel, an augment of the form /t/ is added before the affix (6.1.71 e.g., *viji-t-ya*). The final *it*-symbol in both affixes, *ṇyat* and *yat*, signal *svarita* 'circumflex' accent to the affix (6.1.185). The initial consonant in *ṇyat* distinguishes this suffix from *yat* by providing substitution of *vṛddhi* for the vowel preceding the affix (7.2.115). It also specifies that when a base is obtained from roots *īḍ*, *vand*, etc., by the addition of this suffix (6.1.214), the initial of this base (6.1.187) receives acute accent (6.1.159 e.g., *ī́ḍyam*, *vándyam*). On the other hand, being *ārdhadhātuka*, the affix *yat* signals a *guṇa* substitution for the final *ik*-vowel of the stem (7.3.84) and specifies that the initial syllable of a disyllabic base formed with this affix receives acute accent (6.1.213 e.g., *géyam*).

The initial consonant in the affix *kyap* debars the substitution of *guṇa* and *vṛddhi* to the preceding *ik*-vowel (1.1.5) and also allows *samprasāraṇa* (6.1.15) while the initial of *lyap* signals acute accent for the vowel of the base which immediately precedes the affix (6.1.193 e.g., *prakṛ́-tya*). Thus

1. The examples are cited in the final form, i.e. *Pada*, for convenience.

the four *kṛt* affixes all of which are phonetically realized as *ya* are differentiated by Pāṇini by certain subsequently deletable markers added initially and finally to the actual suffix. By this device the same suffix is made to appear differently in its underlying representations in the grammar. Only as many characteristics are utilized as the number of differentiation required to be explained. The markers signal information on the position of accent in the word as well as further grammatical operation, such as strengthening or the lack of strengthening of the radical vowel, gender of the form derived, etc. The distribution of the different forms of the same affix and the functions they signal (e.g., final syllable bearing acute, grave, and circumflex) are complementary to each other. We may therefore suggest that the different representations are *allos* of one and the same suffixal morpheme.

2. The secondary derivative or *taddhita* affixes derive nominal bases from primary nominal bases (*prātipadika*) as opposed to the primary suffixes discussed above which derive bases from roots (*dhātu*). The number of *taddhita* affixes mentioned by Pāṇini is quite a large one; there are in fact 1110 rules given in the *taddhita* section covering almost two *Adhyāyas*, viz., from 4.1.76 to the end of the 5th *Adhyāya*. We will discuss here only 17 of these affixes all of which are again realized finally in the form of *ya*. They are grouped in five sets on the basis of the *it*-symbols which are added either only finally or in final as well as initial positions.

The set which is distinguished only by the final *it*-symbol includes 7 forms: *yak*, *yaṭ*, *yap*, *yañ*, *yaṅ*, *yal*, and *ya*. The affix form *yak* derives secondary forms in the sense of 'quality' (5.1.119) or 'action' (5.1.124) from nominal bases having *pati* as their final component and also those belonging to the class of *purohita* (5.1.128 e.g., *paurohityam*, *prājāpatyam*). It also derives a secondary form *kaucavāryaḥ* from the nominal base *kūcavāra* (4.3.94) in the sense of 'a person of that place' (4.3.90). The form *yat* is applied to nominal bases *rāja* and *śvaśura* (4.1.137 e.g., *rājanyaḥ*) to derive secondary bases in the sense of 'offspring' (4.1.92); to nominal bases *śūla*, *ukhā* (4.2.17 e.g., *śūlyam*, *ukhyam*) to derive bases in the sense of 'food prepared' (4.2.16). It also derives nominal bases denoting such senses as 'the divinity thereof', 'staying therein', 'coming therefrom', 'belonging to', 'agreeable to', 'bought,' 'a body part', 'modification', 'similar to' and many others. The affixal form *yap* is applied to *dvigu*-compounds having *māsa* as their second member (5.1.82) in the sense of 'aged' (5.1.81 e.g., *dvimāsyaḥ*) and also to the nominal base *rūpa* in the sense of 'stamped' as well as 'praised' (5.2.120 e.g., *rūpyaḥ*).

The affixal form *yañ* derives secondary bases from nominal bases *garga* and others (4.1.105) in the sense of 'descendant' (4.1.98) and 'offspring', and from *keśa* and *aśva* (4.2.48) in the sense of 'collection of' (4.2.37 e.g., *kaiśyam*). In the sense of 'descendant', the nominal base formed of this affix may add further an affix *phak* (4.1.99) which gets the substitution of *āyana* (7.1.2 e.g., *gārgyāyaṇaḥ*). The affix *yan* is added to the nominal bases *brāhmana* and others (4.2.42) in the sense of 'collection of' (e.g., *brāhmaṇyam*), and to nominal bases *sagarbha* and others (4.4.114) in the sense of 'born thereof' (4.4.110 e.g., *sagarbhyaḥ*).

The affix *yal* is applied to a nominal base in which the first element is either *veśa* or *yaśas* and the second element is *bhaga* (4.4.131) in the sense of 'possession' (4.4.128 e.g., *veśobhagyaḥ*). Finally the affix form *ya* is applied to nominal bases *pāśa* and others (4.2.49) in the sense of 'collection of' (e.g., *pāśyā*); to *sabhā* (4.4.105) in the sense of 'good therein' (4.4.98 e.g., *sabhyaḥ*); and to *soma* (4.4.137), *daṇḍa* and others (5.1.66) in the sense of 'deserves' (e.g., *somyaḥ*, *daṇḍyaḥ*).

There are two forms in the set in which the initial consonant is a retroflex nasal: *ṇya and ṇyat*. Of them the *ṇya* form derives secondary bases from nominal bases *kuru* and others (4.1.151) in the sense of 'offspring' (e.g., *kauravyaḥ*) and *ṇyat* is applied to the nominal base *ṣaṇmāsa* (5.1.83) in the sense of 'aged' (e.g., *ṣāṇmāsyaḥ*). There are three forms in which the initial consonant is a palatal nasal:*ñya*, *ñyaṅ*, and *ñyaṭ*. Of them, *ñya* is employed after the nominal base *gambhīra* (4.3.58) in the sense of 'stays therein' (4.3.53 e.g., *gāmbhīryam*) and after the nominal base *vidūra* (4.3.84) in the sense of 'born of that' (4.3.83 e.g., *vaidūryaḥ*). It also denotes, when employed, such meanings as 'a person of that place', 'belonging to it' (4. 3.129 e.g., *chāndogyam*), 'having contact with' (4.4.90 e.g., *gārhapatyaḥ*), 'meant for another' (5.4.26 e.g., *ātithyam*). The form *ñyaṅ* is applied to nominal bases *kosala*, etc. (e.g., *kausalyaḥ*), and to bases termed *vṛddha* (i.e. nominal bases which have a *vṛddhi* vowel in their first syllable) (e.g., *āmbaṣṭhyaḥ*) and to bases with a final *ī*-vowel (4.1.171 e.g., *āvantyaḥ*), in the sense of 'offspring', provided that the nominal bases mean both the country and the warrior race (4.1.168). The affix form *ñyaṭ* is applied to nominal bases meaning a 'society living by the use of weapon', excepting the class of Brahmins and the warriors, especially among the *Vāhīkas*, in 'svārtha', i.e., the same sense as that possessed by the nominal base (5.3.114 e.g., *kṣaudrakyaḥ*).

There are two forms in the set in which the initial consonant is a retroflex sibilant: *ṣyaṅ* and *ṣyañ*. The form *ṣyaṅ* is employed as a substitute in the feminine for the affixes *aṇ* and *iñ* in the sense of a 'descendant' (4.1.78 e.g., *kārīṣagandhyā*, *vārāhyā*) of nominal bases with a heavy penultimate syllable. The form *ṣyañ* is added in the sense of 'quality of it' (5.1.119) to nominal bases *dṛḍha* and others denoting 'particular colours' (5.1.123 e.g., *śauklyam*). There are three forms in the set containing an initial cerebral voiced consonant: *ḍya*, *ḍyat*, and *ḍyaṇ*. Of them, both *ḍya* and *ḍyat* are employed after the nominal base *vāmadeva* (4.2.9) in the sense of 'Sāma introduced by' (4.2.7 e.g., *vāmadevyam*), and optionally, after the nominal base *srotas* (4.4.113) in the sense of 'present therein' (e.g., *srotasyaḥ*). And in this last sense, the form *ḍyaṇ* is applied to nominal bases *pātha* and *nadī* (4.4.111 e.g., *pāthyaḥ*, *nādyaḥ*).

By employing again *it*-symbols only in the final position for some and in both initial and final positions for others, a two-way distinction is made of these affixes. In the initial position the *it*-symbol is either a retroflex or a palatal sound. Each member in each of the sets is differentiated from others by only one marker. For instance, the form *ṇya* is distinguished from *ṇyat* by not having a final consonant; *ṣyaṅ* is distinguished from *ṣyañ* by a different nasal as the final *it*-symbol. The final as well as the initial consonant in all these forms are termed *it* and are dropped after providing for the operations for which they are introduced.

The final *it*-symbol in *yat*, *ḍyat*, and *ṇyat* signals the circumflex accent for the affix element in the nominal bases formed with these affixes (e.g., *rājanyaḥ*, *ṣāṇmāsyaḥ*), whereas the absence of a specific symbol in *ya*, *ḍya*, and *ṇya* specifies acute accent on the affix (3.1.3 e.g., *sabhyáḥ*, *kauravyáḥ*). The symbol *ñ* specifies an acute accent for the first vowel of the bases formed with the affixes marked by it (6.1.197). The symbol that is final in *yan* indicates that the base characterized by this affix receives the acute accent on the vowel of the first syllable (e.g., *bráhmaṇyam*). The final symbol in *yal* signals acute accent for the vowel of the base which immediately precedes the suffix (6.1.159 e.g., *veśobhágyaḥ*), and the symbol *p* indicates grave accent of affixes marked with it. The *it*-symbol *k* provides acute accent for the final syllable.

The final *it*-symbol in *ñyaṭ* signifies that in the feminine the suffix *ṅīp* is added (4.1.15) to the nominal bases from which *ñyaṭ* derives a secondary base (e.g., *kṣaudrakī*). The final symbol in *ñyaṅ* and *ṣyaṅ* specifies that in the feminine the suffix *cāp* (4.1.74) will be added to the nominal bases which possess those affixes (e.g., *āvantyā*, *vārāhyā*). The initial symbol in *ṣyaṅ* and *ṣyañ* specifies that in the feminine the suffix *ṅīṣ* (4.1.41) will be added to nominal bases which possess these suffixes. Since both *cāp* and *ṅīṣ* are provided by *ṣyaṅ*, *cāp* being an *apavāda* rule in the grammar prevails over *ṅīṣ*.

The *it*-symbol *ṇ* in *ḍyaṇ*, *ṇya*, and *ṇyat*; *k* in *yak*; and *ñ* in *yañ*, *ṣyañ*, *ñya*, *ñyaṅ*, and *ñyaṭ* indicate the substitution of *vṛddhi* (7.2.114) for the initial vowel of the stem (7.2.117). The initial *it*-symbol in *ḍya*, *ḍyat*, and *ḍyaṇ*, specifies that the final vowel and the following consonant, if any, of the nominal base are elided before these affixes.

Thus, the different forms of the same suffix are distinguished each from the others, first of all, by the nature of accent they specify for the base (e.g., circumflex, grave, acute); the accent being the same, then by the position where it falls in the bases (e.g., initial syllable, final syllable, penultimate syllable, etc.). They are further differentiated by adding or not adding a feminine suffix and when added, by the kind of feminine suffix (e.g., *cāp* or *ṅīṣ*). They are also distinguished on the basis of whether or not there will be substitution of *vṛddhi* for the initial vowel of the base. We may therefore think of only one suffix here too with several members each having roles complementary to others. Even if they signal the same grammatical operation (e.g., *ñyaṅ* and *ṣyaṅ*), or provide for the same accentual specification (e.g., *yan* and *ñya*) their domain of application is different, i.e., they are applied to different lists of nominal bases. Although the phonological structures of the secondary bases derived by the addition of different suffixal forms appear to be the same, they specify different shades of meaning.

The *taddhita* affixes are distinguished from the *kṛt* affixes. For instance, the *kṛt* affix *kyap* and the *taddhita* affix *yak* have the same *it*-symbol. However, it specifies different operations; in the *kṛt* suffix, it debars the substitution of *guṇa* and *vṛddhi* while it provides for *vṛddhi* substitution in the *taddhita*. There is *ṇyat* which is both a *kṛt* as well as a *taddhita* affix. The two are differentiated by Pāṇini, by placing them in different sections of the grammar so that they do not interfere with each other's operation. This kind of separation of affixes is another device utilized by Pāṇini in his grammar.

3. The denominative affixes are so termed because they derive roots from nouns. The nouns, to which they are added, can fill the position of objects of the verb 'to desire'. We are concerned with only three such affixes here, viz., *kyac*, *kyaṅ*, and *kyaṣ*. They are referred together by the term *kya* (1.4.15). It is a device of Pāṇini to use the same *it*-symbol for all the terms which are members of one set. The symbol that binds them all here is the symbol *k* and the other *it*-symbols differentiate each from the others.

The affix form *kyac* derives roots from nouns in the sense of 'desiring for oneself' (3.1.8). The final *a*-vowel of such nouns will get the substitution of *ī* when the affix *kyac* is added (7.4.33). The verb form thus derived, for instance, *puttrīyati*, is equivalent to a sentence with a verb and an object, *putram ātmanaḥ icchati* 'desires a son for himself'. The affix *kyac* is added also to nouns which function as 'standards of comparison' and will have the meaning 'behaviour' (3.1.10). It derives roots from *namas*, *varivas*, and *citra* in the sense of 'doing' (3.1.19 e.g., *namasyati*). The affix form *kyaṅ* is added to nouns in the sense of 'similar behaviour' when the comparison is meant for the subject (3.1.11 e.g., *śyenāyate*). The affix form *kyaṣ* derives roots from nouns *lohita* and others (3.1.13 e.g., *lohitāyati*).

The final *it*-symbol in *kyaṅ* specifies middle terminations to be added to roots derived by the addition of this affix (1.3.12). The roots ending in *kyac* will add the active terminations (1.3.78), and the final *it*-symbol in *kyaṣ* indicates that roots ending with this affix will optionally add (1.3.90) active terminations (1.3.78). The final *it*-symbol in *kyac* signals that the form derived by the addition of this suffix receives acute accent on the final syllable (6.1.163 e.g., *puttrīyá*).

The denominative affix is distinguished from the *taddhita* affix; the former derives from nouns roots which then add *tiṅ* affixes whereas the latter derives secondary nominal bases from primary nominal bases to which are added *sup* affixes. Similarly, the denominative is differentiated from the *kṛt* affix in that a form derived by the addition of a *kṛt* affix does not further add a *tiṅ* affix.

4. The suffix *yak* derives a passive stem and is applied to roots when the latter are followed by *sārvadhātuka* affixes, i.e., the personal endings (3.1.67),

having the sense of 'state' as well as 'act' (3.1.66). Only the middle terminations are added further to this passive stem (1.3.13 e.g., *āsyate*, *kriyate*). The *it*-symbol in the affix debars the substitution of *guṇa* and *vṛddhi* to the preceding *ik*-vowel. The suffix receives acute accent; however, the roots ending in a vowel are optionally marked by an acute accent on the initial syllable (6.1.195 e.g., *lū́yate*).

5. Finally, the affix *yaṅ* derives intensive stems when added to roots which are monosyllabic and have an initial consonant. The sense of the form is intensity of action or repetition of an action (3.1.22 e.g., *pāpacyate*). Here the affix specifies the reduplication of the first syllable; if the roots begin however with a vowel, then the reduplication involves the second syllable (6.1.9 e.g., *yāyajyate*, *arāryate*). Again because of the affix which is not having *k* as an *it*-symbol, the vowel of the reduplication gets lengthened (7.4.83). The final *it*-symbol specifies the addition of only the middle terminations to stems derived by this affix.

It is clear from the foregoing discussion that Pāṇini has attempted to distinguish two or more morphemes included in a homonymy. For this purpose, he has introduced deletable symbols which signal various functions and also contribute to formal distinctions between the different morphemes. The morpheme which denotes 'Intensive' and the morpheme which denotes 'Passive' are represented by single phonemic shapes. The other three, viz., *kṛt*, *taddhita*, and the denominative, are represented by more than one shape. Since we noted that the different representations within each morpheme are complementarily distributed, they were considered here as allomorphs of a single morpheme. There are however a few instances of allos of two different morphemes having common shapes (e.g., *yat* and *ṇyat* are *kṛt* as well as *taddhita*; *yak* is both *taddhita* and passive).

The morphemes discussed here are arranged in different sections of the grammar (e.g., *kṛt* is treated in the third chapter while *taddhita* figures in the fourth and fifth chapters) and thus contribute towards the removal of confusion among forms in a homonymic situation. They have different functions: *kṛt* derives from roots verbal derivatives such as potential passive participles; *taddhita* derives secondary nominal bases from primary nominal bases, and the denominative derives roots from nouns. They all share one thing in common; they are all derivational morphemes and stems derived by them will receive the designation of *pada* by a further addition of inflectional morphemes.

The formal distinctions in the morphemes have corresponding semantic distinctions. They include such things as the nature and/or position of accents; the modification of the radical vowel either by *guṇa* or by *vṛddhi* processes; the further addition of a gender suffix; the type of gender suffix (e.g., *cāp* as in *āvantyā*, *ṅīp* as in *kṣaudrakī*). The affixes have different meanings: *kṛt* specifies 'verbal activity' and 'necessity of action'; *taddhita* has various senses such as 'modification', 'descendant', 'quality'; the denominative has the sense of 'desire for oneself'; the passive has the sense of 'state' as well as of 'act'; and finally, the intensive has the meaning of 'intensity' and 'repetition' of action. It is noted that although these affixes have different ranges of meaning, each one further distinguishes within itself different shades of meaning. In some cases, the meanings are so different that it may not be correct to term them simply different shades of the same meaning. This is especially true of the *taddhita* affix for which we have noted many meanings.

List of Pāṇini's sūtras referred to in the paper

1.1.5 kṅiti ca
1.3.2 upadeśe' janunāsika it
1.3.3 hal antyam
1.3.5 ādir ñiṭuḍavaḥ
1.3.6 ṣaḥ pratyayasya
1.3.7 cuṭū
1.3.8 laśakvataddhite
1.3.9 tasya lopaḥ
1.3.12 anudāttaṅita ātmanepadam
1.3.13 bhāvakarmaṇoḥ
1.3.78 śeṣāt karttari parasmaipadam
1.3.90 vā kyaṣaḥ
1.4.15 naḥ kye
3.1.3 ādyudāttaś ca
3.1.4 anudāttau suppitau
3.1.8 supa ātmanaḥ kyac
3.1.10 upamānād ācāre
3.1.11 karttuḥ kyaṅ salopaś ca
3.1.13 lohitād iḍājbhyaḥ kyaṣ
3.1.19 namovarivaścitraṅaḥ kyac
3.1.22 dhātor ekāco halādeḥ kriyāsamabhihāre yaṅ
3.1.27 kaṇḍvādibhyo yak
3.1.66 ciṇ bhāvakarmaṇoḥ
3.1.67 sārvadhātuke yak
3.1.93 kṛd atiṅ
3.1.95 kṛtyāḥ prāṅ ṇvulaḥ
3.1.97 aco yat
3.1.106 vadaḥ supi kyap ca
3.1.124 ṛhalor ṇyat
3.1.125 or āvaśyake
3.3.94 striyāṃ ktin
3.3.95 sthāgāpāpaco bhāve
3.3.96 mantre vṛṣeṣapacamanavidabhūvīrā udāttaḥ
3.3.98 vrajayajor bhāve kyap
3.4.67 karttari kṛt
4.1.15 ṭiḍḍhāṇañdvayasajdaghnañmātractayapṭhakṭhañkañkvarapkhyunām

4.1.41 ṣidgaurādibhyaś ca
4.1.74 yaṅaś cāp
4.1.78 aṇiñor anārṣayor gurūpottamayoḥ ṣyaṅ gotre
4.1.92 tasyāpatyam
4.1.98 gotre kuñjādibhyaścphañ
4.1.99 naḍādibhyaḥ phak
4.1.105 gargādibhyo yañ
4.1.137 rājaśvaśurād yat
4.1.151 kurvādibhyo ṇyaḥ
4.1.168 janapadaśabdāt kṣattriyād añ
4.1.171 vṛddhet kosalājādāñ ñyaṅ
4.2.7 dṛṣṭaṃ sāma
4.2.9 vāmadevāḍ ḍyaḍḍyau
4.2.16 saṃskṛtam bhakṣāḥ
4.2.17 śūlokhād yat
4.2.37 tasya samūhaḥ
4.2.42 brāhmaṇamāṇavavāḍavād yan
4.2.48 keśāśvābhyāṃ yañchāvanyatarasyām
4.2.49 pāśādibhyo yaḥ
4.3.53 tatra bhavaḥ
4.3.58 gambhīrāñ ñyaḥ
4.3.83 prabhavati
4.3.84 vidūrāñ ñyaḥ
4.3.90 abhijanaś ca
4.3.94 tūdīśalāturavarmatīkūcavārāḍ ḍhakchaṇḍhañyakaḥ
4.3.129 chandogaukthikayājñikabahvṛcanaṭāñ ñyaḥ
4.4.90 gṛhapatinā saṃyukte ñyaḥ
4.4.98 tatra sādhuḥ
4.4.105 sabhāyā yaḥ
4.4.110 bhave chandasi
4.4.111 pāthonadībhyāṃ ḍyaṇ
4.4.113 srotaso vibhāṣā ḍyaḍḍyau
4.4.114 sagarbhasayūthasanutād yan
4.4.128 matvarthe māsatanvoḥ
4.4.131 veśoyaśa āder bhagād yal
4.4.137 somamarhati yaḥ
5.1.66 daṇḍādibhyo yaḥ
5.1.81 māsād vayasi yat khañau
5.1.82 dvigor yap
5.1.83 ṣaṇmāsāṇ ṇyacca
5.1.119 tasya bhāvas tvatalau
5.1.123 varṇadṛḍhādibhyaḥ ṣyañ ca
5.1.124 guṇavacanabrāhmaṇādibhyaḥ karmaṇi ca
5.1.128 patyantapurohitādibhyo yak
5.2.120 rūpād āhatapraśaṃsayor yap

5.3.114 āyudhajīvisaṅghāñ ñyaṅ vāhīkeṣvabrāhmaṇarājanyāt
5.4.26 atitheñyaḥ
6.1.9 sanyaṅoḥ
6.1.15 vacisvapiyajādīnām kiti ca
6.1.71 hrasvasya piti kṛti tuk
6.1.159 karṣatvato ghaño 'nta udāttaḥ
6.1.163 citaḥ
6.1.165 kitaḥ
6.1.185 tit svaritam
6.1.187 ādiḥ sico 'nyatarasyām
6.1.193 liti
6.1.195 acaḥ kartṛyaki
6.1.197 ñnityādir nityam
6.1.213 yato 'nāvaḥ
6.1.214 īḍavandavṛśaṃsaduhām ṇyataḥ
6.4.65 īd yati
7.1.2 āyaneyīnīyiyaḥ phaḍhakhacchaghām pratyayādīnām
7.1.13 ṅer yaḥ
7.1.37 samāse 'nañpūrve ktvo lyap
7.1.47 ktvo yak
7.2.114 mṛjer vṛddhiḥ
7.2.115 aco ñṇiti
7.2.117 taddhiteṣvacām ādeḥ
7.3.52 cajoḥ ku ghiṇṇyatoḥ
7.3.59 nakvādeḥ
7.3.65 ṇya āvaśyake
7.3.84 sārvadhātukārdhadhātukayoḥ
7.4.33 kyaci ca
7.4.83 dīrgho' kitaḥ

REFERENCES

Katz, J.J. and J.A. Fodor. 1963. "The Structure of a semantic theory." *Language* 39.170-210.

Palmer, F.R. 1977. *Semantics*. London: Cambridge University Press.

PHONOLOGY AND PHONETICS IN ANCIENT INDIAN WORKS THE CASE OF VOICED AND VOICELESS ELEMENTS

George Cardona

1. Prātiśākhya works, it is known, state phonologic rules relating one version of a Vedic text with another. Three such rules are

(1) TPr. 10.2: dīrghaṃ samānākṣare savarṇa-pare

(2) RPr. 2.15: samānākṣare sasthāne dīrgham ekam ubhe svaram

(3) VPr. 4.50: siṃ savarṇe dīrgham

all of which concern collocations of final and initial vowels in elements that are constituents in analyzed Vedic texts (*pada-pāṭha*). According to (1) TPr. 10.2, if a vowel of the samānākṣara class is followed by a vowel savarṇa with it, both together give a single long vowel.[1] For example: *tvacam gṛhṇīṣva antaḥ-itam rakṣaḥ→tvacaṅ gṛhṇīṣvāntaritaṃ rakṣaḥ* (TS 1.1.8.1)[2] 'Take on your skin; any demon has been put away,' *rāsnā asi indrāṇyai→ rāsnāsīndrāṇyai* (TS 1.1.2.2) 'You are Indrāṇī's girdle.' The *-a* and *a-* of the constituents *gṛhṇīṣva* and *antaḥ* are changed to *ā* in deriving *gṛhṇīṣvāntaritaṃ* of the continuously recited text; in the same manner, *-ā a-* and *-i i-* are changed to *ā* and *ī* in accounting for *rāsnāsīndrāṇyai*. Similarly, (2) RPr. 2.15 provides that two homorganic (*sasthāne*) vowels of the samānākṣara set both are combined to give a single long vowel,[3] and according

---

1. (1)TPr. 10.2 comes under the heading TPr. 10.1: *athaikam ubhe*. Rules under this heading let both (*ubhe*) the sounds given as operands change to one (*ekam*). According to TPr. 1.23: *aṅkāra āgama-vikāri-lopinām*, TPr. 1.28: *aṃ vikārasya*, a nominative form is used to designate an augment (*āgama*), an element which undergoes a change (*vikārin*), or one which undergoes deletion (*lopin*), and an accusative form is used to designate a modified entity (*vikāra*). Thus, in TPr. 10.1, the nominative dual *ubhe* (sc. *akṣare*) 'both (sounds)' refers to sounds which are subject to change, the accusative *ekam* 'one' to the result of such change. Similarly, in(1)TPr. 10.2 *dīrgham* 'long vowel' refers to the result of the operation provided for when a samānākṣara vowel is followed by one that is savarṇa with it (*samānākṣare savarṇa-pare*).

2. To the left of the arrow appears the pertinent part of the analysed text (*pada-pātha*), to the right the continuously recited text (*saṃhitā-pāṭha*). I have simplified by omitting accents. Note also that the pada-pāṭha of the Taittirīya-saṃhitā gives compounds such as *antaritam* in two forms, with *iti* after the first: *antaritam ity antaḥ-itam.* I have again simplified by citing only the second form, in which components are separated. Finally, I give the last word of a citation in its prepause form (e.g., *rakṣaḥ*, with *-ḥ*) though in the full text it be followed by elements which condition other variants.

3. RPr. 1.56: *asāv amum iti tad-bhāvam uktaṃ yathāntaram* (*pratīyāt* 53) is a metarule (*paribhāṣā*) which serves to interpret nominatives such as *samānākṣare sasthāne ... ubhe* 'both homorganic samānākṣara' and accusatives such as *dīrgham ekam ... svaram* 'a single long vowel' in rules such as (2)RPr. 2.15. When forms *X-nom.* (*asau*), *Y-acc.* (*amum*

to (3)VPr. 4.50, a vowel of the sim set and a following vowel which is savarṇa with it together change to a single long vowel.[4]

(1) - (3) concern particular sets of vowels, called *samānākṣara* ('simple vowels') in the Taittirīya- and Ṛk-prātiśākhya, *sim* in the Vājasaneyi- prātiśākhya. These texts operate with accepted sound lists (*varṇa-samāmnāya*),[5] and assign class names to groups of sounds in these lists, thus recognizing different sets of sounds. According to

(4) TPr. 1.2: atha navāditaḥ samānākṣarāṇi

(5) TPr. 1.5: ṣoḍaśāditaḥ svarāḥ

(6) TPr. 1.6: śeṣo vyañjanāni

the first nine sounds of the list accepted in this work have the class name *samānākṣara*; the first sixteen sounds are called *svara* ('vowels'); and the rest have the name *vyañjana* ('consonant'). The sixteen sounds referred to in (5)TPr. 1.5 are: *a ā a3 i ī i3 u ū u3 ṛ ṝ ḷ e ai o au*. Of these, the first nine constitute the class of samānākṣara. Further, by

(7) TPr. 1.3: dve dve savarṇe hrasva-dīrghe

each two short and long samānākṣara in the triplets *a ā a3* etc. make up a group of sounds said to be *savarṇa* ('homogeneous') with each other. Thus, *a ā*, *i ī*, and *u ū* are savarṇa sets. Accordingly, (1)TPr. 10.2 provides for the following change -*ă ă*- → *ā*, -*ĭ ĭ*- → *ī*, -*ŭ ŭ*- →*ū*. The set of samānākṣara provided for by

(8) RPr. 1.1: aṣṭau samānākṣarāṇy āditaḥ

consists of the first eigth sounds in the list accepted for the Ṛk-prātiśākhya: *a ā ṛ ṝ i ī u ū*. Moerover, (2)RPr. 2.15 includes a phonetic qualification for the sounds said to undergo fusion: the two samānākṣara in question must be homorganic (*sasthāna* 'having the same place of production'). The set of samānākṣara provided for by (8)RPr. 1.1 and the sim set provided for by

(9) VPr. 1.44: sim ādito' ṣṭau svarāṇām

have the same members: according to (9)VPr. 1.44, the first eight vowels (i.e., *a ā i ī u ū ṛ ṝ*) are called *sim*. In addition, (3)VPr. 4.50 also includes a phonetic qualification, as does (2)RPr. 2.15. For it says a vowel of the sim set and a following vowel change to a single long vowel if the second is savarṇa with the first, and according to

(10) VPr. 1.43: samāna-sthāna-karaṇāsya-prayatnaḥ savarṇaḥ

a sound *b* is said to be *savarṇa* ('homogeneous') with a sound *a* if it has the

are used, one is to understand it to be said that X becomes Y(*tad-bhāvam uktam pratīyāt*); and if there is a possible choice of results, that Y is selected which is closest to the original X.

4. (3)VPr. 4.50 comes under the heading of VPr. 4.49: *athaikam uttaraś ca*: subsequent rules provide that a given sound and one which follows (*uttaraś ca*) both change to a single sound (*ekam*). According to VPr. 1.133: *tam iti vikāraḥ*, a term *X-acc.* (*tam*) designates the result of a modification (*vikāra*), and by VPr. 1.142: *vikārī yathāsannam*, a sound which is to undergo modification (*vikārin*) changes to the one closest to it (*yathāsannam*).

5. TPr. 1.1: *atha varṇa-samāmnāyaḥ* ('Now the accepted sound list') refers to such a list as accepted in this work.

same (*samāna*) place of production (*sthāna*), active articulator (*karaṇa*), and type of articulatory effort in the oral cavity (*āsya-prayatna*) as *a*.

(7) TPr. 1.3 and (10)VPr. 1.43 differ in two obvious ways. The latter concerns sets of sounds, both vowels and consonants, determined by stated phonetic criteria. The former concerns sets of vowels alone, and these sets are not defined in terms of phonetic criteria. Clearly, (7)TPr. 1.3 sets up groups of savarṇa vowels in respect of the operation provided for in (1) TPr. 10.2. Now, this rule is in part an exception to

(11) TPr. 10.15: i-varṇo-kārau ya-va-kārau

according to which *i*-vowels (*i-varṇa*) and *u* (*u-kāra*) change respectively to *y* and *v* when followed by vowels.[6] If the vowel which follows -ĭ or -*u* is one that is savarṇa with it, semivowel conversion does not apply; instead, vowel fusion provided for by (1)TPr. 10.2. takes effect. However, consider the following. The vocative form *agna3i*[7] is followed by a consonant in *agna3i patnīva3s sajūr devena tvaṣṭrā somam piba* (TS 1.4.27) 'Agni with the wives, drink the soma with heavenly Tvaṣṭṛ.' On the other hand, the analyzed text of TS 6.5.8.4 has *agna3i iti āha*, with *iti* following *agna3i*, and from this one should get *agna*3 *īty āha* ([The priest] says "*agna3i*".') of the continuously recited text. But in terms of (7)TPr. 1.3 the -*i* of *agna3i* and the *i*- of *iti* are savarṇa vowels, so that they are eligible for vowel fusion. Were this to apply, one would get **agna*3 *īty āha*, which has to be prevented. The required result *agna*3 *ity āha* is accounted for if semivowel conversion by (11)TPr. 10.15 can apply not only to the -*i* of *iti* (*iti āha*→*ity āha*) but also to the -*i* of *agna3i*: *agna3i iti*→ *agna3y iti*. For, according to

(12) TPr. 10.19: lupyete tv a-varṇa-pūrvau ya-va-kārau

-*y* and -*v* preceded by *a*-vowles are deleted (*lupyete*) before vowels: *agna3y iti* →*agna*3 *iti*.[8] Of course, this is possible only if (11)TPr. 10.15 applies in

---

6. TPr. 9.10: *atha svara-paro ya-kāram* contains a heading valid in later rules: *svara-paraḥ* 'followed by a vowel.' By contextual modification of endings, one understands *svara-parau*, modifying *i-varṇo-kārau*, in (11)TPr. 10.15.

7. This derives from *agne*. Pāṇini's rule 8.2.82: *vākyasya ṭeḥ pluta udāttaḥ* is a heading: under conditions to be stated in following rules, the last vowel of an utterance is replaced by an extra-long high-pitched vowel (*pluta udāttaḥ*). According to 8.2.107: *eco' pragṛhyasyādūrāddhūte pūrvasyārdhasyād uttarasyed-utau*, if the vowel subject to replacement by an extra-long one is *e* or *o* (*ecaḥ*), provided this is not a pragṛhya vowel and the prolation does not apply in calling from afar (*adūrāddhūte*), then the following takes effect: the first half of *e*, *o* (*pūrvasyārdhasya*) is replaced by an extra-long *ā* ([*plutaḥ*] *āt*), the second half by *i*, *u*, respectively. One thus gets *agna3i*. The Taittirīya-prātiśākhya does not have special rules accounting for such a vocative, since it appears as *agna3i* in the analyzed text from which the continuously recited text is derived.

8. According to TPr. 10.24: *na pluta-pragrahau*, prolated vowels (*pluta*) and vowels of the pragraha class do not (*na*) undergo phonologic changes, so that *agna*3 *iti* is not subject to any further change affecting -*a*3. Rules following (12)TPr. 10.19 give information concerning -*y*, -*v* as treated in other dialects. For example, TPr. 10.20: *nokhyasya* says that according to Ukhya -*y* or -*v* preceded by an *a*-vowel is not (*na*) deleted. It is understandable, then, why the Taittirīya-prātiśākhya accounts for an instance such as *agna*3 *ity āha* through an intermediary stage *agna3y ity āha*.

agna3i iti instead of (1)TPr. 10.2, though the latter is an exception to the former. It is to provide for this that

(13) TPr. 1.4: na pluta-pūrvam

says a samānākṣara preceded by a pluta vowel is not savarṇa with another samānākṣara, as would otherwise obtain by (7)TPr. 1.3. The *-i* of *agna3i* and the *i-* of *iti* are thereby not savarṇa, so that (1)TPr. 10.2 cannot apply to *agna3i iti*.

Clearly, whether or not a given *-i* is considered homogeneous (*savarṇa*) with a following *i-* according to (7)TPr. 1.3, (13)TPr. 1.4 depends ultimately on the operation which an *-i* is to undergo. Now, as has been noted, (7) TPr. 1.3 does not concern sets determined explicitly by phonetic criteria, but (10)VPr. 1.43 does. In this connection, consider the passage *mā tvāgnir dhvanayīt* (VS 25.37a) 'Let not the fire cause you to make noise,' to which corresponds *mā tvā agniḥ dhvanayīt* in the analysed text. (3)VPr. 4.50 should account for the *-ā-* of *tvāgnir* here, from *tvā agniḥ*. Of course, for this rule to apply, the *-ā* of *tvā* and the *a-* of *agniḥ* must be homogeneous (*savarṇa*) sounds in terms of the criteria given in (10)VPr. 1.43. However, there is a problem. Long *ā* is a low back vowel, short *a* a mid central vowel. In terms used by Indian phoneticians, the former is open (*vivṛta*), the latter close (*saṃvṛta*), so that they differ in respect of articulatory effort in the oral cavity (*āsya-prayatna*). Consequently, *ā* and *a* cannot be homogeneous by (10)VPr. 1.43. Yet it is true that collocated vowels *-ā̆ ā̆-* give *ā*, just as *-ī̆ -ī̆* and *-ū̆ ū̆-* give *ī* and *ū*: though phonetically different, *ā* and *a* behave in the same manner phonologically. Hence, after saying that *a*-vowels are pharyngeal, the Vājasaneyi-prātiśākhya goes on to say that they are treated as homogeneous with each other (*savarṇavat*):

(14) VPr. 1.72: savarṇavac ca

Consequently, (3)VPr. 4.50 can apply to *-ā a-*, though the two vowels in question are not truly homogeneous.

It is known that a similar procedure is followed by Pāṇini and others. The Pāṇinian rule corresponding to (1) - (3) is

(15) 6.1.101: akaḥ savarṇe dīrghaḥ

whereby a vowel *ā̆ ī̆ ū̆ ṝ̆ ḷ* and a following vowel homogeneous (*savarṇa*) with it are both replaced by a single long vowel (*dīrgha*).[9] By

(16) 1.1.9: tulyāsya-prayatnaṃ savarṇam

a sound *b* is homogeneous (*savarṇa*) with a sound *a* if it is produced with the same articulatory effort at the same place of production in the oral cavity (*tulyāsya-prayatna*) as *a*, and according to

(17) 1.1.69: aṇ udit savarṇasya cāpratyayaḥ

a vowel *a i u ṛ l e o ai au* or a semivowel *y v r l* is a term used to designate a set of homogeneous sounds.[10] Thus, *i* denotes short *i*, long *ī*, and extra-

9. (15)6.1.101 comes in a section of rules headed by 6.1.84: *ekaḥ pūrva-parayoḥ*: these rules provide that one sound replaces both the preceding and following sounds given.

10. The abbreviation *a*Ṇ refers to the sounds given in the first six śiva-sūtra: *a i u* Ṇ *ṛ ḷ* K *e o* Ṅ *ai au* C *h y v r* Ṭ *l* Ṇ (with markers [*it*] shown in upper case Roman symbols).

long *i*3, each with three possible pitches and nasalized or non-nasal. The abbreviation *aK* (abl. sg. *akaḥ*) used in (15) 6.1.101 refers in the first instance to the vowels *a i u ṛ ḷ*; by (17) 1.1.69, then, each of these designates a set of vowels. Now, as Kātyāyana says in his first vārttika on śiva-sūtra 1 (*akārasya vivṛtopadeśa ākāra-grahaṇārthaḥ*), one must recognize that the vowel *a* given in this śiva-sūtra (*a i u* Ṇ) is taught as open (*vivṛta*), in order that, by (17) 1.1.69, it refer to *ā*. That is, once *a* is treated as an open vowel, it can be homogeneous with *ā* by (16) 1.1.9, hence can be used as a class term referring to *ā*. Of course, *a* is actually a close (*saṃvṛta*) vowel. Therefore, having treated *a* as an open vowel throughout his grammar, for phonologic purposes, Pāṇini reinstitutes *a* in its actual value by the last rule of the Aṣṭādhyāyī:

(18) 8.4.68: a a

There are thus instances where phonologic and phonetic considerations are to be balanced against each other. There are several instances such that terms used or statements made in prātiśākhya and śikṣā works might appear to be based only on phonetic criteria but actually reflect phonologic considerations. In this paper, I shall deal with one such case: the use of *ghoṣavat* in prātiśākhyas with reference to voiced consonants alone.

2. The authors of prātiśākhya and śikṣā works correlate sets of sounds with different physical processes, thus accounting for properties of these sounds. Two kinds of processes are distinguished and called *ābhyantarāḥ prayatnāḥ* 'internal efforts' and *bāhyāḥ prayatnāḥ* 'external efforts' in some works, namely those which take place within and without the oral cavity. Thus, the Āpiśala-śikṣā says an effort (*prayatnaḥ*) is of two kinds (*dvividhaḥ*), internal and external:

(19) ĀŚ 3.1: prayatno dvividhaḥ

(20) ĀŚ 3.2: ābhyantaro bāhyaś ca

So far as concerns external efforts, different works recognize different degrees of glottal aperture. Some operate with two degrees, others with three. Consequently, some works recognize three kinds of emitted air, others only two.

2. 1. The Taittirīya- and Ṛk-prātiśākhyas operate with three degrees of glottal aperture. The former begins its description of speech production saying there arises a primitive sound (*śabdotpattiḥ*) in the area between the chest and throat (*kaṇṭhorasoḥ sandhāne* 'at the juncture of throat and chest') as the result of movement of breath in the body (*vāyu-śarīra-samīraṇāt*):

(21) TPr. 2.1: atha śabdotpattiḥ

(22) TPr. 2.2: vāyu-śarīra-samīraṇāt kaṇṭhorasoḥ sandhāne

Places where this sound is finally manifested as perceptibe sound are given:

---

(17)1.1.69 also provides that a sound with a marker *u* (*udit*) refers to a set of homogeneous sounds: e.g., kU designates the stop series *k kh g gh ṅ*. In addition, if a given sound is an affix (*pratyaya*), it is not made a class name (*apratyayaḥ* 'other than an affix').

the chest (*uraḥ*), throat (*kaṇṭhaḥ*), vault of the mouth (*śiraḥ*), the area of the mouth beneath this (*mukham*) and the nasal cavities (*nāsike*):

(23) TPr. 2.3: tasya prātiśrutkāni bhavanty uraḥ kaṇṭhaḥ śiro mukhaṃ nāsike iti.

Further, the air which constitutes this primitive sound is changed into three varieties as it passes through the glottis. If the glottis is close (*saṃvṛte kaṇṭhe*), the variety called *nāda* ('modulated air flow') is produced; if it is open (*vivṛte* [*kaṇṭhe*]), the varietly called *śvāsa* ('unmodulated air flow') is produced; and if the glottis is midway (*madhye*) between close and open, a third variety, called *hakāra*, is produced:

(24) TPr. 2.4: saṃvṛte kaṇṭhe nādaḥ kriyate

(25) TPr. 2.5: vivṛte śvāsaḥ

(26) TPr. 2.6: madhye hakāraḥ

These three are the original matter (*ptakṛtayaḥ*) of which individual articulated sounds (*varṇānām*) are made up:

(27) TPr. 2.7: tā varṇānām prakṛtayaḥ

That is, when an articulated sound is produced (*anupradīyate*), it has nāda, śvāsa or hakāra as material origin (*prakṛtiḥ*), that from which it is made up (*anupradānam*).[11] According to

(28) TPr. 2.8: nādo'nupradānaṃ svara-ghoṣavatsu

(29) TPr. 2.9: hakāro ha-caturtheṣu

(30) TPr. 2.10: aghoṣeṣu śvāsaḥ

the material which goes into making up vowels and voiced consonants (*svara-ghoṣavatsu*) is nāda; for *h* and voiced aspirated stops (*ha-caturtheṣu*) it is hakāra; and for voiceless consonants (*aghoṣeṣu*) it is śvāsa. In addition,

(31) TPr. 2.11: bhūyān prathamebhyo'nyeṣu

remarks that there is more śvāsa (*bhūyān* [*śvāsaḥ*]) in voiceless consonants other than unaspirated stops (*prathamebhyo'nyeṣu*) than there is in these. That is, voiceless aspirated stops and voiceless spirants have more śvāsa incorporated in them than do voiceless unaspirated stops. Note that this does not mean voiced aspirated stops and *h* are produced with less air emitted than one emits in producing voiceless aspirated stops and spirants. Since śvāsa is said to be the material which makes up all voiceless consonants ([30]TPr. 2.10), a distinction is made between those voiceless consonants the production of which involves emitting more air and those the production of which involves emitting less air. On the other hand, hakāra is said to make up only *h* and voiced aspirated stops ([29]TPr. 2.9), not all voiced consonants, so that no distinction need be made between unaspirated voiced consonants and aspirated ones in respect of the amount of hakāra emitted.

11. According to the Tribhāṣyaratna on (28)TPr. 2.8, the term *anupradāna* refers to the root cause (*mūla-kāraṇam*), that is, the material cause of a sound, that matter with which a sound is produced (*anupradīyate*): *anupradīyate'nena varṇa ity anupradānaṃ mūla-kāraṇam/ anupradīyate upādīyate janyata ity arthaḥ*. This is in accordance with what is said in (27)TPr. 2.7. As nāda, śvāsa and hakāra are the original matter of which sounds are made, they are the stuff with which sounds are produced.

The Ṛk-prātiśākhya also distinguishes three degrees of glottal aperture and three varieties of air flow. However, with reference to the air flow variety produced when the glottis is in a state midway between close and open, this text does not use a special term such as *hakāra* of (26)TPr. 2.6. Instead, it speaks of śvāsa, nāda and a combination of these two (*śvāsa-nādau* 'śvāsa and nāda,' *ubhau* 'both'). In

(32) RPr. 13.1: vāyuḥ prāṇaḥ koṣṭhyam anupradānaṃ kaṇṭhasya khe vivṛte saṃvṛte vā/āpadyate śvāsatāṃ nādatāṃ vā vaktr-īhāyām//

(33) RPr. 13.2: ubhayaṃ vāntarobhau

the Ṛk-prātiśākhya describes what happens to the upward moving breath called *prāṇa*, (*vāyuḥ prāṇaḥ*) when there is an effort on the part of a speaker (*vaktr-īhāyām*). This first becomes a primitive sound material (*anupradānam* [*āpadyate*]). Then, as the breath thus transformed passes through the glottis, it is further transformed. Depending on whether the glottis is open (*kaṇṭhasya khe vivṛte*) or close (*saṃvṛte vā*) or between these two states (*ubhayaṃ vāntarā*), the air flow becomes śvāsa or nāda (*āpadyate śvāsatāṃ nādatāṃ vā*) or both of these combined (*ubhau*).[12] These three, śvāsa, nāda and the combination of the two, are then said to be the original matter (*prakṛtayaḥ*) of which articulated sounds are made up:

(34) RPr. 13.3: tā varṇānām prakṛtayo bhavanti

The original matter for voiceless consonants (*aghoṣāṇām*) is śvāsa:

(35) RPr. 13.4: śvāso'ghoṣāṇām

Both śvāsa and nāda combined (*śvāsa-nādau*) make up two kinds of voiced consonants (*ghoṣiṇām*): aspirated stops and a spirant (*soṣmoṣmaṇām*), namely *h*:

(36) RPr. 13.6: soṣmoṣmaṇāṃ ghoṣiṇāṃ śvāsa-nādau

The primitive material of other sounds (*itareṣām*) is nāda:

(37) RPr. 13.5: itareṣāṃ tu nādaḥ

That is, nāda is the stuff of which are constituted vowels and voiced consonants other than aspirated stops and *h*.

In addition,

(38) RPr. 13.19: śīghrataraṃ soṣmasu prāṇam eke

notes that some (*eke*) say the breath (*prāṇam*) is emitted relatively faster

12. (32)RPr. 13.1 is paraphrased in part in the Vṛtti on Vākyapadīya 1.110 (KASI 1.107, p. 177. 1): *vāyuḥ koṣṭha-sthānam anupradānam āpadyate/ sa kaṇṭha-gataḥ śvāsatāṃ nādatāṃ vā* 'The breath becomes an anupradāna located in a cavity, when it has gotten to the glottis, (the breath becomes) śvāsa or nāda.' In his Paddhati on the above (177. 10-12), Vṛṣabhadeva notes that *anupradāna* designates a particular sound into which the breath is transformed (*anupradānam iti dhvani-viśeṣasya saṃjñā/ vāyus tathā pariṇamate*), and that *saḥ* of *sa kaṇṭha-gataḥ* refers to the breath in the form of this anupradāna: when it has gotten to the glottis, it undergoes a change into śvāsa or nāda (*sa cānupradāna-rūpo vāyuḥ kaṇṭha-gataḥ śvāsatāṃ nādatāṃ ca pratipadyate*). Under this interpretation, (32) RPr. 13.1 speaks of the breath undergoing two changes: first to anupradāna, then to śvāsa or nāda. The agreement with (21)TPr. 2.1 and following is patent. Hence, I think it plausible that the cavity (*koṣṭha*) in which the anupradāna is said to be situated (*koṣṭhyam anupradānam*) is the area between the chest and the throat,

(*śīghrataram*) in the case of aspirated stops (*soṣmasu*). That is, given that unaspirated consonants such as *k*, *g* and aspirated ones such as *kh*, *gh* take the same length of time, the latter are produced by emitting air faster than in producing the former, since more air is emitted for aspirated consonants. Though (38)RPr. 13.19 is not identical with (31)TPr. 2.11, the two are nevertheless clearly comparable in that certain consonants are said to involve the emission of more air than others.

2.2. Another description recognizes only two glottal states, open and close, so that one has only śvāsa and nāda, not also a third variety of air flow. Thus, the Catur-ādhyāyikā says that śvāsa is the anupradāna in voiceless consonants (*aghoṣeṣu*), nāda the anupradāna in voiced consonants and vowels (*ghoṣavat-svareṣu*):

(39) CĀ 1.12: śvāso'ghoṣeṣv anupradānaḥ

(40) CĀ 1.13: nādo ghoṣavat-svareṣu

Concerning members of stop series,[13] Patañjali says the following:[14] The first and second members of each series (*vargāṇām prathama-dvitīyāḥ*) are produced with open glottis (*vivṛta-kaṇṭhāḥ*), have śvāsa as their anupradāna and are voiceless (*śvāsānupradānā aghoṣāś ca*); some of these are unaspirated (*eke'lpaprāṇāḥ*), others aspirated (*apare mahāprāṇāḥ*). The third and fourth members of each series are produced with close glottis, have nāda as their anupradāna, and are voiced (*tṛtīya-caturthāḥ saṃvṛta-kaṇṭhā nādānupradānā ghoṣavantaḥ*); some of these are unaspirated, others aspirated. Fifth members of each series are like the third members (*yathā tṛtīyās tathā pañcamāḥ*), except for nasality (*ānunāsikya-varjam*): they have nasality as an additional quality (*ānunāsikyaṃ teṣām adhiko guṇaḥ*). The Āpiśala-śikṣā gives a similar description, though it speaks more generally of all consonants. According to

(41) ĀŚ 4.2: vargāṇāṃ prathama-dvitīyāḥ śa-ṣa-sa-visarjanīya-jihvāmūlīyopadhmānīyā yamau ca prathama-dvitīyau vivṛta-kaṇṭhāḥ śvāsānupradānā aghoṣāḥ

(42) ĀŚ 4.3: varga-yamānāṃ prathame alpaprāṇā itare sarve mahāprāṇāḥ

the first and second members of stop series (*vargāṇāṃ prathama-dvitīyāḥ*), *ś*, *ṣ*, *s*, *ḥ* (*visarjanīya*), ⌒*k*(*jihvamūlīya*), ⌒*p* (*upadhmānīya*) and first and second yamas[15] are produced with open glottis, have śvāsa as their anupradāna and

---

13. As is well known, there are five stop series (*vargāḥ*), in which sounds appear in the order voiceless unaspirated, voiceless aspirated, voiced unaspirated, voiced aspirate, nasal: *k kh g gh ṅ, c ch j jh ñ, ṭ ṭh ḍ ḍh ṇ, t th d dh n, p ph b bh m.*

14. Mahābhāṣya on Pāṇini 1.1.9 (I.61.16-19): *tatra vargāṇām prathama-dvitīyā vivṛta-kaṇṭhāḥ śvāsānupradānā aghoṣāḥ/ eke 'lpaprāṇā apare mahāprāṇāḥ/ tṛtīya-caturthāḥ saṃvṛta-kaṇṭhā nādānupradānā ghoṣavantaḥ/ eke'lpaprāṇā apare mahāprāṇāḥ/ yathā tṛtīyās tathā pañcamā ānunāsikya-varjam/ ānunāsikyaṃ teṣām adhiko guṇaḥ.*

15. A yama is a transitional nasal segment which occurs between a non-nasal stop and a following nasal stop. Details concerning the pronunciation and number of yamas cannot be treated here.

are voiceless; of these, first members of stops series and a first yama are unaspirated (*alpaprāṇa*), all the rest aspirated (*itare sarve mahāprāṇāḥ*). According to

(43) ĀŚ 4.4: vargāṇāṃ tṛtīya-caturthā antasthā hakārānusvārau yamau ca tṛtīya-caturthau saṃvṛta-kaṇṭhā nādānupradānā ghoṣavantaḥ

(44) ĀŚ 4.5: varga-yamānāṃ tṛtīyā antasthāś cālpaprāṇā itare sarve mahāprāṇāḥ

the third and fourth members of stop series, semivowels (*antasthāḥ*)—that is, *y r l v*—as well as third and fourth yamas are produced with close glottis, have nāda as their anupradāna and are voiced; of these, third members of stop series and a third yama as well as semivowels are unaspirated, all the rest aspirated. Further, according to

(45) ĀŚ 4.6: yathā tṛtīyās tathā pañcamāḥ

(46) ĀŚ 4.7: ānunāsikyam eṣām adhiko guṇaḥ

fifth members of stop series are like third ones except that they have the additional property of nasality.

This general scheme is also the one adopted by later grammarians such as Candragomin in his Cāndra-varṇa-sūtra. Thus, according to

(47) CVS 29: vargāṇāṃ prathama-dvitīyāḥ śa-ṣa-sā visarjanīya-jihvāmūlīyopadhmānīyāś ca vivṛta-kaṇṭhāḥ śvāsānupradānā aghoṣāḥ

(48) CVS 30: prathama-tṛtīya-pañcamā antasthāś cālpaprāṇāḥ

(49) CVS 31: itare mahāprāṇāḥ

(50) CVS 32: tṛtīya-caturtha-pañcamāḥ sānusvārāntastha-hakārāḥ saṃvṛta-kaṇṭhā nādānupradānā ghoṣavantaḥ

first and second members of stop series, *ś*, *ṣ*, *s*, *h*, ᳵ*k*, ᳵ*p* are produced with open glottis, have śvāsa as their anupradāna, and are voiceless; first, third and fifth members of stop series as well as semivowels are unaspirated; other consonants are aspirated; third, fourth and fifth members of stop series, *ṃ*, semivowels and *h* are produced with close glottis, have nāda as their anupradāna, and are voiced.

2.3. As shown above (2.2 with n 14), Patañjali uses the term *ghoṣavat* with reference to voiced consonants, *mahāprāṇa* with reference to aspirates. He also uses *nādavat* and *soṣman*, in the Mahābhāṣya on

(51) 1.1.50: sthāne'ntaratamaḥ

According to this metarule, if there is a choice of substitutes for a given substituend, that element occurs in place (*sthāne*) of the substituend which is most similar (*antaratamaḥ*) to it. For example,

(52) 8.4.62: jhayo ho'nyatarasyām (pūrvasya 61, savarṇaḥ 58)

provides that *h* which follows a non-nasal stop (*jhaY*) is optionally replaced by a sound homogeneous (*savarṇaḥ*, [16]1.1.9) with the one which precedes it (*pūrvasya*). Thus, if *hasati* ('laughs') follows *vāg* ('voice') or *triṣṭub* ('triṣṭubh'), its *h-* is optionally replaced by a sound homogeneous with the preceding *-g* or *-b*. One has a choice of replacements, since *k kh gh ṅ* and *p ph bh m* are respectively homogeneous with *g* and *b*, which of course are also homogeneous with themselves. According to (51)1.1.50, one selects the sounds which are closest to *h*, namely the voiced aspirated stops *gh*, *bh*: *vāg ghasati*, *triṣṭub bhasati*. Now, in the Mahābhāṣya on (51)1.1.50 a discussant asks what purpose there is in saying *antaratamaḥ*, with the superlative affix *tamaP*, instead of saying merely *sthāne'ntaraḥ*. Under this formulation, the rule would provide that, if there is a choice of replacements for a given substituend, that one occurs which is similar (*antaraḥ* 'close') to it. Given *vāg hasati*, *triṣṭub hasati*, then, by (52)8.4.62, *h* could be replaced by the voiceless aspirates *kh*, *ph* or by the voiced unaspirate stops *g*, *b*, since *h* is aspirated (*soṣman*) and voiced (*nādavat*). However, since (51) 1.1.50 is formulated as shown, with *antaratamaḥ*, those sounds substitute for *h* which are both aspirated and voiced.[16] Here Patañjali uses *soṣman* and *nādavat* with reference to fourth members of stop series, voiced aspirated stops.

Since nāda is the primitive matter of voiced consonants, it is understandable how these can be characterized as *nādavat* '(a sound) in which there is nāda.' By the same token, vowels also should be characterized as *nādavat*, since nāda is the stuff of which these too are constituted (see [28]TPr. 2.8, [37]RPr. 13.5, [40]CĀ 1.13). Similarly, one might expect both voiced consonants and vowels to be termed *ghoṣavat*, since both are indeed voiced. Consider now the rule

(53) 7.1.39: supāṃ su-luk-pūrvasavarṇāc-che-yā-ḍā-ḍyā-yāj-ālaḥ (chandasi 38)

and what is said in the Mahābhāṣya concerning part of what this provides. According to this rule, nominal endings (*supām*) are subject to certain substitutions in Vedic (*chandasi*). Two of these are as follows: A nominal ending is replaced by zero (*luk*) or by a sound homogeneous with the one which precedes it (*pūrvasavarṇa*). For example, in *ārdre carman* (<*ārdra-i carman-i*) 'on a wet skin', *ārdre* has a locative ending, but *carman* instead of *carmaṇi* lacks this; in deriving the instrumental singular *dhītī* 'thought, hymn' (<*dhīti-ā*), the ending *ā* (*Ṭā*) is replaced by *ī*, homogeneous with the preceding sound *i*. In the Mahābhāṣya on (53) 7.1.39, *carman* is given as an example (*udāharaṇam*) of zero substitution for an ending. A discussant then rejects this, claiming that *carman* is also correctly accounted for otherwise: through *i* being replaced by a sound homogeneous with the preceding *-n*.[17] This meets with the following objection: by proximity (*āntaryataḥ*), *d* would undesiredly be allowed (*dakāraḥ prasajyeta*).[18] That

16. Mahābhāṣya I. 120. 11-13: *atha tamab-grahaṇaṃ kim-artham| jhayo ho' nyatarasyām ity atra soṣmaṇaḥ soṣmāṇa iti dvitīyāḥ prasaktā nādavato nādavanta iti tṛtīyāḥ| tamab-grahaṇād ye soṣmāṇo nādavantaś ca te bhavanti caturthāḥ: vāg ghasati triṣṭub bhasatīti.*

17. That is, one gets *carmann* for *carman-i*. The final *n* of *carmann* is then deleted by a rule (8.2.23: *saṃyogāntasya lopaḥ*) according to which the final consonant of a word which ends in a cluster is replaced by zero.

18. Mahābhāṣya III. 256.16-17, 20-21: *luki kim udāharaṇam| ārdre carman ... naitad asti| pūrva-savarṇenāpy etat siddham ... na sidhyati| yady atra pūrva-savarṇaḥ syād āntaryato dakāraḥ prasajyeta.* Actually, as the Bhāṣya goes on to say (*astu| saṃyogānta-lopena siddham*), the *-d* of *carmand* would be subject to deletion by the same rule as serves to account for *carman* from *carmann* (see n 17).

is, assuming that the ending of *carman-i* is to be replaced by a sound homogeneous with *n*, there are five possible substitutes: *t th d dh n*. By (51)1.1.50, that sound is selected which is closest to *i*, and according to Patañajali, this is *d*. Kaiyaṭa explains that *d* is selected since it is similar to *i* in being non-nasal.[19] Nāgeśa adds that what is meant is: also because *d* is voiced and unaspirated.[20] And indeed, the Bhāṣya makes sense only if *i* is considered voiced and unaspirated, so that *d* alone can substitute for it. Consequently, if *d* is termed *nādavat*, *i* too must thus be termed, and if *d* is characterized as *ghoṣavat*, *i* also must thus be characterized.

That vowels are the voiced sounds par excellence is at the base of a componential analysis referred to in

(54) RPr. 13.15: āhur ghoṣaṃ ghoṣavatām akāram eke'nusvāram anunāsikānām

(55) RPr. 13.16: soṣmatāṃ ca soṣmaṇām ūṣmaṇāhuḥ sasthānena (eke 15)

(56) RPr. 13.17: ghoṣiṇāṃ (soṣmaṇāṃ soṣmatām 16) ghoṣiṇaiva (ūṣmaṇā 16)

which present what some say (*āhur eke*) concerning voicing and aspiration. These persons say *a* (*akāram*) constitutes the voicing of voiced consonants (*ghoṣaṃ ghoṣavatām*) in general; however, anusvāra constitutes the voicing of voiced nasal consonants (*anunāsikānām*). These same teachers say aspirates in general have their aspiration (*soṣmatāṃ ca soṣmaṇām*) through a homorganic spirant (*ūṣmaṇā sasthānena*); but voiced (*ghoṣiṇām*) aspirates have their aspiration through a voiced spirant alone (*ghoṣiṇaiva* [*ūṣmaṇā*]), namely *h*. This is immediately understandable in the following manner. The consonants *c ch j jh ñ y ś* have in common that they are all palatal (*tālavya*). They differ in that *c ch j jh ñ* are stops, whose production involves, occlusion, *y* is a semivowel, whose production involves slight contact bet-

19. Pradīpa V.48. *niranunāsikasyekārasya sadṛśo dakāraḥ*.

20. Uddyota V.48: *ghoṣavattvād alpaprāṇatvāc cety arthaḥ*. In his Laghuśabdenduśekhara (35-36), Nāgeśa notes that the Mahābhāṣya passage considered above shows vowels are characterized by voicing, glottal closure, nāda and absence of aspiration: otherwise, assuming that the ending of *carman-i* is replaced by a sound homogeneous with the preceding *n*, one would get *t* or *d* alternatively and, if vowels are not considered unaspirated, *d* and *dh* as alternates (*ghoṣasaṃvāra-nādālpaprāṇatvam acām/ anyathā ta-dau paryāyeṇa syātām/ alpaprāṇatvānaṅgī-kāre da-dhau paryāyeṇa syātām*). Nāgeśa subsequently notes (36) that it is made clear in the Bhāṣya on 1.4.109 (*paraḥ sannikarṣaḥ saṃhitā*) that vowels are voiced (*acāṃ ghoṣatvaṃ paraḥ sannikarṣa iti sūtre bhāṣye'pi spaṣṭam*). The term used for voice in the pertinent Mahābhāṣya passage is *hrāda*. It is said that a single intervocalic consonant, as in *pacati* 'cooks,' is covered by the voice of the preceding and following elements (I. 355.18-19: *atha yatraikaḥ pacatīty ekaḥ pūrva-parayor hrādena pracchādyate*). Kaiyaṭa explains what is meant: *c* between two *a*'s, which are voiced (*ghoṣavatoḥ*), is perceived as though voiced (Pradīpa II.482: *dvayor akārayor ghoṣavator madhye cakāro ghoṣavān iva lakṣyata ity arthaḥ*). He uses the term *ghoṣavat* with respect to the two *a* vowels.

ween an articulator and a point of articulation, and *ś* is a continuant.[21] Assume now that there are basic elements defined by two characteristics: a place of production and a mode of production. Thus, occlusion at the palate defines a basic unit which we may designate by *C*; slight contact at the same place defines a unit *Y*; and, again produced at the palate, but with a different type of production, we have a unit *Ś*. Further, since vowels are always produced with modulated air (*nāda*), they may be taken to be prototypically voiced. Moreover, since *a* is the first vowel of all accepted sound catalogs, let voicing be designated by *A*. Further, anusvāra (*ṃ*), which is a nasal segment with no fixed place of production in the oral cavity, may be taken to represent voicing with nasality, and *h*, the one voiced spirant, may be said to represent voiced aspiration; let us use *M* and *H* to designate such nasality and aspiration. Now, if we take *C* and *Ś* as defined, with no added properties, we have the stop *c* and the spirant *ś*. If, then, to *C* is added voicing (*A*), represented by the prototypical vowel *a*, we get *j*, the voiced unaspirated non-nasal stop. Similarly, *Y* with voicing gives the semivowel *y*. The voiceless aspirated stop *ch* is constituted by *C* with aspiration as represented by *ś*, the spirant homorganic with palatal stops. On the other hand, the voiced aspirat stop *jh* is gotten from *C* by adding *H*, voiced aspiration, as represented by *h*. The nasal stop *ñ* results from adding to *C* voiced nasality (*M*), as represented by anusvāra. In brief, (54) RPr. 13.15 -(56)RPr. 13.17 give the view of some teachers, who adopted a componential analysis in which features, represented by given segments are added to basic units to give more complex ones. Others (*apare*) did not accept this. Instead, they maintained that aspiration and voicing (*ūṣma-ghoṣau*) arise in the given sounds themselves (*atrotpannau*):

(57) RPr. 13.18: atrotpannāv apara ūṣma-ghoṣau

That is, according to these teachers, voiced and aspirated sounds have voicing and aspiration as properties which inhere in them as individual elements that are not gotten from more primitive sounds through the addition of such qualities.

It is thus recognized that vowels are voiced elements. Moreover, as shown above, Pāṇinīyas characterize vowels as *ghoṣavat*, using a term which refers also to voiced consonants.

2.4. However, the term *ghoṣavat* is not regularly used with reference to vowels. In prātiśākhyas, this regularly designates voiced consonants and is opposed to *aghoṣa*, which refers to voiceless consonants. Thus, (28)TPr. 2.8 uses *svara* and *ghoṣavat* (*svara-ghoṣavatsu*) to denote vowels and voiced consonants. Other rules of the Taittirīya-prātiśākhya explicitly assign the class names *aghoṣa* and *ghoṣavat* to consonants. By

(58) TPr. 1.12: ūṣma-visarjanīya-prathama-dvitīyā aghoṣāḥ

21. See (105)RPr. 13.8 - (108)RPr. 13.9.

spirants (*ūṣman*), *ḥ* (*visarjanīya*)[22] and first and second members of stop series (*prathama-dvitīya*) have the class name *aghoṣa*. However, contrary to this,

(59) TPr. 1.13: na hakāraḥ

provides that *h* is not called *aghoṣa*. This spirant is thereby made a member of a residual set of consonants (*vyañjana-śeṣa* 'remaining consonant') with respect to those termed *aghoṣa*, and by

(60) TPr.. 1.4: vyañjana-śeṣo ghoṣavān

such a consonant is termed *ghoṣavat*. The following Ṛk-prātiśākhya rules assign the class name *aghoṣa* to particular consonants:

(61) RPr. 1.11. antyāḥ sapta teṣām aghoṣāḥ

(62) RPr. 1.12: varge varge ca prathamāv aghoṣau

By (61) RPr. 1.11, the last seven (*antyāḥ sapta*) of the sounds in the spirant class are[23] called *aghoṣa*, and according to (62)RPr. 1.12, the first two (*prathamau*) members in each stop series (*varge varge*) have this name. The Ṛk-prātiśākhya lacks a classificatory rule comparable to (60)TPr. 1.4. It is assumed that, since the class name *aghoṣa* is assigned to a given set of consonants, other consonants will, by virtue of constituting a remainder with respect to these,. be known to be the referents of terms contrary to *aghoṣa*, namely *ghoṣavat* or *ghoṣin*.[24] Indeed, (36)RPr. 13.6 uses *ghoṣin* of voiced aspirated stops and *h*, and *ghoṣavat* is regularly used to refer to voiced consonants in Ṛk-prātiśākhya rules stating phonologic changes.[25]

Moreover, *nādavat*, which Patañjali uses with reference to voiced consonants (see 2.3), is not used of voiced segments in prātiśākhya works. Nor is *śvāsavat* used of voiceless segment.

In this connection let us consider now some phonologic rules and possible ways to restate them. Rules in a section headed by

(63) TPr. 8.1: atha prathamaḥ

state changes which a constituent-final unaspirated stop (*prathamaḥ* 'first stop') undergoes. By

(64) TPr. 8.3: tṛtīyaṃ svara-ghoṣavat-paraḥ

such a stop changes to a voiced unaspirated stop (*tṛtīyam* 'third stop') if it is followed by a vowel or a voiced consonant (*svara-ghoṣavat-paraḥ*). Rules headed by

(65) TPr. 8.5: atha visarjanīyaḥ

state changes which *-ḥ* (*visarjanīyaḥ*) undergoes. By

---

22. For reasons which I cannot discuss here, the Taittirīya-prātiśākhya does not assign *ḥ* to its spirant (*ūṣman*) class.

23. *teṣām* 'of them' in (61)RPr. 1.11 refers to the eight sounds called *ūṣmāṇaḥ* 'spirants' by the preceding rule (RPr. 1.10: *uttare'ṣṭā ūṣmāṇaḥ*), according to which the eight sounds that follow the set of stops in the sound list accepted have this class name.

24. In his comments on (62)RPr. 1.12, Uvaṭa notes that consonants other than those to which the class name *aghoṣa* is assigned bear the class name *ghoṣavat* by virtue of being a remainder (*pāriśeṣyād anyāni ghoṣavatsaṃjñakāni vyañjanāni*).

25. E.g., (72)RPr. 4.2.

(66) TPr. 9.2: aghosa-paras tasya sasthānam ūsmāṇam
if *-ḥ* is followed by a voiceless consonant (*aghoṣa-paraḥ*) it changes to a spirant (*ūṣmāṇam*) homorganic with that consonant (*tasya sasthānam*). Now, as shown in 2.1, according to (28)TPr. 2.8 - (30)TPr. 2.10, nāda, hakāra and śvāsa constitute different groups of sound as follows:

nāda: vowels, voiced unaspirated stops, including nasal stops, and semi-vowels

hakāra: voiced aspirated stops and *h*

śvāsa: voiceless stops and spirants

Using *nādavat*, *hakāravat* and *śvāsavat*, one can formulate rules which are alternative and equivalent to (64)TPr. 8.3, (66)TPr. 9.2:

(67) *tṛtīyaṃ nāda-hakāravat-paraḥ

(68) *śvāsavat-paras tasya sasthānam ūṣmāṇam

(67) provides that a voiceless unaspirated stop changes to a voiced unaspirated stop if followed by a nādavat or hakāravat (*nāda-hakāravat-paraḥ*) sound, that is, by any voiced segment; by (68), *-ḥ* followed by a śvāsavat (*śvāsavat-paraḥ*) sound, that is, by a voiceless segment, changes to the spirant homorganic with that segment.

The Ṛk-prātiśākhya has rules comparable to (64)TPr. 8.3, (66)TPr. 9.2, though this work proceeds differently, treating operations which affect elements according to collocations (*sandhi*) *-V C-*, *-C V-*, etc. According to

(69) RPr. 2.8: eṣa sya sa ca svarāś ca pūrve bhavanti vyañjanam uttaraṃ yadaibhyaḥ/te'nvakṣara-sandhayo'nulomāḥ

(70) RPr. 2.9: pratilomās tu viparyaye ta eva

there are collocations called *anvakṣara-sandhayaḥ*, of which there are two subtypes, called *anuloma* and *pratiloma*. In the first, *eṣaḥ* 'this', *syaḥ*, *saḥ* 'that' and constituent-final vowels are prior members (*...svarāś ca pūrve bhavanti*), and a constituent-initial consonant follows these (*vyañjanam uttaraṃ yadaibhyaḥ*). Thus, *-V C-* is an anuloma anvakṣara collocation. If the same constituents (*ta eva*) occur in reversed order (*viparyaye*), one has a pratiloma collocation: *-C V-*. In pratiloma collocations (*tatra pratilomeṣu*), if the prior members are voiceless unaspirated stop (*prathamāḥ*) they change to voiced unaspirated stops (*tṛtīya-bhāvam ... niyanti*):

(71) RPr. 2.10: tatra prathamās tṛtīya-bhāvam pratilomeṣu niyanti

In another section rules concerning collocations of the type *-C C-* are stated. By

(72) RPr. 4.2: ghoṣavat-parāḥ prathamās tṛtīyān svān

voiceless unaspirated stops followed by voiced consonants (*ghoṣavat-parāḥ prathamāḥ*) change to voiced unaspirated stops of their series (*tṛtīyān svān*). Clearly, (71)RPr. 2.10 and (72) RPr. 4.2 together are equivalent to (64) TPr. 8.3. Similarly,

(73) RPr. 4.31: aghoṣe rephy arephī coṣmāṇaṃ sparśa uttare tat-sasthānam anūṣma-pare (visarjanīyaḥ 24)

(74) RPr. 4.32: tam evoṣmāṇam ūṣmaṇi

are comparable to (66)TPr. 9.2. According to the first of these rules, both rhotacizing and non-rhotacizing *-ḥ* (*rephy arephī ca visarjanīyaḥ*), if followed by a voiceless stop (*aghoṣe sparśa uttare*) that is not itself followed by a spirant (*anūṣma-pare*), change to a spirant homorganic with that stop; the next rule provides that *-ḥ* followed by a voiceless spirant changes to that spirant.[26]

Although, as shown, the pertinent rules of the Taittirīya-and Ṛk-prātiśākhyas are comparable, the terminological substitution which is possible in the former (see [67]-[68]) is not possible in the latter. According to (35) RPr. 13.4 - (37) RPr. 13 śvāsa and nāda make up sounds as follows:

śvāsa : voiceless stops and spirants
nāda: vowels, voiced unaspirated stops, semivowels
śvāsa and nāda combined: voiced aspirated stops and *h*

Patently, one could not properly substitute *nādavantaḥ* for *svarāḥ* in (69) RPr. 2.8. This rule would then include in the anuloma anvakṣara collocations sequences *-C C-* where the first consonant is a semivowel, a voiced stop or *h*, so that (70) RPr. 2.9 would include in pratiloma anvakṣara collocations sequences *-C C-* where the second consonant is one of the above. One could claim that there is nothing wrong with this and that the author of the Ṛk-prātiśākhya was simply clumsy in treating changes in terms of collocations, so that he formulated (71) RPr. 2.10, (72) RPr. 4.2 instead of a single rule

(75) *svara-ghoṣavat-parāḥ prathamās tṛtīyān svān

comparable to (64)TPr. 8.3. And

(76) *nādavat-parāḥ prathamās tṛtīyān svān

would indeed be equivalent to (75). But consider again (73)RPr. 4.31. The rule

(77) *śvāsavati rephy arephī coṣmāṇaṃ sparśa uttare tat-sasthānam anūṣma-pare

cannot be substituted for this. As shown, voiced aspirated stops are made up of both śvāsa and nāda. They would thus be included in the referents of *śvāsavat*, so that (77) would allow a sequence such as *-s dh-* instead of *-r dh-*.[27]

Of course, there is an obvious reason why it is not possible to adopt (77) as an alternative to (73)RPr. 4.31, but (68) can substitute for (66)TPr. 9.2. The Taittirīya-prātiśākhya makes a three-way distinction among nāda, śvāsa and hakāra. The Ṛk-prātiśākhya distinguishes only nāda and śvāsa. Instead of treating the air stream that results when the glottis is midway

26. (73)RPr. 4.31 specifies that the stop following *-ḥ* not be followed by a spirant; (66)TPr. 9.2 does not. However, TPr. 9.3: *na kṣa-paraḥ* provides that the change given in the preceding rule does not occur if *-ḥ* is followed by *kṣ*.

27. For example, the pada-pāṭha to Ṛg-veda 3.11.2c has *agniḥ dhiyā*, from which one should get *agnir dhiyā* of the continuously recited text by RPr. 4.27: *sarvopadhas tu svara-ghoṣavat-paro rephaṃ rephī te punā repha-sandhayaḥ*. According to this rule, a rhotacizing *-ḥ* preceded by any vowel changes to *-r* if it is followed by a vowel or a voiced consonant (*svara-ghoṣavat-paraḥ*).

between close and open as a separately named entity called *hakāra*, it treats it as a combination of nāda and śvāsa, so that *śvāsavat* cannot here refer exclusively to voiceless segments. The Taittirīya-prātiśākhya's system also makes it impossible to substitute one term for another in certain rules. Consider some more rules headed by (65)TPr. 8.5. According to

(78) TPr. 9.9: avarṇa-pūrvas tu lupyate (ghoṣavat-paraḥ 8)

(79) TPr. 9.10: atha svara-paro yakāram

-*ḥ* preceded by *ă* (*avarṇa-pūrvaḥ*) is deleted (*lupyate*) when followed by a voiced consonant (*ghoṣavat-paraḥ*), and changes to -*y* when followed by a vowel (*svara-paro yakāram*).[28] On the other hand, by

(80) TPr. 9.7: okāram aḥ sarvo'kāra-paraḥ

(81) TPr. 9.8: ghoṣavat-paraś ca

the whole of -*aḥ* (*aḥ sarvaḥ*) changes to -*o* before *a*- (*okāram akāra-paraḥ*) and before a voiced consonant.[29] Now, (64) TPr. 8.3 states a noperation that applies to a stop followed by any vowel or voiced consonant, so that it is possible to formulate this alternatively (see (67)) using a term that refers to all voiced segments. However, (78)TPr. 9.9 - (81)TPr. 9.8 state different operations for elements followed by vowels and voiced consonants, so that a similar terminological substitution is not possible, Thus, if (81)TPr. 9.8 were modified to

(82) *nādavat-paraś ca

the rule would at once be overly narrow and too broad: it does not include voiced aspirated stops in the right contexts, and it would allow the change of -*aḥ* to -*o* before any vowel. A rule

(83) *nāda-hakāravat-paraś ca

would provide for the change of -*aḥ* to -*o* also before voiced aspirated stops, but it would still be overly broad in allowing this change before any vowel. Having either *nādavat-paraḥ* of (82) or *nāda-hakāravat-paraḥ* of (83) carry into (78)TPr. 9.9 would let this rule provide for wrong results: it would now allow -*ḥ* of -*ăḥ* to be deleted directly before a vowel. Again, if *svara-paraḥ* of (79)TPr. 9.10 were replaced by *nādavat-paraḥ*, the rule would allow the change of -*ḥ* to -*y* also before voiced unaspirated consonants. The following Ṛk-prātiśākhya rules also concern -*ḥ*:

(84) RPr. 4.25: okāraṃ hrasva-pūrvaḥ (visarjanīyaḥ arephī ghoṣavat-paraḥ 24)

(85) RPr. 2.27: hrasva-pūrvas tu so'kāram (visarjanīyo'riphitaḥ svarodayaḥ 24)

The first provides that -*aḥ* with non-rhotacizing *ḥ* changes to -*o*[30] when

---

28. The -*y* of -*ăy* gotten by (79)TPr. 9.10 is deleted by (12)TPr. 10.19, though prevocalic -*y* is not deleted in all dialects (see n 8).

29. It is not necessary to consider here anything more about the collocation -*o a*- and abhinihita sandhi.

30. Of itself, *arephī visarjanīyaḥ* refers merely to a non-rhotacizing *ḥ*. However, rules such as (84)RPr. 4.25 are interpreted together with a metarule: RPr. 1.67: *sahopadho 'riphita ekavarṇavad visarjanīyaḥ svara-ghoṣavat-paraḥ*. This establishes a convention in

followed by a voiced consonant (*ghoṣavat-paraḥ*), the second that *-aḥ* goes to *-a* before vowels.[31] Substituting *nādavat-paraḥ* for *ghoṣavat-paraḥ* understood in (84)RPr. 4.25 would not make this rule overly narrow, since voiced aspirated stops are constituted in part by nāda in the Ṛk-prātiśākhya description, so that they could be referents of *nādavat*. However, the modified rule would be too broad in allowing the change of *-aḥ* to *-o* before vowels, where, by (85)RPr. 2.27, *-aḥ* should change to *-a*. Similarly, if *svarodayaḥ* 'followed by a vowel' in (85)RPr. 2.27 were changed to *nādavad-udayaḥ*, the modified rule would allow the change of *-aḥ* to *-a* also before voiced consonants.

As shown in 2.2, the Catur-ādhyāyikā and other works recognize only two degrees of glottal aperture, hence operate only with śvāsa and nāda: the former pertains to voiceless sounds, which are all consonants, the latter to voiced sounds, including vowels and aspirated stops and *h*. For *ghoṣavat-svareṣu* 'before voiced consonants and vowels' in

(86) CĀ 2.2: padāntānām anuttamānāṃ tṛtīyā ghoṣavat-svareṣu

then, one could substitute *nādavatsu* and still have a rule providing that constituent-final non-nasal stops (*padāntānām anuttamānām*) are replaced by voiced unaspirated stops before vowels and voiced consonants. Similarly, one could substitute *śvāsavati* for *aghoṣe* 'before a voiceless consonant' in

(87) CĀ 2.40: visarjanīyasya para-sasthāno'ghoṣe

which provides that *-ḥ* before a voiceless consonant is replaced by a consonant homorganic with the following one. But *ghoṣavati* 'before a voiced consonant' of

(88) CĀ 2.54: ghoṣavati ca (akāropadhasyokāraḥ 53, visarjanīyasya 40)

cannot be replaced with *nādavati*. The original rule lets *u* (*ukāraḥ*) substitute for *-ḥ* preceded by *a* (*akāropadhasya visarjanīyasya*) and followed by a voiced consonant.[32] The modified rule

(89) *nādavati ca

would allow this substitution also where *-aḥ* is followed by any vowel, though by

(90) CĀ 2.53: akāropadhasyokāro'kāre (visarjanīyasya 40)

it should apply only if the following vowel is *a* (*akāre* 'before *a*').

In the same vein, consider again (11)TPr. 10.15 (1 with n 6) and

(91) RPr. 2.21: samānākṣaram antasthāṃ svām akaṇṭhyaṃ svarodayam

(92) CĀ 3.39: svare nāmino'ntasthā

By (91)RPr. 2.21, a non-pharyngeal (*akaṇṭhyam*) samānākṣara changes to the semivowel proper to it (*antasthāṃ svām*) when followed by a vowel

---

respect of rules that state operations for non-rhotacizing *-ḥ* followed by a vowel or a voiced consonant (*svara-ghoṣavat-paraḥ*): *-ḥ* and the sound preceding (*sahopadhaḥ* 'with the preceding sound') are treated as a single sound (*ekavarṇavat*). That is, the operations in question apply to *-Vḥ*, specifically to *-aḥ*.

31. *saḥ* 'it' of (85)RPr. 2.27 refers to a non-rhotacizing *ḥ*, mentioned in RPr. 2.24.

32. By another rule, *-au* gives *-o*.

(*svarodayam*); that is, *ṝ̆, ī̆, ū̆* (see (8)RPr. 1.1) change to *r*, *y*, *v* before vowels. According to (92) CĀ 3.39, a semivowel replaces a nāmin vowel before a vowel; the next rule (CĀ 3.40: *sandhyakṣarāṇām ay-av-āy-āvaḥ*) lets *ay*, *av*, *āy*, *āv* substitute for *e*, *o*, *ai*, *au*, respectively, when these are followed by vowels, so that (92)CĀ 3.39 applies to substitute *y*, *r*, *l*, *v* for *ī̆, ṝ̆, ḷ, ū̆*. Clearly, one cannot replace *svarodayam* of (91)RPr. 2.21 with *nādavad-udayam* or *svare* of (92)CĀ 3.39 with *nādavati*: the rules would then allow semivowel conversion to apply also before voiced consonants.

Although one could substitute *nādavat, hakāravat, śvāsavat* for other terms in some phonologic rules of prātiśākhyas, then, this is not always possible. In particular, though vowels and voiced consonants together are involved in some rules, others concern only one or the other of these groups. Such rules require distinct terms referring separately to vowels and voiced consonants: *svara* 'vowel' and *ghoṣavat* or *ghoṣin* 'voiced consonant.' Moreover, voiced consonants are opposed both phonetically and phonologically to voiceless consonants, so that one has also a terminological contrast of *ghoṣavat* versus *aghoṣa* 'voiceless consonant.'

We thus have to do with terms used in two contexts, phonetic and phonological. From the phonetic viewpoint, any segment constituted by nāda, the modulated breath emitted when the glottis is close, can be called nādavat, a term Patañjali uses with reference to voiced stops (2.3 with n 16). And if *ghoṣa* refers to the property of voicing (cf. [54]RPr. 13.15), all voiced segments can be called *ghoṣavat*, a term used both of voiced consonants and vowels (2.3 with n 20). On the other hand, from the phonologic viewpoint, *ghoṣavat* refers to distinctively voiced elements, namely voiced consonants, as opposed to voiceless consonants (*aghoṣa*), and both of these together constitute the class of consonants (*vyañjana*) in opposition to vowels (*svara*). Thus used, *ghoṣavat* and *aghoṣa* have a status comparable to that of terms like *antasthā* 'semivowel' and *ūṣman* 'spirant', which also designate phonologically distinctive sets of sounds.[33]

2.5. One might be tempted to suggest that *ghoṣavat* is used of voiced consonants because these have a particular feature of resonance, called *ghoṣa*, which distinguishes them phonetically from vowels. There is no good evidence to support this view. As shown in 2.1, the Taittirīya-prātiśākhya says nāda is the stuff of vowels and voiced consonants other than *h* and aspirated stops, which are made up of hakāra, and the Ṛk-prātiśākhya says nāda constitutes vowels and voiced consonants other than *h* and aspirated stops, which are made up of a combination of nāda and śvāsa. These texts describe in some detail how nāda, śvāsa and hakāra or the combination of nāda and śvāsa are emitted, but they say not a word concerning any special resonance which one could say is denoted by *ghoṣa*. Further, the Taittirīya-prātiśākhya describes in considerable detail just

33. Moreover, as *ghoṣavat*, *aghoṣa* are used with reference to consonants, for which alone there is a distinction between voiced and voiceless units, so are *hrasva* 'short', *dīrgha* 'long' and *pluta* 'prolated, extra-long' used specifically with reference to vowels. I cannot discuss here rules where *antasthā*, *ūṣman* etc. are used.

how organs are positioned for producing different sounds, but again says nothing which would indicate that it operated with any special resonace called *ghoṣa*. Consider now a representative sample of the descriptions in question. To begin with, the Taittirīya-prātiśākhya distinguishes two kinds of interplay between an articulator (*karaṇa*) and a place of production (*sthāna*). With respect to vowels (*svarāṇām*) a place of production is one where approximation is made (*yatropasaṃhāras tat sthānam*), and an active articulator (*karaṇam*) is one which a speaker brings close to such a place (*yad upasaṃharati*):

(93) TPr. 2.31: svarāṇāṃ yatropasaṃhāras tat sthānam

(94) TPr. 2.32: yad upasaṃharati tat karaṇam

With respect to other sounds (*anyeṣām*), a place of production is one where contact (*sparśanam* 'touching') occurs, and an active articulator is one which a speaker causes to make contact (*sparśayati* 'causes to touch') at such a place:

(95) TPr. 2.33: anyeṣāṃ tu yatra sparśanaṃ tat sthānam

(96) TPr. 2.34: yena sparśayati tat karaṇam

Thus, in producing *i*-vowels (*ivarṇe*), one makes the middle of the tongue approach the palate (*tālau jihvā-madhyam* [*upasaṃharati*]):

(97) TPr. 2.22: tālau jihvā-madhyam ivarṇe

For producing stops of the *c*-series (*ca-varge*), one has the middle of the tongue make contact at the palate (*tālau jihvā-madhyena* [*sparśayati*]):

(98) TPr. 2.36: tālau jihvā-madhyena ca-varge (sparśayati 35)

The spirants (*ūṣmāṇaḥ*)ᴖ̆*k*, *ś*, *ṣ*, *s*,ᴖ̆*p* are produced at the places given for the *k*-, *c*-, *ṭ*-, *t*-, and *p*-series of stops respectively (*sparśa-sthāneṣu* ... *ānupūrvyeṇa*):

(99) TPr. 2.44: sparśa-sthāneṣūṣmāṇa ānupūrvyeṇa

and with the same active articulators. However, the middle of the active articulator (*karaṇa-madhyam*) is now separated (*vivṛtam*) from the place of production:

(100) TPr. 2.45: karaṇa-madhyaṃ tu vivṛtam

That is, the middle of the articulator does not make contact. Semivowels too are described as produced by letting an active articulator make contact at a place of production, but here again only part of the articulator is said to be brought into contact. Thus, according to

(101) TPr. 2.40: tālau jihvā-madhyāntābhyāṃ yakāre (sparśayati 35)

in producing *y* (*yakāre*), one has the edges of the mid-tongue (*jihvā-madhyāntābhyām*) make contact at the palate. On the other hand, some consonants are said to be produced at given places, but no active articulator is mentioned. Thus,

(102) TPr. 2.46: kaṇṭha-sthānau hakāra-visarjanīyau

says *h* and *ḥ* (*hakāra-visarjanīyau*) have the pharyngeal area (*kaṇṭha* 'throat') as their place of production (*kaṇṭha-sthānau*), and

(103) TPr. 2.47: udaya-svarādi-sthāno hakāra ekeṣām

(104) TPr. 2.48: pūrvānta-sasthāno visarjanīyaḥ (ekeṣām 47)

mention that according to some (*ekeṣām* [*mate*]) *h* has the place of production of the beginning of a vowel which follows it (*udaya-svarādi-sthānaḥ*), *ḥ* the place of production of the last part of a preceding vowel (*pūrvānta-sasthānaḥ*). That is, (102)TPr. 2.46 describes *h* and *ḥ* as produced at a neutral place of production—as when *h* is followed and *ḥ* is preceded by *a*—but (103)TPr. 2.47, (104)TPr. 2.48 note the view of some teachers, according to whom these consonants are given the places of production proper to any vowels which may follow and precede. Now, detailed descriptions of how organs are positioned in producing different sounds lend themselves to classifications of modes of production (*karaṇa*) in what may be called broad systems. One of these appears in the Ṛk-prātiśākhya, where

(105) RPr. 13.8: tad-viśeṣaḥ karaṇam

heads a group of rules each of which gives a mode of production (*karaṇam*) which serves to distinguish (*tad-viśeṣaḥ*) groups of sounds. Thus, according to

(106) RPr. 13.10: duspṛṣṭaṃ tu prāg ghakārāc caturṇām

(107) RPr. 13.11: svarānusvāroṣmaṇām aspṛṣṭaṃ sthitam

the production of the four sounds that precede *h* (*prāg ghakārāc caturṇām*) in the sound list adopted for the Ṛk-prātiśākhya — that is, of the semi-vowels *y r l v* — involves slight contact (*duspṛṣṭam*) between articulator and place of production; the production of vowels, *ṃ* and spirants (*svarānu-svāroṣmaṇām*) involves an articulator not making contact (*aspṛṣṭam*) but being held (*sthitam*) near a place of production. And according to

(108) RPr. 13.9: spṛṣṭam asthitam

when other sounds, that is, stops, are articulated, an active articulator makes full contact (*spṛṣṭam*) at a place of production, a contact which is momentary (*asthitam*), the articulator being removed quickly. That is, a three-way distinction is made: full occlusion for stops, slight contact for semivowels, and no contact for vowels, *ṃ* and spirants. Now, leaving aside features of length, pitch and nasality, a given sound's properties are correlated with: glottal aperture, which determines the type of air emitted; mode of production; and place of production. The contrast between ghoṣavat and aghoṣa sounds, as it applies to consonants, cannot be correlated with these in a cogent manner. Thus, voiced unaspirated stops, semivowels and vowels are all described as produced with close glottis resulting in the emission of nāda. But the consonants in question are termed *ghoṣavat* in phonologic rules, not the vowels. Both the Taittirīya- and the Ṛk-prātiśākhya say the glottis is in one state for producing voiced unaspirated stops and semivowels, in another state for producing aspirated stops and *h*; yet all these are termed *ghoṣavat*. Nor is it licit to say that a voiced consonant's being ghoṣavat is a function of its being articulate with a greater degree of closure than for vowels. Surely (102)TPr. 2.46 and (107)RPr. 13.11 agree in saying *h* is articulated with no closure between an articulator and a place of production. Yet in rules of these texts, *h* is termed *ghoṣavat*, vowels are not.

There is, then, only one reasonable conclusion to be drawn. Though *ghoṣavat* ('voiced') and *aghoṣa* ('voiceless') might at first blush seem to be purely phonetic class names, the use of these terms with reference to voiced and voiceless consonants alone is based on a phonological distinction.

REFERENCES AND ABBREVIATIONS

ĀŚ: Āpiśala-śikṣā, in: Śikṣā-sūtrāṇi Āpiśali-Pāṇini-Candragomi-viracitāni, edited by Yudhiṣṭhira Mīmāṃsaka; Ajmer, saṃvat 2024. [Āpiśala-śikṣā: 1-8, Cāndra-varṇa-sūtrāṇi: 24-26]

CĀ: Śaunakīyā Catur-ādhyāyikā: The Atharva-veda Prâtiçâkhya or Çaunakîyâ Caturâdhyâyikâ; text, translation, and notes, by William D. Whitney; *JAOS* 7: 333-615 (1862). [Reprinted: The Chowkhamba Sanskrit Series, vol. XX; Varanasi: Chowkhamba, 1962].

CVS: Cāndra-varṇa-sūtrāṇi; see ĀŚ.

Laghuśabdenduśekhara: Laghuśabdenduśekhara of Śrī Nāgeśa Bhaṭṭa with the Śekhara Dīpaka commentary by M.M. Pt. Śrī Nityānanda Panta Parvatīya, with an introduction by Pt. Gopāla Śāstrī Nene (Kashi Sanskrit Series 27); Varanasi: Chowkhamba, 1954.

Mahābhāṣya: The Vyākaraṇa-mahābhāṣya of Patañjali, edited by F. Kielhorn; third edition by MM K.V. Abhyankar; 3 volumes; Pune: Bhandarkar Oriental Research Institute, 1962, 1965, 1972.

Pradīpa: Kaiyaṭa's Pradīpa on the Mahābhāṣya, in: Śrībhagavatpatañjaliviracitaṃ Vyākaraṇa-mahābhāṣyam [śrīkaiyyaṭakṛtapradīpena nāgojībhaṭṭakṛtena bhāṣyapradīpoddyotena ca vibhūṣitam], edited by Vedavrata; 5 volumes; Gurukula Jhajjar (Rohatak): Harayāṇā-sāhitya-saṃsthānam, 1962-1963.

RPr.: The Ṛgveda-prātiśākhya with the commentary of Uvaṭa, edited by Mangal Deva Shastri volume II: text in sūtra form and commentary with critical apparatus; Allahabad The India Press, 1931.

RV: Ṛg-veda

TPr.: The Taittirīya-prâtiśâkhya with the commentaries of Somayârya and Gârgya Gopâlayajvan, edited by Panditaratnam K. Rangacharya and R. Shama Sastri (Government Oriental Library Series, Bibliotheca Sanskrita No. 33); Mysore: Government Branch Press, 1906.

TS: Taittirīya-saṃhitā

Uddyota: see Pradīpa.

Vākyapadīya: Bhartṛharis Vākyapadīya: die Mūlakārikās nach den Handschriften herausgegeben und mit einem Pāda-Index versehen von Wilhelm Rau (Abhandlungen für die Kunde des Morgenlandes XLII, 4) Wiesbaden: Steiner, 1977.
Vākyapadīya of Bhartṛhari with the Vṛtti and the Paddhati of Vṛṣabhadeva, critically edited by K.A. Subramania Iyer (Deccan College Monograph Series 32), Pune: Deccan College, 1966. [kārikā numbering according to Rau's edition; reference to commentaries according to page and line of Subramania Iyer's edition (KASI)]

VPr.: Vājasaneyi Prātiśākhya of Kātyāyana with the commentaries of Uvaṭa and Anantabhaṭṭa, edited by V. Venkatarama Sharma (Madras University Sanskrit Series No. 5); Madras: University of Madras, 1934.
The Śuklayajuḥ-prātiśākhya of Kātyāyana, critically edited from original manuscripts with English translation of the text by Shrimati Indu Rastogi (Kashi Sanskrit Series 179); Varanasi: Chowkhamba, 1967. [Numbering of sūtras according to Rastogi's edition]

VS: Vājasaneyi-saṃhitā

A SEARCH FOR THE PHONETIC CORRELATES OF HINDI STRESS

Manjari Ohala

INTRODUCTION

In addition to certain common syntactic and morphological features which make India a 'linguistic area', there are also phonological characteristics which many Indian languages share.[1] It has been claimed, for example, that Modern Indo-Aryan languages lack stress entirely (Bloch 1930).[2] In this paper I propose to examine such claims based on data from Hindi.

Among those who think that Hindi has a stress system few have paid attention to its phonetic correlates which makes it difficult to verify the stress assignment rules that have been offered. Those who claim that Hindi has stress agree that it is far weaker than in English, perhaps because unstressed syllables are not as detectably reduced in Hindi as they are in English. Also, unlike English, stress plays a very marginal role in Hindi: no words are differentiated solely by stress (however, see the discussion below). However, stress can be used contrastively, and for many words there is only one syllable that can be made prominent, and even in those three (or more) syllable words where the placement of accent is doubtful there is at least one syllable on which the accent may not be placed.

In this paper I report on the experiments that attempt to discover whether stress exists in Hindi, and if so, how distinctive it is and what its phonetic correlates are.

Although a large number of studies dealing with stress in Hindi have appeared in the past 100 years (Kellog 1875, Grierson 1895, Qadri 1930, Bailey 1933, Scholberg 1940, Firth 1944, Rudin 1958, Arun 1961, Dixit 1963, Mehrotra 1965, Dimshits 1966, Tiwari 1966, Ray 1966, Kelkar 1968, Sharma 1969, Jones 1971), there is still little that is understood about it. Amongst these writers, Grierson, Qadri, Rudin, Dixit, Dimshits, Tiwari, Mehrotra, Ray, Kelkar, Sharma, and Jones give rules for stress assignment.

---

1. This is a revised version of a paper that appeared in L. Hyman (ed.) 1977. *Studies in Stress and Accent.* I am grateful to John Ohala for his helpful comments on this paper as well as for making available to me the facilities of the Phonology Laboratory, University of California, Berkeley. I also thank R.N. Srivastava for the translation of Rudin (1958). I have also benefited from the comments of W.O. Bright, R.P. Dixit and P. Ladefoged. Finally, I would also like to thank my subjects for their patience. Responsibility for the opinions expressed and the data presented rests with me.

2. Also, for example, Scholberg says "The author is not prepared to say it [stress] does not exist, but he is more and more convinced that what there is largely of foreign origin." (1962 14).

The primary problem with all of these studies is that they are entirely impressionistic;[3] they do not make any attempt to check the predictions about stress placement with Hindi speakers nor, in most cases, do they suggest any phonetic correlates of stress so that someone else could check the predictions.

In this paper I will first review five of these algorithms proposed for assignment of word stress in Hindi and then present some instrumental phonetic data on selected words for which the stress patterns have been predicted by these writers, thus showing what the probable phonetic correlates are of what has been identified as "stress".

PHONEMIC STRESS IN HINDI ?

Writers such as Bailey (1933), Mehrotra (1965), Arun (1961) and others have claimed that there are a handful of words in Hindi which are distinguished solely by stress. They cite examples such as:

(1) bəha 'flowed' (past tense) bəha 'cause to flow' (imperative)
gəla 'throat gəla 'melt' (imperative)

Here those in column 1 are claimed to have stress on the first syllable and those in column 2 on the second syllable. However, I would claim that these are homophonous as far as lexical stress is concerned; rather it is the peculiar intonation pattern of imperative sentences which may make the words in the second column phonetically different from those in the first.

This is an empirical question, however, and can easily be tested. To do so I tape-recorded the following two sentences spoken twice each by a native speaker of Hindi.

(2) *ye hɛ ʊska gəla* '*This* is her throat'
tu hi bərəf gəla '*You* melt the ice'

Since in these sentences the initial word is emphasized, both cases of [gəla] get similar intonational contours, thus eliminating any differences due to the imperative intonation itself. These four instances of [gəla] were copied twice and spliced out and randomized onto a separate tape. These 8 samples were then played back to the same informant who was asked to identify which [gəla] belonged to which of the two sentences. The subject reported that they all sounded alike to her and was unable to differentiate them. This shows that the difference between words such as those in (1) is not due to lexical stress.

ALGORITHMS PROPOSED FOR STRESS ASSIGNMENT IN HINDI

The five linguists whose stress assignment algorithms I will focus on here are Grierson (1895), Dixit (1963), Mehrotra (1965), Kelkar (1968),

3. Another problem is that with few exceptions, those writers offering stress rules ignore whatever was done by others in this area. The result is an unnecessary proliferation in the literature of differently phrased but functionally equivalent rules.

and Sharma (1969). I will discuss Grierson's proposals only very briefly and concentrate mostly on the latter four. The rules given by other writers are in general similar to the rules of one or more of these five. Most of the proposed algorithms require reference to the concept of syllable weight which is a function of vowel length and whether the syllable is open or closed.

The earliest algorithm for stress assignment in Hindi was that given by Grierson. Actually his rules were intended to apply not only to Hindi but to Modern Indo-Aryan languages in general. He claimed that "The Indo-Aryan vernaculars closely follow the rules of the Sanskrit stress accent" (139). Here he refers to the rule of Sanskrit accentuation used by European scholars; however, many linguists today question whether such a rule ever existed in Sanskrit or in Modern Indo-Aryan. The rule he gives, in brief, amounts to:

> assign stress to the penultimate syllable if it is long,[4] if it isn't, keep moving backward till you find a long syllable. (If no such syllable is found, the accent is thrown back as far as possible but no further than pre-antepenultimate if the word ends in a short vowel and antepenultimate if it ends in a long vowel.)

This is certainly reminiscent of the Latin stress rule.

Dixit and Sharma explicitly recognize two degrees of syllable weight: light (L) and heavy (H). Sharma, however, implicitly recognizes 3 degrees of syllable weight as can be seen from his rule (3). Heavy $=\check{V}C_1$ and $\bar{V}C_0$, all others are light (i.e. $\check{V}$ is light). Kelkar recognizes three degrees of syllable weight: light, medium and heavy. His light is the same as that of Dixit and Sharma, his medium is $\bar{V}$ or $\check{V}C$ and his heavy is any other syllable type (i.e. $\check{V}C_2$ or $\bar{V}C_1$).[5]

Given below are my versions of the stress assignment rules of Kelkar, Sharma, Dixit and Mehrotra:

Kelkar:

(1) If there is only one maximally heavy syllable, assign stress to it.
(2) If there is more than one maximum, the last but one of the maximally heavy syllables gets the stress.

Sharma:

(1) If there is only one heavy syllable, it gets the stress.
(2) If all the syllables are light, the penultimate is stressed.
(3) If there is more than one heavy, then the last $\bar{V}$ or $\check{V}C$ which is followed by a consonant or syllable gets stress (i.e., if the $\bar{V}$ were word final it would not get stress but if it were followed by a C it would be stressed, e.g. $\bar{V}C\#$; similarly final $\check{V}CC$ would be stressed but $\check{V}C\#$ would not.

4. Grierson seems to equate long and short syllables with long and short vowels.

5. Kelkar also gives rules for locating syllable boundaries in medial consonant clusters, but these need not concern us here.

Dixit:

(1) If all syllables are heavy, or all are light, stress the penultimate.
(2) If there are some light syllables and some heavy, stress the penultimate if it is heavy, if not, keep moving back one syllable till a heavy is found.[6]
(3) If only one syllable is heavy it gets the stress.

Mehrotra:[7]

(1) In two syllable words, stress the second syllable if it is $\bar{V}C_1$ or $\check{V}C_2$, otherwise stress the first syllable.
(2) In a three syllable word, if all three vowels are short, stress the first.
(3) In words with three open syllables, if the penultimate is long, stress it; if not, stress the first vowel.
(4) In words where the first two syllables are open and the last is closed, if there is only one long vowel, it is stressed, otherwise the first vowel gets the stress. (Mehrotra allows here for variation of the following sort: if the final syllable has a $\bar{V}$, then optionally it could be stressed rather than the first syllable.)
(5) In all other types of words including those with more than three syllables, stress either a $\bar{V}$ or a closed syllable, which ever comes first, starting with the penultimate.

In spite of some superficial differences, most of these rules are very similar. For example, Kelkar's and Sharma's first rules are the same as Dixit's third. For words having all syllables of equal weight, Dixit's rule 1, Kelkar's rule 2, and Sharma's rules 2 and 3, would all assign stress in the same way, namely to the penultimate syllable.

Not surprisingly, these rules give similar results for many word types; a sample of these are listed in appendix A. Nevertheless there are cases where, due either to the rule used or the differing degrees of syllable weight recognized, different predictions are given; some examples are given in appendix B.

PHONETIC CORRELATES OF STRESS

Having clarified how various writers' stress algorithms for Hindi differ, it would be of interest to take those cases where their predictions on stress assignment to a particular syllable agree, and see how that syllable differs from other syllables in order to find out what the phonetic correlates of stress in Hindi are. Previous studies of stress in various languages have shown that it can be manifested in a variety of ways: by pitch, duration, intensity, vowel reduction,

---

6. This rule of Dixit's is similar to that given by Grierson.

7. Mehrotra doesn't really give an algorithm but gives a list of words exemplifying different syllable structure and lists where the stress would go for each type. I am here giving the rules I extrapolated from his lists.

degree of aspiration, etc. (Lehiste 1970). In searching for the correlates of stress in Hindi it is reasonable to start by looking at duration and pitch as prime candidates since these are the most salient correlates in some languages. Moreover Kelkar, one of the very few to address the problem of the phonetic correlates of of stress in Hindi has claimed "phonetically the prominence of a tonic or subtonic syllable consists of extra length to the coda nonsyllabics or (in case there is no coda) to the nucleus". This requires some interpretation, however. First, if it was the case that stress was correlated with the heaviest syllable in the word, then it would be pointless to speak about stress, we could just as well talk about short and long syllables. But I think by "extra length to the coda" Kelkar means that the same coda or nucleus would be longer when the syllable containing it gets word stress than when it occurred in a syllable which didn't. Kelkar apparently did not actually make any measurements to test this.

To test this claim, stress was located on 36 words according to Kelkar's rules (and for most of these words stress would be assigned similarly by the other's rules as well). The words were spoken by a native speaker of Hindi in isolation, and also in the frame: [apne——kəha] 'You said———'. The list was read once backwards and once forwards. The utterances were taped on a high quality tape recorder and were processed by a pitch and amplitude meter. The processed signals were written out on paper by an oscillomink. The coda was measured by hand. (The words had been chosen so that the coda or nucleus would be acoustically distinct from their environment and so could be easily measured.)

The results did not reveal any consistent increase in duration for the tauto-syllabic consonant after stressed vowels. For example the [t] in [mətləb] 'meaning' averaged 125 msec. whereas that in [prətyek] 'each' was 177 msec. (both uttered in isolation), just the opposite of what would be predicted by Kelkar. Nor was any consistent increase found in the duration of the vowel which would be considered to be 'stressed' according to Kelkar's rules.

Of course one might object that such measurements do not take into account how duration would be influenced by position in the word and sentences, how many syllables there are in a word, the nature of adjacent segments, etc. This is true, but if all these factors were controlled for we would not be able to carry out measurements since some of these factors determine where stress falls. If we kept them constant then we couldn't vary stress.

The next step was to see if pitch was a correlate of stress. Some 38 words were used. Although a total of 4 informants were used, not all of the words were said by all of the informants, thus the analysis for many words is based on only one informant. Again all the informants were native speaker of Standard Hindi from Uttar Pradesh. The words were put in a context designed to give the word sentence stress. For example, for the word [təmbaku] 'tobacco' the informant would be asked to read the following dialogue:

mera nɔkər təmbaku pita hɛ . 'My servant smokes tobacco'
kya pita hɛ? 'What does he smoke?'
təmbaku pita hɛ. 'He smokes *tobacco*'

The utterances were taped on a high quality tape recorder. For three of the informants the data were processed by a pitch and amplitude meter and written out on paper by an oscillomink. For the fourth informant narrow band spectrograms were made.

The data suggest that in general the syllable which was identified by the above-mentioned writers as the stressed, i.e., the prominent syllable, has a rising pitch on it and a falling pitch on the syllable following it, e.g. [dər-váza] 'door' as given in Figure 1. Sometimes this "stressed" syllable did not have a rising pitch on it but the following syllable did have a falling pitch, e.g. [pɪčʰla] 'last one' given in Figure 2. Also, it was sometimes true that if the syllable identified as the stressed one was short it only had high pitch on it, i.e., higher than immediately surrounding syllables. There were a number of words which had ambiguous pitch patterns, e.g. [əmɪta] 'a proper name',[8] as can be seen in Figure 3. One problem encountered was how to decide when a high falling pitch contour was due to the intended accent or due to the effects of a preceding voiceless stop. Nevertheless, it is possible to offer the generalization that what has been identified as the 'stressed' syllable in a polysyllabic Hindi word is generally the syllable which has a high or rising pitch on it with a falling or low pitch on the immediately following syllable.

More research on this question is needed, however. This paper is offered as only a first step towards finding out the nature of stress in Hindi. To verify that pitch is the primary cue, or at least an important cue for stress in Hindi, tests using synthetic speech are required wherein Hindi subjects can judge the acceptability of synthesized Hindi words where the pitch pattern can be varied without any variation in the other phonetic charac teristics of the word.

EXPERIMENT ON STRESS PLACEMENT

Although instrumental studies would probably be necessary to discover the precise perceptual cues for stress, a simple auditory analysis can nevertheless have some value, at least as a prelude to further more rigorous investigations. I conducted the following study to find out whether stress placement would vary depending on the context in which the word appeared.

I chose 40 words from those given in Appendices A and B. Five native speakers of Standard Hindi read these in isolation, and in the frames: [apne ——kəha] 'you said——', [apne——dekʰa] 'you saw——'. I noted down the syllable I heard as stressed. The words [kəha] and [dekʰa] were to pro-

8. On this word Mehrotra's rules assign stress to the first syllable, and those of the others on the last syllable.

vide a difference in the sentence frame since in [kəha] the first syllable is light and in [dekʰa] it is heavy. Finally, I pronounced the words in these two frames varying the stress and asked the subjects for their preferences. For example:

apne dərvaza kəha 'You said door'
dərvaza
dərvazá

And similarly for the frame with [dekʰa]. The results showed that:

(a) stress did indeed vary from the word in isolation to when it was in a sentence.

(b) In words of VC_1^2VCV structure the short vowel is never stressed. Thus in words such as [pətʰrila] 'stony', [təmbaku] 'tobacco', [dərvaza] 'door', the stress was never on the first syllable.

(c) The heaviest syllable doesn't always receive the stress. All the algorithms discussed earlier place the stress on the first syllable of [mámla] 'affair'. However, 4 out of 5 subjects preferred [mamlá] with the stress on the second syllable.

(d) In sentence frame, if the final syllable is the heaviest, i.e. $\bar{V}C$, then it receives the stress. Thus:

rozgǎr	'job'
kəmzór	'weak'
əkʰróṭ	'walnut'
pučkâr	'cooing sound'

CONCLUSIONS

In trying to find out whether there is any phonetic evidence of stress in a language one must first have a clear notion of what will count as evidence. Instrumental studies of what has been identified as stress in other languages have pointed to pitch contour, segmental and syllable duration, intensity and a few other lesser phonetic features as being the primary signallers of stress. One can therefore ask of the Hindi data: are there any habitual variations in the pitch contour that are not predictable from the over-all sentence intonation, or are there any characteristic variations in segmental duration that are not predictable from the segments themselves or the segmental environment they appear in? Furthermore if one does find such habitual or characteristic variations in these parameters is it the case that deviations from these patterns are unacceptable, unintelligible or foreign sounding?

Using these criteria, I am willing to state definitively that Hindi does have stress phonetically. The basis for this judgement is the finding that there are specific locations in many words which can be made prominent by placing a pitch fall after them and, optionally a pitch rise on them. Although there are instances in which this location of the pitch fall shifts within a single word depending on the context (as is true of stress in English, too) there are also locations in the word that may not receive the pitch fall.

I have not been able to verify the claim that variations in duration are a significant correlate of stress, but I would prefer to be cautious about this conclusion since not all possible duration measurements, using all reasonable controls, have been made. On the other hand, it has been claimed by Hyman (1977), as a universal tendency that languages using long *vs.* short distinction on segments or syllables—as is true of Hindi—will not use duration as a primary cue for stress.

Having established that phonetically stress does exist in Hindi, the next task is to see if there is any rule for assigning it to particular syllables in polysyllabic words, or whether it is completely idiosyncratic. On this issue I think all of the authors cited have captured some of the essential aspects of the stress-assignment rule for Hindi; the rule requires specification of the position of the syllables with respect to the end of the words, and the syllable weight.

The rules provided by writers such as Kelkar, Sharma, etc., do give different predictions for stress assignment for some words. Although I am in no position at present to give a definitive answer in regard to whose algorithm is correct, I think Sharma's seems to work the best.

The general findings—that the stress placement is determined by the position of the syllable in the word and by the syllable weight—fit into the universal claims put forth by Hyman. He claims (following Trubetskoy and others) that stress usually serves a culminative or delimitative function. Culminative in that it marks the presense of some major subunit of the sentence, delimitative in that it may also mark the boundary of that unit. We could say that stress tries to be delimitative in Hindi, but since it is not strictly penultimate (or ultimate) it is at least culminative. Hyman claims that syllable weight is a common factor in stress assignment rules since the speaker needs time to manifest a pitch contour on a syllable—the longer a syllable is (i.e., the heavier it is), the more it lends itself to this.

It may even be possible to elaborate on his model in a way that would account for my finding of the shifting stress seen from the word in isolation condition to the word in sentence context. Overall one could say that the optimal environment for the manifestation of stress is a heavy (i.e. long) syllable on which to put a pitch rise and a syllable following on which to put a pitch fall. Thus when the word [pučkar] 'cooing sound' was spoken in isolation scanning the word from right to left, the location of the pitch rise has to be on the first syllable and the fall on the second However when this word is spoken in the context of a sentence ([apne pučkar kəha]) the pitch rise can be placed on the second syllable and the fall on the following syllable in the next word. Thus in isolation the word has initial stress, but in a mid-sentence context, final stress.

Appendix A

Examples of words where the algorithms of Kelkar, Sharma, Dixit and Mehrotra give the same results.

1.	pə́ttʰər	'stone'	22.	dɪyasəlái	'matchstick'
2.	pətʰríla	'stony'	23.	mə́tləb	'meaning'
3.	gɪrəftári	'arrest'	24.	ə́drək	'ginger'
4.	pakɪstáni	'Pakistani'	25.	rəsói	'kitchen'
5.	dumə́nzɪla	'two storied'	26.	kêsərɪya	'saffron colored'
6.	pərsərgíy (ə)	'suffix'	27.	ɪnsánɪyət	'humanity'
7.	ədálət	'court'	28.	təmáša	'exhibition'
8.	kímti	'expensive'	29.	čəprási	'peon'
9.	kímət	'price'	30.	dərváza	'door'
10.	púrvəǰ	'ancestors'	31.	sɪpáhi	'policeman'
11.	behóš	'unconscious'	32.	kʰɪṛkí	'window'
12.	ríšvət	'bribe'	33.	ləkəṛhára	'wood cutter'
13.	áṭa	'flour'	34.	bʊṛʰɪyá	'old woman'
14.	kʊrsí	'chair'	35.	kəbáṛɪya	'junk collector'
15.	mʊ́škɪl	'difficulty'	36.	həlvái	'sweet seller'
16.	təmbáku	'tobacco'	37.	tə́lɪya	'towel'
17.	mámla	'affair'	38.	dɪkʰái	'seen'
18.	avə́šyək	'necessary'	39.	hɛ́sɪyət	'position'
19.	gusəlkʰána	'bathroom'			
20.	kʰərbúǰa	'melon'			
21.	pərə́mpəra	'tradition'			

Appendix B

Examples of words where the algorithms of Mehrotra, Dixit, Kelkar and Sharma assign stress differently.

1.	Kelkar:	kʰúbsurət	'pretty'	others:	kʰubsúrət
2.	Kelkar:	rézgari	'small change'	others:	rezgári
3.	Kelkar:	ráǰniti	'politics'	others:	raǰníti
4.	Kelkar:	bʰártiy (ə)	'Indian'	others:	bʰartíy(ə)
5.	Mehrotra:	kə́ləm	'pen'	others:	kələ́m
6.	Mehrotra:	ə́mɪta	'proper name'	others:	əmɪtá
7.	Mehrotra:	gə́ṛərɪya	'grass cutter'	others:	gəṛərɪyá
8.	Mehrotra:	ə́mɪya	'raw mango'	others:	əmɪyá
9.	Mehrotra:	kə́la	'art'	others:	kəlá
10.	Sharma:	aširvád	'blessing'	others:	áršivad
11.	Sharma:	ɪtɪhaskár	'historian'	others:	ɪtɪháskar
12.	Dixit:	pakɪ́stan	'Pakistan'	others:	pakɪstán

13.	Dixit:	kəlákar	'artist'	others:	kəlakár
14.	Dixit:	kə́mzor	'weak'	others:	kəmzór
15.	Dixit:	ə́kʰroṭ	'walnut'	others:	əkʰróṭ
16.	Dixit:	púčkar	'cooing sound'	others:	pučkár
17.	Dixit:	gobə́r	'cow dung'	others:	góbər
18.	Kelkar/Dixit:	rózgar	'job'	Sharma:	rozgár
19.	Kelkar Sharma	bʰrəšṭačár	'bad behavior'	Dixit Mehrotra	bʰrəšṭáčar
20.	Kelkar/Medrotra	ándolən	'movement'	Dixit Sharma	andólən
21.	Sharma:	tὲhsildár	'govt. official'	Dixit Mehrotra	tɛhsíldar
				Kelkar	tɛhsíldar or tɛ́hsildar

BIBLIOGRAPHY

Arun, V. B. 1961. *A comparative phonology of Hindi and Panjabi*. Ludhiana: Panjabi Sahitya Akademi.

Bailey, T. G. 1933. *Studies in north Indian languages*. London: Lund Humphries and Co.

Bloch J. 1930. *Introduction to Qadri's Hindustani Phonetics.*

Dimshits, J. M. 1966. *Hindi vyakaran ki roop rekha.* Delhi: Rajkamal Prakashan.

Dixit, R. P. 1963. The segmental phonemes of contemporary Hindi. Austin: University of Texas master's thesis.

Firth, J. R. 1944. Introduction to Harley's Colloquial Hindustani.

Grierson, G. A. 1895. "On the stress-accent in Modern Indo-Aryan Vernaculars". *Journal of the Royal Asiatic Society of Great Britain and Ireland.* 3. 139-147.

Hyman, L.M. 1977. "On the nature of linguistic stress". In *Studies in Stress and Accent* ed. by L.M. Hyman. Southern California Occasional Papers in Linguistics. 4. 37-82.

Jones, W. E. 1971. "Syllables and word stress in Hindi." *Journal of the IPA* : 12.74-78.

Kellog, S. H. 1875. *A grammar of the Hindi language*. London: Routledge & Kegan Paul Ltd. (Reprinted 1965).

Kelkar, A. R. 1968. *Studies in Hindi-Urdu* I. Poona: Deccan College building centenary and silver jubilee series. 35.

Lehiste, I. 1970. *Suprasegmentals.* Cambridge: MIT Press.

Mehrotra, R. C. 1965. "Stress in Hindi." *Indian Linguistics* 26: 96-105.

Qadri, M. S. G. 1940. *Hindustani phonetics.* Villeneuve-Saint-Georges.

Rudin, S. G. 1958. "Nekotorye voprosy fonetiki jazyka xindustani." *Uchenye zapiski instituta vostokovedenija* 13. 232-65.

Scholberg, H. C. 1940. *Concise grammar of the Hindi language.* London: Oxford University Press. (Reprinted 1962).

Sharma, A. 1969. "Hindi word-accent." *Indian Linguistics.* 30. 115-18.

Tiwari, B. N. 1966. *Hindi Bhasha.* Allahabad: Kitab Mahal.

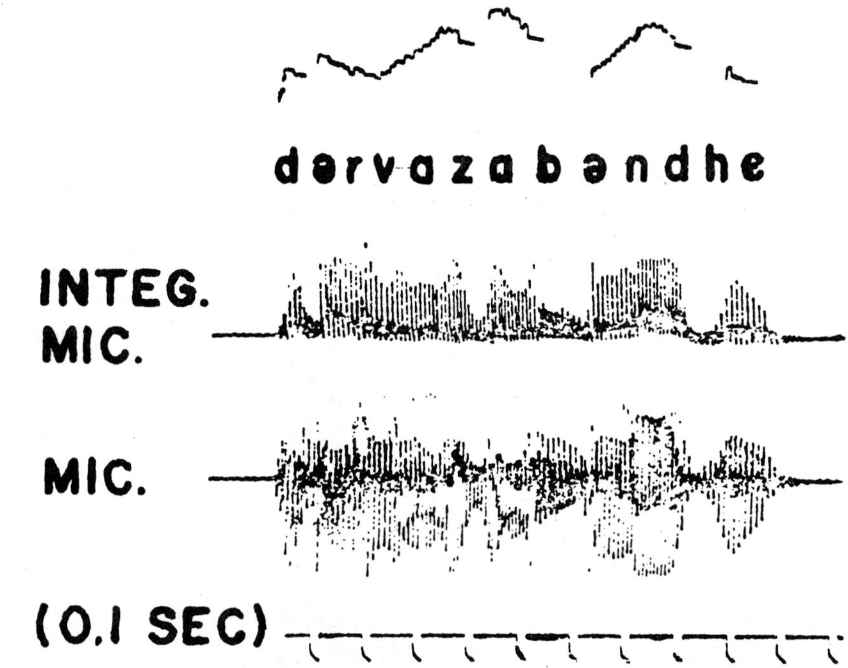

Figure 1. Parameters from top to bottom: fundamental frequency, rectified and integrated microphone signal, (unprocessed) microphone signal, 0.1 sec timing pulse. These data show that the second syllable of [dərvaza] "door" has a rising pitch and the syllable following a falling pitch.

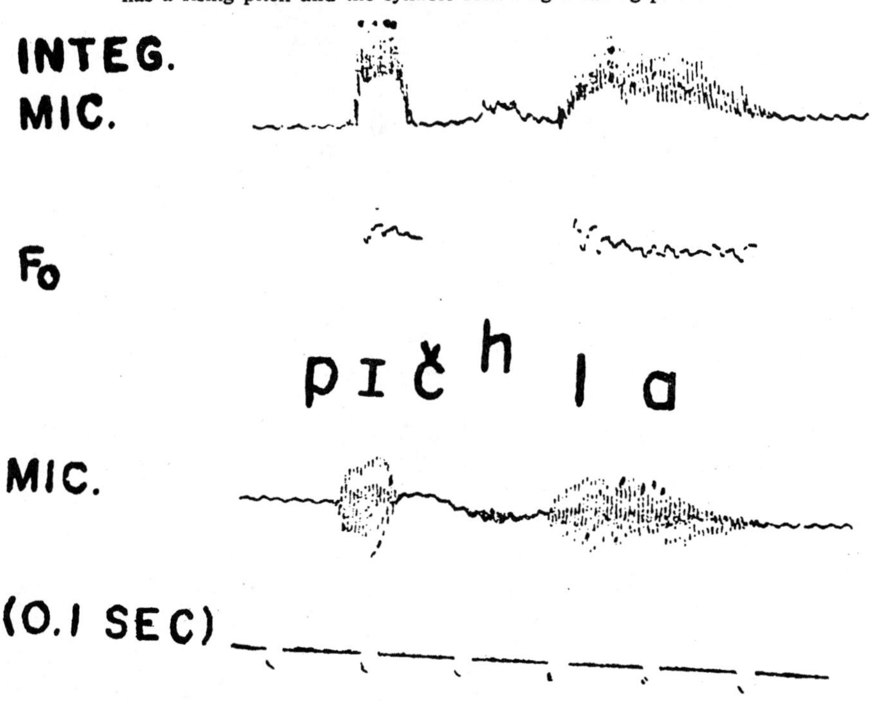

Figure 2. Parameters from top to bottom: rectified and integrated microphone signal, fundamental frequency, (unprocessed) microphone signal, 0. 1 sec timing pulse. These data show the second syllable of [pɪčhla] "last one" has a falling pitch

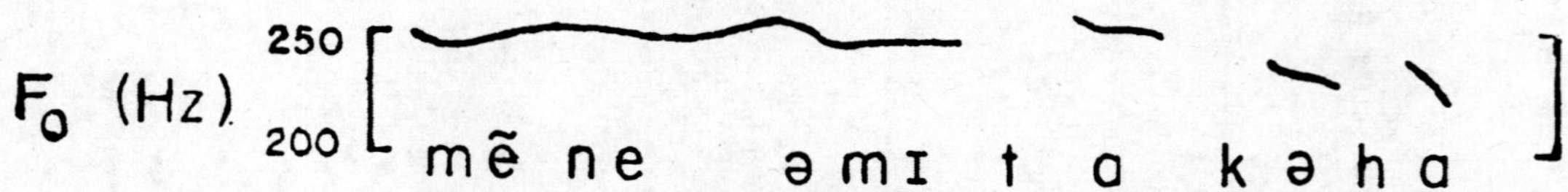

Figure 3. Tracing of the fundamental frequency curve from a narrow-band spectrogram of the word [əmIta] (proper name). Here either the first or the third syllable of the word could be said to have high pitch.

ON CERTAIN PHONOLOGICAL PROCESSES IN SOUTH DRAVIDIAN II

A. Usha Devi

South Dravidian II is a sub-group of Dravidian family of languages, classified by Bh. Krishnamurti. The languages that come under this group are Konda, Pengo, Kui, Kuvi, Gondi, Manda, and Telugu. Except Telugu, all other are tribal languages which do not have scripts.

This paper is concerned with some of the phonological processes common to this sub-group, its analysis is based on the data drawn from the available descriptions. Since no grammar is available for Manda, its phonology has not been taken into consideration. The aim of this investigation is to study and understand the relevance of a contemporary theory of phonology in the light of the Dravidian data.

Recently, many scholars in the field of transformational-generative phonology have shown their interest in a discussion of the "naturalness" of the phonological changes. They rightly claim that to explain the nature and direction of the change is as much essential as formulating a rule. They use the term 'naturalness' to refer to the distinctive features of phonological elements of a language. Accordingly, they have postulated a theory of markedness that provides +, –, U, or M values to features, which are universal. Thus an obstruent unmarked for voice is always voiceless. It is clear that this is based on the phonetic (articulatory and/or acoustic) properties of phonological features.

Schane (1972) has discussed three categories of natural rules, which are assimilative rules, preferred syllable structure rules, and the rules for maximum differentiation. He observes that "there is some kind of hierarchy of preferred syllable structure" and says, "some indications of this hierarchy are presented in the marking convention for syllable structure proposed by Chomsky and Halle (1968)" (Schane 1972: 209). Vennemann (1972) and Ramarao (1975) have made similar observations. Foley (1972, 1977), however, has a different proposal, which is based on 'strength hierarchy', it refers to the abstract phonological relationship, and not to the phonetic properties of segments". He, thus, defines the phonological elements on the basis of their participation in rules.

As mentioned above, while discussing some of the phonological processes of South Dravidian II languages, the paper tries to propose the 'naturalness' of the rules by positing a common strength scale for the phonological features of these languages. The vowel that is lost in the stem final position before a suffix (mostly a plural suffix) is a high back rounded one *u*. This can be seen in the following examples from Konda, Kui and Telugu. Pengo and Gondi have no stem final vowels, but there are one or two examples in Gondi, where word final *u* is observed:

Konda:	kopu	+	ku	→kopku	'braid of hair'
Kui:	koju	+	ka	→koska	'fowl'
Telugu:	kālu	+	lu	→kāḷḷu	'legs'
Pengo:	kozu	+	ku	→kosku	'fowls'
Gondi:	goddu	+	ku	→godku	'cows'
Kuvi:	vegu	+	ka	→veska	'fire-wood'

Word final *-i* is also sometimes lost in Telugu and Konda:

Telugu:	gadi	+	lu	→gadulu	'rooms'
	guḍi	+	lu	→guḷḷu	'temples'
	kōḍi	+	lu	→kōḷḷu	'fowls'
Konda:	peni	+	ku	→penku	'lice'

These languages have vowel insertion (or addition) also either in the form of epenthesis or copying. Through the process of epenthesis, high front unrounded vowel *i* is inserted between the consonants of verbal base and a suffix:

Konda:	ḍig	+	t	→ḍig*it*-	'to get down'	past tense stem
Kui:	kāg	+	t	→kāg*it*-	'to warm'	—do—
Kuvi:	ajj	+	t	→ajj*it*-	'to fear'	—do—
Gondi:	huṛ	+	t	→huṛ*it*-	'to see'	present tense stem
Koya:	ūḍ	+	t	→ūḍ*it*	'to see'	—do—

The vowels that are inserted by copying in Pengo and Konda are *a*, *i*, and *e*.

Pe:	huṛ + t + n + an	→	huṛt*a*n*a*n 'I saw' (perfect)
	huṛ + t + n + ik	→	huṛt*i*n*i*k 'they saw' (")
	huṛ + d + men	→	huṛd*e*m*e*n 'II p. Neg. Imp.) 'don't see' (sg.)

In Konda, copying is not observed in the surface forms but the process of derivation is discussed in detail in Ramarao (1976), where a case for copying is argued and established. Here also the vowels are *e* and *i* and *a*. The following example from the compound verb supports the claim:

Ko:	vāt + suṛ + ta	→	vāt*a*suṛt*a* 'I came and saw'
	vāt + suṛ + ti	→	vāt*i*suṛt*i* 'You (sg.) came and saw'
	vāt + suṛ + te	→	vāt*e*suṛt*e* 'he came and saw'

The process of insertion of vowels in Telugu is slightly different. The vowels involved here, call it a harmony or epenthesis, are *i* and *u*. The low vowel *a* also causes harmony but is not involved in the change.[1]

Te:	gadi + lu	→	gad*u*lu	'rooms'
	gadi + ku	→	gadik*i*	'to the room'
	maniṣi + nu	→	maniṣin*i*	'man (acc.)'
	atanu + i + ku	→	atanik*i*	'to him'
	aḍugu + i	→	aḍ*i*gi	'having asked'
	aḍug (u) + aka	→	aḍ*a*g*a*ka	'without asking'
	aḍug(u) + ani	→	aḍ*a*g*a*ni	'that which is not asked'
	aḍug(u) + ite	→	aḍ*i*gite	'if (one) asks'

Based on these processes, the following strength scale is proposed:

u i a e o
———————→
1 2 3 4 5

The vowel involved in loss is *u* which is considered as the 'weakest' phonological element whereas the strongest one which is not involved in any process is *o*. Other vowels are ranged between the two on the basis of their participation in the observation of rules and their relationship to each other. Obviously the vowels involved in addition are *i*, *e* and *a*. *i* is considered next to *u* as it is involved in many processes, like deletion and addition. *a* is seen in examples given above in more than one language and *e* is seen in copying only in Konda.

Now, let us turn to the consonantal processes. Assimilation and deletion are the two main types of consonantal processes. Nasal deletion and cluster reduction are the two involved in deletion.
Examples:

Nasal Deletion:

Ko:	ambu	+	ku	→	apku	'arrows'
Pe:	prānj	+	ku	→	prācku	'mosquitoes'
Kui	glunj	+	ka	→	gluska	'puddles'
Go:	menj	+	k(a)	→	mesk(a)	'eggs'
Kuvi:	onḍu	+	ka	→	oṭka	'parts'

Cluster Reduction:

Te:	cepp + t + ānu	→	ceptānu	'I say / will say'
	guḍḍu + lu	→	guḍḷu	'eggs'
	ceṭṭu + lu	→	ceṭḷu	'trees'
Ko:	man + n + an	→	manan	'we will stay'
	as + zi	→	asi	'having held'
	ūz + zi	→	ūzi	'having crawled'

1. See Ramarao (1976) for further details.

Pe:	end + den	→	enden	'to dance'
Kui:	tin + n + eru	→	tineru	'they eat'
Kuvi:	jap + p + esi	→	japesi	'let him teach'
	tos + sa	→	tosa	'having shown'

Assimilation is partial or complete; regressive or progressive.

Regressive:

Ko:	rāzu + ku	→	rāsku	'kings'
Pe:	kozu + ku	→	kosku	'fowls'
Kui:	nāj + ka	→	nāska	'villages'
Go:	menj + k(a)	→	mesk(a)	'eggs'
Kuvi:	vanju + ka	→	vaska	'fingers'
Te:	ceruku + gaḍa	→	ceruggaḍa	'sugar cane'
	aḍug(u) + kō	→	aḍukkō	'ask yourself'
Ko:	sur̠ + t	→	suR	past stem of the verb 'to roast'

Progressive:

Ko:	kap + zi	→	kapsi	'having covered'
	as + du	→	astu	'hold'
Kui:	ag + t	→	agd[2]	past stem of the verb 'to be fitting'

Though retroflexion and lateral assimilation are also regressive, they are treated separately with their respective 'marked' features.[3] The examples are:
Retroflexion:

Ko:	kol + t	→	koṭ-	past stem of the verb 'to buy'
	uṇ + t	→	uṭ-	" " " " " 'to eat'
Kui:	in + t	→	iṭ-	" " " " " 'to say'
Pe:	un + t	→	uṭ-	" " " " " 'to eat'
Te:	tin + t	→	tiṇṭ-	" " " " " 'to eat'
	un + t	→	uṇṭ-	" " " " " 'to be'
Kuvi:	hon + t	→	hoṭ-	" " " " " 'to run'

Lateral Assimilation:

Ko:	nil + n	→	ninn	→	nin-	Future stem of the verb: 'to stop'
	mūḷ + n	→	mūṇṇ	→	mūṇ	'to urinate'
Pe:	hal + n	→	hann	→	han--	'to go'

Some other assimilations which are not linked up with any of the above processes are:

2. There are only nine verbs ending in *-g* which have progressive assimilation in Kui.
3. The question of underlying representation has not been looked into in this study.

Te:	pāta + ceppulu	→	pācceppulu	'old chappals'
	vacc + te	→	vaste	'if comes'
	tūc + dām	→	tūddām	'let us weigh'
	kōs + dām	→	kōddām	'let us pluck'
Ko:	in + t	→	iR-	*Past stem*: 'to say'
	tūl + t	→	tūR-	'to be splashed'
Pe:	in + t	→	ic-	'to say'
	hal + t	→	hac-	'to go'
Kui:	tin + t	→	tis-	'to eat'
	jel + t	→	jes-	'to pull'
Kuvi:	ven + du	→	venju	'listen'
	hal + du	→	haju	'go'

By observing the above processes, we may posit the following strength scale for consonants:

$$\begin{array}{cccccc} l & n & c & s & b & p \\ \hline 1 & 2 & 3 & 4 & 5 & 6 \end{array} \longrightarrow$$

l = liquid, n = nasal, c = affricate, s = sonorant, b = voiced stop, p = voiceless stop.

If we look at the above assimilations it is evident that one cannot distinguish between assimilations based on the point and manner of articulation, since both are involved simultaneously. The strength hierarchy not only takes into consideration the inherent strength, but also the other strengths such as positional strength and the strength of a neighbouring element; for both these, sometimes, condition and dominate the change.

If we look into the example of *l* assimilating to *n*, the markedness theory has no way of predicting the change. But the strength scale makes it possible to assume that the phonological element *n* is relatively stronger than *l*. Within the terminology of marking conventions, it may be said that a phonological feature is marked or unmarked not only because of its inherent phonetic content, but also because of its function in the language. According to this, *u* may be considered unmarked and *o* marked, but there is no way to explain or distinguish between *u* and *i* or *e* and *o* if they are treated on the basis of their phonetic characteristics. The strength hierarchy provides potential as well as relative strength to the phonological features not on the basis of their phonetic characteristics but on the basis of their participation in rules.

Now, let us turn to our earlier discussion on 'naturalness'. Ramarao (1975) observes: "Retroflex is a marked feature and it is *progressively marked from obstruents to sonorants and to vowels.* As it is well-known, only Badaga has contrastive retroflex vowels. In any of the Dravidian languages retroflexed consonants are confined to non-initial positions. The distribution also points out that sonorant retroflex consonants are *more marked* than their obstruent counterparts. In Telugu it is hard to find a nongeminate retroflex sonorant contrasted with a non-retroflex sonorant. It is also probably true that a retroflex lateral is more marked than a retroflex nasal. *This suggests that there are also different degrees in markedness*" (p. 43, emphasis mine).

The above passage can easily be interpreted in terms of strength hierarchy. What Ramarao argues for is that the feature retroflex is stronger than other features. And this feature gains more strength when it is added to sonorants and to vowels. Though the theory of markedness does not provide "degrees" such as 'more marked' and 'less marked', Ramarao has recognised the fact that there are different degrees in markedness. If his proposal is acceptable it can be rephrased in terms of strength as:

ṭ ḷ Ṿ

————————→

1 2 3

ṭ = retroflex stop, ḷ = retroflex sonorant, Ṿ = retroflex vowel.

There is some important difference between marking conventions and strength hierarchy. What markedness theory claims as 'unmarked' and 'marked' cannot be equated with the strength hierarchy. The unmarked and marked values are language universal, and they decide the 'naturalness' of the change by their phonetic properties, whereas strength considers universal as well as language particular strengths of 'abstract' phonological features.

Ramarao also observes that it is probably true that the retroflex lateral is more marked than the retroflexed nasal. The feature retroflex is marked for both lateral and nasal, but historical evidence necessitates him to suggest retroflex lateral to be 'more marked' than retroflex nasal. What Ramarao observes as 'more marked' is the 'weak' element from the point of view of strength. But there is some difference between the two values. According to Ramarao the 'more marked' element is a retroflex lateral, and not a plain lateral. But the strength scale separates the retroflex from the lateral, and the plain lateral is a weak element. There is another indication from the languages under discussion that wherever there is an assimilation, retroflex seems to be dominant and powerful irrespective of the strength of a particular phonological element. This is clearly evident when we observe the retroflex lateral assimilating to the following nasal (/mūḷ + n/→/mūṇ + ṇ/),[4] the lateral assimilates to the nasal whereas the nasal assimilates to the retroflexion. The same is found in nasal deletion also, where the nasal is deleted after changing the following dental stop to the retroflex, e.g., /uṇ + t/ → /uṭ/.

4. There is no retroflex lateral as a phonological element in the descriptive grammars of any of the languages, though historical evidence shows the presence of a retroflex lateral. In his Konda grammar, Bh. Krishnamurti has proposed two different laterals as L_1 & L_2 to distinguish the plain lateral from the retroflex. The writer, without getting involved in the controversial discussion on the nature of the 'abstract' underlying representation, uses / ḷ / to explain the retroflexion in the surface forms.

As observed above, it may also be possible to assign strengths not only to segments (which contain feature complexes) but also to individual features. If this is acceptable, then retroflex feature may be separated from other features of the segments in SDr II languages. Thus:

$$\frac{\text{[-retroflex]} \qquad\qquad \text{[+ retroflex]}}{1 \qquad\qquad\qquad\qquad 2} \longrightarrow$$

$$1 \longrightarrow 2 \;/\; 2$$

To conclude, it is clear that Ramarao's observations for historical restructuring of SDr II languages further support the need to revise or strengthen the theory of markedness so as to enable 'degrees' for the marked and unmarked values to be clearly noted. As strength scale is capable of capturing these aspects, it is preferred in the present analysis.

BIBLIOGRAPHY

Arden, A.H. 1969. *A progressive grammar of the Telugu language.* Madras: The Christian Literature Society.

Anderson, S. 1974. *The Organization of phonology.* New York: Academic Press.

Burrow, T. and S. Bhattacharya. 1970. *The Pen o language.* Oxford: The Clarendon Press.

Chomsky N. and M. Halle. 1968. *The sound patterns of English.* New York: Harper and Row.

Foley, J. 1972. "Rule precursors and phonological change by meta-rule." In *Linguistic change and generative theory,* ed. by Stockwell, Robert. P and Ronald K. S. Macauley. Bloomington: Indiana University Press. 96-100.

———. 1977. *Foundations of theoretical phonology.* London: Cambridge University Press.

Israel, M. 1979. *A grammar of the Kuvi language.* Trivandrum: Dravidian Linguistics Association.

Krishnamurti, Bh. 1961. *Telugu verbal bases : A comparative and descriptive study.* Delhi: Motilal Banarsidass.

———. 1969. *Konda or Kubi : a Dravidian language.* Hyderabad: Tribal Cultural & Training Institute.

Patwardhan, S. B. 1935. *First Gondi manual.* London: Society for Promoting Christian Knowledge.

Ramarao, C. 1975. "Dravidian evidence for abstract phonology." In *Osmania Papers in Linguistics.* 1. 30-44.

———. 1976. "Vowel harmony in Telugu." In *Papers in Linguistic Analysis.* Univ. of Delhi. 1:1. 25-35.

Ramarao, K. 1979. Phonology and morphology of Koya language. Unpublished M, Phil. dissertation submitted to Osmania University.

Schane, S. A. 1972. "Natural rules in phonology". In *Linguistic change and generative theory*. ed. by Stockwell, Robert. P. and Ronald K. S. Macauley. Bloomington: Indiana University Press. 199-228.

Usha Devi, A. 1978. A typological study of Dravidian morphophonemics. Unpublished M. Phil. dissertation submitted to Osmania University, Hyderabad.

Vennemann, Theo. 1972. "Sound change and markedness theory. On the history of the German consonant system." In *Linguistic change and generative theory*. ed. by Stockwell, Robert, P. and Ronald K. S. Macauley. Bloomington: Indiana University Press. 230-262.

ACOUSTIC CORRELATES OF WORD STRESS IN MAITHILI

Ramawatar Yadav

1. *Introduction.* Maithili, like most Indo-Aryan languages, is a stress language. However, stress in Maithili is far weaker than in English. Vowel reduction in unstressed positions is not as marked in Maithili as in English. Also, stress in Maithili is less significant; it plays only a marginal role in distinguishing words.

Little has been published on the phonetics and phonology of Maithili. The only studies that I have personal knowledge of are: Jha (1941, 1958); Ingemann and Yadav (1978); and Yadav (1976, 1979a, b, c).

Previous experimental studies of stress in various languages of the world including English have shown that stressed syllables differ from those that are unstressed along at least five parameters: duration, intensity, fundamental frequency, vowel reduction, and vowel quality. Little, however, has been published on the acoustic correlates of stress in modern Indo-Aryan languages of India and Nepal. The present paper investigates three acoustic features (fundamental frequency, relative intensity, and duration) in detail and attempts to determine the probable acoustic correlates of word stress in Maithili.[1]

2. *Experimental Method : Test Material.* For this study, a list of Maithili word pairs was prepared. The word pairs were read three times in isolation and were recorded in the order presented in Table I. The speaker was a native speaker from the Tarai of Nepal. The test words chosen for this study were all disyllabic and of the CVCV type. The word pairs differed primarily in their stress pattern and were of the type in which one word was a noun and the other a causative verb—with the exceptions of ['giro] 'may he fall' and [gi'ro] '(you) cause to fall', which were both verbs. Table I lists the stress pairs used in this study.

Table I: Maithili Stress Pairs

	Fo (in Hz)
['bəča]	'child'
[bə'ča]	'cause to save'
['suta]	'heavy thread'
[su'ta]	'cause to sleep'
['giro]	'may he fall'
[gi'ro]	'(you) cause to fall'

1. This study forms part of Chapter V of Yadav (1979c)

['gəla]	'throat'
[gə'la]	'cause to melt'
['pota]	'grandson'
[po'ta]	'cause to whitewash'

2.2. *Apparatus and Measurements.* Three recordings of each Maithili stress pair were made on an Akai GX reel-to-reel taperecorder in a soundproof studio of the Language Laboratory of the University of Kansas, U.S.A.

Fundamental frequency was measured from narrow band spectrograms by dividing by ten the frequency of the tenth harmonic. In some cases (e.g.[i o u]) where the tenth harmonic was not visible, the fundamental frequency was estimated on the basis of the frequency of the fifth harmonic.

Intensity was measured from intensity tracings produced by the F.J. Electronics Intensity Meter.

Duration was measured on both wideband spectrograms and oscillographic wave forms.

3. *Results and Discussion.* Results of the measurements are given in Tables II-V.

Table II: Peak Fundamental Frequencies (in Hz) of Maithili Stress Pairs.

		Fo (in Hz)			
Word	Vowel	1	2	3	Average
['bəča]	['ə]	131	131	125	129
	[a]	114	120	125	120
[bə'ca]	['a]	134	134	125	131
	[ə]	114	103	108	108
['suta]	['u]	145	145	134	141
	[a]	103	106	131 ??	113
[su'ta]	['a]	131	131	131	131
	[u]	117	111	117	115
['giro]	['i]	134	134	134	134
	[o]	128	128	128	128
[gi'ro]	['o]	117	122	122	120
	[i]	128	128	128	128
['gəla]	['ə]	131	128	128	129
	[a]	114	117	134??	122
[gə'la]	['a]	122	120	122	121
	[ə]	111	114	108	111
['pota]	['o]	145	134	134	138
	[a]	123	100	134	119
[po'ta]	['a]	134	131	134	133
	[o]	106	111	106	108

Table II lists the fundamental frequency (in Hz) measured at the peak for each of the three tokens of each stress pair and their average fundamental frequency. The values show that stressed vowels in Maithili usually have a higher fundamental frequency than the corresponding unstressed vowels. On the average, a stressed vowel in Maithili has a fundamental frequency of 14 Hz higher than the fundamental frequency of an unstressed vowel.

The presence or absence of voicing during consonant environment has an influence upon the fundamental frequency of the adjacent vowel. The fundamental frequencies of vowels in voiceless environments are in general higher than in voiced environments. However, as House and Fairbanks (1953: 110) have concluded:

> ... the effects of consonants upon fundamental frequency, although significant, are probably less than the variations in fundamental frequency natural to the vowels themselves when consonant environments are constant.

Other studies (Peterson and Barney 1952, Lehiste 1961, 1970) have shown that there is also a close connection between the phonetic quality of a vowel and its intrinsic fundamental frequency. Other things being equal, a high vowel has a higher fundamental frequency.

Although the corpus used in this study was extremely limited, both the above-mentioned observations are borne out by the present study. For instance, Table II shows that the stressed ['a] occurring after voiceless consonants [t] or [č] have considerably higher fundamental frequency values than the one occurring after the (voiced) lateral [l]. Also, the intrinsic fundamental frequencies of Maithili vowels (computed from Table II and listed in Table III) show that Maithili high vowels too have higher fundamental frequencies. As a matter of fact, the results presented in Table III show a striking similarity between the intrinsic fundamental frequency values obtained for English stressed vowels by Peterson and Barney (1952) (as reported in Lehiste 1970: 69) and those of the Maithili stressed vowels. This similarity is shown in Figure 1.

Table IV lists the relative intensity (in dB from an arbitrary o) measured at the maximum level for each of the three tokens of each Maithili stress pair and their average intensity. The figures show that the stressed vowels in Maithili have a slightly higher average intensity than the unstressed vowels. On the average a stressed vowel in Maithili has a 3 dB higher relative intensity than an unstressed vowel. This is, however, not a considerable difference as compared to the 4 to 5 dB range established for American English and 12 dB range for Hungarian (as reported in Lehiste 1970: 121).

Previous investigators (Fairbanks, House and Stevens 1950, Fonagy 1966, House and Fairbanks 1953, Lehiste 1961, 1970) have emphasized the connection between the phonetic quality of a vowel and its intrinsic intensity. They have also considered the differing consonant environment (especially the presence or absence of voice) as an important factor in determining the intrinsic vowel intensity.

Considering the limited number of stress pairs used in this study, no claim will be made as to the intrinsic intensity of the Maithili stressed vowels. Nevertheless, looking at the intensity values provided in Table IV, the following observations may be made:

Table III: Intrinsic Fundamental Frequency (Hz) of Maithili Stressed Vowels.

['i]	134 Hz
['ə]	129 Hz
['a]	128 Hz
['o]	129 Hz
['u]	141 Hz

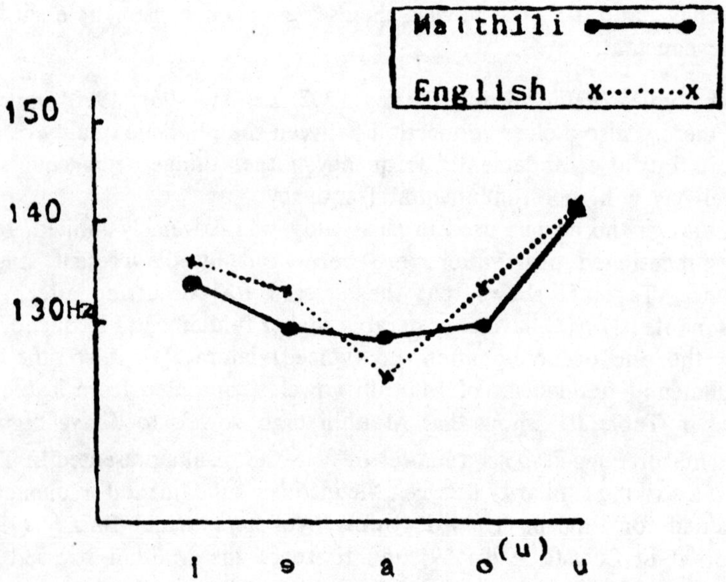

Fig. 1. Peak fundamental frequency values for Maithili stressed vowels (connected line) as compared with the English stressed vowels (dotted line) obtained by Peterson and Barney 1952 (as reported in Lehiste 1970:69).

Table IV: Peak Intensity (in dB) Values for Maithili stress Pairs

Word	Vowel	Intensity (in dB) 1	2	3	Average
['bəča]	['ə]	21.5	23.5	23	23
	[a]	19.5	21	20.5	20
[bə'ča]	['a]	20	22	22.5	21.5
	[ə]	17	18	22	19
['suta]	['u]	21	21.5	22.5	22

	[a]	18.5	18.5	21	19
[su'ta]	['a]	20.5	20	21.5	21
	[u]	17	21	21.5	20
['giro]	['i]	22.5	24	25	24
	[o]	18.5	22.5	21.5	21
[gi'ro]	['o]	22	24	24.5	23.5
	[i]	21	23.5	23	22.5
['gəla]	['ə]	22.5	23.5	23	23
	[a]	18.5	21	20.5	20
[gə'la]	['a]	20.5	22	22.5	22
	[e]	18.5	20.5	20.5	20
['pota]	['o]	21.5	22	22.5	22
	[a]	17.5	17.5	18.5	18
[po'ta]	['a]	20	21	21	21
	[o]	15.5	18	18.5	17

(i) Studies of other languages have shown that in general a high vowel has a lower relative intensity. However, the Maithili stressed high front vowel ['i] has a high relative intensity. This may be so because the presence of the continuous voicing throughout the word ['giro] has caused the intensity to go higher. Similarly, the high relative intensity value of the Maithili stressed high back vowel ['u] may have been so because of the preceding fricative consonant [s] in the word ['suta].

(ii) The low vowel [a] is known to have higher intrinsic intensity. However, the values registered for the stressed ['a] in this study are rather low. This may be explained in terms of the fact that all instances of [a] occur in the second syllable of the word.

(iii) Voicing of the consonant environment is known to increase the intensity of the adjacent vowel. This may be observed in the case of the stressed vowel ['o] in the word ['pota] which has a lower intensity than in the word [gi'ro] even when the stress falls on the second syllable in the latter word. Thus, it appears that voicing of the consonant environment may be a more important factor than the word structure in determining the relative intensity of a vowel.

Table V lists the duration (in msec) of each of the three tokens of the Maithili stress pairs and their average duration. The figures show that all the stressed vowels of Maithili are considerably longer in duration than the unstressed vowels. The greatest durational difference is observed between the stressed and unstressed [o] and [e]: on the average stressed ['o] and ('e) are 76 msec and 60 msec longer in duration than the unstressed [o] and [ə]—with the average ratio of 1.00 to 1.59 and 1.00 to 1.80, respectively. Similarly, on the average stressed ['i], ['u] and ['a] are 47 msec, 40 msec and 34 msec longer than the unstressed (i u a) respectively—with the average ratio of 1.00 to 1.47, 1.00 to 1.70 and 1.00 to 1.18, respectively. On the average an unstressed vowel in Maithili is about 50msec longer in duration than an unstressed vowel.

Table V: Duration (in msec) of Maithili Stress Pairs

Word	*Vowel*	*Duration (in msec)* 1	2	3	Average
['bəca]	['ə]	160	100	80	113msec
	[a]	150	160	190	167
[bə'ca]	['a]	220	240	200	220
	[ə]	70	70	70	70
['suta]	['u]	100	90	100	97
	[a]	220	130	230	193
[su'ta]	[a]	200	190	220	203
	[u]	50	50	70	57
['giro]	['i]	170	120	150	147
	[o]	180	190	220	197
[gi'ro]	['o]	240	220	280	247
	[i]	100	100	100	100
['gəla]	['ə]	160	150	160	157
	[a]	180	180	190	183
[gə'la]	['a]	200	200	230	210
	[ə]	80	80	80	80
['pota]	['o]	160	160	160	160
	[a]	190	140	190	173
[po'ta]	['a]	220	220	220	220
	[o]	50	70	50	57

Duration is a much more robust cue of word stress in Maithili than fundamental frequency since no particular pitch contour can be observed to correlate well with stress. For instance, the word pairs ['giro] and (gi'ro) cannot be differentiated on grounds of pitch since no difference in pitch contour is observed on the narrow band spectrograms: both words have rising pitch on the first vowel followed by a falling pitch on the succeeding vowel. Further evidence that rising pitch cannot be said to be a uniform cue for stress is that both stressed and unstressed [i] and [e] are observed to have rising pitch, while the stressed ['o] and ['u] have only level pitch. Also, both stressed and unstressed [a] and [o] occurring in the second syllable usually have falling pitch; occasionally they have level pitch. Information on duration, on the other hand, is straightforward and unambiguous and all the stress pairs can be differentiated on the basis of duration.

4. *Conclusion.* Much more detailed investigation needs to be made in order to arrive at definitive statements on the acoustic parameters of word stress in Maithili. Nevertheless, the results show that of the parameters investigated in this limited study, duration appears to be the single most important cue. Since relative intensity in itself is not an adequate cue to stress in Maithili, a combination of duration and fundamental frequency, or of all three acoustic features (duration, fundamental frequency and relative intensity in that order) collectively may be associated with what might be termed 'stress' in Maithili.

REFERENCES

Fairbanks, G., A. S. House and E.L. Stevens. 1950. "An Experimental study of vowel intensities". *J. Accous. Soc. Am.* 22:4. 457-59.

Fonagy, I. 1966. "Electro-physical and acoustic correlates of stress and stress perception." *Journal of Speech and Hearing Research* 9 231-44.

House, A.S. and G. Fairbanks. 1953. "The influence of consonant environment upon the secondary acoustical characteristic of vowels." *J. Acous. Soc. Am.* : 25. 105-113.

Ingemann. F. and R. Yadav. 1978. "Voiced aspirated consonants." In *papers from the 1977 Mid-America Linguistic Conference* ed. by Lance, D. M. and D. E. Gulstad Columbia, Missouri : University of Missouri. 337-344.

Jha, S. 1941. "Maithili phonetics". *Indian Linguistics* 8:1. Reprinted edition Vol II (1965), 435-459.

———. 1958. *The formation of the Maithili language.* London: Luzac & Co., Ltd.

Lehiste, I. 1961. "Some acoustic correlates of word stress in American English". *J. Acous. Soc. Am.* : 32, 23-44.

———. 1970 *Suprasegmentals.* Cambridge : The M.I.T. Press.

Ohala, M. 1977. "Stress in Hindi." *Studies in Stress and Accent*, ed. by Hyman, L. M. Los Angeles : Southern California Occasional Papers in Linguistics 4 : 327-338.

Peterson, G. E. and H. L. Barney. 1952. "Control methods used in a study of vowels," *J. Acous. Soc. Am.* 24 : 175-184.

Yadav, R. 1976. "Generative phonology and the aspirated consonants of colloquial Maithili." *Contributions to Nepalese Studies* 4:1, 77-91.

———. 1979a. "The influence of aspiration on vowel duration in Maithili." *South Asian Languages Analysis* 1 157-165.

———. 1979b. "A Fiberoptic study of stop production in Maithili". *Kansas Working Papers in Linguistics* 4 2, 555-69.

———. 1979c. Maithili Phonetics and Phonology. Unpublished Doctoral Dissertation, The University of Kansas, Lawrence, Kansas, U.S.A.

ARCHAEOLOGY, LINGUISTICS, AND ANCIENT DRAVIDIAN

William Bright

The hypothesis that a Dravidian language was spoken by the Ancient Indus Valley civilization of Mohenjo-Daro and Harappa has long been considered highly plausible, and on several grounds. First, the presence of a modern Dravidian language in the hills to the west of the Indus, namely Brahui, is most easily explained if the Brahui are seen as the linguistic descendants of the ancient Indus Valley people. Second, the identification of Dravidian loan words in the Sanskrit of the earliest Vedic texts, by Emeneau and others, indicates that the first contacts between Sanskrit and Dravidian must have occurred when Sanskrit speakers first entered the Indian Subcontinent, i.e., when they arrived in the Indus Valley. Finally, evidence for a Dravidian substratum in many modern Indo-Aryan languages suggests that Dravidian languages once had wide distribution in the northern part of the subcontinent. But if the identification of the Indus Valley language as Dravidian is accepted, many questions still remain, for example: With what other languages was Dravidian in contact, and where, and when? What was the cultural nature of the contact? And what chronology can be assigned to cultural and linguistic shifts in the ancient Indus Valley and adjacent areas?

The eminent archaeologist Dr. Walter A. Fairservis, Jr., author of an authoritative text on Indian prehistory (1975), has recently attempted to offer answers to such questions, in a paper entitled "The consequences of Harappan as a Dravidian language". His method is to present six "axioms" regarding the relationship between archaeology and linguistics, each of which has this general form: "If one finds certain types of cultural assemblages, i.e. collections of material-culture items as recovered by archaeology, then one can infer certain facts about the corresponding languages." Applying these axioms to data from the Indus Valley, Fairservis derives a rather detailed ethnolinguistic prehistory of the area.

I welcome such attempts to coordinate research in linguistics and archaeology; earlier attempts to relate these two fields, in other parts of the world, have been made in recent years by myself (cf. Bright and Bright 1976), and by other scholars (Ehret 1976, Kinkade and Powell 1976). If a set of axioms like those proposed by Fairservis for the Indus Valley were valid, they could have very important application all over the world. Furthermore, because of Fairservis' prestige, I anticipate that other archaeologists may well attempt to apply them. However, they are so vague as to their form, and so unproven as to their validity, that they should not be allowed to go unchallenged. I wish to discuss each of Fairservis's axioms in turn, pointing out both the ways in which they are too vague to be applied easily, and the ways in which they may be contradicted by evidence.

Axiom 1 begins: "Sharply differing cultural assemblages, but contemporary, with significant time depth demonstrated in the local stratigraphy, represent differences of language, whether or not from the same family."

The very words in which the axiom is stated raise problems: even if we assume agreement as to what is allowed to constitute a "cultural assemblage", there will inevitably be room for diverse opinions as to how great a difference must exist in order for things to be called "sharply differing", or about how great a time depth is to be regarded as "significant". However, giving a middle-of-the-road interpretation to these terms, it seems to me that the axiom does not fit well with the facts of several present-day cultures. For instance, in modern Maharashtra, or in a European country like Spain, "cultural assemblages" from an urban center like Bombay or Madrid, as compared with those from a peasant village, could well be seen as "sharply differing", even though contemporary, and even though both would show continuity over "significant time depth"; yet they would both correspond to the Marathi or the Spanish language respectively—or, at most, to different dialects of those languages. Fairservis's Axiom 1 continues:

"If the assemblages are far apart geographically, this can mean fundamental differences in language going so far as to the basic stock.'

Now we encounter another difficulty in Fairservis's wording: "this can mean fundamental differences". The word "can" suggests that the implication either may or may not be valid. I assume that Fairservis believes that it is valid most of the time. But here we may continue our consideration of Spanish language and culture: what if one compares Madrid to a peasant village in, say, Uruguay? (I choose a Latin American country in which the American Indian cultures were extinguished immediately after the Conquest, so that there is no continuity between indigenous and European traditions.) If four hundred years can be considered "significant time depth", then this will be a further counter-example to Fairservis's statement, since both assemblages will, again, correspond to the Spanish language.

Here of course I am comparing "cultural assemblages" in which at least one is from an industrial society. It is possible that Fairservis means his axioms to apply only to pre-industrial society; however, he states no such qualification. We must ask a serious question, to which no answer may be yet available: are correlations between culture and language, whatever they may be, different in industrial societies than they are in pre-industrial ones?

Axiom 2 is: "Sharply differing cultural assemblages without significant time depth demonstrated by local stratigraphies represent different languages but not necessarily different language families."

Here a possible counter-example might be provided by comparing an industrial community with an agricultural community, each founded within the last hundred years in adjacent areas of the United States and of Mexico,

In the United States, even the agricultural communities would show relatively great mechanization, and thus could probably not be considered as "sharply differing". In Mexico, by contrast, many agricultural communities remain relatively unmechanized, by comparison to the industrial cities. But the two types of Mexican community both use Spanish, just as the two communities in the U.S. both use English. The Mexican case thus seems to falsify Fairservis's Axiom 2.

Axiom 3 is as follows: "Moderately differing cultural assemblages which, however, share core traits, may represent dialectal differences of the same language."

Again we have difficulties with Fairservis's wording: first we have to decide what are to be regarded as "core traits", and then we have to deal with the expression "may represent dialectal differences". The use of the word "may" seems to imply an equal and opposite "may not", in which case the "axiom" makes no claim at all. In fact, the only real meaning that can be attached to the "axiom" is that, when moderately differing cultural assemblages share core traits, they USUALLY or NORMALLY represent dialectal differences of the same languages. But such a claim can be tested by imagining an archaeologist of the year 5000 A.D., comparing the remains of 20th century New York, Bombay, and Tokyo. He might conclude that the cultural assemblages from those cities, while "moderately differing", nevertheless shared "core traits", namely those of Western European civilization; but he would be wildly incorrect in concluding that the inhabitants spoke dialects of a single language. If one does not wish to consider industrial civilizations, one can look to ancient Mesopotamia, in which the Akkadians and the Sumerians had virtually the same material culture, although their languages were of completely different stocks: Akkadian was a Semitic language, but the genetic connections of Sumerian are much more obscure.

Fairservis's Axiom 4 is: "Sharply differing cultural assemblages which share trade goods can represent different languages, but can be presumed to have developed a lingua franca."

Here, if we manage to surmount the ambiguity of the word "can", we may consider another modern example: Trade goods from Japan, such as transistor radios, are now found all over the world; but certainly no single "lingua franca" covers the same area.

Axiom no. 5 is as follows: "Stratigraphical representation of the imposition of a new cultural assemblage upon an older one, but which does share a considerable number of traits in common (some of which must be core) demonstrates linguistic integration of some form: for example, the rule of the Indo-European speaking Hyksos elite over the non-Indo-European speaking Egyptians in the Second Intermediate period, or the creation of a pidgin such as Anglo-Indian."

This seems to say that a mixture of cultural elements indicates some kind of linguistic "integration". A possible counter-example is provided by the Navajo, an American Indian tribe of the Southwestern United States, who have adopted many items of European material culture, but are famous for their resistance to linguistic borrowing. Thus, although the automobile has been thoroughly integrated into present-day Navajo culture, the terminology relating to automobiles is provided entirely by new coinages within the Navajo language, not by borrowing from English.

As regards Fairservis's "Anglo-Indian" example, I assume he refers to the variety of English spoken by educated people in India. It is of course true that Indian English shows characteristics derived from the phonology, grammar, and semantics of the Dravidian and Indo-Aryan languages. But linguists use the word "pidgin" to refer to trade-languages, of markedly hybrid origin and of greatly simplified grammar; I doubt if any linguist would apply the term "pidgin" to Indian English. It thus remains unclear what kind of degree of linguistic interaction or "integration" Fairservis has in mind in his Axiom no. 5.

Finally, Axiom no. 6 is: "Cultural assemblage confoımity from site to site demonstrates language conformity."

A modern counter-example might be provided by "cultural assemblages" from opposite sides of certain international borders, e.g., that between France and Germany: one would find little in material culture to correspond to the difference in language. Similarly in India, one might look on opposite sides of the border between Andhra and Orissa; again, the differences in material culture would be minor in comparison to the difference between the Dravidian and the Indo-Aryan language structures. Looking to non-industrial cultures, we have many American Indian examples: thus, in northwestern California, the Yurok, Karok, and Hupa tribes have been famous, since the time of Edward Sapir, for sharing a single culture, while nevertheless speaking languages of three completely separate stocks.

Since Fairservis's axioms contain so many vaguely defined terms, as well as "may's" and "can's", we might assume he intends them as statements of tendencies, rather than as absolute laws. But then, unless some statistical measures of probability are attached to them, it is not clear to me what their value is. My conclusion is not that Fairservis's account of Indus Valley prehistory is necessarily wrong, but rather that it must share the weakness of his axioms. Like many other archaeologists, Fairservis is all too ready to draw linguistic conclusions from archaeological data; and his reputation is such that other archaeologists and historians may well accept his proposals uncritically. Linguists must therefore continue to repeat that the study of potsherds can never, in itself, reveal anything about language. Fortunately, the continuing analysis of linguistic data is constantly adding to our knowledge of prehistoric Dravidian language and culture; I refer in particular to the work of Franklin Southworth (1975, 1978), and to David McAlpin's evidence for linguistic relationship between Dravidian and Elamite (1974, 1975). Our hypotheses of linguistic history must not fly in the face of non-linguistic data, but they cannot be DETERMINED by archaeological considerations.

REFERENCES

Bright, William, and Marcia Bright. 1976. "Archaeology and linguistics in prehistoric Southern California." *Variation and change in language : Essays by William Bright*, 189-205. Stanford, Calif.: Stanford University Press.

Ehret, Christopher. 1976. "Linguistic evidence and its correlation with archaeology." *World Archaeology* 8:1.5-18.

Fairservis, Walter A., Jr. 1975. *The roots of ancient India*. 2nd ed. Chicago: University of Chicago Press.

———. 1977. The consequences of Harappan as a Dravidian language. Cyclostyled. (Paper read at the 76th Annual Meeting, American Anthropological Association, Houston, Texas.)

Kinkade, M. Dale, and J. V. Powell. 1976. "Language and the prehistory of North America." *World Archaeology* 8:1.83-100.

McAlpin, David. 1974. "Toward Proto-Elamo-Dravidian." *Language* 50.89-101.

———. 1975. "Elamite and Dravidian." *Current Anthropology* 16:1.105-15.

Southworth, Franklin C. 1975. "Cereals in South Asian prehistory: The linguistic evidence." *Ecological backgrounds of South Asian prehistory*, ed. by Kenneth A. R. Kennedy and Gregory L. Possehl (South Asia occasional papers and theses, 4), 52-75. Ithaca, NY: South Asia Program, Cornell University.

———. 1978. "Lexical evidence for early contacts between Indo-Aryan and Dravidian." *Aryan and non-Aryan in India*, ed. by Madhav M. Deshpande and Peter E. Hook, 191-234. Ann Arbor: Center for South and Southeast Asian Studies, University of Michigan.

STUDY OF THE INDUS SCRIPT : A BI-LINGUAL APPROACH

Iravatham Mahadevan

1. The Indus Script has so far defied all attempts at decipherment. Indeed many feel that the task is hopeless in view of the limited inscriptional material available for study (about 3500 lines), the extreme brevity of the texts (the average length being 5 signs only), and the absence of bi-lingual texts. However, recent developments in the field provide some basis for cautious optimism. The number of texts is steadily increasing with the discovery of more Harappan sites. Critical editions of the texts and computerised concordances and tables have been recently published facilitating further studies (Parpola *et al* 1973, 1979; Mahadevan 1977). A photographic edition of the original seals and other inscribed objects is being compiled by an international team of scholars with assistance from UNESCO (A. Parpola, B.K. Thapar and M.R. Mughal, in prep.). There is no reason to doubt that further advances will be made when more scholars are attracted to the field with the availability of original texts through reliable editions.

2. Objective studies of the Indus Script have generally proceeded on the basis of frequency counts of the signs and statistical-positional analyses to determine the characteristics of individual signs, to identify sign groups corresponding to words and phrases and to recognise probable syntactical patterns (Hunter, 1934, Knorozov *et al*, 1965, Parpola *et al*, 1969). The direction of writing of the script has been determined with certainty and some progress has been achieved in word division (B.B. Lal 1966, Mahadevan 1977, 1978 with previous references). While these studies constitute the essential groundwork necessary to gain an insight into the nature of the script and the typology of the underlying language, they have not so far led to the actual decipherment of the Indus Script. Experience of earlier successful decipherments of other ancient scripts tells us that after the initial routine analytical work has been completed, it is necessary to look for some external clues 'to break the code' and to get at the meaning of the texts and the phonetic values of the signs. Cartouches containing kings' names in the Egyptian Script, repetetive use of royal titles in the cuneiform Persian and the identification of place names in the Linear-B Mycenaean script are famous examples of such clues leading to their decipherment. One cannot avoid speculation at this stage. Guesses must be made and the wrong ones discarded by a process of trial and error. The only requirements are an open mind and a readiness to acknowledge one's mistakes when these are demonstrated.

3. There are three types of objective external evidence that bear on the character of the Harappan Civilization and the likely contents of the inscriptions in the Indus Script:

(i) *Material remains* from the excavated sites;
(ii) *Pictorial motifs* associated with the inscriptions on seals and sealings; and
(iii) *Ideograms* which are recognizable in the Indus Script.

It is outside the scope of the present paper to deal with the first two types of evidence, which have been exhaustively described in the original excavation reports on Mohenjodaro (Marshall 1931, Mackay 1937), Harappa (Vats 1940) and Chanhudaro (Mackay 1943), and subsequently analysed by competent scholars in the field (Piggott 1950, Wheeler 1960, Fairservis 1967, Allchins 1968). The purpose of the present paper is to draw attention to the possibility of utilising the ideograms in the Indus Script to serve as clues to understand the probable contents of the inscriptions.

4. The Indus Script is basically pictographic in character, even though it is so stylised in the mature form presently available to us that it is not always easy to recognise the objects depicted by many of the signs. However, one has only to inspect the sign lists to see that even in the mature Indus Script there are a large number of signs which are recognizably pictographic (Parpola 1973, 1979; Mahadevan 1977).

5. We know from a study of other ancient pictographic scripts that a picture can be used in three different ways in writing:

(i) As a *pictogram* directly representing the intended object;
(ii) As an *ideogram* representing ideas and concepts associated with, or suggested by the object depicted in the pictogram; or
(iii) As a *phonogram*, that is, as a phonetic sign, which may represent either a whole word, or a syllable or a single phone. A word can be indicated directly by the picture as in the case of a concrete object, or by homonymy as in the case of an abstract concept or an action difficult to pictorialise. Syllables (which may be of any pattern, CV, VC or CVC) or single phones (consonants or vowels) may be indicated either through acrophony (that is, from the initial sounds of the word indicated by the object) or by rebus writing (which employs pictures to represent homonymic words).

6. No viable writing system can be built up through the exclusive use of direct pictograms. Ancient pictographic scripts generally employed a mixture of pictograms, ideograms and phonetic signs. The Indus Script is unlikely to be an exception in this respect. Formal analysis of the script leads us to the same conclusion. The large number of signs rules out the possibility that the script is alphabetic. The Indus Script could be a syllabary; but the extreme brevity of the texts is more consistent with an ideographic rather than purely phonetic script. The fixed relative order of most

of the signs as demonstrated by the Soviet scholars indicates that the signs stand for words rather than mere phonetic units (Knorozov *et al.* 1965). In a syllabary, one should expect a much greater freedom in the distribution of signs within the texts, which is certainly not the case with the Indus Script. Another important clue is the behaviour of sets of independent signs which are graphically similar, but differentiated by slight but deliberate graphic modifications (e.g. the 'fish' group of signs). Signs within each such set have very similar positional and functional characteristics, a pattern which is wholly inconsistent with their interpretation as phonetic syllables sharing the same consonants but with different vowels (as proposed by Hunter 1934, S.R. Rao 1973 and others). The behaviour of such sets of signs can be accounted for only on the basis of their being groups of ideograms with similar but not identical meanings. There is thus a strong probability that the Indus Script consists of word-signs with a fair amount of ideographic content. The presence of phonetic signs based on the rebus principle is also quite probable.

7. Once we recognise the presence of ideograms in the Indus Script, we have in them a visual aid to furnish us with clues to their probable meanings. To begin with, we can select the more easily recognizable ideograms whose pictographic nature is obvious. Such ideograms can then be studied in the light of the following sets of graphic parallels, viz.,

(i) Similar pictograms or ideograms from contemporary pictographic scripts; and
(ii) Symbolism from the later Indian traditions.

8. The Indus Script does not appear to be closely related to the other known contemporary pictographic scripts. Not only are most of the signs graphically independent, but the sign sequences are also unique in the Indus Script proving that the Harappan language is not related to the languages written in the other pictographic scripts. However it is in the very nature of pictographic writing that there should be some similarity in the mode of depiction of the same object even in unrelated scripts. Such similarities of the Indus Signs with those in the Egyptian, Sumerian, Proto-Elamite and the ancient Chinese scripts have been pointed out by Langdon (in Marshall 1931), Hunter (1934), Heras (1953) and others. These parallels can be utilized to recognise the objects depicted by the Indus pictograms. The parallels can further serve to indicate the probable ideographic significance of the signs. In the latter case, however, one has to be more cautious as the range of ideographic meanings will depend on the social and cultural milieu of the users of the script. For example, the pictogram of a 'star' may signify ideographically a 'god' only in a society which practised some form of astral religion. It is also necessary to point out that pictograms or ideograms (even when borrowed from one script to another) will not have the same phonetic values in the two scripts. It is in any case possible to comprehend the pictographic or the ideographic significance of a sign without the intervention of a linguistic medium.

9. The suggested use of parallels from the later times is based, in general, on the well-known continuity of Indian historical and religious traditions and, in particular, on the demonstrated links with the later Indian culture on the basis of the material remains and the pictorial motifs of the Harappan civilization. One can readily cite the examples of the *svastika*, phallic symbolism, veneration of the pipal tree and the serpent, which have survived to this day in the composite Hindu religious practices. It is therefore not unreasonable to suppose that even when the Indus Script ceased to be a writing system, individual ideograms survived in the later tradition and evolved into conventional symbols of various kinds. Such survivals may consist of iconographic elements and religious symbols, royal insignia, emblems on coins and seals, heraldic signs of the nobility, corporate symbols, and totem signs of clans and tribes, etc.

10. The Indian historical tradition has come down to us in two main linguistic streams, viz., Indo-Aryan and Dravidian. It is my view that in looking for parallels to understand the Harappan civilization, it is possible, and even necessary, to search both Indo-Aryan and Dravidian sources for survivals. I have dealt with this matter in greater detail in one of my earlier papers (Mahadevan 1972). To recapitulate briefly, the bi-lingual approach is based on the following premises:

(i) The Harappan seals, in accordance with universal usage, give the names and titles of the owners. It is likely that due to prolonged bi-lingualism and racial fusion in the sub-continent, the more important Harappan names and titles passed into the later Indo-Aryan languages as loan-words or loan-translations.

(ii) It is possible that the later symbols derived from the Indus ideograms were continued to be associated, even though in a conventional manner, with the later forms of the older names and titles represented originally by the Indus ideograms.

(iii) It should be possible to undertake a comparison of such traditional symbols resembling the signs of the Indus Script and names and concepts associated with them in the Indian historical tradition, in an attempt to establish the original ideographic meanings of the signs.

(iv) The results should not be inconsistent with those obtained from a formal textual analysis of the inscriptions.

11. The advantage of the method of bi-lingual parallels is that it is not necessary to make any *a priori* assumption about the linguistic affinity of the Harappan language, since ideograms, as mentioned above, can be directly understood without phonetization. The bi-lingual parallels will help us to comprehend broadly the original meanings of the ideograms and also confirm the validity of such deductions on the basis of the ancient and strongly persistent traditions. I also wish to emphasise the limitations of the method, which is dependent on random survivals and uncertain interpretations of symbols. The diversity of the later Indian traditions would

preclude us from assigning any specific phonetic values to the ideograms of the Indus Script. I however feel that when pursued with due circumspection and caution, the bi-lingual parallels may lead to accumulation of evidence indicating the probable affinity of the Harappan language as well as the general meaning or contents of the texts.

12. I proceed to illustrate the method with the example of a sign  (No.171 in sign-list, Mahadevan 1977). This pictogram appears to represent some kind of a weapon or tool with a toothed head and a long handle. It resembles a 'trident', though the variants recorded in the texts have four or more 'teeth' (Mahadevan 1977: 788). The close graphic similarity of the sign with the Sumerian ideogram *gal* 'great' was noticed quite early (Langdon in Marshall 1931:454, Hunter 1934:209). The probability that the sign in the Indus Script is also an ideogram with a similar meaning is suggested by the considerations that (a) the sign functions grammatically as an attribute, and (b) it is very often found before the 'horned person' sign  (No. 8 in sign-list, Mahadevan 1977), a self-evident ideogram indicating a divine, royal or eminent personage as seen from its variants (Mahadevan 1977: 785). Consequently the paired ideograms 'trident horned person' occurring 40

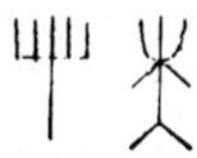

times in the texts (Mahadevan 1977: 171-73) have been interpreted by many scholars as a title meaning broadly a 'great divinity or personage' (Heras 1953:264, Knorozov 1965:20, Gurov 1968:44, Parpola *et al.* 1969:15, Mahadevan 1970:195). The Finnish scholars even drew attention to the parallelism with the later concept of Śiva's trident. But they could not pursue this line of reasoning further as they identified the object depicted by this pictogram as a kind of flower (ixora) and sought to derive its meaning and phonetic value by the method of homonymy. If however the analogy of 'trident' is pursued further, we get an important and wholly independent corroboration of the probable meaning of this ideogram. The most characteristic of the *symbolic* attributes of Śiva is the 'trident'. Hence the names like Śūlin, Śūladhara, Śūlapāṇi and other equivalents. It is significant that the most characteristic *verbal* attribute of Śiva is the epithet 'great' as evidenced by names like Mahādeva, Maheśa, Maheśvara, Parameśvara etc. We can thus set up the following parallelism from the later Indian tradition:

TRIDENT-GOD	:	*Śūla-deva*
= GREAT-GOD	:	*Mahā-deva*
∴TRIDENT = GREAT	:	*śūla = mahā*

The suggestion made here is as follows: The Indus ideogram survived as a symbol in later times and its association with the meaning 'great' was also remembered. When Śiva evolved as the 'great god' of the Hindu pantheon, he also acquired this symbolic attribute, which itself evolved into a weapon (trident) in his hands. The Indian religious tradition has thus preserved in this case the ancient and hitherto unsuspected connection between the symbolism of the 'trident' and its original signification, 'great'. This parallelism provides a wholly independent corroboration of the meaning of the ideogram already suggested by its positional and functional characteristics in the texts as well as by its close graphic similarity with the corresponding Sumerian ideogram with the same meaning. Here is a three-way control on the meaning of the Indus ideogram, which merits serious consideration.

13. Two other aspects of the suggested parallelism deserve notice. The reason why the corresponding pictogram in the Sumerian script was given the ideographic value 'great' is unknown. However, the parallelism would hold good irrespective of the true nature of the object originally depicted by the pictograms in the Indus and the Sumerian scripts. As mentioned earlier, the evolution of the Indus pictogram into a symbol representing a weapon ('trident') might well have been a post-Harappan phenomenon influenced by its association with Śiva. It is also not necessary that the paired ideograms under consideration referred exclusively to a divine entity in the Indus texts. There is no need to infer from them the presence of Śiva or proto-Śiva in the Harappan pantheon. It is probable that the title was in general use by the Harappan ruling classes (priests, nobles, etc.) in exactly the same way as the titles *deva* and *mahādeva* were also used as royal epithets or even as ordinary personal names in later historical times.

REFERENCES

Allchin, B. and R. Allchin, 1968. *The Birth of Indian Civilization.* Penguins.

Fairservis, Jr. W. A. 1967. *The origin, character and decline of an early civilization.* American Museum Novitates, No. 2302.

Gurov, N. V. *et al.* 1968. *Proto-Indica : brief report on the investigations of Proto-Indian texts.* Moscow.

Heras, H. 1953. *Studies in Proto-Indo-Mediterranean Culture.* Bombay.

Hunter, G. R. 1934. "The Script of Harappa and Mohenjodaro and its connection with other scripts." *Studies in the History of Culture* No. 1. London.

Knorozov, Yu. V. *et al.* 1965. *Preliminary report on the investigation of the Proto-Indian texts* (in Russian), Moscow. (Tr. by H.C. Pande) ed. by Henry Field and Edith M. Laird, Florida (1969) (citation from this tr.).

Lal, B. B. 1966. "The direction of writing in the Harappan script." *Antiquity.* 9

Mackay, E. J. H. 1937. *Further excavations at Mohenjodaro,* New Delhi.

———. 1943. *Chanhudaro excavations,* 1935-36, New Haven.

Mahadevan, I. 1970. "Dravidian parallels in Proto-Indian script." *Journal of Tamil Studies.* Vol. II : No. 1.

Mahadevan, I. 1972. "Study of the Indus script through bilingual parallels." *Proceedings of the Second All-India Conference on Draviaian Linguistics.* 1972 (1975). Reprinted in *Ancient Cities of the Indus*, (ed.) Gregory Possehl, New Delhi (1979).

———. 1977. "The Indus Script : Texts, Concordance and Tables". *Memoirs of the Archaeological Survey of India* No. 77. New Delhi.

———. 1978. "Recent advances in the study of the Indus script." Paper read at the Tenth International Congress of Anthropological and Ethnological Sciences, New Delhi. *Puratattva*, No. 9.

———. 1979a. "Indus script in the Indian historical tradition. Mythology to History through Astronomy." *Proceedings of the Seminar on Astronomy as aid to History.* Madras.

———. 1979b. "Terminal ideograms in the Indus script." Paper read at the Seminar on Harappan Civilization. Indian Institute of American Studies at Srinagar. *Harappan Civilization*, ed. Gregory L. Possehl.

Marshall, J. (ed.) 1931. *Mohenjodaro and the Indus Civilization.* London.

Parpola, A. *et al.* 1969. Decipherment of the Proto-Dravidian inscriptions of the Indus Civilization. A first announcement, Copenhagen.

———. 1973. *Materials for the study of the Indus Script, I: A Concordance to the Indus Inscriptions.* Helsinki.

———. 1979. *Corpus of texts in the Indus Script.* Helsinki.

Piggott, S. 1950. *Prehistoric India.* Pelican.

Rao, S. R. 1973. *Lothal and the Indus Civilization.* Bombay.

Vats, M. S. 1940. *Excavations at Harappa.* Calcutta.

Wheeler, R. E. M. 1960. *The Indus Civilization* (2nd ed.). Cambridge.

PART II

Convergence

DEFINITENESS-MARKING IN SOUTH ASIAN LANGUAGES

Colin P. Masica

In this paper, I shall be using the term DEFINITENESS-STATUS as a cover term for all relations of nouns to a discourse—that is: assumed to be known to the listener, or unknown, or part of his general knowledge. Every noun in context unavoidably has such a status, whatever its other properties. It may thus be called a general semanto-syntactic category inherent in all languages, including South Asian languages—or better put, in all discourse. Its overt marking is another matter, and languages differ considerably in the extent of such DEFINITENESS-MARKING as well as in the subcategories distinguished and in the strategies and devices employed. Probably all languages, however, are forced to mark at least some aspect of DEFINITENESS-STATUS at some points in a discourse, whether only "lexically" and facultatively or in a more structured fashion. It is as basic to discourse as pronominalization, to which it is in fact closely related, or as aspect in verbs, to which it is also related.

The differences among languages with regard to DEFINITENESS-MARKING invite the construction of a general typology of DEFINITENESS-MARKING, encompassing all the possibilities, à la Greenberg, according to which individual languages, or groups of languages such as South Asian languages, might be characterized. Although construction of such a typology in its full implications is beyond the scope of this paper, we cannot characterize South Asian languages—or even pose the questions by which they might be characterized—without reference to at least a hypothetical such typology, however crude.

The first element in such a typology has to be a universal theory of the semantic relations involved, derived, not by extrapolation from the marking system of a particular language, but from the general dynamics of discourse as such, which all languages have to contend with, such as linearity.

In such a theory, the traditional terms "definite" and "indefinite" are best avoided. They are too imprecise, and are contaminated by too close association with European article systems, particularly English, where they overlap in confusing ways. They are also insufficient: we need more than two terms. I shall accordingly use these terms—in caps, taking a cue from Comrie 1976—only to refer to *forms* in specific languages—e.g. the Definite Article (English), the Definite Accusative (Turkish), the Indefinite Suffix (Persian).

The first distinction that must be made is between GENERAL and SPE-

CIFIC[1] reference. Among nouns entailing SPECIFIC reference, a second and of course very important distinction is between those UNIDENTIFIED for the listener or reader at first mention and those already IDENTIFIED. Identification may be established by prior mention in the discourse itself in the narrow sense of a given conversation or text, or by its immediate extra-linguistic context, or by the universe of discourse—the total shared knowledge (including cultural assumptions) of speaker and hearer at a given point in the discourse. It is important to remember, however, that both these status-categories share the feature of reference to an actual individual/item or individuals/items (or quantity of a substance—mass nouns present special features that cannot be gone into here) rather than to a type.

Among GENERAL (=NONSPECIFIC) nouns, a further distinction should also be made, namely between those with GENERIC reference—that is, to any or all members of a category as such, and a residue referring not to a category but merely to the idea of the noun in a very vague sense. The latter are typically bound to verbs (as their formal objects) to make one complex idea that is essentially verbal. Examples in English are: catch *cold*, have *lunch*, have *fun*, wash *dishes*, wash *clothes*, clean *house*, make *hay*, take *place*, bear *fruit*. Such NONSPECIFIC NONGENERIC nouns have no independent existence in the discourse apart from the verb.[2] This

---

1. Note that this is starting from the opposite side to the traditional exposition of e.g., the "Functions of the Articles." Regarding the term *specific*, I could have used *specified*, but decided not to on discovering that for some persons that term already means *identified* ("definite"). Givón (1978:293ff) uses the term *referential*, but I find this awkward because we can speak of generic "reference" also, thus leading to "referential" vs. "non-referential" *reference*. A better use of the term *non-referential* might be to restrict it to *nongeneric nonspecific* nouns (which have no independent status in the discourse), thus producing a fully binary typology as follows:

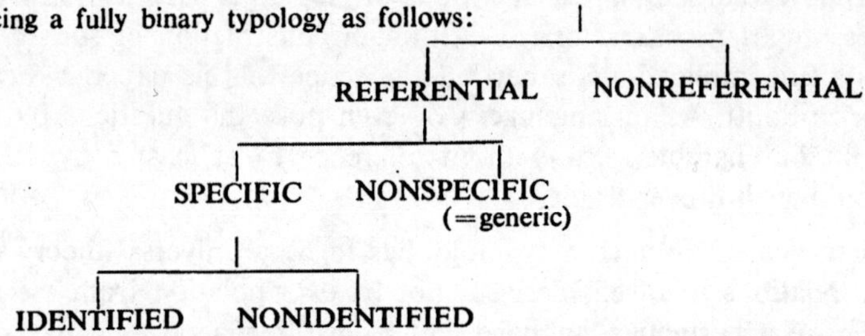

2. It can be held that one criterion for such nouns should therefore be that they be *nonpronominalizable*. By such a criterion some of the English examples given seem to fail, partly because of the ubiquitous *it*—which, however, in addition to referring to an activity in general ("doing it"), may represent confusion with similar collocations involving UNIDENTIFIED-SPECIFIC nouns: e.g., there is something odd about *where shall we have it?* in reply to *Let's have lunch*: a kind of weak syntactic pun. Similarly with *where did you catch it?* after *I caught cold* (cf. *I caught A cold*). Compare **I won't catch it* after *Don't catch cold*. Unmarked plurals are often ambiguously NONSPECIFIC/SPECIFIC UNIDENTIFIED in status in English, South Asian, and other languages, although they can be disambiguated, e.g. *I'm washing SOME clothes*. Note that several expressions do pass the pronominalization criterion nicely: *Did you have fun*? **Yes, we had it Exactly what took place*? **This is what took it It hasn't yet borne fruit*; **Then when will it bear it?* It is my impression that this criterion applies without any such equivocation in South Asian languages.

status-category is one that is often overlooked, but we cannot ignore it in South Asian languages where, due to the importance of noun-verb compounding, it looms very large. A typical text in a modern South Asian language will be found to have a significantly greater number of nouns than, say, its English equivalent. Most of them will be found to be of this category, components of verbal expressions.

The four categories just mentioned can be derived, not only from the general logic of discourse relations, but also from a formal comparison of noun discourse markers and their domains, both across languages and within a given language. It is not that any language has or needs distinct overt markers for all four. The categories emerge from the overlap of markers, constraints on markers, and contrast with zero. In English, for example, the UNIDENTIFIED category is distinguished by the possibility of occurrence of the Indefinite Article *a*, the word *some*, or numerals[3]: the IDENTIFIED category by that of the Definite Article *the*, the demonstratives *this*, *that*, and their plurals, *which*, and possessives; the GENERIC category by that of *a*, *the*, *some*, *any*, numerals[3], or zero, with syntactic restrictions on the second and probably the third and fourth of these (e.g., exclusion from predicate nominal position)[4], and the NONGENERIC NONSPECIFIC category by zero only and apparently, restriction to verbal and prepositional object position. In English also, the indicators cited are in complementary distribution within each category (except for *any* and numerals in the GENERIC category), a feature which is not necessarily true of other languages. The categories and their indicators in English (which are not claimed to be exhaustive, and concerning which there may be some disagreement) may be illustrated by the following sentences:

---

3. I own my insight into the basically UNIDENTIFIED character of numerals to Edith Moravcsik, who kindly sent me a copy of her important paper *Determination* (1969) when I was in the midst of a revision of this paper and could not obtain one. It should be noted that, unlike A or SOME, expressions with numerals can be definitized: e.g., *the four men*. This apparently always requires an additional or special marker: cf. the Hindi-Urdu forms *tiinõ*, *caarõ*, etc. and the special English form *both* (=the two). Although some may disagree, I feel that both numerals and the word *some* (and its equivalents in other languages) can be used in GENERIC contexts also—defining the latter to include statements of a general character. (See Davison 1979.) *Four individuals constitute a quorum. Some snakes* (=some kinds of snakes?) *give birth to live young.*

Moravcsik's basic insight, however, has been missed by a number of persons. Cf Hudson (1965:40): "Since a number is always definite a [definiteness] particle is usually used with a number." What he really means is *specified* (which still does contradict the position I have just taken with regard to GENERIC use of numbers, to be sure)—and the particles concerned are better called *specifying* particles. Again, note the potential for confusion in the term "definite".

4. Exclusion is perhaps too strong, but it is closely approached. One can contrive a sentence, using a relative clause and dummy *it*, such as *It is nevertheless THE lion that is the king of beasts.* THE is of course common enough in its IDENTIFIED marker meaning: *That is the house?* The word ANY involves special proplems which cannot be gone into here.

(1)	They bought *a house* (*some houses/four houses*).	Unidentified Specific
(2)	There is *a dolphin* (are *some dolphins/four dolphins*) in the tank.	Unidentified Specific
(3)	They kept *the house* (but sold the shop).	Identified Specific
(4)	*Which house* did he sell? *That*(*this/our*) *house*.	Identified Specific
(5)	That is *a house*! (interpreting picture for a child)	Generic
(6)	*A house* is not *a home*.	Generic
(7)	They want to protect *the dolphin*.	Generic/(also Identified)
(8)	*The dolphin* is *a mammal*.	Generic/(also Identified)
(9)	*The dolphin is the mammal.	
(10)	*Dolphins* are *mammals*.	Generic
(11)	*Some dolphins* are male and some are female.	Generic
(12)	*Any dolphin* could do that.	Generic
(13)	*Four dolphins* (*any four dolphins*) constitute a quorum.	Generic
(14)	She kept *house* for them.	Nongeneric Nonspecific
(15)	We *house*-sat[5] for them while they were in India.	Nongeneric Nonspecific
(16)	He sells *houses* (i.e. for a living—not some specific houses; cf. *writes, lectures*, etc.)	Nongeneric Nonspecific? or Generic?

We should distinguish here between markers of DEFINITENESS-STATUS proper (e.g., in English, the words *a*, *the. some*, and *any*, along with—probably—the demonstratives), whose function is primarily that, and other indicators of DEFINITENESS-STATUS, which merely imply DEFINITENESS-STATUS in addition to their other functions. All languages have both—unless we exclude the demonstratives and *some*, in which case some languages have only indicators.

Languages adopt varied marking strategies with respect to the four basic status categories. Some elect to mark the basic SPECIFIC/NONSPECIFIC distinction itself, e.g., Vietnamese, where this is accomplished through the use or non-use of classifiers with the noun (Vuong-Gia-Thuy 1975:96-97). An interesting question is whether South Asian languages with classifier systems(primarily Bengali and Assamese) work that way, in view of the fact that these "definiteness particles", as they are sometimes misleadingly called (Hudson 1965:40), also are attached to numerals, including "one" in an Indefinite Article function, and to expressions for "some", e.g. *koyekṭa*. If so, it would give us one indigenous South Asian criterion for sorting out, for example, generic vs. specifying usages (which, as will be seen, is not always easy) on a simple formal basis.

Some languages, particularly those of the type one called *polysynthetic*, incorporate Nongeneric Nonspecific nouns into the verb itself, e.g., Eskimo:

(17) *klipaq* 'bread'—*klipa*lioq 'he bakes bread'
(18) *nusheq* 'knife'—*nushi*ligertog 'he carries a knife with him'

This sometimes occurs even in English, e.g. *to babysit*[5]. In South Asia, it seems to be confined to the Southern Munda languages:

(19) *ti* 'hand'—mai ˀgwi ˀ*ti*gu 'he washed his hands' (Gadba)[6]
(20) *gcaiŋ* 'porcupine'—*m*mo ʔcaiɲke 'I smoke out the porcupine' (Gtaʔ)

Some languages mark only Identified nouns regularly, some only UNDENTIFIED-SPECIFIC nouns (in South Asia a prime example is Sinhala), some both. Possession by a language of only one structuralized marker, however, does not mean that the remaining categories are uniformly unmarked in that language. Every language has lexical devices sufficient to distinguish them where this is crucial, and where context alone does not suffice. However, it is true that, as far as lack of formal marking is concerned, in non-crucial contexts the NONSPECIFIC categories are merged with the UNIDENTIFIED category in the first case and with the IDENTIFIED category in the second.[7]

At the other extreme, either the IDENTIFIED or the UNIDENTIFIED marker, or both (as in English), may be extended to the NONSPECIFIC categories, primarily the GENERIC. Either type of extension can be seen to be a natural enough development of certain analogies the GENERIC has with each. The existence of a genus of things can be taken to be a part of a listener's general knowledge, therefore "identified". Syntactically also, GENERIC nouns often occur as subject-topics, the same as IDENTIFIED nouns. On the other hand a genus can be represented by a typical "unidentified" (though nonspecified) member.

Nevertheless, the primary function of DEFINITENESS-MARKING seems to be *specifying*—which is to say, immediate-discourse-related, anaphoric or counter-anaphoric, rather than generalizing and logical. Extensions of marking to the GENERIC category are a later development (Heinrichs 1954). In languages such as English, these extensions are incomplete, and in competition with each other and with zero, as may be seen from

5. For the benefit of stay-at-home readers, *to house-sit* is a recent American expression, on the analogy of *to babysit*, meaning to occupy and care for someone's house or apartment while they are away, paying utilities but not any rent, or only a nominal rent.

6. I owe these examples to Norman Zide. For a rich collection of examples, see G.V. Ramamurti 1931: *A manual of the So:ra: (or Savara) language* (Madras: Government Press).

7. Unless, of course, either of these is extended to the GENERIC category before its opposite number becomes part of the system, as indeed seems to have occurred in Classical Greek.

examples 5-13 above. Differences in article usage among European languages in this area are notorious:

(21) He's a doctor. (English: Indefinite Article with GENERIC predicate noun)

(22) Es médico. (Spanish; no Indefinite Article with GENERIC predicate noun)

(23) Man is mortal. (English: not all GENERIC subjects take article)

(24) Der Mensch ist sterblich. (German: most GENERIC subjects take article)

The "normal" GENERIC marking can be said to be zero. No language marks the GENERIC category unless it also marks at least one of the SPECIFIC categories. Furthermore no language marks the GENERIC other than by extension of an already structuralized SPECIFIC marker.[8] There are no uniquely GENERIC markers (Moravcsik 1969:71). The qualification "already structuralized" is necessary, and the separateness of the GENERIC category underlined, by the fact that, as Moravssik points out (1969:90), demonstratives, which are always optional IDENTIFIED markers and underlie structuralized markers (i.e. Definite Articles) in many languages, never themselves mark GENERIC nouns. Accordingly, in South Asian languages demonstratives, which as we will see assume many article-like functions, are not used in this context. An apparent exception is the demonstrative called for by the Indo-Aryan correlative construction:

(25) *kuch pakṣii-śaastra-vettaaõkaa mat hai ki pakṣiyõ ke puurvaj tathaa vartamaan pakṣii ke biic kaa jantu hai VAH camgaadar, JISE ham aksar puraane makaanõ kii chatõ par laṭkaa huaa dekhte hãĩ*—'Some ornithologists are of the opinion that the creature between the ancestor of the birds and present-day birds is THE bat which we see often hanging on the ceilings of old houses' (Narayansingh 1958:2)

Extension of marking to the NONGENERIC NONSPECIFIC category would seem to come last of all, perhaps as the last step in the evolution of DEFINITENESS-markers into obligatory markers of nouns as such. In English it is mainly confined to a few idiomatic expressions, such as *He kicked the bucket* or *He bit the bullet.*

The preceding discussion is necessary, though perhaps not sufficient, because English-speakers often do not distinguish between different functions of their articles, especially between the specifying and the generic functions of the Indefinite Article, and sometimes this confusion is carried over into descriptions in English of other languages or general linguistic discussions where such a distinction is crucial. The best medicine for these English-induced perceptual difficulties is simply to observe what languages

8. Leaving the word *any* and its possible counterparts out of consideration. In *any* case, ANY is never a *general* marker of the GENERIC category.

with less ambiguous marking do in various situations. (It is possible that languages may differ in the apparent allocation of certain situations to one category or the other, since it is sometimes possible to view things either way. This implies different semantic perceptions of the situation, however, and we should stretch our imaginations a little to find out what these may be. Again, a massive comparison of different languages in context should help.) Meanwhile we would do well to eschew both the term "definite" (confusing IDENTIFIED and GENERIC) and the term "indefinite" (confusing UNIDENTIFIED-SPECIFIC, GENERIC, and NONGENERIC NONSPECIFIC as well).

The next question our typology must deal with is the devices a given language uses for DEFINITENESS-MARKING purposes. The first thing we should note is that there are a number of devices besides articles which are so employed. One is topicalization, always inherently correlated with IDENTIFIED status and therefore endued with the potential for marking it. Whether by a special particle, shift in position, or some other method, one of the arguments of a sentence is marked as already known. Japanese is a well-known example, replacing subject or object case markers with the topic marker WA:

(26) *koko ni inu ga imasu* 'There is a dog here'
(27) *inu wo motte imasu* 'He has a dog'
(28) *inu WA doko ni imasu ka*? 'Where is THE dog?'
(29) *inu WA chichi ga mimashita* 'As for THE dog, my father saw it'

Languages of the Philippine type manage to combine topicalization with retention of case function indication through the so-called focus construction. The erstwhile case function of the topicalized noun is shown by affixes to the verb, as in Tagalog (Schachter and Otanes 1972:78).

(30) *b-UM abasa ng nobela ANG guro* 'THE teacher is reading a novel' (=actor-focus)
(31) *b-IN-abasa ng guro ANG nobela* 'a/the teacher is reading THE novel' (=object-focus)

Thanks to great flexibility of word order (in contrast with the comparative rigidity of Japanese in this respect, it should be noted), topicalization through word order shifts is an obvious option in most South Asian languages. The subject needs more careful study, in the context of the functions of word order shifts and emphasis phenomena in general. Topicalization is not simply to be equated with sentence fronting, either in South Asian languages or in general (note the sentence-*final* position of the topic in the examples from Tagalog—a verb-initial language). Some fronted expressions are not IDENTIFIED and therefore not topics:

(32) *ek baat mãi ne noṭ kii*—'One thing I noted' (Khanna 1971:29)

Others—in fact, most others—are concurrently IDENTIFIED by some other implication as well, typically oblique case status (see below):

(33) *klark par raajniiti ke in maulik siddhaantõ kaa koii asar nahīī huaa*—'On the clerk these basic principles of politics had no effect' (Shukla 1968:46)

In such an investigation, the phenomenon of appending should not be overlooked. My impression is that it always implies identification:

(34) *adde sangati aaḍadaanik' enduku? avasaramaytee tala taakaṭṭu peṭṭi testaaḍu ḌABBU*—'Why should a woman be concerned with matters like rent? It necessary he would mortgage his head and bring THE MONEY' (Rao 1964:17)

Blank topic markers of the Japanese type do not seem to occur in South Asia proper, although they do turn up in Burmese:

(35) *pa? wùñc̱iñ-ăhlá-HA ăèi-dañ-ḵou mei-t̠hwà-s̱ei-lau?-pa-ṯe-* 'THE surrounding beauty was enough to make (one) forget the severe cold' (Okell 1969:334)

I owe to Junghare 1980 the suggestion that Indo-Aryan relative clauses of the type with the relative marker in *j-* standing first may be taken as a kind of topicalization device—in this case preserving the indication of case function of the noun (hence analogous to a focus construction):

(36) *JO aadmii vahãã khaṛaa hai vah meraa bhaaii hai*—'The man who is standing there is my brother'

(37) *JIS aadmiiko maĩne yahãã dekhaa vah dhobii thaa*—'The man I saw here was a dhobi'[9]

(38) *vidvaan yah bhii maante hãĩ ki JIS saahityik bhaaṣaa kaa apnii bolii se aṭuuṭ sambandh rahtaa hai, voh baṛii sajiiv hotii hai*—'Scholars also think it is the literary language that retains an unbroken connection with its (parent) dialect that has the greatest liveliness' ("Suman" 1960:4)

A whole set of devices is focussed on marking direct objects as IDENTIFIED. Why direct objects in particular? It is claimed (e.g. Chao 1968:76, 343-4; Givón 1978:306) that direct objects are more likely to convey new information—that is, more likely than subjects are, for example, and also more likely to convey new information than old information, thus needing marking more than other positions when they do convey old information. It is difficult to establish this priority in English, the statistical edge of "new" over "old" objects being only a slight one, at least by my counts, but it might at least be agreed that this is the argument of the verb whose DEFINITENESS-STATUS is most uncertain. The edge is greater in languages where NONGENERIC NONSPECIFIC noun objects play an important role in the expression of verbal concepts, such as those of South Asia.

9. Examples (36) and (37) are from Junghare's paper, with spelling modified.

One common such device is the differential employment of cases, such as Accusatives, Nominative, or of special prepositions or postpositions, to mark what are usually called Definite Objects on the noun itself, as in Turkish:

(39) *bir köpek gördüm* 'I saw a dog' (Nominative)
(40) *köpegi gördüm* 'I saw THE dog' (Accusative)

This is highly characteristic of South Asia, being found in some form in Indo-Aryan, Dravidian, Iranian, and even some Tibeto-Burman and Munda languages.[10] As a device, it presents certain problems, however. For one thing, in Indo-Aryan languages the Accusative has merged with the Dative, which has a prior claim to the common suffix when both an indirect object and a definite direct object occur, as in this example from Sindhi, taken from Grierson's collections (LSI VIII.I:28):

(41) *UHO GHOṚO paṭewāle-KHE ḍḍino-athamᵉ*—'I have given that horse to the orderly' (=H. *vah ghoṛaa paṭevaale ko diyaa hai*)

On the other hand, certain constructions, for example object complement constructions, require the suffix on the object whether it is IDENTIFIED or not:

(42) *gaṛeriyõ ke bacce apne jhuṇḍ kii EK bhii bakrii yaa bheṛ KO us or BARHTE dekhkar kaan pakaṛ kar khĩic le jaate hãĩ..*—'The shepherd children on seeing even one goat or sheep going off in that direction grab it by the ears and drag it back'(Varma S.V.2014:258)

In fact, the marker is by no means incompatible with overt indication of UNIDENTIFIED status in other contexts as well:

(43) *HEKIRE bbaṇhe-KHE koṭhe*—'Having summoned a slave..'(Grierson VIII.I:28)
(44) *unhõne EK baalak KO śiṣyõ ke biic khaṛaa kar diyaa*—'He set a child in the midst of the disciples' (Bulcke 1977:116)

This raises the question of whether the category marked is SPECIFIC rather than merely IDENTIFIED. However, absence of the marker is probably more frequent with UNIDENTIFIED SPECIFIC objects:

(45) *jayacand ne...uske saath KUCH daasiyãã rakh dĩĩ*—'J. left some slave-girls with her...' (Gupta 1963:99)
(46) *mãĩ ne EK chatnaar baagh dekhaa*—'I saw a sparse garden'(Raghava n.d.:7)
(47) *vah kuch duuri par EK pattedaar anjiir kaa peṛ dekhkar uske paas gaye..*'And seeing a fig tree afar off, he went to it..'(Bulcke 1977:122)

10. As I have devoted a whole paper to this (Masica 1976), I will confine myself here to brief discussion of some of the problematic aspects of the subject.

NOTE: Another Hindi translation has *vah duur se EK pallavit anjiir ke vṛkṣ KO dekhkar*...A third has *vah duur se anjiir kaa EK haraa peṛ dekhkar*, while an Urdu version has *vah duur se anjiir kaa EK daraxt jis me patte the dekhkar*...Which sounds best?

Moreover, the marker is found on GENERIC objects:

(48) *kiiso KO hii nahı̃ı balki, chipkalii, cuuhe, mẽḍhak aadi nuksaandeh jiivjantuõ kii vṛddhi ko bhii pakṣii rokte hãĩ*—'Not only insects—birds stop the increase of lizards, rats, frogs and other destructive creatures also' (Narayansingh 1958:4) (N.B.: also shows topicalization.)

The real problem, however, is that the question is mixed up with that of object-status itself. DEFINITENESS-STATUS distinctions overlap here with questions of personal vs. nonpersonal nouns, and secondarily of animacy. Personal nouns are more likely to be Agents than Patients, and therefore may need marking to establish Patient status, especially in languages where flexible SOV or VSO word orders may otherwise leave the roles of two juxtaposed NP's unclear. This may explain the indulgence in "definite object" marking—or particularly in definite *personal* object marking—by languages already possessing fullblown article systems (Spanish, Hebrew, Rumanian, Amharic). In South Asia, the device gives the impression of having been extended from personal nouns to IDENTIFIED inanimate nouns, perhaps restructuring itself in the process. Clearly, however, the process has gone further in some South Asian languages, e.g. Hindi, than in others, e.g. Bengali, Telugu, and Malayalam[11], where object *pronouns* referring to *inanimate* objects are generally in the Nominative case, although (as pronouns) certainly "definite."

Another device for marking the IDENTIFIED status of objects is the use of redundant pronouns (affixed or otherwise), as in Swahili:

(49) *niliona mbwa*—'I saw a dog'

(50) *nili-MW-ona mbwa*—'I saw (it) the dog'

In South Asia, this device (which comes entangled in the same matrix of animacy, etc. as the case-marking device) appears to be confined to the Munda languages, e.g. Santali:

(51) *janwariń ńamleKOkhan iń aguKOa*—'If I find (them) the animals, I shall bring them' (Bodding 1925)

(52) *uni ho̱rKO to̱lkedEa*—'They bound (him) that man' (Bodding 1925: 18.30b)

It is possible that it may also occur in the so-called "Complex Pronominalized" Himalayan languages in the Tibeto-Burman family, such as Limbu,

11. For examples see my 1976 paper.

but I have no certain evidence of this. Similarly I have no evidence for its occurrence in Sindhi, the Indo-Aryan language with the most elaborate system of enclitic pronouns.

A device indicating the DEFINITENESS-STATUS of objects that is independent of animacy and case-marking considerations is the difference in *conjugation* found in Hungarian:

(53) *kutyát LÁTOK*—'I see A dog' (Indefinite Conjugation)

(54) *LÁTOM a kutyát*—'I see THE dog' (Definite Conjugation)

To my knowledge, nothing of this kind is to be found in South Asia, but one never knows. Another device—this time not connected with direct objects—which seems to have no analogs in South Asia is the Definite Adjective, once more widespread in Europe, but now surviving in this function only in a few corners of its former domain, one of which is Latvian:

(55) *suns* 'dog/a dog/the dog'
balts suns 'a white dog'
baltais suns 'the white dog' (Lazdņia 1966)

It is remotely related, to be sure, to the topicalizing relative discussed above.

Finally, we should note uses of *word order* other than for topicalization purposes as noted previously. In both Russian and Chinese, for example, an altered word order is one way of conveying UNIDENTIFIED SUBJECT status:

(56) *kèrén lái le* 'The guests arrived' (SV:normal order)

(57) *lái kèrên le* 'A guest/some guests arrived' (VS: Givón 1978:308)

(58) *gosti prijéxali* 'The guests arrived' (SV: normal order)

(59) *prijéxali gosti* 'Some guests arrived' (VS:Borras and Christian 1959: 377ff)

Although we should not rule out possible DEFINITENESS-marking functions of word order in South Asian languages without a more thorough study of the question, they typically resort, as we shall see, to another and more familiar device to mark the UNIDENTIFIED category at least. Sanskrit might seem the most promising field in which DEFINITENESS-MARKING through word order might be discovered, but Staal (1967) reports nothing of this kind (although his book is not specifically addressed to this question, and many grammars of Russian and Chinese ignore the DEFINITENESS-MARKING significance of word order in those languages). My Sanskritist colleagues also report noticing nothing, but one of them, Donald Nelson of the University of Chicago, pointed out to me that *saḥ* and *kaścid* often function respectively like definite and indefinite articles in Sanskrit discourse.

This brings us back to the subject of articles, which even when all of the above alternatives are taken into account, remain among the most common

DEFINITENESS-MARKING devices. They have an advantage over most of the others in that they are not tied to any particular construction or syntactic position, but are free to accompany the noun anywhere. ("Definite Objects" are among those with obvious inherent limitations in this regard.) For this reason articles can also become convenient carriers of other kinds of grammatical information—number, gender, and case, for example—without sacrificing their DEFINITENESS-MARKING function.

What is an article? It is a (usually) unstressed "word" or affix, which may, depending on the language, precede or follow the noun: *LE chien* (French), *DER Hund* (German). *SONO inu* (Japanese). *NEÌJR gǒu* (Chinese) – 'the dog': *câineLE* (Rumanian), *hundEN* (Swedish), *andjing ITU* (Indonesian). *khyi TE* (Tibetan) – 'the dog': *UN perro* (Spanish). *BIR köpek* (Turkish) – 'a dog': *sagı* (Persian), *kalbUN* (Classical Arabic) = 'a dog'. In some languages (e.g., Amharic) the Definite Article attaches itself to the adjective instead, when there is one; in Arabic it goes with both adjective and noun: *al-kalb al-kabīr* 'the big dog'. Because of the close semantic relation between deixis and anaphora, definite articles commonly evolve out of demonstratives and, for similar reasons, indefinite articles evolve out of the numeral 'one'. They may remain undifferentiated from these except for stress, in which case we tend to say the demonstrative or numeral is "*used* as an article." Or there may develop reduced forms for the article and/or strengthened forms for the demonstrative and numeral. In any case, a form need not be totally distinct from all other forms in a language (as does happen to be the case in English) in order to qualify as an article. German is generally considered to have articles—*der, die, das*: these are identical in form to the demonstratives (except for stress) in all cases except the genitive (and dative plural), which is a fairly recent development. Or compare the relations of the Indefinite Article to the numeral 'one' in various languages in the table below:

(60) *'One' and Indefinite Articles*

	count	pronoun	numeral adjective	indefinite article
Old English			ĀN	—(+/-')
Mod English		*ONE*		*A/AN*
Spanish(msg)		*UNO*		*UN* (+/-')
German(msgn)	*EINS*	*EINER*		*EIN*
Chinese	*YI*		*YI-ge**	
Persian	*YEK*	*YEKI,*	*YEK dāne**	Noun – -I (also *Yek*–Noun—i)
Hindi		*EK*[12]		(+/-')
Marathi		*EK*		(+/-')

12. While the Hindi form is not "reduced" when functioning as an article, there are already signs of the development of *strengthened* forms to mean 'one' in some contexts, e.g. *peṛ ke niice* - 'under the tree', *EK peṛ ke niice* - 'under A tree', *EK HII peṛ ke niice* - 'under one tree'. Cf. also *vah/vahii* and *yah/yahii* on the demonstrative side.

Sinhala**	*EKA*			*-EK/AK*
Bengali	*ÆK*	*EKṬI**		
Assamese	*ÆK*	*ÆTA**		
Tamil	*ONR̲U*		*ORU*	
Telugu	*OKAṬI* (*ŌKAḌU*, *OKAṬE*)		*OKA*	
Kannada	*ONDU*	(*OBBA*) *ONDU*		

*classifier may vary
**colloquial standard

Although South Asian demonstratives with article-like functions do not seem to be differentiated in form, numerals with such functions do begin to show some differentiation in Dravidian and Eastern Indo-Aryan (as much as some of their European counterparts), while Sinhala has a fully distinct Indefinite Article (although its suffixed form has sometimes led to its being called something else.)

There is probably no language in the world in which deictics are not used to mark prior identification to at least some extent, and also no language in which unstressed 'one' cannot be used as an "optional indefiniteness marker" (Moravcsik 1969: 88). Does this mean all languages have articles? If not, how do we discriminate? Clearly not by form. It is a question of usage, rather. The dichotomy obligatory/optional is a bit too simplistic, although the question needs more study in South Asian languages: it is possible that in some contexts the use of a DEFINITENESS-marker of the article type may indeed be obligatory. (On the importance of grammatical context see below). There are different degrees of obligatoriness or optionality. At this point we may invoke two rough and ready methods of diagnosis. One is translation-equivalence: a great many 'that's' and 'one's' in South Asian sentences have to be translated by articles: the use of a demonstrative or numeral will be wrong. The second is *frequency*: although Russian, for example, like all languages, sometimes uses 'one', 'this', or 'that' in clarifying discourse status, therefore as "optional" DEFINITENESS-markers, such usage in South Asian discourses will be readily found to be far more frequent. Even if no strictly obligatory usage were to be found, it would miss something of typological importance to class Russian and South Asian languages together without further qualification only on that ground in view of this difference.

Despite all the evidence from earlier stages of European languages, the process of evolution of articles is not well understood (Hodler 1954:13). South Asian languages may currently represent a stage of that evolution where that process can be more readily observed. Investigation of these phenomena in South Asia could therefore help not only our understanding of South Asian languages but also our understanding of larger linguistic issues.

A fourth dimension of our typology must be invoked before we can pose the proper questions for such an investigation. Before proceeding to it.

however, we are forced to take note of an additional complication. Namely, not all definite articles originate from demonstratives (or indefinite articles from the number 'one')—that is, unless we want to make such origin a part of their definition. If not, we have to recognize in the "definiteness particles", as they are usually called (Pattanayak 1972 significantly calls them *specifiers*) of Bengali, Assamese, and Oriya (the commonest being *-ṬA,-ṬI, -JON*; *-TO, -ZON, -KON, -GOR*; and *-ṬA, -ṬI* respectively, all, suffixes) another set of distinctively South Asian articles, derived from classifiers instead of demonstratives.

Not all so-called "articles" are DEFINITENESS-markers. Those of Khasi are merely NOUN-markers, obligatorily attached to every noun and indicating subclasses of the latter.

Finally, we should take care not to assume, when we have identified one mode of DEFINITENESS-marking in a language, that we have the whole picture. Many languages employ several that complement or strengthen one another, for example articles and definite vs. indefinite verb conjugation and word order differences (Hungarian), definite object markers and indefinite articles (Turkish, Persian), definite object markers and definite articles (Amharic). The existence of "definite object" marking in South Asian languages does not preclude the possibility of articles. At the same time it may be admitted that the presence or absence of one mode of marking affects the pressure behind another. The presence of the Definite Suffixes in Eastern Indo-Aryan means there is less pressure for the demonstrative to take on article functions, and less pressure for personal object-marking to generalize into Definite Object marking. If Definite Object marking is weakly developed in Dravidian languages, there is more pressure for article development. (All languages, moreover, including those with differentiated article systems, resort to lexical means of disambiguation of noun discourse status when the customary devices are felt to be insufficient.)

The fourth typological dimension stems from the fact that marking of noun DEFINITENESS-STATUS will in many cases be redundant, because such status is semi-predictable. That is to say, it is strongly correlated with sentence function. Although most of the status-categories can occur in most positions, the probability of it being a particular one in a given position is sometimes very high:

1. "Subjects" tend strongly to represent old information (and coincide with "topics") and thus to be IDENTIFIED in status. Indeed in a typical text or conversation the majority of subjects are pronouns—the ultimate in anaphoric identification. (In certain registers they may also frequently be GENERIC.) This skewing of frequency results from the simple fact that a noun is UNIDENTIFIED only once—when it is first introduced: thereafter in all references it is IDENTIFIED. Added to this are the many bits of information *assumed* in the situation, which can be referred to as IDENTIFIED without such introduction.

2. Subjects of existential verbs constitute the main systematic exception, this being the favored construction for the introduction of new nouns (*There is A WORM in my apple*), and accordingly, typically UNIDENTIFIED-SPECIFIC.

3. Indirect objects (and oblique subjects), locative and genitive nouns—in fact all nouns in an oblique case relation (instrumental, ablative, etc.) other than the accusative are even more likely to be IDENTIFIED-SPECIFIC. That is, *to the landlord* is more common than *to a landlord, in the house* than *in a house, the landlord's son* than *a landlord's son, from the village* than *from a village.*

4. Direct objects have been discussed earlier. They tend to work in the opposite way: *I bought a sweater* (probably more common than *I bought the sweater*). *We had lunch* (probably more common than *We had the lunch*).

5. Predicate nominals tend to favor the GENERIC category: *He is a professor* (more common than *He is the professor*). *That is a custard-apple* (more common than *That is the custard-apple*).

Marking of the status-categories dominant with respect to the above environments can be called redundant. At this point we may—at the risk of some confusion because of the use of the word "mark" in two senses in the same context—invoke the principle of markedness. The dominant status-categories noted above will be the *unmarked* ones; the *marked* categories for each position will be the contrary of these: i.e. UNIDENTIFIED subjects and nouns in oblique relations, IDENTIFIED objects, existential subjects, and predicate nominals. An economy minded language would overtly "mark" only the *marked* combinations, taking the *unmarked* ones for granted. At the very least, we might expect the "marking" process to begin with the *marked* combinations, and only then encroach by analogy onto the *unmarked* ones. (Here it must be noted that articles are more likely—because first of all they are able!—to spread by analogy to unmarked environments than are other kinds of marking.)

In addition to the above, certain modifying elements have the effect, regardless of sentence position, of strongly or always implying a particular discourse status, e.g., possessives and numerals strongly imply IDENTIFIED and UNIDENTIFIED status respectively, while demonstratives *always* imply IDENTIFIED status. Overt marking is needed to reverse the implications of the first two, i.e. *a friend of mine* vs. *my friend, the four men* vs. *four men*, which is not possible with the third (**a that book*). In all three cases, however, any further marking for the status already implied will obviously also be redundant. That is not to say that some languages, consistency-minded rather than economy-minded, may not elect to indulge in such marking. A language may also elect to mark redundantly nouns that are inherently IDENTIFIED, i.e. proper names. (Proper names are similar to pronouns, implying prior identification.) The DEFINITENESS implications of *relative clauses* appear to differ between languages, and need further study, in South Asian languages and generally. (See discussion in Moravcsik 1969 and Junghare's paper.) Note also McGregor's statement (1972:46-47) to the effect that in Hindi the JO clause precedes when the head is IDENTIFIED but follows an UNIDENTIFIED head, which he illustrates with the following two sentences:

(61) *mai EK aadmii se baat kar rahaa thaa JO kal bhaarat jaaegaa*—'I was talking to a man who is going to India tomorrow'

(62) *mai JIS aadmii se baat kar rahaa thaa, vah kal bhaarat jaaegaa*—'The man I was talking to is going to India tomorrow'

This might provide a basis for taking an UNIDENTIFIED relative clause head as *marked* (note the *EK* in Hindi), with IDENTIFIED status otherwise taken for granted, at least in restrictive clause heads. It remains to be seen whether this applies to other South Asian languages, and to Dravidian adjectival participles.

A basic axis in a general typology of DEFINITENESS-MARKING, then, would be one along which a language could be classified according to the semantosyntactic environments in which it elects to mark DEFINITENESS-STATUS, arranged along a scale from the least to the most redundant. Languages with minimal and largely lexical DEFINITENESS-MARKING, such as Yoruba, would fall at one end of the scale, languages with maximal and highly redundant marking, such as Modern Greek (which uses its Definite Article with proper names, possessives, and demonstratives), at the other.

The above-mentioned markedness strictures lead to a more general observation. Implications of IDENTIFIED status are by far the most common, direct objects being the major exception. An economical marking strategy therefore might well give priority to marking UNIDENTIFIED ("specified indefinite") status, and to IDENTIFIED direct objects when they occur, with lack of any marking normally implying IDENTIFIED status elsewhere. This is indeed the strategy South Asian languages appear to have adopted —or at least to have begun with. Such a marking strategy should be distinguished from minimal ad hoc lexical marking: it is economical but structured. South Asian languages thus fall typologically somewhere between Yoruba and Modern Greek, not at the low end of the marking scale.

Compare the following parallel translations of Mk 14:3:

(63a.) (*Greek original*): ḗithen GYNḖ echousa *alábastron* myrou nardou pistikḗs polytelous; kai syntripsasa *tēn alabastron* katecheen *autou* kata tḗs kephalḗs..

(63b.) (*English:KJV*): "..there came A WOMAN having *an alabaster box* of ointment of spikenard very precious: and she brake *the box*, and poured *it* on his head."

(63c.) (*Hindi* : *Bulcke*): EK MAHILAA sangmarmar ke paatr me aslii jaṭaamããsii kaa bahumuulya *itr* le kar aayii. usne *paatr* toṛ kar iisaa ke sir par *itr* ũḍel diyaa.

(63d.) (*Urdu*): EK AURAT jataamaasii kaa besh qiimat xaalis *itar* sang-i-marmar ke itardaan mẽ laaii aur *itardaan* toṛkar *itar ko* uske sir par ḍaalaa.

(63e.) (*Gujarati*): EK STRII jaṭaamãāsiinaa ati muulyavaan attarnii bharelii sangemarmarnii *ḍabbii* laine aavii; ane *e ḍabbii* bhaagiine teṇe tenaa maathaa par *te* reḍayũ.

(63f.) (*Marathi*): KOṆII EK STRII jaṭaamãāsiicyaa bahumuulya sugandhii telaaci alaabaastra *kupii* gheuun aalii; tinẽ *tii kupii* phoḍuun tyaacyaa mastakaavar otilii.

(63g.) (*Bengali*): EKṬI STRILOK sheto pathŏrer patre bishuddho bohumullae jŏtamangshir *ator* loiya uposthito hoilo; *patroṭi* bhangiya she jishur mathae *taha* ḍaliya dilo.

(63h.) (*Assamese*): AEZONI TIROTAI bohumuliya bixuddho zŏtamangsir xugondhi telere bhŏra *aeta tema* loi ahi, *temato* bhangi, teŏr murŏt baki dile.

(63i.) (*Telugu*): OKA STRII mikkili veluvagala acca jaṭaamaansi *attarubuḍḍi* tisikoni vacci, *aa attarubuḍḍi* pagulagoṭṭi *aa attaru* aayana talamida poosenu.

(63j.) (*Kannada*): OBBA STRIIYU bahu biliyuḷḷa acca jaṭaamaansi tailạda *bharaṇiyunnu* tegedukoṇḍu bandu *aa bharaṇiyunnu* oḍedu *tailavannu* atana taliya meeli hoyidaḷu.

(63k.) (*Tamil*): ORU STIRII vilaiyeeṟappeṟṟa naḷatam ennum uttam tailamuḷḷa veḷḷaikkal *paraṇiyai* -k-koṇṭu vantu, *atai* uṭaittu, *anta-t-tailattai* avar ciracinmeel uuṟṟinaaḷ.

(63h.) (*Malayalam*): ORU STRII *oru venkal bharaṇi* vilayeeṟiya svaccha jaṭaamaansi tailavumaayi vannu *bharaṇi* poṭṭiccu avanṯe talayil ozhiccu.

(63m.) (*Santali*): *mit' alabastar-dhiri-cukạk'* asol aḍi damanak' joṭamaṅsi sunum tahẽkantae MIT'ṬEN MAEJIUE hec̃ena : *alabastar-dhiri-cukạk'* rạput'kate uniak' bohok' reye duladEa.

Whatever the general merits of these sentences, it should be noted that they do not follow literally either the Greek or the English, and an interesting pattern is already discernible when they are compared. The UNIDENTIFIED status of the subject is overtly marked in *all* the South Asian versions (although not in the Greek). Turning to the direct objects ("italics") we find less uniformity. The second mention of the box, now IDENTIFIED on that ground, and the second mention of the perfume (where it occurs) are for the most part status-marked by devices other than the use of the Accusative case. Only the Urdu version employs that option, and only with the perfume. (The Tamil and Kannada versions employ the Accusative, but obviously not in that function here, since both IDENTIFIED and

UNIDENTIFIED objects have it—probably as a result of the overgrammaticalized translators' dialect.) The Bengali and Assamese versions use the Definite Suffixes available in those languages. The majority of the versions, including not only all the Dravidian versions but also significantly Marathi and Gujarati, mark the IDENTIFIED objects with anaphoric *demonstratives*. UNIDENTIFIED direct objects are an *unmarked* category, according to our theory, and the first mention of the box (or the perfume) has no status-marker in most of the versions. However, the Malayalam, Assamese, and Santali versions employ what we might begin to call the Indefinite Article here also. Although languages of the Indian mainland may not yet have adopted the strategy of Sinhala, according to which all (singular)nouns not marked Indefinite are deemed Definite (Garusinghe 1962:21), they may be moving in that direction, some faster than others.

Obviously we cannot make such generalizations on the basis of a couple of sentences, translated ones at that. These only serve to raise questions for further and proper study. Such investigation should include: 1. elicitation of contrastive sentences, ideally starting from a uniform set, from native speakers of each language, with context carefully provided; 2. native speaker judgments on substitutions and deletions in sentences thus provided by the first group, and culled from texts, again with context (or with hypothetical contexts also elicited); 3. extensive survey of noun-status marking in texts.[13]

Preliminary investigations tend to confirm the hypothesis that UNIDENTIFIED status in marked environments has come to require an overt marker in South Asian languages, e.g.

(64) Subject: *caar din hue, kaalij mẽ EK prem-patr pakaṛaa gayaa thaa jo EK laṛke ne kisii laṛkii ko likhaa thaa*—'Four days ago, *A* love-letter had been confiscated in the college which A boy had written to some girl' (Shukla 1968:90)

(65) Oblique Position: *aadikavi baalmiiki ke hṛday mẽ kaavya kii sṛṣṭii EK pakṣii ke kaaraṇ hii to huii, jab EK baheliye ke baaṇ se krãũc kaa vadh dekhkar anaayaas unke muke se abhiśaap ke KUCH śabd anuṣṭup chand mẽ nikal paṛe the*—'It was *on account of a bird* that epic poetry

13. In order to conduct such surveys so that the results may be compared, we need a uniform matrix for classifying all nouns in texts. I have indicated the necessary components of such a matrix: 1) the discourse status of the noun: 2) the sentence function (grammatical status) of the noun: 3) the *markedness* relation between the two preceding, derived from the theory as discussed: 4) further semantic properties (personal/nonpersonal: animate/inanimate): 5) presence or absence of overt marking: 6) the particular marking device used. What remains is to suggest some notational symbols for the variables under each of the above, and to illustrate with a short passage how to apply the matrix to a text. Although this was done in one version of this paper and appended at this point, we omit this section here due to lack of space.

was created in the heart of the Ur-poet Valmiki, when, after seeing the curlew's murder by the arrow *of a hunter, some curse words* came out of his mouth spontaneously in the form of a 32-syllable meter' (Narayansingh 1958:k)

Could this development of an "indefinite article" possibly be the result of influence from English? Before hazarding an answer to that question (or better, a speculation) let me inflict another series of parallel Biblical texts:

(66a) '*It is easier for A CAMEL to pass through the eye of A NEEDLE than for A RICH MAN to enter the kingdom of God*' (Mark 10:25)

(66b: Greek origianl): *eukopōteron estin KAMEḶON diá tēs trymaliās TES RHAPHIDOS eiselthein, e PḶOUSION eis tēn basileian tou theou eiselthein.*

(66c: Urdu): *ŨŨṬ kaa SUUII ke naake mẽ se guzar jaanaa is se aasaan hai ki DAUḶATMAND xudaa kii baadshaahii mẽ daaxil ho.*

(66d: Hindi): *parameśvar ke raajya me DHANVAAN ke praveś karne kii apekṣaa, ŨŨṬkaa SUII ke naake mẽ hokar nikal jaanaa adhik saral hai.*

(66e: Gujarati): *DOḶATVAANne devnaa raajyamãã pesvaa kartãã ŨŨṬne SOYNÃA naakaamãã thaine javũ sahel che.*

(66f: Bengali): *isshorer rajje DHONOBANER probesh kǒra opekka SHUCER chidro-pothe UṬER probesh kǒra shǒhǒj.*

(66g: Assamese): *DHONIḶOK issǒrǒr razzǒt homowatǒkoi, BEZIR bindhaidi UTE hǒroki zowai uzu.*

(66h: Malayalam): *DHANAVAAN daivaraajyattil kaṭakkuntinekkaal OṬṬAKAM SUUCIkkuzhayuuṭe kaṭakkunnatu eḷuppam*

(66i: Telugu): *DHANAVANTUḌU deevuni raajyamuloo praveeśincuṭakaṇṭe OṆṬE NUUDIbejjamuloo duuruṭa sulabhamu.*

Whereas in the series in illustration (63) the English Indefinite Article has an equivalent in every South Asian language cited, in series (66) it does in none of them—despite the fact that the grammatical context (oblique case status) normally implies IDENTIFIED unless contradicted by an overt marker. Why the difference? The reason is that these are GENERIC "indefinites" and not instances of UNIDENTIFIED status at all.

Does this mean South Asian indefinite articles are specified indefinites only, and have yet to extend themselves into the GENERIC area, the marking characteristic of which is always zero? Almost but not quite. It is possible to find instances of GENERIC "indefinite" marking, primarily in predicate nominal position:

(67) *bataasii EK choṭii-sii ciṛiyaa hai jo dekhne mẽ abaabiil kii tarah hokar bhii abaabiil nahīĩ hai*—'The *batāsī* is a smallish bird which although looks like a swallow is not a swallow' (Narayansingh 1958: 120)

(68) *vaastav mẽ yah EK saamaajik-manovaigyaanik yaanii lagbhag daar-śanik savaal hai*—'This is really a social-psychological that is to say almost a philosophical question' (Shukla 1968:88)

(69) *vah EK siiniyar guṭband thaa aur aksar raajdhaanii mẽ rahtaa thaa*—'He was a senior factionalist and usually stayed in the capital' (Shukla 1968:87)

Such constructions may indeed show English influence. Or they may be instances of those somewhat borderline situations that enable UNIDENTIFIED markers to get a foothold in the GENERIC area. For that matter. the South Asian Indefinite article also turns up in the (*Unmarked*) direct object position:

(70) *unhõne tatkaal vaais prinsipal kaa pad pane ke lie EK darxvaast likhii*—'He immediately worte an application to secure the post of vice-principal' (Shukla 1968:91)

It is especially because of such cases that we need both extensive textual studies and native speaker judgments. We need textual studies both to turn up a large sample of usage and to establish the frequency of optional usages in each environment. Although the use of the markedness typology involves a scale with discrete points, there is a statistical element also, in that, especially when changing usage is involved, as it well may be in South Asia, it is not just a question of yes or no, but of more or less (and also, one must add, of who and when). Only native speaker judgments—preferably a consensus of several—can determine whether there is (as I suspect there is) a difference (obligatory/optional?) in the usage of EK in (64-65) as against (67-69) and especially (70). The question is, does it make a difference in the meaning if the EK is deleted? Would *laṛke ne...likhaa thaa* mean *THE boy had written*, and *baheliye ke baaṇ se* mean *by THE hunter's arrow*? But does *EK darxvaast likhii* = *darxvaast likhii*?

There is another positional category that deserves some comment here. That is the subject of the existential verb, which we agreed earlier is typically UNIDENTIFIED, which therefore ought to be the *unmarked* category. The South Asian indefinite article is so frequent in this position, however, that there is some question as to whether that view is correct.

(71) *ek śahar thaa. śahar kyaa thaa raajdhaanii thii vah.* 'There was a city. In fact, it was the capital city.' (Saah 1972:17)

(72) *anagaa anagaa OKA uḷḷoo OKA allaripilla vaaḍu*—'Once upon a time there was in a certain village a naughty boy— (Vaasamoorti 1961:3)

(73) *vaaḷḷa iṇṭloo OKA pillipilla undi*—'In their house was a kitten' (Vaasamoorti 1961:6)

Possibly, South Asian languages treat these subjects like any other subjects (i.e. IDENTIFIED unless marked otherwise) rather than as a separate category. There is, after all, not a great deal of difference between a subject of 'be/exist' and of a verb like 'lived'.

(74) *ek ghane jangal mẽ EK bahut baṛaa śer rahtaa thaa*—'In a dense jungal there lived a very big lion' (Saah 1972:17)

That this is a South Asian trait rather than a universal is shown by languages like Russian where the traditional tale begins *Zhil-byl tsar'*—'There once was a king...'

This brings us to the fifth dimension in a typology of DEFINITENESS, which is *area*. Although there are always plausible "universal" justifications for a particular type of DEFINITENESS-MARKING (which mean it could crop up anywhere—and without which it presumably could not happen at all), it typically shows striking areal concentrations. *Topic-markers* are typical of the western Pacific and eastern Asia. There is an obvious *article* area in the Mediterranean and Western Europe. with aberrant phenomena—postposed articles, articles attached to adjectives, etc.—appearing as expected on its fringes. (*Definite adjectives* are probably to be classed among such aberrant article-phenomena: they are concentrated to the northeast of the main article area.) Incorporation of NONSPECIFIC noun objects is especially characteristic of the Americas, while *definite object* marking through case differentiation has a definite center in Central and Northern Eurasia (where it is a feature of both Proto-Uralic and of the earliest Turkic).

IDENTIFIED object marking in South Asia appears to be more developed and utilized in the languages of the northwestern part of the subcontinent (e.g. Hindi and Urdu) than in those of the south and east. It appears as an extension of the Central Asian area, which has also taken in a number of intervening Iranian Languages (including Persian and Baluchi), and in fact to owe something to influences from that quarter. (See Masica 1976.)

If IDENTIFIED object marking is characteristic of an area of which South Asia is a part or at least an appendage, articles, as we have seen, are sufficiently universally motivated to crop up anywhere, and they do appear in widely scattered languages in addition to their particular concentration in the above-mentioned Euro-Mediterranean zone. We have also seen that there are good general grounds on which a marking strategy giving priority to UNIDENTIFIED-SPECIFIC marking might well be adopted. Be that as it may, the Euro-Mediterranean article area seems to have followed a different path of development, with *definite* articles appearing first. Therefore, the indefinite article strategy appears to be not a universal, but a South Asian trait also. Actually, the area involved is larger than South Asia, including also the Persian and Turkish-speaking areas to the northwest. These are the same areas, roughly speaking. with which South Asia shares the "definite object" marking trait. It is conceivable that definite object marking and indefinite article priority go together: they can be seen as complementing one another with regard to the marking needs of *marked* environments. (It is of course possible to have one without the other, as in Sinhala.)

One might speculate that elaboration of definiteness-marking (e.g., spreading to *unmarked* environments, marking more than one status-category, etc.) is related to complexity of communicational needs. It can indeed be observed to increase over time, e.g. in the familiar languages of Western and Southern Europe. Other cases can be cited, however, in which definiteness-marking has been lost—e.g., definite adjectives in Russian. Languages of quite complex societies may have a low degree of definiteness-marking development (Latin, Sanskrit, Russian) while languages of small "simple" societies may have a high degree of it (Samoan, Dakota).

The degree of elaboration also seems to own more to areal and historical factors than to anything else. The Euro-Mediterranean article area, for instance, can be observed to spread in space and time, beginning in the eastern Mediterranean in Hebrew, spreading later to Greek (where articles were absent at the Homeric stage), then to the descendants of Latin, and finally to Germanic and the intrusive Hungarian. The eastern Mediterranean still shows up as a center of article "density" in terms of use in unmarked environments. Northeastern Europe on the other hand remains by contrast an area without articles and of low definiteness-marking in general. Uralic languages such as Finnish, once characterized by definite object marking, have dropped or modified that device on moving into the area.

A key question we must try to answer (through statistical and historical studies) is whether DEFINITENESS-MARKING is increasing in South Asia. If so, we may still ask whether this is: a) related to communicational needs—the development of new registers, etc.: b) influenced by English; or c) the result of the inner dynamics of the areal typology. Of course these answers are not mutually exclusive. There are many issues (some of which I have not had space to go into here, such as the relation between DEFINITENESS-STATUS and aspect/mood[14]). With productively-formulated questions, there is much to be learned both about and from South Asian languages on these matters.

14. See Davison 1979.

REFERENCES

Bodding, P.O. 1925. *Santal folk takes*, I. Oslo: Instituttet for Sammenlignende Kulturforskning.

Borras, F.M. and R.F. Christian. 1959. *Russian syntax*. Oxford: University Press.

Bulcke, Kamil, SJ (trans.) 1979) *Nayaa vidhaan*. 2nd rev. ed. Ranchi: Dharmik Sahitya Samiti

Chao, Yuen Ren. 1968. *A grammar of spoken Chinese*. Berkeley: University of Califoria P.

Comrie, Bernard, 1976. *Aspect*. Cambridge University Press.

Davison, Alice. 1979. Contextual effects on 'generic' indefinites: cross-linguistic arguments for pragmatic factors. Paper presented at 1979 NWAVE Conference, Université du uebec à Montreal.

Garusinghe, Dayaratne. 1962. *Sinhalese : the spoken idiom*. Munchen:Max Hueber Verlag

Givón, Talmy, 1978. Definiteness and referentiality. In *Universals of Human Language*. Joseph H.Greenberg, ed. Vol.4: Syntax. Stanford University Press. 291-330.

Grierson, George. 1919. *Linguistic survey of India*, Vol. VIII. Part 1: Sindhi and Lahnda. Repr. 1968. Delhi : Motilal Banarsidass.

Gupta, Mataprasad (ed) VS 2020, *Prthviraaj raasau* (text and notes). Chirgaon: Sahitya Sadan

Heinrichs, Heinrich Matthias. 1954. *Studien zum bestimmten Artikel in den germanischen Sprachen*. Giessen: W.Schmitz.

Hodler, Werner Oskar Felix. 1954. *Grundzuge einer germanischen Artikelehre*. Heidelberg: C. Winter.

Hudson, D.F. 1965. *Teach yourself Bengali*. London: English Universities Press.

Junghare, Indira Y. 1980. Some discourse considerations in Marathi. Paper presented at 1980 South Asian Languages Roundtable, University of Illinois, Urbana.

Khanna, Navin. 1971. Jii, aap kyaa bannaa caahte hãĩ? *Saptaahik hindustaan*, 26 March 1971. 28-29.

Lazdina, Tereza Budiņa. 1966. *Teach yourself Latvian*. London: English Universities Press.

Masica, Colin P. 1976. Another typological feature common to South and Central Asian languages: identified object marking. Paper presented at the 30th Congreso Internacional de Ciencias Humanas an Asia y Africa del Norte, Mexico City, 1976, and to appear in the Proceedings of the Congress. Also to appear under the title *Identified object marking in Hindi and other languages* in Topics in Hindi Linguistics, Vol. 2 Omkar N.Koul, ed. 1982

McGregor, R.S. 1972. *Outline of Hindi grammar*. Oxford:Clarendon Press.

Moravcsik, Edith. 1969. Determination. Stanford: Working Papers in Language UniversalsN,1.

Narayansingh, Rajeshwarprasad. 1958. *Bhaarat ke paksii*. Delhi: Publications Division, Ministry of Information and Broadcasting Government of India.

Okell, John. 1969. *A reference grammar of colloquial Burmese*. London: Oxford University Press (2 vols.)

Pattanayak, D.B. and G.N. Das. 1972. *Conversational Oriya*. Mysore: (S.Pattanayak).

Raghava, Rangeya, n.d. *Dhartii meraa ghar* (novel). Delhi:Rajpal and Sons.

Rao, Kommuri Venugopala. 1964. Aprayojakuni koopam. (Story included in *Grading Readings in Modern Literary Telugu*, ed. by G.N. Reddy and Dan M. Matson, University of Wisconsin, Madison, 15-21.)

Saah, Kailash. 1971. Iisap kii caar kahaaniyãã. *Saptaahik hindustan*, 26 March 1971. 17, 56.

Schachter, Paul, and Fe Otanes. 1972, *Tagalog reference grammar*. Berkeley and Los Angeles: University of California Press.

Shukla, Srilal. 1968. *Raag darbaarii* (novel). Delhi:Rajkamal.

Staal, J.F. 1967. *Word order in Sanskrit and universal grammar*. Dordrecht (Holland): D. Reidel.

'Suman', Dr. Amba Prasad. 1960. *Krsak jiivan sambandhii brajbhaasaa sabdaavali* Allahabad Ḥindustani Academy.

'Vaasamoorti'. 1961. *Allari goopi adbhuta yaatra* (children's book). Rajahmundry: Addepally & Co.

Varma, Mahadevi. S.V. 2014 (1957). Ghiisaa. (Story included in *Ikkiis kahaaniyãã*, Ray Krishnadas and Vachaspati Pathak, eds. Allahabad: Bharati Bhandar. 257-71.)

Vuong-Gia Thuy. 1975. *Vietnamese in a nutshell.* Montclair (N.J.): Institute for Language Study

SINHALA FOCUSED SENTENCES : NATURALIZATION OF A CALQUE

James W. Gair

Sinhala, an Indo-Aryan language long in contact with South Dravidian languages, has a focusing construction that plays a highly visible role in its grammar.[1] Under names such as "emphatic sentences", "cleft sentences", or "focused sentences" it has been analyzed in various ways in syntactic studies (as in Gair 1970, Fernando 1973, De Abrew, forthcoming) but its distinguishing characteristics are a special, or emphatic tensed form of the verb (EMPH)[2] commonly though not invariably accompanied by rightward placement of the focused constituent, as in the following:

(S1) *mamə giyee gaməṭə*
I go-PAST-EMPH village-DAT
'It was to the village that I went.'

(S2) *gunəpaalə kəranne monəva də*
Gunəpalə do-PRES-EMPH what Q
'What does Gunapala do ? '

These bear an unmistakable resemblance, in both form and meaning, to constructions in several Dravidian languages utilizing a nominal form of the verb as described for Tamil and Malayalam (Lindholm1972), Telugu (Krishnamurti 1974), and Kannada (Schiffman 1979), and exemplified by the following from (Jaffna) Tamil.[3]

---

1. I would like to thank Milan Rodrigo for her help in finding and discussing relevant Sinhala examples, particularly from earlier texts. I have also profited at various points, from discussions with numerous colleagues, especially Leonard Babby, John Bowers, Kamal De Abrew, Wayne Harbert, Barbara Lust, Claudia Ross and Margarita Suñer. None of them is, of course, responsible for any errors or misinterpretations. A shorter paper including many of the points dealt with here, but from a different perspective, was given at the sixth Berkeley Linguistic Society meeting, February 16-18, 1980.

2. In Colloquial Sinhala, EMPH is represented by *-nne* in the present tense and *-e* or *-ee* (added to the past tense stem) in the past tense. Sinhala is a diglossic language, and in Literary Sinhala, the variety used for virtually all written purposes, EMPH is represented by *-nne* or *-nuye* and *-e*. This does not affect the argument of the present paper, however, and except where otherwise noted, this paper deals only with Colloquial Sinhala.

3. Tamil examples used herein are from Sri Lanka (Jaffna) Tamil, since that is the variety for which I have the fullest relevant data. The transcription is as in Gair,

(T1) *naan* *poonatu* *yaaLppaaNattukku*
I go-PAST-NOM Jaffna-DAT
'It was to Jaffna that I went.'

(T2) *cuppiramaniyam* *ceyyiRatu* *enna*
Subramaniyam do-PRES-NOM what
'What is it that Subramaniyam does?'

One obvious difference between Sinhala and the others lies in the verb form. In the Dravidian languages mentioned, it is a nominal form derived from an attributive ("relative") participle by adding person-number endings (characteristically third person inanimate neuter), and it also functions as an action nominal in nominalized clauses (i.e. *maṇi pooRatu* 'Mani's going). In current colloquial Sinhala, however, the emphatic form has another use outside focused sentences; it is the form regularly occurring before *nææ*, the usual negative in verbal sentences :[4]

(S3) *man* *yanne* *nææ*
I go-PRES-EMPH *nææ*
'I don't go.'

It is difficult to subsume these two uses under any single syntactic rule, and syntactic studies have not done so as far as I know, so that we may ignore the use before *nææ* for present purposes.

The Sinhala emphatic form is thus not a clearly nominal form at present. However, though its origin is not entirely clear (contrast Paranavitana 1956, clviii wth Geiger 1938, 134-135) it is probably derived from a form used as an attributive participle through the addition of a third person masculine/neuter ending. Hence the resemblance would have been even clearer at an earlier stage, (and the affix does in fact retain some of that person-number character in the current literary variety).

It is worth noting here that the Dravidian focused sentences cannot easily be regarded as ordinary nominal equational sentences despite the obvious resemblance to the latter, for reasons set forth clearly by Lindholm

---

Suseendira Rajah and Karunatilaka 1979. Examples from other Dravidian languages are from the sources cited and in the transcriptions used therein.

4. There are in fact, sentences with V-EMPH that could be considered to represent another type, or at least a special subtype of focused sentences. These are represented by such sentences as:

arə *enne* *gunəpaalə*
There come-EMPH Gunapala
'The one coming is Gunapala', or 'There comes Gunapala now.'

As in this example, such sentences involve situational deixis and contain an appropriate deictic form. If other focused sentences are given a transformational derivation, they do not fit it neatly, and are distinct in that way as well, but not considering them separately here will not affect the argument. It is interesting however, that they can be considered to have sentences such as SA4, given later, as their forerunners, and they would require treatment in a full study of the history of Sinhala focused sentences.

(1972)—most importantly the variety of kinds of constituents and case markings that can occur in focused position. The same reasoning holds for Sinhala, and since the verbal form lacks the nominal uses of the Dravidian ones, the difference is even greater. However, the resemblance between focused and nominal equational sentences does appear to play a part in the history of the construction, as we shall see.

The close resemblance of the Sinhala and Dravidian constructions, taken with the apparent lack of such forms in Indo-Aryan languages, strongly suggests a Dravidian model, or at the least Dravidian influence on Sinhala. Equally interesting, however, is the way in which Sinhala developed and elaborated the construction once it was acquired, so that it achieved prominence in the grammar, interacting in an intricate way with several other grammatical processes. This paper will concern itself with the general outlines of that development, largely as they are revealed by a comparison of Sinhala with the Dravidian languages mentioned.

Before describing that development, we must characterize its end product: the current Sinhala focusing system.

In recent syntactic studies, Sinhala focus has been treated either as the result of a transformation (as in Gair 1970, De Abrew forthcoming) or as derived from a complex deep structure plus appropriate transformations (Fernando 1973). For present purposes, however, it suffices to restrict ourselves to surface structure characteristics. We will also not deal with the semantics of focus, reserving that for later treatment, except to say that the focused constituent is usually a "focus of contrast" in Chafe's sense (1976, pp. 37-38). We will thus deal with focus only as a syntactic phenomenon and initially restrict ourselves to sentences with a verbal predicator.

There are six relevant interrelated basic characteristics of Sinhala focused sentences, given below as C1-C6.

C1. If the focus is any form other than the verb or some stretch including the verb, the verb will be marked with EMPH.[5] In the following sentences, the focus is underlined :

(S4) *lankaave di* *mamə yanne* *ee gaməṭə*
Sri Lanka-GEN-while I go-PRES-EMPH that village-DAT
'It is to that village that I go while in Sri Lanka.'

(S5) *lankaave di* *ee* *gaməṭə* *yanne* *mamə*
'It is I who go to that village while in Sri Lanka.'

5. I have not specified here which constituents may be focused, but in general they include any phrasal constituent dominated by S or VP. Some details will be found in Gair 1970, but there are additional possibilities, such as some constituents of embedded S's, for which details have not been worked out but are currently under investigation.

(S6) *mamə ee gaməṭə yanne lankaave di*
'It is while in Sri Lanka that I go to that village.'

C2. The focused element is commonly placed after the verb, (Sinhala is an SOV language) but not invariably so. Thus in the following it is not :

(S7) *mamə ee gaməṭə yanne*
I that village-DAT go-PRES-EMPH
'It is to that village that I go.'

(S8) *kohaaṭə də yanne*
where-DAT Q go-PRES-EMPH
'Where are you going?'

The focused element in sentences such as S7 may be additionally marked by prominence in intonation and/or by one of the focus-marking forms to be discussed below. The factors determining whether or not rightward placement occurs are not yet clear, but they appear to include not only "information packaging", but more purely surface considerations. For example, there appears to be a "naked verb constraint"[6], or a reluctance to place the focused constituent rightward if the verb will be in leftmost position as a result. Thus S8 above and S9 seem preferable to S10, though S10 is certainly grammatical.

(S9) *dæn yanne kohaaṭə də*
now go-PRES-EMPH where
'Where are you going ?'

(S10) *yanne kohaaṭə də*
go-PRES- EMPH Where-DAT
'Where are you going?'

C3. There is a set of focus-marking forms including *yi*, *tamaa* and *tamay* 'emphatics', and *lu* "it seems, it is said' (*cf.* Tamil *aam*) which may only occur on the focus. It thus follows from C1 that when they follow any constituent other than the verb, the verb will be marked with EMPH. Thus :

(S11) *eyaa tamay gaməṭə yanne*
he *tamay* village-DAT go-PRES-EMPH
'He is indeed the one who goes to the village.'

but not

(S12) **eyaa tamay gaməṭə yanəwa*
go-PRES-SIMPLE

6. This term is adapted from M. Suñer's "naked noun constraint" to characterize a somewhat similar phenomenon in Spanish.

Note however, that while these forms can only occur on the focus when they do occur, they need not occur for the sentence to be focused. See, for example, S1 and S4-S7, in comparison with S11 or S13-S14 :

(S13) *mamə yanne ee gaməṭə tamay*
I go-PRES-EMPH that village-DAT tamay

(S14) *eyaa yanne ee gaməṭə lu*
he go-PRES-EMPH that village-DAT it-seems
'They say it is to that village that he goes.'

(as we would expect from C2, variant orders are possible for all of these).

Thus, and most importantly, focus may be defined syntactically as the substring with which one of these forms either occurs or may occur without other structural change occurring. For example, a focus-marking form could be added to the focus in S4-S5 without a change in the verb form or any other change being required.[7]

C4. The question-marker *də* (referred to hereafter as Q), regularly used in yes-no questions, is a focus-marking form in the sense of C3 :

(S15) *gunəpaalə gaməṭə də yanne*
Gunapala village-DAT Q go-PRES-EMPH
'Is it to the village that Gunapala is going ?'

(S16) *gaməṭə yanne gunəpaalə də*
'Is it Gunapala who is going to the village ?'

Compare S17, a neutral yes-no question where the focus is not on a form other than the verb :

(S17) *gunəpaalə gaməṭə yanəva də*
Gunapala village-DAT go-PRES-SIMPLE Q[8]
'Is Gunapala going to the village ?'

This is what we would expect from C1 as stated, and the other focus-marking forms may similarly occur following the verb; as in S18-S19.

---

7. There is also a focus-marking emphatic *may*, but this is an emphatic *mə*+ *yi* and is thus a subcase of the latter. Sinhala has forms like *mə* 'emphasis',-(*u*)*t* 'also' which mark "emphasis" of some sort but are not focus-marking forms in the sense in which that term is used here since they do not require clefting (*i.e.*, -EMPH). Note also that the definition of focus here clearly leaves out other phenomena of a kind which have been called "emphasis", or "focus", including "focus", marked by intonational prominence. This distinction is important, as is the distinction between "focus" and "topic", and it will be dealt with at greater length elsewhere.

8. The "simple" form of the verb is the tensed form usually occurring in finite non-focused sentences. For a fuller description of verb forms see Gair 1976 and the references therein.

(S18) *gunapaalə gamətə yanəva lu*
Gunapala village-DAT go-PRES-SIMPLE it-seems.
'They say Gunapala is going to the village.'

C5. There are two main[9] negative forms in independent sentences; *nææ* and *novey*, (with dialectal variants *nemey*, *nevi*); *nææ* was mentioned earlier as the usual negator in verbal sentences, as exemplified in S3 and S20[10].

(S20) *gunapaalə gamətə giyee nææ*
Gunapala Village-DAT go-PAST-EMPH *nææ*
'Gunapala did not go to the village.'

novey is a focal negator, and a focus marking form in the sense of C3:

(S21) *mamə novey ee gamətə yanne*
I novey that village-DAT go-PRES-EMPH
'I am certainly not the one who goes to that village.'

(S22a) *gunəpaalə giyee gamətə novey*
Gunapala go-PAST-EMPH village-DAT novey
'It was not to the village that Gunapala went.'

nææ, on the other hand, cannot negate any constituent other than the verb or a stretch including it.[11]

C6. WH-questions in Sinhala require the occurrence of a WH form and the question marker *də* (Q). WH forms are characteristically focused, and it thus follows from C3 and C4 that *də* will occur following the WH-form. Thus S2, S8-10 and S22-23 below:

(S22) *gunəpaalə mee vædə keruve kohomə də*
Gunapala this work do-PAST-EMPH now Q.
'How did Gunapala do this work?'

(S23) *mokətə də dəen gamətə yanne*
what-DAT Q now village-DAT go-PRES-EMPH
'Why (what for) are you going to the village now?'

---

9. There is a third form, a prefix *no* occurring in embedded S's and on some verb forms in independent sentences, including verbs with EMPH. It is not necessary to deal with it in this paper, however. For details, see Gair, 1970 : 156 and De Abrew, forthcoming.

10. In such sentences, *nææ* is not the focus as the result of any sort of focusing operation, transformational or otherwise, and no recent study has treated it as such to the best of my knowledge.

11. *nææ* may be moved by low-level scrambling rules, but that does not make any form preceding it the focus, and even then it leaves traces of its former location in the form of constraints on what may follow the verb and precede *nææ*. For details, see De Abrew, forthcoming.

This focusing of WH (+Q) has a semi-obligatory character.[12] Quantifier WH forms *kiiyak* 'how many-indef', *koccərə* 'how much' are exceptions, and may occur focused or unfocused with a consequent difference in meaning:

(S24) *miniha siini koccərə gatta də*
man sugar how-much get-PAST-SIMPLE Q
'How much sugar did the fellow get?'

(S25) *miniha siini koccərə də gatte*
man sugar how-much Q get-PAST-EMPH
"How much sugar was it that the fellow got?'

Unfocused WH forms also occur under two other related semantic conditions: in object complements of negated verbs like *dannəva* 'know', *teerenəva* 'understand' and in independent "dubious questions", i.e., roughly with a sense like 'what on earth', 'can it be that...':

(S26) *miniha monəva karənəva də danne nææ*
man what-Pl do-PRES-SIMPLE Q know-EMPH *nææ*
'(I) don't know what he's doing.'

(S27) *gunəpaalə monəva kərənəva də?*
Gunapala what-PL do-PRES-SIMPLE Q
'What (on earth) is Gunapala doing?'

with S27, compare S2 (repeated here):

(S2) *gunəplaalə kəranne monəva də*
Gunapala do-PRES-EMPH what-PL Q
'What is Gunapala doing?'

C1-C6 together constitute a clearly integrated system, and while similar individual characteristics appear in one or the other of the South Dravidian languages or Telugu, none of the latter appear to incorporate all of them, so that the total system has distinctly Sinhala character. The precise manner in which this system developed and the exact sequence in which its separate features appeared is not yet clear, and awaits a more thorough study of the relatively rich inscriptional and written documentation available as material for the history of Sinhala syntax. Also, determining the precise features that might have been borrowed would require more work in comparative Dravidian historical syntax. However, a number of suggestive points emerge from some initial explorations into older Sinhala texts and a feature by feature comparison with the other languages, so that we can at least formulate some likely hypotheses at

12. The association of WH form and Q is so strong that dictionaries such as Carter 1924 and De Zoysa 1964 list them as single entries : *koheedə* 'where', *kohomədə* 'how' etc., and do not list the WH forms alone.

this time. For Dravidian comparison, I will necessarily rely mostly on Tamil, and specifically Sri Lanka Tamil, since I have a greater amount of relevant data available from that language. Otherwise, I have had to rely primarily on the sources cited earlier and on published grammars (from which it is usually difficult to extract the precise information needed). In any case, Tamil and Malayalam would seem for obvious historical reasons to be the most likely candidates for borrowing, and the initial borrowing could well have occurred at a time to make the distinction between those two languages irrelevant.

A comparison with the Dravidian languages on the basis of the available evidence reveals a number of interesting parallels and differences, particularly with regard to the focus-marking forms. Although Lindholm refers to Tamil *-aa* 'question' and *-taan* 'emphatic' as "clitics of focus" (1972, p. 301) they are clearly less restricted than Sinhala *də* and *tamaa* (or *tamay*) as described in C3 and C4 above. Nor does Tamil *-aam* "reportative" behave like Sinhala *lu* in that regard. All of the Tamil forms may occur on forms other than the verb without obligatory clefting, as in the following:

(T3) *avaraa naaLaykku koLumpukku pooRaar*
he-Q tomorrow-DAT Colombo-DAT go-PRES-3 Sg-MASC
'Is it he who is going to Colombo tomorrow?'

(T4) *avartaan naaLaykku koLumpukku pooRaar*
he-EMPH tomorrow-DAT Colombo-DAT go-PRES-3Sg-MASC
'He is going to Colombo tomorrow.'

(T5) *eppavaam avar pooRaar*
when-it-seems he go-PRES-3Sg-MASC
'When did they say he is going?'

In fact, non-clefting seems to be the usual case, and since clefting is also possible there is a possibility for contrast that is not open in Sinhala. Compare T6 for example, with T4:

(T6) *naaLaykku koLumpukku pooRatu avartaan*
tomorrow-DAT Colombo-DAT go-NOM-PRES-3 SG-NEUT he-EMPH
'It is certainly he who is the one who is going to Colombo tomorrow.'

Malayalam *tanne* 'emphatic' and-*oo* 'question' also appear not to be restricted in the same way as the Sinhala forms (for *-oo* Lindholm, 1972, p. 305; for *tanne* Rodney Moag, personal communication). Thus the same possibilities for contrast as in Tamil appear to exist with regard to occurrence with the focus of clefted or non-clefted sentences.[13]

---

13. One should perhaps say with greater precision, "with two kinds of focus, involving both semantic and syntactic differences". This distinction requires more extended

Malayalam *aaNu* 'copula', also called a "clitic of focus" by Lindholm (p. 301) is particularly interesting in that it does seem to be restricted like the Sinhala forms. In fact, Malayalam goes beyond colloquial Sinhala in requiring the occurrence of *aaNu* on the focus of a cleft sentence unless *tanne* already occurs, and this is true even if the question marker *-oo* or a WH form appears :

(M1) *innale baalanaaNoo vannatu*
yesterday Balan-aaNū- Q came-NOM-3SG·
'Was it Balan who came yesterday ?'

(M2) *innale aaraaNu vannatu*
yesterday who-aaNū came-NOM-3SG
'Who was it who came yesterday ?' (Lindholm p. 306)

It is for that reason that Lindholm does not include Malayalam *-oo* and *WH-* as "clitics of focus" but only *tanne* and *aaNu* (p. 305-306). Note however that of the latter two, only *aaNū* is a focus marker in the sense of the Sinhala forms. Its closest equivalent is *yi*, which also has some copula functions.[14]

yi however, does not obligatorily occur in the absence of other focus markers in colloquial Sinhala, nor does it generally occur with *də* 'question'.[15] A comparison of Malayalam with Literary Sinhala, though, reveals a much closer similarity and casts light on the probable development of Sinhala *yi* as a focus marker when not a copula. The obligatory occurrence of *aaNū* actually appears to be part of a more general rule, covering both cleft sentences and the nominal equational sentences that they resemble in other respects. That is, Malayalam, unlike its sister languages, appears to have developed a rule requiring an overt copula even in the present tense, and *aaNū* serves that function.[16]

---

treatment than we can give it here. Note, however, that it is paralleled by Sinhala forms allowing *mə* (fn. 7) vs. those allowing forms like *tamay* or *-yi*. We use "focus" here only for the latter in Sinhala.

14. In current Colloquial Sinhala, *NP NP* equational sentences lack an overt copula, but *NP Adj* sentences obligatorily take *-yi* if the adjective is vowel-final (as most are) :

meekə hoñday
This-one good-yi
'This one is good.'

15. *yi* may co-occur with *də*, but under special circumstances involving, in rough terms, another level of focus, as, for example, when asking for confirmation :

meekə hoñday də
'Is this one really good?'

16. Thus, in an equational sentence :
atu meesa (y) aaNu 'That is a table.' (George, 1971 : p. 10)
compared with Tamil : *atu meesay*. As George points out :

"Malayalam is probably the only Dravidian Language which demands the use of the copula *aaNu* corresponding to *is* or *are* in English. Languages like Telugu do not take

Literary Sinhala has a similar rule (Gair and Karunatilaka 1974, pp.11 and 25). The copula may be a form of *venəva* (Skt. *bhū*) but the usual form, (and currently the exclusive one in focused sentences) is *yi* or one of its variants.[17] Here, as elsewhere, Literary Sinhala reflects an older stage of the language,[18] and to arrive at the present colloquial use of *-yi*, we need only to relax the obligatory nature of its occurrence as copula, leaving it, then, as an optional focus-marking form as in S28, to be compared with S1 :

(S28) *mamə yanne gaməṭay*
Gunapala go-PRES-EMPH village-DAT-*yi*
'It is to the village that Gunapala is going.'

In verbal focused sentences with or without-*yi*, the verb retains its EMPH marking, and with the loss of the nominal character of that affix elsewhere the resemblance between focused and nominal equational sentences is attenuated. Note, however, that while the copula rule was relaxed also in nominal equational sentences, it was not in adjectival equational sentences, where *yi* retains its obligatory character even in Colloquial Sinhala (See S35 and footnote 14). In this respect, then, nominal equational and focused sentences were treated alike.

At present, on grounds of external history, I consider the development of an obligatory copula rule in Sinhala and Malayalam and its application to both focused and equational sentences to be a case of parallel development but the similarity is indeed striking.

Sinhala *də* and the Kannada question marker *-aa* afford another striking parallel. Unlike Tamil *-aa* and Malayalam-*oo*, the Kannada form requires obligatory clefting (Schiffman 1979, pp. 103 and 129-130).[19] Thus :

(K1) *avnaa naaLe uurg hoogoodu*
he-Q tomorrow town-DAT go-PRES-NOM-NEUT
'Is it he who is going to town tomorrow?' (Schiffman, p. 113)

On external historical grounds, of course, the likelihood of cross language influence here is even more remote than for the Malayalam and Sinhala copula, and it must be considered a parallel development. It is interest-

---

such a verb. To be considered complete the Malayalam sentence must have at least an *aa* at the end which function (sic) in place of *aaNu*."

17. Forms of *venəva*, as copula, inflect for tense and number-gender to agree with the subject in Literary Sinhala. Thus :

mama goviyek vemi
I farmer-INDEF be-PRES-ISg.
'I am a farmer.'

yi and its variants, however, do not show agreement. Hence, *mama goviyek yi* (or *goviyeki*).

18. Compare, for example, SAI, given later from a twelfth century text.

19. Judging from the examples given by Schiffman, the verificatory particle-*oo* may also be subject to that rule (p. 132) though this is not stated.

ing to speculate on the reasons for it, but that goes well beyond the confines of this paper.

The obligatory co-occurrence of *də* with WH forms is a distinct Sinhala development, not paralleled in any of the other languages, as is the semiobligatory focusing of WH forms given as C6. Neither, for example apply in Tamil; compare T7 with S29 :

(T7) *enna* *taaRinkaL*
what give-PRES-2 PL
'What are you giving?'

(S29) *oyaa* *denne* *monəva* *də*
you give-PRES-EMPH what Q
"What are you giving?'

As I shall show subsequently, the semi-obligatory focusing of WH forms and the consequent usual adjacent co-occurence of most WH forms and *də* in focused position are later developments than their possible co-occurrence in the same sentence, and clearly both are internal developments.

The interaction of negation and focus in Sinhala is complex, and several aspects of it have recently been treated by De Abrew (forthcoming). The negative *novey* is transparently from *no-* 'negative prefix' plus the third person singular of the copula *venəva*, and its development as a focus-marking form clearly involved the same parallel treatment of equational and focused sentences that we saw in the development of *yi*. Thus *novey*, in addition to its function as a focus negator, also retains its functions as the regular negator of nominal (but not adjectival) equational sentences, as in S32 :

(S30) *meekə* *potak* *novey*
This-one book-INDEF *novey*
'This one is not a book.'

The specialization of *novey* to these two functions in contrast with *nææ* is a later development, like the somewhat different specialization of *yi* since in earlier texts we may find *novey* (or its etymon) where we would currently expect *nææ*.[20]

Two further characteristics of negation in Sinhala deserve mention here, since they show how far the system has developed. First, *novey* may negate an entire sentence (or some stretch including the verb) but the verb appears in its usual form for non-negative independent sentences, and the entire sentence (or that stretch) is in focus. This allows a neat possibility of

20. Thus, from *Amavatura* (12th century) :
mee væni *sihhanadayek* *anekhata* *vanne* *no* *veyi*
This kind lion-voice-INDEF another-DAT be-EMPH not-be-3Sg.
'This kind of a lion voice could not be (i.e., belong) to any other.'

contrast with parallel sentences with *nææ*. Compare, for example, S31 with *novey* with earlier S20 with *nææ* :

(S31) *gunəpaalə gaməṭə giyaa novey*
Gunapala village-DAT go-PAST-SIMPLE *novey*
'It is not the case that Gunapala went to the village
[he did something else]'

Secondly, *nææ* itself has an emphatic form, allowing it to occur as predicator in focused sentences :

(S32) *gunəpaalə giyee nætte gaməṭə*
Gunapala go-PAST-EMPH *nææ*-EMPH village-DAT
'Where Gunapala didn't go was to the village.'

Any of the focus-marking forms may occur with the focused constituent, like *də* in S33, and this includes *novey* as in S34 :

(S33) *gunəpaalə giyee nætte gaməṭə də*
Gunapala go-PAST-EMPH nææ-EMPH village-DAT Q
'Was it to the village that Gunapala didn't go ?'

(S34) *gunəpaalə giyee nætte gaməṭə novey*
Gunapala go-PAST-EMPH *nææ*-EMPH village-DAT *novey*
'It was not to the village that Gunapala didn't go.'

The semantics here, involving differential negation of presupposition and focus, are interesting but must be dealt with elsewhere.

Just as *novey* is etymologically the negative of a copula, so *nææ* is an existential negator, still serving as the suppletive negative for *tiyenəva* 'be, exist (inan.)' and *innəva* 'be, live (anim.)'. This is another striking parallel to Dravidian, in which the same distinction is found, as in Jaffna Tamil *illay* (=*nææ*) and *allay* (=*novey*). Although the morphological material is Indo-Aryan, this is another possible instance of Dravidian influence, though we must proceed with caution here because of other Indo-Aryan parallels.[21] On the other hand, we might wonder whether the Jaffna Tamil preservation of a distinction which seems to be lost in other Tamil dialects is not an instance of reciprocal influence from Sinhala.

Another set of developments, as yet unstudied in detail, has led to a further characteristic of Sinhala focusing system not included in C1-C6; its extension to non-verbal sentences.

Sinhala has a set of tenseless forms showing partial verbal inflection, including EMPH, which have accordingly been called "Quasi-verbs" (Gair

21 The difficulties of reaching definite conclusions as to Dravidian influences underlying the existence of two negatives of this sort have been set forth by B. Lakshmi Bai in her paper at this conference. Also, given the existence of two 'be' verbs and a negative prefix, the likelihood of independent development is quite strong.

1970, p.38). These include *nææ*, *æti* 'might be' and *bææ* 'cannot', and since at least the first two are clearly verb-based etymologically, their inclusion in the system is not surprising.[22]

However, the system has also been extended to adjectives, which do not take EMPH, but appear in focused sentences without the-*yi* which is obligatory for them in predicate position in non-focused sentences (cf. footnote 14). Compare S35 with S36 :

(S35) *adə mee kehelgeḍi honday*
today these bananas good-yi
'These bananas are good today.'

(S36) *adə hondə mee kehelgeḍi*
today good these bananas
'It is these bananas that are good today.'

Adjectival sentences have thus been fully integrated into the system along with verbal ones. For example, the same rules for obligatory focusing with focus markers applies as shown by S38 in comparison with S37 (the absence of *yi* in S37 is accounted for by a separate rule deleting it before *də*—cf. fn. 15).

(S37) *adə mee kehelgeḍi hondə də*
today these bananas good Q
Are these bananas good today?'

(S38) *adə hondə mee kehelgeḍi də*
today good these bananas Q
'Is it these bananas that are good today?'

I have not found equivalents for this extension of focusing constructions in any of the Dravidian languages so far.

There is at least one important characteristic, pertaining to discourse rather than syntax, that differentiates Sinhala focused sentences from those in Tamil at least among the Dravidian languages. It is difficult to define, but might be called a "lower threshold for focus triggering."

That is, the range of situations under which focusing (or clefting) is appropriate is much wider in Sinhala than in Tamil (or than in English for that matter). We might expect as much from what has been said concerning the difference in contrast potentialities between Sinhala and Tamil in relation to some clitics and types of questions, and it stands out very clearly in passages such as the three that follow. They are taken from a

22. *bææ* actually does not inflect with EMPH, but in focused sentence appears as ***bəeri***, which also serves as an adjectival (or relative participle) form. Since it does have participal forms, however, it clearly belongs with the Quasi-verbs, and it is simplest to treat ***bəeri*** in focused sentences as resulting from a spelling-out rule operating on ***bəeəe*** +EMPH or from an equivalent rule.

recent text for Jaffna Tamil for Sinhala speakers (Gair, Suseendirarajah and Karunatilaka 1979), and thus keep both situation and discourse patterns as constant as possible, since they were designed to do so. Focused sentences are marked with (+FOC):

1. Asking a WH-question
   T: *yaalpaaṇattilay atikamaay enna maram irukku?*
   Jaffna-LOC mostly what tree (s) be (PRES-3-NEUT)
   S: (+FOC) *yaapənee vædtpurə monə gas də tiyenne?*
   Jaffna-GEN mostly what trees Q be-PRES-EMPH
   E: In Jaffna, what kind of trees are there mostly?

2. (Another instance of WH)
   T: *avayiTTay eppa colluvinkaL*
   They-REF when say-FUT-2-PL
   S: (+FOC) *eyaalaṭə kavədaadə kiyanne?*
   They-DAT what-day-Q say-PRES-EMPH
   E: When will you tell them?

3. (Yes-No question and reply)
   T: *yaaLpaaNattukku ovvoru naaaLum piLeen*
   Jaffna-DAT every day-EMPH plane(s)
   irukkaa illay. Tiṅkal, putan, veLLi
   be-PRES-3-NEUT-Q No. Monday Wednesday Friday
   kiLamayaLilay mattum piLeen irukku
   day-PL-LOC only plane (s) be-PRES-3-NEUT
   S: *yaapəneetə dawasəgaane aasyaatraa tiyenəva də?*
   Jaffna-DAT daily plane-PL be-PRES-SIMPLE Q
   (+FOC) *nææ, sanduda, badaada, sikuraada vitəray aasyatraa*
   No Monday Wednesday Friday only plane-PL
   tiyenne
   be-PRES-EMPH
   E: Are there planes from here to Jaffna every day?
   No, there are planes only on Monday, Wednesday and Friday.

The foregoing comparison with Dravidian languages shows clearly that while the basic construction may have been the result of cross-language influence, a great deal of internal development took place subsequently. The exact time at which borrowing might have occurred is difficult to determine at present. We have relatively rich documentation for earlier stages of Sinhala going back to at least the second century B.C., but as yet nothing like a comprehensive historical study of syntax based on it. Also, the evidence prior to about 1200 is primarily inscriptional and generally not of such a nature as to include discourse conditions that would invoke the kind of construction we are examining. Such evidence as there is, is often inconclusive or difficult to interpret with confidence. For example, in Sigiri graffiti as early as the eighth century (poetry, but often conversational in tone), sentences with nominal verb forms that are the etymons of our emphatic forms are common (Paranavitana 1956 clxiii) but it is difficult to find clear cases of declarative focused sentences. There are, however, a few examples that appear to be focused WH forms much like modern ones:

(SG1) *ko ja giye himiya yi balam*
where Q (-*də*) go-PAST-NOM lord
siṭiyuyun vanno
COMP looking be- seeming-NOM-PL
NOM-PL -OBL (109, 8th century)
'They seem as if they stood (there) looking backward (wondering) where their lord has gone.'

(SG2) ...*n* [*o*] *balaya yanne kese*
not having look-d go-PRES-NOM how (261, 9th century)
'How does one go away without looking?'

There are also non-focused ones, with non-nominal finite verbs:

(SG3) *sav-abaranin saji giri-hisa siṭihi kumaṭa*
All-ornaments-INST adorned mountain-summit-LOC be. PRES-2sg what-DAT (3, 9th Century)
'Wherefore do you, being adorned with all ornaments, stand on the summit of the rock?'

Difficult as this evidence is to interpret conclusively, it does at least suggest clearly that the construction was present by the time of the graffiti (8th-10th centuries) though functioning less centrally in the grammar than at present.

One of the earliest surviving extended prose texts, Gurulugomi's *Amāvatura* dates from about the twelfth century. (There is, however, some still earlier commentarial material.) That text includes a number of conversational interchanges, and we find what appear to be clear examples of declarative focused sentences. Thus:

(SA1) *sokaśalya buduhu udurāpiyannata nissaha yi*
sorrow-thorns Buddha pluck-out-Nominal-DAT(=INF)
sitannaṭa yæ utsaha upanne (K. Ñ. p. 282)
suitable COMP Thinker-DAT COP effort born-EMPH
'It is to him who thinks 'the Buddha is suitable to pluck out the thorns of sorrow' that effort is born.'

Though the verb form that occurs in sentences like SA1 has been glossed here as EMPH, it clearly retains its nominal character, with both animate and inanimate uses, as shown by SA2 and SA3, in which it clearly occurs as subject:

(SA2) *manaḥ-karma mahatæ yi kiyanne*
mind action important say -EMPH-3SG-Masc-Neut.
nokalakireṇu nam ve (K. Ñ. 53)
not backslide-adj Emphatic Cop-3Sg
'The person who says that the action of the mind is (the) important (thing) will not backslide.'

(SA3) *ovun no sanhinduva baḍu karavuvara*
them-ACC not calmed taxes royal-revenue
ganne daham noveyi (K. Ñ. 103)
take-PRES-EMPH 3SG proper doctrine no-COP-3SG
'It is not proper to take the royal revenue without calming them.'

Thus it is difficult to interpret decisively such sentences as SA4 as either focused or equational, if indeed the distinction is relevant at this period:

(SA4) *vahanse enne saccaka yæ* (K. Ñ. 171)
Sire come-EMPH Saccaka COP
'Sire, Saccaka is coming [or, The one who is coming is Saccaka].'

WH forms are found with and without co-occurrence with *da* (= *də* = Q) as in SA5-SA8. Sentences like SA8 with *də* occuring immediately following the WH form appear to be the exception rather than the rule, making it clear that the modern semi-obligatory focusing of WH does not apply:

(SA5) *koyaṭa giyehi*
where-DAT go-PAST-2 SG (K. Ñ. 136)
'Where did you go?'

(SA1) *mohu koyaṭa yeti*
these (people) where-DAT go-PRES 3Sg (K. Ñ. 189)
'Where are these people going?'

(SA7) *dæn pæviji væ kumaṭa kiyam da*
now ordained been what-DAT say-PRES-1Sg Q (K. Ñ. 76)
'Now that I am a monk why would I say it?'

(SA8) *mese da vaḍane kumata dæ yi kiha*
thus also go what-DAT Q COP say-PAST-3pl(K. Ñ. 145
'Wherefore do you go then? they asked.'

On the basis of this evidence it seems clear that the construction was well established by the time of *Amāvatura* but that the modern system had not yet evolved.[23] Interestingly, except for the possible co-occurrence of

23. Evidence from *Amāvatura* must be interpreted with caution, since the text is an archaizing one largely based on Pali originals (Reynolds 1970 32.33). However, there is no apparent Pali model for focused sentences of the type we are considering. Also there is no obvious Pali model for *də*, and certainly none for its co-occurrence with,

WH and Q, as in SA8, the situation reflected in these examples seems very close to that in Tamil as described earlier, with WH forms occurring both focused and unfocused and the verb form having nominal functions outside of the focusing construction.

The evidence outlined above from Sigiri Graffiti and *Amāvatura* lead to the same conclusion reached by the comparison with Dravidian: The complex modern Sinhala focusing subsystem is the result of a long process of internal development. The precise steps in that development remain to be worked out on the basis of much more textual study, but its general outlines are clear. The focusing construction, once established, was steadily extended in its domain. At the same time, it was, so to speak, regularized so as to subsume that increased domain under an integrated and relatively small set of rules with wide application. It also came to occupy a more central and important place in the overall syntax of the language, by intersecting with an increasing number of grammatical processes. Note that one cannot describe such basic processes as yes-no and WH question formation, negation, or the use of emphatic particles in Sinhala without involving focusing, and at the beginning of this paper I used the phrase "highly visible in the grammar" with that centrality in mind.

The term "adaptation" is commonly used in historical linguistics to describe the alteration of a borrowed form so as to accord more easily with established indigenous structure. Though it is commonly used with reference to phonology, any calque or syntactic borrowing using native material involves the same general process of adaptation in principle, despite the difference in material. The fortunes of the Sinhala focusing construction, which appears to have its origin in borrowing, go far beyond adaptation, however, in that once adapted it was extended and reinterpreted, becoming itself an important factor in further change. For this sort of process I would suggest the term "naturalization", on the analogy of "immigration and naturalization." In these terms, the construction in Sinhala not only immigrated and changed its appearance but went on to become a most important and influential citizen.

WH. Pali influence would thus be looked for in the absence rather than the presence of *də* with WH, but parallel examples were also found in *Sigiri graffiti*. Hence, our conclusions, though limited, seem relatively safe.

REFERENCES

Carter, Rev. Charles. 1924. *A Sinhalese-English dictionary*. New printing, M. D. Gunasena, Colombo, 1965.

Chafe, Wallace L. 1976. Giveness, contrastiveness, definitiveness, subjects, topics, and point of view. *Subject and topic*, ed. by Charles N. Li, 27-55. New York : Academic press.

De Abrew, Kamal K. Forthcoming. *The syntax and semantics of negation in Sinhala.* Cornell University Dissertation.

De Silva, M. W. S. 1979. *Sinhalese and other island languages in South Asia.* Tubingen : Gunter Narr Verlag.

De Zoysa, A. P. 1964. *Dharmasamaya sinhala śabda koṣaya.* 3 Vols. Colombo : Dharmasamaya Press.

Emeneau, Murray. 1956. India as a linguistic area. *Language* 32. 3-16.

Fernando, Madras Siromani. 1973. *The syntax of complex sentences in Sinhalese.* University of London Dissertation.

Gair, James W. 1968. Sinhalese diglossia. *Anthropological linguistics* 10 : 8 1-15.

———. 1970. *Colloquial Sinhalese clause structures.* Mouton : The Hague.

———. 1976. The verb in Sinhala, with some preliminary remarks on Dravidianization. *International Journal of Dravidian Linguistics* 5,2 (June 1976. 259-273.

Gair, James W. and W. S. Karunatilaka. 1974. *Literary Sinhala.* Ithaca, N. Y. : South Asia Program, Cornell University.

Gair, James W., S. Suseendira Rajah and W. S. Karunatilaka. 1979. *Spoken (Sri Lanka Jaffna) Tamil.* Sri Lanka University, Extension Services Press.

Geiger, Wilhelm. 1938. *A grammar of the Sinhalese language.* Colombo : Royal Asiatic Society.

George, K.M. 1971. *Malayalam grammar and reader.* Kottayam, India : National Book Stall.

Gurulugōmi. 1967. *Amāvatura,* ed. by Kōdāgoḍa Ñāṇaloka Sthavirayan Vahanse. Colombo : Gunasena.

Hockett, Charles F. 1958. *A course in modern linguistics.* New York: Macmillan.

Krishnamurti, Bh. 1974. Topicalization/verb inversion transformation. *A generative grammatical sketch of Telugu.* Mimeo.

Lindholm, James M. 1972. Cleft sentences in Tamil and Malayalam. *Proceedings of the First All India Conference of Dravidian Linguists.* ed. by V. I. Subramoniam and Elias Valentine. Trivandrum.

Masica, Colin P. 1976. *Defining a linguistic area : South Asia.* Chicago : University of Chicago Press.

Paranavitana, Senarat. 1956. *Sigiri graffiti.* (2 vols.). Oxford.

Reynolds, C. H. B., ed. 1970. *An anthology of Sinhalese literature up to* 1815. London : George Allen and Unwin.

Schiffman, Harold. 1979. *A reference grammar of Kannada.* Office of Education Report. Washington D. C. : HEW.

THE SYNTAX OF DAKKHINI : A STUDY IN LANGUAGE VARIATION AND LANGUAGE CHANGE*

Yamuna Kachru

1.0. In recent years, studying language variation has become an important aspect of sociolinguistic research as is evident from recent publications such as Fasold and Shuy 1975 and 1977. Another important and related aspect of sociolinguistic research has been the study of pidginization and crealization and the role of these processes in the development of new varieties and/or languages. Several such studies have utilized the data provided by South Asian languages, e.g., Gumperz and Wilson 1977, Southworth 1977. In this study, I would like to discuss the case of Dakkhini which is unique in certain respects. It is possible that Dakkhini went through the stage of intertranslatability as suggested in Gumperz and Wilson 1977 and hence its present syntactic structure. Before discussing the syntax of Dakkhini, it may not be out of place to say something about Dakkhini.[1]

1.1. Dakkhini is a variety of Hindi-Urdu spoken in Andhra Pradesh and other southern states of India. Here I am mainly concerned with the Dakkhini spoken in Hyderabad and adjacent areas of Andhra Pradesh. It is spoken as a first language by the Muslim population of the region, and as a second language by the other communities as well. According to historians and literary scholars, Dakkhini is a transplanted language in that it was brought to the South by the North Indian population that migrated to the South over the centuries. The history of Dakkhini begins after the decision of Muhammad Tughlaq to move his capital from Delhi to Daulatabad (or Deogiri) around 1327 A.D. Daulatabad did not enjoy the status of a capital very long. However, it is believed that when the emperor moved back to Delhi, a large number of people who had arrived in Daulatabad with him found it impossible to return, and settled down in the Deccan. Later, these people and their descendents became parts of the Bahmani kingdom in Gulbarga (established in

---

* I am grateful to the American Institute of Indian Studies for making it possible for me to do the field work in Hyderabad on Dakkhini, and to the Research Board of the Graduate College of the University of Illinois at Urbana-Champaign for providing me with research assistance for the work on Dakkhini.

1. The dates mentioned in this study are based upon the account of Indian history given in Smith 1958. For a discussion of the literary scholars' account of the history of Dakkhini, see Sharma 1972.

1347 A.D.) and the Qutubshahi kingdom in Golkunda (established around 1518 A.D.). It was the Qutubshahi dynasty which encouraged the development of Dakkhini language and literature. From the time of the Bahmanis, the Muslim population in the South had become divided into *mulki*, or native, and *gairmulki* or non-native (Sharma 1972). The *mulki* were proud of their linguistic and literary heritage. They had little knowledge of Arabic or Persian. By the second generation, the non-native population also tended to adopt the language of the native population. The linguistic situation of the area is described by many literary personalities of the period. According to Shah Miraji Shamsul Ushshaq (15th Century), everyone speaks Hindi, no one knows Arabic or Persian.[2] The language in which Ushshaq, Vajahi (1639-1660), Bahri (17-18th Century), Sanati (17-18th Century) and others wrote was referred to as Hindi and Dakkhini. In fact, till the end of the nineteenth century, Dakkhini and Hindi were used to refer to the variety that later became known as Urdu.

Because of the nature of the population that moved to the South and brought Hindi-Urdu with it to the region, scholars have attempted to trace the origin of Dakkhini from not only Khaṛī Bolī Hindi but also Panjabi, Haryani and Bangru. What seems to be clear is that the language spoken around the fourteenth century had certain features of the language and/or dialects that later developed as Panjabi, Haryani and Bangru.

1.2. In the South, Dakkhini came into contact with Marathi, Kannada, and Telugu, probably in that order, as Daulatabad is in Maharastra, Gulbarga is in Karnataka and Golkunda is in Andhra Pradesh. In the language of the literary works of the fifteenth century as well as the current spoken language of Hyderabad, there are many features at all levels that could be traced back to Marathi, Kannada, Telugu, and the other languages mentioned above.[3] I am, however, not concerned here with phonology, morphology and lexicon. I am mainly interested in discussing certain syntactic constructions in Dakkhini which mark it as divergent from the Western (or Standard) and Eastern varieties of Hindi-Urdu. I would like to suggest that the growth of the Dakkhini variety is the result of language contact with Marathi and Dravidian and the subsequent change in language structure that this contract induced. In this connection, I have already discussed the quotative construction in Dakkhini which is almost identical to the quotative construction in Marathi and Dravidian (Kachru 1979). Sentences 1-4 below exemplify the quotative in Dakkhini :

---

2. *we arabii bol naa jaane/ naa phaarsii pachaane*
ye unkũ bacan hiit / sunnat buujhe riit
Shamsul Ushshaq- (15th Century)

zabãã hindawii mujhsũũ hor dehalawii
na jaanũũ arab hor azam masnawii
-Abdal (16th-17th Century)

hindii to zabããc hai hamaarii
-Bahri (18th Century)

3. For example, *nako* as a nagative marker and *-c* as an emphatic marker from Marathi, and *-ãã* as a plural marker from Panjabi.

1. *vo log aaj aate bolke bole.*
Those people today come Qu. said
'They said Qu. they are coming today.'

2. *merii dost biimaar hai bolke maĩ sunii.*
my friend sick is Qu. I heard
'I heard Qu. my friend is sick.'

3. *sab vafaadaar haĩ bolke usko yaxiin hai.*
all honest are Qu. he Dat. belief is
'He believes Qu. all are honest.'

4. *mere bhaaii ku laRkaa huaa bolke mere ku*
my brother Dat. boy happened Qu. me Dat.
Teligraam milaa.
Teligram get
'I got a telegram Qu. my brother had a son.'

The two constructions that I am going to discuss in some detail are the causative and relative clause constructions.

2.0. The causative construction in Standard Hindi-Urdu works as follows. Given a non-causal verb, the first causal is formed by adding a first causal morpheme to the base form of the verb and the second causal is formed by further morphological modifications as in the examples in 5 :[4]

5. H-U

BASE	1ST CAUSAL	2ND CAUSAL
dekh 'see'	*dikhaa*	*dikvaa*
sun 'hear'	*sunaa*	*sunvaa*
hãs 'laugh'	*hãsaa*	*hãsvaa*
bhaag 'run'	*bhagaa*	*bhagvaa*

The syntactic consequence of this morphological process is as follows. If the verb is intransitive, the first causal corresponding to it is transitive, and the second causal is transitive with an additional argument, an initiator agent. The Sentences 6-8 exemplify this :

6. H-U *raaj bhaagaa.*
Raj ran
'Raj ran'.

7. H-U *ratan ne raaj ko bhagaayaa.*
Ratan Ag. Raj DO run caused
'Ratan caused Raj to run (Ratan chased Raj away).

4. The H-U and M prefixed to the examples identify the data from Hindi-Urdu and Marathi respectively. I am grateful to Rajeswari Pandharipande for the information on Marathi.

8. H-U *mãĩ ne ratan se raaj ko bhagvaayaa.*
I Ag. Ratan by raj DO run caused
'I caused Ratan to cause Raj to run (I had Ratən chase Raj away).'

In case the basic verb is 'ingestive' or 'affective', the first causal is double transitive and the second causal takes another additional argument, an initiator agent. The sentences in 9-11 exemplify this :

9. H-U *raaj ne giit siikhaa.*
Raj Ag. song learnt
'Raj learnt the song.'

10. H-U *siimaa ne raaj ko giit sikhaayaa.*
sima Ag. Raj IO song learn caused
'Sima caused Raj to learn the song (Sima taught Raj the song).'

11. H-U *mãĩ ne siima se raaj ko giit sikhvaayaa.*
I Ag. Sima by Raj IO song learn caused
'I caused Sima to cause Raj to learn the song (I had Sima teach the song to Raj).'

In short, causativization results in increasing the valency of the verb by one. Furthermore, the first causal expresses direct causation, the second causal, indirect causation. Neither one has a coercive meaning. Also, the positive causative sentence implies that the caused action, or event, did take place (Kachru 1976).

In Marathi, there are two causal constructions, one non-coercive and the other coercive in meaning as exemplified by 12 and 13 :

12. M *mii tyaacyaakaDuun kaam karavla.*
I he by job do caused
'I had him do the work.'

13. M *mii tyaalaa kaam karaaylaa laavla.*
I he Dat. job do Dat. engaged
'I made him do the work (coercive in meaning).'

Compare the Dakkhini sentences 14-20 with the Marathi examples; Dakkhini seems to have a periphrastic causative with *lagaa* similar to Marathi :

14. *mãĩ naukar se kamraa saaf karne lagvaaii.*
I servant by room clean do engaged
'I had the servant clean the room.'

15. *mãĩ use paise xabuul karne lagvaaungii.*
I him money accept do engage will
'I will make him accept the money.'

16. *vo mujhe iniazaʊr karne nahĩĩ lagvaaegii.*
She me waiting do not engage will
'She will not make me wait.'

17. *vo bacce ko bhaagne lagvaa rae haĩ.*
he child DO run engage ing is (hon.)
'He is making the child run.'

18. *hasan alii se fouziyaa ko paise dene lagvaae.*
Hasan Ali by Fauzia IO money give engaged (hon.)
'Hasan made Ali give Fauzia some money.'

19. *vo mere bhaaii ke zariye dhobii se kapRe dhone lagvaataa hai.*
he my brother by dhobi by clothes wash engages
'He has my brother get the clothes washed by the dhobi.'

20. *alii hasan ke zariye naukar se kamraa saaf karne lagvaayaa.*
Ali Hasan by servant by room clean do engaged
'Ali had Hasan make the servant clean the room.'

This construction does not exist in either standard Hindi-Urdu or the Eastern variety. The semantic distinction that operates in Marathi does not operate in Dakkhini : the construction with *lagaa* is not coercive in meaning. Both the morphological and the periphrastic causatives imply that the initiated agent performed the action or the affected patient underwent the process. The one consistent difference in distribution seems to be that while conjunct verbs participate in the periphrastic construction, the main verb and *kar* 'do' does not. Compare 21/22 with 14-16 above :

21. *vo bacce se bahut kaam karvaatii hai/*karne lagvaatii hai.*
she child by much work do causes do engages
'She makes the child do much work.'

22. *vo mujhse alii kii taariif nahĩĩ karvaayaa/*
he me by Ali of praise not do cause

**karne lagvaayaa.*
do engaged
'He did not make me praise Ali.'

In case of some transitive verbs, the morphological and the periphrastic constructions are in free variation (23-25 below) :

23. *mãĩ dhobii se kapRe dhulvaaii.*
I *dhobi* by clothes wash caused
'I had the *dhobi* wash the clothes.'

24. *mãĩ dhobii ko kapRe dhone lagvaauungii.*
I *dhobi* IO clothes wash engage will
'I will have the *dhobi* wash the clothes.'

25. *mãĩ hameshaa dhobii se kapRe dhulaatii hũũ.*
I always *dhobi* by clothes wash cause
'I always have the *dhobi* wash the clothes.'

The lexical similarity of Dakkhini *lagaa* and Marathi *laav* 'engage' is the first noticeable fact about the construction. At this point, both the morphological and periphrastic constructions seem to be in free variation in Dakkhini. A reasonable assumption is that the periphrastic construction developed in Dakkhini under the 'influence' of Marathi. The absence of semantic specialization suggests either incomplete, or arrested, change. The reasons for this incomplete or arrested development are a matter of speculation at this stage, but, increased contact with the standard varieties may have something to do with it.

3.0 In Standard Hindi-Urdu, there are two strategies of relative clause formation (Kachru 1978). One strategy leads to the correlative type of full relative clause (26 below) and the other to the participial modifier (27 below) :[5]

26. H-U *ve us kaar se kuud paRe jo cal rahii thii.*
They that car from jump fell WH-move ing was
'They jumped from the car that was moving.'

27. H-U *ve caltii huii kaar se kuud paRe.*
they moving car from jump fell
'They jumped from the moving car.'

The full relative clause occurs either preceding or following the main clause or following the NPhd; i. e., these three orders are all possible:

28. (a) Srel – Smain (b) Smain—Srel (c) NPhd—Srel

---

5. The *wh-* and the *C* in the gloss identify the relative and the correlative markers respectively.

the participial modifier, however, must precede the NPhd, There are several restrictions on the occurrence of participial modifiers. However, given a context where both are possible, participials are preferred to full relative clauses. With regard to the order of the full relative clause, in case the NPhd is the subject, the order in 28 (a) is preferred, in case the NPhd is not a subject, the order in 28 (b) is preferred:

In Dravidian languages, full relative clauses are extremely restricted. Typically, participials occur preceding NPhd. As compared to Hindi-Urdu, Marathi has a larger range of participial modifiers similar to Kannada and other Dravidian languages.

Dakkhini exhibits a type of relative clause construction which is closer to participial construction, and also exhibits a marked preference for the order in 28 (a) for all NPhds. Consider the examples in 29-30:

29. *khel rayaa thaa so laRkaa gir gayaa.*
play ing was C boy fall went
'The boy who was playing fell down.'

30. *piyaano bajaa rayaa thaa so laRkaa mere*
Piano Play ing was C boy my
bhaaii kaa dost hai.
brother of friend is
'The boy who was playing the piano is my brother's friend.'

Notice the participial forms in 31-32, and compare the order of Srel and Smain in 33-35 and 36-42:

31. *piyaano bajaataa huaa laRkaa.*
Piano play ing boy
'The piano playing boy.'

32. *piano bajaanevaalaa laRkaa*
piano player boy
'The boy who plays piano regularly (in H-U, could mean the same as 30).'

33. *aap khariide so ghar mere kuu pasand hai.*
you bought C house me Dat. liking is
'I like the house you bought.'

34. H-U *mujhe vah makaan pasand hai jo aapne*
me C house liking is Wh- you Ag.
xariidaa hai.
bought have
'I like the house you have bought.'

35. H-U *aapne jo makaan xariidaa hai vah mujhe*
you Ag. *Wh-* house bought have C me

pasand hai.
liking is
'I like the house you have bought.'

36. *baRe kamre mẽ thaa so mez par vo kitaabãã*
big room in was *C* table on he books
rakh diyaa.
put gave
'He put the books on the table which was in the big room.'

37. *baRe kamrevaale mez par*
big room one table on
'The table in the big room.'

38. H-U *usne us mez par kitaabẽ rakh dĩĩ jo baRe*
he Ag. *C* table on books put gave wh- big
kamre mẽ thii.
room in was
'He put the books on the table which was in the big room.'

39. H-U *usne baRe kamrevaalii mez par kitaabẽ rakh dĩĩ.*
he Ag. big room one table on books put gave
'He put the books on the table in the big room.'

40. *jitte kitaabãã tum diye the utte mãĩ*
as many books you given had that many I
vaapas kar dii.
return do gave
'I returned all the books you gave me.'

41. H-U *mãĩ ne ve sabhii kitaabẽ vaapas kar dĩĩ*
I Ag. *C* all emph. books return do gave
jo tumne dii thĩĩ.
wh- yoy Ag. given had
'I returned all the books you gave me.'

42. H-U *jitnii bhii kitaabẽ tumne dii thĩĩ mãĩ*
as many emph. books you Ag. given had I
ne vaapas kar dĩĩ.
Ag. return do gave
'I returned whatever books you gave me.'

Notice the strong tendency to front the focussed element in Dakkhini as opposed to other varieties of Hindi-Urdu; consider 43-45:

43. *jitte bhii kitaabãã tum diye the mãĩ vaapas*
as many emph. books you given had I return

kar *dii.*
do gave
'I returned whatever books you gave me.'

44. *tumhaare ko dekhne kaun aayaa thaa bolo.*
you DO see who came had tell
'Tell me who came to see you.'

45. H-U *bataao ki tumse milne kaun aayaa thaa.*
tell that you with meet who came had
'Tell me who came to see you'.

Also, note the absence of the ergative construction and its effect on grammatical gender in Dakkhini. The absence of the relative marker is alse noticeable. The total effect of the construction is very similar to the participial modifier construction in Dravidian languages.

4.0. In this preliminary study, I have presented some data from Dakkhini to show that the syntax of this variety differs significantly from the syntax of the standard and eastern varieties. I have also suggested that this variation is due to contact with Marathi and Dravidian. A more detailed study of Dakkhini may be of great interest to linguists working in the area of language contact and language change. Dakkhini is unique in that it has an unbroken literary tradition of over four centuries.

REFERENCES

Fasold, Ralph W. and Roger Shuy. 1975. *Analyzing variation in language.* Washington D. C. : Georgetown University Press.

Fosold, Ralph W. and Roger Shuy. 1977. *Studies in language variation.* Washington D. C. : Georgetown University Press.

Gumperz, John J. and Robert Wilson. 1977. Convergence and creolization: A case from the Indo-Aryan/Dravidian border. In Hymes 1977, 151-168.

Hymes, Dell. 1977. *Pidginization and creolization of language.* Cambridge University Press.

Kachru, Yamuna. 1976. On the semantics of the causative construction in Hindi-Urdu. *The grammer of causative construction: syntax and semantics* 6, ed. by M. Shibatani. Academic Press. 353-369.

Kachru, Yamuna. 1978. On relative clause formation in Hindi-Urdu. *Linguistics* 207, 5-26.

Kachru, Yamuna. 1979. The quotative in South Asian languages. *SALA* 63-79.

Smith, Vincent A. 1958. *The Oxford history of India.* Third Edition, ed. by Percival Spear. Oxford University Press.

Sharma, Sriram. 1972. *Dakkhinī hindī kā sāhitya.* Hyderabad: Dakshina Prakashan.

Southworth, Franklin C. 1977. Detecting prior creolization: An analysis of the historical origin of Marathi. In Hymes 1977, 255-274.

KAMTI TAI : FROM AN SVO TO AN SOV LANGUAGE*

Wilaiwan Kanittanan

Kamti is a Tai dialect spoken by minority groups in Assam and Arunachal Pradesh in India, and in Burma. It belongs to the Tai family which is spoken by over 50 million people in South East Asia, India and China.[1]

In the past, the language has been reported on in Grierson's Linguistic Survey of India (1904) and in a monograph by Needham (1893), intended as a handbook for learning the language. Its lexicon and phonology more recently have been studied by Alfons Weidert 1977 and Jimmy G. Harris 1976. This paper is based on field work conducted by the author over the past 4 years.

Kamti is of special interest because, while other languages of the Tai family exhibit a dominant word order of Subject-verb-object (SVO), it shows a dominant order of Subject-Object-Verb (SOV). It is this aspect of Kamti grammar that is the subject of this paper.

Greenberg 1966 lists a set of characteristics that are common to SOV languages as a type. Of these Kamti exhibits the following :

1. It does not put interrogative words or phrases first in interrogative questions.
2. In comparison, the word order is Standard-Marker-Adjective.
3. It has OSV as the alternative basic order.

These are illustrated in the following sample sentences.

5 2 6 5 1
1. *məəu paa neʔ laa naa*
you fish this want question particle
'Do you want this fish?'

5 1 1 6 2 2 2
2. *khan-wii-hoo neʔ khəə-ləu neu*
comb this how much
'How much is this comb ?'

1 2 4 2 5
3. *khau kau+mai khen mii*
They I obj. marker more rich
'They are richer than I.'

---

*This research was supported by a grant from the Ford Foundation.

1. I would like to thank Dr. John Grima for reading an earlier draft of this paper and offering many valuable suggestions. All remaining errors and problems are the responsibility of the author.

5 5 5 4 2 1
4. *mee man- man+mai khen sɛɛn*
She mother she obj.marker more beautiful
'She is more beautiful than her mother.'

In the normal course of speaking, sentences with nominal subject and object are arranged in the order of SOV as in the following sentences.

5 1 1 6 2 1 6
5. *man wan-phan neʔ ʔau-phee yɔʔ*
He glass the to break past tense particle
'He broke the glass.'

2 5 4 3 1 3 6
6. *kau man+mai khau–saan həu yɔʔ*
I he object marker rice to giver past tense particle
'I gave her rice.'

5 1 6 1 2 2
7. *man wɛ́ɛn neʔ thuk–cəu ɔɔʔ*
She bracelet the to like question particle
'Does she like the bracelet ?'

2 5 4 1 6
8. *kau man-mai han yɔʔ*
I he obj. marker to see past tense particle
'I saw him.'

In the event that the speaker wants to emphasize the nominal object, it can be topicalized and moved to the front of the sentence. Thus the four sentences above can appear in the order of OSV as the following.

1 1 6 5 2 1 6
9. *wan–phan neʔ man ʔau–phee yɔʔ*
glass the he to breeak past tense particle

5 4 2 3 1 3 5
10. *man+mai kau khau-saan həu yɔʔ*
He obj.marker I rice give past tense particle

1 6 5 1 2 2
11. *wɛɛn neʔ man thuk–cəu ʔɔɔ*
bracelet the she to like question particle

5 4 2 1 2
12. *man+mai kau han yɔʔ*
He obj. marker I to see past tense particle

Note that the first Kamti verb final characteristic is also shared by other Tai dialects, which have SVO as the dominant order. And though other Tai dialects out of India do not have OSV as an alternative basic order, it is not an impossible word order. Standard Thai or Siamese has the dominant word order of SVO and OSV is possible with a restrictive rule, i.e. this word order can occur only when "O" or object is definite or specified.

For example :

SIAMESE

13. *bâan lǎŋ níi khǎu ʔɔ̀ɔk-bὲɛp*
house classifer this he to design
'He designed this house.'

14. *bòt – khwaam níi khǎu khǐan*
article this he to write
'He wrote this article.'

15. **bâan lǎai lǎŋ khǎu ʔɔ̀ɔk – bὲɛp*
house many classifier he to design
'*He designed several houses.'
(This sentence is not grammatical.)

The normal version of sentences 13 and 14 are :

16. *khǎu ʔɔ̀ɔk – bὲɛp baân lǎŋ níi*
he to design house classifier this
S V O

17. *khǎu khiǎn bòt—khwàam níi*
he to write article this
S V O

Another dialect, Phake Tai, which is also spoken in Assam, India, also has OSV as the alternative basic order, but its dominant order is S V O. This dialect is mutually intelligible with Kamti Tai. Sentences 5 to 8 are expressed in Phake Tai as the following.

18. *myn ʔau – luu kaa kauk nεʔ*
he to break past tense part. glass the

19. *kau həəu kaa khau—saan hyŋ myn*
I to give past tense particle rice to him

20. *myn wεέn nεʔ thuk-cəəu*
he bracelet the to like question particle

21. *kau han kaa hyŋ myn*
I to see past obj.marker he

When the nominal object is topicalized, it can be moved to the front of the sentence as the following.

22. *kauk nεʔ myn ʔau – luu kaa*

23. *hyŋ myn kau həəu kaa khau – saan*

24. *wεεn nεʔ myn thuk – cəəu*

25. *hyŋ myn kau han kaa*

4
Kamti has *mai*, postpositional with respect to the noun, as its object marker. Phake has *hyŋ*, a preposition. Both have the alternative object
6
markers *neʔ* and *nɛ̆ʔ* (in Kamti and Phake respectively) both occurring
6
after the noun. In Kamti, if *neʔ* is used to mark the object, then *mai* does not occur. Fhr example.

```
      5    4        6    2    5        6
26.   man  nam–ciʔ  neʔ  ʔau–maa       yɔʔ
      He   milk     the  to bring      past tense particle
      'He brought the milk.'

      3       2    3          6    5      2
27.   mee     kau  sin        neʔ  too    kaa
      mother  I    a piece    the  weave  past tense particle
                   of garment
      'My mother wove this.'
```

6
neʔ has the meanings of 'the' and 'this' which is about the same as *níi*, a determiner in Siamese. The same is true of *nɛ* inʔ Phake. *mai*[4] when it occurs as an adverb means 'here'. All this points to the fact that object postposition markers in Kamti are specifiers. In other words they indicate whether the object is specified or definite. Specifiers of this sort occur in postnominal position in Siamese and all Tai languages and not these are postpositions in the accepted sense of that term.

We must note, however, that the fact that these markers occur in Kamti only in SOV sentences is special and marks them as different from ordinary nominal specifiers or demonstratives. There is no restriction on the occurrence of postnominal demonstratives in Siamese, or, as far as I know, in any other Tai language, in SVO sentences.

4
We can then suggest that Kamti does have a set of postposition *mai*
6
and *neʔ*. These occur as object markers in SOV sentences. This shift in
4 6
in status of *mai* and *neʔ* from simple specifiers to postpositions is a development that must have started at the same time as the switch to the dominant order of SOV.

J. F. Needham's samples of Kamti sentences both in his book, *Outline of the Tai (Khamti) Language*, published in 1893, and in G. A. Grierson's *Linguistic Survey of India* show that the state of the language was much the same about one hundred years ago as it is now. That is, SOV was the dominant word order, and SVO was only sporadically used.

Greenberg refers to Kamti in his book *Universals of language* and lists it as an SOV language. He also classifies it as a prepositional language and thus as an exception to general SOV language patterning, in which postpositions are the norm. It is true that prepositions predominate.

However, as we have seen, the language has already developed two post-
4 6
positions—*mai* and *ne*. These two object markers are used extensively in the language.

Aside from not being a rigidly postpositional language, Kamti has another characteristic which is common in SVO languages but rare in SOV languages. That is, the relative clause which modifies a noun follows the noun it modifies. For example :

	5	2	2	1
28.	*həə*	*ʔan*	*kau*	*khaai*
	boat	which	I	sell

	3	2	6
29.	*səə*	*ʔan*	*tin*
	shirt	which	to be torn

Conclusion : It has been shown that SOV is the dominant word order in Kamti while in other known Tai dialects SOV is the dominant one. We may conclude that SVO is the older dominant word order in the Tai family and that Kamti has developed from SVO to SOV. It has also been shown that Kamti contains a set of object marking postpositions.

The traces which show that Kamti is a "new" SOV dominant language are characteristics that are also common among SVO languages. Moreover, it lacks certain characteristics which are common among SOV languages.

REFERENCES

Cornyn, S. William and D. Haigh Roop. 1968. *Beginning Burmese*. New Haven : Yale University Press.

Greenberg, Joseph H. ed. 1966. *Universals of language*. Cambridge (Mass.) : The M. I. T. Press.

Gogoi, Lila. ed. 1971. *The Tai Khamtis*. Chowkham, NE FA.

Grierson, G. A. 1904. *Linguistic survey of India*, Vol. II. Mon-Khmer & Siamese-Chinese families. (Motilal Banarsi Dass, Delhi).

Needham, J. F. 1893. *Outline grammar of the Tai (Khamti)*. Rangoon.

Weidert, Alfons, 1977. *Tai-Khamti phonology and vocabulary*. Wiesbaden : Franz Steiner Verlag.

Gething. Thomas Harris, G. Jimmy Rullavinich, Pranee (ed.). 1976. Phonetic notes on Tai Khamti, *Tai linguistics in honor of Fang Kuei Ld.*

SEMANTIC PARAMETERS AND THE SOUTH ASIAN LINGUISTIC AREA*

M. H. Klaiman

The South Asian linguistic area is widely discussed, but investigation tends to be limited to formal or structural similarities.[1] Conceptual similarities—similarities in semantic structure—are less frequently discussed.[2] One paper to broach thc subject is Verma 1976, in which it has been argued "that 'stativeness' is a fundamental entity of the conceptual structure of Indic languages...which is involved in many structural relations and contrasts, and is (systematically) sought to be expressed through certain structural devices typical of South Asian languages", among which Verma includes "the compound verb, the verbal series based on transitivity, the passive, the indirect subject construction, and to some extent, also a class of participial modifiers..." (Verma 1976: 1). In other words, for some Indic languages, Verma sees such formal distinctions as intranstive/transitive, noncompound/compound verb, and others, as (at least to some extent) expressions of a semantic opposition stative/non-stative. Such a semantic opposition, which obtains expression at the overt level of language structure I shall hereafter refer to as a linguistically significant semantic PARAMETER. My intention in the present paper is to amplify the case for the thesis

---

* I would like to express my appreciation to the sponsors of the Second International Conference on South Asian Languages and Linguistics (Hyderabad, India, January 9-11, 1980) for giving me the opportunity to read this papar before a distinguished audience. For financial, academic, and/or moral assistance I am also grateful to all of the following : the American Institute of Indian Studies, the Indian Institute of Advanced Study in Simla, Pritilata Ghose, Dr. Pabitra Sarkar, Dr. Suhas Chatterjee, Udaya Narayan Singh, Probal Dasgupta, Dr. Omkar N. Kaul, Dr. Peter Hook, Dr. Rafiqul Islam, Dr. Sukumar Sen, Dr. S. K. Upadhyaya, Dr. Norman Zide, Dr. Colin Masica, Dr. Bettchen Barber, and M.M. Sathe. I alone am responsible for errors and other infelicities. The following abbreviations may be noted : cond=conditional, c.p.=conjunctive participle, impv=imperative, Inf=infinitive, G=genitive case, L=locative case, N=nominative case, O=objective case, obj=object—marking postposition, ptc=particle.

1. For instance, Masica's 1976 study of the South Asian linguistic area concentrates on certain formal features, such as word order, presence/absence of causative verbal forms, conjunctive participles, etc. Likewise, the papers in Southworth and Apte 1974, a volume devoted to contact and convergence in South Asia, tend to be concerned mainly with formal manifestations of convergence.

2. For instance, Southworth 1974 : 209 mentions the possibility of semantic convergence in only one paragraph, in which he cites a single example of the sharing of a feature by Dravidian languages and Marathi, namely, the exclusive/inclusive distinction in first person plural pronouns.

that characteristic similarities among South Asian languages at the formal level may be attributable to the sharing of semantic parameters at the conceptual level.

But before the possibility can be convincingly supported that South Asian languages share some degree of conceptual structuring, it must be demonstrated for an adequate number of individual languages that some surface structures express semantic parameters. An obvious heuristic consideration is the identification of semantic oppositions which are most likely to acquire the status of parameters. For South Asian languages, Verma 1976 has already proposed the stative/non-stative opposition. In this paper I should like to suggest and discuss two more oppositions. One of these, the affective/effective parameter, will be discussed later on for the purpose of illustrating cross-linguistic parameter sharing. For the moment I shall merely attempt to support the validity of the notion PARAMETER by demonstrating the significance of a specific parameter in an individual language. The language is modern standard colloquial Bengali; the problem involves the formal distinction between dative/direct subject constructions; the parameter which, I shall argue, is expressed by this distinction is the opposition NON-VOLITIONAL/VOLITIONAL; and the data is taken from my dissertation (Klaiman 1979).

In modern standard colloquial Bengali, so called dative subject constructions are extremely common.[3] They are formally distinguished from the more typical direct subject constructions of the language by certain features. These features include : (a) The marking of the subject (or experiencer) in an oblique case, specifically, the genitive; (b) The nearly absolute or categorical tendency for the finite verb of such constructions to be impersonal (i.e., absence of verbal agreement); and (c) The tendency of these constructions to express certain kinds of activity to the exclusion of others.

To amplify on the last, the semantic range of dative subject predicates in Bengali appears to be distributed among the following six semantic categories :[4]

(1) a. Sensory and Mental Experiences (e.g. "think", "be aware")
b. Emotional Experiences (e.g. "be angry", "like/love")
c. Physical and Biological Experiences (e.g. "be hungry", "hurt")
d. Need/Duty/Obligation (e.g. "need/want", "be proper")
e. Possession/Existence (e.g. "suffice")
f. Happenstance (e.g. "profit", "benefit")

3. *Pace* Masica 1976 : "...a high development of this feature is characteristic of India—perhaps slightly more of Dravidian and slightly less of Bengali..." I suspect Masica may have underestimated the strength of this feature in Bengali.

4. These categories are due to N. McCawley 1976. In Klaiman 1979, a number of Bengali dative subject predicates are listed according to their distribution among these six categories; the listing is only for the purpose of illustration and is not exhaustive.

The following contrastive pair illustrates the usual formal differences between dative and direct subject constructions, respectively :

(2) a. *aamaar anek laabh hoyeche*
my much profit has-become
'I have profitted a lot'

b. *aami anek laabh korechi*
I much profit hove-done
'I have profitted a lot'

In (a) the experiencer subject appears in the genitive case and fails to elicit verbal agreement, while in (b), the experiencer subject takes the direct or nominative case and the verb agrees with it. The two expressions, (a) and (b), are formally and semantically related; they may be described as dative and direct counterparts.

Moreover, example (2) illustrates that most Bengali dative subject predicates and their direct counterparts are complex, consisting of a nonfinite component (such as *laabh*, 'profit', in (2) plus a finite verb. Dative and direct counterparts are usually distinguished by the shape of the finite component, the typical instance being illustrated in (2), in which the finite verb of the dative subject predicate (2a) is an existential verb such as 'become', while that of its direct counterpart (2b) is the verb 'do/make'.

In Bengali, not all, but a great many dative subject predicates have direct counterparts.[5] It is therefore natural to ask why the language needs both types of constructions. In (2), for instance, it appears as if the sentence has the same meaning regardless of whether the speaker selects the dative or the direct counterpart. If one can say the same thing with a direct subject construction, why complicate the grammar with a class of formally idiosyncratic dative subject constructions ?

The answer is that sameness just spoken of is illusory. Dative and direct counterparts, in fact, cannot be interchanged in all contexts. For instance, compare (2) with (3) :

(3) a. *raadhaakrisner bhaagobot gitaa pore aamaar anek*
Radhakrishnan-G Bhagavat Gita read-c.p. my much
laabh hoyeche
profit has-become
'I have profitted greatly by reading Radhakrishnan's *Bhagavat Gita*'

b. **raadhaakrisner bhaagobot gitaa pore aami anek*
Radhakrishnan- G Bhagavat Gita read-c.p. I much
laabh korechi
profit have-done

Many more contextually-conditioned contrasts between dative and direct counterparts can be illustrated (some will be seen below). In examining a large number of such contrasts one can observe a definite pattern, the basis for which appears to have to do with the semantic notion of VOLITIONALITY. That is, it seems that Bengali speakers select the dative subject

5. Of the sixty-odd dative subject predicates listed in Klaiman 1979 (see last footnote), about two-thirds have direct counterparts.

counterpart when an activity is to spoken of as NONVOLITIONAL, while the direct subject counterpart is selected when the activity is to be spoken of as VOLITIONAL. The evidence for this generalization is of several types

First of all, the six categories of activity listed in (1), which represent the semantic range of Bengali dative subject predicateṣ, all pertain exclusively to HUMAN actors or experincers. This is compatible with the volitionality hypothesis since, in most contexts of speaking, nonhumans are not credited with the attribute of conscious choice.

Secondly, volitionality seems to be implicated in differences between the glosses of some dative and direct counterparts, e.g. :

(4)

	DATIVE COUNTERPART	GLOSS	DIRECT COUNTERPART	GLOSS
a.	*buddhi aa-*	'to get an idea'	*buddhi kar-*	'to plan'
b.	*dhoirjo aạch-*	'to be patient'	*dhoirjo dhar-*	'to maintain patience
c.	*majaa laag-*	'to be amused'	*majaa paa-*	'to have fun'
d.	*sojjho ha-*	'to tolerate physically'	*sojjho kar-*	'to put up with'
e.	*casi*	'to need'	*caa-*	'to want'
f.	*cal-*	'to suffice'	*calaa-*	'to make do'
g.	*dos ha-*	'to be at fault'	*dos kar*	'to transgress'

A third type of evidence is the distribution of direct subject counterparts among the six categories in (1). According to my data, in other words, the tendency of dative subject predicates to have direct counterparts varies from category to category. In the second category, Emotional Experiences, it is greater than in the third, Physical and Biological Experiences. This can be related to the real world fact that bodily functions are often involuntary, while conscious control can usually be brought to bear on human emotions. Similarly, comparing the first category (Sensory and Mental Experiences) with the fourth (Need/Duty/Obligation), one notes relatively more direct counterparts in the former. This may be because the notions need/duty/obligation suggest a lack of volitional control, while the notions of sensory and mental experience suggest the possibility of volitional intervention, i.e., one can usually tune in or tune out one's mental processes.

All the above types of evidence are encouraging, but a fully convincing case for the volitionality hypothesis depends on the contrastive behavior of dative and direct subject predicates. Although I am reproducing only some of the evidence here,[6] I believe it will be sufficient for my audience to judge the merits of the case.

EXHIBIT A. Consider the Bengali predicate "to snore". It behaves either as a dative or direct subject predicate without alteration of its shape (as usually distinguishes dative predicates and their direct counterparts):

6. For additional evidence and discussion, see Klaiman 1979.

(5) a. *taar naak ḍaake* b. *se naak ḍaake*
his nose calls he nose calls
'He snores'

The dative and direct counterparts of "snore" are not, however, interchangeable. Only the direct counterpart is possible when a deliberate (volitional) act of snoring is expressed, as :

(6) a. **taar ḍhaṅ kore naak ḍaakchilo* 'He was faking a snore (i.e.,
his pose do-c.p. nose was-calling pretending to be asleep)'

b. *se ḍhaṅ kore naak ḍaakchilo* 'do'
he pose do-c.p. nose was-calling

The contrast in (6) suggests that volitionality plays some role.

EXHIBIT B. With adverbials expressing volition, only direct counterparts can co-occur; dative counterparts are excluded. Although many examples could be given, I shall illustrate with just one : the verb "to conceive", which has both dative and direct counterparts :

(7) a. *aamerikaar film dekhe cheleder anek bhul dhaaronaa hay*
America-G film see-c.p. boys-G many wrong conception becomes
'Boys get a lot of misconceptions from watching American films'

b. *aamerikaar film dekhe cheleraa anek bhul dhaaronaa kare*
boys-N do
'do'

In the context of such an adverbial as *icchaa kore* 'deliberately', only the direct counterpart is possible :

(8) a. **tomaar icchaa kore aamaar sambondhe bhul dhaaronaa hocche*
your deliberately my about wrong conception is-becoming
'You're deliberately misconstruing me'

b. *tumi icchaa kore aamaar sambondhe bhul dhaaronaa korcho*
you are-doing
'do'

EXHIBIT C. Direct but not dative subject counterparts occur in commands :

(9) a. **tomaar onusoconaa hok*! b. (*tumi*) *onusoconaa karo* !
your repentence become-impv. you repentence do-impv.
'Repent'

To be sure, a dative subject predicate can occur in the so called imperative form :

(10) *aami caai, tomaar onusoconaa hok* 'I want you to repent'
I want your repentence become-impv.

But a sentence such as this is not a command; it is a wish.

Commanding by its very nature presupposes the addressee's ability to choose to act or not to act on the speaker's request. This is why commands are normally addressed only to humans and to the more intelligent species of animals and not to inanimate objects. Given that a command presupposes the addressee's faculty of volition, the fact that dative subject constructions cannot occur as commands suggests that dative subjects are semantically nonvolitional.

EXHIBIT D. So far, in Exhibits A-C, we have only seen instances in which the dative counterpart is unacceptable and the direct counterpart, acceptable. As example (3) earlier illustrated, however, the reverse is sometimes the case.

For instance, there are occasions when it is appropriate to represent the subject as the unwilling prisoner of his impulses, as a victim of circumstances. In such a context, a dative subject predicate may be preferred over its direct counterpart, e.g. :

(11) a. *misṭi dekhle aamaar lobh hay* 'When I see sweets, I feel
sweet see-cond my greed becomes tempted'
b. **misṭi dekhle aami lobh kori* 'do'
I greed do

Here (b) is strange because it places the speaker in the position of confessing himself a willful glutton. (a), however, allows the speaker to make the same confession with the face-saving nuance of helplessness.

A dative subject predicate may also be preferred in a context in which the nuance of volitionality conveyed by the direct counterpart would give an absurd reading. Compare the examples in (12) :

(12) a. *taar paa bhaaṅglo* b. *?se paa bhaaṅglo*
his leg broke he leg broke
'He broke his leg'

(a) is a more natural utterance in usual contexts of speaking. (b) implies that the subject deliberately broke his own leg, which is an absurd reading in most contexts.[7] In this example it appears that the dative counterpart is preferred in order to avoid the nuance of deliberateness. This hypothesis finds confirmation in an example of the reverse sort, such as (13) :[8]

(13) a. *?taar upos bhaaṅglo* b. *se upos bhaaṅglo*
his fast broke he fast broke
'He broke his fast'

Unlike leg-breaking, which tends to be a nonvolitional activity, breaking a fast tends to be a volitional activity. (13a) is possible in a context in

7. On the other hand, if one wished to describe a situation in which an individual for some reason deliberately broke his own leg, then (b) would be preferred and (a) would become inappropriate.

8. I owe this insightful example to Udaya Narayana Singh (personal communcation).

which a fasting person is force-fed. In usual contexts of speaking, (13b) is more natural. A comparison of (12) and (13) suggests that volitionality is the parameter according to which speakers choose between native and direct counterparts.

EXHIBIT E. Direct subject constructions can passivize in Bengali, while dative subject constructions cannot. The reason is that passive in Bengali (as in Hindi; see Pandharipande 1978) makes crucial reference to the semantic notion of volitionality. The proof necessarily involves some discussion of Bengali passivization. (The discussion is given in the briefest possible terms here; for further details about Bengali passives see Klaiman 1979.)

Bengali has two passives : an impersonal passive, whose characteristic is the finite verb *jaa*-'go'; and a passive which occurs both personally and impersonally (depending on factors which will not be discussed here; see Klaiman 1979 for details), and whose characteristic is the finite verb *ha*- 'become'.[9] Both passives entail clause nominalization, followed by assignment of one of the matrix verbs just mentioned. Examples of the *jaa*- and *ha*- passives are respectively :

(14) a. *aekṭaa khabor praayi khaborer kaagoje daekhaa jaacche*
one news very often news-G paper-L seeing is-going
'One piece of news is very frequently seen in the newspaper'
(from *Jugantor* newspaper, 10 April, 1979)

b. *aamerikaay iṅreji balaa hay*
America-L English speaking becomes
'In America, English is spoken'

Passive as applied to direct subject counterparts is illustrated in the a-examples of (15), (16), while passive as applied (infelicitously) to dative subject counterparts is illustrated in the b-examples :

(15) a. *alpo kheṭe anek laabh karaa jaabe* (cf. ex. 2b)
less labour-c.p. much profit doing will-go
'A lot of profit can be made without working hard'

b. **alpo kheṭe anek laabh haoaa jaabe* (cf. ex. 2a)
less labour-c.p. much profit becoming will-go
'do'

(16) a. *alpo kheṭe tomaar anek laabh karaa habe*
less labor-c.p. your much profit doing will-become
'You'll make a lot of profit without working hard'

9. Udaya Narayana Singh has mentioned (personal communication) the possibility of a minor third passive construction. It is formally similar to the *ha*-passive, but differs in two ways : (1) its matrix verb is not *ha*-'become' but *aach* 'exist' and (2) it expresses already completed action, e.g. *otaa aamaar deekhaa aache* 'I've already seen that'.

b. **alpo kheṭe tomaar anek laabh haoaa habe*
less labor-c.p. your much profit becoming will-become
'do'

Here only a few examples have been given (for others, see Klaiman 1979) to show that in Bengali, passive can apply to direct but not to dative subject counterparts. One could try to account for this on formal grounds, e.g. by writing an appropriate structural description (SD) into the rule for passive. However, such a solution would fail to account for other types of sentences the passives of which block in Bengali.

For instance, the passive blocks for a sentence whose subject has a nonhuman referent. Just one among many examples which could be given to illustrate this is :

(17) a. *tinṭe naa chaaṛle aamaar samoymoto pouchono hoto naa*
3 o'clock not leave-cond my on-time arriving would-become not
'If I hadn't left at three o'clock, I could not have arrived on time'

b. **tinṭe naa chaaṭle gaaṛiṭaar samoymoto pouchono*
3 o'clock not leave-cond the train-G on-time arriving
hoto naa
would-become not
'If it hand't left at three o'clock, the train could not have arrived on time'

Examples like (17) recall the observation made earlier in this paper that volitionality is primarily an attribute of humans. It is interesting to note that a passive sentence blocks in Bengali even if the subject has a human referent when the predicate expresses a NONVOLITIONAL activity. Here are several illustrations :

(18) *uṛo jaahaajer jaanlaagulo kholaa jaay naa, sutoraañ*
airplane-G windows opening goes not therefore

a. *jaanlaa diye paṛaar bhay nei*
window through falling-G fear is-not

b. *jaanlaa diye poṛte paaren naa*
window through fall-inf you-can not

c. **jaanlaa diye paṛaa jaay naa*
window through falling goes not

'The windows in an airplane cannot be opend, hence
a. one need have no fear of falling out a window'
b. you cannot fall out a window'
c. it is impossible to fall out a window'

(19) a. *omuker boi haariyeche* 'So-and-so has lost his book'
so-and-so-G book has-gotten-lost

b. **omuker boi haaraano hoyeche* 'do'
so-and-so-G book losing has-become

(20) a. *maar khaaoaar par se tin din maatro bãaclo*
beating eating-G after he 3 day only survived
'After taking the beating he only survived three days'
b. **maar khaaoaar par taar tin din maatro bãacaa holo*
his 3 day only surviving became
'do'

(21) a. *omuk ei maatro maaraa giyeche* 'So-and-so just died'
so-and-so just now has-died
b. **omuker ei maatro marao hoyeche* 'do'
so-and-so-G just now dying has-become

It is interesting to compare example (21), which expresses an act of dying, with example (22), which expresses a VOLITIONAL act of dying (i.e. suicide) :

(22) *aattohattaa karaar jonno aeksoṭaa ghumer osudh khelaam, kintu*
suicide doing-G for a hundred sleeping medicine I-ate but
aamaar maraa holo naa, kaaron, ḍaaktaarraa aamaake bããciye tullo
my dying became not because doctors me-O saved
'I took a hundred sleeping pills in order to commit suicide; but I did not die, because the doctors saved me'

In (21) passive blocks, in (22) it does not block. The contrast between the two examples provides especially clear evidence that the passive in Bengali applies only to sentences in which volitional activity is expressed. Given this much, the failure of dative subject constructions to passivize suggests that which has been argued all along, namely, that dative subject constructions express nonvolitional activity and direct subject constructions, volitional activity.

In Exhibits A-E, I have provided several types of evidence for the claim that the formal distinction in Bengali between dative and direct subject constructions is matched at the semantic level by the opposition NON-VOLITIONAL/VOLITIONAL. My purpose has been to illustrate what a semantic parameter is and how it is expressed. This instance should immediately suggest the possibility of cross-linguistic parameter sharing, for an obvious reason: dative-type constructions are typical not only of Bengali but of South Asian languages in general, irrespective of genetic affiliation (Masica 1976). If in one South Asian language (such as Bengali) the presence of this common characteristic can be attributed to a particular semantic parameter, then the possibility may well be pursued that the parameter itself is common to South Asian languages, which is to say, that South Asian languages share some degree of conceptual structuring.

Let us leave the nonvolitional/volitional parameter and consider some evidence for cross-linguistic sharing of another semantic parameter. In the following discussion (taken from Klaiman to appear), the parameter in question is the opposition AFFECTIVE/EFFECTIVE, which to my knowledge was first raised by A.R.K. Zide 1971 in connection with a Munda language, Gorum. The relevance of this opposition for Tamil has also been ably argued for in a dissertation by Paramasivam 1979.

Both writers use the term 'affective', to refer to an action which primarily bears on, or affects, its subject; the term 'effective' refers to an action which does not primarily bear on or affect the subject.[10]

There may be some natural basis to this distinction. It has been claimed for instance, by Barber 1975, that what amounts approximately to the same opposition, effectivity vs. affectivity, is responsible for a well known grammatical phenomenon in Indo-European : the active/middle distinction in verbal inflection (grammatical voice).[11]

What I wish to suggest is that the same parameter may account for a formal peculiarity of causative constructions in Indic languages, especially Hindi (see discussion in Masica 1976), which has heretofore appeared difficult of explanation.

In Hindi causative constructions, the NP referring to the intermediary or noncausal agent is usually marked by the postposition *ko*, provided the underlying noncausal predicate is intransitive. In (23) and (24), the a-examples illustrate the noncausal base and the b-examples, the derived causative :

(23) a. *madhu baiṭhaa* 'Madhu sat'
Madhu sat

b. *yadu ne madhu ko biṭhaayaa* 'Yadu seated Madhu'
Yadu ptc Madhu obj caused-to-sit

(24) a. *madhu royaa* 'Mandu cried'
Madhu cried

b. *yadu ne madhu ko rulaayaa* 'Yadu made Madhu cry'
Yadu ptc Madhu obj caused-to-cry

---

10. That there is an important difference between the intransitive/transitive distinction and the affective/effective distinction is nicely pointed out by Paramasivam 1979 :95 : "...whereas the role of object is crucial in the Intransitive/Transitive distinction in English, the role of subject is crucial in the Affective/Effective distinction in Tamil." For detailed discussion of the affective /effective distinction see Paramasivam and see also Zide 1971.

11. For example, in Greek, according to Barber, when an author "chooses the middle over the active voice for a particular verb, he is expressing what is usually described by Greek teachers as the 'involvement' of the subject in the action—the fact that the agentive subject is also affected in some way by the action." See Barber for complete discussion. Zide 1971:211, on the other hand, denies that affectedness is a version of middle voice. Her denial, however, seems to be based on a definition of middle voice as "the neutralization of the agent/patient distinction." But it seems to me that this is far from an accurate characterization of middle voice in Indo-European. Barber's remarks in particular would indicate that, at least in Greek, middle voice is something quite different.

But when the underlying noncausal predicate is transitive, then the intermediary or noncausal agent is usually marked by a different postposition either *ke dvaaraa* or, alternatively, *se* :

(25) a. *madhu ne kaam kiyaa* 'Madhu worked'
Madhu ptc work did

b. *yadu ne madhu ke dvaaraa kaam karvaayaa* 'Yadu had Madhu do the work'
Yadu ptc Madhu by work caused-ty-do

(26) a. *madhu ne kapṛaa kaaṭaa* 'Maadhu cut the cloth'
Madhu ptc cloth cut

b. *yadu ne madhu se kapṛaa kaṭvaayaa* 'Yadu had Madhu cut the cloth'
Yadu ptc Madhu by cloth caused-to-cut

Other Indic languages which follow this pattern include Bengali. In Bengali, the counterpart of Hindi *ko* is *-ke* and of *ke dvaaraa/se* is *-ke diye*. Otherwise the pattern is identical, e.g. :

(27) a. *modhu boslo* 'Modhu sat'
Modhu sat

b. *jodu modhuke basaalo*
Jodu Modhu-O caused-to-sit
'Jodu seated Modhu'

(28) a. *modhu kaaj korlo* 'Modhu worked'
Modhu work did

b. *jodu modhuke diye kaaj karaalo* Jodu had Modhu do the work'
Jodu Modhu-by work caused-to-do

There are certain transitive predicates whose intermediary or noncausal agents are not marked by *ke dvaaraa/se* in the causative. They are, surprisingly, marked by *ko*—the marker expected when the underlying noncausative predicate is intransitive. Some Hindi examples are given in (29)-(31), and some corresponding Bengali examples in (32)-(34) :

(29) a. *madhu ne khaanaa khaayaa* 'Madhu ate food'
Madhu ptc food ate

b. *yadu ne madhu ko (*ke dvaaraa) khaanaa khilaayaa*
Yadu ptc Madhu obj by food caused-to-eat
'Yadu fed Madhu food'

(30) a. *madhu ne gulaab sũũghaa* 'Madhu smelled the rose'
Madhu ptc rose smelled

b. *yadu ne madhu ko (*ke dvaaraa) gulaab sũghaayaa*
Yadu ptc Madhu obj by rose caused-to-smell
'Yadu had Madhu smell the rose'

(31) a. *madhu ne baat samjhii* 'Madhu understood the matter'
Madhu ptc matter understood

b. *yadu ne madhu ko (*ke dvaaraa) baat samjhaayii*
Yadu ptc Madhu obj by matter caused-to-understand
'Yadu explained the matter to Madhu'

(32) a. *modhu khaabaar khelo* 'Modhu ate food'
Modhu food ate

b. *jodu modhuke (*ke diye) khaabaar khaaoaalo*
Jodu Modhu-O by food caused-to-eat
'Jodu fed Modhu food'

(33) a. *modhu golaap sũklo* 'Modhu smelled the rose'
Modhu rose smelled

b. *jodu modhuke (*ke diye) golaap səkaalo*
Modu Modhu-O by rose caused-to-smell
'Jodu had Modhu smell the rose'

(34) a. *modhu bal paarṭaa bujhlo* 'Modhu understood the matter'
Modhu the-matter understood

b. *jodu modhuke (*ke diye) baepaarṭaa bujdaalo*
Jodu Modhu-O by the-matter caused-to-understand
'Jodu explained the matter to Modhu'

Masica (1976:46) describes this rather limited set of verbs—the causatives of the base verbs *eat, smell, understand* and so on—as DOUBLE TRANSITIVES : verbs which take "a direct and an indirect object rather than a direct object and an instrumental of agent". After reviewing the writers who have noticed the double transitive set of verbs in Hindi, Masica (p. 52) adds : "The common semantic element...in the set of verbs underlying these formations has been noticed by none of the writers mentioned." This common semantic element or feature is said (p. 46) to be that "of taking something into the body or mind (literally or figuratively)". For instance, "eat" obviously refers to an act of taking something into the body. "Smell" also does so, though less obviously. "Understand" seems to refer to an act of taking something, intangible if not tangible, into the mind if not the body. So it seems that the notion "ingestive" captures what is common to the semantics of the relevant base verbs.

At the same time there are certain problems in positing an ingestive set of verbs. For instance, it is problematic to think of a fixed class of verbs as ingestive if there exist verbs whose causatives can go either way (ingestive or noningestive). Here is an example : consider the verb *paṛ* 'study' in Bengali. The formal causative derived from this base may behave in the typical pattern of causatives derived from transitive bases, or in the pattern of causatives derived from so called ingestive bases (i.e., as a double transitive). It depends on the sense :

(35) a. *jodu modhuke diye (jore) ciṭhi paṛaalo*
Jodu Modhu-by loud letter caused-to-read
'Jodu had Modhu read the letter (out loud)'

b. *jodu modhuke hindi paṛaalo*
Jodu Modhu-O Hindi caused-to-study
'Jodu taught Modhu Hindi'

This example is problematic, since the ingestive verb viewpoint suggests that there is a limited but definite class of verbs which are all characterized by a particular semantic feature; *paṛ-* is supposed to be such a verb, and it fulfills the semantic characterization of one; nevertheless the formal causative of *paṛ-*, having either of the possible meanings 'cause to read' or 'teach', behaves differently depending on which is meant. About the only way this can be accounted for under a strict interpretation of the ingestive verb viewpoint is by positing two homophonous verbs *paṛ-*, one (noningestive) meaning "read" and the other (ingestive) meaning "study". The formal causatives of these two verbs, which are also coincidentally homophonous (*paṛaa-*), are to be derived separately. But this is a questionable solution, since it splits one verbal form with two clearly related senses into two separate, supposedly accidentally homophonous lexical items.

A somewhat better way out of this problem would require that the notion of a fixed verbal class be given up. Instead, it could be claimed that the behavior of a given verb in a given context depends on semantics, i.e., whether or not the verb is being used in an "ingestive" sense. However, this modification will still not solve the other problems of the notion "ingestive", which will now be outlined.

For instance, it is questionable whether the notion "ingestive" covers what is common to the samantics of *all* the relevant verbs. Troublesome instances can be cited, such as the Hindi verb 'to wear/put on (e.g., a garment)', pahan-, which behaves like a so called ingestive verb :

(36) a. *madhu ne kamiiz pahanii* 'Madhu put on a shirt'
Madhu ptc shirt put on

b. *yadu ne madhu ko (*ke dvaaraa) kamiiz pahanaayii*
Yadu ptc Madhu obj by shirt caused-to-put-on
'Yadu dressed Madhu in a shirt'

If *pahan-* is to be regarded as an "ingestive" verb then it will not do to interpret the notion INGESTIVE in terms of taking something into the body or mind; one must further stretch the notion to include acts of taking something *onto* the body. The verb "to cry" (ex., 24) is also troublesome, since its meaning is the opposite of "ingestive". A still more problematical example, from Bengali, is :

(37) a. *modhu mad khaaoaa chaaṛlo* 'Modhu gave up drinking'
Modhu liquor drinking left

b. *jodu modhuke (*ke diye) mad khaaoaa chaaraalo*
Jodu Modhu-O by liquor drinking caused-to-leave
'Jodu got Modhu to give up drinking'

In (37), the predicate "leave" behaves like a so called "ingestive" verb, but an act of giving something up is not semantically an "ingestive" act. Hence one is still in a quandary as to how to accurately characterize the semantics of the relevant verbs.

The most stubborn problem of all is why so called ingestive verbs and intransitive verbs behave alike vis-a-vis the marking of the noncausal or intermediary agent in the causative. Under the ingestive viewpoint one would be inclined to posit three classes of verbs : noningestive transitve verbs, intransitive verbs, and "ingestive" verbs. But in their behavior, verbs fall into only two classes. The first consists of intransitive verbs and bases of so called double transitive verbs; their noncausal or intermediary agents are marked in the causative by *ko* (Hindi) or *-ke* (Bengali). The second class consists of all other transitive verbs, whose noncausal or intermediary agents are marked with *ke dvaaraa/se* (Hindi) or *-ke diye* (Bengali). It does not seem possible to account for this by the notion "ingestive", for surely, no one would claim that all intransitive verbs express an "ingestive" act (e.g., the notion "go" is not an "ingestive" notion). However, the sameness in the surface behavior of intransitive verbs and bases of double transitive verbs must be explained if an account of Indic causative morphology is to be even minimally adequate.

The problems above outlined are somewhat similar to problems in other languages for which the affective/effective hypothesis has been formulated. Zide 1971 on Gorum and Paramasivam 1979 on Tamil both observe that the verbs of these languages fall into basic paradigms (as verbs do in Indic). Zide, following the shapes of the verbal infinitives, calls these the *-nuH* and*-u* verb stem types. Paramasivam, using traditional Tamil grammatical terminology, speaks of weak and strong verbal bases. To reconcile the terminology, one may refer to Zide's *-nuH* class and Paramasivam's weak class together as *VI*, while Zide's *-u* class and Paramasivam's strong class may be spoken of together as *V*2. According to both writers, VI and V2 roughly correspond with intransitive and transitive verb, respectively. However, the correspondence is far from airtight.

For instance, Zide points out that some seemingly transitive Gorum verbs behave unexpectedly as VI. In the Gorum sentences, 'The boy feared the tiger' and 'The girl liked the boy', the verbs *fear* and *like* are formally VI even though they are transitive (i.e., even though they take objects within the sentence). Also, Gorum causative verbs, though logically speaking always transitive, are not always V2 in shape. Whether a causative verb is VI or V2 seems to depend on whether or not one speaks of the subject of the base verb as *primarily affected* or *not primarily affected* by the action.

Paramasivam similarly observes that a given Tamil verb may be either

VI or V2 in shape, depending on the sense. He cites, for instance, the Tamil sentences 'The child is kicking its legs' and 'The child is kicking me'. In the former the verb *kick* is VI and in the latter, V2. This is despite the fact that both sentences are transitive, inasmuch as each contains an object in the accusative case.

Both Zide and Paramasivam adopt the solution that, semantically, the VI class represents affective action—action viewed or spoken of as primarily affecting the subject of the base verb—and the V2 class, effective action, or action not spoken of as primarily affecting the subject. For instance, the action of kicking is affective in the Tamil sentence: 'The child is kicking its legs' but effective in 'The child is kicking me'.

Now let's consider how the affective/effective parameter may be applied to Indic. The opposition affective/effective is not based on, but rather transects the grammatical categories intransitive and transitive. This is essential for the analysis of Gorum and Tamil, as we have seen. It is also a useful sort of distinction in Indic, if one is to avoid an inelegant tripartite division of verbs into classes such as noningestive transitive, intransitive, and ingestive.

Moreover, since the affective/effective parameter entails no fixed class or classes of verbs, one can allow for the possibility that a given verb may behave in either of two ways depending on the sense. We have just discussed how some verbs go either way in Gorum and Tamil. An instance in Indic has also been illustrated in example (35). One can claim that the non-causal agent is marked in a certain way in (35a) because the verb is, semantically speaking, effective. It expresses an act which primarily affects some party other than the subject of the base verb "read" (namely, his audience). In (35b), on the other hand, the subject-referent of the base verb is the one primarily affected by the act expressed by the base verb. Consequently the noncausal agent receives a different marking in this sentence.

It is a common problem of Gorum, Tamil and Indic that certain transitive verbs seem to behave as if they were intransitive. For Gorum and Tamil, the affective/effective opposition provides a plausible account for this. The account is also plausible for Indic. Intransitive verbs, having only one argument, the subject, necessarily refer to activities whose affect bears primarily on that party and not on some other. Hence intransitive verbs tend to be affective. The so called ingestive verbs of Indic—"eat", "smell", "understand" and so on—also refer rather clearly to activities the primary effect of which is on the subject. Also a verb such as "wear/put on", whose semantics, as we have seen, are troublesome for the ingestive viewpoint, refers to an act whose affect is primarily on its subject. The behavior of this verb can therefore be accounted for under the affective/effective hypothesis. Smilarily, in (37b), the act expressed primarily affects the subject-referent of the base verb "give up".

For all the above reasons, the affective/effective parameter seems to provide a satisfying account of certain peculiarities of the causative in Indic languages such as Hindi and Bengali. If the above hypothesis is accepted, then the significance of the same parameter with regard to Tamil and Gorum verbal morphology hardly deserves to be treated as a coincidence. Rather, we may be dealing with a characteristic feature of the conceptual structure of South Asian languages, a feature which tends to find expression at the formal level in terms of a distinction in verbal paradigms exclusive of the intransitive/transitive distinction.

I have attempted in this paper to show what a semantic parameter is and how it may be shared. That genetically unrelated South Asian languages demonstrate formal similarities is well known, but the mechanism for sharing of formal features is still poorly understood. The notion of the semantic parameter lays open the possibility that the similarities in question go a lot deeper than the formal level. These days, what with declining belief in the independence of levels of analysis, linguists are becoming increasingly aware of the impracticability of ignoring the level of conceptual structure. The hypothesis that language areas may be definable in terms of the sharing of semantic parameters may be viewed as one manifestation of a growing trend of thought.

REFERENCES

Barber, E.J.W. 1975. Voice—beyond the passive. Berkeley, USA : *BLS* 1.

Klaiman, M.H. 1979. *Volitionality and subject in Bengali : a study of semantic parameters in grammatical processes.* University of Chicago Ph.D. dissertation. In preparation.

———.Arguments against the 'ingestive verb' hypothesis. To appear *Topics in Hindi linguistics* ed. by Omkar N. Kaul. Vol. II. Delhi : Bahri Publications.

Masica, Colin P. 1976. *Defining a linguistic area.* Chicago : University of Chicago Press.

Pandharipande, Rajeshwari. 1978. Exception and rule government : the case of the passive rule in Hindi. *Studies in the Linguistic Sciences* 8:1 Urbana : Department of Linguistics, University of Illinois.

Paramasivam, K. 1979. Effectivity and causativity in Tamil. *IJDL* (Trivandrum, India) 8:1.71-151.

Southworth, Franklin C. 1974. Linguistic stratigraphy of North India. In Southworth and Apte. 201-23.

———.and Apte, Mahadev L. 1974. *Contact and convergence in South Asian languages.* Trivandrum, India : *IJDL.*

Verma, Manindra K. 1976. Typological aspects of the stative in some Indic languages. Paper delivered at the 30th International Congress of Human Sciences in Asia and North Africa, Mexico City, August 1976.

Zide, A. R. K. 1971. Transitive and causative in Gorum, *Journal of Linguistics* 8.201-15.

A NOTE ON SYNTACTIC CONVERGENCE AMONG INDIAN LANGUAGES : THE VERB "TO BE"

B. Lakshmi Bai

The present study attempts to examine the possible convergence of Indian languages with regard to maintaining a formal distinction between existential and equational sentences. For the purpose of this paper a sentence of the type 'x is y' will be called equational and a sentence of the type 'x is' or 'there is x', existential. An equational sentence refers to the identity or quality of a thing or person whereas an existential sentence shows the existence or location of a person or thing.

One way in which a language can distinguish between the two types of sentences is by using a copular form in an equational sentence which is lexically different from the existential verb. A language which maintains such a distinction in positive sentences makes a parallel distinction in negative sentences by employing different negative forms to negate the two types of sentences in question. In classical Chinese (Graham 1967), for example, while the existential verb is *yu*, to indicate the equational relation the final particle *yeh°* is used. The existential verb is replaced in a negative sentence by a corresponding negative verb *wu* meaning 'lack' or 'there is not', while *pu* or *fei* are used to negate an equational sentence. Similarly in Amharic (Ferguson 1972) *allä* is used as present tense existential verb while *näw* functions as present tense copula. The present tense negative existential verb in Amharic is *yälläm* while the present tense negative copula is *aydälläm*.

As distinct from Chinese or Amharic, Indo-European languages like Greek, Latin and German use the existential verb also as a copula of an equational sentence as can be observed from the following examples :

LATIN : viinum bonum est
wine good is
'The wine is good'

acqua est
water is
There is water'

GERMAN : Er ist main Vater
he is my father
'He is my father'

Mein Vater ist zu Hause
my father is at home
'My father is at home'

Er ist nicht mein Vater
he is not my father
'He is not my father'

Mein Vater ist nicht zu Hause
my father is not at home
'My father is not at home'

Both Iranian and Old Indo-Aryan (OIA) use the existential verb *as* also as a copula like the other Indo-European (IE) languages mentioned above. Note, for example, the following sentence from the Rigveda.

tvaṃ hi ratnadhaa asi
thou emph. part. generous are
'Thou art generous'

Similarly in the following sentences from Modern Persian (MP) (Phillott 1919) *ast* is used both as an existential verb as well as a copula of an equational sentence.

iinjaa barra bisyaar ast
here sheep many are
'There are many sheep here'

uu fa'la ast
that workman is
'He is a workman'

As in the positive, so also in the negative MP uses the same negative form *niist* to negate both types of sentences. For example,

maar iin dardaa raa davaa ii niist
but this disease of remedy emph. part. not

'But there is no remedy for this disease'

tuu majnuun niistii
you Majnu not
'You are not Majnu'

As distinct from this, most Dravidian (Dr.) languages make a clear-cut distinction between equational and existential sentences. In the positive the distinction is maintained by using in an equational sentence a copular verb which is lexically distinct from the verb denoting existence or location or by having a zero copula. Observe, the following examples from Malayalam (Ma.) (Asher 1968) and Gondi (Go.).

MA.: Eq. avan joon aaṇa
he John is
'He is John'

Exist. daivam uṇṭa
God exists
'God exists'

Loc. unni viiṭṭil uṇṭa
Unni house in is
'Unni is at home'

Go. : Eq. voor peeḍal (aandur)
he boy is
'He is a boy'

Exist. agu peeḍal mantor
there boy is
'There is a boy'

As can be noticed from the above examples, in both Ma. and Go. the verb *aan/aaṇ* is used in an equational sentence and is different from the existential verb which is *uṇṭ* in Ma. and *man-* in Go.

Dravidian languages keep the two types of sentences apart in the negative also by having two distinct negative forms. For example, Old Tamil (OTa.), Ma. and Kannada (Ka.) have *alla* to negate an equational sentence and *illa* to negate an existential sentence. Similarly Kuvi (Israel 1979), Koṇḍa (Krishnamurti 1969) and Parji (Burrow and Bhattacharya 1953) use *hil, sil* and *cila* respectively to negate an existential sentence, while an equational sentence is negated in these languages by *aa, akay* or *aaˀe*. A few examples of negative sentences from different languages of the Dravidian family are given below:

MA. mohan vivaahitan alla
Mohan married person not
'Mohan is not a married person'

daivam illa
God is not
'There is no God'

PA. ood viled erad
he white not
'He is not a white man'

niir cila
water not
'There is no water'

Ko. kata aaˀed
story not
'It is not a story'

paṭṇam siled
town is not
'There is no town'

Go. iiswar laam aayo
Ishwar tall not
'Ishwar is not tall'

pustak ballat poro sille
book table on not
'The book is not on the table'

The following table shows the existential verb and the copular form used in the affirmative and negative in some of the Dr. languages.

	Positive		*Negative*	
LANGUAGE	EXISTENTIAL	EQUATIVE	EXISTENTIAL	EQUATIVE
O. Ta.	uṇṭu, iru	aaku	illa	alla
Mod. Ta.	iru	ϕ	illa	illa
Ma.	uṇṭa	aaṇa (ϕ)	illa	alla
Te.	uṇḍu	agu (ϕ)	lee-	kaa-
Ka.	iru	ϕ	illa	alla
Tu.	uṇḍ	ϕ	ijji	alla
Pengo	man	aa	hil	akay, aa
Kuvi	man	ϕ	sil	aaˀe
Konda	man	ϕ	sil	aa
Go.	man	aan (ϕ)	sil	aayo
Pa.	men	men (ϕ)	cila	er

According to Graham 'A verb "to be" which serves both as copula and as indicator of existence is almost confined to IE' (1972:225).

As per Graham's generalization, as well as the pattern obtaining in OIA and Iranian one would expect the majority of IA languages not to distinguish between the existential and copular forms. But an examination of Modern IA languages with regard to the linguistic feature in question leads to a clear-cut division of them into two geographical groups. On the one hand, we have the Eastern and Southern IA languages like Nepali, Assamese, Bengali, Oriya, Old Marathi, Konkani, and Sinhalese, which agree with the Dr. languages in maintaining a distinction between existential and equational sentences. On the other hand, we have the western bloc of languages consisting of Hindi, Gujarati, Sindhi, Panjabi and Kashmiri which lack such a distinction.

In Nepali there exist two verbs *cha* and *ho* of which the former denotes existential and the latter is used only in equational sentences as can be seen from the following examples :

cara rukh ma cha
bird tree on is
'The bird is on the tree'

yo kukur ho
this dog is
'This is a dog'

As far as the negative sentences are concerned, Nepali negates both equational and existential sentences by adding the negative particle *na* as is the case in OIA. For example,

tyɔ maanis hoyina
he man is not
'He is not a man'.

cara rukh ma chaina
bird tree on is not
'The Bird is not on the tree'

Bengali has equational sentences which are mostly verbless as opposed to existential ones which have the verb *ach-* 'is'. As pointed out by Ferguson 'most equational sentences are negated by the inflected negative copula *nɔ* while all *ach-* sentences are negated by the invariable negative existential verb *neĩ*' (1972:76). For example,

śe ḍakṭar
he doctor
'He is a doctor'

baba baṛite achen
father home at is
'Father is at home'

śe ḍakṭar nɔĕ
he doctor not
'He is not a doctor'

baba baṛite neĩ
father home at is not
'Father is not at home'

Though normally equational sentences in Bengali are verbless, in certain contexts we find *hɔŏa* being used as a copula as in the following sentences,

cheleṭi holo chatro
boy is student
'The boy happens to be student'

In Assamese, an equational sentence is normally verbless whereas the existential one has the verb *ase*. An equational sentence is negated by *nɔhɔy*, while to negate an existential sentence *nai* is used. For example,

mor naam xiita
my name Sita
'My name is Sita'

mor deuta ghɔrɔt ase
my father home at is
'My father is at home'

mor naam xiita nɔhɔy
my name Sita not
'My name is not Sita'

mor deuta ghɔrɔt nai
My father home at not
'My father is not at home'

Equational sentences in Oriya have either the verb *ɔṭe* or ϕ and are negated by *nuhẽ*. On the other hand, an existential sentence has the verb *ɔch* and is negated by *nahĩ* or *na*. A few examples from Oriya are given below :

mo namɔ siita
my name Sita
'My name is Sita'

mo bapa ghɔre ɔchɔnti
my father home at is
'My father is at home'

mo namɔ siita nuhẽ
My name Sita not
'My name is not Sita'

mo bɔhiṭa ṭebul upɔre nahĩ
my book table on not
'My book is not on the table'

In Old Marathi (Tulpule 1960) the pattern is exactly like the Dr. languages in the sense that equational sentences are either verbless or have a copula *ho* which is distinct from the existential verb *aahe*. Likewise in the negative, there are two distinct sets of negative verbs formed on *asaṇe* 'to be' and *hoṇe* 'to become'. It is the latter set which is employed in the negative equational sentences. For example,

tuu aamca atithi
you our guest
'You are our guest'

kshudhaa naahii
hunger is not
'There is no hunger'

pari hastii navhe
but elephant not
'But it is not an elephant'

he srimukhiice sabda navhtetii he hotii
these mouth of the master words are not these are
'These are the words from the mouth of the master and not these'

Sinhalese has an existential verb *inn.* Equational sentences normally do not have any verb. There are two distinct negative verbs, namely, *naxa* used in existential sentences and *novey* in equational ones. The following examples illustrate the distinction.

meye muduruo xungak innovaa
here mosquitoes plenty are
'There are a lot of mosquitoes here'

meye muduruo naxa
here mosquitoes not
'There are no mosquitoes here'

maage naama siitaa
my name Sita
'My name is Sita'

maage naama siitaa novey
my name Sita not
'My name is not Sita'

As distinct from this, in Hindi, Gujarati, Sindhi and Kashmiri the same verb serves as an existential verb as well as a copula. Similarly one and the same negative particle is used to negate the equational and existential sentences in these languages. The following examples can be noted in this connection.

	Positive		*Negative*
HI. Exist.	mãã ghar par hai mother home at is 'Mother is at home'	Exist.	kitaab mez par nahĩĩ hai book table on not is 'The book is not on the table'
Eq.	ye merii mãã hai this my mother is 'This is my mother'	Eq.	ye kitaab nahĩĩ hai this book not is 'This is not a book'

SI. Exist. hite daaḍhaa macharɔ ahini
here lots mosquitoes are
'There are a lot of mosquitoes here'

Exist. hite macharɔ na ahiṇi
here mosquitoes not are
'There are no mosquitoes here'

Eq. mũhĩjo naalo siitaa aahe
my name Sita is
'My name is Sita'

Eq. mũhĩjo naalo siitaa na aahe
my name Sita not is
'My name is not Sita'

GUJ. Exist. tahmaaro bhaai ghare che
your brother at home is
'Your brother is at home'

Exist. e ophismaa nathi
he office in not
'He is not at the office'

Eq. a saruṇ che
this good is
'This is good'

Eq. a saruṇ nathi
this good is not
'This is not good'

The non-employment of the existential verb also as a copular form and the presence of two different negative forms in the Eastern and Southern IA languages is not quite in consonance with Graham's generalization referred to earlier. This suggests that the IA languages in question have acquired such a distinction at some point in their historical development from OIA. The following observation made by Jules Bloch is significant in this regard: 'Sanskrit received from Indo-Iranian a verb of existence *as* supplemented by the verb 'to become' *bhuu* notably in the future and aorist. Moreover, the present of this second verb being thematic at the same time, progressively assumed the sense of "to be" ' (1965 : 303). The crucial point to note here is not that because the present of the verb *bhuu* was thematic that it gradually assumed the sense of 'to be' but that the derivatives of OIA verb *bhuu* 'to happen', 'to become' besides retaining these meanings and being employed for expressing universal truth have also assumed the function of a copula in the languages of the East and South. Nepali *ho* used regularly as a copula and Bengali *hɔĕ* used in place of a zero in certain equational sentences are both derivable from OIA *bhuu*.

The use of *bhoti, bhodi, hoti* and *hodi* from OIA *bhavati* for stating attributes or for identifying a thing or person is clearly attested in MIA. In Pali (Warder 1963) for example, we find instances of equational sentences not only with *as* but also with *ho* as shown below:

aham asmi brahmaa
I am God
'I am God'

brahmaṇo mahamatto hoti
priest minister is
'The priest is a minister'

Speaking about the use of *as* and *hoti* in Pali, Warder points out that the verb *as* 'to be' asserts with emphasis the existence of something or somebody. On the other hand, *hoti* is not emphatic and is also used to state attributes (1963 : 30).

But though Pali shows evidence of the use of *hoti* alongside of *as* in equational sentences, no parallel distinction between the two negative forms seems to have developed clearly yet. For instance, Pali *natthi* < *na*+ *asti* has both the meanings 'it is not so and so' as well as 'it does not exist'. It is, therefore, likely that the development of a negative substantive verb consisting of the negative particle *na* followed by the derivative of *bhavati*, with the exclusive function of negating an equational sentence, belongs to a period later than Pali.

At the same time, a modern Indo-Aryan language like Bengali has inherited the equational negative as a fossilized form, no longer analysable as the particle *na* followed by a verb, i.e. *na* + *bhavati*, etc. This is so because unlike OIA, in Bengali in general, the negative particle *na* follows the verb. As a result the verb *hɔě* < *bhuu* with the meaning 'become' or when used for expressing universal truth is followed by the negative particle in a negative sentence.

kukurer śiing hɔěna
dog's horns are not
'A dog has no horns'

But as opposed to this, the equational negative marker *nɔy* must be derived from *na* + *hɔy*.

An examination of a few Munda languages shows that while Ho and Khaṛia maintain a distinction between the two types of sentences in question in the same manner as the Dravidian languages do, Santali, Mundari, Savara and Remo do not have such a distinction.

Ho (Burrow, 1915) has the existential verb *mena* which is distinct from the copula or verablizing agent *a*ʔ.

aʔsar oare mena
bow in the house is
'The bow is in the house'

ne diri hambalaʔ
this stone heavy
'This stone is heavy'

While an equational sentence in Ho is negated by *ka*, an existential sentence is negated by replacing the verb *mena* by *bano*.

ne	gara	ka	ikira
this	river	not	deep

'This river is not deep'

alea	hature	penainko	bangkoa
our	village	weaver pl.	are not

'There are no weavers in our village'

Biligiri (1965) in his grammar of Khaṛia speaks of two different forms of 'be' namely *ai* and *heke* both of which are inflected. Of these, the former is an existential verb, whereas the latter is used to identify a person or thing. A similar distinction is made in the negative also. For example, the negative of *aij* 'he is' is *umboṛej* 'he is not', whereas the negative of *heke* 'he is so and so' is *nalege* 'he is not so and so'.

In Santali (Bodding 1929), in the positive, an equational sentence is characterized by the auxiliary *kan*. For example,

aṇḍia	kanae
male	is

'It is a male'

apun	kanae
your father	is

'He is your father'

Bodding says that *kan* does not have the meaning either of existence or of remaining or staying. An existential sentence in Santali has the verb *menak* ʔ. For example,

dokan	menakʔa
shops	are

'There are shops'

The negative counterpart of *menak*ʔ is *banuk* which is derived from the ordinary negative *ba*. But unlike Ho, Santali does not show two distinct negatives. Bodding considers it a strange phenomenon of Santali that it does not possess the negative *ka* which the sister language Ho has.

In Mundari (Langendoen 1967) the verb *menaq* functions both as an existential verb as well as a copula of an equational sentence.

gelea	hora	hature	menaq-a
ten	paths	village-in	are

'There are ten paths in the village'

hodo-ko	maran	menaq	ko-a
man pl.	tall	copula	pl. pro.

'The men are tall'

Similarly in the negative *ban* and its alternants are used to negate both existential and equational sentences.

It is likely that Mundari *ban* and *ka* had distinct functions originally like the parallel forms *bano* and *ka* of Ho, which got lost presumably due to the influence of Hindi.

In Savara (Ramamurti 1931) an equational sentence is verbless whereas an existential sentence has the verb *daku* 'to be'. For example,

vaanen gorzaaṅ-an daku
father-my village in is
'My father is in the village'

anin sukkadom
he healthy
'He is healthy'

But in the negative the same form *teḍ* is used to negate both types of sentences.

ñen bujaa teḍ
I priest not
'I am not a Priest'

bɔrun consuuṅ teḍ
hill in the village not
'There are no hills in the village'

Yet another South Munda language called Remo has the same characteristic as Sora, in the sense that it uses one and the same negative to negate equational as well as existential sentences.

ḍabbu aaṇḍa
money not
'There is no money'

õ?õ aaṇḍa
children not
'There are no children'

maay remo aaṇḍa
he remo is not
'He is not a Remo'

gitina guso aaṇḍa gime
this dog not goat
'This is a dog not a goat'

An examination of a few Munda languages thus disproves Graham's generalization that the employment of the same verb in existential and equational sentences is a characteristic only of Indo-European languages. We have noticed that South Munda languages like Savara and Remo also have a single form used in both the contexts.

The evidence from a language like Remo seems to be significant in making reasonable conjectures regarding the source of influence on the Eastern and Southern IA languages in this respect. The absence of the distinction between the existential and copular form in Remo, which has possible contact only with Oriya and Telugu, both of which have such a distinction, thus suggests that the syntactic feature in question is not necessarily a typical characteristic of the Munda languages.

Since the majority of Dravidian languages including Old Ta. show the existence of two distinct forms in the positive as well as in the negative to distinguish between the existential and equational sentences, we can conclude that it is a characteristic of the Dravidian family of languages. Somewhere during the MIA period a parallel distinction must have developed in the neighboring IA languages and was inherited by the Eastern and Sothern IA languages.

Ferguson (1972) proposes a set of 'universal tendencies' by which languages sharing certain features in common would undergo the same kind of typological shifting over a period of time. He lists twelve features of the verbs of 'being' which are structurally similar in Bengali and Amharic, two languages unrelated genetically as well as in diffusional relationship. On the basis of these shared features, Ferguson sets up a set of 'universal tendencies' pertaining to the existential, copulative and auxiliary functions of verbs. One such hypothesis is worded by him thus: "If Ex. and Cop. are lexically separate and they are in a suppletive relation with verbs meaning 'becoming' and 'stay' then 'become' will be related to Cop. and 'stay' to Ex." (112). The development of copular function by the derivatives of OIA verb *bhuu* 'to become or to happen' in MIA and Mod. IA languages thus is quite natural according to the generalization made by Ferguson.

But one wonders why such a natural development should show up only in a set of languages which are also geographically close to each other. The presence of the distinction in question in languages belonging to three different language families all of which are spoken in a contiguous region offers a strong basis for ascribing the feature to the impact of convergence among them.

It is interesting to note that while on the one hand certain Munda and IA languages seem to have acquired the distinction in question under the impact of Dravidian, there are also instances where a Dr. language seems to have lost it presumably under the influence of neighboring IA languages which do not have such a contrast. For example, Kurukh (Grignard 1924) which has borrowed extensively from Hindi uses the same verb *ra'ana* from Hindi *rahnaa* 'to stay' in both existential and equational sentences as can be seen from the following examples :

eng kiyya ra'a das
my under is
'He is under me'

aasgahi urb ra'anan
he rich is
'He is rich'

Similarly, in negative, *mal* is used in both the contexts. For example,

enghai sangee nee hoo malkar
my with no body is
'Nobody is with me'

em tortaa paddniar urb malkar
our villagers rich not
'Our villagers are not rich'

Similarly, in Kolami (Emeneau 1955) which has come under heavy influence from Marathi, *anḍ* is used both as an existential verb as well as a copula. For example,

ama vaaḍit aṇḍan
that man garden in is
'That man is in the garden'

am maas beerak aṇḍan
that man deaf is
'That man is deaf'

Likewise, *tōt* is used in Kolami to negate both existential and equational sentences.

To conclude, our study shows that the languages of the East and South constitute a solid block in the sense that they keep equational sentences apart from existential ones in the affirmative by having either a zero or a form lexically different from the existential verb, and in the negative by using two different negatives. As this distinction is a widespread phenomenon of Dravidian languages and as the Central and Western IA languages and South Munda languages do not have such a distinction it may be assumed that the Munda languages and the Eastern and Southern IA languages have acquired this distinction under the influence of Dravidian.

REFERENCES

Asher, A. E. 1968. Existential, possessive, locative, and copulative sentences in Malayalam. *The verb 'Be' and its synonyms*, ed. by Verhaar John, Part 2, 88-111. Holland: Reiding Publishing Company.

Biligiri, H. S. 1965. *Kharia : phonology, grammar and vocabulary*. Poona : Deccan College.

Bloch, Jules. 1965. *Indo-Aryan from the Vedas to modern times*. English translation by Alfred Master. Paris : Librairie Adrien Maisonneuve.

Bodding, P.O. 1929. *Materials for a Santali grammar*, Dumka, India : The Santal Mission of the Northern Churches.

Burrow, T. and Bhattacharya, S. 1953. *The Parji language*. Hartford: Stephen Austin and Sons.

———. 1970. *The Pengo language : grammar, texts and vocabulary*. Oxford : Clarendon Press.

Burrow, L. 1915. *Ho grammar with vocabulary*, Calcutta; Catholic Orphan Press.

Emeneau, M. B. 1955. *Kolami : a Dravidian language*. California : University of California Press.

———. 1974. The Indian linguistic area revisited. *International Journal of Dravidianl Linguistics*. Vol. 3. No. 1. 92-134.

Ferguson, C. A. 1972. Verbs of 'Being' in Bengali with a note on Amharic. *The verb 'Be' and its synonyms*. Part 5, 74-114.

Graham, A.C. 1967. 'Being' in Classical Chinese. *The verb 'Be' and its synonyms*, Part 1. 1-361

———. 1972. 'Being' in linguistics and philosophy. *The verb 'Be' and its synonyms*, Part 5. 225-233.

Grignard, A. 1924. *A grammar of the Oraon language*. Calcutta : Catholic Oraon Press.

Israel, M. 1979. *A grammar of the Kuvi language*. Trivandrum : Dravidian Linguistic Association.

Krishnamurti, Bh. 1969. *Koṇḍa or Kūbi : a Dravidian language*. Hyderabad : Tribal Cultural Research and Training Institute.

Langendoen, T. 1967. The copula in Mundari. *The verb 'Be' and its synonyms*. Part 1, 75-99.

Phillott, D. C. 1919. *Higher Persian grammar*. Calcutta : Baptist Mission Press.

Ramamurti, G.V. 1931. *A Manual of the SO:Ra (or Savara) language*. Madras : Government Press.

Tulpule, S. G. 1960. *An Old Marathi reader*. Poona : Venus Prakashana.

Warder, A.K. 1963. *Introduction to Pali*. London : Luzac and Co.

THE QUOTATIVE IN INDO-ARYAN

K. Meenakshi

A majority of Indian languages do not have an indirect construction of the type found in English in clauses connected by *that* to main clauses; instead, they use a quotative marker either before or after the reported speech. The morpheme *iti* (= Lat. *ita*) is used as a quotative marker in Sanskrit. *iti* has a cognate *uiti* in Avestan, where the quotative marker precedes the reported speech, which is the regular feature in Indo-European. The quotative marker *iti* occurs about fifty times in RV.; the quotative follows the reported speech/thought about forty times and only eight times does it precede. The shift in the position of its occurrence has been attributed to contact with a non-Aryan language and the contact is presumed to have taken place in the pre-historic period (Kuiper 1974).

Dravidian languages also have the same type of construction. The general pattern in Dravidian is that the quotative follows reported speech which is exactly the pattern adapted by Skt. even in its earliest stage.

The quotative marker *iti* of OIA has completely disappeared in Modern Indo-Aryan languages and new forms have been acquired by these languages. Sanskrit *iti* is retained in the form of *ti/tti* in Middle Indo-Aryan (MIA) and another morpheme *kiṁti/kiti* (<Skt. *kim+iti*) is used in the Inscriptional Prakrits. Modern Indo-Aryan languages, generally, use two different kinds of forms in such constructions. For instance, Hindi has *ki* and *aisā* (Skt. *īdṛśa*). Gujarati has *ke* and *ɛm* (<Skt. *evam*); Marathi, *ki*, *asa* and *mhaṇūn*; Bengali, *je* (Skt. *yat*) and *boliye*, etc.

An interesting pattern has evolved in the quotative construction of the Modern Indo-Aryan languages. When the morpheme *ki* (< Pkt. *kiṁti* < Skt. *kim+iti*?) is used in any of these languages, it precedes the reported specch and when a newly developed form is used, it invariably follows the reported speech. Though Bengali and Oriya do not use the morpheme *ki*, the morpheme *je* (Skt. *yat*) is found to occur clause initially and the other, newly developed marker, is found clause finally. Thus, when the quotative marker is derived from an Old Indo-Aryan form, it precedes the reported speech and when it is a later acquisition, it follows. Not only in the position of its occurrence, but also in the formation of the new marker itself, one finds a striking similarity between the Dravidian languages and some Indo-Aryan languages, e.g. Marathi *mhaṇūn* and Bengali *bolie*. Both these morphemes are participles from the verb 'to say'. This is exactly how the quotative marker in Dravidian is formed. Tamil *eṉṟu* is a participle from the verb *eṉ* 'say'.

The aim of the present paper is to trace the development of the quotative marker in Indo-Aryan (i.e. from OIA to Modern Indo-Aryan), to describe its various uses and compare it with Dravidian. The comparative study will mainly be restricted to Marathi and Bengali, on the one hand, and Tamil, on the other, as Bengali and Marathi show greater affinity with Dravidian. RV *iti* is used with verbs of speaking, thinking, etc. It generally concludes the reported speech and is followed by the verb; less commonly, the verb precedes. Very rarely both the verb and the quotative precede the reported speech. Occasionally, the quotative is omitted; e.g. *yá indrāya sunavāméty āha* (RV 4.25.4) 'Who says, "let us press for Indra" '; *idam udakam pibatéty abravītana* (RV. 1.161.8) ' "Drink this water," thus you have said.'

Besides the above use, *iti* is also used to denote cause, reason, motive, purpose, etc. in Vedic, e.g.,

tváṣṭā duhitré, vahatúm kṛṇotītidáṁ
viśvaṁ bhuvanaṁ sam eti (RV 10.17.1)

'Tvaṣṭa performs the ceremony of marriage for his daughter, so the whole world is assembled' which may be understood as 'the world is assembled saying to itself, "because Tvaṣṭa..." '

āhuti juhoti mahacchāstram vāk ca manaś
ca prīte udyacchate iti (KB XVIII.5)

'He offers the two oblations of the offering for the choosing (of priests) (thinking) "Speech and mind being delighted shall support the great Sastra." ' *nā pāpaḥ puruṣo yājyo dvādaśāhena ned ayaṁ mayi pratitiṣṭhad iti* (AB IV.24.7) 'No evil man should be sacrificed for with the twelve-day rite (thinking), "Let not this one find support in me." '

The relative pronoun *yat* can also be used, in all such contexts where *iti* is found used above, e.g., *gṛṇé tád indra te śávo yád dhámsi vṛtrám* (RV 8.62.8) 'I praise this mighty deed of thine, that, thou slayest Vṛtra'; *tád yád páyasā śrīṇāti vṛtró vái sóma āsīt* (ŚB) 'That (=the reason why) he mixes soma with milk (is) this: Vṛtra was Soma'; *ā vaha devátātiṁ śárdho yád adya divyam yájāsi* (RV. 3.19.4) 'Bring hither the host of the gods, that thou mayest adore the divine throng'; *tát prāpnuhi yát te prāṇo vātam apipādyātai* (ŚB) "Obtain thou this, that thy breath may pass unto the wind.'

In Classical Sanskrit also, *iti* is used to conclude the direct speech and it is also used to denote the cause, motive, purpose, etc.; e.g. *kathitam avalokitayā madanodyānaṁ gato mādhava iti* (Māl. I.P. 11) 'Avalokita had told me that Madhava had gone to the grove of Kama'; *na cākhyeyam asmai cāṇakyo lekhayatīti* (Mud. I. p. 37) 'He must not be informed that it is Cāṇakya who has it written by him'; *purāṇam ity eva na sādhu sarvam na cāpi kāvyam navam ity avadyam.* (Mālav. I.S1.2) 'All poetry is not good merely because it is old; nor is it faulty because it is new'; *kṣatriyair dhāryate cāpo nārtaśabdo bhaved iti* (R 3.10.3) 'The warriors carry their bow in order to rescue the distressed'; *gṛham asmadīyam kṣīnārtham ity atithayaḥ parivarjayanti.* (Mṛcch. I. p. 19) 'Guests shun my dwelling, because, wealth has vanished from it'; *nīḍo me tava netyevam vivāda udabhūd dvayoḥ* (Kathā. 62.49) 'A quarrel arose between them on account of the nest', lit. "(both of them saying) the nest is mine, not yours".

Yat is used to introduce the direct speech and also to denote cause, motive, etc. In other words, the corelative form *yat* is again used in all contexts where *iti* can occur, e.g. *itaḥ kaṣṭataram kiṁ nu yad vayam gahane vane, diśaś ca na vijānino gantum caiva na śaknumaḥ* (Mbh. I.150.23) 'What can be more miserable than this that we are not able to go out of this dense forest, as we do not know the directions'; *utkarṣaḥ sa ca dhanvinām yad iṣavaḥ sidhyanti lakṣye cale* (Śāk. II). 'It is the highest glory for an archer, that his arrows hit a moving aim'; *taṁ vada yad anyo bhṛtyo vahanāyāsmat sthāne kriyatām* (Panc. 102) 'Tell him that he must appoint some other of his servants instead of me, to be his carrier'; *priyam ācaritam late tvayā me yad iyam punar mayā dṛṣṭā* (Vik.1) 'O creeper, you have done me a service, since she has been seen once more by me'; *kim tavāpakṛtam rājan vane nivasatā mayā...yad ahaṁ tāḍitas tvayā* (R.2.63.38) 'In what have I offended you that you should have slain me ?'; *vajrasāramayaṁ nūnaṁ hṛdayaṁ me na samśayaḥ, apaśyantyā na tam yad vai phalatīdam sahasradhā* (R 2.61.9) 'Certainly my heart is of the hardest stone, since it does not burst into a thousand pieces now that I do not see him'.

The full form of the quotative *iti* is not used in the Prakrit dialects except in the Girnar version of Asokan Inscriptions. In the Prakrit and Pali *ti/tti* is used; *tti* occurs after a word ending in a vowel and *ti* occurs elsewhere; *tti/ti* occurs clause finally, e.g., *jeṇa maṁ bhāṇadi ehi santesi kilintesi tti* (Mṛcch. I) 'Hence she says to me, "Come, you are fatigued, you are exhausted"'; *ayaṁ sikkhā ti bhagavā avoca* (DN. 182.3) 'The blessed one said this is the training.'

(I) *asti ca pa pi vutam sādhu dāna iti.* G. (=*ti* in K; M; D;). 'And it has been said also, "Gifts are meritorious"'

(N) *icchā hi me hevaṁ niludhasi pi kālasi pālatam alādhayeyuvu ti* (Pillar-Edict) 'For my desire is this, that even the time (of respite) has expired, they should attain (happiness) in the other world.'

As in Skt. *ti/tti* is used to denote, the cause, reason, purpose, motive etc. in Prakrit dialects also. E.g., *kiṁ ṇu khu daddurā vaharandi tti devvo pudhavie varisidum sumaradi* (Māl. IV) 'Does it begin to rain on the earth because frogs rattle?'; *athe me janasa paṭivedetha iti* (G. VI. 4-5)=*janasa atham paṭivedaṁtu me ti* (J.D.) 'Reporters are posted everywhere in order to report to me the affairs of the people at any time'; *pasamsā me āgacchatu iti sīlam rakkheyya paṇḍito* (Iti. 67.6). 'The wiseman should practise virtue in order to win praise.'

Besides *ti/tti*, the Inscriptional Prakrits and Pali use another form *kiṁti/kiti* (Skt. *kim+iti*) to denote purpose/motive, reason, etc. This may perhaps be translated simple 'saying to oneself, "what, why;" ' as interrogation has remained a means of marking the different stages of speech in the popular language. When *kiṁti/kiti* is used in the inscriptions, the sentence is generally concluded with *iti.* In Classical Sanskrit, such constructions are not wanting. The form *kim iti* in Sanskrit signifies 'under what pretext', 'with what intention', an action has been done. Consider the following sentences: *tat kim iti tvam uccaiḥ śabdam kṛtvā svāminaṁ na jāgarayasi* (Hit.) 'why don't you wake up the master by making a loud noise?' *kim iti bhāvān āhāraparityāgena tiṣṭhati* (Hit.) 'Why (=with what motive) do you sacrifice your food?'

Although the form *kiṁti/kiti*, in the Inscriptional Prakrits, is generally used to denote the purpose/motive of an action, it is also used as a simple quotative marker. *kiṁti/kiti* always occurs clause initially and the construction is concluded with *iti* occasionally, e.g.

(D) *tasa us idaṁ mūlam ya vaciguti kiṁti ātpapāsaṁdapūja va parapāsaṁdagarahā va no bhava* (G. XII). 'But its root is this, viz. guarding (one's) speech, (i.e.) that neither praising one's own sect nor blaming the other sects should take place on improper occasions.' (K. Sh.; and M. have *kiti* for *kimti*).

(I) *ta samavāyo eva sādhu kiṁti anamamnasa dhamman suṇaru ca susumsera ca.* (G. XII). 'Therefore concord alone is meritorious, (i.e.) that they should both hear and obey each other's morals.' (K; Sh., and M. have *kiti* and conclude with *ti.*)

(L) *etāya athāya ayam dha* (*ṁ*)*malipī lekhāpita kiṁti ciram tiṣṭheya iti* (G. VI). 'For the following purpose has this script on morality been caused to be written, (viz.) that it may last long.'

Thus, OIA, *iti* is retained generally in the form of *ti/tti* in MIA dialects. In addition, the Inscriptional Prakrits make use of a form *kiṁti/kiti* (<Skt. *kim+iti*) which has all the semantic functions of the earlier quotative *iti.* The quotative *ti/tti* is completely lost sight of after the Apabhramśa stage. From the earliest stage of modern Indo-Aryan languages one finds newly acquired markers playing the role of the OIA quotative. None of these is the direct descendant of the OIA *iti.* Each one has a morpheme of its own and they are not cognates.

The morpheme *ki* is found in all modern Indo-Aryan languages except the Eastern ones and functions as a quotative. The introduction of the morpheme *ki* into Hindi is said to be under the direct influence of Persian and its acceptance by the majority of Indo-Aryan languages is explained as the result of the confusion between Persian relative pronoun *ke* and Skt. interrogative *kim* (Kellogg 1972: 316).

Persian *ke* is used to introduce reported speech, and also to denote cause, purpose, etc. Consider the following sentences: *man guftam ke fardā bekhāna šuma me oyam.* 'I said, "I will come to your place." ' *mam īnjā āmadam zirā ke šumā mārā khaste būdīd.* 'I have come here because you had asked us to come.' *maqusada ke in kitab inja avasda am in bud ke besuma ihda kunam.* 'The purpose for which I brought this book was to present it to you.'

The morpheme *ki* always precedes the reported speech or thought. In MIA the morpheme *kiṁti/kiti* also generally precedes the reported speech. It is likely that *ki* of Modern Indo-Aryan is the direct descendant of *kiṁti/kiti* which is derived from Sanskrit *kim+iti* a combination of interrogative *kim* and the quotative *iti.* The morpheme *ki* forms a uniform pattern in all modern Indo-Aryan languages. It regularly occurs before the direct speech in all these laguages, which is the regular pattern in IE languages and to a certa'n extent in the Vedic as well.

The morpheme *ki* is generally used to introduce reported speech, and other functions such as cause, motive, etc. are denoted by other morphemes. Generally, the quotative marker *ki* is used with verbs of saying, knowing, believing, hearing, etc. Consider the following sentences:

(H) *usne mujhse kahā ki vah kal āegā.* 'He said he will come tomorrow.'

(Guj.) *te ne em bolyo ke te no (māro) nāno bhāī pās theyo.* 'He said that his younger brother had passed (the examination).'

(Mar.) *mi aikle ki tumhi ḍhākyās jāṇār āhāt.* 'I heard that you are going to Dacca.'

(P) *me suṇīa e ki tusi əmrīka ja rəeo.* 'I heard that you are going to America.'

Besides *ki* these languages have another morpheme which occurs invariably *after* the reported speech: *aisā* (H), and *asā/aisa* (Mar.) which are derived from Sanskrit *īdṛśa* are used as quotative, although Sanskrit *īdṛśa* is never used in such constructions. Consider the following :

(H) *vah mujhse milne āyā thā aisa usne mujhse kahā.* 'He said he came to see me yesterday.'

(Mar.) *tumhi dhākyās jāṇār, asā mi aikle.* 'I heard you are going to Dacca.'

Though both *ki* and *aisa* are used, the *ki*-construction is more frequent in Hindi.

Gujarati has a morpheme *em* (<Skt. *evam*). It occurs after the direct speech, e.g. *māro (te no) nāno bhāi pās theyoem te bolyo.* 'He said that his younger brother has passed in the examination.' It retains the original position of Sanskrit *evam* in a sentence.

Bengali, Oriya and possibly the other eastern Indian languages do not use *ki.* Instead, some other morpheme is used. Bengali has the morpheme *je* (derived from the Sanskrit relative pronoun *yat*) which precedes the reported speech. Unlike *iti* which can be shifted to either clause initially or finally, *yat* has a fixed position in Sanskrit. Bengali *je* also has a fixed position and it always occurs before the direct speech like the morpheme *ki* of Hindi and other languages. Consider the following :

āmi sunecchi je āpni ḍhakāy jācchen. 'I have heard that you are going to Dacca.' *tini bolchilen je kāl tini apnar bāṛi jāben.* 'He was saying that he would go to your house tomorrow.'

(O) *mū sunichi je tume bambe jaucha.* 'I have heard that you are going to Bombay.'

(O) *se kɔ hile je aji barsat hebɔ.* 'He said that it will rain today.'

Besides *je*, Bengali has another form, namely, *bole* (<*bol* 'say'). This form is used as a quotative and it occurs always after the direct speech like Hindi *aisa*; e.g., *āpni ḍhākāy jācchen bole ami sunecchi.* 'I have heard you are going to Dacca.' *kāl tini apnār bāṛi jāber bole bolchilen.* 'He was saying that he would go to your house tomorrow.'

Marathi too has acquired a new form in addition to *ki* and *asā*. Its formation is similar to Bengali *bole*. This form *mhaṇūn* (<*mhaṇ* 'say') in Marathi, like Hindi *aisa*, or Bengali *bole*, occurs after the direct speech; e.g. *tumhi ḍhākyās jāṇar mhaṇūn me aikle.* 'I heard that you are going to Dacca.'

The formation of *bole* (B), *bole* (O), *bhanun* (Nepali), *mhaṇūn*(Mar.), etc. is very similar to the formation of the quotative in Dravidian languages. The quotative in Dravidian is a participial form from the verb of "saying" and it always occurs after direct speech. For instance, the quotative *eṉṟu/eṉa* of Tamil is a participial form of the verb *eṉ* 'say'. Telugu has the form *ani* from the verb *an* 'say'; Malayalam has *ennu* from the verb *ennuka* 'to say' and all these languages use the quotative only after the reported speech:

nāṉ uṉṉai nāḷaic cantikkiṟen eṉṟu avan coṉṉāṉ. 'He said, "I will meet you tomorrow."'

(Ma.) *avaṉ nāḷa varām eṉṉu paraññu.* 'He said, I will come tomorrow."

The occurrence of the quotative *eṉṟu/eṉa* is attested right from the earliest literature, that is, the Sangam literature in Tamil. The morpheme *eṉa* is far more frequent in early texts.

The other functions of Sanskrit *iti* and *yat*, such as motive, reason, etc. have been taken by newly acquired forms in modern Indo-Aryan languages. Each language has invented a form of its own. Though they serve to denote the same function, the forms used are not cognates. For instance, Hindi uses *kyõki*, *islie*, etc., in such contexts. E.g., *mujhe āpne bulāyā islie* (*isvāste*) *mɛ̃ āyā hũ/mɛ̃ yahā̃ āyā* (*hũ*) *kyõki āpne mujhe bulāyā* 'I came here because you called mɛ.'

(Guj.) *əme tɛ̃mni vat jota həta kārəṇ ke əme sathe naṭək jova jəvana həta.* 'We were waiting for them because we were going together to see the play'; *tə me məne bolavi eṭle hũ avi.* 'I came here because you called me.' *teo pan e maṭe khay che ke khorak pacən thay.* 'They eat pan so that food can be digested.'

(Mar.) *tumhī bolāwle, mhaṇūn me ālo.* 'I came because you called me.' *he mī tujhyasāṭhi āṇle/he mī tulā mhaṇūn āṇle.* 'I brought this for you.' *mī mhaṇāle mhaṇūn he kām karāylā have asānahi* 'This work need not be done because I have told (you) to do it.'

(B) *āmi aphis jābo bole beriyechi.* I have come out for going to the office.' *āpni dākechen bole esechi.* 'I have come because you called me.' *ami bolchi bolei je a kaj korte hobe tay nay.* 'It is not that this work has to be done because I am saying so.'

The Dravidian participial form from the verb of "saying" used in concluding reported speech, is also used to denote cause/reason, motive/purpose, etc. like Sanskrit *iti.* The use of Tamil *eṉṟu/eṉa* in such semantic situations is attested right from the earliest period.

kaḷiru paṭiṇṭuṇṭeṉa-k-kalaṅkiya... (Puṟam. 23) 'the water became turbid because the elephant entered the pond and drank the water.'

nī varavillaiy eṉṟu avaṉukku-k-kōpam 'He is angry because you did not come.' *uṉakku eṉṟu itai vāṅkiṉēṉ.* 'I bought this for you.'

(Te.) *nī māṭa nilabeṭṭukō lēdani nēnu kōpangā unnānu.* 'I am angry because you did not keep up your word.'

To sum up, the *that* complementizer in Indian languages may either behave as a quotative marker or subject|object complementizer or serve to denote a cause and effect relationship between the clauses so connected. In Sanskrit, *iti* behaves as a quotative marker and as an object complementizer, *yat* behaves as subject and object complementizer, and both are used to connect clauses showing cause and effect relationship.

There is a shift in the placement of Sanskrit *iti.* The regular pattern in IE is that the quotative precedes the reported speech. In the case of Sanskrit, this pattern is reversed even in the Rigvedic period.

Of the two MIA quotatives, the place of *ti/tti* is like that of Sanskrit *iti,* but *kiṁti/kiti* precedes the reported speech. The original function of *iti* has been carried out by both these morphemes. The quotative *ti/tti* disappears completely from the scene after the Apabhraṃśa period.

Modern Indo-Aryan languages have invented new forms which serve as quotative and have all the functions of the earlier quotative. The new forms are neither the direct descendants of OIA quotative morphemes nor are they cognates.

The form *ki* is found in almost all the Modern Indo-Aryan languages, excepting the Eastern ones. The introduction of this morpheme is said to be under the direct influence of Persian, due to a confusion between the Sanskrit interrogative *kim* and the relative pronoun *ke* of Persian. This theory appears to be far fetched, when we see the history of the quotatives as traced above. In MIA, the morpheme *kiti/kiṁti* serves as a quotative marker. There is every possibility that the same morpheme is retained as *ki* in modern Indo-Aryan languages. The position of occurrence of *ki* supports this contention, as *kiti/kiṁti* always occurs before the quotation, whereas newly invented forms always follow the reported speech. This is also true of the Bengali quotatives : *je*, which is a descendant of Sanskrit *yat*, always precedes the reported speech and *bole*, a newly acquired form which is unrelated to any of the older morphemes, always follows.

Bengali, Oriya, Nepali, and Marathi have acquired a new form. B. *bole*, and Mar. *mhaṇūn* are participles from verbs of saying, i.e. B. *bol* and Mar. *mhaṇ*. In Sanskrit, the verb of saying or its derivative was never used as a quotative, but the quotative in Dravidian languages is a participle from the verb of saying. The quotative always occurs after the reported speech in Dravidian. It is interesting to note that it is the peripheral languages of Indo-Aryan which have adopted the model of Dravidian both in forming the quotative and in its placement.

It is very difficult to say the exact period in which this took place. There is no evidence for such forms occurring in the language up to the Apabhraṃśa period. The invention of these forms by Bengali or Marathi must therefore have happened sometime during the Old Marathi or Bengali stage. Tracing these forms backward in Marathi and Bengali might prove fruitful. Although the forms in Bengali and Marathi discussed above clearly show that they are formed exactly in the same manner as the Dravidian, their adoption into the languages appears to be very late, even though the contact situation was existing right from the early period. This might be taken as a clue in deciding the time span involved in the diffusion of linguistic features. It appears that if the change involved is only the shift in the placement of a particular morpheme, then it is adopted quickly. If it involves a morphological or syntactical feature, then it is very slow. One may hasten to add here, that this is not the definite answer to the question of the lateness of the formation of these particular in Bengali and Marathi. It is possible that the contact situation arose once again in the early stages of the development of these languages, as Marathi and Bengali/Oriya are geographically contiguous to the Dravidian language speaking area.

ABBREVIATIONS

Asokan Inscriptions. D = Dhauli; G = Girnar; J = Jaugada;
K = Kalsi; M = Mansehra Sh = Shahbazgarhi

AB = Aitareya Brāhmaṇa

B = Bengali

DN = Dighanikāya

Guj. = Gujarati

H = Hindi

Hit. = Hitopadesa
Iti = Itivuttaka
KB = Kausītakī Brāhmaṇa
Kathā. = Kathāsaritsāgara
Lat. = Latin
Ma. = Malayalam
Māl. = Mālatīmādhavam
Mālav. = Mālavikāgnimitram
Mar. = Maraṭhi
Mbh. = Mahābhārata
Mṛcch. = Mṛcchakaṭikam
Mud. = Mudrārākṣasam
MIA = Middle Indo-Aryan
OIA = Old Indo-Aryan
O = Oriya
P = Panjabi
Panc. = Pancatantra
Puṟam = Puṟanāṉūṟu
R = Rāmāyaṇa
RV = Ṛgveda
Rat. = Ratnāvali
Śāk. = Abhijnāna śākuntalam
ŚB = Śatapathabrāhmaṇa
Satta. = Sattasai
Te. = Telugu
Vik. = Vikramorvaśīyam

REFERENCES

Basak, Radhagovind. 1971. *Gāthā-saptaśatī* (Edited and translated). Calcutta : Asiatic Society.

Bloch, Jules. 1934. *L'Indo-aryen du Veda aux temps modernes.* Paris : Libraire d' Amerique et d'orient. Adrien Maisonneuve. Revised and translated by Alfred Master, 1965. *Indo-Aryan from the Vedas to modern times.*

Burgess, J. 1883. *Report on the Elura Cave temples and the Brahmanical and Jaina caves in Western India.* London : Archaeological Survey of Western India.

Hultzch, E. (Ed.) 1969. *Imscriptions of Asoka.* Corpus Inscription Indicarum. (New Ed.) Vol. I. Delhi-Varanasi.

Kellogg, S. H. 1972. *A grammar of the Hindi language* (1st Indian Edition). New Delhi : Oriental Books Reprint Corporation.

Kuiper, F.B.J. 1974. *The genesis of a linguistic area, IJDL.* I. 135-153.

Lambert, H. M. 1971. *Gujarati language course*. Cambridge : Cambridge University Press.

Macdonell, A.A. 1971. *A Vedic grammar for students*. (Reprinted) Bombay-Calcutta-Madras : Oxford University Press.

Permiola, V. 1958. *A grammar of the Pali language*. Colombo : Aquinas University College.

Sen, Sukumar. 1953. Historical syntax of middle Indo-Aryan *IL*. 13. 462-463.

Sircar, D.C. (Ed.) 1965. *Select inscriptions*. Vol. I. Calcutta : University of Calcutta. 207, 208.

Speijer, J.S. 1973. *Sanskrit syntax* (Reprint). Delhi : Motilal Banarsidass.

Woolner, A.C. 1972. *Introduction to Prakrit*. (Reprint) Delhi: Motilal Banarsidass.

LANGUAGE CONTACT AND LANGUAGE VARIATION : NAGPURI MARATHI

Rajeshwari Pandharipande

0.0. Introduction.

In recent years, it has been argued variously (Bailey and Shuy 1973, Bickerton 1971, DeCamp 1971, Labov 1969, etc.) that the metatheory of language should incorporate variation into the core of language study. Empirical studies of Haugen 1953, Gumperz 1971, and others question the traditionally accepted monolithic concept of language. Diachronic as well as synchronic aspects of variation are discussed (Bell 1976, Hock and Pandharipande 1978, Kachru 1976, 1978, and Weinreich 1953). With this upsurge of studies on language variation, languages spoken by bilinguals have come to be looked upon in a very different light. Mutual 'interference' of the languages spoken by bilinguals is now regarded as a natural outcome of linguistic convergence (Fishman 1972). Bilingualism, among other sociological factors such as sex, class, etc., thus plays an important role in bringing about variation in language. The dichotomy between monolinguals' 'pure' vs. bilinguals' 'impure' / 'deviant' speech is questioned.

In this paper I propose to discuss the case of a variety of Marathi (traditionally known as *Nāgpurī* Marathi) spoken in an area on the north-eastern border of Maharashtra State, India. This variety of Marathi is traditionally labelled as 'deviant' since it differs significantly from the Marathi spoken in other parts of Maharashtra. No systematic research has been done to answer questions such as (i) in what sense does Nāgpurī Marathi differ from other varieties of Marathi and (ii) what is the reason for these differences. The goals of this paper are : (a) to point out the linguistic features of Nāgpurī Marathi which separate it from other varieties of Marathi, (b) to demonstrate with illustrations that the linguistic features which mark Nāgpurī Marathi as different from other varieties are shared by Hindi, (c) to argue that the Hindi-Marathi bilingualism on the northeastern border of Maharashtra is responsible for the differences in the speech of Marathi speakers in that area, and (d) to show the relevance of bilingualism for the theory of language change.

1.0. Nāgpurī Marathi.

A majority of people living in the northeastern part of Maharashtra are bilingual, i.e., they use Marathi and Hindi. The neighboring state, northeast of Maharashtra, is Madhya Pradesh where the language is Hindi. Marathi spoken in the northeastern region differs significantly from Marathi spoken in other parts of Maharashtra. These differences are observed at various linguistic levels such as vocabulary, syntax and semantics.

The linguistic features which separate the language of the northeastern part of Maharashtra from the rest of the state can be conventionally called the markers of this variety of Marathi (popularly known as Nāgpurī Marathi from Nagpur, the major city in northeastern Maharashtra).

A close examination of the data shows that the linguistic features which mark Nāgpurī Marathi (hereafter NM) are commonly shared by Hindi, the other language known by the Marathi speakers in that area. It will be argued with illustrations that the only plausible explanation for the above mentioned variation in Marathi is that the Marathi spoken in the northeastern part of Maharashtra acquired certain linguistic features from Hindi as a result of a long language contact situation. Because of the absence of such bilingualism in other parts of Maharashtra, the other varieties of Marathi did not acquire features similar to NM.

It will be pointed out the traditionally accepted theory of transformational grammar fails to account for such a linguistic situation. In this study I hope to demonstrate that the case of the variation in Marathi supports the claim that sociological factors such as bilingualism play an important role in language change.

1.1. Variation in Marathi.

There are three major varieties of Marathi: (i) the Northeastern variety of Marathi (NM) as described in section 1.0, (ii) the Southern variety of Marathi spoken in the southern part of Maharashtra bordering Andhra Pradesh on the eastern side and by Karnataka on the western side, where the languages spoken are respectively Telugu and Kannada—both members of the Dravidian family of languages and which have considerable influence on this variety of Marathi (Gumperz 1971), and (iii) the Northwestern variety of Marathi, traditionally known as *Puṇerī* Marathi, after the major city, Puṇe. This city has been traditionally one of the mojor centers of education and culture in Maharashtra. This area is geographically separated from the Hindi speaking area to the northeast and the Telugu and Kannada speaking areas to the south. *Puṇerī* Marathi has less borrowings from other languages as compared to NM and the Southern varieties. *Puṇerī* Marathi is traditionally considered the 'pure' (šuddha) form of the Marathi language.

Although NM differs from both *Puṇerī* Marathi and the Southern varieties of Marathi, I shall compare NM only with *Puṇerī* Marathi (PM hereafter). The difficulty in using the Southern varieties of Marathi as a norm arises from the fact that any reference to the linguistic features of those varieties calls for an analysis of the origin (i.e., Marathi vs. Dravidian; (i) Kannda (ii) Telugu) of their linguistic features.

2.0. LINGUISTIC FEATURES : VOCABULARY.

In this section I shall discuss the vocabulary which separates NM from PM (and also other varieties of the language) and show that NM shares this vocabulary with Hindi spoken in the Nagpur area.

The following chart is divided into four sections. The first presents the items as they occur in PM. The items in the second section are semantic equivalents from NM and the third section lists the items in Hindi. The fourth section gives the gloss of the items in sections (a) – (c). Notice that the vocabulary items in NM (section b) are different from those in PM (section a). Also notice that the vocabulary in NM (section b) is similar to that in Hindi (section c)

		a PM	b NM	c Hindi	d Gloss
NOUNS :					
	1.	*piŝvī*	*zolā*	*jholā*	'bag'
	2.	*ghar*	*makān*	*makān*	'house'
	3.	*divā*	*battī*	*battī*	'lamb'
	4.	*viḍā*	*pān*	*pān*	'betel leaf folded with spices inside'
	5.	*dār*	*darwāzā*	*darwāzā*	'door'
	6.	*lāz*	*ŝaram*	*ŝarm*	'bashfulness'
	7.	*anthrūṇ*	*bichānā*	*bichaunā*	'bed'
	8.	*varṣa*	*sāl*	*sāl*	'year'
	9.	*mɛtrī*	*dostī*	*dostī*	'friendship'
	9*a*.	*viŝrāntī*	*ārām*	*ārām*	'rest'
ADJECTIVES :					
	10.	*prāmāṇik*	*imāndār*	*īmāndār*	'honest'
	11.	*veḍā*	*pāgal*	*pāgal*	'crazy'
	12.	*viŝeṣ*	*khās*	*khās*	'special'
	13.	*rikāmā*	*khālī*	*khālī*	'empty'
	14.	*kaṭhīṇ*	*muŝkil*	*muŝkil*	'difficult'
VERBS :					
	15.	*bhī-ṇe*	*ḍar-ṇe*	*ḍar-ṇā*	'to fear'
	16.	*barḷ-ṇe*	*bak-ṇe*	*bak-nā*	'to blab'
	17.	*varṣa-ṇe*	*baras-ṇe*	*baras-nā*	'to rain'
	18.	*visar-ṇe*	*bhul-ṇe*	*bhūl-nā*	'to forget'
	19.	*āvar-ṇe*	*sameṭ-ṇe*	*sameṭ-nā*	'to collect'
ADVERBS :					
	20.	*ajibāt*	*bilkul*	*bilkul*	'at all'
	21.	*haḷu haḷu*	*āste-āste*	*āste-āste*	'slowly'

The chart also sh ows that the vocabulary which NM shares with Hindi is not restricted to any particular grammatical category but rather, it includes nouns, verbs, adjectives and adverbs. The above chart is a fairly small sample of the vocabulary commonly shared by Hindi and NM. However, it may be observed that in general the vocabulary items commonly shared by NM and Hindi are related to every-day life.

2.1. Compound Verbs.[1]

Speakers of NM are often accused by speakers of PM of using *vicitra* 'strange' compound verbs. Although Marathi has compound verbs, the process of combining a main verb with an operator (also called explicator or vector verb) is not totally free. In other words, certain combinations of main verb + operator are totally blocked in PM. However, these combinations are freely used in NM. Consider the following examples :

	a PM	b NM	c Gloss
22.	**gheūn ghe-ṇe* take take	*gheūn ghe-ṇe* take take	'to take for oneself'
23.	**deūn de-ṇe* give give	*deūn de-ṇe* give give	'to give for someone else'
24.	**mhaṇūn de-ṇe* say give	*mhaṇūn de-ṇe* say give	'to say out'

In PM, as a rule, a verb cannot function as both a main verb and an operator within the same compound verb. In examples (22) and (23) the verbs *ghe-ṇe* 'to take' and *de-ṇe* 'to give' are used as main verbs as well as operators; column (b) shows that the restriction does not hold in NM. Examples (25) and (26) show that such combinations are allowed in Hindi. Also, notice that the combination in (24) is allowed in NM and also in Hindi (27).

	a NM	b Hindi	c Gloss
25.	*gheūn ghe-ṇe* take take	*le le-nā* take take	'to take for oneself'
26.	*deūn de-ṇe* give give	*de de-nā* give give	'to give for someone else'
27.	*mhaṇūn de-ṇe* say give	*kah de-nā* say give	'to say out'

1. Compound verbs : A compound verb is a verb + verb sequence functioning as a unit where generally the first verb is the main verb and the second verb is an auxiliary or explicator. E.g.,

   deūn ṭākṇe (Marathi)
   give drop
   'to give in order to get rid of'

Here the main verb is *de-ṇe* 'to give' and *ṭāk-ṇe* 'to drop' is an auxiliary verb (explicator). For further discussion on compound verbs in Hindi and Marathi, refer to Y. Kachru 1966, Kachru and Pandharipande 1979, and Pandharipande 1978.

2.2. Conjunct Verbs.[2]

A number of conjunct verbs which are freely used in NM are totally absent in PM. The data show that such conjunct verbs in NM are formed on the analogy of conjunct verbs in Hindi. Consider the following examples (28-30). Notice that NM uses verbs which are semantically similar to those in the conjunct verbs in Hindi. The nouns used in NM are also commonly shared with the Hindi conjunct verbs in column (c).

	a PM	b NM	c Hindi	d Gloss
28.	*viśrāntī gheṇe* rest take	*ārām kar-ṇe* rest do	*ārām kar-nā* rest do	'to take rest'
29.	*rāgāv-ṇe,* *rāg ye-ṇe* anger come	*ghussā kar-ṇe* anger do	*gussā kar-nā* anger do	'to get angry'
30.	*thaṇḍī asṇe* cold be	*thaṇḍī paḍ-ṇe* cold fall	*thaṇḍ paṛ-nā* cold fall	'to be cold'

2.3. Adverbs.

Both in Hindi and Marathi an adverb is derived by adding instrumental suffixes (i.e., H. *se* 'by, with, etc.' and M. *ne* 'by' to a noun. (Example (31) in column (a) shows, however, that not all adverbs are derived by this process.) Examples (31)-(33) show that adverbials in NM are formed by adding the instrumental suffix *ne* 'by' of PM to Hindi nouns. Thus the adverbial forms in NM (section (b)) share the nouns with Hindi (column (c)) and the instrumental suffix with PM (column (a)).

	a PM	b NM	c Hindi	d Gloss
31.	*sāvkāś*	*ārāmā-ne* rest inst.	*ārām se* rest inst.	'in a leisurely manner'
32.	*kaṣṭāne* effort+inst.	*muśkilī-ne* difficulty-inst.	*muśkil se* difficult-inst.	'with great difficulty'
33.	*ānandāne* happiness+inst.	*khuśī-ne* happiness-inst.	*khuśī se* happiness-inst.	'happily'

---

2. Conjunct verbs : A conjunct verb is a noun + verb sequence functioning as a unit. E.g.,

stutī karṇe (Marathi)
praise do
'to praise'

For further discussion see Damle 1911 and Y. Kachru 1966.

3.0. Transfer of Fixed Collocations (Idioms)[3].

NM has some idioms which it does not share with PM but which it shares with Hindi. A close examination of the data shows that the Marathi words in the idioms in NM are the exact semantic equivalents of the words in the Hindi idioms. This phenomenon of loan translations from one language into another is commonly observed in a bilingual's speech. Haugen 1953 discusses loan transfers from English into Norwegian in the speech of Norwegians who had settled in the U.S.A. Kachru 1978 discusses the same phenomenon in connection with Hindi-English bilingualism in India. Consider examples (34)-(37a). (34), (35), (36), and (37) are fixed collocations (idioms) in NM which are absent in PM. (34a), (35a), (36a), and (37a) are the Hindi counterparts of (34), (35), (36), and (37), respectively.

(34) NM : *ghussā/rāg thaṇḍā hoṇe*
anger cold become
'For anger to become cold' (for anger to vanish)

(34a) Hindi : *gussā ṭhaṇḍā honā*
anger cold become
'For anger to become cold' (for anger to vanish)

(35) NM : *jivāne mārūn ṭāk-ṇe*
life-inst. kill drop
'to kill'

(35a) Hindi : *jān se mār ḍāl-nā*
life-inst. kill drop
'to kill'

(36) NM : *X lā khušī ho-ṇe*
X dat. happiness happen
'for X to become happy'

(36a) Hindi : *X ko khušī ho-nā*
X dat. happiness happen
'for X to become happy'

(37) NM : *āplyā gallīt kutrā paṇ šer*
one's alley in dog also lion
'A dog is a lion in his own alley.'

(37a) Hindi : *apṇī galī mẽ kuttā bhī šer*
one's alley in dog also lion
'A dog is a lion in his own alley.' (i.e., one always acts stronger in one's own neighborhood.)

4.0. Syntax.

In what follows I shall discuss three syntactic constructions which NM shares with Hindi but not with PM. First, the progressive construction in

3. Collocations : The term collocation is used in the Firthian sense. See Firth 1957. Also, see Kachru 1965.

NM is absent in other varieties of Marathi. PM expresses the progressive aspect of a verb by adding /t/ to the verb stem, which is then followed by an appropriate form of the verb *as-ṇe* 'to be' (Damle 1911). Consider the following examples :

(38) PM : *tī gāṇa mhaṇat āhe*
she song say-prog. is
'She is singing a song.'

(39) PM : *mula kāma karat/karīt āhet*
boys work do-prog. are
'The boys are doing the work.'

PM does not allow the use of the verb *rāh-ṇe* 'to be' as an auxiliary in a progressive construction. Thus the following sentences are ungrammatical in PM.

(40) **tī gāṇa mhaṇūn rāhilī āhe*
she song say prog. is
'She is singing a song.'

(41) **mula kāma karun rāhilī āhet*
boys jobs do prog. are
'The boys are doing the jobs.'

However, (40) and (41) are grammatical sentences in NM. NM allows both types of progressive constructions, i.e., that of (38) and (39) and that of (40) and (41), but the type of progressive construction in (40) and (41) which is blocked in PM is the most natural and preferred in NM. In other words, although speakers of NM do not rule out sentences such as (38) and (39) they use the progressive construction in (40) and (41) in their own speech.

The use of the verb *rāh-ṇe* 'to be' as an auxiliary to express the progressive aspect (cf. NM (40) and (41) is shared with Hindi. In fact, the only way to express the progressive aspect in Hindi is by using the verb *rah-nā* 'to be' (Kachru 1966, Vajpeyi 1959). (H. *rah-nā* 'to be' is a cognate of the M. verb *rāh-ṇe* 'to be'.) Consider the following examples in Hindi :

(42) *vah gānā gā rahī hɛ*
she song sing prog. is
'She is singing a song.'

(43) *laṛke kām kar rahe hɛ̃*
boy jobs do prog. are
'The boys are doing the jobs.'

Both in Hindi (42) and (43) and NM (40) and (41) the auxiliary verbs *rah-nā* (Hindi) and *rāh-ṇe* (Marathi) are in their respective perfective forms. (For a description of the perfective forms in Hindi, see Kachru 1966, and for the perfective forms in Marathi, see Damle 1911).

4.1. NEGATION IN FUTURE TENSE.

A sentence in future tense is negated in PM by changing the form of the verb, which is then followed by the negative verb *nāhī* 'not' (Damle 1911 : 696). Consider the following examples :

(44) PM : *āmhī udyā mumbaīlā zāu*
we tomorrow Bombay to will go
'We will go to Bomay tomorrow.'

Negation :

(45) PM : *āmhī udyā mumbaīlā zāṇār nāhī*
we tomorrow Bombay to will go not
'We will not go to Bombay tomorrow.'

Notice the change in the verb from *zāu* 'will go' (44) to *zāṇār* 'will go' (45). The following example (46) shows that if the verb form *zāu* 'will go' (44) is retained and the negative verb is inserted before the verb then the resulting sentence (46) is ungrammatical in PM.

(46) **āmhī udyā mumbaīlā nāhī zāu*
we tomorrow Bombay to not will go
'We will not go to Bombay tomorrow.'

In contrast to PM, NM allows both types of negation as observed in (45) and (46). In fact sentences such as (46) are commonly used by speakers of NM. Consider example (47).

(47) NM : *āmhī udyā mumbaīlā* {*nāhī zāu* / *zāṇār nāhī*}
we tomorrow Bombay to {not will go / will go not}
We will not go to Bombay tomorrow.

Now consider Hindi sentences (48) and (49). (49) is the negative counterpart of (48). Notic that in Hindi, as in NM, the negative particle *nahī̃* 'not' is inserted before the main verb and the main verb *jāẽge* 'will go' remains unchanged.

(48) Hindi : *ham kal bambaī jāẽge*
we tomorrow Bombay will go
'We will go to Bombay tomorrow.'

(49) Hindi : *ham kal bambaī nahī̃ jāẽge*
we tomorrow Bombay not will go
'We will not go to Bombay tomorrow.'

4.2. NEGATION OF *pāhije* 'TO WANT'.

NM behaves similarly to Hindi with respect to a negative construction of another type. In PM the verb of wanting is *pāhije* 'to want', which when negated is replaced by its negative counterpart *nako* 'do not want'. Thus the verb *pāhije* 'to want' cannot be retained in a negative sentence as is evident from the following sentences.

(50) PM : *malā cahā pāhije*
I-dat. tea want
'I want tea.'

Negation :

(51) PM : *malā cahā nako*
I-dat. tea do not want
'I do not want tea.'

Notice that in the negative sentence (51), *pāhije* 'to want' is replaced by *nako* 'do not want'. If *pāhije* 'to want' is retained and the negative verb *nāhī* 'not' is inserted before it as in (52) it is ungrammatical in PM.

(52) **malā cahā nāhī pāhije*
I-dat. tea not want
'I do not want tea.'

In contrast to this, NM allows both types of negation, i.e., (51) and (52). In fact, the negative construction in (52) is much more natural for speakers of NM and is preferred.

An investigation of the Hindi data shows that the negation in Hindi (in the above context) is exactly the same as in (52) in that the verb of wanting, *cāhiye* 'to want' is retained in a negative sentence and the negative particle *nahī̃* 'not' is inserted before the verb.

(53) *mujhe cāy cāhiye*
I-dat. tea want
'I want tea.'

Negation :

(54) *mujhe cāy nahī̃ cāhiye*
I-dat. tea not want
'I do not want tea.'

5.0. SEMANTICS.

Another ground on which NM differs from PM is the semantics of some verbs. A number of verbs in Marathi (both PM and NM) and Hindi are cognates. However, they are not always semantically similar to each other. The semantic range of the verbs in PM is more restricted than the semantic range of their counterparts in NM and Hindi. Between Hindi and NM, the semantic range of the verbs in NM is less restricted (more extended) than Hindi.

Consider the following chart of verbs in PM and Hindi. Notice that in example (55) the cognates *bhaṭak-ṇe* 'to roam around' (PM) and *bhaṭak-nā* 'to get lost' (Hindi) do not share the meaning at all. In (56) and (57) the verbs in PM express only one meaning which is commonly shared by their counterparts in Hindi. However, the additional meaning expressed by the Hindi verbs in (56) and (57) is not shared by their counterparts in PM.

PM	Gloss	Hindi	Gloss
(55) *bhaṭak-ne*	a) 'to roam around' b) *'to get lost'	*bhaṭak-nā*	a) 'to get lost' b) *'to roam around'
(56) *mil-ṇe*	a) 'to get' b) *'to meet'	*mil-nā*	a) 'to get' b) 'to meet'
(57) *pakaḍ-ṇe*	a) 'to catch' b) *'to hold'	*pakaṛ-na*	a) 'to catch' b) 'to hold'

Examples (55)-(57) show that the semantic range of these verbs in Hindi is more extended than PM.

In contrast to the above, consider the chart of examples (58)–60). The verbs in (58)—(60) are from NM and they are the cognates of the verbs in (55)–(57). Notice that the verbs in NM (58)–(60) express the meanings conveyed by verbs in both PM and Hindi.

(58) *bhaṭak-ṇe*	(a) 'to roam around' (PM) (b) 'to get lost' (Hindi)
(59) *miḷ-ṇe*	(a) 'to get' (PM and Hindi) (b) 'to meet' (Hindi)
(60) *pakaḍ-ṇe*	(a) 'to catch' (PM and Hindi) (b) 'to hold' (Hindi)

6.0. EXPLANATION.

In the preceding sections, it was pointed out that NM differs from PM (and other varieties of Marathi) in terms of a number of linguistic features at different linguistic levels. It has been pointed out that these identificational features of NM are shared by Hindi. Thus we can conclude that NM is recognized as a distinct variety of Marathi on the basis of the linguistic features which it shares with Hindi, another Indo-Aryan language.

The question arises then as to why NM developed certain linguistic features in common with Hindi when other varieties of Marathi failed to do so. The most plausible hypothesis is one which takes into account Hindi-Marathi bilingualism at the northeastern border of Maharashtra. This provided a language contact situation, as a result of which Marathi spoken in this area borrowed a number of linguistic features from Hindi.

Therefore, NM shares a number of linguistic features with Hindi lacking in the other varieties of Marathi. This hypothesis is the most plausible one or two grounds :

(i) It provides a straightforward explanation for the development of certain linguistic features in NM which are similar to Hindi. Within this hypothesis, the vocabulary (2.0) and syntactic features (4.0—4.2) which are commonly shared by Hindi and NM can be labelled as borrowings from Hindi into Marathi. Also, the compound verbs, conjunct verbs, adverbs, and fixed collocations (idioms) in NM (sections 2.1—3.0) can be clearly noted as loan translations of their Hindi counterparts.

(ii) It abides by a more general axiom of linguistics, i.e., languages in contact become more and more like each other. Thus it is based on an independently motivated theory of linguistic convergence of languages in contact.

7.0. Problems and Questions.

In this paper I have shown that NM developed certain linguistic features as a result of linguistic convergence. Thus it can be inferred that two languages known by a bilingual are not learned and stored up completely separate from each other, but rather they influence each other. The question arises then as to how the grammar of the mother tongue of a bilingual should be described. For example, the description of the grammar of Marathi spoken by a Hindi-Marathi bilingual will not be complete unless the rules of the other language (Hindi) are incorporated into it. It is not clear at this point just how these two sources (i.e., Hindi and Marathi) of the bilingual's mother tongue (i.e., Marathi) should be formally represented.

This paper is also relevant for the theory of language change. If the language change (in this case the development of certain linguistic features similar to Hindi) is to be described within the generally accepted theory of transformational grammar, then it will have to be described in terms of rule loss, addition, and simplification. However, the transformational theory fails on two grounds. There does not seem to be any motivation within the grammar of Marathi which would have allowed one variety of Marathi to coin new vocabulary. Recall the chart in section 2.0. It shows that there are no gaps in the language, since PM has the vocabulary equivalent to that in NM and Hindi. Notice also that the innovation of certain types of constructions such as progressive (section 4.0) and negation (sections 4.1 and 4.2) is not justifiable in terms of simplification or necessity. PM as well as NM already have syntactic constructions equivalent to the ones in Hindi. Therefore, these innovations do not simplify but rather, complicate the grammar of NM. As a result of those innovations NM has two of each kind, instead of one (sections 4.0—4.2).

Any explanation of the above phenomenon within the transformational grammar fails to explain why these changes occur at all. In other words, the transformational theory of grammar fails to acknowledge the fact that the changes took place in NM due to Hindi-Marathi bilingualism.[4] Thus the discussion here supports the claim made in earlier studies by Kachru 1965, Labov 1970, Haugen 1953, etc. that sociological factors play a crucial role in language change and therefore, an adequate theory of language change should be made dynamic enough to accommodate those factors.

The discussion in this paper (recall sections 4.0—4.2) points out that NM has more than one construction available to perfom the same grammatical function. For example, recall section 4.0, where it is shown that NM allows both types of progressive construction. Similarly, both types of negation are (sections 4.1 and 4.2) allowed in NM. The questions that arise are : (i) whether or not these constructions (borrowed and native) are in free variation in the speech of speakers of Nāgpurī Marathi. In other words, whether or not these constructions are mutually interchangeable in all contexts, and (ii) whether there are extralinguistic factors which determine the choice of one as opposed to the other. Answers to these questions are essential to determine linguistic as well as extralinguistic functions of the variation created in NM because of Hindi-Marathi bilingualism.

REFERENCES

Bailey, C.I.N. and Roger W.Shuy, eds. 1973. *New ways of analyzing variation in English* Washington D.C. : Georgetown University Press.

Bell, R.T. 1976. *Sociolinguistics.* New York : St. Martin's Press.

Bickerton, D. 1971. Inherent variability and variable rules. *Foundations of Language* 7.457-92.

Bokamba, E.g. 1975. The Impact of multilingualism on language structures : The case of Central Africa. *Studies in Language Learning.* B.B. Kachru, ed. Urbana-Champaign: The Unit for Foreign Language Study and Research of the University of Illinois.

Damle, M. 1911. (1965 edition). *Shastriya Marathi vyākaraṇ.* Puṇe : Sawlaram āṇi manḍaḷī

Decamp, D. 1971. Toward a generative analysis of a post-creole speech continuum. In *Pidginization and creolization of languages,* ed. Dell Hymes, pp. 349-70. Cambridge : University Press.

Ferguson, C.A. 1959. Diglossia. *Word* 15 : 325-40.

Firth, J.R. 1957, 1964. *Papers in linguistics* 1934-1951. London : Oxford University Press.

Fishman, J.A. 1972. *The sociology of Language.* Rowley, Mass. : Newbury House Publishers.

Gumperz, J.J. 1971. *Language in social groups.* Edited by Anwar S. Dil. Stanford : Stanford University Press.

Haugen, E. 1953. *The Norwegian language in America.* Philadelphia : University of Pennsylvania.

Hock, H. and R.Pandharipande. 1978. Sanskrit in the pre-Islamic socio-linguistic context of South Asia. *International Journal of the Sociology of Language.* 1.11-25.

Kachru, B.B. 1965. Indian English: a study in contextualization. In C.E. Bazell, et. al., eds., *In memory of J.R. Firth* 255-87. London : Longmans.

4. It needs to be mentioned here that Hindi spoken in the Nagpur area is also influenced by Marathi. As a result, it has developed a number of linguistic features different from Hindi spoken in other parts (Uttar Pradesh, Bihar, etc.) of the country.

———. 1976. Indian English : a sociolinguistic profile of a transplanted language. In *Studies in Language Learning*. Vol. 1 : 2.

———. 1978. Toward structuring code-mixing : an Indian perspective. In Kachru and Sridhar, eds., *Aspects of sociolinguistics in South Asia*. Special issue of *International Journal of the Sociology of Language*, 16.27-46.

Kachru, Y. 1966. *An introduction to Hindi syntax*. Urbana : Dept. of Linguistics, University of Illinois. (mimeo)

——— and R. Pandharipande. 1979. Toward a typology of compound verbs in selected South Asian languages. Paper presented at the Conference on African Linguistics held at University of Illinois, Urbana.

Labov, W. 1970. *The study of language in its social context*. Studium Generale 23. 30-87.

Pandharipande, R. 1978. Nativization of loan words in Marathi. Paper presented at the Summer Meeting of Linguistic Society of America, held at the University of Illinois, Urbana.

———. 1978. On the syntax of compound verbs in Marathi. Paper presented at the Annual Meeting of American Oriental Society held in St. Louis.

Vajpeyi, K. 1959. *Hindi shabdānushāsan*. Banaras.

Weinreich, U. 1953. *Languages in contact*. The Hague : Mouton.

ENGLISHIZATIÓN OF ORIYA*

B.N. Patnaik
and
Ira Pandit

During the last five hundred years Oriya came in contact with a number of Indian and foreign languages including Marathi, Hindi, Persian, Portuguese and English. Of these, the language which has influenced Oriya the most significantly and extensively is English. The concern of this paper is to identify some of the forms in use in contemporary Oriya which have English sources.

Though Oriya has borrowed extensively from English, scholars who have worked on the development of the former have paid very little attention to this phenomenon. All one finds in the entire bulk of linguistic literature on Oriya on the subject are lists of a few words borrowed from English and some scattered, though sometimes insightful, observations here and there. Since the scope of the study is vast and very little work has been done, the present paper reports a study of an exploratory nature.

The data of the present study are from the written variety of Oriya and have been collected mostly from the following kinds of texts : sports reports, film journals, advertisements, thrillers, and both popular and scholarly writings on political and economic topics. Thus for the most part the study is based on the language of newspapers and periodicals. Since Oriya periodical literature is barely a hundred years old, and thrillers, film journalism, write-ups on sports events are of even more recent origin, it is expected that a study of the language used in texts of these kinds will be directly relevant to the needs of the present paper. Literature on science and technology has not been included in the corpus because even now there is hardly any literature in these subjects in Oriya.

The influence of English on Oriya is discernible at various levels and is not confined to the lexicon. This influence is most transparent at the level of vocabulary, but a careful study reveals that it goes far beyond vocabulary. The syntax of Oriya has been influenced and so have been the punctuation, the linguistic etiquette and the narrative mode. The present paper concentrates on the impact of English on the lexicon and the syntax of Oriya, on

*We are indebted to Professor R.N. Srivastava, Professor S.K. Verma and Dr. A.C. Pandey for making useful suggestions on the subject during the discussions we had with them, though we could not, we must admit, incorporate all their suggestions.

its linguistic etiquette and its punctuation system. The impact of English on the phonology of Oriya is beyond the scope of this study because the corpus here is confined to the written variety. Though English has significantly modified the narrative mode in Oriya, this subject also has been excluded from the present study partly because it is felt that it deserves a full-length treatment, and partly because the issues at this level relate more to stylistic choices than to purely linguistic forms.

LEXIS

A considerable number of English words have been borrowed by Oriya and most of them are now widely used both in speech and in writing. They are usually written in the Oriya script. It is not so much the number of borrowed words as the wide variety of contexts in which they are used that shows the extent of the influence English has had on Oriya at the lexical level. Given below is a list of English words currently used in Oriya. The list is by no means exhaustive; it is merely suggestive.

Articles of daily use : torch, battery, brush, lantern, electric, switch, glass, cigarette, etc.

Furniture : desk, bench, table, stool, dressing table, etc.

Crockery : cup, plate, dish, etc.

Names of dishes and related words : omelette, cutlet, chop, biscuit, peppermint, dinner, breakfast, dining hall, dining table, hotel, etc.

Fashion and dress : pant, shirt, coat, suit, maxi, mini, ear-ring, ring, armlet, snow, powder, blouse, hairpin, fashion, etc.

Games, sports and other modes of entertainment : cricket, football, hockey, badminton, volley (i.e. volley-ball), penalty, referee, umpire, handball, batting, bowling, circus, cinema, theatre, radio, harmonium, etc.

Names of diseases and related words : typhoid, cholera, pneumonia, injection, quinine, potash, stretcher, doctor, nurse, compounder, medical, hospital, etc.

Means of transport and related words : rail, motor, cycle, bus, launch, motor-boat, motor-cycle, truck, car, jeep, town, bus, tube, tyre, handle, spoke, brake, bell, petrol, road, canal, etc.

Words related to education : school, college, master, headmaster, principal minor, matric, I.A., B.A., M.A., pass, fail, pencil, rupper, nib, pen, chalk, slate, etc.

Law and administration : office, officer, peon, orderly, municipality, police, inspector, collector, S.D.O., bank, cheque, card, coupon, block, secretariat, jail, warden, jailor, kine house, court, judge, court-fee, degree, dismiss, etc.

Literary criticism : tragedy, comedy, novel, hero, drama, villain, romantic, absurd, etc.

The English words 'head', 'full', and 'half', as Haripriya Misra (1975:51) points out, are now being used as prefixes in Oriya. Words like *hed pandita* 'head-master', *hed gumastā* 'chief accountant', *hed kirāni* 'head clerk', *hāph cā* 'half-cup tea', *hāph chuti* 'half holiday' *phul ṭāim* 'whole time', etc. are commonly used.

A couple of observations regarding the spelling of the English loan words may be in order here.

Oriya has three letters in its alphabet to represent the dental, the retroflex and the palatal *s* sounds, though in speech it makes use of only one *s* sound, namely the dental /s/. A very large number of English loan words containing the *s* sound are spelt with the letter that represents the dental *s* in Oriya. However, in some cases, the dental /s/ in the /st/ cluster is always spelt with the letter represening the retroflex *s* in this language and the same holds for the English loan words like *master*, *stretcher*, *station*, etc.

Oriya has a single *j* sound, which in writing is represented by two symbols. One occurs in words like *jibā* (go), *jadi* (if), *je* (the complementizer), and the other, in words like *janibā* (know), *jaya* (victory) and *jibana* (life). All the English loan words containing the /dž/, /ž/ and /z/ sounds are spelt in Oriya with the letter which occurs in the second set of words given above.

Oriya does not distinguish betweeen long and short /i/ in speech, whereas in writing these are represented by two different symbols. *Puri* (name of the temple city) and *puri* (an item of food) are both pronounced alike, but spelt differently; the first carries the marker representing the long /i/ and the second, the short /i/. All English loan words containing the /i/ sound are spelt with the marker representing the short /i/.

It may be noted that the vast majority of borrowed lexical items from English are substantives; very few English verbs have been borrowed and even these are all used as nominals or predicative adjectives in Oriya. For instance, consider the use of *pass*, *fail*, *argue*, and *settle* in the following :

(1) *rāma pās karichi*
pass has done
'Rama has passed in the examination'

(2) *hari phel heichi*
fail has been
'Hari has failed in the examination'

(3) *mu tuma sange ārgu karibi nāhi*
I your with argue will do not
'I will not argue with you'

(4) *se kathā kana setil helā?*
that thing what settle was
Was that matter settled?'

In the structures above, *pās*, *phel*, *ārgu* and *setil* have not been used as verbs : *pās* and *ārgu* occur in the nominal slot in the compound verb form constructions, while *phel* and *setil* are used as predicative adjectives.

In a situation like this, when substantives are borrowed but not verbs, it is only to be expected that some Oriya verbs may acquire new collocations. This, indeed, has happened. For instance, the transitive verb *māribā* 'hit' in some non-standard varieties collocates with *gol* 'goal' in the context of the game of football, whereas in the standard variety the di-transitive verb *debā* 'give' takes this as object. Similarly the verb *karibā* 'do' collocates with *ran* 'run' in the context of cricket in the standard variety, whereas in at least some non-standard varieties the verb *pitiba* 'beat' collocates with it.

A few Oriya verbs appear to be acquiring new grammatical properties. *ṃilita hebā* 'meet' which normally does not take animate NP as subject seems to be acquiring this feature, under the influence of English, as evident from the following :

(5) *mu tānka sahita brekphāst tabul re milita heli*
I his with breakfast table at met
'I met him at breakfast.'

Similarly, the verb *bhala lagibā* 'like' which takes the so-called "dative" subject, normally does not take a human NP as "object", but now it seems to be acquiring this feature as (6) below would show. In (6), *bhala lagibā* takes the first person pronoun "object" *mu* 'I'. That the acquisition of this feature on the part of the verb *bhala lagibā* is due to English is clear when we consider the fact that (6) and (7) are translation-equivalents.

(6) *mu kana tumaku bhala lāgichi?*
I you PP like
(Literally : 'Have I appealed to you?')

(7) 'Do you like me?'

Thus it is evident that the borrowing of English lexical items by Oriya has not only resulted in the expansion of the Oriya lexicon, but also in some subtle changes in the feature complex of some Oriya lexical items.

SYNTAX

Whereas borrowing at the level of lexis is by and large need-based, it is not so at the level of syntax especially when the recipient language has a history of a thousand years. If a few syntactic patterns have come into use in Oriya as a result of its contact with English, it is not because these patterns are needed to fill any "syntactic gap" in the language. Borrowing of syntactic patterns is one of the consequences of a language-contact situation which involves, especially, a dominant non-native language and a native language.

It appears that contact with English has influenced the syntax of Oriya in two ways : (a) a few syntactic forms have come into use in Oriya, and (b) some syntactic patterns which existed in Oriya but were very infrequently used, have started being used quite often.

The following syntactic patterns in use in contemporary Oriya are due to English :

(i) reported speech construction with *je* as the reported speech marker (henceforth RSM).

Oriya uses two syntactic patterns to express reported speech which roughly are as follows :

(8) reported material—*boli*—main clause.

(9) main clause—*je*—reported material.

(9) is due to English whereas (8) has been in use ever since at least *Catura Binoda*, an eighteenth-century Oriya prose classic.

A sentence in direct speech, informally speaking, can be "converted" into its corresponding indirect speech form by : (a) adding either *boli* or *je* to the structure, (b) replacing the first and the second person pronouns in the quote with the appropriate third person pronouns, and (c) applying the subject-verb agreement rules in the quote following the changes introduced into it by (b). If *boli* is used as the RSM, then the quote must precede the main clause with *boli* coming at the end of the quote, and if *je* is chosen in place of *boli*, then the main clause must precede the quote with *je* coming at the beginning of the quote. For example, consider the following.

(10) direct speech : *hari kahilā, "mu kataka jibi".*
Hari said I Cuttack will go

(10a) indirect speech : *hari kahila je se kataka jiba.*
(10b) " " *kataka jiba boli hari kahila*

It may be noted here that contrary to the claim of Mohapatra and Das (1972 : 260), the sequence-of-tense rule does not operate in Oriya ; this language does not have forms corresponding to the English "will-would", "shall-should", etc.

(10a) itself seems to have given rise to a form of direct speech in Oriya in which *je* does not have the function of the indirect speech marker, though it is still used in the structure. An example of this pattern is given below.

(10c) direct speech: *hari kahilā je "mu kataka jibi".*

As forms of indirect speech both (10a) and (10b) are acceptable, though the users of the language show a strong preference for (10b). (10c) as a form of direct speech has certainly come to stay, though it is still not very frequently used.

(ii) restrictive relative construction with the relative *j-* contiguous to the head noun.

In contemporary Oriya three types of restrictive relative constructions are in use: (a) the participial relative, (b) the typical Indo-Aryan, and (c) the "Indo-European" type (Masica 1972 : 199). An example of each is given below.

(11) *cori karithibā* *pilā* (+main clause predicate)
theft do+PERF+REL PART boy

(12) *jou pilā cori karichi sei pilā* (+main clause predicate)
REL COREL

(13) *sei pilā, jie cori karichi* (+main clause predicate)
DEM REL
'The boy who has committed a theft...'

(11) and (12) have long been in use in the language and (13) is of recent origin. Sentence (13) has the following construction: the relative clause is placed to the immediate right of the head noun which it modifies, the head noun carries the distant demonstrative marker '*se*' (that), the relative pronoun occurs at the head of the relative clause, and the main clause predicate follows the relative clause. This construction which is clearly similar to the relative clause construction in English has emerged in Oriya as a result of its contact with English.

It may be noted here, however, that this construction does not seem to have gained wide acceptance among the speakers of the language. It has low frequency of occurrence in written Oriya, though apparently in the speech of the English-educated elite of Orissa its use is not so infrequent. (iii) non-restrictive relative construction with the relative clause in the post-head position.

Present-day Oriya uses two types of non-restrictive constructions: (a) one that resembles the typical Indo-Aryan variety of the restrictive relative construction, and (b) one that is largely similar to the so-called "Indo-European" type of restrictive relative construction, Given below is an instance of each.

(14) *jou gāndhiji sārā jibana ahimsā barata abalambana*
REL whole life non-violence
karithile sei gāndhiji sesa re ātatāyi ra guli re male.
adopted COREL end in assassin POSS bullet by died.
'Gandhiji who had spent his whole life in the cause of non-violence finally died because of an assassin's bullet'

(15) *rāma bābu jie oḍiā re anargala baktrutā dei pāranti,*
Rama HONF REL Oriya PP fluent speech give can
prakrutare oḍiā nuhanti.
really oriya
'Rama Babu who can deliver speeches in fluent Oriya is not really an Oriya'

The structure (15) is due to English. One significant fact about this construction is that it does not make use of the so-called "correlative" morpheme, and it is indeed in this that it is structurally different from the "Indo-European" restrictive relative construction. This structure is decidedly more frequently used, both in speech and writing, than the restrictive relative construction (13) which, as pointed out earlier, has also come from English.

(iv) possessive phrase in the form: object of possession—possessor. Yet another syntactic form which has come into Oriya from English is represented by the following:

(16) *pratnatatwa bibhāg, bhārat sarkār*
archaeology department, India Government
'Department of Archaeology, Government of India'

In this possessive phrase, the genitive morpheme *ra* does not surface and the object of possession NP precedes the possessor NP, the two being separated by a comma. The characteristic Oriya genitive phrase construction, however, is represented by the following:

(17) *bhārat sarkaranka ra pratnatatwa bibhāg*
+HONF GEN

where the possessor NP precedes the object of possession NP and the genitive morpheme *ra* relates the two. (17) is the dominant form in Oriya. (16) is used in the written form in such formal and semi-formal contexts as radio announcements, addresses on envelopes, advertisements, pamphlets, sign boards, posters, and administrative circulars. Especially in official communications this form is widely used. It is rarely used in speech.

If these forms have arisen in the language as a result of its contact with English, some syntactic patterns which existed in Oriya but were used infrequently, are now being used more frequently as a result of the contact. Two such forms are the passive construction and the parenthetical construction.

In general, in Oriya, the active construction is and has always been far more frequently used than the passive. The passive form is used more frequently now than at any time prior to the contact of Oriya with English, which may lead one to think that this syntactic pattern has been borrowed from English. This is not the case, since examples of the passive construction can be found in inscriptions dating back to the early part of the sixteenth century. Consider the following, for instance (Tripathi 1962:301):

(18) *je parikshyā āna gita nāta karāile jāni se jagannāthanka droha karai.*
'If a steward causes other songs to be recited be it known he rebels against Lord Jagannath.'

(18) is an instance of the so-called "impersonal passive". The passive verb *jāni* in sense of "be it known" may have gone out of use in most parts of Orissa but is still used in this sense among the sevakas of the temple of Lord Jagannath at Puri. Passive sentences can be found in *Catura Binoda* also. Given below is an instance (D. Mahanty 1978 : 48):

(19) *puṇḍarika paṇḍā ku kundarekhā prāpata helā.*
'(The girl) Kundarekha was given to Pundarika Panda.'

Traditionally Oriya has favoured the use of the passive construction without the agentive phrase; this is still, by and large, the case, though in present-day Oriya one does find instances of passive sentences containing the agentive phrase. Earlier, the colloquial *dei* (by) derived from Sanskrit *dwārā* (Nanda Sharma 1968:271) and the formal *Kartruka* (by) derived, again, from Sanskrit were the agentive post-positions in such constructions and *dwārā* was generally used as the instrumental postposition. Contemporary Oriya does not make use of *kartruka*, uses *dei* only in informal discourse, and almost exclusively uses *dwārā* in semi-formal and formal uses. The choice of a single postposition *dwārā* in place of *dei/dwārā* and *kartruka* in agentive phrases in which the agent is not always an individual or a group but often an impersonal agency such as a social or political institution, may be due to English which consistently uses the preposition *by* in this structure. Apart from this, the Oriya passive construction does not seem to have been influenced by English.

The increase in frequency of the use of the passive in modern Oriya could, however, be attributed to the impact of English. There are contexts in which English often prefers the use of the passive and in those contexts modern Oriya also shows the same preference. For instance, the passive construction is now widely used in Oriya in official communication, in administration and law in general. A letter for a favour addressed to one's employer, to cite one example, states the request in the passive *mote diājāu* 'may it be given to me' rather than in the corresponding active *mote diantu* (give +HONF me).

The parenthetical construction, like the passive construction, is not new to Oriya. One of the inscriptions that Tripathy (225) has studied contains an example of a parenthetical clause. This inscription dates back to the thirteenth century. The clause is not separated from the rest of the sentence with either vertical lines or brackets as a clause of that kind would be in modern Oriya, but that is because punctuation markers were hardly ever used in the inscriptions. The construction under reference is the following:

(20) *...baghamarā bārabāti bhumi ekādasa rudra bhikshyadeba bhumi samaṃdhe...*
'With regard to the Baghamara land (which was granted) for offering of food (in charity) in honour of the eleven Rudras' (translation, Tripathy (226).

In (20) *ekādasa rudra bhikshyādebā bhumi* is in parenthesis, modifying *baghamarā bārabti bhumi* in the manner of a non-restrictive relative cause.

However, parenthetical constructions were rarely used in Oriya prior to its contact with English. Though such constructions have never really become popular in Oriya, they are certainly used far more frequently now than ever before.

LINGUISTIC ETIQUETTE

English has modified the system of linguistic etiquette in Oriya significantly. In both written and spoken Oriya one comes across terms of greeting, expressions of gratitude, regret, forms of address which can be attributed to contact with English.

Mahapatra and Das (1972:44) observe that in modern Oriya society women use the surname of their fathers before marriage and that of their husbands after marriage, and correctly attribute it to the influence of the West on Oriya society coming through English. Earlier, this was not the practice. In general, no surname was used for women, though sometimes the general word *debi* (literally 'goddess') was used after the names of Brahmin women and *dei* (which may be the colloquial form of *devi*) or *dāsi* (the latter meaning 'female slave') after the names of non-Brahmin women *debi* and *dāsi* were used for both the married and the unmarried alike. *debi* is now in use as a form of address indicating respect to the addressee irrespective of the caste she belongs to.

In addition to the suffix *debi*, other terms of address now used in Oriya are "Mr.", "Miss", Mrs. and *kumāri* (equivalent of "Miss") and *srimati* (equivalent of "Mrs."). "Ms." has not come into use in the language. One finds frequent use of these terms in crime fiction, film journals and the literature that depicts the life style of the urban, educated middle class and the rich. Formal use of the language still does not favour the use of the English "Miss", "Mrs.", or "Mr.", and would prefer their respective equivalents *kumāri*, *srimati* and *sri/srijukta*. No matter what term is used, however, the very mode of addressing women with such terms is due to English.

Expressions of greeting like *suprābhāta* 'good mornig', *susandhyā* 'good evening', *subharatri* 'good night', etc. are mostly found in detective fiction, film magazines and other popular periodicals. These are hardly ever used in speech. These are avoided in serious writing also except when the author's intention is to use them as a device for characterization. Some authors use them for satirical purposes.

The loan-translation term *dhanyabāda* 'thank you' as a means of expression of gratitude and also as a politeness expression is now a part of Oriya. Its use is restricted to the highly educated and sophisticated section of the society. Members of this society use the term only when they communicate among themselves. A bureaucrat, for example, may use the term *dhanyabāda* to express his thankfulness to his superiors, equals and even immediate subordinates both in and out of his office, but the same person is most unlikely to use this term while speaking to his cook or servant at home even when the latter deserves, on occasion, special courtesy.

There are at least two expressions of apology which have come into Oriya from English by way of loan translation: *kshyamā karibe* 'excuse me' and *mu dukshita* 'I'm sorry'. In the same way, *dayākari*+*V-honorific* (as *dayakari sunantu, āsantu, basantu,* etc. meaning 'please listen, come, sit,' etc.) has come into Oriya from English and is used for the purpose of making a request. These are all used in formal situations.

sār 'Sir' as a form of address seems to have already become a part of Oriya. It is used both in speech and writing, though more often in speech than in writing. The urban and semi-urban population use it widely to address teachers, administrators, and others who hold high rank and wield power. Unlike *sāheb* which is a loaded word, *sār* is almost neutral as a term of address. In the colonial days *saheb* and *mem sāheb* were used as terms of address by the natives working as menials in British households for their master and his wife. Now these terms are used mostly by servants and people of lower social status when they address their master and his wife who are of course no longer British. These terms are on their way out and with greater democratisation of the society they will disappear altogether.

PUNCTUATION

If there is any aspect of Oriya where the impact of English has been really sweeping, it is punctuation. Punctuation is an important feature of written Oriya, today, but it was not so prior to the contact of Oriya with English, Except for *purṇa birām* (full stop) there was no punctuation. marker in ancient Oriya. The full stop was indicated by a vertical line, although in poems there was the use of the double vertical lines, to indicate *purṇa birām*. This was so even till the eighteenth century.

Absence of punctuation markers, observes Tripathy (1962:35), is one reason why the ancient Oriya inscriptions dating back to the thirteenth, fourteenth and fifteenth centuries are often difficult to interpret. This is also true of ancient Oriya poetry. Some poets, of course, consciously exploited the absence of punctuation markers for artistic purposes. A line from the eighteenth century major poet Upendra Bhanja's *Baidehisha Bilāsa* will demonstrate this:

(21) *bihara kānana kara ālingana ku*

(21) is ambiguous. The meanings of (21) are as follows:

(21a) 'Wander (with her) through the forests and embrace (her)'

(21b) 'Cut off (her) ears and do not embrace (her)'

In this poem Lord Rama sends the message (21) to his brother Lakshmana through the demoness Surpanakhā who willingly carries it thinking that it means (21a) and when he receives the message Lakshmana immediately cuts off her nose which is what Rama wanted him to do, as he reads the meaning (21b) into it. The sentence can be easily disambiguated by using a comma after *kāna* (ear) to yield the message (21b), or after *kānana* (forest) to yield the meaning (21a). The verb *bihara* which is ambiguous can now be understood as "cut off" or "wander" depending on whether the comma is after *kāna* or *kānana*. Similar instances occur elsewhere in the poetry of Bhanja and his contemporaries.

Punctuation markers came into use in Oriya only after its contact with English. Modern Oriya uses all the punctuation markers that English uses and these have the same value in both the languages with one notable exception. In place of the dot which is used as the full-stop in English, Oriya still uses a vertical line. (The double-vertical lines in use in ancient Oriya has gone out of existence.) The rules governing the use of punctuation markers are by and large the same for both English and and Oriya. Some differences are as follows: (a) The comma is used in Oriya after the complementizer *je* in a sentence like (22) which is not possible in English as evident from the incorrectness of the English version of (22).

(22) *rāma ebe jānilā je, pruthibi gol*
'*Rama recently learnt that, the earth is round.'

(b) In both restrictive and non-restrictive constructions in Oriya, the comma is used after the head word and at the end of the relative clause when the relative clause immediately follows the head word. In English the comma can be used this way only in the non-restrictive relative construction.

(c) In Oriya, when the complement clause using *je* as the complementizer precedes the main clause, a comma is used to separate the two as in (23). This does not happen in English. A comma cannot occur where it is in the English version of (23).

(23) *pruthibi je gol, ehā sata.*
'*That the earth is round, is true.'

The use of abbreviated forms and initials in contemporary Oriya is due to English. Abbreviated forms for *mister* and *doctor*, for instance, are used in Oriya. Mostly the *visarga* sign with two connected circular marks, one above the other (:) or two dots one above the other (:), is used in the abbreviated forms in Oriya whereas in English a dot is used. However, the single dot marker is also used in Oriya. Using initials is not a popular practice among the Oriyas. and it may be noted that initials are used in Oriya only for the male members of the society.

The case of the *visarga* may be interesting. Oriya did not have any punctuation markers in the past other than the *daṇḍā* (vertical line) and borrowed all the punctuation markers from English except the *visarga* which, incidentally, it did not use as a punctuation marker at all. The continuing use of the single *daṇḍā* marker need not be regarded as unusual because it was used in the language before the borrowing took place. What is surprising is the use of the *visarga* sign in a place where the dot would be expected to be used, considering that the *visarga* was never used as a punctuation marker and that Oriya did not make use of the abbrevialed forms in the past.

In conclusion, it may be observed that the impact of English on Oriya is not merely confined to the addition of a number of lexical items to the language. New collocations have arisen in the language modifying the strict sub-categorization features and the selectional restrictions of at least some Oriya verbs, new grammatical forms have come to the language and at least some grammatical forms, which existed in the language but were hardly ever used, have come to be used much more frequently. New items have been added to the system of linguistic etiquette in Oriya and almost an entire system of punctuation has come into existence in the language.

REFERENCES

Bloomfied, Leonard. 1933. *Language*. London : George Allen and Unwin Ltd.

Gumperz, John J. 1975. On the ethnology of linguistic change. *Sociolinguistics*. The Hague : Mouton and Co.

Hockett, Charles F. 1958. *A course in modern linguistics*. New York : The Macmillan Company.

Kachru, Braj B. 1975. Towards structuring the form and function of code mixing : an Indian perspective. *Studies in Linguistic Sciences*. vol. 5, no. 1, Spring.

Kelley, Gerald. 1975. The status of Hindi as a lingua franca. *Sociolinguistics*. The Hague: Mouton and Co.

Mahanty, Banshidar. 1978, *Oḍiā bhāsara utpatti o karma bikās* (in Oriya). Cuttack : Friends' Publishers. (Second edition).

Mahanty, Debendra (ed.). 1978. *Catura binoda* (in Oriya). Cuttack: Friends' Publishers.

Mahapatra, Narayan and Sridhar Das. 1972. *Sarbasāra byākaraṇa* (reprint). Cuttack : New Students' Store.

Masica, Colin 1972. Relative clause in South Asia. In Paul M. Peranteau et al (eds). *The Chicago which hunt*. Chicago. Illinois: Chicago Linguistic Society.

Mishra, Haripriya. 1975. *Historical Oriya morphology*. Varanasi : Bharata Manisha.

Mishra, Pandit Binayak. 1972. *Oḍiā bhāsāra purātatwa* (in Oriya). Cuttack: Friends' Publishers. (Second edition).

———. 1975. *Odiā bhāsāra itihāsa* (in Oriya). Cuttack : Cuttack Students' Store. (Revised edition).

Nanda Sharma, Pandit Sri Gopinath. 1968. *Odiā bhāsātatwa* (in Oriya), Cuttack : New Students' Store. (Second edition.)

Tripathy, Kunj Bihari. 1962. *The evolution of Oriya language and script*. Cuttack (now Bhubaneswar) : Utkal University.

CLASSIFICATION OF POLAR VERBS IN SELECTED SOUTH ASIAN LANGUAGES

Udaya Narayana Singh, K.V. Subbarao
and
S.K. Bandyopadhyay

0.1. In the recent literature on Compound Verbs (henceforth, CV) in Indo-Aryan languages (cf. Singh 1979a; 1979b), it has been suggested that polar verbs (usually the first member in a CV sequence) could be classified according to lexical cooccurrence restrictions on polar-vector combination. Although it would be more expl anatory to find semantic restrictions on these combinations, it is our belief that no meaningful work can be done in this direction if a large-scale survey of lexical constraints is not undertaken in languages with CV-combinations. Besides, such studies could also throw light on patterns of frequency-based distribution of compound verbs in a contiguous linguistic area (cf. Hook 1977 for a different basis of such a distribution of CVs in IA languages), and could also help in identification of vectors from a set of probable vectors, and in their grading. All this would provide lexicographers preparing verb-dictionaries of these languages with much useful data. In spite of the fact that such studies have a number of points in their favour, few linguists have attempted to classify polar verbs using this criterion. On the other hand, a number of studies done with varying degree of success touching on the problem of defining vectors formally as well as functionally have appeared in recent times (cf. Hook 1974, 1978a, 1978b; Masica 1976; Dasgupta 1977; Subbarao 1979; Annamalai 1979; Bhat 1979).

0.2. It is the purpose of this paper[1] to look into cooccurrence restrictions on polar-vector combination in selected South Asian languages spoken over a large but contiguous area in order to find answers to the following questions :

i. What is the relative frequency of occurrence of major vectors in IA languages? How do the Dravidian languages fare in such a frequency-count?

---

1. We are extremely grateful to Dr. Peter E. Hook for offering many valuable suggestions. The first phase of this work was presented at a Seminar on Lexicography at CIH, Agra in December, 1979, and it has been listed in the references as Singh 1979b. We are thankful to Mr. S. Panigrahi who helped us in computing our data in the initial stages.

ii. Can vectors in South Asian languages be graded in any meaningful way that throws light on the nature and extent of 'lexical emptying' (Masica 1979) undergone by them?

iii. Can polar verbs be classified according to vectors they combine with, and on the basis of how many they can occur with? Would the grammatically possible combinations in these languages be limited compared to vast logical possibilities?

iv. Do South Asian languages show striking similarities in the patterns of polar verb classification, or are they very different from each other? What would a relative frequency-distribution map of CV-formation in IA languages look like, if it is based on list-frequency counts? Would it confirm the findings of Hook (1977) which was based on a text-frequency count?

1.1. The following South Asian languages have been included in the present study: Assamese, Bengali, Hindi, Maithili, Oriya, Punjabi and Telugu (abbreviated in tables and appendices as A, B, H, M, O, P and T, respectively). Although we wished to concentrate mainly on Indo-Aryan languages, it was felt that such a study would be incomplete unless it was viewed in contrast with CV-formation in Dravidian. Telugu was taken as a representative of Dravidian languages for several reasons. First, this was the only Dravidian language on which the authors had first hand information. Secondly, in terms of 'linguistic area', it was the nearest to the IA languages included in this work, and this would help us in looking into the nature of CV-formation over a contiguous area. Thirdly, while presenting arguments against a theory that traced the origin of CVs in IA to Dravidian, Masica (1976:144) remarked that CV-formation in the former seemed to be more developed than in the latter. Then he speculated and we quote (Masica 1976:145): "Even if Dravidian turns out to be somewhat poorer in the number of different explicators in use (due perhaps to a very late elaboration of the category in Indo-Aryan)—and we do not know for sure—those it has may be heavily used. This is certainly the case with Telugu *poo-*. The question is an open one". We wanted to test whether what Masica said about Dravidian in general and Telugu in particular was true for GO (*poo*— in Telugu) as well as other vectors.

1.2. The 'probable' vectors that have been included in the work have been given at the end of this paper in Appendix I. They include the follwing or their 'parallels': TAKE, GIVE, GO, DIE, RISE, SIT, COME, FALL, THROW, KEEP, MOVE, SEE, KILL, COME-OUT, BRING-OUT, HOLD and BRING. Not all of these are functional in all of these languages. For instance, our restricted data seems to show that Assamese lacks MOVE, Maithili THROW, and Oriya BRING-OUT and THROW. Similarly, SEND, COME-OUT and BRING-OUT were found to be missing in Bengali. It must be noted here that for Telugu, we have not included RISE and COME in this study because of lack of time for going into the details of CV-formation in Telugu. We must also note that the 'probable' vectors that turned out to be non-vectors in this survey may actually function as vectors if the corpus of polar verbs is enlarged. Therefore, we do not claim any finality of judgement as regards to their vectorship.

1.3. The polar verbs dealt with number 117, and they include 54 intransitives and 63 transitives (plus a few double-transitives and causatives). These have been listed in Appendix II. We started with 200-odd verbs to find out semantic parallels in all the languages under investigation. For the IA languages, we wanted especially to identify verbs that would be similar in both form and meaning. We soon realized, however, that it would not be possible to gather a large number of verbs if we insisted on both. Moreover, since we had included Telugu, semantic parallels were the only ones we could depend on. Actually we used the same criterion in the selection of vectors as mentioned in 1.2. above. For instance, we grouped *phEl/pEl* in Bengali/Assamese, *Daal* in Hindi, and *saT* in Punjabi under THROW. It should be noted that the word "parallel" assumes special importance for several reasons. Although some polars show identical or similar forms in all or most of the included IA languages, they also show slight differences in their shades of meaning. Such forms had to be retained because it was impossible to get verbs in sufficient number with exactly identical semantic shading for all these items across languages. We could illustrate with a few examples as to why we call them "(semantic) parallels." Although *dhok/meru* in Assamese (item 63 in Appendix II) is parallel to words for 'cover' in other languages, *meru* means something more : 'wrap'; *phaT/phuT* (item 35) which has a general meaning of 'break' is used in Punjabi only in slang to mean 'drive (some one) away (from a group or a place)'. Similarly, we have taken Telugu *raayaDam* 'apply' to be parallel to 'anoint' (item 58) in other languages. *khaT* (item 8) would normally mean 'work/labour', but in Punjabi, it is associated with 'earning'. Although other IA languages have a special verb for 'leak/ooze out' (item 16), Oriya has *bOh* which means both 'flow' and 'leak'. Compared to this, we have taken Telugu *kaaraDam* which literally means 'drip'. Then there are verbs such as *thOk* in Bengali which means 'be tired' (item 20) which can occur only as a polar in a CV-sequence where the vector is GO. If we want to avoid such set collocations, we have to include conjunct verbs—in this case *klaanto+hOwaa* 'tired-be'. The latter would have a wider choice of vectors. In such other cases, both options have been chosen, and the widest range of vectors has been accepted. There are about 22 instances where even in IA languages, conjunct verbs had to be accepted as parallels to simple verbs in other languages. The item number and languages in which conjunct verb parallels were found include the following : 1 (B), 7, (A B), 8 (A H), 20 (A B), 23 (B), 24 (A), 36 (A), 37 (A), 41 (O P), 44 (A B), 46 (A), 48 (A), 51 (A), 52 (O), 56 (A B), 64 (P), 65 (A), 69 (A B), 76 (A), 88 (A), 90 (A B), and 109 (B). Ideally, we should have taken simple verbs only or items where all the languages concerned had conjunct verbs. Anyone trying to do so would soon realize, however, that it was a very difficult task. Moreover, as yet we do not know whether conjunct verbs take fewer vectors than their simple verb counterparts. It has been our experience that in most cases, where the same language had the option of taking either of the two for a particular item, it showed the same vector-participation for both. Notice that in the case of Telugu, conjunct verbs could not be avoided. In as many as 22 out of 117 items, the parallels were conjuncts. In fact, one would guess that if the list of polar verbs were enlarged, the chances of finding conjunct parallels would be still greater.

2.1. Of the earlier classifications of polar verbs, the only serious attempt has been that of Hook 1978a. While looking into this classification, one must keep in mind that it was more or less semantically motivated, although data concerning lexical cooccurrences have also been taken into account here. This classification deals only with Hindi polar verbs. The author himself admitted that it was "highly approximative if not actually misleading" (Hook 1978a:144). This typology of polars is given in the following table :

CLASS	NATURE	VECTOR	EXAMPLES
*hu*waadi	Intrn	GO	*ho*; *baiTh; uTh*, etc.
*ru*waadi	Intrn	GIVE	*ro*; *hans*; *cal; muskaraa*, etc.
*samjh*aadi	Trn	GO &TAKE	*samajh*; *jaan*; *maan*, etc.
*li*yaadi	Trn, Refl	TAKE	*le*; *khaa; dekh; chin*, etc.
*di*yaadi	Trn	GIVE	*de; nikal; phenk*; *choR*, etc.
*kar*aadi	Trn	TAKE&GIVE	*kar; karaa; rakh*, etc.
*jaa*di	Exceptional	—	*jaa; bhuul* (*jaa*); *le* (*aa*); *bajaa* (*laa*) etc.
*cah*aadi	Stative	None	*caah; rakh; kahlaa*, etc.

TABLE 1 : Classification of Hindi Polar Verbs as in Hook 1978a.

This is surely an incomplete suggestion. We have shown its shortcomings elsewhere (Singh 1979a; 1979b), and therefore skip a discussion here. A student of the semantics of Hindi verb could, at a later date, elaborate, modify or reject this proposal. In the following paragraph, however, we wish to show the difference between such typologies and our method of classification.

2.2. In order to find the restrictions on lexical combination of CVs in these languages, we first tabulated all polars with all the probable vectors and checked and re-checked these with native speakers[2] of these languages.

2. To start with, for Bengali, Telugu and Assamese, the authors themselves served as informants, but soon these data were checked with a number of native speakers of these languages and new data were collected from others. Many served as informants at different stages of data collection, but we received valuable assistance particularly from the following : Jayantimala Devi (Assamese), Bichitra Kumar Guha (Bengali), Harbir Arora (Hindi and Punjabi), Dipti Mishra (Hindi), Jaya Singh (Maithili), Prabodh Nayrayan Singh (Maithili), Panchanan Mohanty (Oriya), Sabyasachi Panigrahi (Oriya), Ravinder Gargesh (Punjabi) and Sarala Subbarao (Telugu). We are thankful to these and all others who helped us in more than one ways.

We did face a problem of opinion variation as we checked our data-sheets with informants from different mother-dialect background but speaking the same language. We must admit also that in certain cases, even when the same informant was asked about combinatory possibilities of these polars and vectors a second time, there were slight differences. In some cases, the common reaction was : "the combination is okay, but it does not sound elegant." In these instances, we retained the combinations. In case of unsure combinations, we eliminated such CVs. Normally, the informants were asked to supply proper contexts in borderline cases. After that, one or more Compound Verb Tests[3] were applied to determine genuineness of a particular combination. Although we do not claim to have been able to rule out all the variations completely, cases of opinion variation were so few and restricted that we do not believe they will seriously affect our main thesis.

2.3. The first and major classification of polars on the basis of the final data-sheet can be established by answering the following question : With how many vectors can a particular polar occur ? If a language had all 18 vectors, there would be 19 total possibilities. The total is one more because there may be verbs that never participate in CV-formation. Hook (1978a: 144) gave a few such verbs; they are listed in the last category (*cah*aadi) in Table 1 above. Similarly, in our list, Assamese[4], Oriya[5] and Punjabi[6] have polars which are non-participants or "Zero-Vector". Probably, if we enlarged our corpus, we would find such verbs for other languages under investigation also. There could also be polars which occur with only one vector, and this vector could 'potentially' be any one of the 18 mentioned in Appendix I. We could call such polars Mono-Vector verbs. Thus logically there could be 18 sub-types of mono-vector verbs. It would be equally logical to expect to find verbs which could occur with all the vectors in a particular language. These would be *n*-vector polars. One can also imagine that some polars might take any particular combination of two or three or more vectors. The logical possibilities of how many sub-types of polars there could be between Mono- and *n*-Vector types in a language will depend naturally upon the value of *n* in a particular language, i.e., on how many vectors a language has. We have learned from our data-sheets that Bengali has 15 vectors, Oriya 16, and other IA languages 17 each. We have been able to take only 8 Vectors in Telugu, Therefore, for the present, let us assume that Telugu has only 8 vectors. Note that we do not claim here in any case that these languages do not have more vectors than 8, 15, 16 or

3. The tests include the following: Do-Insertion, Verb Interrogation, Negation, Until, By-the-time, Phrasal Verb, Apprehension, Contradiction, Compound Verb Reduction and Incompletion among others. (See Hook 1974; 1978b, Singh 1979a; Singh and Bandyopadhyay, 1978).

4. Swing, Taste and Leave (Intrn) in Assamese.

5. Swing, Fill in/Insert in Oriya.

6. Call/Drive a cart in Punjabi.

17—whatever be the number given. An enlarged corpus may show more vectors to be functional, and some we have ourselves excluded (such as LEAVE in Punjabi). Now, let us compute the maximum possibilities under each of the combination-types here :

COMBINATION-TYPES	MAXIMUM POSSIBILITY				
	18-*vector*	17-*vector*	16-*vector*	15-*vector*	8-*vector*
Mono-Vector	18	17	16	15	8
Two-Vector	153	136	120	105	28
Three-Vector	816	680	560	455	56
Four-Vector	3060	2380	1820	1365	70
Five-Vector	8568	6188	4368	3003	56
Six-Vector	18564	12376	8008	5005	28
Seven-Vector	31824	19448	11440	6435	8
Eight-Vector	43758	24310	12870	6435	1
Nine-Vector	48620	24310	11440	5005	—
Ten-Vector	43758	19448	8008	3003	—
Eleven-Vector	31824	12376	4368	1365	—
Twelve-Vector	18564	6188	1820	455	—
Thirteen-Vector	8568	2380	560	105	—
Fourteen-Vector	3060	680	120	15	—
Fifteen-Vector	816	136	16	1	—
Sixteen-Vector	153	17	1	—	—
Seventeen-Vector	18	1	—	—	—
Eighteen-Vector	1	—	—	—	—
Non-Participant	1	1	1	1	1
Total	262144	131072	65536	32768	256

TABLE 2 : Logical Possibilities of Types of Polar-Verbs Calculated on the Basis of their Occurrence with *n*-Number of Vectors *r*-at a time

2.4. Our obvious next task is to find how many of these logical types and subtypes are grammatically possible in these seven South Asian languages, restricting our attention to the 117 polars mentioned earlier. In particular it would be interesting to know if there is an upper limit on the maximum number of vectors that a particular polar can take. In other words, are there polars that occur with all the vectors of a language ? Similarly, how many of each of these subtypes are actually realized grammatically ? These questions are answered in the following table showing the total number of grammatical possibilities under each combination-type in these language :

VECTOR-TYPES	A	B	H	M	O	P	T
Mono	5	2	1	6	3	1	1
Two	6	4	7	10	8	8	4
Three	10	12	13	11	10	12	8
Four	15	14	16	16	13	15	8
Five	6	12	13	3	7	14	8
Six	5	15	16	5	5	8	7
Seven	4	9	6	—	4	5	3
Eight	1	7	6	2	3	8	—
Nine	1	5	—	—	—	5	—
Ten	—	4	2	—	—	1	—
Eleven	—	1	—	—	—	—	—
Twelve & above	—	—	—	—	—	—	—
Non-Participant	1	—	—	—	1	1	—
Total	54	85	80	53	53	78	39

TABLE 3 : Grammatically Possible Polar-Types in Seven South Asian Languages Based on 117 Polars as in Appendix II.

2.5. Regarding the above table, a few things should be noted. First, for the six IA languages, an eleven-vector combination seems to be the upper limit for polar verbs. Secondly, although Hindi and Maithili appear to show gaps for nine-vector and seven-vector combination slots respectively, these types do exist in those languages. (See Singh, 1979a for seven-vector combinations in Maithili.) The only thing one has to do is to enlarge the corpus and track them down. Thirdly, in all the languages, the maximum polar subtypes seem to be roughly between three-to-five vector combinations. This increases to six-vector combinations in Bengali and Hindi because in these two, the maximum number stretches to as much as ten/eleven. However, we should not restrict our attention to the total number of subtypes only because this number may be deceiving to an extent. It is possible that although the number of subtypes in a particular slot is less than that of another, there may be more polar verbs opting for the former than for the latter. Take, for instance, the case of Assamese mono-vector (total subtypes : 5) and two-vector (subtypes : 6). Of the 117 polars, about 20% in Assamese opt for the former, whereas only about 11% fall in the latter group. Therefore, to get the true picture of the amount of polar-participation, we need to look into a table such as follows :

TYPES	A	B	H	M	O	P	T
Mono	20%	8%	8%	16%	7%	9%	4%
Two	11%	8%	14%	26%	20%	18%	3%
Three	27%	12%	17%	31%	26%	16%	13%

Four	23%	17%	20%	18%	21%	13%	13%
Five	6%	10%	13%	3%	11%	17%	15%
Six	4%	13%	17%	4%	7%	11%	20%
Seven	4%	12%	5%	—	3%	4%	32%
Eight	1%	10%	5%	2%	3%	7%	—
Nine	1%	5%	—	—	—	3%	—
Ten	—	4%	2%	—	—	1%	—
Eleven	—	1%	—	—	—	—	—
None	3%	—	—	—	2%	1%	—

TABLE 4 : Polar-participation in Vector-combinations of Different Length Calculated from 117 (the bottom column is for the non-participant polars).

It is clear from this table that 68% to 98% of the polars fall somewhere between the mono- and the six-vector types in IA languages. A detailed break-up of what percentage of the verbs fall in these slots could be given here : Assamese (94%), Bengali (68%), Hindi (88%), Maithili (98%), Oriya (97%) and Punjabi (89%). As expected, Hindi and Punjabi show similarities in this respect. However, the fact that as many as 32% of the polars in Bengali opt for combinations higher than six-vector is surprising. It shows that the degree of lexical emptying of verbs used as vectors (which is closely related to the 'number' of active vectors) has taken place in Bengali more than in any other language. We will shortly list other evidence in support of this contention. From this viewpoint, CV-formation in Bengali would seem to be more developed than in other IA languages. Another point worth taking note of is the steady increase in the number of polars participating in mono- to seven-vectors in Telugu. In fact, it only confirms that although Telugu has fewer vectors, it makes the maximum use of what it has. The pattern is incidentally very different from that of IA languages.

3.1. The tables given earlier do not tell us whether a limited set of vectors recur again and again in all these combination-types or almost all the vectors occur equally frequently. For this reason, we calculated the relative frequencies with which these vectors enter into the making of combination-types and subtypes. In the following table, the top line under the language names shows the maximum number of times a particular vector can occur in combination-types in these languages. These maximum numbers are the same as the total polar-types in these languages shown in table 3 earlier :

	A	B	H	M	O	P	T
	(53)	(85)	(80)	(53)	(53)	(77)	(39)
a TAKE	68%	76%	74%	57%	47%	81%	41%
b GIVE	49%	49%	58%	51%	66%	68%	—

c Go	66%	76%	68%	51%	62%	56%	74%
d DIE	9%	49%	41%	42%	2%	14%	59%
e RISE	17%	60%	29%	26%	11%	4%	—
f SIT	6%	61%	70%	28%	23%	53%	51%
g COME	26%	21%	16%	15%	66%	38%	—
h FALL	30%	25%	25%	21%	17%	32%	10%
i THROW	49%	51%	31%	—	—	22%	74%
j KEEP	19%	20%	29%	15%	9%	34%	—
k MOVE	—	38%	16%	13%	68%	31%	—
l SEND	2%	—	1%	6%	2%	8%	—
m SEE	2%	11%	4%	2%	2%	9%	57%
n KILL	6%	5%	5%	6%	2%	9%	54%
o COME-OUT	8%	—	3%	4%	2%	5%	—
p BRING-OUT	6%	—	—	2%	—	1%	—
q HOLD	6%	4%	16%	6%	4%	22%	—
r BRING	13%	4%	1%	2%	28%	—	—

TABLE 5 : Relative Frequency of Occurrence of Probable Vectors in Terms of their Participation in Polar-Type Formation.

3.2. On the basis of above table, we could grade the vectors into the following classes: (i) Very Frequent, (ii) More-or-less Frequent, and (iii) Infrequent Vectors. We found that the unsure responses of informants centered around the third category of vectors most of the time. Moreover, they also contribute to the increase in the length of the combination-types in certain languages. In the first category, we have put those vectors that have at least about 49%-54% occurrence. In the third category are vectors that occur in less than 10% of the combination-types. The rest are in the more-or-less frequent category. Here is the graded table of vectors :

LANGUAGES	VERY FREQUENT	MORE-OR-LESS FREQUENT	INFREQUENT
Assamese	*Take Go, Give, Throw*	*Fall, Come, Keep, Rise, Bring*	*Die, Come-out, Sit, Kill, Bring-out, Hold, Send, See*
Bengali	*Take, Go, Sit, Rise, Throw, Give, Die*	*Move, Fall, Come, Keep, See*	*Kill, Hold, Bring*
Hindi	*Take, Sit, Go, Give*	*Die, Throw, Rise, Keep, Fall, Come, Move, Hold*	*Kill, See, Come-out, Bring, Send*

Maithili	*Take, Give, Go*	*Die, Sit, Rise, Fall, Come, Keep, Move*	*Send, Kill, Hold, Come-out, See, Bring-out, Bring*
Oriya	*Move, Give, Come, Go*	*Take, Bring, Sit, Fall, Rise*	*Keep, Hold, Die, Send, See, Kill, Come-out*
Punjabi	*Take, Give, Go, Sit*	*Come, Keep, Fall, Move, Throw, Hold, Die*	*See, Kill, Send, Come-out, Rise Bring-out*
Telugu	*Go, Throw, Die, See, Kill, Sit*	*Take, Fall*	

TABLE 6 : A Three-way Grading of Vectors Depending on their Frequency of Occurrence.

There are few things in the above table that could be pointed out. Notice that in all the Indo-Aryan languages, TAKE, GIVE, and GO are very frequent. DIE, SIT, FALL, RISE and COME are also reasonably frequent as Tables 5 and 6 show. Only in four instances do they come in the infrequent category : DIE and SIT in Assamese, DIE in Oriya, and RISE in Punjabi. But there are a few vectors that fall in the infrequent category almost invariably. These include : KILL, COME-OUT, BRING-OUT, HOLD (in Hindi/Punjabi, HOLD is not infrequent), SEE (except in Bengali), BRING-OUT (except in Assamese and Oriya) and SEND. These are the vectors that are worth watching. It seems likely that with time they will either disappear (probably leaving a few traces on set collocations), or will undergo greater lexical emptying, and become more and more frequent. Compared to these, FALL, KEEP and MOVE are already moving towards greater frequency.

3.3. If we now look into the frequency of occurrence of vectors that have already undergone a considerable degree of lexical emptying, the distribution in Table 5 will be further confirmed. This time, we want to know with what percentage of the 117 polars in these languages TAKE, GIVE, GO, DIE, RISE, SIT, COME, FALL and THROW can occur. We could then find out the mean of vector-employment in these languages to test whether what Masica 1976 guessed about the use of vectors in Dravidian languages was correct. In the following frequency-table, for Telugu, the mean has been calculated on the basis of only the six vectors that were studied :

VECTORS	A	B	H	M	O	P	T
TAKE	63%	71%	65%	61%	37%	74%	50%
GIVE	65%	51%	53%	55%	50%	53%	—
GO	62%	79%	70%	55%	59%	73%	86%
DIE	4%	44%	31%	33%	1%	9%	80%

RISE	9%	56%	24%	15%	6%	3%	—
SIT	3%	59%	61%	17%	14%	45%	65%
COME	19%	17%	13%	10%	59%	32%	—
FALL	17%	22%	24%	15%	17%	30%	4%
THROW	46%	50%	29%	—	—	15%	83%
Mean	(32)	(50)	(41)	(33)	(30)	(37)	(61)

TABLE 7 : A Comparative Table Showing Frequency of Occurrence of Major Vectors. (In each case, the total possibility of occurrence was taken to be 117).

The findings in the above table do confirm Masica's guess noted earlier. Moreover, what he said particularly about Telugu GO is borne out by the fact that it has 86% occurrence compared to 55% to 79% in Indo-Aryan languages. If we leave out Bengali and Punjabi, GO occurs only 55% to 62% of the time in other IA languages. Note that given a chance of forming CV, Telugu would use it almost twice as frequently as Assamese, Maithili and Oriya. Only Bengali, followed by Hindi, could be said to be somewhere near Telugu in this respect. Interestingly, Table 6 too would show that Bengali and Telugu had the maximum number of very frequent vectors—7 and 6, respectively, whereas others had only 3 to 4 in this category. These then further evidence that among the Indo-Aryan tongues, Bengali has the most developed CV-pattern, which is even comparable to Dravidian language CVs.

3.4. What makes all these counts more meaningful is the fact that both the frequency-count of chances of CV-formation (cf. Table 7) and the frequency of vector-participation in combination-types (cf. Table 5) show great similarities and more or less the same distributional pattern. To be doubly sure of our results, we have also looked into CV-formation in these languages in another way. We have already seen that not all the languages employed the same number of vectors. However, for all of them, the number of polars taken was the same. Now, one can easily find out how many instances of compound verbs have been actually formed out of the total number of polars 117 times the number of vectors employed (which varies between 8 in Telugu to 17). This will give us an idea of the comparative frequency of realization of CV-formation. Consider the following table:

	A	B	H	M	O	P	T
No. of vectors	17	15	17	17	16	17	8
Maximum possib.	1989	1755	1989	1989	1872	1989	936
CVs okayed	370	608	512	334	412	492	605
% realized	19%	35%	26%	17%	22%	25%	65%

Table 8 : Percentage of Realization of CV-formation Calculated out of 117 into Number of Vectors Employed.

This is the comparative picture of CV-formation in these seven South Asian languages that emerges from a study of list frequency counts of polar-vector combination. We could divide the total number of combinations okayed into CVs with intransitive and those with transitive polars. It would also be very interesting to compare our results with the findings on comparative frequency distribution of CVs in IA in Hook 1977. The difference between the two approaches is that while we based our calculation on list frequency, in the latter work distribution of CVs was determined on the basis of frequency of occurrence of such combinations in two sets of texts. First, a region-wise distribution map was prepared on the basis of five sentences (227, 234, 235, 236 and 237) given in 'Standard lists of words and sentences' in Grierson's *LSI.* The focal points in these sentences were the following verbs used in these five sentences : PUT, GIVE, TAKE, BIND and DRAW. Another text was 370 of about 500 translations of the Biblical Parable of the Prodigal Son into languages and dialects spoken in India. Here too, five points in the story were identified where one could count whether the verb concerned was a CV. In short, these points were as follows : (1) *Give* me my share..., (2)...he *went* to a far country, (3) ...he *spent* all that he had, (4) ...a mighty famine *fell...,* and (5)...he *sent* him to graze his flocks. The distribution maps that he prepared on the basis of these two texts (which we will call "Sentences" and "Parable", respectively) showed several things. First, in the IA area, the Western Hindi region employed CVs on more occasions than the others. This was closely followed by the Bihari (including Maithili) and Punjabi speech-areas in that order. Finally, if we leave out Kashmiri, Western Pahari, Sindhi, Gurjarati, Marathi and Konkani, i.e., the areas not included in the present study, the Eastern NIA languages, especially Bengali, Assamese and probably Oriya also had the lowest occurrence of CVs in these texts. Hook 1977 used these findings successfully in arguing against both Dravidian origin of CVs in IA and a theory that might suggest that CVs in IA originated as a result of an areal pressure exerted by other language-families in the Asian region. Hook (forthcoming) uses them in what he calls "probable conceptualizations of dialect". It would be beyond the scope of our work to evaluate his conclusions, but it must be noted that a distributional map based on list frequency counts of CVs in IA would show a very different pattern from the distribution maps given in Hook (1977 and forthcoming). Consider the following table which should make the differences in pattern obvious :

	A	B	H	M	O	P	T
Intransitives	154	202	174	141	143	164	229
Transitives	216	406	338	193	269	328	376
TOTAL, cf, table 8 :	370	608	512	334	412	492	605
SENTENCES (×10)	160	160	540	500	—	460	—
PARABLE	.20	.20— .37	.53— .79	.57— .64	.20— .25	.53— .63	— —

TABLE 9 : Distribution Based on List-frequency Compared with Hook's (1977) Maps on the Basis of Two Texts : SENTENCES (which we multiplied by 10) and PARABLE.

In the above table, we multiplied the percentages of CV-employment as given in Hook 1977 to make them comparable to our numbers. The original percentages could be compared with realization of CV-employment as given in our Table 8. Hook's figures and our findings in Table 8 would show similarity in case of Assamese. The similarity ends there. In our study, we find Bengali to have overtaken Hindi in CV-use, and compared to Bihari (here represented only by Maithili) it is twice the total possibilities. Punjabi here seems to be closer to Western Hindi than it was supposed to be. Surprisingly, Oriya has a greater chance of using CVs than Assamese and Maithili. However, Telugu has the highest possibilities. Now, without going into an evaluation of conclusions Hook 1977 draws on the basis of his findings, we would only pose a question to the students of India as a linguistic area : In the event of text-based and other types of frequency-counts showing divergent, if not contradictory trends, which one should we accept as the basis of theorizing in favour of a particular origin of areal pressures? Since Telugu and other Dravidian languages have left a number of traces of such pressures on Oriya and Bengali syntax, and since in our findings the latter show remarkably high chances of CV-employment which could be taken as comparable to Telugu, does this not strengthen the case for the Dravidian origin of CVs in IA? We leave this question open for further research.

3.5. We must look into one more aspect of CV-formation and polar verb classification in South Asian languages which we so far did not touch upon. Notice that Table 3 does not tell us anything about similarities, if any, in subtypes of the languages concerned. In other words, we have not discussed so far whether, for instance, all or some of these languages show identical subtypes under mono- to *n*-vector combination-types. Is it the case, that there is a greater degree of similarity in this respect, in spite of the fact that these languages differ in the nature, number and frequency of vector-use? We have, in Appendix III, given the differences in polar-type and subtype formation in these languages. In the following table, we show how much similarity actually exists across languages of South Asia. We have included only those subtypes here that occurred in more than two languages included in this survey. Here, for the sake of convenience, instead of vector names, labels such as 'a' to 'r' have been used. A quick look at either Table 5 or Appendix I will help the reader in finding out as to what stands for what :

TYPES	A	B	H	M	O	P	T	TYPES	A	B	H	M	O	P	T
I a	√	√	—	√	—	—	—	III abc	√	—	√	√	—	√	—
b	—	√	—	√	√	—	—	abf	—	—	√	√	—	√	—

c	√	√	√	√	√	√	√	abi	√	√	√	—	—	—	—
II ab	√	—	√	√	√	√	—	abj	√	—	—	√	—	√	—
ac	√	—	—	√	—	√	√	ach	—	√	√	√	—	—	—
ce	—	√	√	√	—	—	—	cgh	√	√	√	√	√	√	—
cf	—	√	—	√	√	√	√	chk	—	√	—	√	√	—	—
cg	√	√	√	√	√	√	—	IV abcf	—	√	√	√	—	—	—
ch	√	√	√	√	√	√	—	abcg	√	—	—	—	√	√	—
ci	√	—	—	—	—	√	√	abdf	—	√	√	√	—	√	—
ck	—	—	—	√	√	√	—	acdf	—	√	√	√	—	—	—

TABLE 10 : Similar Patterns in Polar Subtype Formation in Combinations I (Mono) to IV (Four) Where at Least Three Languages Show Identical Classes.

We may add to these two more subtypes from five- and six-vector combinations. They include 'abcfi' (in B, H, P) and 'acdefh' (in B, H, M). Apart from these 24 similar patterns, there are at least 29 subtypes where at least two languages show similarities. These could be listed in the following table :

LANGUAGES	TYPES AND SUBTYPES
A, B	abdei
A, H	abcj; cegh
B, H	ceh; abfi; cefg; abefi; abcfij; abdefi; abdfijk
B, M	cde
B, O	cegk; cghk
H, M	co; abdfjq; abcdefhk
H, P	bc; cfh; abcdf; abcfg; abcfj; abcfjk; acfgh
M, P	abfn
O, P	abfk; acfk; abcfgk
P, A	acgh
P, T	afim

TABLE 11 : A List of 29 Instances Where Only Two Languages Show Similarities in Polar-type Formation.

Notice[7] that out of a logical possibility of 622848 polar subtypes in these seven languages (which include four 17-vector, one 16-vector, one 15-vector and one 8-vector language), 99.3% is ruled out when we see (in Table 3) that only 442 combination-types have been found acceptable. We consider it very significant that of these 442 subtypes all of which could potentially have been very different from each other, about 12% (as given in Tables 10 and 11 above) show similarities. Of these 53 similar subtypes, 29 are found similar at least in two languages, 15 in three languages, 3 in four languages, 2 in five languages, 3 in six languages, and at least 1, i.e., mono-vector with GO was found in all the seven languages. Could so much similarity be accidental? We presume the answer is negative[8].

4.1. In conclusion we summarize the aspects of Compound Verb Formation in South Asian languages that we discussed in this paper. We have shown the relative frequency of occurrence of major vectors in IA (Table 7) and also found that they behave in more or less the same way in respect of participation of polar type and subtype formation (Table 5). Except for TAKE and FALL, Telugu vectors were found to be much more frequent than the vectors in IA languages. The highest frequency of occurrence of all was that of GO in Telugu. We found that only Bengali, followed by Hindi, could come anywhere near to Telugu in the frequency of vector-employment (Table 7). On the basis of these frequency-counts, we graded the vectors in South Asian languages into three categories : Very Frequent, More-or-less Frequent and Infrequent verbs (Table 6). Here too, Telugu and Bengali were found to have more vectors in the first category compared to other languages. It was observed that barring a few exceptions, there were a few vectors which underwent lexical emptying only to a limited extent, and these might become either extinct or quite frequent in course of time. These included KILL, COME-OUT, BRING-OUT, HOLD, SEE, BRING and SEND. Some have already moved in the latter direction, namely, FALL, KEEP and MOVE. We have shown that instead of classifying polar verbs into a few categories (paying attention to semantico-lexical restrictions) in only partial manner (Table 1), a classification based purely on lexical cooccurrence restrictions could be thought of and that such a classification would throw light on a number of phenomena. In fact, the latter type of classification could be used as a basis for later studies on semantic restrictions on polar-vector combination. Our typology should also help lexicographers preparing verb dictionaries of these languages. We have also seen that of the logically possible combination-types (Table 2) only .7% would be grammatically possible (Table 3). Moreover, in at least

7. We could not include another table of comparative frequency here because of lack of space. This would have shown a detailed break up of frequency of occurrence of these vectors separately for intransitive and transitive polars.

8. That polar subtypes are not formed randomly, and that they followed a pattern could be seen in Tables 10 and 11, but even Appendix III would show some kind of system in formation of these combination-types.

12% of these grammatically possible subtypes, these South Asian languages show pattern-similarities (Tables 10 and 11). We have also demonstrated that our list frequency counts and the distributional map of CVs in North India prepared by Hook 1977 basing his study on two texts show entirely different results (Tables 8 and 9). Finally, we have argued that normally the majority of polars participate in mono- to six-vector combinations only (Table 4), and that they are not likely to have twelve-vector combinations and above. At least, there are no polars that occur with all the vectors.

APPENDIX I

A Comparative List of Probable Vectors in Seven South Asian Languages

	A	B	H	M	O	P	T
a TAKE	lo	ne	le	le	ni	lE	kon-
b GIVE	di	de	de	de	de	de	—
c GO	zo	jaa	jaa	jaa	ji	jaa	poo
d DIE	mOr	mOr	mar	mar	mOr	mar	caa(wa)
e RISE	uth	oTH	uTH	uTH	uTH	uTH	—
f SIT	bOh	bOs	bETh	bais	bOs	bETh	kuurcoo
g COME	Oh	aaS	aa	aa(y)	aas	Oo	—
h FALL	pOr	pOR	paR	paR	pOR	pE	paDa
i THROW	pEl	phEl	Daal	—	—	saT	weyya
j KEEP	rOkh	raakh	rakh	rakh	rOkh	rakh	—
k MOVE	—	cOl	cal	cal	caal	cal	—
l SEND	pOtho	—	bhej	paThaa	pOthaa	p'ej	—
m SEE	dEkh	dEkh	dekh	dekh	dekh	dekh/vekh	cuuDa
n KILL	maar	maar	maar	maar	maar	maar	campa
o COME OUT	ulo	—	nikal	kikal	baahaar	kikal	—
p BRING OUT	uluu	—	(nikaal)	(nikaal)	—	kaD	—
q HOLD	dhOr	dhOr	dhar	dhar	dhOr	t'ar	—
r BRING	On	aan	laa	aan	aan	(lOo)	—

APPENDIX II

A List of Polar Verbs (117 in Number) Included in this Work

INTRANSITIVES (54)	A	B	H	M	O	P	T
1. ‘grow’	gozu	{utpOnno-kOr,upjaa, phOlaa}	upjaa	upjaa	phOL	ug	peraga
2. ‘hang’	olOm	jhol	jhuul, laTak	laTak, jhuul	jhuul	ch’ul	weelaaDa
3. ‘be drowned’	dub	Dob	Duub	Duub	Dub, buR	Dub	munaga
4. ‘open’	khol	khol	khul	khul	khol	khul	terawa
5. ‘run’	lOr, dowr	douRo	daoR	daug	dOuR	dauR	parigetta
6. ‘crumble’	khOh	dhOSaa	DhEh	Dhah	dhOs	T’E	paDipoo
7. ‘be digested’	hOzOm + ho	hOjom + ho	pac	pac	hOjOm + heb	pac	araga
8. ‘labour’	khOt, kaam + kOr	khaaT	khaT, šram + kar	khaT	khOT	khaT	paniceyya śraminca
9. ‘be less’	kOm	kOm	ghaT	kam	kOm	k’aT	tagga
10. ‘fall down’	khOh	khOS	gir	khas	khOs	T’E	paDa
11. ‘come’	Oh	aaS	aa	aay	aas	Oo	raa
12. ‘sleep’	xo	So	so	suut	so	sOo	paDukoo
13. ‘rise’	uth	oTh	uTh	uTh	uTh	uTh	leewa
14. ‘sit’	bOh	bOS	bETh	bais	bOs	bETh	kuurcoo
15. ‘get wet’	tit	bhej	bhiing	bhiij, tiit	tint	p’ij, p’ig	taDisi + poo
16. ‘leak/ooze’	nigOr	co^{n}aa	cuu	cuu	bOh	co, cu	kaara
. ‘ ’	pOr, Or	pOR	paR	paR	pOR	pE	paDa
18. ‘prick’	bindh, xomo	be^{n}dh, phoT	gaR, cubh	gaR	gOL	cub	gucca, guccu + koo

Appendix II (Continued)

	A	B	H	M	O	P	T
19. 'swing'	dol	dol	Dol	Dol	doL, jhul	Dul	uuga
20. 'be tired'	bhaagOr + lOg/kho	thOk, klaanto + hO	thak	thaak	thOk	thak	alawa
21. 'bear fruit'	lOg dhOr	phOl	lag phal	phar	phOL	phal phul	panDa
22. 'dress up'	xOz	Saaj	saj	saj	sOjaa	saj	alankarinca, alan-karimpa + baDa
23. 'lie down'	baagOr	gORaa So gaa + Elaa	leT	leT	soi	leT pE	paDu + koo
24. 'feel'	lOg/bodh + hO	laag	lag	lag	laag	lag	anipinca
25. 'rot'	pOs	pOc	saR	saR	sORh, pOc	saR	kuLLa
26. 'bend down'	haaol	jho^{n}k	jhuk	jhuk	no^{n}i	c'uk	wanga
27. 'burn'	zOl	jOl	jal	jar	jOL	jaL	manDa
28. 'go'	zo	jaa	jaa	jaay	ji	jaa	weLLa
29. 'stay/remain'	thOk, rO	rOh	rah	rah	rOh	rE	unDa
30. 'move'	(zo)	cOl	cal	cal	caal	cal	naDawa
31. 'fly'	ur	oR	uR	uR	uR	uR	egara
32. 'dance'	nOs	naac	naac	^{n}aac	naac	nac	naaTyam + ceyya
33. 'be trapped'	phO^{n}s	phaa^{n}S	pha^{n}s	pha^{n}s	phOs	phas	cikku + koo
34. 'be torn'	phOT	che^{n}R	phaT	phaT	phaaT	phaT	wiraga
35. 'break'	phOn	bhaan phaaT	phuuT	phuuT	phuT	phuT TuT	baddalu + awa
36. 'be unnerved'	sOk + kho	bhORkaa	bhaRak	baaR^{a}k	huruR	p'aRak	koopinca
37. 'be under'	sEpaa + kho	caapaa + pOR	dab	dab	dOb	dab	aNaga
38. 'ring'	bOz	baaj	baj	baj	baaj	baj	mooga
39. 'stop'	ro	thaam	ruk	ruk	rok OTOk	khaR	aaga
40. 'run away'	pOlo	paalaa, phaag	bhaag	bhaag	pOLaa, bhaag	p'aj	parigetta
41. 'shout'	si^{n}Or	cE^{n}caa	cillaa	cikar	cillaa, rORi + chaaR	ciik, rOoLaa + pOo	arawa

Appendix II (Continued)

	A	B	H	M	O	P	T
42. 'jump'	zopiu	laaphaa	kuud	kuud, phaan	kud, De^{n}	Tap	genta
43. 'laugh'	hO^{n}h	haaS	ha^{n}s	ha^{n}s	hOs	has	nawwa
44. 'be angry'	khOn/obhi-maan + hO	raag/obhi-maan + hO/kOr	ruuTh	ruus	rus raag	rus	koopagincukona
45. 'cut'	kOt	kaaT	kaT	kaT	kOT	kaT	naraka + baDa
46. 'be glued'	zoraa + lOg	joR	juR	juR	joR	juR	atukkoo
47. 'melt'	gOl	gOl	gal	gal	meLe, tOrOL	gaL	karaga
48. 'move away'	aa^{n}tOri + bOh	SOr	khisak	ghasak	ghunc	khisk	jaraga
49. 'distribute'	bhOgo	baa^{n}T	ba^{n}T	ba^{n}T	baaNT	baND-eyaa + jaa	pancabaDa
50. 'die'	mOr	mOr	mar	mar	mOr	mar	caccipoo
51. 'leave'	Eraai + zo	chaaR	chuT	chuuT	chaaR	chuT	bayaludeera
52. 'be printed'	sOpo	chaap	chap	chap	chOpaa + heb	chap	mudrimpa + baDa
53. 'come out'	olo	bero	nikal	nik^{a}l	baahaar	nikal	bayaludeera
54. 'come down'	nOm	naam	utar	ut^{a}r	olhaa	utar	diga
TRANSITIVES (63)							
55. 'scatter'	sitik, sOtiu	chiTkaa	chiTak	chiT^{a}k	chiTik	Dul, khiND	baddalawa
56. 'vomit'	bOmi + kOr ulOti + hO	ograa, bomi + kOr	ugal	ug^{a}r, ugil	ugaal, baanti + kOr	ugal	kakka
57. 'get'	po	paa	paa	paay	paa	lab	ponda
58. 'anoint'	ghOh, xOn	maakh	mal	mal	boL	mal	raaya
59. 'mince'	kut	kot	kuuT	kuuT	kuT	kuT	danca, rubba
60. 'scrape'	khuroo, so^{n}s	caa^{n}ch	khurac	khurac	aampuR	khurac	giyya
61. 'fry'	bhOz	bhaaj	bhuun	bhuj	bhaaj	taL	weeyinca
62. 'uproot'	ughOl	opRaa	ukhaR	ukhaR	uppaR	paT	tempa
63. 'cover'	dhOk, meru	Dhaak	Dhak, oRh	Dhak, ORh, jhaa^{n}p	ghoR	oR	weesukoo
64. 'turn over'	lutiu	olTaa	ulaT	ulT/unT	olOTaa	puTThaa + kar	tiraga + baDa

Appendix II (Continued)

	A	B	H	M	O	P	T
65. 'prepare bed'	bisOnaa + pOt/kOr	bichaa paat	bichaa	ochaa	bichaa	bichOo	parawa
66. 'avoid'	Er	ERaa	Taal	Taar	TaaL	Taal	tappinca
67. 'cheat'	thOg	ThOkaa	Thag	Thag	ThOk	Thag	moosa + paDa/ —ginca
68. 'keep'	rOkh	raakh	rakh	rakh	rOkh	rakh	unca
69. 'test'	pOrikkh— yaa + kOr	porikkhaa + kOr	aajmaa	ajmaa	pOrOkh	ajmOo	pariikSinca
70. 'see'	dEkh	dEkh	dekh	dekh	dekh	vekh dekh	cuuDa
71. 'throw'	pEl	phEl	phe^{n}k	phe^{n}k	phing, pho-paaR	saT/suT/siT	weyya
72. 'send'	pOthO	paaThaa	bhej	paThaa	pOThaa	p'ej	pampa
73. 'cross'	paar + hO	tOr	tar	tar	tOr	tar	daaTipoo
74. 'encircle'	dEr, aagur	gher	gher	gher	gher	k'er	cuTTu + kona
75. 'scatter'	sOtio	choRaa	phElaa	chiRiyaa	binch-chaaR	khiND	paraca
76. 'overtake'	paar + hO	Topkaa	Tap	Tap	TOp	Tap	genta
77. 'dig out'	khond, rok	kh^{n}oR, khnoT	khodh	khodh	khoL	khod, paT	tawwa
78. 'bury under'	pot, gOz	po^{n}t, gaaR	gaaR	gaaR	pot	gaD	paata
79. 'count'	gOn, likh	gon	gin	gan	goN	giN	lekka + peTTa
80. 'wreathe'	gOth	gaa^{n}thaa	guu^{n}th	guu^{n}th	gunth	gund	gucca
81. 'sort out'	bOs	chaa^{n}t, baach	chaa^{n}t, cun	chaa^{n}T	baach	chaND	eera
82. 'stitch'	taa^{n}k + di	Taa^{n}k	Taa^{n}k	Taa^{n}k	Taank	Tan	kuTTa, Taakaa + weyya
83. 'fill/insert'	thaah	ThaaS	Thuus	Thuus	Thus	tuR, T'u	nimpa
84. 'push'	thEl	ThEl	dhakel	Thel	Thel	t'ak	toyya
85. 'carry'	korhiu	bO	Dho	Dho	bOh	T'o	moyya
86. 'milk'	khiro	do	duuh	duuh	duh	co	pitaka
87. 'read'	pOrh	pOR	paRh	paRh	pORh	paR	cadawa
88. 'taste'	saakhi + so	caakh	cakh	cakh, ciikh	caakh	cakh	ruci + cuuDa
89. 'suck'	sos	coS	cuus	cuus, cobh	cus, cucum	caT	piilca
90. 'frighten'	bhoi + dekho/ khuu	DOraa bhOe + paa	Daraa, waa	Daraa	DOraa	DarOo	bhaya + peTTa

Appendix II (Continued)

	A	B	H	M	O	P	T
91. 'swallow'	gil	gel	gil	giiR	giL	lOngOo	minga
92. 'drag'	tOn	Taan, khe^{n}c	khii^{n}c	ghii^{n}c	TaaN	khic	laaga
93. 'give'	di	de	de	de	de	de	iwwa
94. 'fill'	bhOro	bhOr	bhar	bhar	bhOr	p'ar	nimpa
95. 'plaster'	lEp/xOn	lep	niip	niip	lip	lip	raayaa/tuDawa
96. 'call/shout'	mOt	haa^{n}k	haak	haa^{n}k	haank	hOokaa + lOo	arawa
97. 'buy'	kin	ken	xariid	kiin	kiN	kharid	kona
98. 'sing'	go	gaa	gaa	gaa	gaa	gOo	paaDa
99. 'chew'	cubu	cibaa	cabaa	cabba	cobaa	cab	namala
100. 'build'	xOz	gOR	gaRh	gaRh	gORh	k'aR	cekka
101. 'hold/keep'	rOkh, dhOr	raakh, dhOr	rakh, dhar	dhar, rakh	dhOr, rOkh	t'ar	unca, paTTukoo
102. 'eat'	kho	khaa	khaa	khaa	khaa	khaa	tina
103. 'win'	zik	jet	jiit	jiit	jit	jit	gelawa
104. 'bring-Caus. (2nd)'	Ono	aanaa	mangwaa	mangwaa	mOgaa	mangOo	teppinca
105. 'help win'	zikO	jetaa	jiitaa	jiitaa	jitaa	jitOo	gelipinca
106. 'feed'	khuu	khaawaa	khilaa	khuyaa	jhuaa	khilOo	tinipinca
107. 'pray'	zOp	jOp	jap	jap	jOp	jap	japinca
108. 'cut'	kOt	kaaT	kaaT	kaaT	kaaT	kaT	koyya
109. 'join'	zoro	joR/jog + hOr	joR	joR	joR	joR	ataka
110. 'melt-Caus.'	gOla	gOlaa	galla	galla	gOlaa, tOrOlaa	galOo	kariginca
111. 'dislodge'	aatOroo	SOraa	khiskaa	ghaskaa	ghunce	khiskaa	jarapa
112. 'distribute'	bhOgo	baa^{n}tT	baa^{n}T	baa^{n}T	baanT	baND	panca
113. 'kill'	maar	maar	maar	maar	maar	maar	koTTa/campa
114. 'leave'	ER	chaaR	choR	choR	chaaR	chaD	wadala
115. 'print'	sOpo	chaap	chaap	chaap	chaap	chaap	accu + weyya
116. 'take out'	ulio, uliaai + On	ber + kOr	nikaal	nikaal	baahaar + kOr	kaD	tiyya
117. 'bring down'	nomo	naamaa	utaar	utaar	olhaa	lOo	dimpa

APPENDIX III

A List of Dissimilar Polar Subtypes in Seven South Asian Languages
(where 'a' to 'r' refer to vectors as listed in Appendix I)

TYPES	ASSAMESE	BENGALI	HINDI	MAITHILI	ORIYA	PUNJABI	TELUGU
MONO	e;o			d;h	g		
TWO	aj		af	ad;cd	ah;bk		cm
THREE	aij;aip;	acd;ace;	bcf;bcn;	abd;abn;	abk;abr;	abh;acf;	afm;cdf;
	bcg;bci;	adh;aef;	cdg;cef;	acg;cdh;	bck;bek;	afh;bch;	cdi;cdm;
	bdn;cgn	bdi;bkn	ceg	dek	bgk;cfk;	coq	cfn;cim;
					cgk;egk		cmn;dim
FOUR	abce;	abdi;	acde;	abcd;	abck;	abcg;	cdfi;
	abch;	abhi;	acef;	abde;	abgk;	abfg;	cdhi;
	abci;	acdi;	acfh;	abdr;	abkr;	abfj;	cdin;
	abcj;	aceh;	achi;	abfl;	bcgk;	abfk;	cfim;
	abcr;	achm;	bcfj;	abgj;	bgkr;	abgi;	cimn;
	abim;	cdfh;	bdfi;	abgp;	cdgh;	acdh;	dfin;
	abir;	cefk;	bdfj;	acdm;	cgko;	acfg;	dimn
	abjr;	cegk;	cdeh;	bejl;	cgjk	acgk;	
	bchi;	cghk	cfhk	bejn;		achk;	
	bcir;			cdeg;		cdgk	
	cegi;			cdko;			
	cgho			cfjl			
FIVE	abchi;	abcei;	abcfk;	abceg;	abcgk;	abcdh;	acdmn;
	abcil;	abfik;	abdfk;	abdef;	abcgr;	abchj;	acfim;
	abcir;	acdeg;	acdfh;	abfjq	abfgr;	abcij;	acimn;

APPENDIX III (Contd.)

	abfip; abfjp	acdek; acefk; acegh; cdegh; cefgh	acdgh; adefh; aegkq		abgkr; bcfgk; bcgkl; bgjkn	abegh; abfjl; acdfg; achkl; bcdhn; bfijk	adfim; adfin; adimn; cdimn; cfimn
SIX	abcdiq; abcegi; abcehi; abcehq; abchir	abcdek; abcdik; abcefk; abcfik; abdfik; abefik; acdefg; acdfgh; acefim; acfijk; bcdefi; cdefgh	abcdef; abcdfj; abcdij; abdfij; abefio; abfijq; abfjlq; acefij; acfghk; adefhn; adfkmq	abcgiq; abdefh; abdekh;	abcghr abcgik; abcgkr; abfghr; abgkqr	abcefq; abcfgk; abfgiq; abfjma; acceghq; aijkmq	acdfim; acdfin; acdimn; acfimn; adfimn; cdfimn; dfhimn
SEVEN	abcdhio; abceghi; abcghij; abhijqr	abcdefi; abcdefk; abcdefr; abcefik; abcgikm; acdefhj; acdefik; acefikm	abcdefh; abcdfiq; abcfijq; abdfijq; acdfimq	—	abcegkr; abcfgkr; abcgkqr; bcefgkm	abcdghk abcgijk abdfhjq abfhijl bcghkjq	acdfimn acdhimr cdfhimn
EIGHT	abcdgijn	abcdefij; abcdefik; abcdeijk; abcdfijk;	abcdefgi; abcdfijm; abcfijkq; abdfhijq;	bcdefghk	abcegjkr; abcfghjk; abcfgjkr	abcdfijq; abcfghjo; abcfgikn; abcfgjkl;	—

APPENDIX III (Contd)

		abcefijk; abefijkq; abefhijm	abdfijkq			abcfhijq; abcjkmoq; abfghikm; abfijkmq	
NINE	abcfghijo	abcdefgij; abcdefijm; abcdefikn; abcefgijk; acdefhikn	—	—	—	abcfghkoq; abcfgijnq; abcfgjknq; abcfhijmq; abcgjklnq	—
TEN	—	abcdefghij; abcdefijkm; abdefijknr; acdefgimqr	abcdefijikn; abcdfijkqr	—	—	abcdfhkln	—
ELEVEN	—	abcdefgijmq	—	—	—	—	—

REFERENCES

Annamalai, E. 1979. Aspects of aspect in Tamil. *IJDL*, 8.2:260-7.

Bhat, D.N.S. 1979. Vectors in Kannada. *IJDL*, 8.2:300-9.

Dasgupta, Probal. 1977. The internal grammar of compound verbs in Bangla. *Indian Linguistics*, 38.2:68-85.

Hook, Peter E. 1974. *The compound verb in Hindi.* Ann Arbor: Center for South and Southeast Asian Studies, University of Michigan.

———. 1977. The distribution of the compound verb in the languages of North India and the question of its origin, *IJDL*, 6.2:336-51.

———. 1978a. The Hindi compound verb: what it is and what it does. *Readings Hindi-Urdu Linguistics*, K.S. Singh, ed. New Delhi: National. 130-57.

———. 1978b. perfecting a test for the perfective: aspectual parallels in Russian, Lithuanian, Modern Greek, Hindi and Pastho. *University of Michigan Papers in Linguistics*, 2:4.89-104.

———. Forthcoming. Some uses for probabilistic conceptualizations of dialect space. *Spoken and written language in South and Southeast Asia.* ed. Herman H. van Olphen. Austin: Department of Oriental and African Languages and Literatures, University of Texas.

Masica, C.P. 1976. *Defining a linguistic area : South Asia.* Chicago: The University of Chicago Press.

Singh, Udaya N. 1979a. *Some aspects of Maithili syntax : a transformational generative approach.* Ph.D. Dissertation: The University of Delhi.

———. 1979b. Dictionary-representation of polar verbs on the basis of their combinability with vectors in Maithili. Paper presented at the Seminar on Lexicography. Agra: Central Institute of Hindi.

———. and S.K. Bandyopadhyay 1978. Some aspects of interrogation in Bengali, Assamese and Maithili. *Papers in Linguistic Analysis, II* : 19-34.

Subbarao, K.V. 1979. Secondary verbs in Telugu. *IJDL*, 8:2.268-72.

MORPHOLOGICAL CONVERGENCE IN THE KHONDMALS: (PRO) NOMINAL INCORPORATION

Sanford B. Steever

What I plan to do in this essay is explore the verbal morphologies of South Central Dravidian (SCDr) and South Munda (SM) languages to ascertain the extent to which areal convergence has taken place between the two groups. Both SCDr and SM have well articulated verbal morphologies: we measure the degree of elaboration by the number and variety of morphemes that may appear in a verb form. We may view morphological complexity in SCDr and SM as an isogloss that simultaneously sets them apart from surrounding Indo-Aryan and Dravidian languages and joins them together, forming a miniature linguistic area. To assess this putative convergence, we concentrate on the incorporation of nominal and pronominal elements in verb forms. Serveral scholars, notably Friend-Pereira 1909, Emeneau 1945, Bloch 1946, and Ramakrishna Reddy (mimeo.), have suggested the exercise of Munda influence on Dravidian as the major cause in the formation of this miniature linguistic area in the Khondmals of Orissa. While the singularity of the incorporation of nominal and pronominal elements into verbs is sufficient to separate the SCDr and SM languages from surrounding languages, we attempt to make explicit the nature of this areal confluence both by discovering the synchronic principles governing the process of incorporation and by determining the course of development that these special verb forms took in the history of their respective language families. The results of this two-pronged task will aid us making clear the nature of this areal convergence as independent innovations in one or both families or as a borrowing from one into the other.

To the casual observer, the verbal morphologies of many South Asian languages may appear deceptively simple and tame. A verbal base may occur with a derivative affix such as a causative morpheme; to verbal bases, derived or simple, are appended morphemes indicating tense and agreement with one NP, usually the subject. Non-finite verbs often lack morphemes that express shifters such as tense and person. Subject-verb agreement seems straightforward: a finite verb agrees with at most one NP whether the system is nominative-accusative or ergative-absolutive. Malayalam and colloquial Sinhala lack overt subject-verb agreement altogether. This humdrum stereotype comes to grief when we examine the intricacies of many SM and SCDr languages in the Khondmals.

Example sentences taken from the SCDr language Kūi (Winfield 1928) and the SM language Sōrā (Ramamurti 1931) illustrate the variety of 'exotic' conjugations found in SCDr and SM. Conjugations are enumerated by the number of special, non-inflectional morphemes that may be incorporated into verb forms. Verbs in both languages may affix a morpheme that indicates motion (M) relative to the action denoted by the main verbal base, as in Kūi (Winfield 1928: 113)

(1) *īru vīe meh-ka-d-eru gina?*
you tomorrow see-M-fut-2pl ques
'Will you go and see tomorrow?'

and in Sōrā (Ramamurti 1931: 28)

(2) *'i-' gij-a.*
M-see-imp
'Go and see.'

The motion morpheme *'ij* in Sōrā also functions as an independent verb that means 'go' but does not follow the regular pattern of compound verbs, which require the intervention of the characteristic morpheme *-le* of the conjunctive participle. The Küi motion morpheme *-ka* does not function independently as a verb in the modern language.[1] Verbs in both languages may affix morphemes that indicate the iteration, frequency (F), distribution of the result of the action denoted by the main verb base as in Kūi (Winfield 1928: 113).

(3) *eanju dehane pālu vip-ki-t-enju.*
he many time shoot-F-pst-3sg masc
'He shot many times over.'

and in Sōrā (Ramamurti 1931:28)

(4) *anin gu-' gu·-lo:-t-en.*
he R-call-F-fut-II
'He calls (me) frequently.'

In Sōrā frequency of an action is signalled by the simultaneous suffixation of the morpheme *-lo*: and the reduplication of the verb base to which it is suffixed *gu-'gu.* 'call call' from *'gu.* 'call.' Finally, a verb may incorporate morphemes that signal the direct or indirect object of the action denoted by the main verb; that is, the verb is conjugated for nominal objects as well as nominal subjects. Sentence (5) comes from Kūi (Winfield 1928: 102)

1. It is argued in Steever 1980 that **icakku* 'move' (DED 397) provides the motion morpheme due to the alternation of *-ka-* with *-icaka-* in the motion conjugation of Kūi. **tā/tara* 'give to 1st or 2nd person' (DED 2526) provides the transition particle; and **vā/vara* 'come' provides the consecutive action morpheme (DED 4311). These three verbs, and perhaps others such as **cel/cen* (DED 2286) 'go' c.f. *cay cended* 'he died' in Parji, were fully inflected verbs in Proto-Dravidian that were suffixed directly onto verb bases unadorned by participial morpemes.

(5) *ī cinḍa nāi tōṛenja nāngi cī-a-t-enju.*
this cloth my friend to me give-lst sg-pst-3sg masg
'My friends gave me this cloth.'

Here the morpheme *-a-*, incorporated directly after the verbal base *cī* 'give' indicates the indirect object of the verb as 1st person. Consider the Sōrā sentence (Ramamurti 1931:44) in (6)

(6) *anin 'gij-iñ-t' e:n.*
he see-lsg-pst-II
'He saw me.'

What is remarkable in examples (5) and (6) is that the verbs are conjugated for their *objects* as well as their subjects, the morpheme for the object appearing between the verb stem and the tense morpheme. The study of the objective conjugations in SCDr and SM and their viability as an isogloss is the immediate goal of this paper. For a verb to be conjugated for two or more of its nominal arguments is a rarity in the South Asian *Sprachbund*; so much so that object conjugations in adjacent, genetically unrelated languages suggest areal influence.

Sapir (1911) noted that verbs which incorporate nominal objects fall under one of two headings: *polypersonal verbs* and *noun-incorporating verbs*. The first is an inflectional process (Stankiewicz 1962) whose operation is obligatory; the incorporated morphemes are often clitic pronouns: and the nominal objects are referential. Noun-incorporation, on the other hand, is normally an optional process which derives verbs by compounding noun stems with verb stems; the incorporated morphemes are normally noun stems; and the incorporated nominals need not be referential. The rules governing the formation of polypersonal verbs are *agreement* rules whereas the rules governing the formation of noun-incorporating verbs are *compounding* rules: the domain of the former is morphological while that of the latter is lexical. To anticipate our major conclusion: the objective conjugation in SCDr represents polypersonal verbs while the objective conjugation in SM more nearly approximates to noun-incorporation. To see that this is so we must place the rules governing the formation of the objective conjugation in each language family within the context of more general principles governing the expression of verbal categories in each family. When the synchrony and the diachrony of these special verb forms have been made clear, we can start to assess the nature of the influence of one language on another.

I wish to point out some of the apparent similarities between the object conjugations to indicate why a detailed comparison of the two systems is of interest. I shall take Kūi as paradigmatic of SCDr and Sōrā as paradigmatic of SM. Kūi verbs which incorporate the motion particle *-ka-* cannot also incorporate the object morpheme *-ta-*; likewise, Sōrā verbs that incorporate the deictic particle *-ai-* 'towards the speaker' cannot incorporate object morphemes. The conjunctive participle in each language cannot incorporate pronominal objects. The object morphemes occur between the verb base and tense morphemes in both languages. In Kui, a direct object, and indirect object (including the so-called 'dative-subjects') may be incorporated. In Sōrā, a verb may incorporate a direct object, an indirect object and a locative object. Verbs belonging to the third conjugation class in Sōrā may incorporate 'dative-subjects.' Kūi verbs incorporate one object at a time (the reason for this appears below); Sōrā verbs may incorporate upwards of three or four. Other differences are that in Kūi object incorporation is limited to the first and second persons while in Sōrā nominal object of all persons are eligible for incorporation. Incorporated objects in Sōrā may be reflexive, but they may not be reflexive in Kūi. In Kui one morpheme, *-ta-*, indicates the presence of an object, be it first or second person, singular or plural, direct or indirect; while a zero morph covers the remaining cases. In Sōrā, on the other hand, each incorporated object is differentiated according to person and number (although not to grammatical relation); each incorporated noun has its own form. The incorporation of *-ta-* is obligatory in Kūi if its structural description is met. Incorporation of objects in Sōrā seems to be optional although Ramamurti (1931:142) notes that incorporation seems to be becoming obligatory for incorporated pronominal objects. The appearance of an independent pronominal object along with the object-incorporating verb is not redundant in Kui, whereas it is felt to be redundant in Sōrā.

First Sōrā. Many verbs in Sorā incorporate two or more objects in addition to showing agreement with their subjects. Consider the following sentences.

(7) a *'jum-te*
eat-fut-I-(3sg masc)
'He eats.'

b *'ber-te-nn̥*
talk-fut-II-(3sg masc)
'He talks.'

c *'togəl-t-iñ.*
night-fut-III-lsg
'It will night me.' i.e., 'I shall be overtaken by night.'

(8) *'kina:-te:-n.*
tiger-fut-II-(3sg masc)
'He tigers.' i.e., 'He acts the tiger.'

(9) a *'nam-kid-te-n-a·i.*
seize-tiger-fut-II-Prox (lsg)
'I shall seize a tiger.'

b *'kina·-n 'nam-t-am.*
tiger-def seize-fut-2sg
'A tiger will seize you.'

c *am-'kid-t-am.*
catch-tiger-fut+III-2sg
'A tiger will catch you.'

(10) *'amboi-' si:-l-am-ji* *pə'ren.*
wipe-hand-pst-2sg-3pl *perhaps.*
'Perhaps they have bribed you.'

(11) *'pan-ti- 'dar-iñ-te:-n.*
bring-give-rice-1sg-pst-II-(3sg masc)
'He brought and gave me rice.'

(12) *aŋ-'gan-su:ŋ-'byi-na-ba.*
cause-enter-house-woman-opt-1pl
'Let us make the woman enter the house.'

(13)a (PrV) + V + $(N)^n$ + TNS + CJG + PrN (subject)
b (PrV) + V + $(N)^n$ + TNS + PrN (object) + PrN (subject)

There are three conjugation classes in Sōrā; the active, (1) in (7a); the reflexive (II) in (7b); and the impersonal (III) in (7c). The order of morphemes in a verb varies with the conjugation class chosen and the morphemes expressed: two major patterns are given in (13a) and (13b). Preverbs such as the negative and the causative (12) always precede the base of the verb. Derivation from one lexical class to another is very free in Sōrā (Ramamurti 1931: 25); for example, the noun *'kina'* 'tiger' is inflected as a noun in (9b) but as a verb in (8). Most lexemes which are not exclusively verbal have two morphological forms: (i) a *base* from that occurs when the lexeme occurs unbound and (ii) a *compounding* form that occurs when the lexemes combine with other lexical roots to form compound words. Note that the base form *'kina'* 'tiger' contrasts with the compound form *'kid.* Large lexical compounds may be formed and, as such, are neutral with respect to the syntactic frame they appear in. We may determine their grammatical category membership only when they have been inflected as nouns, verbs, or adjectives through the affixation of nominal, verbal, or adjectival desinences to the compound lexeme. The process appears to be optional as a comparison of (9b) and (9c) suggests. It is very rare to find the same lexeme both incorporated into a verb and free, but Ramamurti mentions somc cases (1931:142).

(14) *ñen ti-iñ.*
1sg give-1sg-imp
'Me, give me.'

Examples (11) and (12) illustrate compound verbs with two incorporated 'verbal' elements. Example (11) is a compound lexeme made up of two verb roots, one noun, and one pronoun: the entire compound is put in the past tense and conjugated as a class II verb. Despite variation in the order of incorporated nominals with respect to the morphemes denoting tense and designating conjugation class, the incorporated object nominal always precedes the incorporated subject nominal: it is the mirror-image of the SOV order of free elements in Sōrā clause structure. The compounding process embraces nouns and pronouns alike: Sōrā personal pronouns have both a base and a compounding form, e.g. *ñen* 'I' (free) versus *iñ* 'I' (compounded). Although these Sōrā verbs seem to present a patent case of what Sapir (1911) called *noun incorporation*, two facts forestall us from making a hasty conclusion. All incorporated nouns are treated as third person, while incorporated pronouns may be first, second, or third person: there is no distinction between noun, pronoun, and proper name in the first and second persons. Since persons is an inflectional category, Sōrā noun-incorporation must be considered an inflectional process to the extent that it takes first and second person nominals as its operands. All referential nouns express the category of person.

The referential properties of compound lexemes in Sōrā serve to promote the hypothesis that Sōrā noun-incorporation shares some features with polypersonal verbs. Cross-linguistically, if a verb incorporates a referential object, it will incorporate a non-referential object; if it incorporates an animate object, it will incorporate an inanimate object; if it incorporates a definite object, it will incorporate an indefinite object. But not necessarily vice versa. Also the third person is incorporated before either the first or sceond persons. Incorporated nominals in Sōrā may be referential, and unlike English compounds such as *secretary-treasurer* and *washer-dryer* in which each member of the compound must refer to one and the same individual or object, may have a reference that is independent of the reference of other nominals incorporated in the same compound. This is frequently observed in the case of *dvandva* compounds in many Indic languages, e.g. Sinhala *de-mau-piyo* 'parents' (='two'+'mother'+'father') and Tamil *mēṭu-paḷḷam* 'potholes' (='bluff'+'pit'). When a nominal lexeme associated with a referring device is compounded with a verbal lexeme and the whole is conjugated in the appropriate class, the resulting verb form is a *de facto* polypersonal verb. The fact that the process is optional keeps us from declaring it to be an inflectional process, which is a defining characteristic of polypersonal verbs.

Below is presented a tentative reconstruction of the genesis of polypersonal verbs in Sōrā. Because of the close derivational relationships among verbs, adjectival participles, and appellative nouns in many Indic languages, it is difficult to tell whether a compounding process similar to the one encountered in Sōrā existed either in Proto-Munda or in Proto-Austroasiatic or whether it is an innovation in Sōrā.

Due to these derivational relationships, a new compounding process that applied at first to verbs could spread quickly to nouns and to adjectives. The order of bound morphemes in Sōrā verbs reflects the word order of Proto-Austroasiatic, namely VOS; while the order of free words in Sōrā follows the areally dominant SOV word order. The appearance of operators such as negation and causation before the verb base is consistent with VOS word-order. The fact that incorporated nominals precede incorporated pronominals in the modern Sōrā verb may be attributed to the fact that antecedents (at least in the third person) normally precede anaphors. Contact with the dominant SOV word-order of South Asia inaugurated a change from the old VOS word-order to the present day SOV clause-order. This change was carried out by a transformation that may have been present in Proto-Austroasiatic as an optional rule: the effect of this rule's operation was to move NPs from post-verbal to pre-verbal position. This rule seems to have become obligatory for subject NPs and optional to some extent for other NPs. The exact nature of this rule is difficult to discern: is it a *Topicalization* rule, a *Pronominalization* Rule, or a *Copy* Rule (with subsequent *Deletion*)? Sentences such as (9b) when compared with (9c) suggest a movement rule such as Topicalization; those nominals which do not undergo Topicalization, as in (9c) become amalgamated with the verb root. Sentences such as (14) suggest a Copying rule (rules of pronominalization may be considered as a proper subset of copying rules in that the former copy *some* of the features while the latter copy *all* the features). As Szamosi (1974) has shown, Copying rules such as *Clitic-Copying* are *Agreement Rules*: our analysis of object-conjugating verbs in Sōrā depends crucially on how we treat this rule which places an NP from post-verbal to pre-verbal position. One could argue that Movement rules are, in fact, Copying rules that leave behind zero-copies (traces in Chomsky' recent terminology). Choosing between these two rule types is not a trivial task of selecting between two labels; however, more profound analyses of Sōrā syntax must be made before we can make such a decision. Let us propose a rule *Left-Copying* with the caveat that the structure of the rule may be a movement rule, even though the outputs are the same.

(15) Left-Copying

S.D.	[X...	V	$NP^{(object)}_i$	$NP^{(subject)}_j$	...Y]
	1	2	3	4	5 ⇒
S.C.	[1 4j# 3i#	2	3t	4t	5]
			[+copy]	[+copy]	

Conditions: (i) # represents Chomsky-adjunction
(ii) [+copy] may be realized as ϕ.
(iii) Optional for objects, obligatory for subjects.

When the rule of Left-Copying became obligatory under the reinforcement of the areally dominant SOV word order, the post-verbal nominals lost their syntactic mobility and became ankylosed with the verb base. With the loss of syntactic mobility, the compounding forms of the nominals arose through the application of sandhi rules (perhaps extended from a pre-existing process of compounding nouns with nouns). The fact that tense morphemes now follow the verb plus nominal compound suggests a shift in the basic word-order template of Sōrā from VOS to SOV: perhaps the tense morphemes are old temporal adverbs (as Ramamurti's remarks (1913: 27) suggest about the distant future in Sōrā).

The rule of left-copying is remarkably simple when viewed as a rule that combines a descriptive predicate with a referring device. The proposition in (16a) represents the sentences in (16b) and (16c) without operators and predicates for tense and definite articles.

(16) a MAN (x) : GO (x) b *The man goes.*

c *L'homme, il va.*
art man he go-pres-3sg
'The man goes.'

(17) *itən-a·sən amən tij-am?*
what-for you give-you
'What for *you*, should I give you;'

The transformation of Left-Copying may be equated with McCawley's *NP-Substitution* transformation (McCawley 1973: 115) or with Wasow's (1979) *Substitution* transformation, both of which have the effect of combining a descriptive predicate with a referring device. The main difference in the Left-Copying rule is that the descriptive predicate is copied to *all* occurrences of the variable it binds rather than just to some (usually to the variable that co-commands the predicate). Sentence (16b) is an example wherein the predicate MAN is copied onto only the co-commanding variable; whereas the French sentence (16c) shows an example wherein the predicate (or its pro-form) is copied onto all occurrences of the variable it binds. Sentences (14) and (17) suggest that Sōrā behaves like French whereas the other examples suggest it behaves like English. What is extremely important to note is that the difference between polypersonal verbs and noun-incorporation is a difference the application of the NP-Substitution rule to all bound variables versus the application to some bound variables : the distinction is one of gradience, not of mutual exclusion. The sentences in (14) and (17) suggest a change (original or innovated?) in the applicability of NP-Substitution from some cases to all cases in Sōrā.

The present discussion of the objective conjugation in Kūi encapsulates protracted and detailed arguments presented in Steever (1980) and adds new evidence for the position taken there.

When a finite verb in Kūi occurs with either a first or a second person object, direct or indirect, an invariant morpheme, the *Transition Particle* is incorporated into the verb form between the verbal base and the negative morpheme slot. Finiteness is defined in terms of tense : besides the past and non-past tenses, the transition particle may occur with the imperative and the hortative (both covertly marked for non-past); with adjectival participles and tensed dative-subject verbs. The transition particle cannot cooccur with the adverbial (conjunctive) participle, the infinitive, or the motion morpheme (in cases where the environments for the incorporation of both are met, the motion particle is chosen); in the compound tenses, the transition particle is incorporated in the finite auxiliary verb (the same is true of pronominal incorporation in Sōrā compound tenses). When the environment for the incorporation of the transition particle is met, incorporation is obligatory. If it is not met, a zero object morph is incorporated : the transition particle is expressive of the inflectional category of *person* (Stankiewicz 1962). The transition particle never expresses a reflexive relation, in keeping with the Pan-Dravidian constraint that only third person NPs may serve as antecedents for the reflexive pronoun *tān* (Proto-Dravidian **tān/tan*); consequently, the transition particle can never appear in a verb whose subject is the first person inclusive plural since, no matter whether the object were construed as first or second person, the resulting relation between subject and object would be reflexive.

There are only two morphemes in the objective conjugation : (i) the transition particle *ta* (alternating with *tara*) and (ii) a zero object morph. The first morpheme covers four cases : (i) third person subject and second person object : (ii) third person subject and first person object; (iii) first person subject and second person object; and (iv) second person subject and first person object. This conjugation is minimal in that it has two morphemes and that there are no distinctions of plurality, gender, honorification or direct versus indirect object. The transition particle is subject to grammatically conditioned allomorphy : (*C*)*a* occurs in the affirmative while (*C*) *ara* appears in the negative. There is also phonologically conditioned allomorphy, the existence of which can be traced to the distinctive underlying shape of the verb root to which the transition particle is suffixed. There are four underlying shapes a verb root can assume in Kūi : (i) disyllable root ending in *-i*; (ii) monosyllabic root ending in a glide; (iii) monosyllabic root ending in a voiced consonant; and (iv) all other monosyllabic roots. The following chart summarizes the allomorphy of inflectional morphemes relative to the type of base.

(18)	BASE	A	B	C	D	E
I:	/lāki/	*lāk-a*	*lāk-ara*	*lāk-a*	*lāki-t-amu*	*ega/epka*
II:	/jā-/	*jā-ta*	*jā-tara*	*jā-pa*	*jā-t-amu*	*epa/eppa*
III:	/kōy-/	*kō-a*	*kō-ara*	*kō-va*	*kō-t-amu*	*nōva/nōc-pa*
IV:	/nog-/	*nog-da*	*nog-dara*	*nobga*	*nog-d-amu*	*inba/ic-pa*

Roman numerals designate Winfield's (1928) numerical classification of Kūi verbal bases : /lāki/ means 'sacrifice', /jā/ means 'beg', /kōy/ means 'reap', /nog/ means 'wash', /egi/ means 'rise', /ep/ means 'reach', /nōy/ means 'ache', /in/ means 'say.' Column A gives the allomorphy of the transition particle in the affirmative; Column B gives it in the negative. Column C is the infinitive; Column D is the 1st plural exclusive affirmative past. Column D gives non-causative and causative pairs : note that in IE and IVC a metathesis between labial and velar stops has taken place. There are two other possible allomorphs for the transition particle: *ḍa* and *ja* depending on whether the underlying form of class IV verbs ends in a retroflex or an alveolar consonant.

There is no formal distinction in the 1st and 2nd person pronouns between accusative and dative: this distinction has been neutralized in favour of what was historically the dative. The rules that assign the transition particle are indistinguishable from other agreement rules in Kūi ; infix the transition particle if the object of a finite verb is first or second person. An independently needed rule governing the distribution of reflexive pronouns will bleed those instances where the transition particle would result in a first or second person reflexive relation. I note that the rule that assigns the first person plural inclusive pronouns (as opposed to the first person plural exclusive) also must refer crucially to the person of the object of the speech act, namely the second person addressee. Finally, the transition particle behaves as if it were a defective class II verb : a class II verb that lacks non-finite morphology. This would help to explain why the transition particle cannot cooccur with the motion morpheme : the transition particle would have to assume a non-finite form, namely the verb base, which the lexicon of Kūi does not provide it with. Treating it as a verb with no non-finite morphology would allow us to predict its morphological position in the verbs of Kūi by relying on the existing rules that specify the order of verbal morphemes in any verb forms. However, the transition particle seems to be devoid of lexical content, perhaps being related to the class II verb *tapa* 'bring'.

Before I broach the question of the history of the objective conjugation in SCDr, let me illustrate it with some concrete examples.

(19) a *īra* *ānu* *eariki* *cī-i.*
this I to them give-fut+lsg
'I will give this to them.'

b **īra* *ānu* *nīngī* *cī-i.*
this I to you give-fut+lag
'I will give this to you.'

(20) a *īra* *ānu* *nīngi* *cī-a-i.*
this I to you give-T-fut+lsg
'This I will give to you,'

b **īra* *ānu* *eariki* *cī-a-i.*
this I to them give-T-lsg
*'This I will give to you to them.'

(21) *āneŋ* *nī* *keydiŋ* *mrīn-ja-t-aŋ*
I your hand press-T-pst-lsg
'I pressed your hand.'

(22) *evan* *nāḍeṅgata* *sītki-da-t-un.*
he upon me blow nose-T-pst-3sg
'He blew (his) nose on me.'

(23) *paji* *mṇiʔiya* *tīni* *kōṛi* *ṭaka* *ṭaki* *prā-ta-mu.*
pig change-avp three 20 rupee for sell-T-imp
'I will change into a pig and you will sell me for 60 rupees.'

The sentences in (19) and (20) come from Kūi; sentence (21) comes from Pengo (Burrow and Bhattacharya 1970 : 82) ; sentence (22) comes from Maṇḍa (Ramakrishna Reddy 1980); and sentence (23) comes from Kūvi (Israel 1979 : 284).

The step-wise development of the transition particle and the objective conjugation is abstracted from Steever (1980). A variety of compound verbs in Proto-Dravidian could be formed by suffixing an aux verb to the *verb base* of the lexical verb. The use of the verb base as an inflectable form is still found in Kūi (Steever 1980) and in Parji (Burrow and Bhattacharya 1953:45). Both Old Kannada and Old Tamil (from Caṅkam Tamil to Medeival Tamil) allowed other verbs to be affixed directly to the verbal base : e.g. Old Tamil *pō-tara* 'come' (='go'+'give to 1st/2nd person'); Old Kannada *sar-tara* 'join' (='join'+'give to you or me'), *pō-tara* 'come' (='go' +give to you or me') (Ramachandra Rao 1976). In Medieval Tamil, this process ends and some auxiliary verbs such as *tā/tara* are used solely as metrical fillers, c.f. *nikaZtara* 'happen' in *Rāmāyana*, *Ayottiya Kāṇṭam*, *Mantirappaṭalam*, verse 60, line 1. Among the auxiliary verbs that could be suffixed directly to verbal bases were **tā/tara* 'give to 1st or 2nd person'; **icakku* 'move'; **cel/cen* 'go' (see Parji *cay cended* 'he died' (Burrow and Bhattacharya 1953)); **vā/vara* 'come'; and others. The transition particle arises from a combination of a main verb's base form and a finite form of the auxiliary verb **tā/tara* 'give to 1st or 2nd person'; the compound thus formed was a benefactive compound verb. Whenever the first or second person indirect object of verb benefited from the action of that verb, **tā/tara* was optionally suffixed to the verbal base of that verb. Since **tā/tara* was (and remains in many daughter languages) an independent verb, its suffixation in benefactive compounds seems to have been merely optional. Evidence from Old Telugu (Bh. Krishnamurti pers. comm.) suggests that this idiom was preserved intact in SCDr; e.g. Old Telugu *ētencu* 'come' (='go'+'give to 1st or 2nd person). **tā/tara* contrasted with two other verbs of giving in the Proto-language: **cī* and **koṭu*. The existence of Old Tamil *pōtara* 'come', Old Kannada *pōtara* 'come' and Old Telugu *ētencu* 'come' corroborate my earlier hypothesis (Steever 1980) that the verb base to which **tā/tara* was suffixed to produce a compound verb meaning 'come' would be a verb that meant 'go', such as *pōka* 'go', not a verb meaning 'come', such as **vā/vara*, as Emeneau's (1945) etymology requires.[2]

2. We cannot agree with Mahadevan's (1971 : 72) reinterpretation of the Old

The benefactive compound verb became a polypersonal construction when the incorporation of **tā/tara* was generalized from *some* instances which met its structural description to *all* instances. That is, the rule ceased being optional and became obligatory when the existential quantifier ($\exists$:x) in the rule description was replaced by a universal quantifier ($\forall$:x). Because its incorporation became obligatory, it lost its paradigmatic contrast with other verbs of giving, namely **cī* and **koṭu* (mutual substitutability requires freedom of substitution in order to factor out what they share in common). Over time, the lexeme **tā/tara,* obligatorily incorporated in finite verbs which had 1st or 2nd person benefactive objects, lost its association with the semantic prime GIVE which figured some prominently in the benefactive meaning of the compound. No doubt, the semantic range of the dative case, which included recipient of an action, redundantly assumed some of the semantic burden of the benefactive construction. Later, it assumed the entire responsibility for benefactive-recipient feature which triggered the incorporation of the morpheme **tā/tara* : before it was merely a sufficient condition for the application of the rule, now it became a necessary and sufficient condition. Most auxiliary verbs, because they modify event variables or propositions, tend to appear only in positions which receive tense morphemes : hence **tā/tara* lost its non-finite morphology. Compare this

---

Tamil verb *tā/tara* 'give to 1st or 2nd person' as expressing either 'seize' or 'take'. In such phrases as :

(a) *tenūr* *tanta* *kōn.*
Tenur give-ajp king
'The king who gave us (his people) Tenūr.'

it is quite natural that the poet should address the king, the poem's subject, directly in this genre of praise poetry. The greatest liberty permissible in translating *tā/tara* might be 'bring'. Obviously a king cannot give his people a town unless he has gained title to it either by inheritance, alliance, or conquest. The notion of seizure is derived from attendant circumstances, not from the inherent content of the word.

Nor can we agree with the reinterpretation of *Tolkāppiyam* 29 such that *tanmai,* the traditional term for first person, is extended to mean reflexive relations in the third person. Mahadevan requires this in order to derive 'seize' via 'the king gives himself Tenur'. But in Tolkāppiyar's terminology, *tanmai* can refer only to the role of the speaker. The following defines *tanmai* :

(b) *tanvinai* *uraikum* *tanmaic* *col.*
self-ăct express-ajp tanmai word
'A word with the quality of tanmai expresses tanvinai'.

The term *tanvinai* 'self-act' in defined is terms of the paradigamatic speech situation : there is in any given speech-act only one active role, namely that of the speaker. The term *tanvinai* refers so the speaker in any speech-act, the active participant; hence, *tanmaiccol* is any word that is expressive of the speaker, that is expressive of the category of first person.

Emeneau's (1945) etymology and my etymology (Steever 1980) cannot sustain Mahadevan's interpretation : *tanmai* must refer to first person; therefore, *tā/tara* must refer to 'give to first or second person'.

with English modal auxiliaries which lack participial and infinitival forms. The verb **tā/tara* split into the transition particle and the class II verb *tapa* 'bring'. Once incorporation was obligatory, the extension of morphophonemic rules governing the allomorphy of bound morphemes next to the verb base such as the infinitive and present verbal participle to the newly formed transition particle was a natural process, resulting in the allomorphy of the initial consonant of the transition particle. The alternation of *ta* with *tara* in the presence of the negative morpheme was inherited from Proto-Dravidian : Emeneau (1945) recognized that each verb may have two bases, the alternation between which is governed by tense and negation. Being bound to the verbal base, the transition particle now appeared in a context (non-initial syllable) in which the distinction between long and short vowels was neutralized in favour of the latter.

The change consists in this : a condition on the lexical insertion of the lexeme *tā/tara* to replace the semantic prime GIVE *just in case* the indirect object refers to a participant in the speech event (i.e. 1st or 2nd person) became an agreement rule in Kūi, Kūvi, Pengo, and Maṇḍa. Later in several languages, the distinction between the dative and accusative case in the first and second persons was neutralized. In Kūi, Kūvi, Pengo, and Maṇḍa, it was neutralized in favour of the historical dative case : this immediately extended the objective conjugation from indirect objects to direct objects in the first and second person. The performative hypothesis (Sadock 1975) predicts that the unmarked object case for the participants of the speech act will be the indirect object (dative) rather than the direct object : the speaker of the performative clause is in the subject role; the utterance he produces is in the direct object role; and his addressee is in the indirect object role. The assignment of dative case to all animate 1st and 2nd person objects was merely a generalization. It may be that socio-linguistic factors aided this change; it is less face-threatening (Brown & Levinson 1977) to address one's audience in the role of indirect object than direct object. This neutralization is carried on in Pengo: all animate nouns, regardless of person, have a single accusative-dative form. In Kūvi (Joy Reddy) all non-exclusively deictic pronouns (anaphoric pronouns) have a single accusative-dative form. 1st and 2nd person pronouns and the 3rd person reflexive pronoun. I note that in Koṇḍa (Krishnamurti 1969) the neutralization of these two cases has gone the other way: it is the historical accusative case which prevails. This may be the main reason why the objective conjugation has atrophied in Koṇḍa,[3] with only a few relics in verbs such as *si-daṭ* 'give to me.' Joy Reddy (1979:5) notes one dialect of Kūvi in which the accusative case seems to have won out : it would be rewarding to discover the fate of the transition particle in that dialect of Kūvi. Thus, the objective conjugation was originally restricted to the dative case objects

3. I wish to thank M. B. Emeneau for drawing my attention to the relics of the transition particle in Koṇḍa.

(note that first person and second person dative-subjects also trigger incorporation of the transition particle) and only later spread to the accusative objects via neutralization. The one slender thread of evidence for this is the following phrase, taken from Lingam Letchmajee's Kūi grammar (Letchmajee 1902 : 41).

(24) *mimma* *sūḍa* *mannanju.*
you-acc see-ajp be-3 masc
'The man who has seen you.'

The form *mimma* 'you' is an old accusative pronoun in Kūi; while Winfield (1928) also lists these old forms, none of his examples appear in contexts that would require the incorporation of the transition particle. Sentence (24), with a past adjectival participle, is just such an environment: the verb appears without the transition particle in the presence of the accusative pronoun. Since Letchmajee did not recognize the systematic status of the transition particle, calling it an 'emphatic' particle, we cannot assign too much weight to this evidence. Instead of (24), we would expect *mimma sūḍa man-ja-anju,* where *-ja-* would be the transition particle if the objective conjugation applied equally to Proto-Dravidian direct and indirect-objects.

Thus, SCDr evolved polypersonal verbs from a Proto-Dravidian benefactive construction. Since the major aspect of the change was the generalization of the application of the rule from some to all the instances in which it could apply, rendering a syntactically optional process a morphologically obligatory one, it is difficult to see how Munda influence might have caused, since the so-called objective conjugation in Sōrā is itself optional. There appear to be sources for each construction in each family and the hypothesis of borrowing seems to be weakened considerably thereby. If compounding was not a Proto-Munda rule, then the appearance of noun-incorporating verbs was triggered by generalizing a topicalization rule upon contact with the domidant SOV word-order of the South Asian continent.

What changes would have to occur to make the two systems more comparable? What follows is a thought-experiment. The Dravidian system cannot really change since there is no obvious source from which new objective morphemes can be derived. I note that this case is probably unique in the world: the evolution of polypersonal verbs from a verb rather than from clitic pronoun. The Dravidian system cannot really change through simplification since there are only two morphemes left and two morphemes are the minimum number required for the expression of an inflectional category, such as person. The Sōrā system might change if examples such as those in (14) and (17) prevailed in such a way as to splinter the general lexeme-compounding process into two rules: polypersonal verbs for pronominal objects and noun-incorporation for all other nominals. Since it is highly marked for a rule of noun-incorporation to have referential operands and to have 1st or, 2nd person operands, the only way the Sōrā rule could change is to stop applying to first and second person pronouns. The rule, which is at its zenith of generalization, affecting virtually every nominal in Sōrā, could only change through a loss of its generality, shedding the most marked cases (i.e. 1st and 2nd person first, then animate NPs, then referential NPs) first. This would reduce the comparability of the SCDr and the SM system.

While we have rejected the hypothesis of exercise of direct influence of SM and SCDr on one another in the formation of these various exotic conjugations in the Khondmals, it is nevertheless tantalizing to examine more closely the paralinguistic and linguistic surroundings that seem to provide an enriched soil in which new and complex verb forms may grow.

The exotic conjugations and synthetic tenses arose in SCDr as the phonological boundary between the two elements of Proto-Dravidian explicator compound verbs eroded, fusing the auxiliary verb with the preceding verb base. These fused auxiliaries were later reinterpreted as a variety of derivational and inflectional morphemes. The process seems to have started with **icakku* 'move', then with **ta/tara* 'give to 1st or 2nd person', and most recently with **vā/vara* 'come' according to the extent each has undergone phonological levelling. It is hoped that detailed studies such as the present one will be interpreted in the context of changes of entire verbal systems so that systematic comparison may be made with the evolution of exotic SM conjugations. Only in this way may we begin to uncover the forces that have given shape to a distinctive, miniature linguistic area in the Khondmals.

ACKNOWLEDGEMENTS

I wish to thank K. Paramasivam of American College for pointing out the existence of Old Tamil verbs such as *pōtara* 'come'. M.B. Emeneau's comments on Steever 1980 prompted me to sharpen and refine my arguments. M. Israel was generous with his personal library and first-hand knowledge of South-Central Dravidian, improving greatly the data base and quality of this paper.

Thanks are also due to Bh. Krishnamurti who organized the conference for which this paper was prepared and who drew my attention to Old Telugu *ētencu* 'come', thereby allowing me to place to change of auxiliary verb into inflectional morpheme within the last 800 years. Thanks also to Bill Bright, Peter Hook, Hal Schiffman, Nick Masica, and B. Ramakrishna Reddy for their comments and encouragement on this paper. I alone claim responsibility for the opinions and errors here in.

ABBREVIATIONS

acc —accusative case
art —article
ajb —adjectival participle
avp—adverbial participle
cause—causative
F —frequentive
fut—future
imp—imperative
M —motion particle
masc—masculine
opt—optative
pres—present tense
pst —past tense
ques—question
T —transition particle

1sg —first person, singular
2pl —second person, plural
I —Sōrā verb conjugation
II —Sōrā reflexive conjugation
III —Sōrā impersonal conjugation

REFERENCES

Bloch, J. 1946. *Structure grammaticale des langues dravidiennes*. Paris : Maisonneuve.

Brown, P. and S. Levinson. 1977. Universals of sociolinguistic use. In E. Goody (ed.), *Questions and politeness*. Cambridge University Press.

Burrow, T. and S. Bhattacharya. 1953. *The Parji language*. Hertford: Stephin Austin & Sons. Ltd.

———. 1970. *The Pengo language*. Clarendon : Oxford University Press.

Friend-Pereira, J. E. 1909. *A grammar of the Kūi language*. Calcutta : Bengal Secretariat Book Depot.

Israel, M. 1979. *A grammar of the Kūvi language*. Trivandrum : Dravidian Linguistics Association.

Kamparāmāyaṇam, Ayōttiyā Kāṇṭam. 1958. Edited by Vai. Mu. Kōpālakiruṣṇamācāriyar. Cennai : Vai. Mu. Ko. Kampeni.

Krishnamurti, Bh. 1969. *Koṇḍa or Kūbi : A Dravidian language*. Hyderabad : Tribal Cultural Research and Training Institute.

Letchmajee, L. 1902. *An introduction to the grammar of the Kui or Kandh language*. Calcutta : Calcutta Christian Observer.

Mahadevan. I. 1971. Tamil Brahmi inscriptions of the Sangam age. In R. Asher (ed.), *Proceedings of the second international seminar on Tamil*. Madras: ITI.

McCawley, J. 1973. *Grammar and meaning*. Tokyo : Taishukan Press.

Ramachandra Rao. B. 1976. Auxiliaries in literary Kannaḍa. Paper presented at *Seminar on auxiliaries in Dravidian languages*. Annamalainagar : Centre for Advanced Studies in Linguistics.

Ramakrishna Reddy, B. 1980. Person deixis and the verb in Manḍa. Paper presented at Second International Conference on South Asian Languages, Hyderabad. Hyderabad:Osmania University.

Ramamurti, G. V. 1931. *A manual of the Sōrā (or Savara) language*. Madras: Government Press.

Steever, S. 1980. The genesis of polypersonal verbs in South-Central Dravidian. *IJDL* 9.337-373.

PART III
Diglossia

SOME SYNTACTIC DIFFERENCES BETWEEN SPOKEN AND WRITTEN TAMIL

E. Annamalai

All languages exhibit differences at all levels of the grammar between their spoken and written forms in varying degrees, showing that the written language is not a transcription of the spoken (Vachek 1973). One must make a distinction between the written language and writing of the spoken language, as the latter is evidenced in the conversations of creative writings and teaching materials. The written language is typically characterised in expository prose. There is a sizeable literature describing the linguistic features of the written language, particularly of special registers like scientific and legal writings. The syntactic features which characterize the written language are generally probablistic and not absolute in nature in the sense that a feature is more likely or less likely to occur in the written language than in the spoken language. Some such characteristics one finds in the literature have a low frequency of truncated sentences, but relatively a high frequency of complex sentences with multiple embeddings and of impersonal sentences such as passive.[1] This paper discusses some other syntactic features which characterize the written Tamil (WT). They may be true of the other languages also. These features are claimed to be characteristic of WT on the basis of the intuitive evaluation of its speakers and not of empirical enumeration from representative sample texts.

The third personal proximate singular pronoun is substituted in the spoken Tamil (ST) as a proform for words that cannot be lexicalized at the particular moment in the conversation.

1. ST (a) kumaar rompa itu paṆNuraan.
   kumar much it does
   'Kumar does "it" much.'

   ST (b) nii periya ivanoo ?
   you big he-Q
   'Are you a big "he" ?'

This use of a proform without the antecedent present linguistically is not possible in WT.

1. The syntactic passive in Tamil is exclusively a characteristic of the written language and perhaps in all languages the passive in present tense with first person agent is an exclusive characteristic of the written language.

The illocutionary force such as promising, warning, etc. in ST is conveyed through adverbs and clitics and not by explicit performative verbs. WT, on the other hand, can use performative verbs also.

2. ST (a) naan onakku niccayam paNam tarreen.
I you-to certainly money give-pres
'I will certainly give you money.'

WT (b) naan unakku paNam tarukiReen enRu uRutikuuRukiReen.
I you-to money give-pres. that promise
'I promise that I will give you money.'

Verbs of certain specific communicative acts are not lexicalized explicitly in ST. Instead, the general verbs of communication and mental state like *en*, *col* 'say', *nene* 'think', etc. are used as predicates of embedded full sentences. These sentences represent the direct speech or mental state of the speaker. WT, on the other hand, has lexicalized specific verbs, which take infinitive complements rather than full sentences.

3. ST (a) naan pookamaaTTeenneen.
I go-will not-said
'I said I wouldn't go.'

WT (b) naan pooka maRutteen.
I go-to refused
'I refused to go.'

4. ST (a) naan neettee varaNumnu paatteen/nenecceen.
I yesterday-(emph.) come-must-that saw/thought
'I considered/thought that I should come yesterday itself.'

WT (b) naan neeRRee vara tiTTamiTTeen/virumpineen.
I yesterday-(emph.) come-to planned/wanted
'I planned/wanted to come yesterday itself.'

As the above sentences indicate, the use of direct speech is relatively more frequent in ST than in WT.

5. ST (a) naan kumaare cinimaavukku vaanneen; avan carinnaan.
I Kumar-acc movie-to come said; he OK-said
'I told Kumar, 'come to a movie'; he said 'O.K.'

WT (b) naan kumaarai cinimaavukku vara conneen/kuuppiTTeen;
I kumar-acc movie-to come-to said/invited
avan ottukkoNTaan.
he agreed
'I told/inivted Kumar to come to a movie; he agreed.'

The component sentences of a sentence with indirect speech as 5(a) are loosely concatenated in the sense that they have undergone less number of syntactic processes. The sentences which are less syntacticized in this sense (Givón 1979) are more common in ST.

The difference in the extent of syntactization is found also in constructions other than the quotative ones. Take, for example, the relative clause (RC) formation in Tamil. There are three ways, viz. tagging, pronominalizing and participialising, which are respectively less sentential in nature (Annamalai 1969). The first one, the tag RC, is almost like two consequent sentences in a discourse. The second one, the pronominal RC, connects two sentences more cohesively by replacing the fully specified NP in the embedded sentence with a pronoun. The third one, the participial RC, does not have all the constituents of a sentence and deletes the relativised NP and does not inflect the verbs for person-number-gender.

6. (a) neettu oru payyan vantaanee avan iNNekkum vantaan.
yesterday a boy came-tag. he today-also came
'A boy came yesterday, you know, he came today also.'

(b) neettu enta payyan vantaanoo anta payyan iNNekkum vantaan.
yesterday which boy came that boy today-also came
'Whichever boy came yesterday, he came today also.'

(c) neettu vanta payyan iNNekkum vantaan.
yesterday came-pa boy today also came
'The boy who came yesterday came today also.'

The tag RC is rare in WT.

Another instance of differential syntactization is the conditional sentence. The conditional clause in ST may occur without any conditional morpheme and it is just like a full sentence with PNG and only the intonation indicates that it is non-finite. This is not possible in WT.

7. (a) nii poone naan aTippeen.
you went I hit-will
'I will hit you if you go.'

(b) nii poonaal/poonaay enRaal, naan aTippeen.
you went-if I hit-will
'I will hit you if you go.'

Similarly, the absence of a complementizer in the following sentence is more colloquial.

8. (a) ivaru yaaru teriyumaa ?
he who know-Q
'Do (you) know who he is ?'

(b) unakku ivar yaar enRu teriyumaa ?
you-to he who comp know-Q
'Do you know who he is ?'

The nominalized sentences are most common in ST than derived nouns. This again shows that ST uses structures that are closer to sentences and have undergone lesser number of syntactic processes.

9. (a) naan amerikkaavukku poonatu upayookamaa iruntatu.
I America-to go-part.-it useful was
'My going to America was useful.'

(b) en amerikka payaNam upayookamaaka iruntatu.
my American visit useful was
'My American visit was useful.'

10. (a) ivan amerikkaavukkaaka oLavu paakkiravan.
he America-for spying-pres-adj-one
'He is one who spies for America.'

(b) ivan amerikka uLavaaLi.
he American spy
'He is an American spy.'

Syntactic differences similar to the ones discussed above between spoken and written varieties exist also between informal and formal styles of a language. The formal speech on a public platform or a classroom lecture in Tamil, for example, has the characteristics of the written language. It may be noted that Brown and Levinson (1978) observe that nominalizations such as 'the President's denial' are more formal than sentential complements such as 'that the President denied.' This suggests that the kinds of syntactic differences under discussion are not attributable to the difference in the medium[2] but to the style, which is determined by the social relation between the participants in the speech event. The formal style is indicative of social distance, i.e. lack of familiarity, between the participants.

That the syntactic differences are indicative of language use in a particular social situation will explain the striking similarities between the syntactic differences discussed above and those claimed by Bernstein to exist between the restricted and elaborated codes of working and middle classes respectively. According to him (1971: 42, 115), the elaborated code has a high proportion of subordination, complex verbal system, passive voice, contingency forms, hedges, conjunction and uncommon adjectives and adverbs, and low proportion of personal pronouns, tag questions, metaphors, idioms and traditional phrases. The difference may not be due to role difference, as suggested by Bernstein, in the working class and the middle class families, but due to difference in the contextualization of the language, as suggested by Kay (1977). The elaborated code, like the written language and the formal style, is used between, and intended for, people who may have less of shared knowledge and thus is less contextualized and more explicit. Kay

2. It is not exactly the medium, as any form of speech could be written down. The differences a re perhaps due to the textual nature of the expository prose.

observes that the language of primitive socieites, which do not have separation of specializations and so have more shared knowledge among their members, exhibits the features of the restricted code.

The lack of explicitness in syntactic relation between sentences, i.e. the lesser extent of syntacticisation, is suggested by Givón (1979) for the earlier stage in the evolution of language. He proposes a pragmatic state of language, when the sentences are loosely cancatenated and a syntactic state, where the sentences are fused and suggests there might be a correlation between these states and the evolutionary stages of the language as well as between oral and written styles.[3]

It is tempting to say that the syntactic fusion of the language of the later stage in the evolution may be due to the development of writing, which is bound by space and time, the latter being due to the fact that it is a slower medium; that this medium perhaps brought about fusion and reduction of sentences; and that the functional aspect of the written language, which is typically used to communicate with people who are not part of the immediate context and shared universe, and the absence of prosodic and paralinguistic cues made the syntactic relations to be expressed explicitly. But it cannot be true as there are so many unwritten languages with a great amount of syntacticisation. The syntactic differences must then be motivated by social factors in language use.

Annamalai, E. 1969. *Adjectival clauses in Tamil.* University of Chicago, Unpublished Ph.D. Thesis.

Bernstein, B. 1971. Class, code and control. *Theoretical studies towards a sociology of language.* vol. 1. London: Routledge and Kegan Paul.

Brown, Penelope and Stephen Levinson. 1978. Universals in language usage : Politeness phenomena. In Esther N. Goody (ed.) *Questions and politeness : strategies in social interaction.* Cambridge: Cambridge University Press.

Givón, Talmy. 1979. From discourse to syntax : Grammar as a processing strategy. In Givón (ed.) *Syntax and semantics,* vol. 12. *Discourse and syntax.* New York: Academic Press.

Hale, Kenneth. 1975. *Gaps in grammar and culture.* Lisse : The Peter De Ridder Press. Reprinted from M. Dale Kinkade et al (eds.). *Linguistics and anthropology.* In honour of C.F. Voegelin.

Kay, Paul. 1977. Language evolution and speech style. In A.G. Blount and M. Sanches (eds.) *Sociocultural dimensions of language change.* New York: Academic Press.

Vechek, Josef. 1973. *Written language : General problems and problems of English.* The Hague: Mouton.

3. Hale (1975) exemplifies the lack of syntactic process in Walbiri, where the relative clause is formed by adjoining it to a sentence rather than to a noun phrase. It lacks the attraction rule and therefore the embedded relative.

DIGLOSSIA IN BENGALI

Suhas Chatterjee

Ferguson in his classic paper 'diglossia' (1959) offered us a conceptual tool which enables us to study the typology of one kind of linguistic variation. I utilize in this paper Ferguson's characterization of diglossia (1959) to examine his statement that Bengali represents a case of standard-with-dialects, and not of diglossia (1963). This will necessarily involve me in considering how the linguistic activity of the Bengali speech-community is structured in terms of the range of functions and relations (Hymes, 1962) existing in the total set of a linguistic repertoire (Gumperz, 1962, 1964) of a community. In the light of the situation that Bengali presents, I also raise a question if it is correct to say, as Ferguson did, that in a diglossic situation 'the superposed variety, the vehicle of a large and respected body of written literature' must necessarily be of 'either of an earlier period' or 'taken from another speech community.'

It is commonly held that the linguistic repertoire of the Bengali speech-community has three distinct elements in it. Firstly, there are the regional dialects. Secondly, there exists the Calcutta colloquial, called *Colit Bhasa* (CB = current language), which though originated in and around Calcutta, has gained the status of the standard colloquial. Lastly, there is the literary language consisting of two varieties, the first of which is called *Sadhu Bhasa* (SB = pedantic language), and the second is popularly equated with CB, the colloquial standard. Since the SB variety of written Bengali is largely on the wane, and since the same name CB is used to designate two varieties, viz. written and standard colloquial, it is assumed by laymen and scholars alike that CB has emerged as the standard Bengali, which is used for all written and spoken purposes. Chatterji (1926) entertained this notion. Besides, since Ferguson observes that Bengali, instead of coming within the realm of diglossia, represents a situation of standard-with-dialects, it is legitimate to infer that he also accepts that CB, both written and as standard colloquial, represents a single system of code, and is distinct from SB.

Singh (1976) conducted a survey in Delhi regarding the use of SB and CB and concluded that since these two varieties play complementary functional roles they should be considered as portraying a diglossic situation. I tend to feel that the use of Bengali in Delhi does not depict the situation in West Bengal and Bangladesh. This, however, does not lessen the value of Singh's study. My study will primarily be restricted to the use of Bengali by those who reside in West Bengal and Bangladesh.

It must be admitted that the SB variety of written Bengali, though losing its ground very fast, has still some use in limited spheres; though the extent of its use has not been measured by any scholar, the fields of its use are known. These are: compilation of some text books for schools and colleges, and in some cases writing some books on some specialized subjects like philosophy and law. In these areas, of course, the use of SB overlaps with the use of CB. However, the invitation cards for traditional rituals and ceremonies are almost invariably written in SB. Some newspapers, though publish all their news items in CB cling to the use of SB for editorials.

The restricted use of SB, coupled with the currency of the term CB to mean both the standard colloquial (hereafter SC) and the formal spoken and written varieties which are theoretically based upon SC, has not only contributed to the growth of the widespread misconception that SB is practically dead, but also has hindered the path of our understanding the nature of relationships between the different varieties of Bengali. It seems pertinent to look into the features that are popularly believed to bind all varieties of CB together and at the same time keep SB apart. Chatterji (1926, 1961) stated that the features that differentiate SB from CB are those of pronominal and verbal morphology. The present author treated elsewhere (1962) all the details of differences between these levels of Bengali. It would, therefore, suffice here to sum up the salient aspects of these differences:

(i) The verbal stems in both SB and CB show generally the same type of morphophonemic alternation. In a small number of cases these are different, but CB forms can be systematically derived from the SB forms by the application of substitutional rules.

(ii) The phonological shape of morphophonemic alternants of verbal inflectional morphemes are characteristically different at the two levels. But the CB forms are always systematically derivable from the SB forms by phonological substitutional rules.

(iii) The distribution of the stem alternants are somewhat different at the two levels. The phonological differences of inflectional allomorphs account for this difference.

(iv) The deviance of phonological shape of morphemes is not limited to verbal inflections alone. It is a regular feature of distinction between SB and CB, and thus is applicable in other categories of morphemes and lexical items. For illustration, the vocalic sequence / ia / of SB is regularly replaced by / e / in CB. Thus, SB postpositions / dhoria / 'along with', / koria / 'by means of', /bolia/ 'for' appear as / dhore/, /kore/ and /bole/ in CB. To take another illustration, SB forms can have / u / and / a / as nuclei of two consecutive syllables. But in analogous forms in CB the nucleus of the second syllable is changed to / o / . Thus, while we get forms like / mula / 'radish' and / juta / 'shoe' in SB; in CB these become / mulo / and / juto / respectively. The categorization of all kinds of Bengali into two broad divisions, viz. SB and CB tends to imply, on the one hand, that all sorts of SB are similar to each other as are all sorts of CB amongst themselves, and, on the other, that no form of SB has similarities in CB. Both of these implications are wrong.

Consider the following four sentences, of which A and C are CB sentences and B and D are SB sentences:

A. *mOra*[1] *phul-gache*[2] *jol*[3] *chiToleo*[4] *tar*[5] *šukno*[6]
dead[1] flower-plant-on[2] water[3] sprinkled-even-if[4] its[5] dried[6]
Daler[7] *kuRigulo*[8] *ar*[9] *phul*[10] *hoe*[11] *phuTe*[12] *oThe na*
branch-of[7] buds[8] again[9] flower[10] becoming[11] having blossomed does not[12]

'If water is sprinkled on a dead flower-plant the buds on its dried branches will not again blossom into flowers.'

B. *mOra phul-gache jol chiTaileo tahar šukno Daler kuRiguli ar phul hoia phuTia uThe na*

C. *mrito pušpo-brikkhe bari šincOn korleo tar šuško šakhar korokgulo punorae pušporupe prosphuTito hoe oThe na*

D. *mrito pušpo-brikkhe bari šincOn korileo tahar šuško šakhar korokguli punorae pušporupe prosphuTito hoia uThe na*

The CB sentences, A and C, agree with each other in so far as the *Colit* grammatical features are concerned, and on these counts they differ from SB sentences B and D. But from the point of view of communicational function these *Colit* features are not as important as they are beleived to be. Let us note here that substitution of SB features for CB features of sentences A and C gives us the SB sentences B and D. However, A and B sentences are very close as are C and D sentences—both structurally and from the point of view of communicational function.

A close scrutiny of the different prevalent forms of Bengali will convince one that there are legitimate structural criteria—both grammatical and lexical—that can be employed to sub-divide SB and CB into two subcategories each. Before I proceed with substantiating my claim for sub-dividing SB and CB, for convenience of discussion, let me name the subclasses that I propose to set up. The proposed subclasses in each of SB and CB are: H (high) and L (low). Thus, we get a set of four subvarieties: HSB, LSB, HCB, LCB. The last subvariety, viz. LCB is very similar to SC, if not hundred per cent identical with it. Hereafter, LCB will be used to mean both SC and LCB, and SC will be used only when specific reference to a spoken aspect is especially called for. Of the four sentences illustrated, LCB is represented by A, LSB by B, HCB by C, and HSB by D.

There is no doubt that vocabulary selection plays a dominant role in deciding subvarieties as H or L. I will return to the question of importance of lexis; for the present, let me point out that HCB makes use of some grammatical devices that are characteristically present in HSB but absent from LSB and LCB. Since it is not possible here to list these exhaustively, a few representative examples are cited. Thus, the primary derivational suffixes / -onio /, / -tobbo /, and / man / as are found in words like / dOršonio / 'worth seeing', / grohonio / 'worth accepting', / gontobbo / 'should be gone to', / drošṫobbo / 'deserves to be seen', / cOloman / 'in the process of moving', / khioman / 'in the process of being decayed' are very frequent in both HSB and HCB, but are conspicuously absent in LSB and LCB. Similarly, the secondary derivational suffixes like / šu / , / išnu / and / ban / as in words like /jiggašu/ 'desirous of knowing', / pipašu / 'desirous of drinking', / khoišnu / 'continuing to be decayed', / colišnu / 'continuing to move', / pranoban / 'full of life', / bOloban / 'full of strength' are not met with in LSB and LCB, but are very common in HSB and HCB. Many more morophological evidences of this nature could be cited to show that HCB agrees with HSB and not with LCB. Again, HCB like HSB makes use of a large number of Sanskritic type of compounds. Speaking about syntax, at least the passive construction, which is prevalent in both HSB and HCB but is absent from both LSB and LCB, can be cited as an example. In the passive construction in question the agent takes / dara / or / kortrik / , / and the predicate is adjectival which is formed from Sanskritic verbal roots with the addition of past participial suffix / -to /. Thus, in both HSB and HCB we meet quite often sentences like / rabon ramkortrik nihOto hOn / 'Ravana was killed by Rama', /ei biššošOŋšar bogobankortrik srišTo/ 'This universe was created by God', /baŋgla baŋgaliderdara kothito hOe / 'Bengali is spoken by the Bengalees', and so on.

Besides these grammatical differences, we must look into the important area of vocabulary or lexis. The rules in question involve selectional norms regarding paradigmatic and syntagmatic relations. We all know that the paradigmatic relations refer to the relations 'in absentia' and the syntagmatic relations, to the relations 'in presentia'. In the sphere of paradigmatic and syntagmatic selectional norms of lexis, one can characterize HCB as maintaining indelible marks of HSB, and generally avoiding day-to-day conversational norms. With regard to paradigmatic aspect of lexical selection, HCB like HSB makes use of a vast number of such Sanskritic lexical items as have more than one paradigmatic substitute having co-referential meaning; for instance, one can use for 'eye' / cokkhu / , / nOeon / or / nettro /; for 'head' / mOstok /, or /šir/; for 'leg' / pOdo/ or / cOron /; for 'sun' / šurjo /,/ robi/bhanu /,/ tOpon / / bhaškOr / and a dozen others; similarly for 'water / jOl / nir / , / šolil /, /bari / , / ombu / and many others. But in LSB and LCB no such co-referential options are available, where for each of the contents an equivalent *tadbhava* derivative or a colloquially current *tatsama* is normally used. Thus, LSB and LCB will use for 'eye' / cokh / , for 'head' / matha /, for 'leg' / pa/, for 'sun' / šurjo/ and for 'water / jOl /. It is not hard to see that these differences of paradigmatic selectional norms would naturally have consequential effect upon the syntagmatic selectional norms as well. In other words, variants tend to be selected in co-occurrent clusters and these at the LCB and HCB levels vary characteristically. Thus, in LCB we have / cokher šamne / 'in front of the eyes', / nicu matha / 'lowly placed head', / pa duTo / 'the two legs', but for the same meanings one has to use in HCB / cokher šOmmukhe /, /nOto mOstok / and / pOdojugol / respectively.

I am aware that all matters relating to lexical choices are traditionally shelved off into the realm of registeral and stylistic varieties of the same code. However, I tend to hold that referential equivalences of paradigmatic and syntagmatic lexical alternates revealing such a widespread variation, as HCB and LCB demonstrate together with the grammatical differences that these two forms of Bengali display, adequately substantiate the relegation of HCB and LCB to two different codes.

For a diagnostic determination of diglossia and for its proper study Ferguson employs a set of nine parameters. These are (i) function, (ii) prestige, (iii) literary heritage, (iv) acquisition, (v) standardization, (vi) stability, (vii) grammar, (viii) lexicon, and (ix) phonology. Of these, the grammatical and lexical differences between HCB and LCB have already been discussed. Speaking about phonology, we should make a summary statement that HCB and LCB do not show a significant difference. Using the remaining parameters of Ferguson, I delineate below the status of HCB and LCB.

Function

Ferguson observes that one of the most important features of diglossia is the specialization of function for H and L. So far as the function of HCB and LCB is concerned, one must note that the use of HCB is restricted to one set of situations and LCB to another. The situations where one is appropriate, the other is generally considered inappropriate. The complementary role of the two varieties with very little overlapping are being indicated below with a list of the situations where each is used:

	HCB	*LCB*
1. Public address of all sorts	x	
2. Scripted Speech	x	
3. News Broadcast	x	
4. News Journals	x	
5. Creative literature except novels, dramas and short stories	x	
6. Narrative description in novels and short stories	x	
7. Formal letters	x	
8. Class lectures	x	
9. Dialogues in novels and dramas		x
10. Informal personal letters		x
11. Conversation with family members		x
12. Instruction to workmen, servants and subordinates		x

Ridiculous or sometimes comical will be the effect if the norms of situational selection between the two are violated.

PRESTIGE

Ferguson notes that in all diglossic communities speakers regard H as superior to L in a number of respects. The speakers of Bengali accord a very high status to HCB and comparatively a lower status to LCB. This is evident from the fact that even a speaker who is very competent in LCB will often complain that he does not have a considerable command of good Bengali. All that this means is that he does not have a commendable mastery over HCB. The feeling of superiority of HCB is generally backed by notions that it is the only fit medium to express thoughts logically, valuably and beautifully, whereas LCB is for ordinary day-to-day non-significant use. It may be mentioned incidentally that this attitude of superiority of HCB and non-superiority of LCB is even transferred to English written and spoken by the Bangalees leading them to resort to a verbose style.

LITERARY HERITAGE

In Bengali there exists a considerable amount of written literature and the speech-community holds it in high esteem. The contemporary literary production is almost invariably limited to HCB, but things were different before. There existed a vernacular literature going back to the tenth or eleventh century. This literature, written in different dialects, was limited to poetic composition, and prose-writing was conspicuously absent. The introduction of printing press by the Christian missionaries in the first decade of the nineteenth century ushered in an era of writing Bengali prose. The pioneers of Bengali prose used SC as the model of their writing, as will be evident from a study of their works (Chatterjee and Chatterjee, 1979). But soon the trend, which was considered unworthy of serious writing and was given a casual status, swung towards a mode, based on the one that was carved out for it through its use in the vernacular literature that existed before. This mode yielded to increased use of elements of Sanskrit, which, as the medium of religious rituals and as the symbol of high culture, has all along been cultivated. This mode of writing grew into what is known as SB. Towards the last quarter of the nineteenth century there arose a movement under the championship of Rabindranath Tagore for making the art of writing and formal speaking portray the spoken form. Without going into the details of this movement, one can state that this movement was successful in introducing once again the common CB features that the pioneers of Bengali prose used; but, the bulk of the vocabulary, grammatical derivation, and compounding that mattered most remained Sanskritic, as before. It is, therefore, an illusion to consider this mode as representing SC, since in both form and function it replicates SB. HCB, therefore, is nothing but SB with those SC features which we have discussed before. Neither the writers nor the readers feel it bad or improper to incorporate words, phrases and grammatical constructions that are not used in SC.

Acquisition

SC is learnt from its oral use. The children in and around Calcutta learn it automatically, since it is the variety they hear quite often. It should, however, be mentioned that children residing in this locality whose parents have non-SC background may learn another dialect in addition to SC. The adults and children of regional dialect areas gain either no efficiency or considerable efficiency depending upon the different socio-cultural contexts in which they spend their lives. One should note, however, that regional dialect speakers who are literate can learn SC by reading and imitating dialogues in dramas and fiction. But HCB cannot be acquired from its oral use. Children and adults do hear HCB, but it is hardly possible to acquire any competence in HCB without formal schooling.

Standardization and Stability

No further explanation is perhaps needed to prove that standardization in Bengali has been, uptill to-day, of a bi-modal type. The demarcation between SC and HCB is very sharp and rather stable. The mixing of the two, however, takes place. But in the native tradition this is looked down upon. The existence of the native term *guru-cOnDali* where the first component means 'high' and the second 'low', proves that mixing of modes takes place, and at the same time indicates that this practice is not encouraged. Despite the prevalence of different norms of codification (Garvin, 1959; Garvin and Mathiot, 1969; Ferguson, 1968; Haugen, 1966) for SC and HCB in recent times there has set in a two-fold mechanism of elaboration seeking to fulfil the needs for modernization (Ferguson, 1968) of the language. Due to the said two-way process, firstly words of day-to-day usage are gaining entrance in the discourse, and secondly, H words are gaining currency in the ordinary, everyday discourse (Chatterjee and Chatterjee, 1979). Undoubtedly the middle-class elites are the agents of this recent trend of change but the non-educated masses, who emulate the former, are very slowly acquiring this new mode of CB. Although the mass-media have still remained embroiled in the age-old cannons of good usage, the challenges that have been thrown open by the mass-literacy programmes are expected to make clear and visible inroads upon these norms. In one word, Bengali is surely moving towards a unimodal standardization but it has by no means yet traversed the path and reached the goal.

I tend to believe that HCB and SC should be considered as representing two different codes on the basis of the parameters that Ferguson has outlined. Pride and Holmer (1972) suggest that three main criteria can be employed to decide if one linguistic code is different from another. The three criteria are: linguistic structure, intelligibility and social function. I have demonstrated already that, on the basis of linguistic structure and social function, HCB and SC can both be assigned to two different codes. Let me discuss here the question of intelligibility.

In a culture, such as that in which Bengali is used, where high prestige is accorded to the written word, the linguistic forms that are traditionally encountered in the forms of writing become imbued with feelings of dignity and refinement. In contrast to this, those that are used in day-to-day conversation acquire an inferior status. These levels of usage are learned by natives as part of their total cultural experience. SC is learned naturally. However, HCB can never be acquired without formal education. The persons who receive formal education acquire a dual functional use, viz. both HCB and SC uses. Thus, due to their cultural conditioning, of which education forms a vital part, they learn to differentiate between what in the community's linguistic repertoire are regarded as highly valued and what carry undignified overtones. In sharp contrast to this, those who are denied the opportunity of formal schooling can never master those aspects of the community's linguistic repertoire that is associated with values of high presitge. Therefore, the situation that obtains in Bengali is neither similar to what obtains, for example, in Zũni that Newman (1965) describes nor to the kind of code-switching that Blom and Gumperz found in a Norwegian community. In both Zũni and the Norwegian community code-switching takes place, as does in Bengali, among those, who, due to their formal schooling, control both HCB and SC. Non-intelligibility does not enter into the picture in any one of these cases, since most of the people control the entire range of two respective codes, viz. sacred and slang in case of Zũni, Ranamål and Bokmål in case of Norwegian, and HCB and SC in case of an educated Bengali. However, in the Bengali community the people who control only SC suffer from the constraint of not being able to understand HCB, not to speak of using it effectively. This goes to prove that what is popularly conceived as CB is, in fact, composed of two mutually unintelligible codes which co-exist in the community's total linguistic repertoire.

I have a feeling that all the Indo-Aryan languages of India, except perhaps Hindi-Urdu, are typically more or less analogous to Bengali, in this respect. An educated person, by virtue of his formal schooling, acquires H of the respective community's linguistic repertoire in areas where a non-educated individual knowing only L suffers limitations owing to his inability to control H. Since L is learnt naturally a person who acquires competence in H is equally at home in L; but the reverse is not true.

Finally, since Bengali literature conforming to the HCB norm is of fairly recent origin and since it is a product of the Bengali speech-community I think it pertinent to pose the question if Ferguson's characterization of H as belonging 'to an earlier period or of another speech community' is justifiable.

REFERENCES

Blom, Jan Petter and John J. Gumperz. 1972. Social meaning in linguistic structure : cod switching in Norway. *In Directions in sociolinguistics : the ethnography of communication.* ed. by John J. Gumperz and Dell Hymes. 407-434.

Bloomfield, Leonard. 1927. Literate and illitrrate speech. *American Speech.* 2.432-438 Reprinted in Dell Hymes (ed.), 1964. *Language in culture and society.* New York Evanston, and London: Harper and Row, Publishers.

Chatterjee, Suhas. 1962. *A study of the relationships between written and colloquial Bengali* (unpublished doctoral dissertation): Connecticut: Hartford Seminary Foundation, Hartford,

——— and Sipra Chatterjee. 1979. The problem of standardization of Bengali in a socio cultural perspective, a paper presented in a seminar on "The Language Movements in India in the Twentieth Century" organized by the Central Institute of Indian Languages, Mysore 6, India.

Chatterji, S.K. 1926. *The origin and development of the Bengali language.* Delhi: Motilal Banarsidass.

———. 1967. *Saral bhasa prakas bangla byakaran.* Calcutta 9: Vak sahitya.

Ferguson, Charles A. 1959. Diglossia. *Word* 15.325-340 (Reprinted in Dell Hymes (ed)., 1964. *Language in culture and society.* New York, Evanston, and London: Harper and Row, Publishers. Also in Dil, Anwar S, 1971. (Selected and introduced by) *Language structure and language use,* Essays by Charles A. Ferguson. Stanford, California: Stanford Univeristy Press.

———. 1963. Problems of teaching language with diglossia. *Georgetown University Monograph Series on Languages and Linguistics.* Monograph No. 15. Report of the thirteenth annual round table meeting, Georgetown University Press, Washington, D.C. 1962. pp.165-177. Also in Dil Anwar S, 1971. (Selected and introduced by) *Language structure and language use. Essays by Charles A. Ferguson.* Stanford, California: Stanford University Press.

———. 1968. Language development. In Joshua A. Fishman, J. Dasgupta and Charles A. Ferguson (eds.), 1968. *Language problems of developing nations.* New York: John Wiley & Sons, pp. 27-35. Also in Dil Anwar S, 1971 (Selected and introduced by) *Language structure and Language use. Essays by Charles A. Fergnson.* Stanford, California : Standard University Press.

Garvin, Paul L. 1959. The standard language problem concepts and methods. *Anthropological Linguistics,* 1(2):28-21. Also in Dell Nymes (ed.). *Language in culture & society.* New York, Evanston and London : Harper and Row, Publishers.

——— and Madeleine Mathiot. 1960. The urbanization of the Guarani language—a problem in language and culture. In Anthony F.C. Wallace (ed.), *Men and cultures,* pp. 783-730. Philadelphia: University of Pennsylvania Press.

Gumperz, John J. 1962. Types of linguistic communities. *Anthropologica Linguistics* 4.1 28-40.

———. 1964. Linguistic and social interaction in two communities. In John J. Gumperz and Dell Hymes (eds.). *The ethnography of communication. Amercian Anthropologist* 66, 6, pt. II:137-154.

Haugen, Einar. 1966. Dialect, language, nation. *American Anthropologist,* vol. 68, pp. 925-935.

Hymes, Dell. 1962. The ethnography of speaking. Thomes Gladwin and William C. Sturtevant (eds). *Anthropology and human behaviour.* pp. 13-53. Washington. D.C.: Anthropological Society of Washington.

Newman, Stanley. 1955. Vocabulary levels : Zuni sacred and slang usage. *Southeastern Journal of Anthropology*, 11:345-354 (Reprinted in Dell Hymes (ed.), 1964. *Language in culture & society*. New York, Evanston and London: Harper and Row, Publishers.

Pride, J.B. and Janet Holenes, 1972. (ed.) *Introduction to socio-linguistics*, pp. 7-11. Penguin Books Ltd.

Voeglin, C.F. 1960. Causal and non-causal utterances within unified structure. In Thomas A. Sebeok (ed.). *Style in language*. pp. 57-69. New York: John Wiley and Sons.

TYPOLOGY OF DIGLOSSIA AND ITS IMPLICATIONS FOR LITERACY

M.W. Sugathapala De Silva

This paper is a by-product of the work I did in South India and Sri Lanka during 1974-6 with a view to ascertaining if there existed any relationship between certain linguistic cleavages obtaining in the region and the level and definition of, and the attitudes to, literacy in the respective communities. The major analysis of my investigation has not yet been written up but some of the findings have been reported in three publications pertaining to it (De Silva 1976, 1977, 1979). In those publications I have treated the linguistic cleavages in question as products of *Diglossia.* I shall attempt to justify the use of the term *Diglossia* to refer to those non-congruent communities in the course of this paper. How this lack of congruence might be set out as a typological statement and what relationships exist between such a typology and the domain of literacy will then be examined.

There is little evidence for making a strong claim that diglossia, as obtaining in South India and Sri Lanka, is the sole or principal determiner of the low level of literacy in the respective communities. Causes of illiteracy are many and not all of them are knowable. Among the knowable are factors such as poverty, the need for child labour as a means of economic survival, the inefficiency or the impracticability of the machinery for enforcing the laws governing compulsory schooling and the rigidly hierarchical stratification of the society.

This last factor, namely, the hierarchical stratification of the society, however, has some bearing on the people's concept of prestige, esteem, propriety and formality with which the use and maintenance of the linguistic duality in question is much enmeshed. A claim could, therefore, be made—weak though it may appear—that there is some relationship, casual or symbiotic, between the level and definition of, and the attitude to, literacy in the community and the sociolinguistic structure of that community. Concepts of prestige, formality, propriety, etc. do not have identical meanings in all communities. The differences in their definitions correspond significantly to the differences in the definition of, and attitude to, literacy.* Exploring some of these differences and relationships is the prime purpose of the present exercise.

*It must be stated in parentheses that while the definition of and attitude to literacy are sociolinguistically determinable in this way, any explanation of the level of literacy in a community is governed by many factors outside sociolinguistics. Only a part of the community's level of literacy is directly related to its sociolinguistics of literacy, i.e. the definition of and the attitude to the subject.

I should like to address myself first to the subject of diglossia typology. When he brought into focus some differences, particularly in origin, practice and stability, between his four defining situations, Ferguson (1959: references to repr. 1964) obviously envisaged the existence of various types of diglossia within his broad framework. In Ferguson's classic definition of diglossia (1964: 435), the prestige variety is said to be characterized by eight features: it is (i) divergent (ii) highly codified (iii) superposed (iv) a vehicle of a respected body of written literature (v) learnt through formal education (vi) used for most written purposes (vii) used for formal spoken purposes and (viii) not used by any sector for ordinary conversation. In South India, and indeed in the whole of South Asia, the only diglossia whose prestige linguistic usage is characterized by all eight features is the Tamil situation. Other comparable situations differ in one (in this case, vii) or two (vii and viii) of the eight characteristics. In a typological inquiry, the first issue that must be decided on is, do we emphasise the sharing of a vast number of similarities (here 6 out of 8), or do we regard the smaller number of differences (1 or 2 out of 8) as the more significant factor. Ferguson's original paper (1959) and subsequent research on his defining situations (Moulton 19 62; Householder 1962; Stewart 1962; etc.) show that these eight features are not shared in equal measure by all of them.

The Tamil situation is governed by the convention that the classical format must be used in formal speech. How far this requirement is realised in actual practice, in the Tamil situation or any other diglossia, is irrelevant; what is of sociolinguistic significance is the prevalence of a belief which dictates an unquestioned allegiance to the classical norm for formal use. In the Telugu and Sinhalese situations, however, formal speech does not require the use of the classical norm. There, the classical norm is restricted to the written literature. (This is not to deny that the knowledge of the literary vocabulary and grammar exercises an influence on the educated formal use of the language.) Among the Kannada speakers, too, there is no rigid belief that formal speech must be conducted entirely in the classical format. One is led to believe, in addition, that the classical, prestige form of Kannada is the vernacular of a particular sector of the community. Kannada, then, is an instance where Ferguson's criterion viii would be violated. (I do not propose to discuss the implications of this characteristic in Kannada for defining "speech community".)

There are two alternative ways of looking at these sociolinguistic complexes One would be to restrict the use of the term *diglossia* for the Tamil-like or Arabic-like situations and invent new names for the Telugu-Kannada-Sinhalese types. Such an approach would mean emphasising the differences rather than the many similarities. This approach, worked to its logical conclusion, could even disallow the labelling of one or two of Ferguson's own defining languages as diglossic situations. The alternative would be the simpler approach—simpler than inventing new labels—which would emphasise the sharing of the majority of features. This approach would treat all the instances mentioned so far as diglossic, allowing the differences to characterize subcategories or types within the general complex of diglossia. I favour this alternative, for the evidence is still strong for distinguishing diglossic situations from non-diglossic situations. Within a framework of diglossic versus non-diglossic, all the instances named above qualify for the former appellation. This would not require adulterating Ferguson's original definition; it might be modified minimally to read thus:

> Diglossia is a sociolinguistic phenomenon which manifests itself in a relatively stable language situation in which, in addition to the primary dialects of the language (which may include a standard or regional standards), there is a divergent, highly codified (often grammatically more complex) superposed variety, the vehicle of a respected body of written literature, either of an earlier period or in another speech community, which is learned largely by formal education and is used for most written and, usually, formal spoken purposes but is not generally used by any sector of the community for ordinary conversation.

Variations in the spectrum of diglossic situations vis-à-vis stability and the relative prestige of the varieties involved are motivated by the conditions that promulgate their emergence. In some diglossic situations, like Tamil and Arabic, the high variety is universally upheld as the prestige variety owing to its religio-cultural-associations. In diglossic situations whose emergence is religio-culturally determined there persists the belief that the high variety is unquestionably superior and purer. Attempts are, therefore, made to perform according to the prestige model in appropriate formal circumstances. To the extent that this belief is held by the community virtually without exception, there is stability with respect to the sociolinguistics of the phenomenon. Religio-cultural pressure to recognise the classical variety as the prestige form forces the community to regard modern and colloquial form as incorrect and impure. This syndrome has been captured in a paper by Schiffman where he attempts to relate the diglossic cleavage in Tamil to the concepts of purity versus pollution in the Tamil-speaking Hindu society (Schiffman 1979). Although their classical literature has been religious in theme, the acceptance of the classical format as the high variety in the Sinhalese, Telugu and probably Kannada communities, on the other hand, does not derive from a basically religio-cultural consideration of such dimensions. There, the ascendancy of the classical norm as the literary format was motivated by the availability of codified compendia of grammar, the rise of nationalism and the search for putatively purer strata in the history to serve as the nations' symbols and illustrious heritage. These, however, are conditions on which disagreement may prevail without endangering socio-cultural retrieval or national liberation. The absence of a factor (such as religion or holy scriptures) to command total dedication is responsible for the polemics on the use of the classical norm as well as for the failure of that norm to dominate formal spoken languages. The implications of associating the high variety with a high caste vernacular in a caste-based society are considerable for the widespread cultivation of the literary norm, as is evident in the Kannada situation where the Sanskritized classical norm is said to be a Brahman vernacular.

The impact of the differences in origin upon the stability, prestige and possible future developments in diglossic situations have been briefly dealt with in Ferguson's paper itself. 'Diglossia may develop from various origins and eventuate in different language situations'. (Ferguson 1964: 429). Ferguson's description of the origins of his four defining situations (429-30) read in conjunction with his tentative prognosis (437) and Moulton, Householder, Stewart, etc. referred to before should yield a hypothesis essentially similar to the claim made here. The differences in the functions and prestige between the two varieties in the Greek (Householder 1962), Swiss (Moulton 1962) and Haitian (Stewart 1962) situations are easily relatable to their diverse origins.

A comparison of these different types of diglossia would lead to the following conclusions. In situations where the high variety is chosen for religio-cultural reasons, it is universally accepted that the high variety is superior to the vernacular forms. Even the 'progressive' elements in the community voice their criticisms of the status quo sparingly. A comparatively stable situation, therefore, exists. The high variety is used for most literary and formal spoken purposes. Departures from the prestige norm are more a result of insufficient mastery of it than deliberate attempts to create new standards. The belief in the superiority of the high form dominates. In situations where the high variety is a product of classical revivalism for nativistic or similar reasons, however, there is no universally shared allegiance to the high norm. This gives rise to polemics on standard usage and the classical versus vernacular debate develops into a war of persuasion. New standards, usually compromises between the two, emerge sooner or later, and situations may be created where both the classical form and the vernacular form may be used equally for literary purposes. The very nature of the origin of these situations ensures that the classical norm is not fully exploited in speech, however formal, although its influence on the formal spoken lexicon is always evident. Then there is a third type. In instances where, in addition to classical revivalism, there appears a respectable sector of the community with a vernacular similar to the classical form, the hierarchical organization of the society forces the community to an ambivalent situation. On the one hand the implications of classical revivalism give rise to polemics and a search for new standards and, on the other hand, the well-entrenched social hierarchy, characterized by its own prestige elements, forces the community to accept the high norm as the undisputedly superior form of language. It is evident from our present knowledge of the sociolinguistics of the Greek, Swiss and several other non-Indian situations that their special properties and attributes would add considerably to the typological distinctions so far outlined, but they fall outside the scope of the present paper.

Between the Sinhalese and Telugu situations which I have placed in the second type there is one significant difference which owes itself to the way purism has worked in the two communities. For reasons I have discussed elsewhere (De Silva 1979), purism in Telugu has been overcome by more forceful intellectual campaigns for modernizing the standard usage. In Sinhalese, however, the power of purism still dominates with modernists making a considerable effort. As a result of this, diglossia in Telugu is diminishing, while an air of uncertainty or indeterminacy seems to characterize the standard usage in Sinhalese. This distinction illustrates how different social pressures may cause different linguistic developments in basically unstable diglossic situations.

As I have attempted to show in the above discussion, South Asian diglossia consists of a number of types. Tamil is essentially a *stable* diglossia, within the broad meaning I have given to the concept of stability. In contrast, Telugu and Sinhalese are cases of *unstable* diglossia. As a consequence of certain social pressures on these unstable situations, Telugu is now of a *diminishing* kind, while Sinhalese has developed an *indeterminate* character with regard to norm specification. In Kannada, in which the allegiance to the classical norm is sometimes confined to the literary usage and sometimes extends to formal speech allegedly through Brahman influence, there is an *ambivalent* situation displaying some vacillation between the Tamil and Telugu types.

The notion that the classical norm is not prescribed for the putatively formal domains in Telugu and Sinhalese needs a brief comment. It is probably the case that formality is conceived differently in different communities, and this difference can be attributed to prestige and cultural conditions which are regarded as the communities' inheritance. As Schiffman (1979) has rightly observed, formal situations have so far been defined, decidedly circularly, as those requiring the use of the classical norm. Non-linguistic constituents of formal situations might not be universally alike and need careful examining. In such an examination, the concept of formality might appear to be different between the Tamil community and the Sinhalese or the Telugu community. If that were to happen, the existing *a priori* statement that Sinhalese and Telugu do not use the prestige variety of language for formal purposes will have been falsified.

I now move on to literacy, perforce very briefly. Models for, and the practice of, literacy that prevail in different diglossic situations are much enmeshed with the typological variation I have attempted to outline. In comparatively stable diglossic situations (e.g. Tamil) the classical format constitutes the undisputed literacy model, and the teachers strive to teach it faithfully. As a result of social changes and changes of values, the occasional murmur and dissatisfaction with the *status quo* might be heard, but with little impact. In unstable diglossic situations, however, an attitude of ambivalence prevails in the sphere of literacy. In the Telugu and the Sinhalese communities, for example, there have been numerous organized attempts to define and redefine the literacy norms during the past several decades. This difference is reflected in some attitudinal observations I have made and reported on in the works already cited.

My 1974-5 investigations revealed that almost all the Tamil speakers that answered my questionnaire defined literacy as the ability to read and write *correctly*. Yet, only 50% of the Kannada speakers, 30% of the Sinhalese speakers and 20% of the Telugu speakers held a similar view. Here again, what the Tamil speakers meant by "correctness" was not necessarily compatible with the notion of correctness held by those others. Almost every Tamil speaker defined correctness as "the observance of the correct rules of spelling and grammar", while only 45% of the above proportion of the Kannadigas, 15% of the Sinhalese and 10% of the Telugus contributed to that view. Seventy per cent of all the Telugus questioned were happy to define literacy as the ability to read and write, without invoking any correctness criterion. Fifty per cent of the Kannadigas and 50% of the Sinhalese held that view also. All Tamil speakers, on the other hand, insisted on the classical basis for correctness. In the Sinhalese and Telugu communities there was a dithering minority—20% in the former and 10% in the latter—who were not able to decide whether "correctness" was an essential ingredient of literacy.

It was found in my survey that every primary school child made mistakes of various kinds and that even grown up writers were not immune to violating the classical rules. Despite this, the Tamil community in general, and its educational system in particular, held steadily to a stable set of beliefs as evinced by the above survey results. In the Telugu community, however, a period of discussion and debate has openly questioned the comparable set of beliefs and has now resulted in the acceptance of a standardized *vyāvahārika* as a viable literacy model to replace or to alternate with *grānthika*. The vyāvahārika movement is not greatly resisted nowadays. This is reflected exactly in the Telugu statistics where 70% did not require the observance of the classical norm in literacy while 10% did. Due to recent events and openness of debate, Telugu diglossia has changed from an "unstable" diglossia to a "steadily diminishing" one. A clear example of an unstable diglossia is Sinhalese. Despite decades of polemics and discussions, Sinhalese diglossia does not show signs of changing from instability to a diminishing one. Here, vociferous puristic influences are the cause of the present situation (De Silva 1967, 1979). Again, this volatile character is clearly reflected in the Sinhalese statistics.

The lesson to draw from all this is that for the prevalence of a settled literacy model the community must converge in the direction of a settled set of beliefs vis-à-vis prestige, etc., either by accepting the classical norm totally (as in Tamil) or by healthily diminishing the overtones of the cleavage (as in Telugu). In the former, the literacy model is taught universally for the sake of formal accuracy; in the latter, the literacy model is stripped of its formal constraints for the sake of creativity. (This aspect of the teaching of literacy is beyond the scope of the present task, however.) In indeterminate diglossia, however, the literacy model is unsettled but is constrained by some pressure for recognizing the classical format. This indecision is not in the best interests of the learner, and many a working day of the policy makers is spent on defining and re-specifying models at the expense of more useful educational activity. The Sinhalese situation furnishes various reports of successive committees on standardization in justification of this statement.

In stable diglossia, classroom teaching of literacy adheres to an agreed code of conduct. In a somewhat different way this is so in diminishing situations also. In the former, teachers—even those whose own writings may occasionally fall short of the aspired ideal—make wholehearted attempts to correct pupil errors in terms of the prescribed model. In the latter, "errors" are identified only minimally, and a consistent approach is usually maintained. Both contrast significantly with indeterminate diglossia. In my survey alluded to above, I had the occasion to have ten pages of randomly selected compositions in each of the languages Tamil, Telugu, Kannada and Sinhalese, written by pupils aged 10-11, marked independently by ten teachers of each language. In the ten pages of Tamil, all ten teachers found 79 errors; there was also agreement as to the breakdown of these 79 into spelling, grammatical and lexical. A similarly consistent marking was made by the Telugu teachers who found four to five mistakes. These mistakes were, by and large, co-occurrences of classical bases with modern affixes. Contrast with these the Sinhalese results. There the teachers' disagreements placed the number of mistakes between 101 and 197. In Kannada, too there was a variation that ranged from 148 to 153 (certainly less varying than in Sinhalese). I reckon that the Sinhalese marking variation is an interesting reflection of the inconsistency in the teaching model in a volatile and unstable, yet forcibly maintained, linguistic duality.

Owing to constraints on space, I am forced to leave unexpanded the implications of diglossia typology for the definition of literacy and social attitudes to it. Polemics in unstable situations like Sinhalese and Telugu arise as a consequence of their nativistic origins with no pervasive religio-cultural motivation. Whether this instability can result in diminishing the cleavage depends on the powers exercised by militant purism. What is most lamentable in all South Asian diglossic situations is that the vernacular is far from being recognized as a realistic medium of higher literacy, and until this is achieved, literacy is bound to remain an elitist activity in which the lower strata of the society has little role to play.

References

De Silva, M.W.S. 1967. Effects of purism on the evolution of the written language. *Linguistics* 36.5-17. Nov. 1967.

———. 1976. *Diglossia and literacy*. Mysore: Central Institute of Indian Languages.

———. 1977. Problems of literacy in diglossic communities. In *Language and literacy: current issues and research*, ed. by T. P. Gorman. Tehran: International Institute of Adult Literacy Methods.

—. 1979. *Vernacularization of literacy: The Telugu experiment*. Hyderabad: International Telugu Institute.

Ferguson, C.A. (1959) 1964. Diglossia. In *Language in culture and society*, ed. by D. Hymes. New York: Harper and Row.

Householder, Jr., F.W. 1962. Greek diglossia. In *GURT* 15.109-132.

Moulton, W.G. 1962. What standard for diglossia? The case of German Switzerland. In *GURT* 15.133-148.

Schiffman, H. 1979. Diglossia and purity/pollution in Tamil. *Contributions to Asian Studies* 11.98-110.

Stewart, W.A. 1962. Functional distributon of Creole and French in Haiti. *GURT* 15. 149-162.

(*GURT : Georgetown University Round Table in Languages and Linguistics*).

SANSKRIT GRAMMARIANS ON DIGLOSSIA

Madhav M. Deshpande

1. Modern linguists led by Charles Ferguson have developed the concept of "diglossia" and have studied instances of diglossia in South Asia and elsewhere. From an objective point of view, the phenomenon of diglossia or polyglossia is not an uncommon phenomenon, and ancient India must have had its own kind of diglossia. However, when one searches for evidence of indigenous awareness of diglossia or indigenous conceptions of diglossia, the investigation gets more complicated and we have to make the best of the available bits of information. In my recent monograph *Sociolinguistic attitudes in India: An historical reconstruction*, I considered the indigenous conceptions of diglossia in their sociolinguistic context. In this paper I will deal with notions related to diglossia and their sociolinguistic implications in the works of Sanskrit grammarians.

2. Certain valuations concerning different kinds of linguistic usage are seen in the Vedic literature. The Vedic Aryans did not always fully understand the languages spoken by their non-Vedic enemies and these enemies were branded *mṛdhravācaḥ* 'those whose language was obscure and unintelligible.'[1] While the Aryan language was called *devī vāk* 'Divine language, the goddess of speech',[2] the language of the non-Vedic enemies was sometimes called *asuryā vāk* 'demonic language'[3], an expression which has often a moral as well as a linguistic connotation. The Vedic poets also make a distinction between the literary language and the commonplace usage. In *RV* 10.71.2 we are told that like men cleansing corn flour in a sieve, the Vedic poets create the literary language.[4] The implication is that the creation of a literary language involves a conscious process of selection and elimination of many features found in the colloquial usage. In the *Brāhmaṇa* texts, one comes across further indications of linguistic valuations. In the *Śatapatha Brāhmaṇa* (3.1.5.11) a Brahmin is warned against speaking like a *Mleccha* 'a barbarian'.[5] A Brahmin should not speak in a degenerate manner. Referring to Vrātyas, the so-called pre-Vedic and non-Vedic Aryans, the *Brāhmaṇa* texts tell us that though these folks are not initiated in the Vedic religion

1. *Ṛgveda*: 1.174.2; 5.29.10; 5.32.8; 7.6.3; 7.18.13 and 10.23.5.
2. *Ṛgveda*: 8.100.11.
3. *yāṁ hy anya-manā vācaṁ vadaty asuryā vai sā vāg a-deva-juṣṭā, Aitareya-Brāhmaṇa*, Ānandāśrama edition, Vol. I., Poona, p. 161.
4. *saktum iva titaunā punanto yatra dhīrā manasā vācam akrata, Ṛgveda*: 10.71.2.ab.
5. For a discussion, see Deshpande (1979: 105, 107).

(*adīkṣitāḥ*), they speak the language of the initiated (*dīkṣita-vācaṁ vadanti*)[6]. This indicates a certain cleavage between the linguistic usage of those who were Vedic Aryans proper and those who were not. The diglossic markedness most probably had a close parallel in the social and religious life. Therefore, the Vrātyas who violated the expected norms stand out as an important exception.

3. The Sanskrit grammarians inherited these kinds of valuations. However, Pāṇini (around 500 B.C.) was not interested in describing diglossia as such, but only the upper or the elite portion of the diglossic spectrum, and the known Vedic usage. He refers to regional and scholastic variation, (Deshpande 1978) as well as mentions certain usages restricted to caste and sex.[7] Though there are sufficient indications of the existence of diglossia, there is no direct treatment of it.

As I discussed elsewhere, the period between Pāṇini and his successors like Kātyayana and Patañjali was marked by vast religious and political changes in India and these changes are often reflected in the changed grammatical and other conceptions held by these later grammarians (Deshpande 1978: 95 ff.; 1979: 4-17). From Kātyāyana (about 300-200 B.C.) onward, the existence of diglossia emerges as a very significant factor in the minds of the Sanskrit grammarians and one detects a number of conceptions relating to it.

4. While, for Pāṇini, the regional and scholastic variation in Sanskrit was quite important, guarding the whole of Sanskrit against the current popular usage emerges as the principal aim for Kātyāyana. Thus Kātyāyana de-emphasizes the value of dialectal variation noted by Pāṇini and turns it into optional or free variation. As long as both the dialectal usages are correct Sanskrit usages, they are both equally acceptable to Kātyāyana and their dialectal restrictions are of no avail to him (Deshpande 1978: 84 ff.) He wants to use Pāṇini's grammar to draw a dividing line between what he considers to be the proper usage on the one hand, and degenerate imporper usage, on the other. He says:[8]

While the relationship between words and meanings is established by the usage in the world [of a certain word] to denote a certain meaning, the science of grammar [only] makes a

---

6. *Pañcaviṁśa-Brāhmaṇa*, XVII.1.9. Ghose (1934: 12) prefers the reading *dīkṣitā* in the place of *adīkṣitā*, on the basis of a single Dacca manuscript, and takes the passage to mean that Vrātyas could speak the language of the initiated only after their initiation. According to A.C. Banerjea (1963: 147), the passage "conveys the idea of the restraining of speech by the Vrātyas in spite of the fact that they were not initiated, as according to the *Śatapatha-Brāhmaṇa* (III.2.2.27) the *dīkṣita* restrains speech and speaks falteringly." He adds (p. 150): "It has connection with the pronunciation of the Aryan language." Referring to the *Pañcaviṁśa-Brāhmaṇa* passage *durukta-vākyaṁ duruktam āhuḥ* (XVII. 1.9), Banerjea (p. 153) says: "The Vrātyas in their ceremonies spoke wrongly a sentence which was rightly uttered in the contest of the orthodox rites."

7. Cf. Pāṇini 8.2.83 (*pratyabhivāde' śūdre*).

8. *Vārttika* 1 (*siddhe śabdārtha-sambandhe lokato'rtha-prayukte śāstreṇa dharma-niyamaḥ yathā laukika-vaidikeṣu*), *MB*, Vol. I., pp. 6-8.

regulation concerning the religious merit [produced by the linguistic usage], as is commonly done in worldly conventions and Vedic rituals.

According to Kātyāyana, only the proper Sanskrit usage, as sanctioned by the grammarians, produces religious merit (*dharma*). He explicitly says that the usage of Sanskrit backed by the science of grammar produces prosperity, and that this is similar to the proper use of Vedic words in rituals. Any violations of the norms set by the grammarians and lapses into colloquial degenerate usage lead to social and religious downgrading. By giving the proper usage of Sanskrit the status of Vedic words, Kātyāyana has intensified the significance of preserving the proper Sanskrit usage and has indicated the widening diglossic gap between the proper élite Sanskrit usage and the more popular forms of the Aryan language. I am using the term "diglossic" here from the conservative point of view of the Sanskrit grammarians who refused to ascribe the Prakrit or Apabhraṁśa languages the status of separate languages. From their point of view, this was not really a bilingual situation, but rather a diglossic situation, where the non-élite people in the society were believed to speak a degenerate form of the élite language. [Here I wish to stick close to the more conservative scope of the term 'diglossia' as used by Charles Ferguson, and not accept the wider scope of the same term as found in the work of other linguists, e.g. Joshua Fishman, which includes a functionally motivated bilingual situation within its scope.] Elsewhere I have contrasted this conservative view of the Sanskrit grammarians with the more liberal views held by the Buddhists, the Jainas and others (Deshpande 1979: 22 ff.) Kātyāyana says that this degenerate usage by the non-élite folks is due to their inability (*aśakti*) to produce proper usage.[9] These are reflections of the social psychology of those days.

5. Patañjali's *Mahābhāṣya* not only provides explanations of Kātyāyana's statements, but adds significant details reflecting the contemporary linguistic situation and the attitudes of the Sanskrit grammarians concerning this situation. While Kātyāyana seems to be asserting the need of speaking proper Sanskrit at all times, we see a distinct change in Patañjali's work. He emphasizes the need for the proper Sanskrit usage at the proper time, and not at all times. He refers to the passage in the *Śatapatha Brāhmaṇa*[10] which tells us that the Asuras ("demons") speaking incorrect words *helayo helayo*, apparently for the proper Sanskrit words *he arayaḥ he arayaḥ*, were defeated by the gods. Patañjali believes that it was the "degenerate" (= "incorrect") linguistic usage by the demons at a sacrificial performance which led to their defeat. He further illustrates this point:[11]

9. *ḷkāropadeśo yadṛcchāśaktijānukaraṇa-pluty-ādy-arthaḥ*, *Vārttika* 1, on the *Śiva-sūtra ṛ-ḷ-K*, *MB*, Vol. I., p. 19.

10. *te' surā helayo helaya iti kurvantaḥ parābabhūvuḥ*, *MB*, Vol. I., p. 10. Also see: Deshpande (1979: 105, 107).

11. *yad apy ucyate ācāre niyama iti yājñe karmaṇi sa niyamaḥ | evaṁ hi śrūyate | yarvāṇastarvāṇo nāma ṛṣayo babhūvuḥ pratyakṣa-dharmāṇaḥ parāpara-jñā vidita-veditavyā adhi-*

The restriction on the [proper] usage [of words] also applies only in the context of sacrificial performances. Thus it is heard. There were great...sages named *Yarvāṇastarvāṇa*. These respected sages spoke *yarvāṇastarvāṇa* instead of speaking the proper Sanskrit words such as *yad vā naḥ* and *tad vā naḥ*. However, they did not use these degenerate forms during sacrificial performances. On the other hand, the demons used degenerate linguistic forms even during a sacrificial performance, and hence they were defeated.

This passage gives us a concrete instance of diglossic variation: *yad vā naḥ* and *tad vā naḥ* on the one hand and *yarvāṇastarvāṇa* on the other hand. This variation is an example of contextual and functional code-switching. However, there is also a social dimension to this discussion. It shows that while some segments in the society could shift their style of speech in different contexts, the other segments did not and perhaps could not shift in the same way. This placed these latter elements also at a lower ritual status from the Brahmanical point of view. Patañjali explicitly warns a Brahmin not to use degenerate linguistic usages during a sacrificial performance and be subjected to a purificatory penance.[12]

6. On Kātyāyana's statement that these degenerate usages are due to the speaker's incapacity (*aśakti*), Patañjali gives the following examples:[13]

Due to incapacity, a Brahmin woman
said *ḷtaka* instead of saying *ṛtaka*.
A Brahmin woman said *ḷtaka*.
A girl said *ḷtaka*.

Patañjali seems to imply that girls and women were prone to speak the degenerate form of the language. There is other kind of evidence in the works of Kātyāyana and Patañjali to show the increasingly lower respect for women (Deshpande 1979: 100, n. 48). The reason for this degenerate usage by women in Patañjali's opinion is *aśakti* "incapacity, inability". Women are deemed to lack the ability that men possess. It would be interesting to compare the linguistic status of women with the sages Yarvāṇastarvāṇa. While these women, including the Brahmin women, uniformly spoke the "degenerate" form of the language, the sages had the ability to switch codes. Hence Patañjali probably would not ascribe *aśakti* "incapacity" as the reason for the contextual degenerate usage of the sages, although it is obviously clear that such élites normally spoke a form of Apabhraṁśa or Prakrit at home and spoke proper Sanskrit only in the context of a sacrificial performance.

7. Given such a linguistic spectrum, with one end of the spectrum being the proper Sanskrit and the other end being considered to be the degenerate *apabhraṁśa* or *apaśabda* usage, what is the function of a grammar such as Pāṇini's *Aṣṭādhyāyī* ? While the more common word for grammar is *vyā-*

---

gata-yāthātathyāḥ | te tatrabhavanto yad vā nas tad vā na iti prayoktavye yarvāṇastarvāṇa iti prayuñjate | yājñe karmaṇi punar nāpabhāṣante | taiḥ punar asurair yājñe karmaṇy apabhāṣitam | tatas te parābhūtāḥ |, *MB*, Vol. I., p. 11.

12. *āhitāgnir apaśabdam prayujya prāyaścittīyāṁ sārasvatīm iṣṭim nirvapet iti | prāyaścittīyā mā bhūmety adhyeyaṁ vyākaraṇam |*, *MB*, Vol. I., p. 4.

13. *aśaktyā kayācid brāhmaṇyā ṛtaka iti prayoktavye ḷtaka iti prayuktam | brāhmaṇy ḷtaka ity āha | kumārī ḷtaka ity āha |*, *MB*, Vol. I, p. 19.

karaṇa "explanation, analysis", the word for grammar brought into focus by Patañjali is *śabdānuśāsana* "regulations concerning words" (Deshpande 1979: 100). Following Kātyāyana, Patañjali also states that while the function of communicating meaning may be feasible by using either the proper Sanskrit words (*śabda*) or by using the degenerate forms (*apa-śabda*), the science of grammar makes a regulation that, for the sake of religious merit, the meaning should be communicated only by using the proper Sanskrit words and not by using the degenerate forms.[14] If a proper Sanskrit word and a degenerate word have the same meaning, then a word backed by the science of grammar (*śāstrānvita*) makes the other word unacceptable. For instance, the word *devadatta* being properly enjoined by grammar (*śāstrānvita*) makes the degenerate form *devadiṇṇa* unacceptable.[15] The word "grammar" in these discussions refers exclusively to the traditional Sanskrit grammar. From the hierarchical point of view of the Sanskrit grammarians, the degenerate Apabhraṁśa usage has no grammar at all (Deshpande 1979: 9-14).

8. The discussion concerning the status of the standard of the proper Sanskrit usage in Patañjali's *Mahābhāṣya* sheds light on the position of Sanskrit within the contemporary diglossic and linguistic spectrum. Patañjali says that only the usage of the *śiṣṭas* "cultured people, élites" is to be considered the standard Sanskrit usage. Patañjali says:[16]

Who are the *śiṣṭas* ?
[They are] the grammarians.
How is it ?
The correct use of words presupposes the science [of grammar], and the grammarians are knowers of the science [of grammar].
But, if the correct use of language presupposes the science [of grammar], and if grammar presupposes the correct use of language, then this [definition] becomes circular. Circular [arguments] do not stand valid.
Then, [we define *śiṣṭas*] by their way of life and place of residence. That particular way of life is [found] only in the province of Āryāvartta. ...[It lies] to the east of the Ādarśa mountain, to the west of the Kālaka forest, to the south of the Himalayas and to the north of the Vindhyas. Those Brahmins who live in this Āryāvartta, the land of the Aryans, who just

14. *samānāyām artha-gatau śabdena cāpa-śabdena ca dharmaniyamaḥ kriyate śabdenaivārtho'bhidheyo nāpa-śabdeneti* /, *MB*, Vol. I., p. 8.

15. *samāne cārthe śāstrānvito' śāstrānvitasya nivartako bhavati / tad yathā / devadatta-śabdaḥ devadiṇṇa-śabdaṁ nirvartayati* /, *MB*, Vol. I., p. 20.

16. *ke punaḥ śiṣṭāḥ ? vaiyākaraṇāḥ / kuta etat ? śāstrapūrvikā hi śiṣṭiḥ, vaiyākaraṇāś ca śāstrajñāḥ / yadi tarhi śāstra-pūrvikā śiṣṭiḥ śiṣṭi-pūrvakaṁ ca śāstram, tad etad itaretarāśrayam bhavati / itaretarāśrayāṇi ca (kāryāṇi) na prakalpante / evaṁ tarhi nivāsataś cācārataś ca / sa cācāra āryavartta eva / kaḥ punar āryāvarttaḥ ? prāg ādarśāt, pratyak kālaka-vanāt, dakṣiṇena himavantam, uttareṇa pāriyātram / etasminn āryāvartte āryanivāse ye brāhmaṇāḥ kumbhī-dhānyā alolupā agṛhyamāṇa-kāraṇāḥ kiṁcid antareṇa kasyāścid vidyāyāḥ pāraṁ gatās tatrabhavantaḥ śiṣṭāḥ / yadi tarhi śiṣṭāḥ śabdeṣu pramāṇam, kim aṣṭādhyāyyā kriyate ? śiṣṭa-parijñānārthā aṣṭādhyāyī/ katham punar aṣṭādhyāyyā śiṣṭāḥ śakyā vijñātum ? aṣṭādhyāyīm adhyīyano' nyam paśyaty anadhīyānaṁ ye cāsyāṁ vihitāḥ śabdās tān prayuñjānam / sa paśyati-nūnam asya devānugrahaḥ savbhāvo vā, yo'yaṁ na cāṣṭādhyāyīm adhīte, ye cāsyāṁ vihitāḥ śabdās tāṁś ca prayuṅkte / nūnam ayam anyān api jānāti-ity evam eṣā śiṣṭa-jñānārthā aṣṭādhyāyī-iti* /, *MB*, Vol. II., p. 174.

store a basketful of grain, who are selfless and have attained the highest wisaom in some branch of learning for its own sake, they are the *śiṣṭas*.
If these *śiṣṭas* are the decisive standard for [correctness of] words, what is the function of Pāṇini's grammar ?
Pāṇini's grammar aims at helping one recognize the normative speakers of Sanskrit, the *śiṣṭas*.
How can the normative speakers of Sanskrit be recognized by means of Pāṇini's grammar ?
One who is studying the grammar observes another person who is not studying it, but who is using the words which are taught in it. He observes—It must be either his inherent nature or divine grace that this person who does not study Pāṇini's grammar uses correct forms which are taught in it. He must also know other [correct] forms [which are not directly taught by Pāṇini's grammar].
Thus Pāṇini's grammar aims at helping one recognize the normative speakers of Sanskrit.

This discussion shows us how the Sanskrit language from the Vedic times upto the time of Patañjali had gradually moved to an extreme end of the Indian linguistic spectrum. It was mainly restricted to the sacrificial and academic activity of the learned Brahmins of Āryāvartta. Women and non-Brahmins are not the normative speakers of Sanskrit. Sanskrit being so removed from the linguistic behaviour of the masses, and being restricted to a highly contextual domain, it would be difficult to say that there was any true diglossia, in the original narrow sense of the term, i.e. various layers within the usage of Sanskrit. The only difference one can make is between the frozen use of Vedic Sanskrit and the contemporary literary and academic use by the learned Brahmins. The frozen use of Vedic Sanskrit had no productive aspect. The gap between Sanskrit and Prakrits or Apabhraṁśas being extremely wide, their mutual relationship must be viewed really from a bilingual perspective, rather than from a diglossic perspective.

Patañjali's discussion actually helps us distinguish between fact and fiction concerning the use of Sanskrit and Prakrits. The Sanskrit dramas, where the upper-class males always speak Sanskrit and everydbody else always speaks some form of Prakrit, create an illusion that there were actual conversational situations where one person would speak Sanskrit and the other person would speak Prakrit, without any code-switching. The likelihood of such actual conversational situations was very little. The Sanskrit dramas were written and performed for a learned Sanskrit-knowing audience, who always had access to Prakrits, and not for monolingual Prakrit audiences who did not always have direct access or even passive understanding of Sanskrit. Patañjali presents a more realistic picture when he says that even the learned sages spoke Prakrit or Apabhraṁśa in all colloquial contexts, implying that such a sage would most probably speak in Prakrit to his wife and other-non-learned acquaintances. The choice of Prakrits as media by the mass-oriented religions such as Buddhism and Jainism also indicate that the masses did not have a clear access to or understanding of Sanskrit The Sanskrit dramas in this respect are not very close to the contemporary reality of language-use, but represent perhaps the idealized expectations on the part of Sanskrit authors concerning who ought to and who ought not to speak Sanskrit.

9. For Patañjali, the proper Sanskrit usage and the degenerate usage of the Aryan language by the masses not only form two extreme ends of the diglossic spectrum, these two are mutually exclusive. This is reflected in his discussion concerning the proper way to formulate a grammar of Sanskrit:[17]

If one teaches the correct Sanskrit words, then once the proper Sanskrit word *guaḥ* "cow" is taught, it is [automatically] understood that words like *gāvī* are degenerate forms. If one teaches all the degenerate forms, then once words like *gāvī* are taught, it is [automatically] understood that words iike *gauḥ* are correct Sanskrit words. Which is better? Because of its brevity, it is better to teach correct Sanskrit words. The teaching of correct Sanskrit words is economical, while the teaching of degenerate forms involves prolixity. Corresponding with each correct Sanskrit word, there are many degenerate forms. Consider the following example. Corresponding with the correct Sanskrit word *gauḥ*, the degenerare forms are *gāvī, goṇī, gotā, gopotalikā*, etc. [Teaching of the correct Sanskrit words also] means accomplishing the explanation of whai is desirable (*iṣṭa*).

This discussion brings out the following main points. There are more degenerate forms or Prakrit and Apabhraṁśa forms corresponding to a given correct Sanskrit form. The proper Sanskrit forms and the degenerate forms are mutually exclusive. While the proper Sanskrit forms are considered to be desirable, the degenerate Apabhraṁśa forms are considered to be undesirable. This is comparable to the characterization of the speakers. While the speakers of correct Sanskrit are *śiṣṭas* "cultured people, élites", the speakers of the degenerate Apabhraṁśa forms are *aśiṣṭas* "uncultured people". Thus from the Brahmanical point of view, the diglossic and linguistic distinctions are inseparably linked with cultural distinctions. However, a modern linguist must appreciate the fact that, shorn of sociocultural overlays, Kātyāyana and Patañjali frankly admit that both Sanskrit and Apabhraṁśa are equally capable of communicating the same message in the same way. The difference between these two diglossic strata is important to Sanskrit grammarians for sociolinguistic reasons. The later grammarians and theologians are perhaps more orthodox than Patañjali, and their linguistic theories show a deeper influence of the socio-religious and theological considerations.

10. There are some significant views expressed in Bhartṛhari's *Vākyapadīya* regarding the relationship between Sanskrit and Apabhraṁśa, and the way an Apabhraṁśa word or a degenerate word conveys its meaning. Bhartṛhari's work is a great compendium and he often presents all sorts of mutually conflicting alternative views without telling us which view is his own. Therefore, we are not ascribing these views to Bhartṛhari himself. According to what to me seems to be the dominant view presented by Bhartṛhari, an Apabhraṁśa word or a degenerate form lacks the proper grammatical pro-

17. *yadi tāvac chabdopadeśaḥ kriyate, gaur ity etasminn upadiṣṭe gamyata etad gāvy-ādayo' pa-śabdā iti| atha apa-śabdopadeśaḥ kriyate, gāvy-ādiṣūpadiṣṭeṣu gamyata etad gaur ity eṣa śabda iti | kim punar atra jyāyaḥ ? laghutvāc chabdopadeśaḥ | laghīyāñ chabdopadeśaḥ | garīyān apa-śabdopadeśaḥ | ekaikasya śabdasya bahavo'-pa-bhraṁśāḥ | tad yathā | gaur ity asya śabdasya gāvī goṇī gotā gopotalikādayo' pabhraṁśāḥ | iṣṭānvākhyānaṁ khalv api bhavati| MB*, Vol. I., p. 5.

cessing.[18] According to this view, the degenerate forms cannot convey meaning directly the way proper Sanskrit words can. The degenerate forms spoken by a person remind the listener of the proper Sanskrit forms and then these reminded Sanskrit forms convey the particular meaning.[19] Since the degenerate forms have not been accepted by the linguistic élites as being proper forms, they are not like synonyms of proper Sanskrit words.[20] The use of Apabhraṁśa is compared by Bhartṛhari to child language. He says that just as the mother recognizes the proper words from the incomplete and deformed pronunciation of her child, the same way an élite listener understands the proper words even when he hears the degenerate forms.[21]

Bhartṛhari's theory is not totally untenable, if we realize that he has a hierarchical conversational situation before him, where the speaker speaks a degenerate form of language, and the listener is an élite person, a speaker of the high variety of that language. It is proposed that given such a situation, the élite listener is reminded of the proper Sanskrit forms and that he understands the message in terms of these reminded proper Sanskrit forms. This is somewhat comparable to recent investigations concerning bilingual situations. For instance, Lovins (1974: 244) points out: 'In listening to unfamiliar foreign sounds, we try to relate what we hear to possible surface forms in our own language'. She further states that a speaker of a given language, in perceiving and reproducing the sounds of a foreign language, substitutes for them those that he takes to be "closest" in his own language. Given a diglossic or a bilingual gap between a speaker and a listener, this process of approximating the received linguistic material to one's own system is very natural. However, Bhartṛhari does not explicitly say that a speaker of Apabhraṁśa, when he hears the proper Sanskrit words, is also reminded of the corresponding Apabhraṁśa words and understands the message through this filter. He does not state this, probably because, from his hierarchical Brahmanical perspective, this may mean legitimizing the "fallen" Apabhraṁśa. However, there is a more sober view found in his work, when he says that due to prolonged use of the degenerate Apabhraṁśa forms among the deficient (*viguṇa*) people, these degenerate forms come to possess some kind of direct communicating ability and that for these people, the proper Sanskrit forms cease to be mean-

---

18. *śabdaḥ saṁskārahīno yo gaur iti prayuyukṣite|*
tam apa-bhraṁśam icchanti viśiṣṭārtha-niveśinam || *VP*, I., 148.

19. *te sādhuṣv anumānena pratyayotpatti-hetavaḥ |*
tādātmyam upagamyeva śabdārthasya prakāśakāḥ || *VP*. I. 150, and
evaṁ sādhau prayoktavye yo' pa-bhraṁśaḥ prayujyate |
tena sādhu-vyavahitaḥ kaścid artho' bhidhīyate || VP, I. 153.

20. *na śiṣṭair anugamyante paryayā iva sādhavaḥ |*
na yataḥ smṛti-śāstreṇa tasmāt sākṣād avācakāḥ || *VP*, I. 151.

21. *ambāmbeti yathā bālaḥ śikṣamāṇo' pabhāṣate |*
avyaktaṁ tad-vidāṁ tena vyakte bhavati niścayaḥ || VP, I. 152.
Lovins (1974:244).

ingful (*teṣāṁ sādhur avācakaḥ*).[22] Bhartṛhari and his commentators state that while the proper Sanskrit words are the essential "juice" (*rasa*) or sap of the Aryan language, the degenerate Apabhraṁśa forms are like dead wood.[23] From the same hierarchical perspective, Bhartṛhari charges that the Divine Sanskrit language has been variously mutilated by the deficient people, and that there can be no legitimate status for the Apabhraṁśa usage.[24] As pointed out earlier, it is not totally clear how much of the above constitute Bhartṛhari's own views. In any case, these are some of the dominant views around 400 A.D. The systems of Nyāya and Mīmāṁsā essentially echo the same hierarchical perspective, though they hold different theological views concerning the communicative function of language (Deshpande 1979: 12, 17-21). This hardening of the orthodox Hindu views may be explained as a reaction to the equally hardened positions held by the Buddhists and the Jainas.

11. In conclusion, it may be said that the linguistic theories held by the Sanskrit grammarians were produced within a certain historical context and one clearly sees in them reflections of the time and place in which they were produced, as well as ıeflections of the sociocultural position held by these grammarians. Their perspective is hierarchical and also fully justifiable within the Brahmanical traditions. They are not unique in being so bound by their own historical situation; every other known tradition of linguistic analysis is also invariably bound by its own historical situation (Deshpande 1979: 124, n. 293). Every linguistic theory has its own preconceptions, and like investigating the sociolinguistic background of a language, it is also instructive to investigate the sociohistorical background and preconceptions which go into the making of linguistic theories, whether ancient or modern.

REFERENCES

Banerjea, A.C. 1963. *Studies in the Brāhmaṇas*. Delhi: Motilal Banarsidass.

Deshpande, Madhav M. 1978. Pāṇinian grammarians on dialectal variation. In *Brahmavidyā. Adyar Library Bulletin*, 42.61-114.

———. 1979. *Sociolinguistic attitudes in India : An historical reconstruction*. Linguistica Extranea, Studia 5. Ann Arbor: Karoma Publishers, Inc.

Ghose, N.N. 1934. *Indo-Aryan literature and culture*. Calcutta: The Book Company.

22. See: Note 20.

23. *evaṁ hy āha—ṛjīṣam etad vāco yaḥ saṁkāra-hīnaḥ śabdaḥ* /, the commentary *Vṛtti*, and *niṣpīḍita-rasasyāgre rasaḥ sāraḥ / yad anyat kiṭṭaṁ sa ṛjīṣaḥ / ye vāco' pa-bhraṁśāḥ kiṭṭasthānīyāḥ ṛjīṣāḥ, sādhavas tu sāra iti* /, the commentary *Paddhati*, See: *Vākyapadīya of Bhartṛhari with the commentaries Vṛtti and Paddhati of Vṛṣabhadeva*, edited by K.A. Subramania Iyer, Deccan College, Poona, 1966, p. 42.

24. *daivī vāg vyavakīrṇeyam aśaktair abhidhātṛbhiḥ* /, *VP*, I. 155ab.

Lovins, J.B. 1974. Why loan phonology is natural phonology. In *Natural Phonology*, pp. 240-250. Chicago: Chicago Linguistic Society.

MB, *Mahābhāṣya by Patañjali*. Edited by F. Kielhorn. Poona, 1980. Revised edition by K.V. Abhyankar, vol. I, 1962, vol. II, 1965. Vol. III, 1972. Poona : *Bhandarkar Oriental Research Institute*.

VP, *Vākyapadīya*, by Bhartṛhari. Edited by K.V. Abhyankar and V.P. Limaye. University of Poona Sanskrit and Prakrit series. vol. 2. 1965. Poona: University of Poona.

SINHALA DIGLOSSIA REVISITED
OR
DIGLOSSIA DIES HARD*

James W. Gair

In 1959, Charles A. Ferguson published an important paper called "Diglossia," in which he defined diglossia as: (p. 336)

> **'...a relatively stable language situaŧion in which, in addition to the primary dialects of a language (which may include a standard or regional standards) there is a very divergent, highly codified, (often grammatically more complex) superposed variety, the vehicle of a large and respected body of written literature, either of another period or in another speech commuuity, which is learned largely by formal education and is used for most written and formal spoken purposes, but is not used by any sector of the community for ordinary conversation.'**

Subsequently, I carried out some investigation of diglossia as it obtained in Sinhala (Sinhalese), the majority and official language of Sri Lanka (formerly Ceylon) (published as Gair 1968), and I was able, some twelve years after my first observations, to observe some of the changes that had taken place in the interim. Though relatively short, that time span seems long enough, under current conditions of rapid change, to allow some tendencies to emerge. In rereading Ferguson's work, I was struck with how many important insights there were, often couched in a few sentences, that I had overlooked and noticed only after that later work, and in particular by his comments on the stability of diglossia in view of the apparent persistence of it in Sinhala. What I propose here is to outline some factors that seem to operate, whether positively or negatively, to maintain it, and along the way to discuss some of the changes that have taken place in some varieties of Sinhala. My remarks can best be regarded as an interim report and in part as a program for further research.

In commenting on the stability of diglossia, Ferguson noted some trends that could possibly lead to its demise: (p. 338)

> **'Diglossia seems to be accepted and not regarded as a "problem" by the community in which it is in force, until certain trends appear in the community. These include**

***This paper is a revised and expanded version of one by the same title given at the First International Conference on South Asian Languages and Linguistics, Urbana, July 1978. In making revisions, I have profited by discussions with Willem Pet and Carol Rosen.**

trends toward (1) more widespread literacy (whether for economic, ideological, or other reasons), (2) broader communication among different regional and social segments of the community (e.g., for economic, administrative, military or ideological reasons) (3) desire for a full-fledged standard national language as an attribute of autonomy or sovereignty.'

All of these trends apply strongly in Sri Lanka. There is an impressive mother tongue literacy rate (approximately 80% overall and over 90% in some districts). Moreover, as Table I shows, unusually high literacy for a third world country is a relatively longstanding phenomenon, so that this factor has had some time to operate.

TABLE 1. MOTHER TONGUE LITERACY IN SRI LANKA

1881-1963 (Population over 5 yrs.)

Year	*All*	*Male*	*Female*
1881	17.4	28.9	3.1
1891	21.7	36.1	5.3
1901	26.7	42.0	8.5
1921	39.9	56.4	21.2
1946	57.8	70.1	43.8
1953	65.4	75.9	53.6
1963	71.9	79.4	63.8
1971 (Population over 10 yrs.)			
Overall :	78.1	85.2	70.7
Rural :	75.9	83.8	67.6
Urban :	85.6	87.5	81.5

Source : 1953 Census and 1970 *Statistical Pocketbook* for 1881-1963, 1971 data from the Population of Ceylon (*Census monograph*) 1971

The twentieth century history of Sri Lanka is largely one of increased social mobility and democratization, accelerated since independence. In particular, individual participation in government and direct communication between the individual and agencies or officials has increased tremendously. In sum, I would consider it to be, in relation to the region, a remarkably open society. The state-operated Sinhala radio service is active, the largest circulation newspapers and magazines are in Sinhala and find a large and receptive audience, and book publishing is Sinhala is impressive (though somewhat curtailed by the recent paper shortage).[1]

Sri Lanka has instituted a national language policy, particularly since the official Language Act of 1956, calling for the use of Sinhala as an official

1. A good overview of the reading public can be gained from the Marga Institute Survey. (See references)

language, largely at the expense of the colonial language English and to some extent of minority languages (some official provision has subsequently been made for the reasonable use of Tamil, the major minority language, but I shall not be concerned with that, and the complex issues involved, in this paper.) This policy has been energetically implemented. Though there is still a great deal of what has been called the "unostentatious" use of English in government and commerce (Fernando 1977, following De Souza 1969), government servants are required to be able to carry out their work in Sinhala, and must deal with correspondence in it. Furthermore, education from the primary level through tertiary is officially (and overwhelmingly in actuality) in the mother tongue, with some few exceptions such as medicine.[2]

Nevertheless, despite the strong presence of all three trends, Sinhala diglossia shows few if any signs of weakening. Before dealing with this question it will be useful to review briefly my earlier (1968) statement of varieties as background. The varieties in Sinhala diglossia were given as:

(1) *Literary Sinhala.* The chief defining characteristic is Literary main verb forms, particularly the subject-verb agreement lacking in other varieties. Generally, these verb endings will entail the other grammatical and lexical features of Literary. It should be noted that this is the variety characteristic of virtually all written Sinhala, not just of literature per se.

(2) *Spoken Sinhala*, lacking Literary verb agreement, but with two main varieties: (a) *Formal Spoken*, making use of one, and usually more, grammatical features of Literary (other than verb agreement) with relative consistency. It characteristically makes considerable use of a formal lexicon shared with Literary. (b) *Colloquial* the language of ordinary conversation.

Perhaps needless to say, there are further varietal distinctions, such as the geographic ones within Colloquial, within these varieties. For present purposes, we can view this as a three-variety schema, with Literary corresponding to Ferguson's *H*, Colloquial to his *L*, and Formal Spoken to the intermediate variety for which he makes provision. I had taken the agreeing verb endings as the primary defining mark of Literary, and further observation and discussions with native speakers have confirmed their salience in that respect. Certainly their use entails other Literary characteristics, while the reverse is not the case.[3] The partial summary in Table 2 illustrates the differences in verbal affixes and agreement between the varieties.

---

2. A more detailed account of these developments may be gathered from Fernando 1977 and Gair 1980.

3. De Silva (1974) has questioned Formal Spoken as a distinct level, to which I have reacted elsewhere (1978), but in any event language with those characteristics is used by speakers for a variety of formal or relatively formal purposes, and the sharpness of its distinction from Colloquial does not matter for present purposes.

TABLE 2. VERB AND PRONOUN FORMS AND AGREEMENT

Present Tenses 'I go, you go', etc.

	COLLOQUIAL		LITERARY	
Pers./No.	Subject	Verb	Subject	Verb
1s.	*mamə*	yanəwa	*mama*	*yami*
2s.	*ohee, oyaa, um̃bə*		*tō, oba*	*yahi*
3s.	(M,F) *eyaa*		(M) *hē, hetema*	*yayi*
	(F only)*ææ*		(F) *ōtomō, o*	
	(Inan.) *eek*		(Inan.) *eya*	
1pl.	*api*		*api*	*yamu*
2pl.	*oheela, oyaala, um̃bəla*		*topi, obalā*	*yahu*
3pl.	(Hum, An.) *eyaala*		(Hum.; An.) *owuhu*	*yati*
	(Inan.) *eewa*		(Inan.) *ēwā*	*yayi* (=3s)

Past Tense (Third person Human only)

	COLLOQUIAL Subject	Verb	LITERARY Subject	Verb
3sM.	*eyaa*	*giyaa*	*hē*	*giyēya*
3sF.	*eyaa*		*ōtomō*	*giyāya*
3pl(M,F)	*eyaala*		*owuhu*	*giyoya*

NOTE: In Colloquial, doubled vowels indicate length. Literary forms are transliterated.

In examining some of the causes of diglossic persistence in Sinhala and some of the changes that have occurred within varieties, it will be convenient to proceed under the three rough headings of (1) prestige and acceptance, (2) varietal functions, and (3) effects of literacy. I will also attempt to relate the persistence of diglossia in Sinhala to some more general considerations and propose a partial typology of diglossia for that purpose.

PRESTIGE AND ACCEPTANCE

Literary Sinhala is the vehicle of an impressive body of literature going back to the tenth century (and beyond, but the earlier literature has been lost save for inscriptions and some graffiti of literary quality). It is essentially the language of that earlier literature as revived in the eighteenth century after a break in the tradition, partly in reaction to colonial learning. It was thus an important symbol of the Sinhalese heritage to those educated in the vernacular, notably the Sinhalese teachers, the Buddhist clergy and Ayurvedic physicians, the three props of the *Swabhasha* movement culminating in the language act of 1956. (See De Silva 1974, and particularly 1967 for a more detailed account.) De Silva feels that "the polemics on the 'purity' of Sinhala have ensured that the Literary variety is not widely recognized as a symbol of the Sinhalese heritage" (1976: 53) and states that "people, when questioned individually, have shown comparatively little enthusiasm for the continuation of diglossia in the Sinhalese community." (p. 101). Yet, as he himself notes, there is no organized movement against it (*ibid.*). There have been authors and scholars, some very well known, who have employed the colloquial variety for purposes for which Literary is customarily used, but such attempts have not been widely emulated, and efforts at forming movements for the purpose have not met with much success. Nor is it a simple matter of prestige or enthusiasm. The written style has significant overtones to which a wide spectrum of the public appears to be sensitive, and they are expected in the appropriate contexts. (An example confirming this is the way in which a dramatist, like Simon Nawagatthegama, in his recent widely popular ironic historical drama *Subha saha Yasa*, can make extremely effective use of the resonances resulting from an interplay of styles.) Also, even if Literary *per se* is not a symbol of the Sinhalese heritage, the Sinhala language itself is, and most people simply accept Literary as the "real" variety of it. In fact, my (unquantified) observations suggest that diglossia is simply accepted as a given, and in a culture with a traditionally high regard for learning, the written variety is one sign of it.

There may be, however, a great deal of uncertainty as to what constitutes proper Literary Sinhala. As De Silva (1980) showed by giving a number of teachers a text to correct, there is wide, if not wild, variation in what is considered correct or incorrect. Nevertheless, this uncertainty, whatever its ultimate effects on the language itself, does not seem to translate into any doubt that *some* form of Literary Sinhala should be used for any serious written purpose.

Similarly, in relation to language standardization, there are disputes, often acrimonious, between advocates of different types of Sinhala. Since these involve educational policy and textbooks, they often gain considerable public attention, but they are essentially about the proper nature of Literary Sinhala and not its elimination. Thus, for example, they may include disputes as to the proper form of grammatical endings, but not the propriety of their existence.[4]

Particularly important is a factor which is lacking: Literary is not clearly identified with any social group or cultural feature regarded negatively by a large share of the population (compare, for example, Brahmin Sanskritized Tamil). Though it may have been advanced by a nativizing elite of sorts which in any event seems to have been widely respected and not resented, it is not the property of any caste, class or group, save of course those educated in the

4. Broadly stated, these disputes are often between a group harking back to the poetic language of the thirteenth century, with the use of inherited words, and others advocating a style allowing more Sanskrit borrowings. Interestingly, both styles have roots in the earlier literature. We thus now find sets of synonyms, often with the same ultimate source, such as *dharmaya* vs. *dama* (Colloquial *darume*) 'dharma'; *hala* vs. *śālāwa* (Colloquial *saalaawa*) 'hall'; *basa* vs. *bhāṣāwa*(Colloquial *baasaawa*) 'language'; and *osu* vs. *auṣadhya* (Colloquial *beet* or *behet*) 'medicine'. Ironically, as the examples show, current Colloquial forms are often closer to the Sanskritic ones.

vernacular. Furthermore, widespread education in Sinhala is generalizing, not narrowing that group. Put otherwise, a command of that variety is a result of effort and ability, not opportunity or privilege.

Varietal Functions

One striking aspect of Sinhala diglossia is the sharp limitation in the functions of Literary, and this restriction is more marked than in the cases described by Ferguson, as a glance at Table 3 will show.

Table 3. Functions of H and L—Sinhala and others

	Ferguson's Chart		Sinhala	
	H	*L*	*H*	*L*
Sermon in church, mosque, or temple	X			F
Instructions to servants, waiters, workmen, clerks		X		C
Personal Letter	X		(X)	F-C
Speech in Parliament, political speech	X		(X)	F
University Lecture	X			F
Conversation with family, friends, colleagues		X		C
News broadcast	X		X	
Radio "soap opera"		X		C
Newspaper editorial, news story, caption on picture	X		X	
Caption on political cartoon		X		C
Poetry	X		X	
Folk literature		X		?
Government documents, forms	Not given in Ferguson		X	
Novels (non-conversational parts)			X	
(conversational parts)				C
Airline announcements			X	

For Sinhala, *L* has been further specified as: F = Formal Spoken, C = Colloquial.

? "Probably, but insufficient observation as yet."

( ) "Sometimes, often under special circumstances."

In fact, it is even more so that Ferguson allowed for in his definition, since Formal Spoken, not Literary, is the language of "most...formal spoken purposes." Though the overall distribution of functions among varieties seems not to have changed significantly, there has been much elaboration and expansion of functions in Sinhala as a whole, particularly since the Official Language Act. C. Fernando has summed this up nicely in discussing the place of English (1977: 348):

> The most striking feature marking the use of English and Sinhala in present-day Sri Lanka is the invasion by Sinhala of almost all the areas held by English alone.

She further remarks, concerning the effects on Sinhala (p. 358):

> In sum, what is more strking about present-day Sinhala is, firstly, the enormous and impressive functional elaboration it has undergone, and secondly, the very substantial influence of English upon Sinhala. These two phenomena are, of course, related...

Setting aside the nature and extent of English influence, which operates differently in different varieties, that functional elaboration represents largely the extension of Sinhala into official and technical domains, where "technical" should be taken to include not only technology proper, commerce, and aspects of agriculture, but education, including the social sciences and the more westernized of the liberal arts (as opposed to traditional oriental learning where Sinhala already held sway), and western medicine (as opposed again, to the traditional, indigenous variety). As a whole, these might be conveniently referred to as "imported" functions. One result is a great expansion in occasions on which such matters require public presentation or discussion in an impromptu or seemingly impromptu manner; i.e., university lectures, conferences, and radio presentations such as panel discussions or interviews on matters such as agriculture, medicine and health education, and economic policy. There are two features that make full-blown Literary unsuitable for such purposes. First, it is difficult for most, even the educated, to produce it in a spontaneous, extended fashion with correctness, though there are *virtuosi* who can do it. The verbal endings, involving agreement not found in Colloquial, seem to cause particular difficulties on this score, along with some other special rules of Literary. Secondly, Literary is fundamentally a written variety, and the use of full Literary forms seem to militate against a sense of spontaneity, and result in distancing or an air of impersonality. This seems also to render it unsuitable for occasions on which the audience, even though passive, is to be engaged in some sense. Thus Literary may be suitable for news broadcasts and even airline or train announcements, but not for political speeches or exhortations (note that we are talking here only of oral presentation). The simplest strategy, then, is to use the proper lexicon both for technical purposes and to give the necessary formality for public presentation, and to employ as well some Literary grammatical features within a basically spoken grammar.[5] What this process will result in, in terms of the schema given earlier, is essentially Formal Spoken. Furthermore, whatever English influence there may be, this usage is also an extension of a tradition by which Formal Spoken, or its ancestor, was used for public debates and Buddhist sermons at least as far back as the nineteenth century. (It is also noteworthy that English lexicon is rare in such uses, though there

5. No extensive data-based study of the features actually used and their frequency has been carried out to my knowledge, but it would seem that the simplest ones to use are those possible by making essentially one-to-one substitutions from Colloquial, *i.e.*, those that are least redundant in De Silva's (1970 and 1974) sense, such as the substitution of Literary postpositions (see Gair 1968 for details).

may be Sanskritized calques on English aplenty, whereas in informal discussions among colleagues, carried out in Colloquial, English loans abound.) It is also interesting that lyrics of popular songs, including the now omnipresent rock, show formal characteristics, as do political songs, however scurrilous (at least to the opposition). In short, public presentation tends to bring forth formal characteristics. Some formal oral presentations, ritualized in a general sense, such as acknowledgements and introductions of events or speakers, call for Literary, even if impromptu. Here the function of the Literary style seems to be to call attention to the occasion rather than the message.[6]

On the other hand, as soon as one puts pen to paper, he is likely to produce Literary, or the best approximation he can muster. Exceptions would be where Literary endings would have too great a distancing effect, as in letters to acquaintances, sometimes resulting in such phenomena as a letter essentially in Spoken, bracketed by Literary. Official or formal correspondence and reports, however, require Literary.

In sum, a large share of the increase in communication resulting from social mobility and what can loosely be termed modernization is being handled by other varieties than Literary, and particularly by Formal Spoken, which, with some adaptation, is quite adequate to the purpose. Thus strong pressure to replace H by some form of L for those functions is lacking, at least until such a time as greater demands are made upon a wider segment of the population as writers. Even there, widespread free mother tongue education mitigates the problem by increasing the number with a competence reasonably adequate to those demands. What effects increase in the volume and number of producers of Literary is having on that variety remain to be seen. (What is needed, of course, is an investigation along the general lines of Fries' now much neglected *American English Grammar.*) Also, this specialization means that there is no direct competition between H and L across any significant range of functions, as might be the case where H and L have overlapping functions with the choice between them in that range determined by other, largely social, factors. Such seems to be the case, for example, in Haitian Creole versus French. The closest Sri Lankan analogue is not Literary versus Spoken, but English versus Sinhala for a sector of the population.

Effects of Literacy

De Silva (1970, 1974) has pointed out that the added grammatical complexities of Literary can be regarded as redundancies from the point of view of Colloquial, and it is true that once a native speaker knows the script, the major bar to understanding is lexical, a point substantiated by his tests showing that those with a limited command of Literary have little difficulty in comprehension once lexical adjustments are made. An implication of this

6. The flourishing Sinhala drama requires separate treatment, since there are different schools involving different styles.

is that we can expect little reaction against diglossia from the literate population in their role as receivers. As noted earlier, though, change could occur as a result of increased demands on that wider population for written correspondence and in education. It would seem that weakening could take place in two ways. The written variety could approach the spoken and merge with it. De Silva (1974) has pointed to a number of "hybridisms" in Literary Sinhala, most of which are mistakes from a puristic standpoint. If they become cumulative and systematically recurrent, they could weaken the sharp line between varieties. At present, however, they seem to lack that systematic, general character, though often explicable in terms of the intrusion of Colloquial habits. Also, the verb agreement system would have to go, by losing its saliency in some fashion. One possibility here may be found in what can be called a "nominalizing strategy". Sinhala has both nominal and adjectival sentences without an overt verb and in which the copula may properly be a non-agreeing form. It also has a rich system of nominalizing devices. It is possible to combine these features so that something that might be stated in a sentence with an agreeing verb is in fact said in one with a nominalized sentence subject and a nominal or adjective as predicator. The copula may then be a non-agreeing form or a third person singular form to agree with the nominalized subject. In either case, the complexities of verb agreement are then avoided. Newspapers, for example, though written in a kind of Literary, seem to show a lower incidence of agreeing endings than one might expect *a priori*, and this seems explicable as the result of that strategy. One result is that there are whole stretches of sentences that differ little if at all from possible sentences in Formal Spoken. This, together with an increased exposure to the Formal Spoken used for formal purposes, might have the required weakening effect, particularly as that variety continues to develop for a variety of uses.

The second possibility for the weakening to take place would be for the Spoken simply to replace the Literary, perhaps as the result of a movement engendered by the increased demands on the population as writers, through bureaucratic exigencies and otherwise. This would be more effective if given a democratizing rationale, but at present there are few if any signs of it.

On the contrary, it seems that in the short run at least, literacy and education are strengthening Sinhala diglossia. One factor involved was mentioned earlier, in that H becomes even less the property of an elite. Also, the variety sees greater use and exposure to it is vastly increased. Where H is restricted to a largely classical literature, it may become *de facto* a kind of museum piece, impinging little upon the consciousness of the population apart from a small group of custodians of the cultural heritage. Where, however, it is not only the medium of official writing in an increasingly democratized and bureaucratized state, but the medium of the printed mass media widely and eagerly read by a large literate population (as is the case), as well as of a popular prose literature (such as the popular novels that account for a large and apparently profitable share of Sinhala book publishing), the situations is quite different. There is indeed a large and active Sinhala reading public (See, for example the Marga Institute study), so that the Literary variety is becoming more familiar and diglossia even more of an established fact.

Indeed, the Sinhala case suggests that a high percentage of literacy may not pose a serious immediate threat to diglossia if it is achieved steadily over a period of time; that is, if there is at no time a sudden dramatic upsurge in the number of people who have to struggle with limited success to master H, as could be the case where there was a sudden drive for literacy as the result of the exigencies of modernization. Such a development could produce not only widespread dissatisfaction, but strong practical imperatives for displacing H in the interests of immediate needs for wider communication. In the Sinhala case, however, a large section of the population has been gradually habituated to the acceptance of H, and, as we have seen, they have been called on more in their capacities as receivers than producers.

Before concluding, I would like to relate the Sinhala situation to some general observations concerning the stability of diglossia in relation to fundamentally different kinds of diglossic situations, and in doing so to propose a partial typology of diglossia in terms of the population using L as their everyday language *vis-à-vis* that using or acknowledging H.

In particular, I would suggest that we distinguish between two general types of diglossic situations, building on a distinction that was in fact implicit in Ferguson's paper and in his examples. In what I propose calling Type I, or "congruent" diglossia, H and L are varieties of the same language, and the speech communities for H and L are essentially coterminous (I will avoid the problem of defining "same language" here, except to say that the varieties are recognized as such, which suffices). H is not used by some other speech community, as their standard or otherwise, and while all speakers of L may not have a full command of H, they do recognize it as the H, or "proper" or "real" variety of their language. Type I diglossia is represented graphically in Table 4. There may be sub-varieties, both regional and functional of L, including a standard or standards, and these possibilities are represented by dotted lines in Table 4.

TABLE 4. TYPE I. (CONGRUENT) DIGLOSSIA

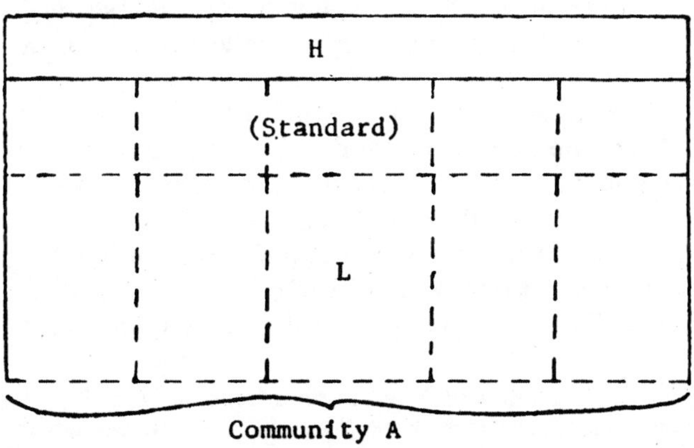

Examples of Type I diglossia are Sinhala, Tamil and Arabic (In increasing order of regional, varietal distinctions in L.) In Type I, H is likely to be essentially an older written or at least literary form of the language, and thus is the case with all examples of which I am aware (This does not, of course exclude changes within H or require that contemporary H be precisely like some earlier actually employed variety).

In Type II, or "included" diglossia, represented in Table 5, only a portion (community A) of the speech community using or recognizing H is diglossic. H is also employed by some other speech community (Community B) and in fact is characteristically the standard language of that community, for whom it is likely to be a part of continuum of functional varieties, and for whom there may be regional varieties as well, (both possibilities again indicated by dotted lines).

TABLE 5. TYPE II (INCLUDED) DIGLOSSIA

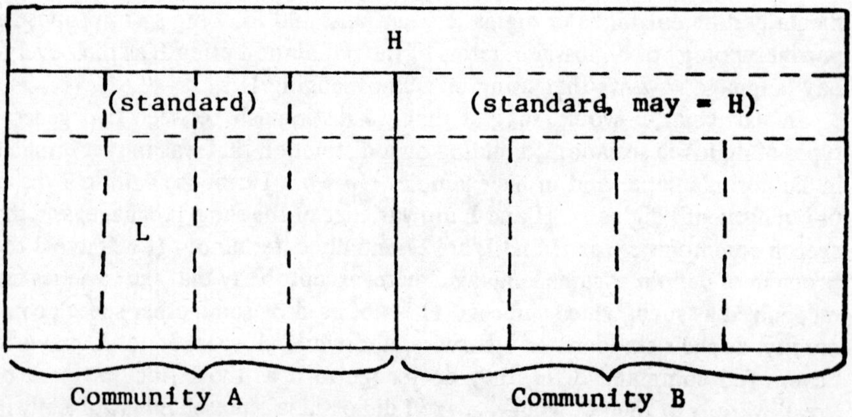

Examples of Type II include Swiss German, where H is Standard German, Haitian Greole, where it is French, and Havyaka Kannada (Ullrich-Baylis, 1974) where it is Standard (Brahmin) Kannada, among many others. The fact that H as used by Community A may actually differ to a greater or lesser degree from the standard of Community B does not concern us here. For example, Jamaican Standard English differs from British English, but it is felt to be the same; that is, British English is the professed model (De Camp 1971).

In both Type I and Type II diglossia, H and L are varieties of the same language. There are similar situations where they are different languages. This is commonly the case in colonial and post-colonial situations, for example. Such situations of functional bilingualism have been called diglossia, but there is good reason to employ some other term, such as "diglossic bilingualism" for them, since the dynamics of change are potentially quite different from either Type I or Type II true diglossic situations.[7] I shall not pursue

7. Diglossic bilingualism will characteristically look like Type II in Figure 5, except that the language of Communities A and B are different languages rather than the same

this further here, save to remark that not only do factors of language allegiance bearing on stability operate differently, but the hybridization affecting L and/or H in diglossia is different in important ways from the convergence that may affect L in diglossic bilingualism.

Now, returning to diglossia proper, a number of factors affecting the stability of diglossia operate very differently in Type I and II situations, such as those relating to language allegiance, solidarity, and sense of identity. In Type II diglossia, stability is affected by the sense of identity of Community A (the L-using group) versus Community B. The Swiss Germans, foı example, have a high degree of pride in their language and a strong sense of identity. As Moulton (1962) points out, this is a factor in the stability of Swiss German diglossia. In such situations, L is unlikely to be displaced by a merger with H. On the other hand, if a sense of pride and identity become associated with a cultural assertivist and anti-outsider movement, diglossia could be threatened by the displacement of H by some variety of L for Community A, but this seems unlikely where H has high functional value as the language of wider communication, as is commonly the case. What we might get instead is a more complex situation with a literary form of L operating side-by-side with (old) H for Community A. To some extent this appears to have happened in Switzerland.

In Type I diglossia, the situation is quite different, and the continuation of diglossia may depend on the extent to which the community feels H to be a repository and symbol of their cultural heritage. Such is the case in Arabic, where H is felt to be not only prestigious, but divine, and the only "real" form of the language as well as a symbol of Arabic cultural unity. As we have seen, Sinhala falls into this category as well, though less strongly. In such cases, anti-H movements cannot be tied to irridentist sentiments and movements. Rather, the relevant factor is the relation of the H-commanding community to the remainder of the society. Where that group represents an elite or powerful political faction definable in other terms as well, a revolutionary or democratizing movement can be in part an anti-H movement. Something of that sort appears to have happened in Greece, with a newer democratic government moving to eliminate the official status of *Katharévusa* (though Greek diglossia seems to have been precarious in any case). An interesting example of another possibility is Tamil, in which an anti-elite movement had as its aim not the elimination of diglossia, but a change in the nature of H, particularly by substituting "pure" Dravidian Tamil forms for Sanskritic

---

language. Logically, there could be diglossic bilingualism parallel to Type I as well, *i.e.*, in which two languages were confined to a single speech community, but I do not know of any instances.

Type I and II, together with diglossic bilingualism, do not exhaust the possibilities, though other situations may be reducible to combinations of them. For example, the situation regarding Latin in relation to the vernaculars in early renaissance Europe seems to have been Type I diglossia with regard to the Romance-speaking countries, but diglossic bilingualism in relation to, say, England and Holland.

forms with their Brahminic overtones. In Sinhala, as we have seen, anti-H movements have not been able to attach themselves to any other widespread social movement, and have lacked strength thereby. Also, the controversy over the proper nature of Literary Sinhala has not taken on any strong caste or regional character, though it has not been entirely free of such overtones. Thus anti-H movements have had to base themselves on more nebulous aspects of educational democratization or on efficiency, causes not very capable of arousing strong sentiments in the general public for the elimination of H.

Ferguson pointed out that H "may succeed in establishing itself as a standard only if it is already serving as a standard in some other community and this diglossic community, for reasons linguistic and non-linguistic tends to merge with that other community" (p. 437). Or, in our terms, this could occur only in Type II situations.[8] Connected with this is the narrowness of functional specialization of H, likely to be much greater in Type I than in Type II situations. In Type I diglossia, H, existing only within the L-using community, can be limited to a narrow subset of functions, as is the case in Sinhala. In Type II, however, H by virtue of its use elsewhere as a standard for a wider range of functions, is likely to possess a ready-made set of associated functional varieties for wider use. These can easily seep over into the L-using community leading to an overlap between H and L in some functions, as when H is used in day-to-day contact with outsiders. This seems to be a common mechanism by which H becomes the spoken standard of the L-using community. It is also only in Type II that we find the post-creole continuum, with the complexities and uncertainties that it entails.

In Type I diglossia, it appears that the demise of diglossia can take place in one of two ways, which we have already discussed in relation to Sinhala. That is, it can be overthrown or go out of use in favour of L, perhaps displaced by some literary form of L, as was the case with Latin in Romance speaking Europe or Sanskrit in India (though the process may take a long time and include successive revivals). This is the possibility envisioned by Ferguson (p. 437) "by which H may fade away and become a learned or liturgical language studied only by scholars and specialists and not used actively

8. Ferguson's observation appears to hold true in general but there are some near counter examples. For example, it appears that in 19th century Italy, only a very small proportion of the population at the time of independence could speak the variety that was to become the standard, though it was clearly a recognized literary standard (having earlier displaced Latin over a period of time). This appears to be a possible case in which a literary variety in a diglossic situation served as the basis for a later generally accepted standard. One could argue, however, that this was really a case of Type II diglossia, since that H was Tuscan-based. This and similar cases need further close study in terms of the framework proposed here. Even if they do require some revision of Ferguson's statement to make it represent the unmarked case, they do not invalidate the general statement that the fate of diglossia is affected differently in Type I and II situations. (I am indebted to Carol Rosen for the account of the Italian situation, for which further details may be found in: Tullio De Mauro, *Storia linguistica dell' Italia Unita*. Bari. Laterza, 1970.)

in the community." As we have seen, this apppears unlikely to occur with Sinhala in the near future, and a long term but widespread increase in literacy may deter the process.

The second manner of demise is the blurring and gradual disappearance of the lines between H and L. In this case, H can be absorbed into L, being restructured so as to become the higher variety in a continuum. As we have seen, hybridization and the nominalizing strategy are possible mechanisms by which this could occur in Sinhala.

At present, Sinhala diglossia, as an example of Type I in which none of the diglossia-threatening factors operate very strongly, appears stable. At the same time, L seems to be becoming richer in terms of functional varieties, though some regional differences may be weakening. A standard spoken variety seems clearly to be developing, based largely on the regional varieties of the southwest, but not exclusively on that of the capital (and largest) city, Colombo. As we noted earlier, Formal Spoken is developing an increased range and flexibility as it fulfils a wider range of functions. The drama is flourishing to an amazing degree, with dialogue in L in most styles, but both imaginative and technical prose continues to be overwhelmingly in Literary, save for the conversational stretches in fiction which are, however, set in a Literary frame. Certainly Sinhala gives no support to Wexler's semi-serious suggestion that the term diglossia "should be retained to describe a speech community with a high percentage of illiterates" (1971, p. 337).

In any event, in the Sinhala case as in many others, diglossia, as Ferguson implied, dies hard.

References

De Camp, David. 1971. Toward a generative analyis of a post-creole speech continuum. In *Pidgninization and creolization of languages*, ed. by Dell Hymes. 349-370. Cambridge: Cambridge University Press.

De Silva, M.W.S. 1967. Effects of purism on the evolution of the written language. *Linguistics* 36.5-17.

———. 1970. Some thoughts on linguistic redundancy. *Modern Ceylon Studies.* 1.147-155.

———. 1974. *Convergence in diglossia: the Sinhalese situation.* In Southworth and Apte, 60-91.

———. 1976. *Diglossia and literacy.* Mysore: Central Institute of Indian Languages.

———. 1980. Typology of diglossia and its implications for literacy. Paper presented at the Second International Conference on South Asian Languages and Linguistics, Hyderabad, India.

De Souza, A.T.A. 1969. The teaching of English, 4. *The Ceylon Observer*, April 21.

Ferguson, Charles A. 1959. Diglossia. *Word* 15.325-340.

Fernando, Chitra. 1977. English and Sinhala bilingualism in Sri Lanka. *Language in Society* 5.341-360.

Fries, Charles C. 1940. *Amrican English grammar.* New York: Appleton-Century-Crofts.

Gair, James W. 1960. Sinhalese diglossia. *Anthropological linguistics* 10, 8, 1-15.

———. 1974. (with W.S. Karunatilaka) *Literary Sinhala.* South Asia Program, Cornell.

———. 1978. Review of Southworth and Apte. *Language* 54.461-465.

———. 1980. English and Sinhala in Sri Lanka since independence : tradition in the midst of change. Paper presented at the Association for Asian Studies meeting, Washington D.C., March 1980.

Marga Institute. 1974. The Sinhala reading public. *Marga Research Studies* 4.

Moulton, William G. 1962. What standard for diglossia ? the case of German Switzerland. Georgetown: *Report of the 13th Annual Roundtable on Linguistics and Language Studies*, 133-144.

Southworth, Franklin C. and Mahadev L. Apte, eds. 1974. Contact and convergence in South Asian languages. *International Journal of Dravidian Linguistics*, Special Issue. Ernakulam, India.

Ullrich-Baylis, Helen. 1974. Morphological coexistence : a key to linguistic convergence In Southworth and Apte, 224-230.

Wexler, Paul. Diglossia, language standardization and purism : parameters for a typology of literary languages. *Lingna* 27.354

DIGLOSSIA IN AFRICA

Bruce C. Johnson

I. Introduction

In an article published twenty years ago, Charles Ferguson described a type of language situation, 'diglossia', that he hoped would be one element in a general typology of language situations (Ferguson 1959; 1968). This general typology still awaits development, but the notion of diglossia found ready acceptance among linguists and other scholars who have found it applicable to many language situations, particularly in Asia, Europe, and the West Indies. My purpose in this paper is to identity those language situations in Africa which can be characterized as diglossic. First, however, I will make some more geneial comments on diglossia and on Africa. Diglossia is defined by Ferguson as

'...a relatively stable language situation in which, in addition to the primary dialects of the language (which may include a standard or regional standards), there is a very divergent, highly codified (often grammatically more complex) superposed variety, the vehicle of a large and respected body of written literature, either of an earlier period or in another speech community, which is learned largely by formal education and is used for most written and formal spoken purposes but is not used by any sector of the community for normal conversation.' (1959:336).

In this paper, the definition of diglossia is based on my interpretation of Ferguson's original paper. In the first place, diglossia is a type of language situation.[1] Ferguson has defined 'language situation' as "the total configuration of language use at a given time and place" (i.e., in a community) (Ferguson 1966:309). In every community there are in use a number of language varieties, and these may be said to constitute the linguistic repertoire of the community.

The essential characteristics of diglossia, for my purposes, can be outlined as follows: a language situation is diglossic if—

(1) the linguistic repertoire of the community consists of two major (in some sense) varieties or 'terms' (and any number of minor terms);

(2) the two terms are "very divergent", yet still (in some sense) varieties of the same language. (The varieties are not necessarily mutually intelligible,

1. The term diglossia has gained some currency in another, expanded, sense as the language situation "in societies which employ separate dialects, registers, or functionally differentiated language varieties of whatever kind" (Fishman 1972:92, for example). So defined diglossia is an aspect of essentially all language situations and thus no longer refers to a type of language situation. Cf. Gilbert 1975:235-236.

but the language distance between them is relatively slight and/or members of the community consider them to be varieties of one language.);

(3) the functional distribution of the varieties is such that one (H) is used for most written and formal spoken purposes, while the other (L) is used for ordinary conversation;

(4) while L is acquired in the 'normal' fashion of vernacular varieties, H is not the mother tongue of any sector of the population of the community, but rather is learned later in life (i.e., is 'superposed'), largely through formal education;

(5) the two varieties, H and L, are structurally and functionally compartmentalized; that is, any utterance in the community can be unequivocally identified as being in H or in L, and, furthermore, speech contexts are clearly divided by members of the community into those for which H is appropriate and those for which L is appropriate.

I have included attribute 5 which, though not explicit in Ferguson's definition, I feel was intended. A complete list of the defining attributes should include the following: that the situation is "relatively stable"; that H is highly codified; that H is the vehicle of a large and respected body of written literature; and perhaps that members of the community regard H as superior to L.

The defining attributes serve to distinguish diglossia from other types of language situations. Thus, for example, attribute (1) distinguishes diglossic situations from those in which there are more than two major terms. Similarly, attribute (2) distinguishes diglossic situations from multilingual situation on one hand and from more purely monolingual situations (i.e., where the language distance between varieties is less than "very divergent") on the other. Attribute (3) distinguishes diglossia from situations in which one of the two major terms is restricted to intergroup purposes, or in which both varieties are used for written purposes, for example. Attribute (4) distinguishes diglossia from situations in which H is the vernacular of a sector of the community, or in which H is superposed but learned informally. Attribute (5) distinguishes diglossia from situations characterized by fluidity rather than compartmentalization. In a 'fluid' situation, H and L are ends of a continuum, structurally and functionally, rather than discrete varieties.

There are other characteristics of diglossic situations that are not defining attributes because their presence or absence does not make a situation non-diglossic, but which rather seem to provide for a sub-classification of diglossia. In particular, consider the provenance of H. H may originate either in "an earlier period or in another speech community". What seem to me to be three distinct types of diglossia can be defined on this dimension. I will illustrate them with the four 'defining languages' of Ferguson 1959.

In the first type, which I will call 'classical' diglossia (slight pun intended), H represents an earlier stage of the language, though it is not necessarily a direct ancestor of L. Classical diglossia is typified by Arabic. Greek belongs here too, as does Tamil. Where H originates in another speech community, there seem to me to be two distinguishable types. The clearer case is one in which L is a creole based on the language of which H is the standard variety. I will call this type 'creole' diglossia, and it is represented by the Haitian Creole example. In the third type, H originates in one speech community and has been superposed on an L which in some sense is not in that speech community. Swiss German is an illustration. It seems to me that what makes this a diglossic situation, while other German dialect areas are standard-with-dialects situations, is that German Switzerland is separated by major political boundary from the area in which standard German is for some groups a vernacular. I call this type 'border' diglossia, for want of a better term, because its recognition depends on the definition of boundaries between 'speech communities'. Other non-defining attributes of diglossia, which could serve for sub-classification, include whether H is grammatically more complex than L; the number and types of varieties of L (whether there is a standard L, for example); the number and types of other languages in the community repertoire; and the proportion of the community that actually uses H.

Africa. Africa is the second largest continent and the third most populous, with a population of about 450,000,000 and an area of 11½ million square miles. It is thus over nine times the size of India with less than three-fourths the population.

The most striking linguistic fact about Africa is its multilingualism, in both senses of the word. In the first place, there are many languages spoken in Africa—certainly more than a thousand, though no exact figure can be advanced. In the second place, most Africans regularly use two or more languages in their daily activities. In a region in which many languages are spoken, there will be a balance between individual multilingualism and cultural isolation. In Africa, the balance is heavily with the former.

These many languages are, of course, not equally represented in terms of geographical spread, numbers of speakers, or patterns of use. In particular, the northern quarter of the continent is dominated by one language, Arabic, which is also easily the most widely spoken language in Africa. It is the mother tongue of perhaps 80 million Africans and is also widely used as a second language and as a liturgical language. In addition to Arabic, there are more than fifty other languages with more than a million speakers in Africa.

Several of these (Arabic, English, French, Portuguese, and Afrikaans) have been 'introduced' into Africa in historical times. Others (Amharic and Tigrinya (Semitic languages of Ethiopia) and Malagasy (the Austronesian language of Madagascar) are generally regarded as introduced languages, although the periods of their introduction are not documented. The indigenous (i.e. non-'introduced') languages of Africa all belong to four major genetic groupings, which furthermore are not found natively outside of Africa. These groupings are Afroasiatic (less Semitic), Congo-Kordofanian, Khoisan, and Nilo-Saharan. Politically, Africa is today divided among fifty independent nations. However, virtually every area of the continent came under

European domination at some period. The colonial legacy is still a factor of major significance in Africa, linguistically as well as socially and economically.

The next section of my presentation consists of a survey of diglossia in Africa. I should point out right away that diglossia, narrowly construed, is not widespread in Africa, and my survey is intended to be exhaustive. I will identify instances of diglossia and briefly describe cases representing the three types defined above. In the third section I will discuss 'triglossia', a term modeled on diglossia that has been coined to refer to what I see as the most widespread and in some sense basic type of African language situation. I will then conclude by considering the prospects of diglossia in Africa.

II. Diglossia in Africa

A. Classical diglossia

(1) *Arabic*. The most familiar and best documented instance of diglossia in Africa is of course the Arabic-speaking area of northern Africa. This is the situation to which Marcais applied the term 'diglossie' and, as part of the Arab world, is one of Ferguson's defining languages. Since the general characteristics of this situation are familiar, I will not review them here, beyond noting that the intermediate, mixed forms of the language noted by Ferguson are becoming more noticeable. See, for example, El-Hassan 1977.

(2) *Geez*. A second African example of classical diglossia is from the Semitic-speaking area of Ethiopia, where diglossia existed for many centuries, but which is now post-diglossic.

Geez was the dominant language of the kingdom of Aksum (Axum) which was founded in the first century A.D. in northern Ethiopia by immigrants from southern Arabia. Aksum was Christianized in the fourth century and flourished until the ninth century.

Geez is attested as a written language from this period, but experienced a literary 'Golden Age' in the 14th to 16th centuries. By this time, Geez was no longer a spoken language, having been superseded by Amharic, Tigrinya, and the other Ethio-Semitic tongues. The exact relationship of Geez to the modern vernaculars is still a matter of discussion. It is possible that Geez was a superposed H well before the fall of Aksum. In any event, diglossia was well established by the fourteenth century and continued through the nineteenth century. Geez held a practical monopoly as the written language and was also the liturgical language of the Ethiopian Orthodox Church. Literary production was considerable and highly regarded. Ullendorff refers to the Kebra Nagast (Glory of the Kings), composed in the 14th century, as "not merely a literary work, but—as the Old Testament to the Hebrews or the Koran to the Arabs—it is the repository of Ethiopian national and religious feelings, perhaps the truest and most genuine expression of Abyssinian Christianity" (1965:144). The extent to which Geez was used for 'formal spoken' purposes outside the liturgy is not clear. However, Amharic's status as the language of the royal court is indicated by its epithet 'language of the kings' (lisana negast). An anecdotal bit of evidence is the following: When the German scholar Ludolf was pursuing his Ethio-Semitic studies in 17th century Rome his principal consultant was Abba Gregory, an Ethiopian priest, who at that time knew no European language. Ludolf knew enough Geez to be able to converse with Gregory in that language, "at first an unaccustomed task to Gregory" (whose mother tongue was Amharic) (Ullendorff 1965:10; cf. Cooper 1976:289).

The situation began to change during the reign of the emperor Theodore (Tewodros) II, 1855-68. He changed the language of the royal chronicles from Geez to Amharic and generally promoted the literary use of Amharic "as a plank in his general programme of imperial unification" (Ullendorff 1965:155). This process has continued. Amharic's position as the official and national language has solidified and expanded (Cooper 1976). Increased westernization brought first French, then Italian, then English into the national repertoire. Geez remains the liturgical language of the Ethiopian Church, and production in certain traditional poetic forms in Geez continues. While the prestige of Geez remains high, knowledge and use of it is receding.

B. Creole diglossia

(1) KRIO. Krio is an English-based creole language with perhaps 100,000 native speakers in and around Freetown, the capital of Sierra Leone. Krio is also widely used as a lingua franca throughout Sierra Leone.

Freetown was founded in 1787 as a resettlement point for persons of African origin from England and the New World (primarily Jamaica and Nova Scotia) and, after the abolition of slavery, for 'recaptives' liberated from slave ships on the high seas. Their descendants, known as Creoles, constitute the greater part of the mother tongue speakers of Krio, though there have been accretions from other sources as well.

Krio is in a diglossic relationship with English. English is the official language of Sierra Leone, the language of education, the predominant language for written purposes and for formal or public use by educated Creoles. Two forms of English can be distinguished: standard British English and Sierra Leone Modified English, possibly an emerging local standard (Berry 1961:1).

The functional range of Krio is "largely intimate and oral". "It is used as the normal means of communication in Creole homes" though "the appropriate occasions for Krio in Sierra Leone society can involve delicate nuances of etiquette" (Jones 1971:68). Its use is discouraged in the schools. There has been some literary production in Krio, but this is largely due to the efforts of a few individuals and it is not clear whether it will increase or decrease in the future. There is not an established orthography for Krio. Krio is used to a limited extent on government radio, in official and private publication, and is the primary language of public address. These functions of Krio are due to its position as a major lingua franca in a multilingual nation.

There is another Krio-speaking community, numbering about 4,000, at Banjul in the Gambia.

(2) OTHER INSTANCES OF CREOLE DIGLOSSIA

a. MERICO. The language situation in Liberia parallels that in Sierra Leone. An English-based creole, sometimes called Merico, is in a diglossic relationship with English. Merico is the first language of the Settlers, descendants of Afro-American immigrants. Its use is "largely restricted to home and informal situations". English is the official language and may be spreading at the expense of Merico, as Hancock reports that "many parents discourage their children from speaking Merico" (Hancock 1975:249).

b. CRIOULO. Crioulo, a Portuguese-based creole, is the lingua franca of Guinea-Bissau and has a community of mother tongue speakers in Bissau, the capital. Portuguese is the official language. Other dialects of Crioulo constitute the general vernacular of the Cape Verde Islands and are also in a diglossic relationship with Portuguese.

c. THE PORTUGUESE CREOLE OF THE GULF OF GUINEA. A situation of creole diglossia exists on the island of Sao Tome. On the associated island of Principle, the creole has given way to Portuguese in this century, so that the situation is one of standard-with-dialects (Valkhoff 1966:85). On the island of Annobon, the creole has been hispanicized to some extent and may be in a diglossic relationship with Spanish (Hancock 1977).

d. FRENCH CREOLE. A French-based creole is spoken in the Mascarene Islands of the Indian Ocean (Mauritius, Réunion, the Seychelles, and dependencies) and is everywhere in contact with French. The situation is complicated, however, by the presence of South Asian languages and English. On Réunion, an overseas department of France, (metropolitan) French is the official language and creole is the lingua franca. The creole is said to be "highly variable and undergoing gallicization" (Hancock 1977:380). On Mauritius, Creole is the lingua franca, but the home language of only 30% of the population. French is "the language associated with the elite" (Baker 1972:15), the medium of instruction in the schools up to Standard IV, and widely used in the media. English has been the official language since 1810, but does not seem to be widely used. 60% of the population have a South Asian language as mother tongue. In the Seychelles, Creole is the predominant mother tongue. French and English are official.

C. Border diglossia

(1) SWAHILI. Swahili is probably the most widely spoken indigenous language in Africa. It exists in such a wide array of varieties that seemingly any type of language situation can be illustrated with Swahili. At the risk of

some oversimplification, I will sketch out an illustration of border diglossia from this tapestry.

The homeland of Swahili as a mother tongue is the East African coast where it is spoken in a number of dialectal forms in coastal communities and on the offshore islands from Somalia to Mozambique. These 'coastal dialects' are quite divergent and not all mutually intelligible. As the predominant trade language of the coast, Swahili spread widely into the interior as a lingua franca. The importance of Swahili was recognized by the colonial administrations who gave it official or quasi-official status that further enhanced its utility and spread.

During the 1920's, a movement arose for the standardization of Swahili: the development of a written standard variety, free of dialectal and orthographic variation, to be used for educational and other official purposes. This standardization was primarily the work of the Inter-Territorial Language (Swahili) Committee, supported by the colonial governments of Kenya, Tanganyika, and Uganda. This organization continued through a number of changes in name and place and today is the Institute of Swahili Research at the University of Dar es Salaam. Today there exists a standard variety of Swahili which is the medium of a large and growing body of publication (educational, technical, and literary), widely used in the East African press and broadcasting, and is the official language of Kenya and Tanzania. The basis of the standard variety, as a result of an inter-territorial conference held at Mombasa in 1928, was Kiunguja, the dialect of Zanzibar town. While the standard variety began to take on characteristics of its own, leading to its appellation 'Kiserikali' ('governmentalese'), it is still classifiable with Kiunguja. "It is of considerable importance that the dialect associated with Zanzibar and not that of Mombasa is most widespread in Kenya " (Gorman 1974: 398).

Thus there exists in the Swahili-speaking coastal areas of Kenya a sort of diglossic situation wherein the local Swahili dialect, Kimvita or some other, is the home and community language and standard Swahili is used for some educational purposes, in the mass media, and for wider communication. The situation is less than clear-cut due to the presence of English in several H functions and to the fact that, at least in urban areas, the local dialects are merging with or being replaced by the standard.

(2) AFRIKAANS. Afrikaans is an Indo-European language spoken as a first language by approximately five million persons, primarily of European origin, in the Republic of South Africa and neighboring countries. It is descended from the Dutch of Dutch immigrants who settled in South Africa after 1652, and was adopted as a first language by many Hottentots (the indigenous population of the Cape), Coloureds (persons of mixed race), and settlers of French and German origin. It is also spoken as a second language by native speakers of English and Bantu languages.

As a result of some phonetic and lexical changes and considerable morphological and syntactic changes in Afrikaans, it is no longer mutually intelligible with Dutch (Valkhoff 1966:194). The main features of Afrikaans were probably established by 1750. This rapid differentiation can be attributed to the accession to the language of a large number of speakers of other language backgrounds and the weak presence of the metropolitan standard. English replaced Dutch as the official language on the British occupation of South Africa in 1795, further weakening the links to metropolitan Dutch.

A diglossic situation existed in the Afrikaans-speaking community from the period, not clearly definable and in any case no doubt variable, at which Afrikaans ceased to be a 'normal' dialect of Dutch until the early 20th century. Afrikaans was a typical L, unstandardized, unwritten, non-prestigious, used primarily as a home and community language, and to a certain extent for inter-group purposes. Standard Dutch was the H variety, the literary and religious language. Official functions were fulfilled by English and/or Dutch, depending on time and place.

The situation is now post-diglossic due to the promotion of Afrikaans. Die Genootskap van Regte Afrikaners, founded in 1875 to promote the use of Afrikaans, reflected the growing Afrikaner nationalism. The association published a monthly magazine and encouraged translations and original literary production. With self-government and the beginning of Afrikaner political domination, events moved quickly. In 1909, a language academy, the Afrikaanse Akademie, was founded. In 1914, Afrikaans replaced Dutch in the schools and, in 1924, in the Reformed Church. In 1925, Afrikaans became a co-official language, with English, of the Union of South Africa. In that same year a standard dictionary of Afrikaans was begun, and in 1933 the Bible appeared in an authorized Afrikaans version. Today, standard Dutch is not a major term in the language situation in South Africa (Coetzee 1967).

(Note: In classifying this situation as border diglossia, I have considered Afrikaans to be a dialect of Dutch that was politically and geographically isolated. There is another possible interpretation, however. Valkhoff's characterization of the evolution of Afrikaans as 'creolization' is now widely accepted, outside South Africa at least. On this basis the Afrikaans/Dutch situation could be considered an instance of creole diglossia.)

III. Language Situations Resembling Diglossia

This concludes my survey of diglossia in Africa. I said at the start that the examples were few. It can now be appreciated that, with the exception of Swahili, all of the examples involve introduced languages. The simple explanation for both of these facts is that writing is a relatively recent introduction to most of Africa, and the written channel is still primarily allocated to introduced languages.

Indigenous African languages have not developed H varieties, or otherwise acquired them. In part, there has not been sufficient time since the beginning of writing in these languages for "a large and respected body of written literature" to develop. In part most of what we consider "formal spoken purposes" were also introduced and are still largely associated with introduced languages.

Some non-introduced African languages do have divergent literary varieties which resemble H varieties in some respects. Three examples are briefly described below.

Kingozi. The Swahili have a written literature that spans a period of at least four centuries. The principal literary form was poetry and it was traditionally written in a distinctive variety known as Kingozi. It is not clear whether or not Kingozi was ever a vernacular variety. Sacleux described it as "a free form which aims at purism and archaism, drawing for this purpose from the northern dialects" (Sacleux 1939:386, quoted in Harries 1962: 14; my translation). At any rate, "it was, as early as the 18th century, a literary *koine*, a common medium for literature accessible to all Swahili-speaking peoples" (Knappert 1979:107). I have not considered Kingozi as a diglossic H variety (a) because it was not the sole written variety, sharing this function with Arabic, and (b) because it is not clear that Kingozi was used for formal spoken purposes beyond the fact that traditional poetry was often rendered orally, as at the "*diriji*, or poets' contest, where the leading bards of the day would be invited to compose on the spot, taking the floor one after another to recite their compositions in which they would criticize one another as well as the political and economic conditions of the day" (Knappert 1979: 264). Today, other Swahili varieties, as well as Kingozi, are used in the composition of poetry.

Ekyevugo. Although the definition of diglossia specifies a literate society, Ferguson has suggested "that a similar situation could exist in a non-literate community where a body of oral literature could play the same role as the body of written literature" in the defining languages (1959:337). In traditional African communities, there is often a distinctive variety of the language the use of which is restricted to certain ceremonial occasions.

For an example, the Hima of Uganda have a form of oral literature, the ekyevugo, which is "a poem composed in praise of the author's heroism in battle.... These recitations, or praise poems, are the principal artistic expression of the Bahima" and there were "certain occasions on which it was necessary for a Muhima to recite a praise poem which he had composed." These occasions included "when a man was given a chieftainship by the Omugabe [king]; when he dedicated himself to the Omugabe for service in battle; and when he visited his future father-in-law the night before his marriage" (Morris 1964:12-13). The variety of the ekyevugo is distinct from that of ordinary conversation to the extent that "an educated Muhima is usually unable to understand a large part of an ekyevugo" (Morris 1964:26). There are lexical differences, in part because everyday nouns are avoided and replaced by figurative equivalents, as well as differences in phonetics and morphology.

Union Igbo. In the third case, a written variety which is quite divergent from any spoken variety of the language is conscously developed. Union

Igbo is one African example. Igbo is a Congo-Kordofanian language spoken in several dialects by several million people in southern Nigeria. When Christian missionaries faced the problem of selecting a written variety for Igbo, they chose to construct a new variety out of elements drawn from five divergent dialects. Union Igbo was never spoken but was used in some publications, including the first translation of the Bible into Igbo. Emenanjo has aptly characterized Union Ibgo as a "fascinating but still-born Igbo Esperanto...manufactured at Egbu in Owerri between 1905 and 1912 by the superhuman intelligence and misguided over-enthusiasm of Archdeacon Dennis. It lives only in the old Bible (1975:116-117).

A similar example is the mission-promoted "standard" form of Kingwana, a Swahili dialect spoken in Zaire. "This...artificial form of the language stands about half-way between Standard Swahili and the up-country dialect of Swahili which is actually spoken" (Polomé 1967:26). "It is exclusively literary, for no one, not even the missionaries, speaks this basic Swahili" (Harries 1955:14, quoted in Whiteley 1969:76).

Because diglossia narrowly constructed is peripheral to the language situation in Africa, and because this seminar is concerned, broadly speaking, with the typlogy of language situations, I will outline another type of language situations, triglossia, which is much more characteristic of sub-Saharan Africa.

Triglossia (Abdulaziz 1972, Whiteley 1972) refers to the language situation of a community whose linguistic repertoire consists of three major terms which are typically distinct languages and can be characterized as follows:

A. a vernacular language used for oral intragroup purposes,
B. a superposed lingua franca used for communication between mother-tongue groups, and
C. a world language used as a vehicle for international communication.

Both B and C are used in education, in the media, and for official purposes. The allocation of functions between B and C varies from area to area, and may not always be well-defined.

As diglossia is typified by the language situation in the Arab world, so triglossia is typified by the language situation in Tanzania where A are the approximately 100 vernacular languages, none of which is spoken natively by (much) more than 10% of the population; B is Swahili, the regional lingua franca and the official language since independence; and C is English, which is still "the dominant language of official business, commercial and legal transactions, and higher education. It is also a language through which almost all world literature and technological and scientific information is acquired" (Abdulaziz 1972:204).

The following tables present data concerning the language situation at Larteh, Ghana, a triglossic community on the other side of the continent. The three major terms are

A. the Larteh dialect of Hill Guan, the vernacular of the community;

B. the Akuapem Twi dialect of Akan, the majority language of southern Ghana; and
C. English, the official language.

The data derive from the Linguistic Survey of Larteh (LSL), an interview survey conducted in 1969 (Johnson 1975).

TABLE 1. COMMUNITY LINGUISTIC REPERTOIRE
(LSL sample, percentages)

Language	*Total sample* N: 330	*Lartehs* N: 286
Hill Guan	93	100
Akan	98	98
English	49	46
Ga	33	33
Adangme	18	19
Ewe	10	8
Hausa	5	4
(and 12 other languages)		

TABLE 2. INDIVIDUAL LINGUISTIC REPERTOIRES
(LSL sample, Lartehs only percentages)

L	2	Larteh only
LT	33	Larteh & Twi
LTO	19	Larteh, Twi, & Other
LTE	22	Larteh, Twi, & English
LTOE	23	Larteh, Twi, Other & English

(Other = one or more languages other than Larteh, Twi, or English)

TABLE 3. FUNCTIONAL DISTRIBUTION OF LANGUAGE
(LSL sample, Lartehs only, percentages)

Function	*Larteh*	*Twi*	*English*	*Other*	*N*
father	98	2	0	1	272
home	97	5	0	1	285
friends	93	19	2	2	284
recreation	87	18	7	4	273
market	86	50	1	9	243
work	70	47	10	5	175
church	28	87	6	1	253
write	11	94	72	8	159
school	19	66	70	3	119

Tables 1 and 2 indicate the degree of multilingualism in the community: many languages are known and most people know more than one. Table 3 illustrates the functional distribution of the languages as it appeared in response to the LSL questions. Note that languages other than the three major terms were infrequently mentioned.

The simple explanation for the prevalence of triglossia in Africa is that the multiplicity of vernaculars motivates the development of regional lingua francas and that European languages became established in administration and education during the period of colonial domination. The European languages have maintained their position after independence because of their prestige and utility, because of the support of the educated elite, and because they are not ethnically marked.

Both Whiteley and Abdulaziz make use of the concept of diglossia in characterizing triglossia. Whiteley, speaking of Kenya, sees English as H and Swahili and the vernaculars as L. Abdulaziz, speaking of Tanzania, describes triglossia as interlocking diglossias with English an H to Swahili's L, and Swahili in turn an H to the vernacular L's. This reflects the status achieved by 'diglossia' in sociolinguistic thought and the felt need for typoligical concepts. However, it would be better if triglossia were established as a new typological element, independent of diglossia and defined in terms of the same types of attributes: community repertoire, functional allocation, and language distance.

IV. Summary

In this paper, I have surveyed the few instances of diglossia in Africa, and suggested the reason for their scarcity. I briefly described another type of language situation, triglossia, which is more characteristic of sub-Saharan Africa. In both types of language situation there is a considerable degree of language distance between the varieties used for written and formal spoken purposes and those used for ordinary conversation, with concomitant implications for education and social mobility.

I do not feel that diglossia will be any more frequently encountered in Africa in the future. Where there is substantial literacy in vernacular languages, it is too broadly based for the literary variety to depart significantly from the spoken form. Continued loyalty to the ethnic tongues, increasing education and social and geographical mobility, and the entrenched status of European languages all point ot the continued spread of triglossia.

References

Abdulaziz Mkilifi, M.H. 1972. Triglossia and Swahili-English bilingualism in Tanzania. *Language in Society* 1.197-213.

Baker, Philip. 1972. *Kreol: a description of Mauritian Creole*. London: C. Hurst.

Berry, J. 1961. English loanwords and adaptations in Sierra Leone Krio. *Creole language studies II*, ed. by R.B. Le Page, 1-16. London: Macmillan.

Coetzee, A.J. 1967. South African literature. *Encyclopaedia Britannica* 20.985-987.

Cooper, R.L. 1976. The spread of Amharic. *Language in Ethiopia*, ed. by M.L. Bender et al., 289-301. London: Oxford University Press.

Emenanjo, E.N. 1975. Central Igbo—an objective appraisal. *Ibgo language and culture*, ed. by F.C. Ogbalu and E.N. Emenanjo, 114-137. Ibadan: Oxford Univeristy Press.

Ferguson, C.A. 1959. Diglossia. *Word* 15.325-340.

———. 1966. National sociolinguistic profile formulas. *Sociolinguistics, ed.* by Wm. Bright, 309-324. The Hague: Mouton.

———. 1968. Introduction. *Georgetown University Round Table Selected Papers in Linguistics* 1961-1965, ed. by R.J. O'Brien, 74. Washington: Georgetown University Press.

Fishman, J.A. 1972. The sociology of language. *Advances in the sociology of language* I, ed. by J.A. Fishman, 217-404. The Hague: Mouton.

Gilbert, G.G. 1975. Review of *The sociology of language*, by J.A. Fishman. *Language* 51.234-236.

Gorman, T.P. 1974. The development of language policy in Kenya with particular reference to the educational system. *Language in Kenya*, ed. by W.H. Whiteley, 397-453. Nairobi: Oxford University Press.

Hancock, I.F. 1975. Some aspects of English in Liberia. *Perspcctives on Black English*, ed. by J. Dillard, 248-255. The Hague: Mouton.

———. 1977. Repertory of pidgin and creole languages. *Pidgin and creole linguistics*, ed. by Albert Valdman, 362-391. London and Bloomington: Indiana University Press.

Harries, L. 1955. Swahili in the Belgian Cango. *Tanganyika Notes* 39.

———. 1962. *Swahilj poetry*. Oxford: Clarendon Press.

Johnson, B.C. 1975. Stable triglossia at Larteh, Ghana. *Ohio State University Working Papers in Linguistics* 19.93-102.

Jones, Eldred. 1971. Krio: an English-based language of Sierra Leone. *The English language in West Africa*, ed. by John Spencer, 66-94. London: Longman.

Knappert, Jan. 1979. *Four centuries of Swahili verse*. London: Heinemann.

Morris, H.F. 1964. *The heroic recitations of the Bahima of Ankole*. Oxford: Clarendon Press.

Polome, E.C. 1967. *Swahili language handbook*. Washington: Center for Applied Linguistics.

Sacleux, Ch. 1939. *Dictionnaire swahili-francais*. Paris : Institut d'Ethnographie.

Ullendorff, Edward. 1965. *The Ethiopians: an introduction to country and people*. London: Oxford University Press.

Whiteley, W.H. 1969. *Swahili: the rise of a national language*. London: Methuen.

———. 1972. Sociolinguistic surveys at the national level. *Georgetown University Monograph Series in Language and Linguistics* 25.167-180.

DIGLOSSIA VERSUS BIDIALECTALISM: HINDI IN FIJI AND IN EASTERN UTTAR PRADESH

Rodney F. Moag

0. INTRODUCTION. No term has been more widely used in the sociolinguistic literature in the past two decades than "diglossia." For a couple of reasons, the label has been applied to many situations which fail to meet all of the criteria set up in Ferguson's (1959) "defining" article. Firstly, some scholars have oversimplified the original formulation, focusing on only one or two of its many aspects. Fishman (1968:261) and Hymes (1974), among others, have taken functional distribution as the only 'defining characteristic'. This allowed them to extend the term to functional distribution between separate languages rather than limiting it to that obtaining between varieties of the same language as Ferguson intended (1959:435). Functional distribution exists, in some degree, wherever two languages or varieties are involved, thus it can hardly serve, in itself, to distinguish one type of language situation from another. What is significant, as will be shown below, is whether the distribution is mutually exclusive (as in diglossia) or overlapping (as in bidialectalism, and probably bilingualism). Since neither the original article (Ferguson 1959) nor subsequent works sought to define other language situations with the same clarity and completeness, there has been no corrective to date for those who would overgeneralize the term and its concepts.

Studies of the phenomenon of diglossia in South Asian languages have, in general, concentrated on the internal linguistic differences between the supposed H and L varieties without critical examination of whether or not these cases met all of the defining sociolinguistic criteria set forth in the Ferguson article. Weinreich distinguished between 'linguistic differences' and 'social differences' (1953:89), pointing out that the two generally coincide. There is, however, a third group of differences involving such factors as language function, language acquisition, prestige and other support mechanisms which form a middle ground between purely linguistic and purely social differences, which I shall refer to as 'sociolinguistic differences'. It is the basic position of this paper that these 'sociolinguistic differences' are primary so that pure linguistic differences are reflexes of these sociolinguistic and social differences, and not vice versa.

I shall support this major point, and address the two shortcomings of other treatments of diglossia mentioned above, by a common device, i.e. by comparing diglossia with the language situation most similar to it, namely that of a standard language with dialects. By bringing to bear all of the dimensions used in Ferguson (1959), I will both clarify the large number of defining features of diglossia, and their interdependent nature, and show that nearly all of these are functional in distinguishing diglossia from the sometimes very similar situation of bidialectalism. Three main conclusions will be presented: (1) that aside from certain features of the lexicon, linguistic differences cannot serve as "defining features" of diglossia, and that diglossia and bidialectalism can only be distinguished on the basis of sociolinguistic characteristics; (2) that the sociolinguistic differences between these two language situations may be summarized in terms of two superordinate features of 'mutual exclusivity' and 'skewedness of distribution'; and (3) that transporting a language beyond its homeland can lead to processes which institutionalize and stabilize diglossia.

The methodology employed will be the application of distinctive feature analysis. The basic principles of this method are well-known through their application to phonological analysis by Jakobson and others. Application of this approach to the classification of language situations has already been tested with encouraging results by the author in a taxonomy of English-using societies (Moag forthcoming a). The two language situations examined in detail are those of Hindi in the South Pacific nation of Fiji, which I have described elsewhere (Moag 1977:vi) as diglossia, and the situation with respect to Hindi in selected districts of India's Eastern Uttar Pradesh state, from whence the largest numbers of immigrants emigrated to Fiji as indentured laborers, particularly during the early years of indenture of 1879-1900 (Gillion 1962:207-208). I am indebted to Dr. B.G. Mishra, director of the Central Hindi Institute, for the original suggestion that the situation of Hindi in Eastern U.P. represented a case of bidialectalism rather than diglossia. My subsequent research suggests that his evaluation was correct, though for somewhat different reasons than he had originally put forward.

1. The Distinctive Features of Diglossia. Table I contains a matrix drawing together all of the "defining features" of diglossia mentioned in Ferguson (1959). The matrix contains designations for the 'high' and 'low' varieties, since most of Ferguson's statements took the form of coordinate sentences juxtaposing the characteristics of both varieties. Though this type of exposition clearly laid out an internal description of diglossia, it did not lend itself to ready comparisons with other types of language situations. A total of 18 features have been derived from a careful reading of the nine sections of the original paper. These could alternatively be counted as 22, if one considers the two or more subdivisions within each linguistic feature separately. Among all of these, only the feature of "stability" refers only to the characteristics of the situation and not to the comparative traits of the two varieties of the language (Ferguson 1959:433).

If the two designations in each row of the matrix are viewed as values of a single dimension which can be plotted on a continuum, the 13 sociolinguistic features may be seen to fall into two categories, those representing digital distinctions versus those representing analog distinctions. Nine of the features form binary oppositions where one variety is 'X', while the other is 'non X' or, stated differently, one variety occupies the full span of the continuum, the other has no place on it at all. 'High' (hereafter designated 'H') has official recognition; 'low' (hereafter designated 'L') has none at all. Formal activities require the use of H only, and proscribe that of L. Similarly, all writing requires the use of H, and excludes the use of L, the one exception being the minute and peripheral category of political cartoons. In terms of acquisition, L is the mother tongue for all members of the speech community; H is the mother tongue for no one. Hence, formal learning takes place for H only, never for L. As a result, full and spontaneous command is achieved only in L, not in H. With regard to what I have termed "support mechanism," the H variety has great prestige, the L variety absolutely none. This is based on the further binary oppositions that H has both historicity and a tradition of formal grammatical study, while L has neither. Finally, H alone is the vehicle of the great literary tradition; L in no wise is.

A smaller set of four sociolinguistic features represent a pattern in which the distribution on the two varieties along a continuum is highly skewed, one variety occupying nearly the full range, the other relegated to a very small area at one end. Thus, the vast majority of the speech community controls and uses a single speech variety, L, while only a small percentage use both H and L. L has a broad functional territory consisting of several macro-domains; H has very limited functional territory of a few micro-domains. Spoken activities are overwhelmingly dominated by L, whereas H has a very restricted role in them. Lastly, the bulk of informal learning takes place with respect to the L variety, with a relatively minor amount occurring with respect to the H variety. Since these four continua, and the highly skewed distribution of the two varieties along them, seem easy to visualize, I have not included graphic representations of them here.

2. Diglossia and Bidialectalism Compared. Table II presents a matrix in which the contrastive features of the two language situations are plotted side by side. As in Table I ratings are given for each of the two varieties functioning in each language situation, the designation for the lower status 'vernacular' variety on the left, that for the more prestigious 'standard' variety on the right. In a few cases, the entries under diglossia in this matrix do not replicate exactly those found in Table I. This was necessary in order to give a more accurate picture of the role of the 'standard' variety in Fiji where, being a communal language, it is embedded within a larger code matrix in which English has an overarching role as a language of intercommunal contact at both the formal and informal levels (Moag and Moag 1977:3, also Moag forthcoming b). English in India, on the other hand, functions increasingly as a foreign language, (Moag forthcoming a), particularly in the Hindi speaking areas, thus giving Standard Hindi a much less restricted range in formal activities there. As will be seen below, these minor discrepancies in the interest of accuracy do not affect the general conclusions of the paper for as Ferguson (1959:436) says, "the situation is only slightly complicated by the

presence of Sanskrit and English for certain functions of H..." in treating diglossia in Tamil.

Data on Hindi diglossia in Fiji was drawn from the author's three years research and teaching there (1975-78). Data on the language situation in the selected districts of Eastern U.P. was drawn from a number of sources: (1) from written sources on Avadhi and Bhojpuri, the two dialects/languages spoken natively there, (2) from consultation with Hindi-speaking linguists familiar with the area, and, (3) from informal interviews with numerous native speakers of both dialects during a field trip to the villages and towns of the five Eastern U.P. districts from which the majority of early indentured laborers to Fiji emigrated. The abbreviations for the language varieties in Fiji are fairly transparent, FH for Fiji Hindi (the L variety) and SH for Standard Hindi (the H variety). The designations for the two varieties in the Eastern U.P. districts reflect local terminology. TB stands for *TheTh bolii* literally 'pure speech', the label used throughout the region for local village dialect as opposed to the standard language. KB stands for *khaRii bolii*, the name of the Western Hindi dialect on which the standard language is based. The standard is also often referred to as *skuul kii bhaashaa*, 'school language'.

Two main principles will be documented in the point by point discussion which follows. It will be shown that where diglossia shows mutual exclusivity between the two speech varieties with respect to a particular dimension, bidialectalism will show overlap. Secondly, where the two varieties show highly skewed distribution in a diglossic situation, bidialectalism exhibits a less skewed, and more balanced distribution along the same dimension.

2.1. LANGUAGE POLICY AND DEMOGRAPHY. The difference between official recognition of the two varieties is digital (of kind) in diglossia and analog (of degree) in bidialectalism. SH is officially recognized in Fiji as the approved medium of instruction in Indian schools up through class three, as a subject of study through high school, as a debate language in parliament, and in various ways as the official medium of Indian culture in the country. Key government reports are published in it, and an examination in it may be taken by non-Indian civil servants. The policy with regard to FH, however, has been to give it no recognition whatsoever. In fact, a special committee of the Ministry of Education in 1978 voted not to allow FH at all in the curriculum of special Hindi classes being developed for non-Indians for purposes of national integration. Even nongovernmental bodies such as the Fiji Broadcasting Commission refuse to allow any FH in their official operations, though their announcers immediately switch to it the moment the microphones are off.

The standard variety (KB) also has full recognition in Eastern U.P., hereafter abbreviated EUP. It is the official language of the state, used in nearly all state government activities, the medium of instruction in government schools, as well as a subject of study, through undergraduate university level and is the ordinary medium on all of the stations of All India Radio in the region. The thing which sets the bidialectalism of EUP apart from the diglossic situation in Fiji, as the matrix shows, is that a certain amount of official recognition is extended to TB as well. Avadhi and Bhojpuri are bona fide subjects of study in several area universities, with departments founded in some. A Bhojpuri Institute was established in Patna in the late 1970s, and both Bhojpuri and Avadhi are recognized in the country's decennial census. Unlike Fiji, where broadcasting is a government-chartered monopoly, on the model of the BBC, radio is state-run in India. Thus we may infer official recognition in the fact that a half hour of programming goes out daily in the local version of TB from All India Radio centers in Allahabad, Banares, Gorakhpur and Lucknow directed to villagers. Some of these forms of official recognition are plainly in acknowledgement of the considerable degree of language loyalty toward TB on the part of many speakers. This loyalty is further evidenced by the fact that private associations exist in cities such as Hyderabad, outside the home territory, of émigré speakers who seek to preserve and promote their interest in Bhojpuri.

In terms of the population segment involved(Feature 2), the present generation of Fiji Indians are all native speakers of FH (Moag 1977:V), whereas only a small cultural elite know and use SH. I have written elsewhere (Moag 1978:137) that most Fiji Indians do not get sufficient grounding in SH in school to be able to read it, or even to produce sentences in it orally with confidence. This is in keeping with Ferguson's definition (1959:436) that, "Literacy in the community is limited to a small elite." This also illustrates how a transported language may become subject to those conditions which preserve diglossia when functioning in a society where another language is truly dominant, as English is in Fiji.

In the EUP districts, on the other hand, a much larger segment of the populace is proficient in the standard variety. With KB being the only language of instruction in schools, the literacy figures' for the area may be taken as a rough index of the percentage of the population controlling KB effectively. This is represented in Table II by the designation "all secondary school graduates" one of the categories suggested by Kloss (1966:15) in his scale of bilingualism. This is undoubtedly somewhat conservative, since a fair percentage of those completing only primary school would also have meaningful functional ability in KB. Indeed, the standard variety is in such wide use that many with little or no education achieve high degrees of oral competence in it through informal means (see Sec. 2.3 below).

The vernacular variety in bidialectalism is not everyone's mother tongue, as it is in diglossia. Those living in the rural villages of EUP speak TB natively, but many today in the towns of the region, particularly among the middle class, speak KB natively. This is partly due to a process of dialect shift, for one finds passive bidialectal children of native TB speaking parents in towns now exhibiting the same patterns of nonreciprocal languages of communication as that of many passive bilingual first generation immigrant children in the U.S. It was my informal observation that this switch to KB is less prevalent in the big cities of the region such as Banares, than in the district towns. The subject of dialect shift in EUP is one which needs rigorous investigation. The other significant source of native TB speakers is the small but growing cadre of members of state and national civil services who frequently transfer from post to post.

2.2. FUNCTION. It has become conventional to measure language use in terms of 'domains', a construct articulated by Fishman (1968:251-2) encompassing role-relationships, locales, and settings.

In both language situations, the vernacular variety occupies a set of several macrodomains—family, informal social contacts, shopping, and for many, work. Also in both language situations the standard variety takes up relatively less territory than does the vernacular one, when Mackey's (1968:563) factors of duration and frequency are figured in. The distinction between diglossia and bidialectalism with respect to this feature is two-fold. Firstly, the functional territories of the two varieties are mutually exclusive in diglossia (Ferguson 1959:431) whereas they are overlapping in bidialectalism. This means that the sum of the domains and subdomains occupied by the two varieties in a diglossic situation will equal the total functional territory of the language, but that in bidialectalism, the sum of the domains and subdomains occupied by the two varieties will be greater than that occupied by the language as a whole.

This difference in the functional distribution of the two varieties is also reflected in the criteria for code selection in the two language situations. The choice of which variety to use is conditioned by the activity in diglossia (Ferguson 1959:431), while in bidialectalism the choice is made on a combination of criteria including situational factors plus the code repertoire of the addressee, a factor which Platt (1977:371) found to operate among bi- and multilingual ethnic Chinese in Singapore and Malaysia. Diglossia implies a single cohesive speech community with respect to the L variety. A speaker never has to stop and ask himself whether or not the person he is addressing knows FH; that is a given. The only consideration is whether or not it is appropriate in the particular situation. Bidialectalism involves two overlapping speech communities, and even though the situational factors be right for its use, the speakers must first assess whether or not a particular addressee knows TB before using it.

2.2.1. USE IN FORMAL VERSUS INFORMAL ACTIVITIES. Features 4-7 compare the language use patterns in the two language situations according to distinct, largely independent, dimensions. The first, formal versus informal activities, forms a true continuum, with gradients of greater or lesser formality all along its length. The second, written versus spoken activities, constitutes a basic bi-polar opposition, though in rare cases written and oral language use for the same speaker occur simultaneously. It will subsequently become clear why it is important to separate these two dimensions of language use. Here, it is important to recognize that the concept of activities is a significantly different way of analyzing language use than is the concept of domains. Each domain, and even subdomain, will have many varied activities which occur within it, and each will have a distinctive ratio of formal activities and informal activities. Further, some will have a high proportion of written activities, others will not. Therefore, though domains tend to be predominantly formal or informal (Platt 1977:370), each type of activity treated below cuts across the category of domains. The domain of education, for example, is overall formal in nature, which calls for the use of the H variety in a diglossic situation, but organized sports are of a sufficiently informal nature usually to occasion the use of the L variety. At the same time some writing may occur in conjunction with these sports which would, naturally, require the use of H.

A 6-point scale was devised for plotting Features 4-7, using: none, some, moderate, considerable, extensive, and full. The scale is my own, and the assigned designations are not based on statistical data.

Use in formal activities (Feature 4) shows a digital distinction in diglossia versus an analog one in bidialectalism. Formal activities include both written and spoken usage, though to different degrees (see Features 6 and 7). Typical of diglossia, SH reigns supreme in all formal activities where Hindi is used in Fiji, in religious observations, public speeches, written activities, and broadcasts. Even the least within them, such as political cartoons, humorous asides, and advertisements permit no use of FH. The writers of Hindi commercials for the Fiji Broadcasting Corporation's ten daily hours of Hindi programming insist on using the complex forms of the numbers found in SH in quoting bargain prices, despite the fact that most of the audience does not understand them, and they themselves often have to look them up in the dictionary. The relatively low use factor for SH in Feature 4 results partly from the extensive role of English in formal activities in Fiji.

In the bidialectal situation in EUP, TB does find some use in formal activities, including some written use (see Feature 12), use on the radio (see above), and use in some public functions. For instance, after this author delivered an address in KB describing his research on Fiji Hindi and its parent dialects before a cultural association in Banares, the chairman delivered the vote of thanks in the vernacular (TB), something which could never have happened in the diglossic situation of Fiji. The vast majority of formal activities in EUP are, of course, carried out in KB.

Use in informal activities (Feature 5) shows an analog distinction in both language situations. This is largely due to the place which the standard variety has in the light entertainment media, particularly films and filmsongs. In keeping with the general principle of shared territory and indistinct functional boundaries in bidialectalism, several films have been made in TB.[1]

1. The literacy figures for the five districts in question, as well as for U.P. as a whole, are given below:

%Literate persons	*Total*	*Male*	*Female*
*Gorakhpur	19.8	30.4	8.2
*Jaunpur	21.2	34.5	8.1

Occasional records of Bhojpuri songs have also been released.[3] It is only the films and pop songs in the standard language which find their way to Fiji, but even the light entertainment materials which are locally produced are in SH. The majority of informal activities, leaving light entertainment aside, in both situations feature the use of the vernacular variety. In EUP, again in keeping with the shared territory principle, KB is used for all informal contacts with those who are not members of the primary (TB speaking) speech community. EUP informants reported using TB only with those from their own home district, or from adjacent districts known to have the same dialect Students in EUP school and university hostels, for example, use KB with fellow students from districts geographically or linguistically removed from their own. The intuitive reasons given for this were the avoidance of embarrassment over linguistic differences, and possible misunderstandings. The latter seems quite improbable given the high intelligibility between variants within the same dialect, and even across the Bhojpuri-Avadhi border which runs through Azamgarh, one of the districts visited. It seems much more likely that the principle in operation is that of maintaining the distinction pointed out by Gumperz (1977) of the "we code" versus the "they code." According to this analysis, use of TB (we code) would signify solidarity, whereas use of KB (they code) would indicate social distance.

One is reminded here of the dimensions of "power" and "solidarity" as used by Brown and Gillman (1960) and others in the analysis of the use of pronouns and other address forms. When the dimension of power operates, as in traditional societies, the choice of pronoun is fixed, being determined by the role relationship between speaker and addressee. Such situations are characterized between unequal relationships in which individuals receive the familiar (hereafter, 'T') forms, but must give the polite (hereafter, 'V') forms, or vice versa. The dimension of solidarity, typical of more modern societies, features reciprocal pronoun use, with members of the same social groups all using T forms with one another, and those who have no special bond of group membership like the family, employees of the same firm, members of a hobby or fraternal association, etc., using V forms with each other. The hall mark of the solidarity dimension is that pronoun usage is dynamic.

+Faizabad	19.3	29.7	8.1
+Ghazipur	20.1	30.7	9.3
+Azamghar	19.1	30.0	8.2
+U.P.	21.7	31.5	10.6

Sources

**Union Primary Census Abstract* Series 1 India Part II-A(ii), 1971, pp. 266-267.
+*Primary Census Abstract* Part X-B Series 21, U.P., 1971, p. i. Faizabad, Ghazipur, Azamghar.

2. Dr. R.R. Mehrotra of Banaras Hindu University has supplied the following Bhojpuri film titles: Ganga Maiya Tohe Piyari Charhibe, Bidesiya, Dangal, Lagi Nahin Chhute Ram, and Mai Ka Lal.

3. Mehrotra has also provided the names of some records containing Bhojpuri folksongs: Nathani Banavay De Soneki Balama, Tori Bali Hai Umariya, Gangapar Ki Gujariya, Babua Rahita Hamare Ganv, Samdhan Tora Joban Hai Bara Majedar, Lahanga Uthay Ke Kahe Chalelu, Bhauji Tor Bahiniya Khilari, and Hamar Khaiba Ki Jiyan Karaba.

Acceptance into a group is signified by the changeover from mutual V to T and the deepening of a personal friendship may be signified in modern European languages such as German and Italian by mutual consent to shift from reciprocal V to reciprocal T forms.

It is instructive to compare the parameters of pronoun choice in power-governed versus solidarity-governed societies to those conditioning the choice of variety in diglossia versus bidialectalism. In power-governed relationships the choice of pronoun is predetermined by the role relationship—parent to child, employer to employee, officer to common soldier, and so on—just as in diglossia the choice of variety is determined by the type of activity (Ferguson 1959:431). Interestingly, a number of the activities requiring H such as religious sermon, radio newscast, university lecture, etc., involve nonreciprocal one-way communication. In situations where two-way communication occurs in the context of diglossia, one wonders if the code use is always reciprocal, or whether non-reciprocal use of H might be used to mark a power relationship. I have observed this taking place in multilingual situations where a speaker would use a high prestige language such as English in giving instructions to an underling, who might well respond in the communal language, the original speaker then turning back to address his colleagues in Hindi. The fact that pronoun choice in solidarity-governed relationships is determined by the presence or absence of shared membership in some group is reminiscent of the "we code" "they code" distinction mentioned earlier. In the bidialectal situation, however, "we group" membership is determined by regional origin and therefore, unlike pronoun usage, code selection is fixed and nondynamic. It is not possible to draw a college friend from another district into the "we group" by switching to reciprocal use of the "we code" since he does not command the variety. Nonreciprocal code use across generations in reference to the special case of dialect shift was mentioned earlier.

2.2.2. Written versus Spoken Activities. Writing covers a full range of activities from highly formal literary efforts, documents, and reports, through less formal notices and advertisements, to highly informal personal letters and grocery lists. Ferguson (1959:435) writes that it is typical of diglossia that "...[H] is used for most written...purposes." The one exception, where the L variety is used, is in political cartoons. As mentioned earlier, only SH is used in writing in Fiji with absolutely no place for FH. Once again the principle of shared territory applies in the bidialectalism of EUP. The literary heritage of TB will be discussed later (sec. 2.4). Some contemporary literature is published in Bhojpuri, c.f. the stories of Girja Shankar Rai, and the newspaper *maaTii ka gamak* was published until recently. Facts are represented in the designations for Feature 6. Here, too, the difference between the two varieties is digital in diglossia but analog in bidialectalism.

Spoken uses of language are predominantly informal in nature, as opposed to the preponderence of written activities which are formal. However, the two are not directly complementary to one another with respect to the distribution of formal versus informal activities, for there tends to be considerably more formal activities in the spoken sphere than there are informal ones in the written sphere, particularly in traditional societies which support diglossia. This points up why it was necessary to separate these two interacting but independent dimensions into four features for the sake of completeness.

The difference between use in spoken activities (Feature 7) for the two varieties is an analog one in both language situations. As with the population segment involved and with use in informal activities, the distribution in spoken activities is highly skewed in the case of diglossia, and more balanced in bidialectalism. In fact, according to the 6-point scale employed, only one degree of difference exists between the use of TB and KB. This is due to the lingua franca function served by KB in EUP, described above.

2.3. LANGUAGE ACQUISITION. In both language situations, the vernacular variety is learned first, the standard variety second (Feature 8). Moreover, the vernacular variety is learned through informal means in both situations. The first difference is seen in the way in which the standard variety is learned (Feature 9). The more limited uses of the standard in diglossia mean that children in the society are far less exposed to it, and especially for the need to acquire it, until the "critical age" of language learning (Lenneberg 1967: 176). Even when those children who go to school are exposed to the H variety from the outset of the educational process, it is learned principally through formal study which results in a limited level of competence in it (Feature 10). This accounts for Ferguson's assertion (1959:432) that "The speaker is at home in L to a degree he almost never achieves in H." Diglossia is somewhat like the foreign language situation in terms of the total dependence on formal learning and the limited competence achieved, except for the close genetic relationship between the two varieties.

Bidialectalism on the other hand, is more like the second language, or bilingual situation in its patterns of acquisition. Because of the relatively high degree of use of the standard variety, the child becomes exposed to it, and the need to learn and use it, well before the critical age. Therefore, many children in EUP achieve full competence in KB, becoming able to handle a range of activities in it. Sreedhar(1976:372) has characterized Naga Pidgin, a reduced variety of Assamese functioning as a second language in Nagaland, as 'almost a second mother tongue' to many who use it. Thus, because of the overlapping functions of the two varieties, areas of language competence in the two are duplicated, that is, the bidialectal speaker can handle many of the same activities in both TB and KB. The areas of language competence tend to be mutually exclusive in diglossia. It will be shown below how this distinction is reflected in the lexicons of the two varieties (see 2.5.2).

2.4. SUPPORT MECHANISMS. Prestige (Feature 11) in many ways represents the sum of the other features in this category. I take the position, following Fishman (1968:261-2), that the prestige of each variety is determined by the functions which it serves, and not vice versa. This would seem to be Ferguson's position, also, judging from the ordering of sections in his article—1. Function, 2. Prestige, etc. (1959:430-1). Once again the distinction between the two varieties is digital in diglossia and analog in bidialectalism, at least for the cases examined here. Ferguson appears not to count a digital distinction between the prestige of the two varieties as characteristic of diglossia for he writes (1959:431), "Even where the feeling of the reality and superiority of H is not so strong, there is usually a belief that H is somehow more beautiful, more logical, better able to express important thoughts, and the like." It must be remembered that two of the four defining languages cited by Ferguson, Greek and Haitian Creole, were already clearly moving away from diglossia toward a unified standard based on the L of their respective capitols (1959:436). The prognostication for Arabic was for a very slow development toward separate regional standards. Indeed, if the functions of language have as deterministic a role in the prestige which a language, or variety, enjoys (this still remains to be thoroughly tested), then the fact that L, or even a mixed variety, is used for functions such as writing in the press (Greek) or formally entertaining guests (Haitian creole de salon) means that there have been shifts in function which have paved the way for the kind of status-raising of L necessary to alter the language situation away from true diglossia.

It seems useful in this regard to attempt to distinguish prestige from language loyalty. Other things being equal, one will naturally have an emotional attachment to his mother tongue, however humble its status. Subsequent formal learning, and exposure to values of the wider society outside the home may either submerge or support this attachment. The fact that Classical Arabic, for example, has the extremely exalted position of being the language of the Q'ran, forces the vernacular dialects into a correspondingly denigrated position. Where the standard language is viewed as the mother tongue of another group, from which the diglossic speech community is, and wants to remain culturally and/or geographically distinct, then the kind of "we code" "they code" dichotomy mentioned earlier is possible. Ferguson (1959:435) mentioned that using the L variety in places where L is customary would, in some cases, be seen as "in some sense disloyal to the community." I have been told that Fiji Indians studying at universities in India use Fiji Hindi among themselves, apparently for similar reasons. Thus, it seems possible to have language loyalty of a kind without prestige and I suggest, therefore, that in the light of the foregoing arguments a binary opposition in prestige may be taken as a defining characteristic of diglossia.

Literary heritage (Feature 12) is typologically like prestige in that the distinction between the varieties is one of kind in diglossia versus one of degree in bidialectalism. This is not clearly shown in the matrix, as it was felt to be useful here to document the particular types of literature in each variety. What is really being plotted in this feature is the existence of a serious literary tradition. Ferguson writes (1959:431) "...for the speech community as a whole it is only the poetry in H that is felt to be 'real' poetry."

The existence of 'some' serious literary heritage for TB in EUP is well-documented. Everyone knows that the original Rama Carita Manas is in Avadhi. The majority of entries under Bhojpuri and Avadhi literature in

Grierson (1903:46 and 1904:12-13) are folk, hence nonserious literature, but more recent discussions of the literary heritage of these languages/dialects are covered in Tiwari (1960 xxvii) and Saksena (1937:9) respectively, and in a more detailed way for Bhojpuri by the extensive work of Krishan Dev Upadhyaya. It must be borne in mind that Avadhi and Bhojpuri are to a considerable extent, standard languages with regional dialects in their own right (see Saksena 1937:19 and Tiwari 1960:xxxiv). This, coupled with their degree of serious literary heritage, plus the occasional role which they play in written and formal activities outlined above, gives TB a mid-level position on a scale of prestige.

When TB-speaking immigrants settled in Fiji, two things happened which caused their vernacular variety to take on the taint of illegitimacy, and therewith a negative prestige value. Firstly, being so far from their land of origin, and with parents who were often illiterate, the first generation of Fiji-born Indians were cut off from the literary heritage and other factors which underpinned the positive prestige for the regional dialects in India. Secondly, the varied regional dialects rapidly underwent processes of dialect leveling and borrowing which produced a new homogeneous "koinéized" (Samarin 1966) variety which was neither Avadhi nor Bhojpuri in character, though having elements from each. This new amalgamated variety which also has absorbed a few elements from Western Hindi, probably through Bazar Hindustani (see Moag 1979:) comprised an independent set of norms often referred to locally as *fiijii baat* and which I have referred to as Fiji Hindi (Moag 1977). Some details of the koinéization of FH are presented in Moag (1979:114 ff) and I have posed an outline of the stages of the process itself in Moag (unpublished). As a result of their loss of Indian roots, and of the distinctively Fiji character of their mother tongue, Fiji Indians came to regard SH not as a different, and now elevated, regional standard (as it is seen in EUP), but as the true form of their language. This gave rise to the universally held view in Fiji that FH is a corruption of the true language brought on by their forefathers' lack of education and humble rural background.

This negative prestige rating for FH persists, and there have been no developments such as expansion of functional territory or the elevation of group traditions for quasi-political purposes, which could contribute to eventual status-raising for FH as has occurred for some once deprecated languages such as Sranan Tongo in Surinam (Voorhoeve 1971:307). There has so far been no serious study of any component of the oral literature of the Fiji Indian community as was done for Guyana (Vatuk 1964) and for Surinam (Arya 1968), but the author's very tentative investigations suggest that there is no body of ritual songs, tales, or even proverbs within FH itself which might provide a focus for such status raising. Ritual songs seem to be in EUP dialects while most proverbs are in SH.

The standard variety is regarded as a suitable vehicle for serious literary effort in both language situations as well as the medium for popular literature and culture. The degree to which the average citizen actually participates in the production or consumption of either type of literature in Fiji is limited by the overarching role of English there. This accounts for the superscript '2' denoting a secondary high prestige for SH in the matrix. This is a phenomenon which may be typical of immigrant communities in nations where English, or some other language, is dominant. Platt (1977:375) found that the high prestige of Mandarin among the Chinese communities of Singapore and Malaysia was secondary to that of English. Because of the relatively low literacy rate in Hindi mentioned earlier, the reading of Hindi books and magazines is limited in Fiji, though greater in the countryside than in towns (Siegel 1973), but Hindi films and the songs so prominently featured in them are universally popular. Two weekly newspapers are published in Hindi (contrasting with two dailies in English) and there is a fair amount of local composition of 'ghazals' and popular love verses and songs.

KB has the preeminent role in both the consumption and production of serious literature in EUP, with Hindi literature taught in every secondary school and university in the region. Hindi books, magazines, and newspapers are printed and read on a massive scale, far in excess of those in English. Thus, while a small elite might rate English higher in prestige than their own standard language, the speech community as a whole would rate Hindi as equal to or higher in status than English.

The designations for 'type of standardization' (Feature 14) have also been chosen to provide more detailed information than required to demonstrate the basic distinction between diglossia and bidialectalism. The meaningful dimension in this respect is the presence of formal standardization. Once again, the distinction between the two varieties is digital in diglossia (H has it, L does not) and analog in bidialectalism (the standard has a greater degree, the vernacular a lesser degree of it) at least in the case studied here.

A similar contrast exists in terms of 'historicity' (Feature 15)—FH has it, SH does not—while KB has more, TB less. The standard language in both situations is linked to great traditions in India's past. The high culture of the Muslim courts of Agra, Delhi, Lucknow and so forth as well as the role of Hindi as the modern vehicle of the ancient Hindu philosophical, religious, and scholarly Sanskritic traditions, either separately or together, furnish all Hindi-Urdu speakers with a sense of being connected through the standard language to the best elements of a great past. The feature of historicity is one first employed by Stewart (1962); though he abandoned it in his revision of his classification of language types (1968), I have included it here since it would seem to be a somewhat independent dimension from that of literary heritage, though the two may in many cases be intertwined.

The role of 'type of variation' (Feature 14) as a support mechanism is less obvious than that of the other four features plotted in this category. Here again the designations were chosen to reveal some of the interesting, if not wholly relevant, details of the specific situations studied. This has the price of obscuring the basic distinction which the paper seeks to draw between language situations which may be typed as diglossia and those which may be typed as bidialectalism. The essential difference seems to be that variation in the standard variety for most members of the speech community in diglossia is related to competence level, whereas it is generally speaking not so in the case of the standard with regional dialect. This competence-based variation stems from the limited and specialized functions of the H variety, and more importantly from the fact that it is acquired mainly through formal learning and largely after the 'critical age'. Other types of variation may also exist in H in some cases, but they will not be a defining feature of diglossia. In the particular case studied here, learners of SH in Fiji all bring essentially the same mother tongue (FH) to the task. In Arabic, however, where there are distinctive regional varieties of the L variety, or where the mother tongue of a particular social group is distinctively marked, as with the Bedouins all across the Arabic speaking zone, those regional and/or social variations would also be reflected in the H variety, but such types of variation would be common to both varieties, whereas the competence-based variation proposed here as one defining feature of diglossia, must be limited to the H variety only.

There would seem to be two measurable indices of competence-based variation in the H variety, (A) grammatical errors and (B) lapses, i.e. unintentional codemixing of L forms. The frequency of occurrence of both errors and lapses will vary from speaker to speaker, thus providing dual indices of the competence level of individial speakers as well as the degree of variation in the competence level of the speech community as a whole in the H variety. I know of no empirical studies of these two phenomena with these goals. De Silva in this volume reports on a study of errors in the written varieties of Tamil and Sinhalese, but his purpose was to demonstrate the stable nature of the H variety in the former as evidenced by teachers' agreement on what constitutes an error in student performance versus the instability in the H variety of the latter where there was no general concord among teachers as to what constitutes ungrammatical Sinhalese. The author has heard both grammatical errors and codemixing of FH in varying degrees in the SH performance of Fiji Indians, but has made no effort to quantify them.

2.5. LINGUISTIC FEATURES. Ferguson described the differences in the internal structure of the two varieties in terms of the commonly accepted categories of grammar, lexicon, and phonology. These have been treated in features 16-18 in Table II. Specific aspects of these broad categories appear in lettered subentries, A., B., etc. but it is probably more accurate to count each as a discrete feature, so that in actual fact seven linguistic features are contained in the matrix, not three.

It will be noted that the entries for six of the seven linguistic features are identical for both language situations. Only 'Domain Specific Lexicon' varies between diglossia and bidialectalism. This means that the other six features cannot, as is suggested by Ferguson (1959), be defining features of diglossia. The individual features are discussed in the three ensuing subsections.

2.5.1. GRAMMAR. The standard language in both cases studied has "grammatical categories not present in L" (Ferguson 1959:433). Hindi has both a simple and a continuous present tense whereas both FH and TB have a single present form. Hindi (SH or KB) has a distinction between the present and the past subjunctive verb forms; both vernacular varieties have a single form which functions for both cases.

Grammatical categories are frequently reflected in the inflectional system. This accounts for Ferguson's second observation about the comparative grammar of the two varieties, H "...has an inflectional system of nouns and verbs which is much reduced or totally absent in L" (1959:433). Hindi has grammatical categories of gender and of number for nouns which are overtly marked by inflectional endings in several, though not all, noun classes. TB and FH have a single uninflected category for all nonhuman nouns, and overt marking of gender only occurs in a small number of human nouns, though the same is true of human nouns in the standard language. The inflectional system for verbs presents a somewhat more straightforward case in that Hindi overtly marks all verbforms for gender and number, with most marked for person as well. The inflectional systems for TB and FH, with a few exceptions, show person, but not gender or number.

Overall, the verb system of FH shows somewhat fewer grammatical categories and inflectional endings than does that of TB, owing to the koinéization process which the former has undergone (described in Moag unpublished). In the indicative tenses, the categories of first and second person, present in the parent TB dialects, have been collapsed into a single 'near person' or 'non-third person' category with the result that these tenses have only two possible inflectional endings in FH, compared to three in TB, as compared with eight in the standard language. Nevertheless, the observations which Ferguson made regarding the comparative grammar of the two varieties (see above) hold equally for the two language situations studied here, hence cannot be taken as defining features of diglossia.

2.5.2. Lexicon. Ferguson (1959:434) gives examples of paired lexical items in the four defining languages where both members represent the same semantic territory but "...use of one or the other immediately stamps the utterance...as either H or L." Such pairs, however, also exist (against the backdrop of the larger shared vocabulary) between two regional dialects of the same language, or between a regional dialect and a standard. The author documented some 70 paired items for the diglossic situation between SH and FH in Fiji (Moag 1977:277-279). Later research in EUP showed that nearly all of these pairs were also operative for bidialectal speakers there. A few additional pairs were also found, and it appears that the number of pairs operating between TB and KB may be somewhat higher than that for the diglossic situation in Fiji, though the limited time in EUP did not allow for an exhaustive study.

If the existence of lexical pairs does not distinguish the two language situations, the existence of certain domain-specific, or registral, vocabulary in both varieties does. Ferguson clearly recognized the connection between the mutually exclusive functional territories of the two varieties and the types of vocabulary which each contained, H has "...technical terms and learned expressions which have no regular L equivalents, since the subjects involved are rarely if ever discussed in pure L" (1959:434). In bidialectalism, the fact that the standard and the vernacular varieties share significant overlap in their functional territories, in the case studied here literary activity and every-day life, for reasons outlined earlier (see 2.2) means that there is shared vocabulary in areas which in diglossic situations are likely to be the exclusive province of one or the other variety. Thus TB has a certain number of learned expressions, though not as many as the standard language, and KB has roughly as much popular and homey vocabulary as TB. Technical vocabulary is, however, restricted to KB, for it is the standard language alone which is used in the domain of science and technology. There is, in effect, no technical and scientific register in SH in Fiji, as English occupies this domain there. It can be seen from the foregoing that registral vocabulary is the one feature of internal linguistic structure which shows a distinction between diglossia and bidialectalism.

2.5.3. PHONOLOGY. In both language situations the two varieties comprise a single phonological system with the vernacular constituting the basic system, and the additional features of the standard forming a parasystem. Thus this aspect of the phonology (Ferguson 1959:435) cannot be taken as a defining feature of diglossia. The principle additional features in both cases are (1) the existence of two alveolar fricatives /s/ and /š/, and (2) the existence of a voiced-voiceless opposition in the apicoalveolar fricative resulting in the extra phoneme /z/ which is merged with /dž/ in both TB and FH.

Ferguson makes a second, but related, observation about phonology in diglossic situations, namely "If 'pure' H items have phonemes not found in 'pure' L items, L phonemes frequently substitute for these in oral use of H, and regularly replace them in tatsamas." (Ferguson 1959:435). These are really two separate points since the first relates to the pronunciation of H, the second to the pronunciation of H items borrowed into L. Specific data was not gathered on the amount of vernacular borrowing from the standard, nor of the form of tatsamas in the two cases studied. The upshot of the first part of the observation is that oral H will vary from written H in certain predictable ways.

Though this mother tongue transfer in oral performance of the standard may be common to both language situations, it has somewhat different implications in each case. In bidialectalism, it results in a marked regional accent, since those from another region where the standard is spoken natively will have a distinct phonological system in which all the phonemic contrasts are realized in oral performance, so that the phonology of the standard is the basic, and not a parasystem. Native speakers of TB in the selected districts (as well as areas further East having other varieties of TB with the same phonological system) do have a marked recognizeable regional accent, clearly traceable to the kind of LI interference just mentioned. As is true with any regional accent in whatever standard language, there will be those who assiduously preserve it as a badge of their regional identity, and those who purposely expunge it in order to cultivate an unmarked pronunciation which, supposedly, allows them greater mobility within the society as a whole.

In diglossia, whereas there may be some regional or social pronunciation differences common to both H and L (see above), mother tongue interference in the pronunciation of H will be seen in all speakers, and there will be no model or motivation for anyone to 'correct' his pronunciation. At least where the language occupies what may be regarded as its home territory, the reference group providing the normative model for H is a wholly internal one. There is no external group of native speakers, such as that in bidialectalism, which provide an alternative model which may either be aped or eschewed. In cases of transported diglossia, however, there is a duality of reference groups. The primary one is definitely internal, comprised of the small elite who actively control H to some degree of proficiency. Speakers of H from the original homeland make up a secondary, and external, reference group and are commonly taken, though often mistakenly, as native speakers. An added factor in transported diglossia can be the sound system of another language dominant in the society. Thus the facts that (A) speakers in the movies and radio programs imported from India distinguish /s/ and /š/, and use /z/ rather than /dž/ in certain items, and (B) the fact that both oppositions are encountered in English at an early age, both function to pave the way and to create pressure for conscious correction of the use of FH phonemes in SH items.

The final aspect of phonology (Feature 18C) is mentioned by Ferguson. It would seem to be a characteristic of regional dialects and standards, whether they be in a relationship of bidialectalism or diglossia. As a result of independent development in the more recent past, sound changes will have taken place in one which either did not occur, or took place differently, in the other. Many TB items contain /r/ where the corresponding item in KB shows /l/. This results in paired items of alternative pronunciations. They function much like the lexical pairs described in 2.5.2 above in that the use of the /r/ variant or the /l/ variant immediately marks an utterance as TB or KB respectively.

Since the /r/ alternants were common to most of the TB varieties brought to Fiji, they were preserved in the dialect leveling and koinéization processes resulting in the formation of FH. Consequently, the same pairs operate between FH and SH as between TB and KB. The author found some twenty (Moag 1977:281-282) items functioning in both situations. It would be interesting to learn whether such paired pronunciations of items exist in other cases of diglossia not studied here.

3. Conclusion. I have tried to show in the foregoing pages that a large number of dimensions must be used to distinguish one language situation from another. I have demonstrated that the principle distinctions between

diglossia and its nearest typological relative, a standard with regional dialects, involve sociolinguistic rather than pure linguistic features. It was shown that these two language situations may be distinguished in terms of the macro features of digital versus analog distinctions, and skewedness of distribution. It was shown that (1) where the distinction between the two language varieties is digital in diglossia, it will be analog in bidialectalism, and (2) where the distinction is analog in both, it will be highly skewed in diglossia, and less so in bidialectalism. Finally, I have documented that when a language is transported outside its home territory, factors come into play in the new situation which tend to institutionalize and perpetuate diglossia. It is hoped that this very modest beginning will spur further studies of the important area of sociolinguistic typology.

TABLE 1. CLASSICAL DIGLOSSIA

Feature	Low Variety	High Variety
I. POLICY AND DEMOGRAPHY		
1. Degree of official recognition	none	full
2. Segment of population using each	total	small educated elite
II. FUNCTION		
3. Functional territory	broad	limited
4. Activities in which used	informal	formal
5. Use in writing	none	full
6. Use in speaking	extensive	some
LANGUAGE ACQUISITION		
7. Order of acquistion	first	second
8. Type of learning	informal	formal
9. Proficiency achieved	full	limited
IV. SUPPORT MECHANISMS		
10. Prestige	none	high
11. Literary heritage	folk	classical
12. Standardization	(informal)	formal normative
13. Stability	(+)	
V. LINGUISTIC FEATURES		
14. Phonology	basic system	para/sub system
15. Grammar	somewhat simplified	complex
16. Lexicon beyond common core	homey, local	technical, learned

TABLE 2. TWO LANGUAGE SITUATIONS COMPARED

Feature	(India, Hindi Bidialectalism) TB(L)	KB(H)	Fiji, Hindi Diglossia FH(L)	SH(H)
I. POLICY AND DEMOGRAPHY				
1. Degree of official recognition	some	full	none	some
2. Population segment involved	total rural	school leavers	total	cultural elite
II. FUNCTION				
3. Range of domains	broad	considerable	broad	moderate
4. Use in formal activities	some	extensive	none	some
5. Use in informal activities	extensive	some	extensive	some
6. Use in writing	some	extensive	none	some
7. Use in speaking	considerable	moderate	extensive	some
III. LANGUAGE ACQUISITION				
8. Order of acquisition	first	second	first	second
9. Type of learning	informal	formal/informal	informal	formal
10. Degree of competence achieved	full	full	full	moderate
IV. SUPPORT MECHANISMS				
11. Prestige	mid	high	negative	high[a]
12. Literary heritage	folk, serious	serious, popular	none	serious, popular
13. Type and degree of standardization	slight informal	full formal Sanskritized	full informal	full formal non-Sanskritized
14. Major basis of internal variation	regional	communal	rutal-urban	competence
15. Historicity	+	+	+	+
V. LINGUISTIC FEATURES				
16. Grammar				
(a) Grammatical categories	fewer	full set	fewer	full set
(b) Inflectional system	reduced	full	simplified	full
17. Lexicon				
(a) Semantic paired items	marked vernacular alternates	marked standard alternates	marked vernacular alternates	marked standard alternates
(b) Domain-specific vocabulary	homey, some learned —	homey, learned technical	homey, — —	— learned some technical
18. Phonology				
(a) System	basic system	parasystem	basic system	parasystem
(b) Results of cross-varietal interference	none	regional accent	none	some H-phoneme replacement

(c) Phonological paired items	marked vernacular alternates	marked standard alternates	marked vernacular alternates	marked standard alternates

REFERENCES

Arya, U. 1968. *Ritual songs and folksongs of the Hindus of Surinam.* Leiden: E.J. Brill.

Brown, R. & A. Gilman. 1960. The pronouns of power and solidarity. In *Style in language*. ed. by T.A. Sebeok. pp. 253-276. Cambridge: MIT Press.

Ferguson, Charles A. 1959. Diglossia. Reprinted in *Language in culture and society*, ed. by Dell Hymes. pp. 429-439. New York: Harper & Row. 1964.

Fishman, Joshua A. 1968. The relationship between micro-and macro-sociolinguistics in the study of who speaks what language to whom and when. Reprinted in *Language in sociocultural change*. ed. by Anwar S. Dil. Stanford: Stanford University Press.

———. 1971. The sociology of language: an interdisciplinary social science approach to language in society. In *Advances in the sociology of language*. vol. 1, ed. by Fishman. pp. The Hague: Mouton. 1971.

Gillion, K.L. 1962. *Eiji's Indian migrants.* Melbourne: Oxford University Press 1962. (reprinted 1973).

Grierson, Sir George A. 1903. *Linguistic survey of India*, vol. V. Indo-Aryan family, eastern group, Part II, specimens of the Bihari and Oriya languages. Delhi: Motilal Banarsidass, (Reprint) 1967.

———. 1904. *Linguistic survey of India*, vol. VI:Indo-Aryan family, mediate groups. specimens of the eastern Hindi language. Delhi: Motilal Banarsidass, 1967 (Reprint).

Gumperz, John J. 1977. The sociolinguistic significance of conversational code-switching. *RELC Jaurnal* vol. 8: 2.1-34.

Hymes, Dell. 1974. *Foundations in sociolinguistics : an ethnographic approach.* Philadelphia: University of Pennsylvania Press. 1974.

Kloss, Heinz. 1966. Types of multilingual communities: a discussion of ten variables. In *Explorations in sociolinguistics*. ed. by Stanley Lieberson. Pp. 7-17. Bloomington, IN: Indian University Press. 1966.

Lenneberg, Eric H. 1967. *Biological foundations of language.* New York: John Wiley & Sons, Inc. 1967.

Mackey, William F. 1968. The description of bilingualism. In *Readings in the sociology of language*, ed. by Joshua A. Fishman. pp. 554-584. The Hague: Mouton.

Moag, Rodney F. 1977. *Fiji Hindi, A basic course and reference grammar.* Canberra: Australian National University Press. 1977.

———. 1978. Vernacular education in Fiji. *The South Pacific Journal of Teacher Education*, vol. 6:2, 134-140.

———. 1979. The linguistic adaptations of the Fiji Indians. In *Rama's banishment : a centenary volume on the Fiji Indians*, ed. by Vijyay Mishra. Pp. 112-138 Auckland: Heinemann 1979.

———. Forthcoming: (a) English as a foreign, second, native, and basal language:a new taxonomy of English-using societies. To appear in *The new Englishes*. ed. by J.B. Pride. Rowley, MA: Newbury House.

—. Forthcoming:(b)The life cycle on non-native Englishes: a case study of Fiji and the South Pacific. To appear in *Other tongue : English in non-native contexts*, ed. by Braj B. Kachru.

—. Unpublished:Koineization, what is it and isn't: a case study of Fiji Hindi and its parent dialects. Paper presented at the 3rd roundtable on South Asian Language Analysis, University of Illinois, March, 1980.

Moag, Rodney F. & Louisa B. Moag. 1979. English in Fiji, some perspective and the need for language planning. In *New varieties of English : issues and approaches,* ed. by J.C. Richards. (Occasional Papers No. 8) June 1979. Pp. 73-90. Singapore: SEAMEO Regional Language Center.

Platt, John. 1977. A model for polyglossia and multilingualism (with special reference to Singapore and Malaysia). *Language in Society* 6.361-378.

Saksena, Baburam. 1937. *Evolution of Awadhi* (2nd ed. 1971). Delhi: Motilal Banarsidass.

Samarin, William J. 1971. Salient and substantive pidginization. In *Pidginization and creolization of languages,* ed. by Dell Hymes. 117-140. London: Cambridge University Press.

Siegel, Jeff. 1973. A survey of language use in the Indian speech community in Fiji. Unpublished field study for the Culture Learning Institute, East-West Center, Honolulu, and Practicum Project for ESL 730, May, 1973.

Stewart, William A. 1962. Outline of linguistic typology for describing multilingualism. In *Study of the role of second languages in Asia, Africa, and Latin America,* ed. by Frank A. Rice. pp. 15-25. Washington DC: Center for Applied Linguistics.

———. 1968. A sociolinguistic typology for describing national multilingualism. In *Readings in the sociology of language,* ed. by Joshua A. Fishman. Pp. 531-545. The Hague Mouton.

Tiwari, Udai Narain. 1960. *The origin and development of Bhojpuri.* Calcutta: The Asiatic Society.

Vatuk, Ved Prakash. 1964. Protest songs of East Indians in British Guiana. *Journal af American Folklore* 77.220-235.

Voorhoeve, Jan. 1971. Varieties of Creole in Surinam: church creole and pagan cult languages. In *Pidgintzation and crealization of languages,* ed. by Dell Hymes. Pp. 305-315. London: Cambridge University Press, 1971.

Weinreich, Uriel. 1953. *Languages in contact: findings and problems.* New York: Publications of the Linguistics Circle of New York, No. 1 (Reprinted 1963, The Hague).

DIGLOSSIC VARIATION IN TAMIL FILM AND FICTION

Harold Schiffman and S. Arokianathan

The Tamil writing system like most indigenous Indian writing systems is derived from Brahmi script, and is a syllabic, rather than alphabetic, system. This means that the basic symbols of the system represent a consonant plus the vowel /a/, while any other consonant-vowel combinations are made with the basic symbol (plus inherent /a/) together with secondary vowel symbols added to it. Initial vowels are also represented with special symbols, since the secondary symbols are only used for the vowels following a consonant.

INVENTORY OF SYMBOLS. The Tamil writing system has a smaller number of symbols than any other Indian script, since Tamil has no aspirated series of consonants, and also does not distinguish phonologically between voice and voicelessness in consonants. Phonetically voiced segments do occur—for example, following a homorganic nasal, all consonants are voiced. Furthermore, intervocalically, stop consonants are voiced and lenis, so that each stop consonant has three variants: a voiceless, tense (but unaspirated) variant that occurs in initial position and when geminated, e.g. /kakku/ 'vomit' is [kakkï]; a voiced variant that follows nasals, e.g. /avankaL/ 'they' is [avəŋga], and a voiced, lenis, sometimes fricative variant that occurs intervocalically, e.g. /pookalaam/ 'let's go' is [pōrəlã]. This is true for all the six stops /p, t, ɽ, T̲/, c, k/, each of which is written with only one symbol in the Tamil orthography. Since the phonetic variants are in a state of classic complementary distribution, there is never any problem with the representation of Tamil words of native Dravidian origin.

The Tamil writing system, however, was devised for and is still used to represent a variety of Literary Tamil (LT) that has changed very little for several centuries (since the 13th century, when the grammarian PavaNantimunivar composed his grammar *nannūl.*) Some minor changes involving certain violations or relaxations of *sandhi* rules have crept into usage, but many other changes in the phonological shape of Tamil lexical items have occurred since the 13th century; indeed many are recorded in inscriptional evidence from as early as the 5th century, but in standard (grammatical) writing these changes are never represented. The kinds of changes we are referring to have been documented in various places by various scholars (Shanmugam Pillai 1960, Zvelebil 1964, Schiffman 1979a, Annamalai 1976, Gnanasundaram 1980).

These changes can be formally represented as a set of historical phonological rules that have been gradually added to the phonological grammar of Tamil such that all native speakers of Tamil apply them when speaking in a casual unmonitored style. We recapitualate them in Appendix I.

It may seem strange to be discussing the Tamil writing system and its relationship to phonetic changes that are not represented by it, if such changes never appeared in print. In fact, however, modern social-realism writers *do* often attempt to represent the modern spoken language in their writing, namely, in the *dialogues* of novels, and short stories. When they do, they are faced with a number of problems that are the real subject of this paper. What is of interest to us is that these representations are only rarely purely phonetic, i.e., they usually are not congruent with a narrow phonetic transcription of modern colloquial speech, although portions of any given representation may be quite narrowly phonetic.

Our goal here is to delineate the factors that mediate between standard orthography and narrow phonetic representation in modern writing and to see whether any general rules emerge that may have bearing on writing systems in general, as well as illuminate the kind of sociolinguistic factors that are reflected in this kind of variation.

1. CONSERVATISM. A very important consideration in evaluating a writing system is how far it goes with a phonetic representation—should the spelling reflect the most colloquial, natural speaking style or should there be some restraints on "pure" phonetic representations? There are also many graduations between "pure" spoken Tamil and "pure" Literary Tamil so that intermediate styles often convey some sociolinguistic information, such as whether the speaker is educated, whether the speaker considers the topic to be more formal, or, more importantly, whether the speaker is of higher status than his/her interlocutor, etc. Every speaker of every language uses forms that she/he considers to be beyond the pale of natural, casual speech, and when brought to their attention, speakers often deny that they even use or used such forms. Many Tamil speakers, for example, pronounce the LT /veeNTaam/ 'don't want/need' [væ:ṇã] in their own relaxed colloquial speech, yet they stigmatize this pronunciation in the speech of others, and deny its validity in their own speech, claiming that the only acceptable spoken form is something like [ve:ṇḍã] (which of course differs from the LT pronunciation only in the nasalization of the final vowel, i.e. by the application of rule no. 2, cf. Appendix).

All of these considerations seem to be related, and for want of a better label, we will call this factor, one of many anti-phonetic factors, CONSERVATISM. Conservatism in a diglossic language like Tamil has many dimensions, and not only at the Literary and of the scale. Here we are dealing primarily with conservatism at the spoken end of the scale, since, "true" conservatism would advocate out-and-out Literary forms.

What we are dealing with here is the problem of how to choose one variant of a lexeme as a 'standard' when in fact there is no standard, and variation is the rule. To obscure this variation is to obscure important sociolinguistic factors and cues that speakers consider important, while at the same time recognizing that at the bottom end of the continuum of styles (the 'basilect') there are forms that are stigmatized and considered vulgar or in poor taste by practically all speakers and would only be represented if the writer wanted to portray a speaker as vulgar or coarse or common.[1]

2. READABILITY. Another convention that is anti-phonetic is what we might call readability or recognizability. If writers write purely phonetically, and this spelling differs significantly from standard orthography, readers are required to read out loud to hear what the speech sounds like in order to understand it. But if some forms are spelled in the conventional way, readers can read the representation without trouble. Thus, in representations of English dialects, e.g. southern American speech, an utterance like "I know he is going to do it" might be spelled (e.g. in a comic strip) "Ah knows he gonna do it" where *I* becomes *ah*, *s* is added to *know*, *is* is deleted, *going to* becomes *gonna*, but *know* itself is not spelled *noze*, because the spelling *know* is required for readability or recognizability. A string of spellings like 'Ah noze heze gonna duwit' is not easily decipherable. Part of this factor may be a subfactor of:

3. GENERALITY. If writing is made close to the forms recognized by more speakers of more dialects, the writer does not lose his/her audience. This is a factor mitigating against spelling reform in modern English—any reform now would tend to reflect the dialect of dominant regions or classes, such as the eastern US or southern England, to the deteriment of other subcommunities of English speakers. Similarly, any reform of Tamil spelling today based on mainland non-Brahman Tamil dialect will leave behind a number of social and geographical communities, most notably mainland (Indian) Brahmans and Sri Lanka (Ceylon) Tamils of all castes, whose speech is quite different from mainland NBr. speech. Many of these latter speakers understand mainland NBr. because they hear it on the radio and in imported Tamil films, but whether they would be comfortable having to write it is another question.

4. SILENT SPEECH. A fourth factor weighing against pure phonetics is one we will call for the moment *silent speech* or the *irrealis* factor for want of a better term. For instance, when a Tamil writer wants to represent unspoken language as in a dream, (even a daydream,) something other than spoken representations are used, even though it is not clear that Tamils dream in something other than the spoken language. But perhaps because it is not uttered aloud, i.e. not 'spoken', Spoken Tamil is not used. We are not sure that all writers observe this convention, but in one work examined, Jayakantan's *yuka canti*, one of the characters, while thinking over a difficult problem during a night of troubled sleep, does her thinking in Literary Tamil. Conversely, foreigners' attempts to speak Tamil (and perhaps the representation of any language other than Tamil) are sometimes represented in very colloquial Tamil. In the novel *vaaSingTanil tirumaNam* ("Marriage in Washington) by Caavi, which depicts a Brahman wedding taking place in Washington, D.C.,

1. Shakespeare does this with his buffoons and oafish louts, while other characters are typically portrayed as speaking in a very refined manner.

and involves non-Tamils who are preseumably speaking English, their speech is represented in a very colloquial spoken style, although the Tamils themselves are speaking a more LT form. This convention differs quite radically from the way French speakers are represented as speaking French in an English novel, for example. In the latter, the speech of Frenchmen (speaking French) is given as a very foreign sounding English interlarded with conventional French expressions (mais oui, monsieur, sacre bleu, naturellement, n'est-ce pas etc.), while French speakers speaking English are given heavy French accents (Zis ees vairy eenteresteeng, m'sieur).[2]

A fifth factor that causes deviation from phoneticization is that of *markedness* or *stereotypicalization*. It has been noted elsewhere (Schiffman 1979b) that when Tamil speakers, usually non-literate speakers or semi-literate speakers, attempt to speak LT they use the strategy of interlarding their ST speech with certain stereotyped LT forms that everyone recognizes as Literary Tamil, and that give enough of a LT flavor to 'mark' the speech as something higher than spoken. These 'marked' forms are conventions recognized by speakers as giving the proper flavor, even though the whole utterance may be more ST than LT. Similarly, some spoken forms are also recognized as typically spoken, e.g. *Num* 'must' instead of LT *veeNTum* or *puTi* 'like' for LT *piTi*. Salting an utterance with these 'marked' spoken forms likewise insures that speakers will understand that the utterance is primarily a spoken one without jeopardizing the readability of the whole passage.

6. ARGUMENTATIVE FORCE. A sixth factor used in both writing and films has to do with the emotional or argumentative force of an utterance or discourse. At a crucial point in the plot, where the author wants to insure that the readers/hearers grasp the full intent of the situation, Literary Tamil forms usually prevail. This is because the utterance is usually emotionally forceful or significant. If the scene is highly emotional, however, indicating confusion and great distress on the part of one or more characters, spoken forms may then erupt, as it were. Thus emotional factors tend toward phoneticity while forceful argumentation is anti-phonetic. Labov (1972: 208) indicates that "styles can be ranged along a single dimension, measured by the amount of attention paid to speech" and that during excited speech, when speakers are highly involved emotionally, they have little attention available to monitor what they are saying. Thus casual forms surface because speakers are not controlling as carefully what they say.

TECHNICAL ASPECTS

Aside from the social factors mitigating against a 'pure' phonetic representation of Tamil speech in modern prose writing, there are a number of technical aspects of the Tamil writing system that, barring a reform of the orthography and introduction of new symbols, constrain and restrict the range of possible phonetic representations.

2. *Mary Worth*, Seattle Times, April 3, 1977.

One of the most obvious problems facing the Tamil writing system, even before there was a modern novel with colloquial Tamil in it, was what to do about borrowed words that do not fit the pattern of native Dravidian morpheme structures, such that voiced stops appear not following nasals only, but in initial positions of words. (As we have already noted, Tamil orthography has no symbols for distinguishing voiced from voiceless consonants). Tamil has borrowed extensively from Indo-Āryan (Sanskrit, Prakrits, Hindustani, Marathi) as well as from other Dravidian languages that have initial voiced consonants (Kannada, Telugu) and from Portuguese, French, and English as well. In order to represent some of these sounds, a supplementary set of symbols, called *grantha* letters, was devised. Some of these grantha letters are still in use to represent sounds such as *s*, *š*, *kš*, *j*, and *h*. These sounds are found mainly in Indo-Aryan loan words, but some Portuguese and English loans are written with these sounds as well.[3] The interesting thing about such borrowings with initial voiced consonants is that such items do not usually contrast with native items that do have voiceless consonants, so that there is usually no problem (except for a few like *palam* 'measure of weight' vs. *balam* 'strength, and *paavam* 'sin' vs. *baavam.* 'nature, condition, idea, imagination'). Usually the correct pronunciation can be deciphered from the context; there is a problem of misunderstanding. Usually this lack of distinction does not raise anything more than trivial problems and we discuss it no further here.

The real problem arises in native colloquial Tamil words that must be spelled differently from literary Tamil items in order to convey the immediacy or intimacy or sociocultural complexity or whatever is involved in motivating Tamil writers to write colloquial speech in general or in particular in the dialogues of modern novels and short stories.

What is a problem here is not that Tamil orthography is not adequate for the representation of sounds found in colloquial speech (despite Zvelebil 1964: 261).[4] The problem is that the modern writers' representation of spoken Tamil appears to be inconsistent, unstandardized, and in fact underutilizes possibilities inherent in the writing system. We have already examined some

3. *Jannal* 'window, from Portuguese *janela*; *hooTTal* from English 'hotel', usually pronounced [o:ṭlu].

4. Zvelebil feels that if Tamil is to modernize it must develop a means of representing certain phonetic material currently unrepresentable by the existing writing system, e.g. nasalization. In actuality, nasalization is predictable in spoken Tamil so that a sequence written *-um* is automatically interpretable as [ũ] by any native speaker. This is true of all the VN combinations in final position except Vṇ, which speakers know to add a final *u* to, rather than nasalize the vowel; that is /kaaN/ 'see' becomes [ka:ṇu] etc. More difficult to represent would be the fronted [æ] vowel found after velars preceded by front vowels, e.g. [paḍikkyæ] 'to study' for LT /paTikka/ etc. But most of these phonetic pecularities are in fact predictable from the structure of the word and so will automatically be pronounced thus by speakers reading a representation of them in a modern work They are in fact so automatic that most speakers are not conscious of them, and even apply these phonetic rules when speaking other languages, e.g. English.

social factors that cause fluctuations from one pole to another in supposedly spoken representations of the language. What now needs to be sorted out is whether, once all these social factors are taken into account, there are still many unexplained phenomena. This is an interesting question for a number of reasons, not the least of which is that if Tamil is ever to modernize its writing system so as to incorporate more of the changes that have occurred since the 13th century, some rationale for deciding how to represent phonetic forms not now represented must be agreed upon.

Inconsistent Phoneticization

We have already discussed a number of factors that influence the way a writer chooses to represent speech. Some of these mitigate against phoneticization while others mitigate in favour of it. When all these extralinguistic factors are taken into account, however, there are still some fluctuations that remain unexplained. One of the most obvious areas of inconsistency is in treating grammatical morphemes differently from lexical morphemes. For example, in our data there recurs a string of morphemes that in speech would be approximately [nene^{1}-ci^{2}-ka^{2}-ṇũ^{4}] '(someone) must^{4} think^{1} for/to-oneself^{3} (past)'^{2}. In almost all cases, with exceptions that we will discuss later, this string is usually written (in the dialogue of modern novels) *ninai-ccu-kka-ṇum*, that is, the grammatical morphemes are represented as phonetically as they can be in the Tamil script. But the lexical verb stem *ninai* 'think, hope' although phonetically pronounced [nene], is represented in its historically older, i.e. literary form.[5] One might say that /ninai/ is the 'underlying' form of /nene/but it is not clear that the historical rules that convert LT to ST are still phonologically operative in Spoken Tamil (rules 4 and 5; see Appendix I). On the other hand, in a language system like that of Tamil, where fluctuation between literary and spoken forms goes on for all literate and semi-literate speakers all their lives, the reality of the literary forms cannot be denied, and to claim that /nene/ is the underlying form because it is always [nene] in the basilect, overlooks the fact that forms like [nenai] or [ninai] also occur when 'higher' norms are in use. The factor that is obviously operative here is that of recognizability of morphemes mentioned earlier (no. 2). What is not clear, however, is why lexical morphemes must be kept recognizable while grammatical morphemes can be represented phonetically. It may be that lexical morphemes have some different kind of psychological reality than do grammatical morphemes, as evidenced by the English example using 'know' earlier—the 'grammatical' morpheme 'going—to' can be converted to 'gonna' but 'know' must be kept recognizable.

In Tamil *writing*, then lexical morphemes are usually spelled in the literary form while grammatical morphemes are usually spelled in a more phonetic way. There are counterexamples in our data, however, and we as yet have no satisfactory explanation, although we can make recourse to some of our

5. The LT form of this utterance would be /ninai-ttu-koLLa-veeNTum/.

extralinguistic social factors for an approximate or impressionistic explanation.[6]

The variations between the poles of LT and ST in film scripts are somewhat different that the variations in dialogues of modern fiction, although some factors remain the same. Part of the difference has to do with the fact that film dialogues are in fact *spoken* by actors standing in front of cameras, while dialogues in modern fiction are of course written. When an actor learns a part for a film, in most cases the script presented to him/her is in Literary Tamil. The actor or actress (unless the film is a historical or puranic film, where LT is used throughout) has to convert the LT script into spoken Tamil on the spot. This involves some mental or psychological operations that are somewhat difficult to understand, partly because they are not verifiable—we cannot observe the mental operations, but only the result of the operations.

When a writer puts Tamil into a dialogue, s/he has time to plan, using the criteria already elaborated, whether the representation will be completely spoken/phonetic or whether it will be somewhere else on the scale in order to achieve some desired effect (emotional, social, formal, etc.). The writer also has the problem of readability to contend with, while the actor has in effect the opposite problem—making a written form into a spoken form.

One of the things we observe in the sound track of the film *tankappatakkam* is that (all other factors such as emotional, social, formal, etc. being equal) actors are not always capable of instantly converting a phrase into colloquial Tamil. They sometimes begin a word in LT and in mid-word begin applying rules. Once they begin, however, they always continue to convert the rest of the word. They never stop in the middle of a word and finish it in LT style, which (apparently because of readability) sometimes happens in modern fiction. In other words, the conversion of a word from LT to ST starts at the end of the word and seems to move to the front, e.g. we can have the various stages:

LT ninai—ttu—koLLa—veeNTum

'someone must think/consider (to/for oneself)'

stage 1 :	ninai	ttu	koLLa	veeNum	
stage 2 :	ninai	ttu	koLLa	Num	(rule 7)
stage 3 :	ninai	ttu	ka	Num	(rule 9?)
stage 4 :	ninai	ccu	ka	Num	(rule 3)
stage 5 :	nene	ccu	ka	Num	(rules 4, 5)

At some point the nasalization rule (2) also applies, probably as early as stage 2, but perhaps not until the last stage. Although we were originally tempted to conclude that rules 1-9 were somehow hierarchical, and would

6. Or, as Labov points out, 'Whenever a subordinate dialect is in contact with a superordinate one, linguistic forms produced by a speaker of the subordinate dialect in a formal context will shift in an unsystematic manner towards the superordinate.' (Labov 1971, in Hymes 1971:450).

be applied in a certain order to give a scale of gradations, we did not find that the rules applied in any scale of order, and the reason is obviously to be found in the progressive application from end of word/utterance to beginning. Rule 7 applies first because an environment to which it can apply presents itself in the final portion of this utterance. Rule 9 applies next (if this is in fact the causative factor here) because the environment is right for it, and it is the second-last morpheme in the utterance. Rule 2, nasalization, seems to be one that we would expect to apply first, since it applies in word-final position, but for some reason its application is held in reserve until a real spoken 'flavor' is desired. It seems to be strongly 'marked' for spoken style, and is at least one rule that is hierarchized as we surmised more of the rules might be. In some of our written materials, however, an occasional utterance begins with the application of one of the conversion rules (lowering, for instance) and ends in a more LT style, for example, with the word /kuṛantai/ 'child' where rule (4), lowering, converts the first vowel to /o/ but the expected conversion of the final /ai/ to /e/ by rule (5), monophthongization, does not occur. Several times in one discourse this odd form, /koṛantai/ halfway between LT and ST, occurs, in violation of the general principle just established that lexical morphemes are spelled in the LT way or in the ST manner for some sort of sociolinguistic effect. This calls for a different kind of explanation, one that has to do with Tamil script. The secondary symbol for the vowel /e/ in Tamil is written *before* the consonant it follows. Since /e/ is rare in the middle of a word, it almost always appears (is written) at the beginning of a word. Writing /e/ for /ai/ at the end of a word, even when /ai/ is a grammatical morpheme (accusative marker) violates this visual norm for some speakers/readers. However, this argument lacks force since in compounds involving second elements that begin with /e/, the symbol for /e/ will appear word-internally, e.g. /avarkaL^1-ellaarum^2/ 'all^2 of them^1' i.e. There are also words like /eṇṇey/'oil' that contain an 'internal' /e/. However, it is still true that the appearance of orthographic /e/ in places it is not expected to appear does have a strange effect on the visual impression of the word.

The conclusions drawn in this paper are based on analysis of texts of Tamil fictional writing as well as the filmscript of a Tamil movie. Ideally it would be helpful if examples of fluctuation between written and spoken styles could be illustrated with examples from these texts, showing the correlation between the fluctuation and the factors we have outlined. Limitations of space prevent us from doing this, but we present below a diagram that attempts to illustrate how the various pro-phonetic and anti-phonetic factors work like vectors, sometimes drawing the utterance toward the literary pole, sometimes working against an opposite factor to average out the utterance to an intermediate stage, and sometimes overriding all other factors to push toward a completely phonetic pole. Thus an average discourse, if plotted on a graph with formal Literary Tamil as the top of the scale, and spoken as the bottom, will resemble a wave, rising and falling as various factors influence the choice of forms. If several anti-phonetic factors co-occur, the flavor will be strongly literary; if several phonetic factors co-occur, the opposite pole will be strongly represented, and an intermediate variety may occur as the result of a pro-phonetic and an anti-phonetic variable neutralizing each other (Fig. 1).

FIGURE 1

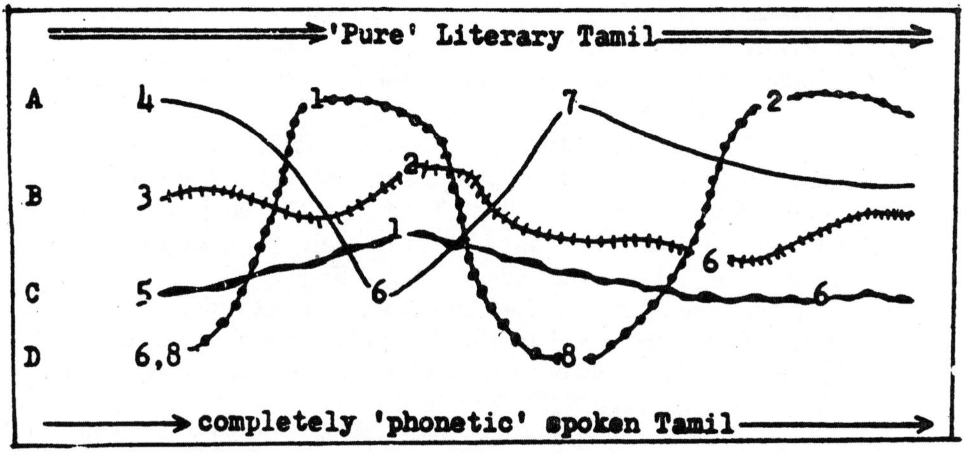

Segment of discourse: sentence, word, etc.

A, B, C, D: Representations of different speech events by different writers.

1 to 8: Factors mediating between the polarity of extremely phonetic spoken Tamil and 'pure' Literary Tamil:

1. *Conservatism.* Primarily used to reflect status differences in speech of various characters: 'refined' vs. 'coarse, vulgar' speech.
2. *Readability.* Helps readers to recognize lexical morphemes they already know, while giving the flavor of spoken language in the grammatical morphemes.
3. *Generality.* Literary forms are usually known over a wider area, so that a spoken form that is closest to LT will be chosen over a little-known dialect form.
4. *Silent speech.* Language of dreams, daydreams, thinking to oneself may be portrayed differently, either more Literary or more Spoken than the rest of the dialogue.
5. *Non-native speech.* Foreigners' speech (when not a transliteration of English, etc.) may be rendered as very colloquial in style.
6. *Stereotypicalisation.* Certain forms are 'marked' as Literary or Spoken and are used to upgrade or downgrade a discourse, without having to resort to conservatism or phoneticization.
7. *Argumentative force.* At a crucial moment in the plot, when the speech of a certain character must be heavily weighted, LT forms will prevail.
8. *Emotional force.* At extremely emotional moments in the plot, more 'phonetic' forms tend to prevail.

APPENDIX

Rules converting LT to spoken Tamil.

(1) *Rounding* of the vowel preceding final /m/, e.g. LT/maram/→ST/marom/ 'tree'

(2) *Nasalization* of a vowel preceding final/m/ and /n/, and deletion of nasal segment, e.g. LT /marom/→ST/marõ/
LT /avan/→ST /avẽ/ 'he'

(3) *Palatalization* of /nt/ and /tt/ to /nc/ and /cc/ respectively following the vowels /i, e/ and the semivowel /y/. e.g. LT /paTitteen/→ST /paTicceen/

(4) *Lowering* of the high vowels /u/ and /i/ to/o/ and /e/ respectively if followed by a single consonant and the vowel /a/;
e.g. LT /ilai/ 'leaf'→ST /ele/ 'ibid.', LT /utavi/→/otavi/ 'help'.

(5) *Monophthongization* of the sequence /ai/ to /e/everywhere except in final position in a monosyllabic word: LT /mar̤ai/→ST /mar̤e/ 'rain'. In a monosyllable such as LT /vai/ a final enunciative /u/ is added that is converted to /i/ by another rule; LT /vai/→ST /vayyi/ 'keep'.

(6) *Final vowel shortening*. All final long vowels (except clitics) are shortened: LT /paTicceen/→ST /paTiccẽ/ 'I studied' (nasalization by rule 2). Otherwise, e.g. if followed by some other morpheme, they remain long, e.g. /paTicceen-aa?/ 'Did I study' ?

(7) *Deletion* of short vowels and intervocalic /v/ and /k/ after the second syllable. LT /pooyviTTeen/→ST /pooyTeen/→/pooyTẽ/ 'I definitely left.'
LT /pookiṟeen/→ST /pooreen/→ /poorẽ/ 'I go."
LT /ooTivanteen/→ST /ooTiyaantẽ/ 'I came running'.
LT /irukkiṟeen/→ST /irukkreen/→ /irukkrẽ/ "I am."

(8) *De-alveolarization*. Merger of /ṟṟ/ with /tt/ and /ṉṟ/ with /NN/. The alveolar consonants of LT are merged with the dentals /tt/ and retroflex /NN/ in ST: LT /aaṟṟukku/→ST /aattukku/ 'to the river'.
LT /oṉṟu/ 'one thing'→ST /oNNu/.

(9) *Deletion* of final /L/ and /l/[7] and non-final /l/, /r/, and /L/ before obstruents. LT /niinkaL/→ST /niinka/ 'you plural'; LT /paartteen/→ST /paatteen/→ /paattẽ/. Some pre-obstruent /l/'s and /L/'s are already converted to stops in LT which are then homorganized in ST: LT /keeL+kkiṟ-een/→ /keeTkiṟeen/→ST [keekkrẽ] 'I ask.'

---

7. The spread of this rule is morphologically restricted in that it does not apply in nouns, e.g. LT/ST /camayal/ 'cooking' but does apply in verbs, e.g. /vantaal/→/vantaa/ 'if someone comes', /aanaal/→ST /aanaa/ 'but' ('if it becomes').

REFERENCES

Annamalai, E. 1976. Standard spoken Tamil: some observations. In *Studies in dialectology*, ed. by R.V. K. Thampuran, vol. I, No. 2. Trivandrum: Department of Linguistic (mimeo).

Beck, Brenda E.F. 1979. *Perspectives on a regional culture : essays about the Colmbatore area of South India.* New Delhi: Vikas Publishing House Pvt. Ltd.

Gnanasundaram, V. 1980. The role of diglossia in the emergence of standard spo ken Tamil. Paper presented at the Second International Conference on South Asian Language and Linguistics held in the Department of Linguistics, Osmania University, Hyderabad, January, 1980.

Labov, William. 1972. *Sociolinguistic patterns.* Philadelphia: University of Pennsylvania Press.

———. 1971. The notion of system in creole languages. In *Pidginization and creolization of languages*, ed. by Dell Hymes. London and New York: Cambridge University Press.

Schiffman, Harold. 1979a. *A grammar of spoken Tamil.* Madras: Christian Literature Society.

Schiffman, Harold. 1979b. Coimbatore Tamil. In Brenda Beck (ed.), pp. 111-128.

Shanmugam Pillai, M. 1960. Tamil—literary and colloquial. In *Linguistic diversity in South Asia. International Journal of American Linguistics* 26:3. ed. by Charles Ferguson and John Gumperz.

Zvelebil, Kamil. 1964. Spoken language of Tamilnad. *Archiv Orientalini* 32:3.237-64.

OUR CONTRIBUTORS

H. S. ANANTHANARAYANA, Department of Linguistics, Osmania University, Hyderabad 500 007, India.

E. ANNAMALAI, Central Institute of Indian Languages, Manasagangotri, Mysore 570 006, India

S. AROKIANATHAN, Department of Linguistics, Tamil University, Thanjavur, Tamilnadu, India.

S. K. BANDYOPADHYAY, Department of Linguistics, University of Delhi, Delhi 110 007, India.

WILLIAM BRIGHT, Department of Linguistics, University of California, Los Angeles, CA 90024, U.S.A.

GEORGE CARDONA, Department of Linguistics, University of Pennsylvania, Philadelphia, PA 19174, U.S.A.

SUHAS CHATTERJEE, 32, Amherst Street, Calcutta, 700 009, India. (Died in May 1985).

ALICE DAVISON, Department of Linguistics, University of Illinois, Urbana-Champaign, Illinois 61801, U.S.A.

MADHAV DESHPANDE, Department of Linguistics, University of Michigan, Ann Arbor, Michigan 48109, U.S.A.

M. W. S. DE SILVA, Department of Language, University of York, York Y01 500, United Kingdom. (Died in May 1980).

JAMES W. GAIR, Department of Modern Languages and Linguistics, Cornell University, Ithaca, New York 14853, U.S.A.

HANS HENRICH HOCK, Department of Linguistics, University of Illinois, Urbana-Champaign, Illinois 61801, U.S.A.

BRUCE C. JOHNSON, 107, Woodcrest CV, Chapel Hill, NC 27514, U.S.A.

YAMUNA KACHRU, Department of Linguistics, University of Illinois, Urbana-Champaign, Illinois 61801, U.S.A.

WILAIWAN KANITTANAN, Department of Linguistics, Liberal Arts Faculty, Thammasat University, Bangkok, Thailand.

M. H. KLAIMAN, Division of Linguistics, La Trobe University, Bundoora (Melbourne) VIC 3083, Australia.

B. LAKSHMI BAI, Department of Linguistics, Osmania University, Hyderabad 500 007, India.

IRAVATHAM MAHADEVAN, 'Vaijayanti', 112, Chamiers Road, Nandanam Extension, Mardas 600 035, India.

COLIN P. MASICA, Department of South Asian Languages & Civilization, University of Chicago, Chicago, Illinois 60637, U.S.A.

K. MEENAKSHI, Centre for Historical Studies, School of Social Sciences, Jawaharlal Nehru University, New Delhi 110 067, India.

RODNEY F. MOAG, Department of Linguistics, University of Michigan, Ann Arbor, Michigan 48109,U.S.A.

MANJARI OHALA, San Jose State University, San Jose, California, U.SA.

RAJESHWARI PANDHARIPANDE, Department of Linguistics, University of Illinois, Urbana-Champaign, Illinois 61801, U.S.A.

IRA PANDIT, D. R. College (Delhi University), Delhi 110 007, India.

B. N. PATNAIK, Department of English, Indian Institute of Technology, Kanpur 208 016, India.

UDAYA NARAYAN SINGH, Department of Linguistics, University of Delhi, Delhi 110 007, India.

SANFORD B. STEEVER, Department of Linguistics, The University of Chicago, Chicago, U.S.A.

K. V. SUBBARAO, Department of Linguistics, University of Delhi, Delhi 110 007, India.

A USHA DEVI, Department of Linguistics, M. S. University of Baroda, Baroda (Gujarat), India.

KASHI WALI, Syracuse University, Syracuse, NY 13210, U.S.A.

RAMAWATAR YADAV, Department of English, Tribhuvan University, Kathmandu, Nepal.

K. S. YADURAJAN, Central Institute of English and Foreign Languages, Hyderabad 500 007, India.

LANGUAGE INDEX

ABBREVIATIONS: f = and the following page; n = footnote; (n) = and footnote

ERRATA

[b = from bottom of text; t = from top of text; fn = footnote]

Page	*Line*	*For*	*Read*
8	1t	derivation	derivations
,,	4	a question	question
14	21t	dependent of	dependent on
18	1 9t	as category	as a category
19	12t	constructio	construction
24	5b	than	then
28	9b	NP's	NPs
35	9t	suggest	suggests
78	2t	resonace	resonance
85	5t	of of	of
,,	11b	controlled for	controlled
,,	5b	speaker	speakers
116	66	phonetization	phoneticisation
123	22-23t	a hypothetical such	such a hypothetical
127	8t	? caiŋke	ʔ caiŋke
,,	11t	DENTIFIED	IDENTIFIED
128	16t	Moravssik	Moravcsik
129	16b	b-UM abasa	b-UM-abasa
130	8t	It	If
,,	16b	*voh*	*vah*
131	1t	common such	such common
131	2t	Accusatives	Accusative
132	6t	*kiiso*	*kiiṛð*
133	16t	Lazdni	Lazdiṇa
135	1b	it.	it,
145	17t	Prthviraaj	Pṛthviraaj
,,	21t	*Grundzuge*	*Grundzüge*
,,	,,	*Artikelehre*	*Artikellehre*
,,	13b	*paksii*	*pakṣii*
146	4t	*krsak*	*kṛṣak*
,,	4t	*sabdaavali*	*śabdaavalii*
152	5b	now	how
153	16b	gunəplaalə	gunəpaal ə

165	5t	crealization	creolization
,,	2b	descendents	descendants
166	fn3	nagative	negative
169	4t	*iniazavr*	*intazaar*
	6t	fhr	for
177	21t	nɛ in ?	nɛʔ i n
179	fn 3	papar	paper
192	4b, 7b, 9b, 13b, 14b	VI	V1
213	21t	*te ne*	*teṇe*
245	3t	Masica 1979	Masica 1976
247	15b	*nikal*	*nikaal*
276	21t	Chomsky'	Chomsky's
277	16b	difference the	difference in the
281	11t	some	so
283	16b	domidant	dominant
285	4t	ajb.	ajp.
318	13t	whai	what
325	2t	Present Tenses	Present Tense
327	7b	that	than
337	7t	identity	identify
354	11t	in	an
371	18t	[pōrəlã]	[pōγəlã]
,,	19t	T/	T
372	8b	2nd	end
377	4t	that	than